North
Kingstown
Free
Library

This Book Has Been Added
to the Collection

In Honor Of
Aldo Smith

In Recognition of
Volunteer Service
to the
North Kingstown Free Library

1996

DATE			

BAKER & TAYLOR

Sail and Power

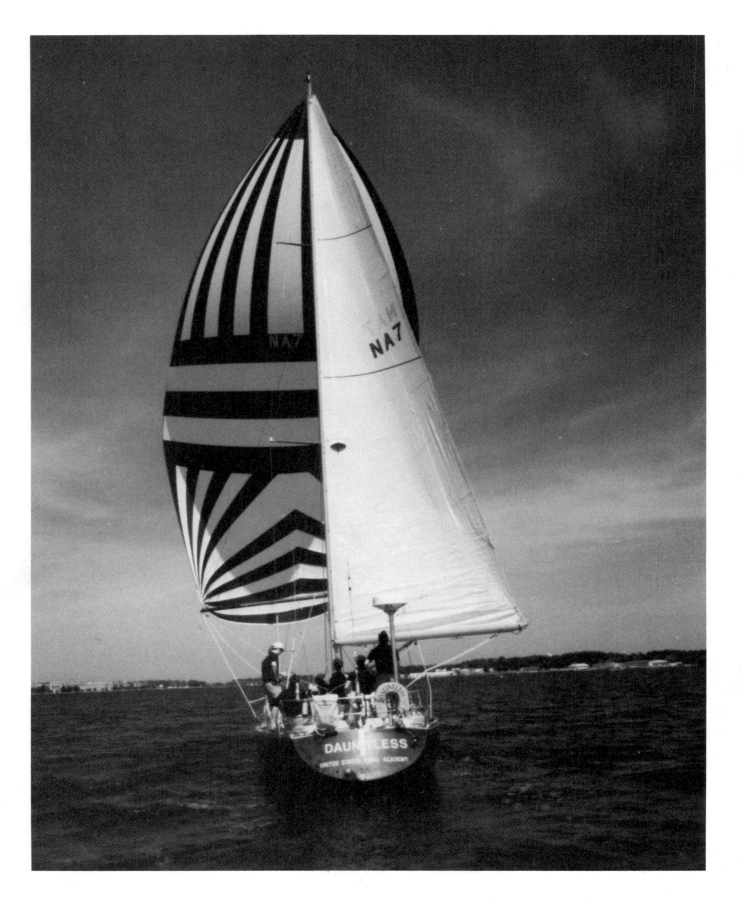

Sail and Power

Fourth Edition

The Official Textbook at
the U.S. Naval Academy

by Richard Henderson
with William E. Brooks III

Naval Institute Press
Annapolis, Maryland

Copyright © 1967, 1973, 1979, 1991
by the United States Naval Institute, Annapolis, Maryland

Library of Congress Cataloging-in-Publication Data

Henderson Richard, 1924–
     Sail and power : the official textbook of the United States Naval
Academy / by Richard Henderson ;   with William E. Brooks III. -- 4th
ed.
        p.   cm.
     Includes index.
     ISBN 1-55750-359-1 (alk. paper)
     1. Sailing.   2. Seamanship.   I. Brooks, William E., III.
II. Title.
GV811.H365   1991
623.88--dc20   90-23229

Printed in the United States of America
on acid-free paper ♾

9 8 7 6 5 4 3 2

First printing

In memory of
Captain Alexander G. B. Grosvenor, U.S. Navy
who, in such a short time, contributed so much
to the Naval Academy sailing program

Contents

A mid-Atlantic chance encounter between *Rattlesnake*, a USNA training ketch en route to Plymouth, England, and the destroyer *John Hancock* (DD 981) in the summer of 1986. The photo was taken by LCDR Don Loren, USNA class of 1974 and executive officer of the destroyer.

We teach sailing and seamanship here at the Naval Academy for one purpose: to make competent seamen of our midshipmen, who will be the naval leaders of the future. . . . We send them to sea to learn the fundamental characteristics of the professional seaman: a deep-seated sense of humility in the face of nature and her master.

—Captain John B. Bonds, USN (Ret.), former Commodore, Naval Academy Sailing Squadron/Commanding Officer, North Severn Naval Station

Preface

The primary purpose of this book is to instruct the U.S. Naval Academy midshipmen in the essentials of small-boat handling and seamanship under sail and power. The book is intended as well to serve as a text for Navy-wide training. In addition, *Sail and Power* has proven a useful source of instruction for the general public, because sailing and boat handling are dealt with in general terms, and most of the boats discussed (with the exception of the Naval Academy's Yard patrol craft) are highly representative of types commonly used by civilian yachtsmen.

In the first edition of *Sail and Power*, Bartlett S. Dunbar wrote the powerboat portion of the book, but this section has now been changed extensively and reorganized. In addition, the entire book has been updated and expanded with the inclusion of the following new material: basic sailing hydrodynamics; recent theory on rigging and sails; a new class of Lasers and tips for Laser sailors; J-24s; 420 dinghies, and a new class of YPs (two different types within this class); the magnificent Navy 44s; new methods of man overboard recovery; additional information on heavy weather; new winches; recent spinnaker theory; instrumentation; boat management in heavy weather offshore; gasoline auxiliary engines; towing; offshore equipment lists; additional marlinspike seamanship; hull stability; a new section on outboards and inboard/outboard drive boats; new reefing techniques. There is also a new chapter on the rules of the road, a new chapter on the general fundamentals of powerboat handling, new Naval Academy power craft, the circumnavigation of Delmarva training cruise, medical and damage control kits, and so forth. The last two editions of this book would not have been possible without the considerable help of William E. Brooks III, formerly an instructor in the Department of Seamanship and Navigation at the U.S. Naval Academy. I also appreciate the numerous fine photographs (some of them sequential) that Bill Brooks has contributed.

While some may argue that instruction in sail is not essential to the training of naval officers, there is no question that it is highly desirable. There is nothing like sailing to bring one into close contact with, and to develop a real love and respect for, the sea. In addition to improving and broadening skills in boat handling and seamanship, sailing helps build resourcefulness, general nautical knowledge, the ability to make quick decisions, team spirit, and the ability to give and take orders. Furthermore, sailing and racing under sail encourage an understanding and sensitivity towards the wind, tide, and waves, which are, after all, the seaman's environmental elements.

There was a time when yachtsmen wondered whether naval officers could really sail, but not so today. Great emphasis is now put on sailing at the U.S. Naval Academy, and its training program is recognized as one of the finest in the world. The effectiveness of this training has been demonstrated by many outstanding, seamanlike offshore passages by Naval Academy yachts and numerous victories in prestigious racing events. Especially noteworthy is the Navy's prowess in intercollegiate sailing—for example, repeatedly winning the coveted McMillan and Kennedy trophies and the North American Intercollegiate Championships. *Sail and Power* is a basic text for Naval Academy training, and the authors are gratified for whatever help the book has been in introducing the midshipmen to the fundamentals of seamanship.

Many people have been helpful and encouraging to the authors in their preparation of this book. We are especially grateful to the following for their support and assistance in the preparation of the first three editions: Captain Robert D. McWethy, Roger C. Taylor, Lieutenant Karl R. Witschonke, the late Captain Jacob J. Vandergrift, Lieutenant (junior grade) Stuart A. Finlay, Commander Christopher Weaver, Lieutenant Paul Dodson, Lieutenant Commander Bruce McLaughlin, Lieutenant W. G. Furnholm, Chief Warrant Officer M. Kerekesh, Gary Jobson, Graham Hall, Bert Wylds, and Captains Richard C. Ustick, the late Alexander G. B. Grosvenor, and John Bonds, who took up where Alex Grosvenor left off. In preparing the fourth edition of *Sail and Power*, Captains L. W. Hewlett, Stephan Woodall, S. E. (Skip) Wright, Don McCrory, John Bonds, and Commander Chip Barber and members of their staff provided support and insight into the new Navy 44s and the new class of yard patrol craft. In particular, the authors would like to thank Charles Ogletree, John White, Jack Quinn, Louise Burke, Lieutenants Kenneth Rome and Lee Price, Steve Podlich, Dan Rugg, and Gary Brodie for their assistance with updates to the sailing portions of the book and Warrant Officer Dave Fannon, ENCS Ernest Patterson, BMC Michael J. Harris, and Jack Reynolds for their considerable help in preparing the new chapters on the yard patrol craft. We would also like to thank the staff of the Division of Professional Development at the Naval Academy and the many YP craftmasters and their fine crews from the Naval Station Annapolis who granted the authors frequent access to their craft and answered numerous questions. In addition, the authors wish to thank Contemporary Books, Incorporated, for permission to use many drawings from my books *Hand, Reef, and Steer*, two diagrams from the *Racing-Cruiser*, and one from the *Cruiser's Compendium*. Also, we are grateful to the International Marine Publishing Company for allowing the use of drawings from my books *Sailing in Windy Weather* and *Sailing at Night*.

Richard Henderson

Sail and Power

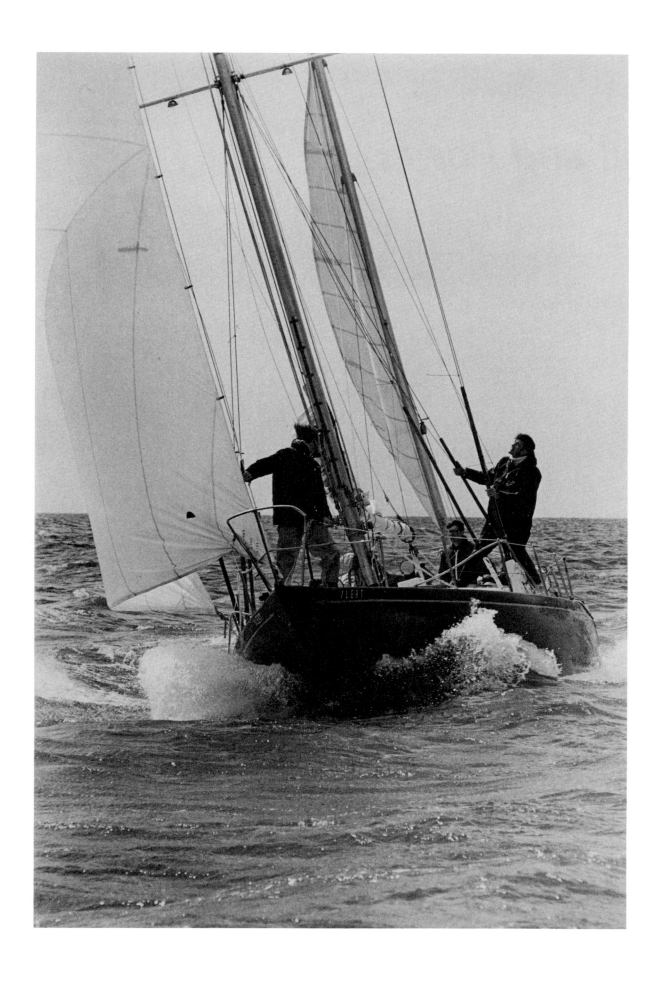

1.
Terminology

A prime prerequisite to boat handling is the ability to use the correct nautical language. The language of the sailor is not an affectation, but a traditional and functional means of communication. Improper use of nautical terms by a sailor is not only lubberly, but it can result in dangerous misunderstandings. As Joseph Conrad wrote in *The Mirror of the Sea*: "To take liberty with technical language is a crime against the clearness, precision, and beauty of perfected speech."

Since the boating novice is apt to be confused by an initial overdose of nautical terms, this chapter will serve merely as an introduction to the subject. More terms will be introduced in subsequent chapters, and all are indexed at the end of the book. When a new term is first introduced in the text, it will be italicized and explained or defined, and because definitions will seldom be repeated, the reader should familiarize himself with each new term the first time it is used.

To begin with, boats are traditionally thought of as being feminine, and they are referred to as *she* or *her*. A boat's front is her *bow* or her *fore* part, and her back end is her *stern* or *after* part. When we move towards the bow we say we are going *forward*, but when moving towards the stern, we are going *aft*. When one object on a boat lies farther aft than another object, we say the first object is *abaft* the second. Facing forward, the left side of a boat is the *port* side, while the right is the *starboard* side. *Amidships* is the middle of a boat, halfway from side to side or from bow to stern. *Athwartships* means across a boat, as opposed to *fore and aft*, from bow to stern. The *thwarts* or seats in a rowboat run athwartships, but the *keel* or main structural member at the bottom runs fore and aft.

Figure 1-1 shows the system used for expressing *bearings* or directions in which objects are observed from a boat. If an object lies *on the port beam* it is said to be *abeam*, at right angles to the keel (on the port side in this case). Should the object lie halfway between *dead ahead* and abeam, it is *broad on the bow*, or if halfway between abeam and *dead astern*, *broad on the quarter*. As the diagram shows, the distance around the boat is divided into 32 *points*, 8 points from dead ahead to abeam, and 8 points more to dead astern, or a total of 16 points halfway around the boat. If a buoy or some other object bears between dead ahead and broad on the bow, we say it bears one, two, or three points on the bow.

1-1. Directional terms. The same system is used on the starboard side.

If it bears between broad on the bow and on the beam, it is one, two, or three points forward of the beam. From abeam to broad on the quarter, the object bears one, two, or three points abaft the beam; while from broad on the quarter to dead astern, it bears one, two or three points on the quarter. This is explained in the diagram.

Figure 1-2 deals with boat nomenclature. The boat illustrated is a typical, traditional, sloop-rigged, deep-keel *day sailer* (without any living accommodations and intended for short-range sailing), having a *ballasted* or weighted keel. This kind of boat with her simple sloop rig is often called a *knockabout*. When we step on a boat we *board* her or go *aboard*. If we should drop or throw something over the side, we throw it *overboard*. Any part of the boat that extends beyond or is attached outside of the *hull*, the main body of the boat, is said to be *outboard*. If the object is inside the hull or near the boat's center it is said to be *inboard*.

When we board a knockabout we step on her *deck*, the flat surface at the top of her hull. Where the deck joins the *topsides* or upper sides of the hull, there is a low *toe rail* to prevent the *crew*, those who man the boat, from sliding overboard when the boat is *heeled*, tipped by the force of the wind when sailing. On small open boats (without decks), the extreme top of the sides is called the *gunwale* (pronounced gun'l). The large opening in the deck abaft the mast that accommodates the *helmsman*, who steers the boat, and the crew is called the *cockpit*. The fore-and-aft benches in the cockpit are called *seats*.

The knockabout is *sloop*-rigged—having one *mast* (vertical pole) supporting two sails, the *mainsail* and the *jib*. The mainsail's *foot* or bottom is secured to the *boom*, a horizontal pole hinged at its forward end to the mast with a fitting called the *gooseneck*. Poles used to spread sails are called *spars*. The sails are *hoisted* or pulled up the mast with *lines* (ropes) called *halyards*. They are pulled in or let out with lines called *sheets*. Halyards and sheets collectively are called *running rigging*, while the wire ropes that hold the mast upright and keep it straight are called *standing rigging*. Those wires that support the mast fore and aft are called *stays*. The *permanent backstay* is at the stern, and the *headstay* (outer stay) and *forestay* (inner stay) are at the bow. The wires that give lateral support are called *shrouds* and they attach at or near the rail to metal straps called

chainplates and on the mast to metal straps called *tangs*.

The helmsman of a knockabout steers with a *tiller*, a wooden stick or handle that attaches to the *rudder*, a flat, underwater plate hinged to the *after* (back) end of the keel. The flat after part of the stern is called the *transom*, while the overhanging part of the stern below the transom is called the *counter*. Around the cockpit there is a low railing called the *coaming*, which helps keep water from washing into the cockpit. The coamings on each side of the cockpit converge and meet just abaft the mast. Here they are raised slightly, and they are often referred

1	mainsail
2	jib
3	head
4	foot
5	luff
6	leech
7	tack
8	clew
9	battens
10	reef points
11	spreader
12	boom
13	forestay
14	headstay
15	backstay
16	shrouds
17	jib halyard
18	jibsheet
19	mainsheet
20	sampson post
21	chock
22	toe rail
23	coaming
24	bilge pump
25	tiller
26	transom
27	counter
28	rudder
29	keel
30	ballast
31	topsides
32	load water line
33	deck
34	cockpit seat
35	barney post
36	forestay plate

1-2. Sailboat nomenclature.

to as *washboards* or *splashboards*. On the bow is a *samson post* or *deck cleat* to which a docking line, anchor line, or towline may be fastened. These lines are led through the bow *chocks* (shown in the diagram) to prevent the lines from *chafing*, or rubbing the rail.

At the bottom of the cockpit there are *floorboards* on which the crew stands. Floorboards are not to be confused with *floors* or *floor timbers*, which are constructional members bolted to, and running athwartships across the top of, the keel. These members often tie in with the *ribs* or *frames*, the

framework pieces that rise from the keel upward, and to which the boat's planking is fastened. Below the floorboards is the *bilge*, the inside bottom of the boat, which often contains, but should be kept clear of, bilge water. The place at which the bottom of a round-bottom boat curves upward to become its sides is called the *turn of the bilge*. On a V-bottom boat the bottom and sides join at a definite angle, and this is called the *chine*. Constructional parts for wooden hulls are shown in figure 1-3.

On *cruising boats*, those having cabins or roofed-over shelters with living accommodations, the cabin

1	cockpit well	9	stem	17	false keel	25	deck shelf
2	companion ladder	10	rib or frame	18	rudder straps	26	carlin
3	cabin beams	11	bilge stringer	19	deadwood	27	keel bolt
4	hanging knee	12	keel	20	rudder stock	28	fastenings
5	mast partners	13	mast step	21	horn timber	29	clinker planks
6	rail	14	ballast keel	22	stern knee		or lap-strake
7	deck beams	15	floor timbers	23	doorway	30	carvel planking
8	clamp	16	cabin sole	24	bulkhead		

1-3. Hull construction.

floorboards are usually referred to as the *cabin sole*. *Bulkheads* are the athwartships walls with or without doorways. They divide a cabin for privacy, but their primary purpose is to stiffen and strengthen the hull. They are essential on fiberglass boats that customarily have few, if any, ribs. In the cabin there are *bunks* or *berths* (beds), the *galley* (kitchen), and *head* (toilet). The part of the cabin that sticks up above the deck is the *cabin trunk* or *deckhouse*. If the after end of the trunk is raised, it is often called the *doghouse*. If there is no cabin trunk, we say the boat is *flush-decked*. Holes or openings through the deck or cabin trunk that may be closed with covers are called *hatches*. The large hatchway through which we enter the cabin is called the *companionway*, and we climb down the *companion ladder*. We say we are going *below*, never downstairs. Small windows in the cabin that may be opened or closed are called *portholes*. Those that cannot be opened are called *port lights*.

Figure 1-4 shows thirteen frequently used terms that describe the shape or dimensions of a hull. The *load waterline* (L.W.L.) is the line on which the boat floats. The hull is submerged below this line. *Tumble home* is the inward curving of the topsides, while *flare* is the outward slant of the topsides, usually at the bow. *Deadrise* is the vertical distance of the upward slant of a boat's bottom. If the bottom is flat, she has no deadrise. *Entrance* is the forward part of the immersed hull, while the *run* is the after part that sweeps upward towards the stern. *Forefoot* is the immersed part of the bow, between the load waterline and the fore end of the keel. *Draft* is the distance measured vertically from the L.W.L. to the deepest part of the keel's bottom. We say that a knockabout, for instance, *draws* four feet. *Sheer* is the horizontal curve from bow to stern along the rail. With *conventional sheer* the *freeboard*, height of the rail above the water, is lower amidships than at the bow or stern. Some boats, however, have a *straight sheer*, in which freeboard is constant, or a *reversed sheer*, where the freeboard is highest amidships. *Beam* is the maximum width of a boat. The rest of the terms in figure 1-4 should be self-explanatory.

1 length overall
2 load water line
3 sheer
4 freeboard
5 run
6 overhangs
7 entrance
8 forefoot
9 deadrise
10 flare
11 tumble home
12 beam
13 draft

1-4. Descriptive terms for the hull.

A. mainsail B. jib C. foresail
D. fore staysail E. mizzen

cat

schooner

sloop

cutter

yawl

ketch

1-5. Common fore-and-aft rigs.

Today's most common sailing *rigs* (the system or arrangement of masts and sails) for *yachts* (pleasure boats) are shown in figure 1-5. All these rigs are called *fore-and-aft* rigs as opposed to *square* rigs. The latter have sails, approximately square-shaped, that hang from *yards*, horizontal spars running athwartships that may be swung fore and aft to a limited extent only. Fore-and-aft sails may be pulled into a true fore-and-aft position, and their forward edge is attached to a mast, stay, or semi-fixed location. All the sails shown in figure 1-5 are *Marconi* or *jib-headed* except the mainsail (pronounced mains'l) of the *cat boat* and the *foresail* (pronounced fors'l) of the *schooner*. The *heads* (top edges) of these sails are attached to a *gaff*, a spar that may be hoisted

aloft (high off the deck), and thus these sails are said to be *gaff-headed*. The cat boat has her mast *stepped* (put in place) far forward, and she carries no jib (the foremost sail). Like the cat boat, *cutters* and *sloops* are single-masted, but they carry jibs. The cutter's mast is stepped much farther aft than the sloop's, and the cutter often carries a *forestaysail* (pronounced forstays'l) in addition to her jib. *Yawls*, *ketches*, and *schooners* each have two masts, although the schooner may have more than two. Yawls and ketches are quite similar, except that a ketch's *mizzen* (the aftermost sail) is much larger and farther forward than a yawl's, which is almost always abaft the helm or rudder post. Notice that the schooner's mainsail is the aftermost sail.

7

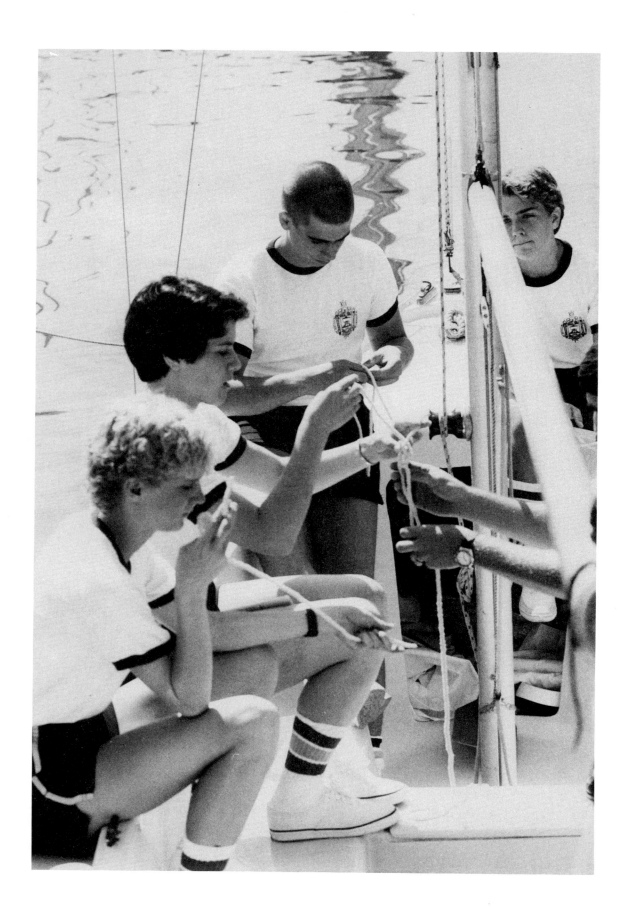

2. Elementary Seamanship

Seamanship is a very broad term used to cover a variety of subjects, including general boat-handling, steering and maneuvering, managing a vessel under adverse conditions, and *marlinspike seamanship*, or knots, splices, and general ropework. This chapter is merely an introduction to the subject; more advanced seamanship and other areas of the subject will be introduced in later chapters.

Small-boat safety

Every sailor should constantly be conscious of safety. Boating is a relatively safe activity, but hundreds of people die every year as a result of careless seamanship. To begin with, every sailor should be able to swim well. He should be able to float with his clothes on for at least five minutes.

Personal gear should include a knife and boat shoes, the latter with soles especially designed to grip a slippery deck (see figure 2-1). A knife is not only extremely useful for numerous small jobs around a boat, but it might be needed to cut a line in an emergency. The sailor's knife usually has a locking *marlinspike*, which is handy for splicing and can be inserted into the eye of a shackle screw to tighten or loosen it (see figure 2-1).

Small open boats should carry Coast Guard-approved life preservers (at least one for each person on board), an anchor and anchor line, a large bailer or bucket for removing bilge water, and oars with oarlocks or a paddle. In addition, a small day sailer should have a *chart* (nautical map) of the local area, tools (at least a screwdriver and pliers), a horn or whistle, spare parts (shackles, pins, etc.), a small compass, extra line, waterproof tape, twine, lubricating oil, a sponge, and a flashlight.

Many small boats, particularly certain *dinghies* (small, open rowing or sailing boats, often used as tenders and carried aboard larger vessels), have little initial stability. Boarding one of these boats

9

folding marlinspike

2-1. Boat shoes and knife.

should be done with caution. To some extent, stability can be judged by looking at the hull form. A flat-bottomed skiff or a beamy dinghy with flotation tanks on either side should be fairly stable or *stiff*, as sailors often say, but a boat with a narrow bottom and slanting sides, the dory form, will tip quite easily, or be *tender*. Never board any kind of small boat by stepping on her gunwale, and never jump aboard. Keep your weight amidships as much as possible. Avoid standing up in a small boat, and don't overload her, especially when the water is rough.

A   blade vertical

Basic rowing

With the increasing use of the outboard motor for small boats, there seems to be a diminishing interest in the skill of rowing. Handling a boat with oars, however, is one of the basics of good seamanship, and no one can call himself an accomplished boatman until he has learned to row well. To acquire this skill, he must not only have instruction but regular practice.

B   begin to twist
                                      or feather blades
                                      for extra power

2-2. Rowing.

The simple principle of the rowing stroke is shown in figure 2-2. In step A the oarsman, with arms extended in front of him and the oar handles held side by side, dips the oar blades into the water. In step B he pulls the oar handles towards his chest and leans backwards slightly. This action causes the blades to move aft, which naturally makes the boat move ahead. At the end of this stroke, the blades are lifted from the water and are then brought back to the position shown in step A.

Notice in step B that the blades enter the water almost vertically, but as they are pulled aft, they are twisted somewhat, which adds much to the power and effectiveness of the stroke. This is called *feathering* the oars. When the blades leave the water at the conclusion of step B, they should be almost flat or horizontal and remain in that position until just before they enter the water again.

A common mistake made by beginners is to raise the oars out of the water with the blades vertical, which usually results in the oarsman being splashed with spray, or to dip the blades in the water when they are flat or horizontal. This often results in the oarsman losing his balance and falling over backwards, since the blades will not *catch* or have any resistance against the water.

Another sure way of recognizing a beginner is to seem him use the "paddlewheel stroke." This is

when the oarsman lifts the blades up high in the air and then sinks them unnecessarily deep in the water so that the oar blades describe great circles like windmill sails. Actually, the blades should be sunk only deep enough to get a good bite in the water, and on a calm day they should be lifted only a few inches above the surface.

When carrying one or more passengers in a dinghy, see that the boat is properly *trimmed*, so that she is not excessively down by the bow or the stern. This sometimes involves moving the oarlocks to another thwart, but it makes a tremendous difference in the ease with which the boat may be rowed. A boat should generally be trimmed so that she is slightly lower at the stern than at the bow.

Turning a rowboat is accomplished by pulling harder on one oar than on the other. A quick turn can be made by dragging one oar or even reversing the stroke direction of one oar while the other is driving the boat ahead. Backing down is done by reversing the stroke direction of boat oars. When landing alongside a vessel or pier, do not land bow first but turn the boat (into the wind if possible) so that you land side to side. *Unship* or take in the oar on the side that will face the vessel or pier in plenty of time. The other oar may be dragged with the blade held vertically to make the boat turn. When within several feet of landing, *unship your oarlock* which faces the side of the vessel or pier. Failure to do this has caused many gouges in the topsides of boats. Keep the outboard oar in use to hold the boat steady until all passengers have disembarked. Before leaving the boat, be sure oars and oarlocks are unshipped and stowed. Oars should be stowed flat normally with at least one end under a thwart. Be sure the oarlocks are lashed to the boat so that they won't be lost.

Rowing in the conventional manner requires that the oarsman face aft; thus, a final word of advice is that he should constantly turn his head around to look where he is going. To facilitate holding a straight course, try, if possible, to line up a near object aft with a distant object aft so that you have a range along which you can sight.

Capsizing and righting

Although capsizing can usually be avoided with proper care, all small dinghies and boats with *centerboards* (a fore-and-aft board or plate that can be lowered through a trunk or well on the centerline to increase the boat's lateral resistance, as in figure 3-7) are subject to turning over. Most boats capable of being capsized, and all small rowing or sailing boats at the U.S. Naval Academy, have built-in flotation to prevent sinking after a capsizing or swamping. The cardinal rule after turning over is to *stay with the boat.* Even if you are an excellent swimmer, hang onto your capsized boat and don't strike out for a "nearby" shore. Distances can be deceptive when you are in the water, wind and current are hard to predict, and you have a much better chance of being spotted when you are with your boat.

To recover from a capsizing, the overturned boat must be *righted* or turned upright, and then she can be bailed out. A small nonsailing dinghy will sometimes *turn turtle* or completely upside down. She can usually be righted easily, however, if you lean backwards, grip the bottom or keel with your fingers, and exert pressure downwards at the gunwale with your knees or feet. A sailboat is usually more difficult to right because the weight of her mast and wet sails must be lifted up out of the water. Most sailboats will lie on their side with the sails resting

on the water's surface, but some with extreme beam, excessive flotation, or metal masts that can fill with water may have a tendency to turn turtle. Try not to let any sailboat turn bottom side up, because in this position she is very difficult to right and is subject to damage. If the water is shoal, her mast may get stuck in the mud. To avoid turning turtle, stand on the centerboard immediately after capsizing. If another crew member is present, have him attach a float, a life preserver for instance, to the masthead. This float should be made fast to the halyard, in such a way that the float may be hauled down after the boat is righted and bailed out.

As soon as possible after capsizing, don life jackets. Some small boats carry Coast Guard-approved kapok cushions in lieu of life jackets. The cushions with long grab straps may be worn over the chest and stomach and one handle strap around the neck and the other around a leg so that the hands are left free. Don't put one of these cushions on your back as it will tend to float you face down. Although cushions are legally allowed as PFDs (personal flotation devices) on boats less than 16 feet in length, and they are even allowed as Type IV (throwable) PFDs on larger craft, they are inferior to life jackets, ring buoys, or other devices that are designed for no other purpose than to keep a person afloat, face up.

Not long after capsizing, equipment will begin to float out of the cockpit and start to drift away. Try to gather it up and lash it or otherwise secure it to the boat, but do not swim any great distance away from the boat in pursuit of a floating object. The bailing bucket should be tied to the boat with a *lanyard* (short rope).

Figures 2-3 and 2-4 show the procedure for righting a small sailboat. Lowering the sails will make the operation much easier. (With some very small modern sailboats having ample flotation, it is not necessary to lower the sails before righting. See section on Lasers in chapter 7.) The sails should be loosely *furled* and *stopped*, rolled or bundled up and tied to the boom, and also the mainsheet should be pulled tight and cleated down to prevent the boom from falling off the deck. Lower the centerboard if it is not already down and climb up on it. Stand on the centerboard with your feet near the boat's bottom to prevent the board from breaking, and then lean backwards while holding on to the boat's rail or gunwale. With sails down, the boat should roll back

11

upright. Since the waterfilled boat will have little stability, she may want to keep rolling beyond the vertical and capsize again in the opposite direction. Once she is upright, it is a matter of splashing, rocking, or bailing the water out of the cockpit with a crew member on each side for counterbalance. If the boat has ample flotation, the crew member on the windward or upwind side can climb aboard and bail much more effectively. If you are alone, you may be able to board the boat by climbing over her stern. Should a rescue craft come along, try to right your boat before accepting help, because a boat coming alongside a capsized sailboat can damage the rigging and get a floating line caught in her propeller. If the water is very cold, however, immediately board the rescue craft before your boat is righted. The rescue craft should never attempt to tow a capsized boat

until she has been righted. More will be said on the subject of rescue from a motor boat in the chapter entitled "Boat Handling under Power."

Basic hull stability

To understand why some small sailboats will capsize and others will not, we must understand the relationship between the *center of buoyancy* (CB)

2-4. A buoyant boat capsized. The sailor has climbed onto the centerboard immediately to prevent the boat from turning turtle. Notice that he has put his weight fairly close to the boat's bottom to avoid bending or breaking the board. It will not be necessary to lower sail to right a boat this small.

12

2-3. Righting after capsizing. If float (life preserver, for example) is fastened to masthead to prevent boat from turning upside down, secure float to halyard so that it can be pulled down after boat is righted.

and the *center of gravity* (CG). The center of buoyancy is the center of all forces keeping the boat afloat, in effect the geometrical center of the underwater volume of the hull. The center of gravity is the center of the boat's weight and all weights on board (including the crew). The positions of the CB and CG for typical centerboard boats and keel boats having ballasted (weighted) keels are shown in figures 2-5, 2-6, and 2-7. It can be seen in figure 2-5 that as the boat heels, the CB shifts to leeward to the center of the submerged hull. Since the CG acts downward and the CB acts upward, there is a force called a righting moment attempting to keep the boat upright.

It is important to understand the concept of a force moment, since it plays an important role in both stability and boat balance (to be discussed in chapter 6). A moment can be thought of as a rotating force acting on a lever arm some distance from the axis of rotation. The magnitude of the moment is found by multiplying the length of the arm by the force acting in a direction that is perpendicular to the arm. If you were using a lever to lift a 200-pound rock, for example, you could figure that more than 50 pounds of downward force would be needed at the end of a lever measuring four feet from the fulcrum (axis of rotation) to the lever's end in order to lift the rock. This same sort of rotating force occurs when a sailboat heels, as the forces acting through the CG and CB create the righting moment. The farther the two centers are apart, the greater the righting arm (corresponding to the lever arm) and therefore the greater the boat's stability.

All boats derive form stability from the shifting of the CB to leeward when heeling occurs, and the greater the boat's beam, the farther the shifting of the CB at moderate angles of heel. When a centerboard boat reaches a high angle of heel, however, the gap between the two centers becomes narrower. This reduces the arm length—as shown in figure 2-5—until the CG is directly over the CB, and any further heeling will result in a capsize. On the other hand, a keel boat develops a long righting arm, not only through her beam but through her deep ballast, which keeps the CG low.

Figure 2-6 and 2-7 show the approximate positions of the CB and CG of the Naval Academy knockabout and the 44-foot Luders yawl, two fairly typical keel boats. It may surprise some readers that the CG is above the CB; nevertheless, a normal keel

13

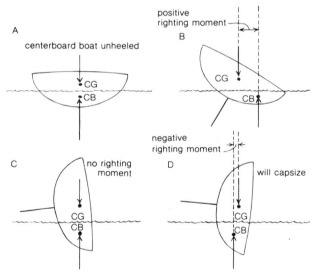

2-5. Center of buoyancy and center of gravity for a centerboard boat.

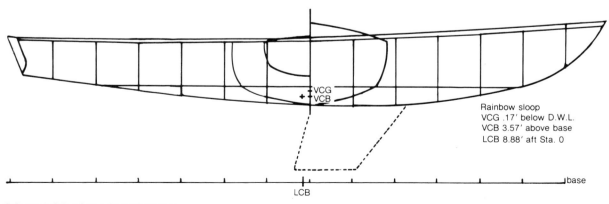

Rainbow sloop
VCG .17' below D.W.L.
VCB 3.57' above base
LCB 8.88' aft Sta. 0

2-6. CG and CB of the knockabout.

2-7. CG and CB of the Luders yawl.

30' W.L. Yawl, MK II
VCG .65' below D.W.L.
VCB 4.64 above base
LCB 16.25 aft Sta. 8

boat's CG is considerably lower than that of an unballasted centerboarder. This feature—together with reasonably high freeboard—gives the keel boat a greater *range of stability*, meaning that it can heel a great deal farther than a centerboarder without capsizing.

Typical keel boats have about one-third to one-half of their *displacement* (total weight) consigned to keel ballast, and this will normally result in a CG that is positioned at or slightly below the load waterline (contact line where the water meets the hull). This relatively low CG coupled with a proper hull form will give the yacht sufficient stability to right from an extreme (mast in the water) angle of heel. A stability range of at least 120 degrees is desirable for an offshore yacht.

Figure 9-6 is a graph showing the approximate curve of righting moments through various angles of heel for the Navy 44. This curve indicates that at a heeling angle of 130 degrees the boat still has a positive righting moment tending to rotate the yacht back to the upright position.

Basic marlinspike seamanship

Rope is almost constantly in use on all boats, particularly sailboats, and so learning to knot and handle it is of prime importance. Every sailor should know at least the basic knots shown in figure 2-11, and he should learn to make a *whipping* and an *eye splice* shown in figures 2-12 and 2-13. Of course, he should also know how to cleat and to coil lines. These operations are shown in figures 2-8, 2-9, and 2-10.

A variety of fibers are used for making rope: manila, hemp, linen, sisal, and coir, but presently the most popular rope fibers are the synthetics—nylon, Dacron, and Kevlar. These are exceptionally

Method B may be used on a halyard but a sheet should never be hitched unless a slippery hitch is used.

2-8. Belaying on a standard cleat.

2-9. Slippery hitching on a cleat.

strong, very resistant to chafe, and will not rot. Nylon is excellent for anchor or tow lines because it is quite elastic, but this characteristic makes it poor for most other uses. Dacron has very little stretch and therefore is very good for sheets and halyards. Although tremendously resistant to stretch, Kevlar has proven somewhat brittle and subject to sun degradation and chafe. These problems are minimized when Kevlar is used as a core with a covering or sheath of Dacron.

In cleating a line it is customary to start off with a round turn on the cleat and then to follow this with criss-cross wraps, as shown in figure 2-8A. Finishing off with a hitch, as shown in 2-8B assures that the line will not jump off its cleat. This is a

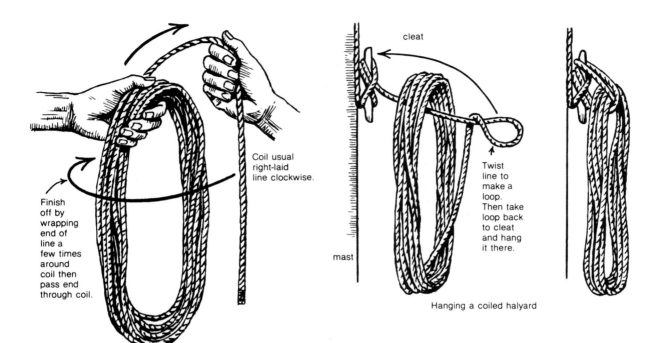

Coil usual right-laid line clockwise.

Finish off by wrapping end of line a few times around coil then pass end through coil.

cleat

mast

Twist line to make a loop. Then take loop back to cleat and hang it there.

Hanging a coiled halyard

completed coil

2-10. Coiling lines.

dangerous practice, however, if the line has to be released in a hurry, because it will often swell and jam when wet. Synthetic lines are not as likely to swell, but it is a good practice never to hitch a sheet unless a slippery hitch (figure 2-9) is used.

The knots illustrated in figure 2-11 are self-explanatory. They are shown tied loosely for clarity but should be pulled tight. The square knot is used most often to tie reef points or *sail stops* (sail lashings usually of cloth). The hitches shown are most often used to secure a line to a post or part of the rigging. When it is necessary to prevent the knot from sliding, a rolling hitch is used. The sheet bend is the best simple knot for joining the ends of two lines, while the fisherman's bend makes a line fast to the ring of an anchor. Undoubtedly the most essential knot is the bowline, which is used for a great variety of purposes, such as attaching sheets to the jib or making a line fast to almost any object. The great advantage of a bowline is that it cannot jam.

Whipping consists of wrapping the end of a line with twine to keep it from unraveling. There are several ways to do this, but the one illustrated, called *needle whipping*, is probably the most permanent. It requires a heavy sailmaker's needle and twine. It consists of a series of round wrappings of the thread followed by diagonal weavings of the thread along the *lay* or twisting of the rope strands. This is explained in figure 2-12.

There are several kinds of splices but the *eye splice* illustrated (figure 2-13) is probably the most useful. The first series of tucks or interweavings of the strands (A, B, and C in the diagram) is the most difficult. Step 3 often gives the beginner the most trouble, but difficulty can be avoided if it is kept in mind that the strands are always tucked from right to left. In step 3 the entire splice is turned over, but strand C is still tucked from right to left. In making the tucks, be sure that no two ends go through the same strand openings. A splice in a synthetic line should have at least four series of tucks. After the first series, it is a simple weaving operation where A, B, and C each go over their neighboring strand and under the following strand. Before turning in the last series of tucks, the splice should be tapered. This is done by cutting about half the fibers out of each strand prior to tucking them. After the last tuck, pull each strand end tight and cut it off flush with the rope. To give it a smooth, finished appearance, roll the splice under your foot. Ragged whiskers may be burnt off with a match.

Overhand Knot

Square Knot
(correct)

Granny Knot
(incorrect)

Figure Eight Knot

A QUICK, SURE WAY TO TIE A BOWLINE

hold
loosely

standing part

A

pull
back and up

end of line

loop will
form

B

end now
to left of
standing part

pass end under
standing part
and up through
loop

C

finished
bowline
(pull tight)

16

extra hitch
for safety

Clove Hitch

an extra wrap
around post is
often desirable

Two Half Hitches

will
not
slip

Rolling Hitch

Sheet Bend

anchor
ring

Fisherman's Bend

2-11. Knots, hitches, and bends. (All knots are shown tied loosely for clarity, but they should be pulled tight.)

1

large needle

heavy thread
or twine

end of thread

overhand knot

2

under strand

end of
thread

3

Weave thread
back and forth
following lay
of line.

under strand

4

Finish off with two half hitches around
thread. Pull knot tight and down between
the strands. Cut off.

cut line

Put needle
through strand

2-12. Whipping.

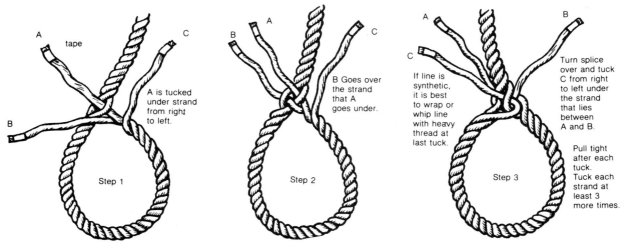

2-13. Eye splice for 3-strand twisted line. (The first series of tucks are illustrated.)

In addition to the seaman's knife with its small spike (figure 2-1), there are several other basic tools used by sailors. The twine used for the whipping shown in figure 2-12 is commonly coated with beeswax (in stick or block form) to prevent drying and rot. The work with the large sail needle is made easier by using a *palm* (a thick leather band that fits around the hand and holds a sewing thimble next to the palm of the hand), which performs the same function as a seamstress's thimble. A large marlin-spike made of tapered steel is used for opening the wire strands when splicing wire rope. Since the metal marlinspike may damage fiber line, a similar device called a *fid* is made of wood and is used exclusively with fiber line. Both these tools are shown in figure 2-14. A special metal fid in the form of a long hollow tube is used in conjunction with a small metal pusher (figure 2-14) to splice braided synthetic lines made of nylon or Dacron. Splicing braided line is entirely different from splicing three-strand twisted line (figure 2-13). The technique for splicing braided line is adequately explained in the instruction booklet that accompanies each splicing kit.

While modern synthetic lines in some respects make the work easier on board a sailboat, their increased strength does not ease the burden placed on the crew attempting to adjust the rigging or trim a large sail. A mechanical advantage is gained through the use of a number of different devices. A *turnbuckle* (see figure 6-15) is a simple opposing-screw arrangement that can provide tremendous power in adjusting standing rigging. Geared

2-14. Splicing aids.

winches come in a variety of sizes and also provide significant mechanical advantages when hoisting or trimming sails. A very common method of obtaining an increase in power is the use of a combination of line and blocks to form a *tackle* (pronounced tay-kle). Figure 2-15 shows two examples of tackles and the resulting theoretical mechanical advantage. Notice that mechanical advantage is determined by the number of rope parts at the block that moves.

It is important to handle and care for all lines properly. Not only will proper care make them last longer, it will also give your boat a smart, seaman-like appearance. The following tips will help keep lines in excellent condition.

• Keep all lines clean. Wash dirt or sand out with clean, fresh water. Never use detergent on natural fiber lines. A very mild liquid soap can be safely used on synthetic lines. Always rinse thoroughly and allow line to dry before stowing.

• Coil lines neatly without kinks. A kink, especially under a load, can quickly weaken fiber line and it will ruin wire rope.

2-15. Tackles.

• Use chafing gear to prevent fraying. Never work a line over a sharp or rough surface.

• Use the right line for the job. Make sure that the blocks are the correct size for the line in use. One rule of thumb is that a block's sheave diameter should be at least six times a Dacron line's diameter.

• When a line or wire rope becomes worn, do not hesitate to replace it. Never endanger a crew member or a piece of equipment by using line that is not capable of handling a strain.

In addition to various types of line, wire rope is commonly used on board sailboats for both standing and running rigging. Wire rope is described by the number of strands and the number of wires in each strand. A 7 × 19 wire rope has 7 strands with 19 wires in each strand. For a wire rope of the same diameter, a 7 × 19 rope is much more flexible than a 7 × 7 rope, which has only 7 wires in each of its 7 strands.

Because of the heavy loads placed on wire rope, it is important to handle wire carefully and conduct frequent inspections for broken wires or signs of excessive strain.

Anchoring

One of the basic skills required of a seaman is the ability to anchor a boat properly. Anchoring and handling *ground tackle* (anchors and related gear) is a lengthy subject, and only the rudiments will be touched on here.

Figure 2-16 shows anchor nomenclature and a group of the most commonly used, nonpermanent anchors. These are the ones that are put over temporarily and, when not in use, are pulled up and usually stowed on the forward deck. Permanent

2-16. Anchors.

anchors, such as the mushroom type, are often left on the bottom for years and are used for offshore moorings. Of the anchors shown in figure 2-16, only the Navy anchor is unsuitable for a small boat. It has no stock so that it can be pulled into the hawse pipe of a large ship. In the smaller sizes, the Navy anchor doesn't have enough weight to dig in properly, and it can turn over on its side. The yachtsman's anchor is subject to fouling if the boat swings in a complete circle around her anchor so that the line wraps the exposed fluke (see figure 2-17). The Danforth anchor is a popular anchor in the Annapolis area, for it is especially effective in soft sand and sticky mud. One must be sure, however, that this anchor does not merely lie on the bottom, but that it digs in thoroughly by putting a strain on the line.

The holding power of an anchor depends on two principal factors aside from its design: its weight and the *scope*, or length of its *rode* (anchor line). The greater the anchor's weight and the longer the scope, the greater the holding power. As a general rule, the most effective length of scope is six or seven times the depth of water where the boat is anchored. A simple rule of thumb for weight is one-half pound per foot of overall length for a light anchor (one used only for temporary anchoring in fair weather—sometimes called a "lunch hook"), and one pound per foot of overall length for a heavy anchor (one expected to hold for a considerable time in heavy weather). Of course, this rule depends on the type of anchor. Danforth and plow anchors generally need not be as heavy as the yachtsman's type.

When preparing to anchor a small boat, stand in the bow with the neatly coiled anchor rode shackled or tied with a fisherman's bend to the anchor ring (see figure 2-11). Then the boat is headed into the wind, and when she has stopped all forward motion, gently lower the anchor into the water making sure your feet are well clear of the coiled rode. Never throw it in, for it can easily foul its line. When the anchor's crown strikes bottom, let the boat drift backwards and *pay out* or *veer* (let out) scope

gradually, keeping a slight tension on the line until the anchor flukes can bite into the bottom. Then *snub* the line, stop it from running out by taking a turn around the bow cleat. This should cause the flukes to dig in deeply and make the anchor hold effectively.

When raising or *weighing* the anchor, pull in on the line until it lies straight up and down. At this time, there is a minimum of scope and the anchor has little if any holding power. Then a hard tug up on the line will pull the anchor's *shank* (shaft) up and break the flukes out of the bottom.

If the anchor is difficult to break out, additional force may be applied to the line, once it is straight up and down, by taking a turn or two on the cleat and *swaying* on it or applying force laterally by pulling up on the line between cleat and chock.

19

2-18. Trip line.

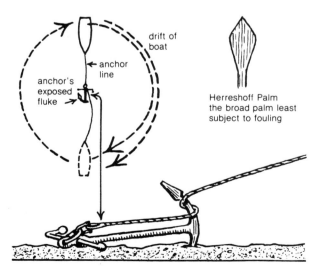

2-17. Fouled anchor.

Such action, making the rode from chock to anchor completely vertical, is a most persuasive technique. Or the anchor may be sailed out by heaving in to up-and-down, belaying, and setting a headsail and backing it to blow the bow off. With the anchor line straight up and down, any motion of the boat applies tremendous force to the line.

Sufficient scope is important for holding power because when the line makes a small angle to the bottom (when it is nearly parallel to the bottom), this causes the anchor to dig in. In many of today's crowded harbors, however, it is not always possible

to let out all of the scope one might desire. It is of the utmost importance to have *swinging room*, or room to clear other anchored boats no matter what direction the boats are swung by the current or wind. Small boats should be anchored in shallow water so that they will need relatively little scope to achieve the aforementioned ideal scope to depth-of-water ratio (6 or 7 to 1). If large boats cannot veer sufficient scope due to crowded conditions, their heavy anchor should be used. When veering scope be sure to take into consideration and allow for the rise or fall of the tide. After anchoring, take bearings on various stationary objects so that these may be checked later to see if the anchor is holding.

If the bottom is rocky, it is often wise to rig a *tripping* line, a line tied to the anchor's *crown* (see figure 2-18), so that the anchor can be broken out flukes first in the event it becomes jammed between two rocks. The free end of the trip line is often buoyed (attached to any floating object) and left overboard to float directly above the submerged anchor. Then if the anchor cannot be pulled up with its rode in the conventional manner, it can be done with the trip line.

Elementary steering

Small boats are usually equipped with tillers for steering, while larger boats usually have steering wheels. A normal tiller turns the rudder directly, its length providing leverage, while a wheel sometimes has a worm gear or is rigged in some other way to give the *helmsman* (steersman) a mechanical advantage. As a rule, tillers are quicker and more sensitive, while wheels are more powerful and require more movement to make the boat respond.

Figure 2-19 shows how the turning of the *helm* (wheel or tiller) affects the turning direction of the boat. A helmsman turns his wheel in the direction he wants his boat's bow to turn when moving ahead. This is similar to steering an automobile. But with a tiller the reverse is true. The helmsman pushes the tiller in the opposite direction from that in which he wants his bow to turn. When moving backwards the stern follows the direction in which the rudder is turned.

An important point the helmsman should always keep in mind is that the rudder is effective in turning the boat only so long as the boat is moving ahead or backwards. The more *way* she carries, or the faster she moves, the more effective is the rudder. Steering

2-19. The helm.

20

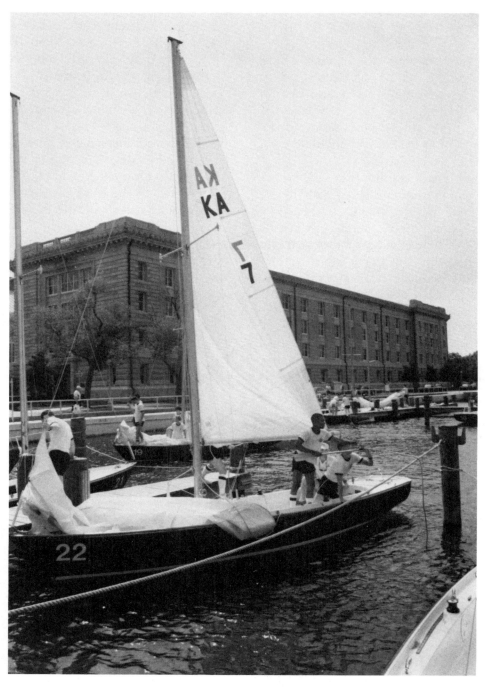

2-19a. A knockabout landing downwind. Coming into the pier bow first with sails still up risks damage to the boat should the wind pick up. There is also the risk that the main boom will jibe suddenly in which case the young midshipman reaching for the stern lines may find himself overboard in Santee Basin.

a boat under power with single or twin screws and also the fine points of helmsmanship under sail will be discussed in subsequent chapters.

Shoal water

A good seaman always attempts to familiarize himself with the waters in which he sails. Knowledge of local topography, water depths, landmarks, the location of shoals, channels, and channel markers are readily obtained from government charts. Every boat above the size of a small dinghy should carry a chart of the area in which she sails.

A study of local charts will not only give proper orientation, but will prevent needless groundings. It is especially desirable to avoid running aground in a deep-keel boat. Center-board boats usually can be freed quite easily by raising the board, provided care is taken to see that the boat is not blown farther onto the shoal, but keel boats are more difficult to get off. If a keel boat is driven hard aground, it is usually a wise practice to lower all sails so that the boat will not be driven farther aground. After the situation is studied and the exact shape of the shoal is obtained from the chart or from soundings taken around the boat or from a dinghy, then if the boat is headed in the right direction, sail may be hoisted and sheeted in to cause heeling and to drive her off.

There are several methods of freeing a boat. If she is small she might simply be poled off. If she has power she might be backed off or driven ahead after the vessel has been turned the right way. Placing all crew members on the bow often lifts the keel off the bottom. Of course, heeling the boat by sail, by putting the crew on one side, or putting a man on the end of the main boom and then swinging it out over the water help decrease the boat's draft. An effective method of freeing a vessel is by *kedging.* This means that an anchor is carried out some distance from the vessel by someone wading or going in a dinghy; then the anchor line is hauled on or winched in until the vessel is moved. If all these methods fail, it is necessary to wait until the next high tide or for a tow from a power boat. Remember that a power boat can damage a boat that is hard aground when trying to tow her off.

Shoals and channels are marked with *buoys* or channel markers. The end papers of this book show the principal types of navigational aid buoys, including the unlighted and soundless ones. It will be noted that they are painted solid or in combinations

of red, green, and white (orange and yellow colors are used for regulatory markers and special aids—see end papers). The age-old expression for understanding U.S. channel markers is *Red, Right, Returning.* This simply means that when returning to the harbor (from seaward), you leave a red marker on your right or starboard side. Of course, the reverse is true when leaving the harbor. The red is left to port. The end papers show *mid-channel* and *junction* or *obstruction* buoys also. The former mark the middle of a channel and should be passed fairly close on either side. Junction or obstruction buoys can be passed on either side but should be given a wide berth. As shown in the illustrations, the topmost band of color indicates the preferred channel. In compliance with a modern international agreement, black has now been changed to green on navigation aids, with the exception that mid-channel

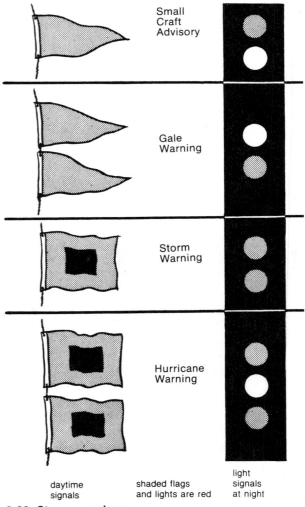

Small
Craft
Advisory

Gale
Warning

Storm
Warning

Hurricane
Warning

daytime
signals

shaded flags
and lights are red

light
signals
at night

2-20. Storm warnings.

markers have had their vertical stripes changed from black to red. New red and white mid-channel buoys will be spherical in shape or have a red spherical top mark.

Local weather

In the Annapolis area during the summer months, the most frequent wind direction is from the south or southwest. This area is frequently under the influence of the *Bermuda high*, a region of high barometric pressure near Bermuda whose winds rotate around the high in the clockwise direction. This brings warm, moist, southerly winds up the Chesapeake Bay. Warm weather is often relieved by highs dropping down from Canada. These usually bring cool, dry, gusty northwest winds. Low-pressure cells with their cyclonic or counterclockwise rotation bring bad weather. These travel, as does the entire weather system in the middle latitudes, from west to east. Exact paths of the lows depend on the direction of the steering currents aloft, but they often curve toward the northeast as they approach the Atlantic coast. When these lows pass to the north of Maryland, they cause only brief but sometimes violent periods of stormy weather, and these are usually accompanied by rapidly *veering* winds (changing clockwise) that bring clear northwesters. But when the low-pressure cells pass to the south of Maryland, the wind *backs* (changes counterclockwise) from south to northeast and often there is a lengthy period of stormy, rainy weather. This is

known as the "northeaster," and it will often last for two or three days, perhaps longer.

Figure 2-20 shows storm-warning signals that are displayed at most boating centers or weather stations and, of course, at the Naval Academy. These warnings should be heeded. Even if conditions look clear at the moment, it is likely that bad weather will soon arrive. Quite often boats are used when the small craft warning is up, but this should be done only with great caution and never by a beginner sailing alone.

The greatest weather hazard in the Annapolis area is the frequent midsummer thunderstorm. It results from the rapid rising of warm moist air that is lifted aloft either by local surface heating or the approach of a *weather front* (the boundary between air masses of different temperature and moisture content). Usually, thunderstorms associated with a *cold front* (cold air advancing against warm air) passing over your locale produce the most severe weather, and they can be very widespread along most of the front, which is usually oriented northeast to southwest.

Occasionally, a *squall line* of low, dark clouds will precede the front and bring a short-lived but particularly vicious blow. It is comforting, however, that weather forecasts will nearly always give ample warning of approaching fronts. Sometimes a less stormy *warm front* (warm air advancing against cold air) will arrive in advance of the cold front. High-altitude and then lower-altitude clouds filling in generally from westerly or southwesterly directions can give plenty of visual warning (see the accompa-

2-21. Cirrus clouds, "mares' tails" (over 25,000 ft.) If thick, often advanced forerunners (24 hours or more) ahead of a front.

2-22. Altostratus clouds (about 19,000 ft.) Gray sheet often warns of approaching warm front.

2-23. Cirrocumulus, "mackerel sky" (over 20,000, ft.). Can predict approach of warm front in unstable air.

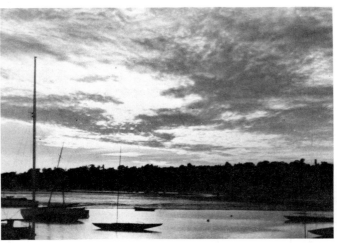

2-25. Altocumulus clouds (over 12,000 ft.). Like sheep. Can warn of cold front in unstable air.

2-24. Cirrostratus clouds. Whitish sheet (over 20,000 ft.) often causing halo around sun. Can warn of approaching warm front.

2-26. Nimbostratus clouds (with fractostratus below). Dark rain cloud (about 3,000 ft.).

nying photographs of clouds). Thunderstorms at the cold front especially can produce spectacular towering clouds called *thunderheads* or *cumulonimbus clouds* (shown in figure 2-30). They are fully or past fully developed after reaching an altitude that causes their tops to fan out into flaring anvil shapes.

Local surface heating produces the generally less severe air-mass thunderstorm. These storms most often develop over land to the west and they usually occur in the late afternoon of a hot, humid day. Frequently, they can be spotted a long way off because of vertical cloud developments that may form into distinctive thunderheads. Cumulus clouds, the white, puffy "cotton wool" type of clouds, indicate fair weather, but be alert for a thunderstorm when they begin to tower upward and especially when they turn dark at and under their bases. Static on the radio will also indicate that a thunderstorm is not far away.

If you are far away from a protected harbor, reef down, set a small staysail or lower sails when a thunderstorm seems imminent. Don't wait for the last moment before taking action. When sail is lowered, it may be advisable to anchor or run before the wind under bare poles provided there is plenty of sea room to leeward. Boats with powerful engines can power slowly into the wind. Thunderstorms can be severe, but usually they don't last long.

2-27. Stratus clouds (about 1,500 ft.). Gray sheet.

2-29. Cumulus clouds (over 4,000 ft.). Fair weather unless extreme towering up.

2-28. Stratocumulus clouds (with cumulus below). Globular rolls (about 8,000 ft.).

2-30. Cumulonimbus clouds. "Thunderhead" (thunderstorm cloud) can reach height of cirrus.

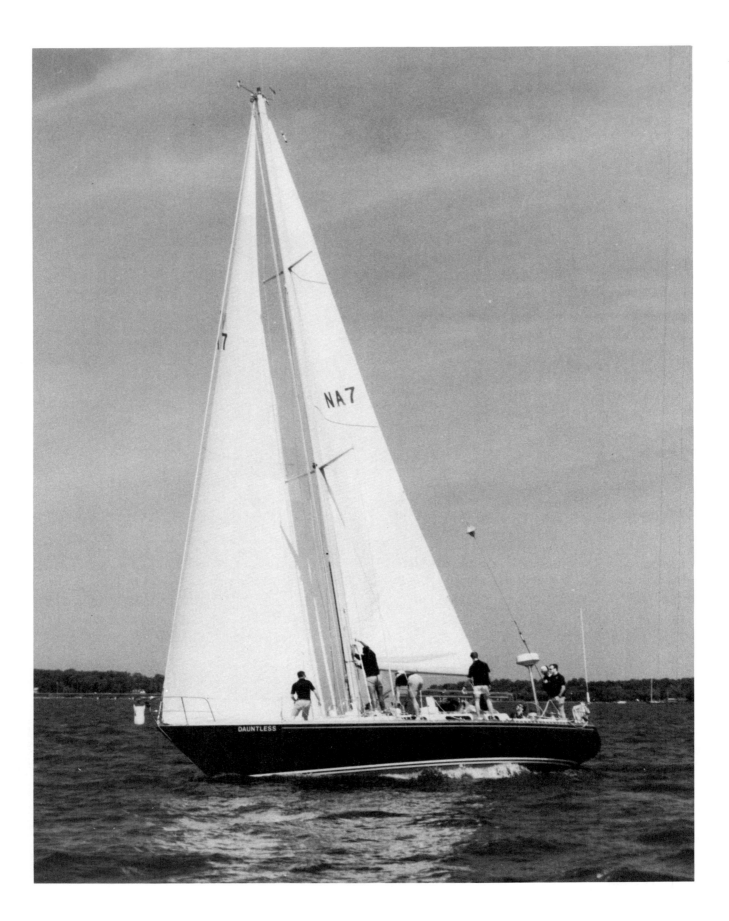

3.
Theory of Sailing

*T*his chapter describes the general fundamentals of sailing, such as the points of sailing, general sail positions, turning maneuvers, elementary aerodynamics, and hydrodynamics. Practical details, specific procedures, and the fine points of steering will be discussed in chapter 5.

Points of sailing

A sailboat's directional heading with respect to the wind is called her *point of sailing*. There are five basic points of sailing: *running, broad reaching, beam reaching, close reaching*, and *beating*. These are illustrated in figure 3-1 along with the approximate sail positions for each point of sailing. When the wind is from dead astern to approximately two points on the quarter (see figure 1-1), the boat is running. When the wind comes from two points on the quarter to approximately one point abaft the beam, the boat is broad reaching. With the wind abeam the boat beam reaches. But with the wind ahead of a half point forward of the beam until the wind bears approximately three points forward of the beam, the boat close reaches. When the average boat sails with the wind broad on her bow, she is beating. As the wind comes from farther ahead, the sails begin to flap or *luff*, and they become increasingly ineffectual until the boat is *head to wind* (headed directly into the wind) at which time they are totally ineffectual. A sail that is not luffing is said to be *full* (full of wind). The term *luffing* can be applied to the boat herself, as well as to individual sails.

The sail positions shown in figure 3-1 are achieved by adjusting the sheets, which pull the sails in towards the boat's centerline or allow them to swing out to a more athwartships position. When the sheets are pulled in, the sails are said to be *trimmed*; when the sheets are let out, they are said to be *cracked, started, eased*, or *slacked*, to use the terms in increasing order. The word *trim* is also used to indicate whether or not a boat's sails are in exactly the right position for a given point of sailing, a vital factor for speed—as, for example, "Her sails are well trimmed," or "She is trimmed too flat."

In figure 3-1, the topmost boat is shown running. She is also said to be sailing *before the wind, off the wind* (also applied to reaching), *sailing free* (with sheets eased), or sailing with *a fair wind*. The illustration shows her jib hanging limply because the wind is from nearly dead astern, and the mainsail is

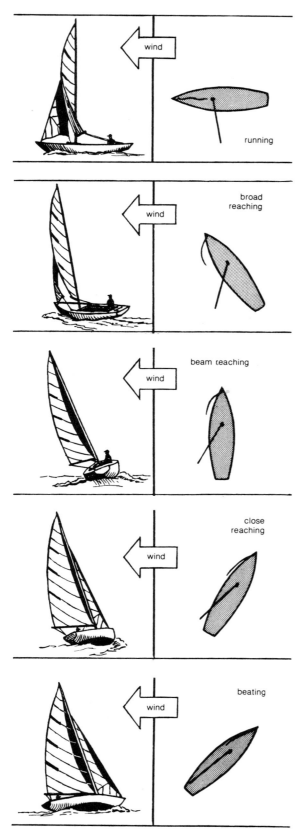

3-1. Points of sailing.

blanketing the jib or blocking off its wind. The jib might be made to *draw* (fill with wind) if it were *wung-out* or pushed out on the opposite side from the mainsail. The boat then would be said to be sailing *wing and wing.* (The term is usually applied to a schooner sailing with her foresail and mainsail on opposite sides.) Notice in the illustration that the *main boom* (mainsail's boom) is let out so that it is almost athwartships. When a boat is running with the wind nearly dead astern, her boom is let out as far as it will go without chafing against the aftermost shroud. As the boat is gradually turned towards the wind, her sheets are slowly trimmed until, when beam reaching, her jib and main boom are about halfway in, roughly 135° to the wind or 45° to the boat's centerline. When close reaching, the sheets are trimmed still closer, somewhere between the beam-reaching position and about 10° from the boat's centerline.

On various points of reaching, especially when beam reaching or sailing slightly farther away from the wind, boats usually achieve their highest sailing speeds. Some lightweight boats having planing hulls and flattish bottoms will gain considerable speed by *planing* or lifting up on their bow waves and skimming over the top of the water rather than plowing through the water like a boat with a *displacement hull* (a deep, heavy hull). At most times when boats are traveling at their highest speeds, sails must be trimmed a little flatter than normal. This is due to the *apparent wind,* which is explained in figure 3-2. Since the boat in the diagram is moving ahead at 4 *knots* (nautical miles per hour), she causes a 4-knot wind from directly ahead. The *true wind* or actual wind is 9 knots from slightly forward of the beam; thus the apparent wind is a resultant of these two forces (boat-speed wind and true wind), which in this case is blowing at 11 knots from broad on the bow. Sails should always be trimmed to the apparent wind. To put it very simply, the faster a boat travels (unless dead before the wind), the closer her sheets are trimmed. This becomes especially evident when the true wind is nearly on the beam.

When beating, a boat's sails are trimmed quite flat. Very generally speaking, this is to within about 10° or less of the boat's centerline. (Mainsails are sometimes trimmed to the centerline.) The average modern boat intended for day sailing or cruising-racing can be made to sail to within about 45° of the wind. Strictly cruising types will not sail quite this close, but some racers will sail closer than this. Progress directly to *windward* (upwind) is accomplished by making a series of *tacks* or zigzag courses towards the windward destination. On the zig course, the sails lie to one side of the boat, and on the zag course, they are swung by the wind to the boat's opposite side. With the sails on the port side and the wind blowing from the starboard side, the boat is said to be on the *starboard tack*, and she is on the *port tack* when the wind comes from the port side and the sails lie to starboard. Obviously, with an average boat that can *point* or head up to within 45° of the wind, the highest heading on the starboard tack will be at right angles to the highest heading on the port tack. Other terms for beating are *sailing close-hauled*, *sailing to windward*, *tack-ing*, *on the wind* or *hard on the wind*, and *by the wind*. *Full and by* means beating, with the emphasis on keeping the sails full rather than on heading as close to the wind as possible.

Turning maneuvers

There are two ways a boat can turn from one tack to the other. First, she may *luff* or *head up* into the wind and continue turning through the eye of the wind until her sails fill on the other tack. This is called *coming about* or *tacking*. Secondly, she may *bear off* or head away from the wind until the wind is dead astern and then continue turning until the wind suddenly swings her sails across to the boat's opposite side. This is called *jibing* or *wearing ship*. To put it simply, a tack is an upwind turn with the bow swinging across the wind, causing the sails to flap; but a jibe is a downwind turn with the stern crossing the wind and the sails suddenly filling on their opposite sides and swinging across the boat. These turns are illustrated in figures 3-3 and 3-4. Specific procedures involved in tacking and jibing will be discussed in chapter 5.

Prior to making the final tack when beating towards a windward destination, there arises the question of exactly when to tack in order to arrive at the mark in the quickest time without sailing any extra distance or having to make additional tacks. If the boat can be brought about at the proper moment so that she is pointed directly at the windward mark on her final tack, she is said to be *fetching* or *laying* the mark. This final approach tack that brings the close-hauled boat directly to the mark lies on an imaginary line called the *fetch line* or *lay line*. This is explained in figure 3-5. If the helmsman tacks his boat too soon, before reaching the fetch line, then

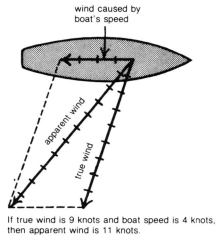

wind caused by
boat's speed

apparent wind

true wind

If true wind is 9 knots and boat speed is 4 knots,
then apparent wind is 11 knots.

3-2. Apparent wind. (Any mention of wind in this book refers to true wind unless specifically called apparent wind.)

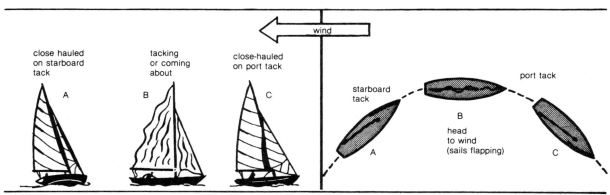

wind

close hauled
on starboard
tack
A

tacking
or coming
about
B

close-hauled
on port tack
C

starboard
tack
A

head
to wind
(sails flapping)
B

port tack

C

3-3. Tacking.

he has *under-stood* the mark (he is heading *below* it) and must tack twice again. On the other hand, if he waits too long before tacking and sails beyond the fetch line, he has wasted time and distance. In this case he has *over-stood* the mark (he is heading too far *above* it). Assuming that the boat can sail to within 45° of the wind, then the proper time to tack is when the mark bears abeam or lies at right angles to the boat's centerline if there is no *current* (flow of water). The foregoing discussion has been concerned with only the final windward tack when approaching a mark. Planning windward courses and the general strategy of beating will be discussed in chapter 11, "Basic Racing."

Aerodynamics of sailing

It is not difficult to understand how a boat sails before the wind. To quote an old saying of sailors, "Even a haystack will sail downwind." But understanding how a boat can sail against the wind is not so easy. The force that drives a sailboat to windward is similar to the force that gives *lift* to an airplane's wing or, to be more exact, a glider's wing. The sail is actually an airfoil stood on end. The airfoil characteristic is achieved by building a fore-to-aft curve into the sail, which we call *draft* or *camber*. This curve is parabolic, having its greatest amount of curvature closer to the *luff* or forward edge of the sail, but the curvature flattens out or becomes straighter near the *leech*, the after edge of the sail. An explanation of how draft is built into a sail will be given in chapter 6.

When a boat reaches or beats to windward, the air flows around her sails from luff to leech. As the wind meets the luff, it splits to form a flow to windward of the sail and another flow to *leeward*

(on the downwind side). The molecules of air to leeward move faster than those on the opposite side of the sail as they race back to rejoin each other at the leech. The reason for this behavior, according to a recent revival of the circulation theory of lift, is that a circular current around the sail partially blocks the flow to windward and reinforces it to leeward. In any event, the flow is considerably faster to leeward, and the pressure is lowered on the sail's downwind side. This is in accordance with a physical law known as Bernoulli's principle, which tells us that in fluid motion wherever the velocity of flow is high the pressure is low. A simple demonstration of this principle is shown in figure 3-6. Water (or any fluid) is forced through a constricted pipe with pressure gauges in three locations as illustrated. The pinched-in area of the pipe accelerates the flow and lowers the pressure as shown by the lower water level in the middle gauge.

The lowering of pressure on a sail's leeward side creates a suction pull that acts approximately at right angles to the surface of the sail (see figure 3-7). If the boat is close-hauled, most of this suction pulls the boat to leeward and a small amount pulls her forward. All boats intended for windward sailing, however, are designed to resist making *leeway* or being blown sideways but to resist as little as possible being pulled forward; thus, for the most part, the suction pull can only draw the boat ahead.

Resistance to making leeway or *lateral resistance* is supplied by one of the means illustrated in figure 3-8. All Naval Academy boats are equipped with either keels, centerboards, or daggerboards the last two of which may be raised or lowered as shown in the diagram. Figure 3-9, which compares a child on a sliding board to a boat close reaching, perhaps

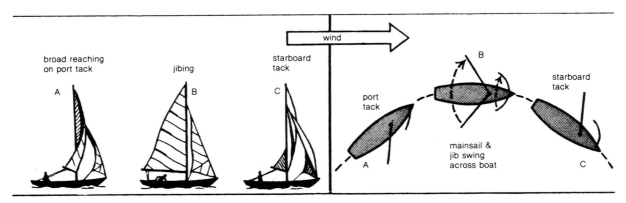

3-4. Jibing.

gives the simplest explanation of how lateral resistance forces the boat ahead.

Up to this point we have been discussing the aerodynamic forces acting on a single sail, but the addition of another sail in close proximity to the first has a considerable influence on these forces. A correctly trimmed jib set just ahead of a mainsail creates a narrow space, often called a *slot*, between the jib's leech and the mainsail's luff. Much of the airflow passing to leeward of the mainsail must first pass through this slot. (See figure 3-10.)

The mainsail is, in at least one respect, made more efficient aerodynamically by the jib because a proper slot helps eliminate a turbulent flow on the mainsail's leeward side. Air passing through the slot helps keep the flow attached to the lee side of both the jib and main. When sails are improperly adjusted and the slot is too narrow, however, the mainsail will be *backwinded* and detrimentally affected as shown in figure 3-11. Some quite recent investigations into sailing aerodynamics have given rise to the theory that the mainsail is not only affected beneficially for the most part by the jib, but more important, the jib is helped considerably by the mainsail. The latter alters the wind flow against the forward sail to allow higher pointing ability, and also more flow is diverted to the jib's leeward side to increase the velocity and thus lower the pressure there.

The fine points of jib trimming will be discussed in chapter 6.

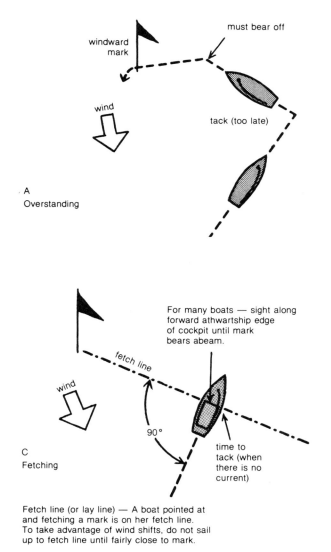

A
Overstanding

C
Fetching

Fetch line (or lay line) — A boat pointed at and fetching a mark is on her fetch line. To take advantage of wind shifts, do not sail up to fetch line until fairly close to mark.

3-5. Fetching the windward mark.

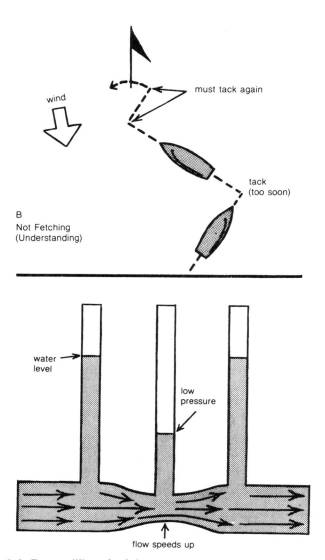

B
Not Fetching
(Understanding)

3-6. Bernoulli's principle.

Sail and Power

Sails alter the direction and velocity of the wind flow. They may do this in a beneficial way so as to give maximum drive to a boat, or they may do it in a harmful way so that they lose their drive or disturb the wind of other sails in close proximity. We have seen examples of disturbed air in the blanketed jib of figure 3-1 and the backwinded mainsail of figure 3-10. *Backwind* is the turbulent air that flows off a sail's leech and is deflected to windward. The blan-

ket or *wind shadow* is the resulting turbulence and partial absence of air when the wind is blocked off or a *lee* is formed by a sail or other object. More will be said about disturbed air in chapter 11, "Basic Racing."

Sails can only reach maximum effectiveness when they have the proper shape, especially draft, and when they have the correct *angle of incidence* (angular position to the wind). Figure 3-12 shows two close-hauled boats sailing about 45° to the wind. On one boat, the mainsail is not trimmed close enough and its luff extends too far to leeward so that the wind blows directly on its lee side causing it to luff or flap. In this case, the sail is said to be *luffing*, and the forward component of the suction pull is partially destroyed. The other boat in the diagram shows the other extreme; it is trimmed too flat. In this case, the sail is partially *stalled*. Instead of the leeward airflow being relatively smooth it becomes detached, and *eddies* or reverse currents are formed to leeward of the leech. The most effective angle of incidence lies somewhere between the stalling and luffing angles, and this

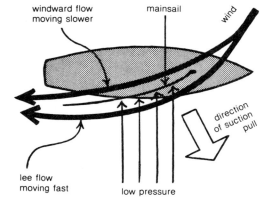

3-7. Leeward side suction.

32

3-8. Lateral resistance.

depends, of course, on the heading of the boat and the trim of her sails. This will be discussed in chapters 5 and 6.

Hydrodynamics of sailing

While aerodynamic forces are acting against a boat's sails, similar hydrodynamic forces are working against her hull and appendages (keel or centerboard and rudder) under the water. The flow of water around a sailboat's submerged appendages is also comparable to the flow of air around an airplane's wings, and the *angle of attack* or incidence that the flow makes with the axis of a keel or centerboard creates lift as well as drag forces like those acting on a wing. The angle of attack, usually referred to as the leeway or *yaw angle* on a sailboat, is a small one—normally three to seven degrees when she beats or reaches. Should the angle become much greater, leeway will be excessive, and the flow may become detached and turbulent. When this occurs the hydrofoil (underwater appendage) is partially stalled, at which time lift decreases and drag increases enormously. Figure 3-13 illustrates the lift-drag forces at work on a keel. Notice that lift acts at right angles to the water's force or flow, while drag, which is resistance to forward movement, acts parallel to the direction of the flow.

Fin keels or centerboards that have *high aspect ratios* (those that are deep but short in the fore-and-aft direction) have proven to be highly efficient, for they supply a maximum of lateral resistance at a minimum cost in resistance to headway (see figure 3-14). Such a deep, short appendage having a streamlined section has a high *lift-drag ratio*, because a long leading edge on a hydrofoil helps produce effective lift, while a short length reduces area and thus skin friction or *wetted-surface drag.* There is nothing new about high-aspect-ratio appendages, but nowadays we are seeing a greater use of short fin keels on *racing-cruising sailboats* (those types similar to the Navy 44s or other ocean racers).

Although there are advantages in short fin keels

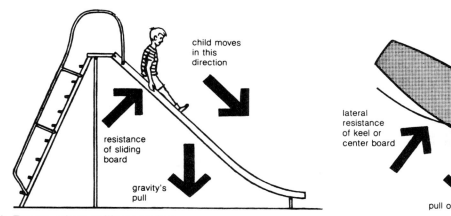

3-9. Forces when sailing upwind.

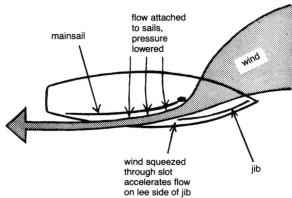

3-10. A proper jib slot.

3-11. Jib backwind.

wind direction

air flow

air flow

Luffing due to insufficient sail trim or from pointing too high.

Stalling, due to trimming the sail too flat.

3-12. Luffing and stalling.

course

water force

keel

yaw angle

center line

drag

lift

resultant

wind

3-13. Keel/water force.

34

3-14. A PJ seen out of water. This Sparkman-Stephens design exemplifies the modern racer-cruiser with a short fin keel and separated rudder. The hull shape of this particular class has been influenced by the IOR handicap rule, which has encouraged relatively shallow bottoms, great beam amidships, and a pronounced tumble home.

in terms of speed and efficiency, steering control can be adversely affected. When the keel is extremely short, steering may become overly sensitive, and the boat may be difficult to hold on a steady course. This difficulty can be alleviated, however, by separating the rudder from the after end of the keel and moving it aft as far as possible. There, the rudder can be attached to a *skeg* (a short appendage abaft the keel as shown in figure 3-8E), or it can be a free-standing *spade* rudder, which is held only by its rudder stock. This is the type used on the Naval Academy knockabouts (see figure 7-1). A great advantage in a keel-separated rudder is that its location as far aft as possible permits the maximum distance from the boat's vertical turning axis to the rudder's center of pressure. Such an arrangement gives the greatest possible arm length for steering leverage. A possible disadvantage in a separated rudder, however, is that the rudder cannot be used to give the keel camber to increase lift when beating to windward (more will be said about this when helm balance is discussed in chapter 6). Furthermore, spade rudders are subject to early stalling, and so they may require a slightly different steering technique. This will be discussed briefly in the section on knockabouts in chapter 7.

The two principal sources of underwater drag are from wetted-surface resistance and *wavemaking resistance*. The former source predominates at low to medium speeds, while the latter causes the most drag at high speeds. When a boat moves through the water, her bow pushes up a mound of water and other waves are formed farther aft. As boat speed increases, the length of these waves increases until the boat sits in the *trough* (hollow) between two waves with one *crest* (peak) at her bow and another crest at her stern. At this point, the boat has insufficient length to make longer waves, and so her speed theoretically is limited to the speed of a wave equal in length to her waterline. This is called *hull speed*, and it is equal to 1.34 times the square root of her waterline length. In actuality, it is possible for a boat to exceed her hull speed but only if she planes or partially planes, lifting up and riding on the surface of the water as described earlier. Light-displacement dinghies such as the Lasers and 420s plane very easily in good breezes, but even relatively heavy-displacement ocean racers can plane to a very limited extent by *surfing* momentarily in strong winds with sizable following seas.

Skin friction under water is caused not only by surface area but also by the roughness and unevenness of a boat's bottom. If the boat is to be raced, every effort should be made to obtain a smooth, fair bottom. Underwater protuberances should be minimized with the use of flush through-hull fittings, whenever possible, and the bottom should be faired with filling compounds and thoroughly sanded before application of bottom paint. When antifouling bottom paint is used on boats left afloat, it is usually helpful to sand the final coat of paint with fine wet and dry sandpaper to remove the brush strokes. A very fine film of slime may not be harmful to speed, but weeds or barnacles on a boat's bottom can be disastrous. It is more important to obtain smoothness in the forward half of the hull than the after half, because forward, the water flow is mostly *laminar* or more closely attached to the hull surface.

4.
Rules of the
Road

*O*n today's crowded waterways, it is important not only to know the various rules that govern boat traffic, but also to know which rules apply and where. Vessels making passages along the coast will very often have to comply with two sets of rules, the Inland Rules and the International Rules. The former rules apply to U.S. inland waters, while the latter apply on the high seas. The new boundary lines between inland and international waters are drawn closer inshore than the old lines, roughly parallel to the shoreline, and at the entrances to all major harbors, rivers, and bays.

Separate parts of the rules cover right-of-way situations for boats under sail and those under power. The first two sections of this chapter will discuss converging situations between sailboats, and the last section will discuss the converging of power boats. Incidentally, a sailboat using her engine for propulsion is considered a power boat. A sailboat has the right of way over a power boat except when overtaking it. Also, a sailboat must keep clear of vessels fishing* with nets, lines, or trawls, and it is against the rules to interfere with a large ship in a narrow channel. Details of International Rules and Inland Rules are shown in appendixes A and B, respectively.

Steering and sailing rules for sailboats

Formerly, rules covering the converging of sailboats were quite different for inland and international waters, but in 1981 a change brought the two sets of rules into close agreement. These are basically similar to the USYRU racing rules shown in chapter 11.

Rule 12 of the International Rules (also the Inland Rules, except for one word, "and") reads:

(a) When two sailing vessels are approaching one another, so as to involve risk of collision, one of them shall keep out of the way of the other as follows:

(i) when each has the wind on a different side, the vessel which has the wind on the port side shall keep out of the way of the other;

(ii) when both have the wind on the same side, the vessel which is to windward shall keep out of the way of the vessel which is to leeward;

---

* The phrase "vessels engaged in fishing" means any vessel fishing with nets, lines, trawls, or other fishing apparatus which restricts maneuverability, but does not include a vessel fishing with trolling lines or other fishing apparatus which do not restrict maneuverability.

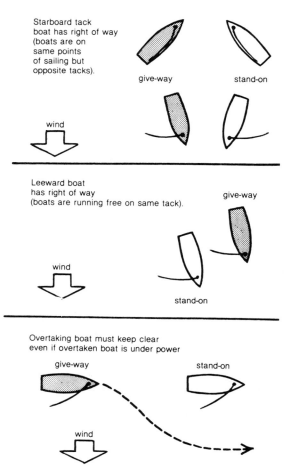

Starboard tack boat has right of way (boats are on same points of sailing but opposite tacks).

give-way   stand-on

wind

Leeward boat has right of way (boats are running free on same tack).

give-way

wind

stand-on

Overtaking boat must keep clear even if overtaken boat is under power

give-way   stand-on

wind

4-1. Right-of-way situations for boats under sail under the Inland and International Rules.

4-2. On opposite tacks. NA 9 has the right of way, of course, since she is on the starboard tack, and she must hold a reasonably steady course so that the port tack yawl can take evasive action. There should be a crew member stationed at the mainsheet of the port tack boat in case the mainsail needs slacking to help the boat bear off. This is especially important in fresh winds.

(iii) if a vessel with the wind on the port side sees a vessel to windward and cannot determine with certainty whether the other vessel has the wind on the port or on the starboard side, she shall keep out of the way of the other.

(b) For the purposes of this Rule the windward side shall be deemed to be the side opposite to that on which the mainsail is carried, or in the case of a square-rigged vessel, the side opposite to that on which the largest fore-and-aft sail is carried.

A situation not covered under the preceding rules would arise if a sailboat overtakes another sailboat on the same tack and the same point of sailing when neither is to windward of the other. In this case, the overtaken boat is privileged (now called the stand-on vessel) and has the right of way. The overtaking boat is burdened (now called the give-way vessel) and must keep clear. In any converging situation the privileged, or stand-on, boat must hold

her course until there is no longer any danger of collision. If a sailboat is equipped with an auxiliary engine, the only time she is considered a sailboat is when she is propelled by sail alone.

Common sense and courtesy should be exercised at all times on the water. A sailboat skipper should never demand his right of way when converging with a large ship in constricted waters. In fact, as said earlier International Rules and Inland Rules strictly forbid sailboats to hamper large power vessels in a narrow channel. Boats that are not racing should attempt to stay out of the way of boats that are racing, even though the former may have the right of way. (Boats racing can usually be identified by a class flag attached to the permanent backstay and often a similar flag attached at the bow.)

Lights and shapes (International Rules)

Sailboats over 23 feet long, and all powerboats, except those under 23 feet whose maximum speed does not exceed seven knots, are required to carry red, green, and white navigation or running lights when underway between sunset and dawn, in order that they may be seen by other vessels. These navigation lights include red and green side lights, a white stern light (also a yellow stern light if towing a vessel), and a forward mast light (called "mast-head lights" in the rules). A sailboat under 23 feet long only needs to show a flashlight or lantern under the International Rules, but if possible, she should display normal running lights. To reiterate, these rules also permit a powerboat under 23 feet with a maximum speed of seven knots or less to carry only a single all-around white light, but she should have additional side lights if possible. Running lights have definite sectors or arcs of visibility, which are shown in figure 4-3. If there is any possibility that a boat will be taken offshore, she should be fitted with lights that meet the requirements of the International Rules, because these lights must be used on the high seas and they may be used on inland waters. Figure 4-4 shows International Rule lighting for motorboats and sailboats. When the engine is running on an auxiliary sailboat, the 20-point white light forward must be turned on, but when under sail alone, this light must be off.

Under International and Inland Rules, there is a lighting option that enables a sailing vessel under sail to carry (in addition to her normal side lights and 12-point stern light) a 32-point red light over a 32-point green light at the masthead, sufficiently separated so as to be clearly distinguished and visible for two miles (on vessels less than 164 feet). A further option for boats under 65.6 feet is the carrying of the stern light and side lights combined

4-4. Required lights for motorboats and auxiliary sailboats under International Rules. These are required on the high seas and may be shown on U.S. waters. A sailing vessel may also show optional red over green 32-pt. lights with 2-mile visibility (if she is under 164 feet long) at or near the top of the mast. A sailing vessel under 65.6 feet has the option of carrying the stern light and side lights combined in a single multisector light at the masthead. If this is done, the above-mentioned red over green optional lights may not be used. A power-driven vessel under 39.4 feet has the option of carrying an all-around white light and side lights.

in a single multisector light at the masthead. This option has been added because normal side lights are often obscured by sails. The Inland Rules also allow a high-intensity flashing white light that may be used as a distress signal. If you are on a sailboat, it is often wise to shine a flashlight on the sails when converging with another vessel at night.

If you are in shallow water and decide to anchor at night, you must turn off the running lights and display an anchor light. This is a white, 32-point

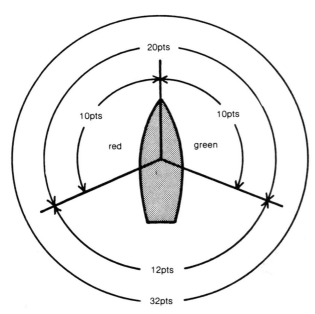

4-3. Arcs of visibility for running lights.

light normally displayed on the forward part of the vessel.

A careful lookout should be kept at night, even in uncongested waters. When you spot another vessel, her approximate course can usually be determined by looking at her lights. If the after white light can be seen, she is moving away from you. If her red and green lights show simultaneously, she is headed directly toward you. If only one red or green light can be seen, you are looking at her side or at her starboard or port bow as she approaches you at an angle. The course of a large ship can be determined with further accuracy by looking at her masthead and range lights, which are white mast lights, one forward and one aft with the after light being higher than the forward one. If these lights are widely separated, the ship is not headed very close to you; if they are close together, the ship is headed toward you. When the masthead light and range light line up vertically, then obviously the ship is headed directly toward you.

When the lights of a distant vessel are spotted, the possibility of collision should be determined by taking bearings on her. If the bearing holds steady and the light becomes more and more distinct, then you are on a collision course. When the other vessel has the right of way, obviously you must change course. If you have the right of way, you hold your course, but make certain that the other boat sees you by shining a light on your sails or superstructure. In close passing situations, it is a good idea to be prepared to use a sound signal (one that cannot be mistaken for any other signal authorized in the rules), and to see that flares are readily available.

The rules of the road also require that certain black shapes be hoisted during the day. For instance, a vessel proceeding under sail with her engine running shall exhibit forward where it can best be seen a conical shape, apex downwards. Under Inland Rules this requirement is not necessary when the vessel is less than 12 meters long. Also, an anchored vessel shall exhibit in the fore part a ball shape. Details of the International and Inland Rules can be found in appendixes A and B.

Steering and sailing rules for powerboats

When operating under power, whether or not sails are set, a sailboat must comply with those regulations governing motor vessels. She is no longer a sailboat. The applicable International Rules of the Road and Inland Rules of the Road are in appendixes A and B. Therefore, the explanation here will be brief.

In addition to knowing which boat has the right of way in meeting, overtaking, and crossing situations, the skipper of a boat under power must be familiar with the maneuvering whistle signals prescribed by International and Inland rules.

The diagrams in figure 4-5, A–F, illustrate the six basic situations encountered by vessels under power under Inland Rules, the rules that apply in Chesapeake Bay. International Rules are similar except that the overtaking vessel sounds a different signal (see Sound and Light Signals in appendix A). The proper reaction to each situation should become instinctive to the skipper.

In figure 4-5A, both vessels are passing to port of each other, which is preferable in this situation. Each has signified her intent by one short blast of the whistle. At night the masthead light and red (port) side light would be visible to each.

In figure 4-5B, both vessels are headed directly toward each other. In this situation, the rule is that each shall turn to starboard and pass on the port side of the other. Each has signified her intent to do so by one short blast of the whistle. Both are burdened and both are obliged to alter course. At night, both side lights (red and green) and the masthead light would be visible to each before altering course, and the red side light and masthead light would remain visible after course alteration.

In figure 4-5C, the vessels are going to pass to starboard of each other. Each has signified this to be her intent by two short blasts of the whistle. Both are burdened, but neither has to alter course. At night, the masthead light and green (starboard) side light would be visible to each.

Figures 4-5D and 4-5E illustrate overtaking situations. (To be considered an overtaking, rather than a crossing, situation, the overtaking vessel must be at least two points or more abaft the beam of the overtaken vessel.) In both cases the overtaken vessel (b) is privileged and must maintain course and speed, while the overtaking vessel (a) is burdened and must alter course. In figure 4-5D, vessel (a) should signify intent to pass to port of vessel (b) by sounding two short blasts. If such a passage is clear, and acceptable to vessel (b), she should answer with two short blasts and the passing will be effected. In

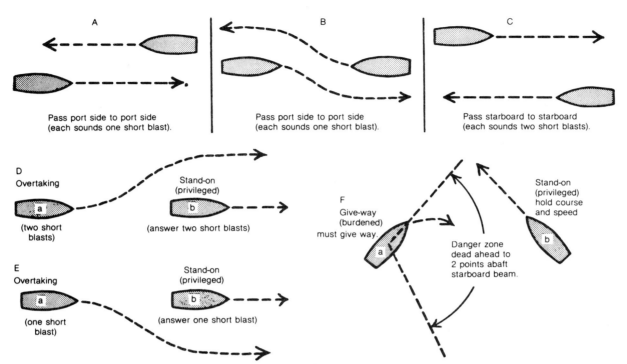

A

Pass port side to port side
(each sounds one short blast).

B

Pass port side to port side
(each sounds one short blast).

C

Pass starboard to starboard
(each sounds two short blasts).

D
Overtaking

a

(two short blasts)

Stand-on
(privileged)

b

(answer two short blasts)

E
Overtaking

a

(one short blast)

Stand-on
(privileged)

b

(answer one short blast)

F
Give-way
(burdened)
must give way.

a

Danger zone
dead ahead to
2 points abaft
starboard beam.

Stand-on
(privileged)
hold course
and speed

b

4-5. Inland Rules for motorboats or sailboats under power. When vessels meet head on or nearly so, each vessel passes on the port side of the other unless the courses of such vessels are so far to starboard of each other as not to be considered meeting head and head.

figure 4-5E, vessel (a) should signify intent to pass to starboard of vessel (b) by sounding one short blast. If the passage is clear and acceptable to vessel (b), she should answer with one short blast. If, in either case, the initially proposed passage is dangerous, vessel (b) should sound the Inland Rules danger signal of five or more short blasts. After passage is clear, vessel (b) would sound the proper answering signal.

In the crossing situation diagrammed in figure 4-5F, two vessels are approaching each other at right angles or obliquely in such a manner that there is a risk of collision. Vessel (a), which holds the other to starboard, is burdened and should maneuver to keep clear either by altering course to starboard, slowing, or both. She may signify this to be her intent by sounding one short blast. Vessel (b), which holds the other to port, is the privileged vessel and is obliged to maintain course and speed. This intent should be signified by one short blast. At

night, vessel (a) would see the masthead light and red (port) side light of vessel (b), while (b) would see the masthead light and green (starboard) side light of (a). In studying these situations, see Rule 16 through 18 of the Inland Rules (appendix B).

For vessels under power, the Steering and Sailing Rules of the International Rules of the road are essentially similar to those of the Inland Rules. Rules 13, 14, and 15 of the International Rules (see appendix A) cover the overtaking, head-on, and crossing situations shown in figure 4-5. The terms "stand-on" and "give-way" correspond to the "privileged" and "burdened" terms used in the text above.

Although the Inland rules and the International Rules are similar in most respects, there are certain minor differences primarily in lighting and sound signals. It is therefore important that the crew of vessels proceeding offshore know the boundary lines between inland and international waters.

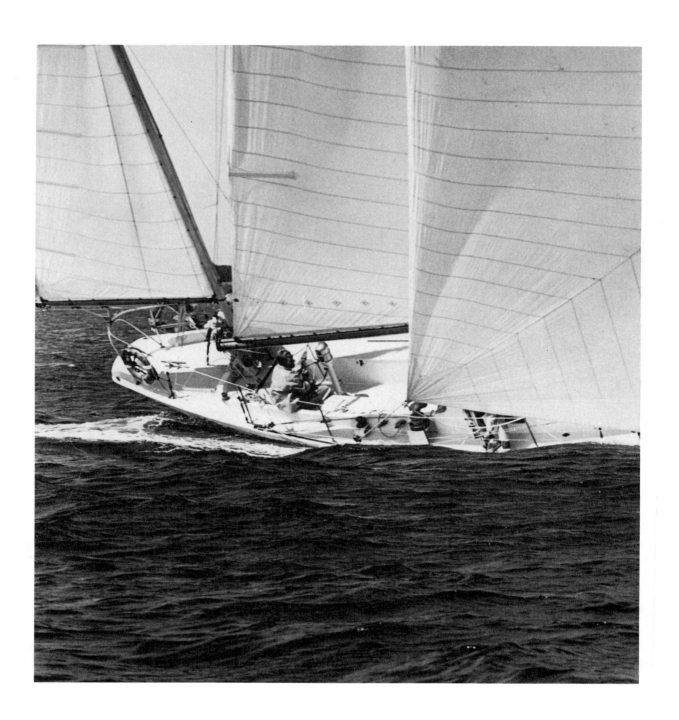

5.
Helmsmanship and Maneuvering Under Sail

A thorough knowledge of the fine points of sailing can only be acquired after a great deal of practice and experience under sail. Before actually handling a boat, however, the beginner should study the basic principles of maneuvering, helmsmanship, and sail trim. With some preliminary reading, he will learn a great deal faster and avoid many pitfalls.

Wind direction

In chapter 2 we examined the simple rudiments of steering with a tiller or wheel. Obviously, this is a prime prerequisite of sailing. Another prerequisite is the determination of wind direction. Just as you can't control a boat's heading without knowing how her steering gear works, you can't properly trim her sails without knowing from what precise direction the wind is blowing.

Wind direction can be detected by carefully observing the water's surface. Small ripples move in the same direction as the wind; however, do not be misled by the movements of larger waves. Quite often the larger waves are controlled by a previous wind, and their movement doesn't indicate the direction of a new wind that has recently *shifted* or changed its direction. Watch the movement of the smallest ripples to determine the present wind.

Other signs of wind direction are flags flying; smoke from ships, chimneys, or cigarettes; and the heeling as well as the sail trim of other boats. If anchored by the bow, boats and ships will lie with their bows pointed directly into the wind unless their heading is controlled by a strong current. The most effective means of determining wind direction and observing momentary shifts is by using wind indicators, shown in figure 5-1. The *masthead fly* and *wind sock* illustrated are carried at the top of the mast where they are either permanently secured or are hoisted into position with a flag halyard when needed. A very useful indicator is the masthead-mounted Windex vane, which has two projecting reference arms, each angled aft at about 30 degrees to the boat's centerline. These arms show approximately the boat's optimum close-hauled sailing angle, and the vane should be more or less aligned with one arm when beating. *Telltales* are short pieces of yarn, thread, or ribbon tied to the shrouds about seven feet above the deck. They are easy to watch and respond instantly to even the lightest breeze. Remember, though, that wind indicators on a moving boat do not show the true wind, but only the apparent wind.

Sight is not the only sense used to determine wind direction. Most experienced sailors develop a sensitivity to the feel of the wind. They can detect slight shifts and velocity changes by feeling the breeze on their cheeks, necks, arms, or hands. Of course, this is particularly valuable when sailing at night. More will be said of this in chapter 12.

Sailboat maneuvering at dock or anchorage

The fine points of sailing should be practiced in open water, where there is enough *sea room* (ample room for maneuvering) to hold a fairly long *board* (tack or leg to windward). But before reaching open water, a boat must be sailed from her dock or mooring, which nearly always involves tight maneuvering in crowded anchorages or other constricted areas. It is therefore very important to understand the basic principles of sailboat control. This involves *gaining way* (picking up speed), *killing way* (slowing down), turning, and holding a straight course.

Before getting *underway* (a vessel is considered underway when not anchored, made fast, or aground), a boat should be headed into the wind so that when her sails are hoisted, they will merely flap and not drive the boat ahead before she is ready to get underway. If she is at a mooring (permanent anchor), she is probably already lying head to wind, but if she is made fast to a dock or pier, she will probably have to be swung into the wind by *casting off* (releasing) her stern line. This is shown in figure 5-2. After the sails are hoisted and the boat is ready

to leave, she is shoved straight back with the rudder *amidships* (held straight or on dead center). When she is well clear of the dock, the rudder is put over to the right or left to swing the bow in the opposite direction (since the boat has sternway), as illustrated in figure 5-2 (also see figure 2-19, The Helm). The sails will begin to draw, because the boat will turn so that the wind is broad on the bow. Putting the helm over too soon will result in the boat gaining headway too soon, which might cause her to strike the dock before she can be turned away from it. After the boat has stopped drifting backwards, the helm is turned the opposite way because the boat will begin to move ahead as her sails fill. Notice in the diagram that the jib is *backed* or pulled in by its windward sheet so that it is trimmed from the wrong side. This will cause the bow to fall off, away from the wind, very rapidly. When the boat has gained headway and if she is clear of the dock, the windward jibsheet is released and the jib is trimmed on the boat's leeward side.

The same procedure is followed when a boat leaves a permanent mooring. The mooring line is simply cast off and left afloat. Getting underway when anchored involves the same basic principles. Sail is hoisted while the boat is head to wind, the anchor is hauled in until the line lies straight up and down, then the anchor is broken out and hauled aboard, the jib is backed to make the bow fall off in the desired direction, and then the sheets are trimmed in on their proper side as the boat gains headway.

wind sock (cloth) usually attached to a flagstaff

masthead fly (metal, plastic, or cloth on wire frame)

shroud

ribbon

telltales

thread

5-1. Wind indicators.

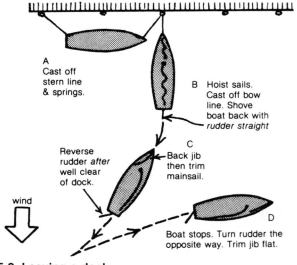

A Cast off stern line & springs.

B Hoist sails. Cast off bow line. Shove boat back with *rudder straight*

Reverse rudder *after* well clear of dock.

C Back jib then trim mainsail.

wind

D Boat stops. Turn rudder the opposite way. Trim jib flat.

5-2. Leaving a dock.

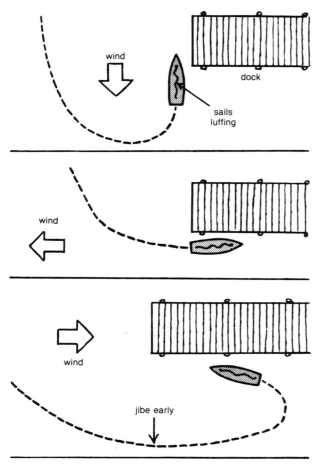

5-3. Approaching a dock under sail (in a weak current).

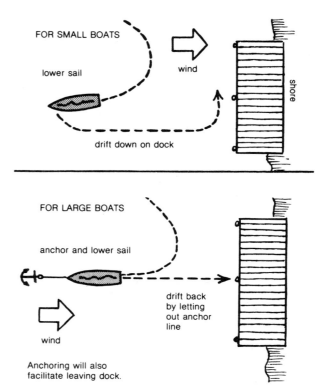

45

There are a few times when it might be advisable to hoist sail downwind instead of when head to wind; for instance, when the boat is in a very constricted docking area or if a strong current has swung the boat's stern into the wind when anchored or moored. In these cases it is best to drift with the wind or current or sail away under jib alone until the boat is clear of docks and obstructions, then head as close to the wind as possible before hoisting the mainsail.

Leaving the windward side of a dock under sail usually presents a problem. The boat must be moved so that she is headed into the wind while sails are hoisted. She might be moved by *warping* (moving her with lines) or kedging with the anchor, or by paddling if the boat is small and the wind is light. No matter how she is moved, her bow should be fairly near the wind. If she cannot be brought directly head to wind, great care should be taken to see that her boom does not strike anything on the dock and the sheets do not catch on dock *pilings* (posts) or cleats.

Figure 5-3 shows the proper approach when landing at a dock under sail. Notice that in all five situations the boat is turned into the wind and held there with sails flapping until headway is lost. This maneuver is called *shooting*, and it is also used when anchoring, picking up a mooring, or landing alongside another boat. Helm control is very important when shooting for a dock or mooring. If the wheel or tiller is turned suddenly and to its full extent, the boat's *way* or momentum is partially killed because a rudder rapidly jammed to one side acts somewhat like a brake. If it is desired to make a long shoot, the helm is eased over slowly, and the boat carries a lot of way or coasts a long distance before coming to a stop. A boat's weight or displacement will have a great bearing on how much way she carries also. A heavy boat, such as a Navy 44 or Luders yawl, will carry away for a very long distance compared to a light boat, such as a 420 dinghy or Laser. The exact distance a given boat will shoot under any given conditions will vary greatly and can only be determined by experience.

A boat's momentum also depends on conditions of wind and water. In a strong wind and rough water, a boat will carry less way. The strength and direction of the current must be noted, because naturally this will have a great effect on the boat's speed (not through the water but over the bottom).

Since the latter part of a "shoot" will be at very slow speeds, any current will affect the maneuver out of all normal proportion. A boat with a favorable current under her seems to shoot forever. Many an otherwise well-planned maneuver has been spoiled because it was only when the boat slowed down in a shoot that a small but significant current announced its presence to a surprised skipper by taking over the situation. Even the best of sailors sometimes misjudge a boat's shooting speed and distance. When this happens, if the boat is carrying too much way, do not attempt to land at the dock or pick up the mooring, but bear off, sail away, and try the approach again. Notice in figure 5-3 that the shooting boats are never aimed directly at the dock, but they are landed almost parallel to the dock or in such a manner that they can easily be turned away from the dock at the last minute if they are carrying too much way. Occasionally it is necessary to make a direct, right-angle approach to the middle of the dock so that the landing must be made bow first. This can be very dangerous in a large, heavy boat, and it should be avoided if possible. If unavoidable, however, a very slow approach should be made. It is better to have the boat stop short than carry too much way. If she stops short without quite reaching the dock, a crewman stationed on the bow can often throw a line to someone standing on the dock. In a small, light boat a fast landing, with too much way, is not quite as serious, though it is certainly most unseamanlike. A crewman can sit on the foremost part of the bow facing forward with a leg on each side of the jibstay so that he can *fend off* (push off) with his feet just before the bow makes contact with the dock. Falling short and having to make another try is far preferable to risking damage to the boat and injury to the crew.

There is another basic method of slowing a boat down to land at a dock or pick up a mooring besides shooting into the wind. This is to slack the sheets while on some point of sailing between close-hauled and a beam reach. A close reach is the optimum heading. With sheets slacked and sails luffing on a close reach, no power is being applied to the boat, and she will lose headway. If more headway is

desired during such a maneuver, the sheets need simply be trimmed back in. The amount they are trimmed back in will correspond to the amount of power applied to the boat. By alternately trimming in and slacking the sheets to achieve the desired amount of luffing, precise speed control can be attained, and the boat can be eased slowly up to a dock or mooring buoy.

The reason why a close reach is the optimum heading for this maneuver is that wind shifts can then be responded to merely by adjusting the trim of the sails, while maintaining the same heading. By contrast, if the boat were luffing along close-hauled, and the wind shifted more ahead during the maneuver, the option of trimming in for more power would be lost, and the only way to gain headway would be to head off, which would take the boat away from the desired course to her dock or buoy. If, on the other hand, the boat were luffing along on a beam reach, and the wind shifted farther aft, then the option of continuing to luff the sails would be lost, and the only way to slow down would be to head up, again heading the boat away from her desired maneuvering course. Significant wind shifts are common in harbors, where this kind of maneuvering is likely to be done.

The following basic principles of sailboat maneuvering should always be kept in mind:

• For maximum *steerageway* or rudder control, keep way on the boat. Remember that the rudder is only effective when the boat is moving.

• Quick rudder action will slow a boat, but slow rudder movement will enable the boat to carry way for a long distance.

• Heading into the wind or releasing sheets so that the sails flap will stop headway.

• Sails should be hoisted or lowered when the boat is heading into the wind.

• When maneuvering a centerboard boat, see that the centerboard is all the way down, otherwise she will make leeway, especially at low speeds.

• When making a sharp turn, allow for some stern skid. During such a turn the bow turns in one direction and the stern skids somewhat the opposite way. This is important to bear in mind when landing alongside a dock or another boat. Stern skid is more apparent on flat-bottomed centerboarders.

• When headway is lost after unsuccessfully shooting for a dock or mooring, back the jib to make

EFFECT OF A PUFF ON APPARENT WIND

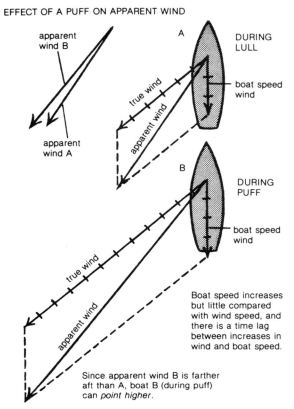

Boat speed increases but little compared with wind speed, and there is a time lag between increases in wind and boat speed.

Since apparent wind B is farther aft than A, boat B (during puff) can *point higher.*

5-4. Wind puffs. A puff is a sudden increase in the wind's velocity, usually within a small area and of short duration.

THE RADIATING PUFF OR CATSPAW

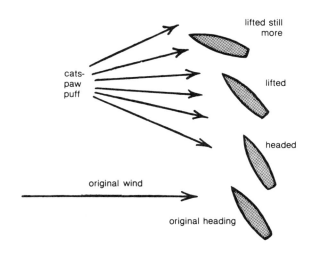

47

the bow fall off in the desired direction. If the boat has no jib, wait until she drifts backwards, and then reverse the rudder as explained in chapter 2 under "Elementary Steering."

• If the boat has too much way on when shooting for a mooring, she can be slowed by pushing her main boom forward so it goes *aback* or fills from the wrong side.

• Maneuvering in constricted areas should be done under a reasonably *balanced* sail plan. This means that the boat should neither have too much sail forward nor too much aft, but a sail plan that will permit the easiest possible steering. Balance will be discussed in the next chapter.

• Remember that a boat tends to carry a lot of way when she is heavy and is moving fast against a light wind in smooth waters. On the other hand, a light boat moving slowly against a strong wind in rough waters carries very little way.

• Remember that even a small current is the

biggest single factor affecting a boat's speed when getting underway or landing.

• The speed of a boat may be controlled precisely by putting her on a close reach and adjusting the sheets to luff the sails to produce the desired power.

Windward helmsmanship

The concern when sailing to windward is to sail the boat as close to the wind as possible but at her best possible speed on this point of sailing. If you sail her too close, her sails will begin to shake at the luffs, and you will feel her begin to slow down. On the other hand, if you bear off too far, the boat will pick up speed, but will not gain as much distance to windward as she could. Beating is always a delicate balancing of these two factors, *pointing* (heading as close as possible to the windward objective) and *footing* (sailing through the water as fast as possible). When you sail too high so that you accentuate the gain to windward at a sacrifice of speed, you are said to *pinch*; when you sail too low, at a good speed but at a sacrifice to windward gain, you sail too *full.* Usually, under normal conditions, the best windward course lies somewhere between pinching and sailing too full. Making a boat do her best to windward is always an interesting challenge. Since the conditions of wind and sea that produce the challenge change continuously, the problem of getting to windward never loses its appeal.

Some winds are relatively steady, but most winds vary constantly in direction and velocity. A temporary increase in velocity over a limited area is known as a *puff*, and it appears as a dark patch of ripples

5-5. Use of wind indicators when beating. The optimum angle is the angle between apparent wind and the boat's most efficient heading when beating. The broad angle shown might be for a cruiser beating in choppy seas.

darting across the water's surface. Most puffs allow a boat to point higher because they cause the apparent wind to blow from more on the beam. This is explained in figure 5-4. Some puffs are the radiating type, often called *catspaws*, which are also shown in the diagram. This type will force the helmsman to bear off when he first feels the puff, but then he is *let up* or allowed to point increasingly higher as he sails through the puff.

The wind nearly always fluctuates in direction as well as velocity. When the breeze blows from farther ahead (more from the bow) and forces the helmsman to bear off, this change in wind direction is called a *header*, but when it blows from farther aft (more on the beam) enabling the helmsman to point higher, it is called a *lift*. Fluctuations in direction can be detected immediately by watching the masthead wind indicator and particularly the telltales on the windward shrouds. When they swing more abeam, the helmsman should point up, but when they swing more ahead he must bear off. This is illustrated in figure 5-5.

The skilled, experienced helmsman uses all of his senses when sailing a boat to windward. In addition to watching the telltales, he watches the luffs of his sails. When they begin to flutter or luff in normal winds or sailing conditions, he is generally sailing too high and must bear off. The experienced helms-

man also keeps a constant lookout for puffs on the water on his windward bow. When the water darkens with ripples from a puff, he is then ready to head up when the boat first feels its effect. He uses his sense of hearing when listening to the sound of the bow wave. A clearly audible bow wave indicates that the boat is moving at her best speed, while only a slight murmur of the wave suggests that perhaps the helmsman is pinching slightly or perhaps the sheets could be better trimmed for more speed. A good helmsman also uses his sense of balance as well as his vision to detect a change in the boat's angle of heel. When beating, a boat should heel to leeward at least slightly, but the heel should not be excessive. For the average boat, if the lee rail begins to *bury* (dip in the water), the boat is heeling too far. This can result in loss of speed and even a capsizing in a centerboard boat. Excessive heeling can be controlled in two ways: by heading up or pointing higher, or, as a last resort, by slacking the main sheet so that the mainsail beings to luff.

Another aid to helmsmanship is luff telltales. These are usually wool or acrylic yarns taped to the jib on both sides or threaded through the sail about ten inches abaft the luff at about a third of the luff's length up from the tack and at higher and lower positions. The sail cloth is normally transparent enough to see the yarn on the leeward side as well as the windward side of the sail except in direct sunlight. Most racing jibs have a small Mylar window near the 1/3 luff length position so that the yarns can be read when the sun makes the sail appear opaque. One should try to sail so that the yarns are streaming directly aft rather than fluttering wildly or twirling around. If the windward yarn twirls, bear off, but if the leeward yarn twirls, head up a bit.

Perhaps the most important sense a skilled helmsman uses is the sense of feel or touch, often called the *tiller touch*—though, of course, it applies to steering with a wheel also. This is sailing "by the seat of the pants" or sensing when the boat is going to windward at maximum efficiency. Of course, this ability can be acquired only after a good deal of practice. The average, properly balanced boat will have a slight *weather helm* or tendency to turn into the wind in moderate breezes (this will be discussed in the next chapter). The weather helm will exert a light pull or pressure against the helmsman's hand. This pressure will increase as the wind freshens and heels the boat, or it will decrease when the wind slackens and causes a smaller angle of heel. In the former case, the helmsman should relax his pressure on the helm and let the boat point up until he senses that she is beginning to lose speed or until he sees her sails start to luff. When the helm pressure slackens, however, he should bear off slightly to see if the boat will pick up a little speed.

Good helmsmanship to windward is really a matter of experimentation. The helmsman should alternately point up or prod the wind to see if she won't sail just a little higher without slowing down, and then, as soon as she shows signs of slowing down, bear off a little to see if she won't sail a little faster.

Figure 5-6 illustrates how the helmsman uses all his senses when beating to windward. Notice that the illustration shows a useful visual sign that has not been discussed, the sagging of the jibstay. Ordinarily, the jibstay should be set up tight for best efficiency to windward, but it will always sag off to leeward slightly. When the boat is sailing full and by, the sag will be most pronounced, but when she is being pinched the stay will be almost straight. Thus, if there is considerable sag the helmsman should point up somewhat, but with little or no sag he should fall off a little. This aid to the helmsman should not be relied on in rough water because as

the boat *pitches* (rocks fore and aft), the mast will move forward and aft somewhat, causing the jibstay to slacken and tighten accordingly.

When sailing into a *chop* (a short, steep sea) the helmsman should sail his boat full and by, because wave action tends to kill headway. The boat must be given enough power to drive through the waves. Also, in very light airs the boat should not be sailed extremely close to the wind. She should be kept footing to minimize leeway and to take advantage of a stronger apparent wind. In a moderate breeze, however, most boats can be sailed *fine*, or quite close to the wind. Rudder action in light airs should be slow and gentle, but in moderate breezes the helm of a small boat can be turned quite rapidly to respond to lifts and headers. With large, heavy boats a slower action must be used. Remember that excessive rudder angles have a braking effect.

In a strong or puffy breeze, the helmsman should be ready to release his mainsheet at a moment's notice. In a small, capsizable centerboarder, the

Watch luff yarns.

Watch sag of jibstay.

Watch and listen for shaking sails at luffs.

Watch telltales.

Watch and feel angle of heel.

Feel puffs on face.

Watch for puffs on water.

Listen for more or less sound from bow wave.

Feel balance of helm (weather or lee helm). In light airs use only two fingers on tiller of small boat.

5-6. Aids to helmsmanship through the senses.

49

5-7. Cleating the mainsheet.

mainsheet should be held in hand. If its pull is too great, a turn may be taken around a cleat as shown in figure 5-7. On larger boats jam cleats may be used (see figure 5-7). It is perfectly permissible to cleat the mainsheet on a large keel boat that will not capsize, but, as you will recall from chapter 2, it is a dangerous practice to hitch the mainsheet on a cleat, unless a slippery hitch is used. As previously mentioned, wind may be spilled from the sails by luffing up, and naturally this method of righting an excessively heeled boat should be used before the mainsheet is released so that distance can be gained to windward. Sheets should be slacked only as a last resort. Keeping a boat *on her feet* (as upright as possible) by luffing up sharply in the puffs is known as *feathering*. By using this technique, a skillful small-boat sailor can gain a much greater distance to windward than can a sailor who merely slacks his sheets to keep upright.

To summarize, here is a list of tips for the windward helmsman:

• Watch the water for puffs. Head up in them. In the radiating type, bear off when first entering the puff then head up.

• Watch the telltales for wind direction changes. Head up when they swing farther abeam, and bear off when they swing farther ahead.

• Watch the luffs of sails. When they begin to flap, the boat is usually being pinched. There are two exceptions to this. In a heavy breeze, the mainsail can be trimmed less flat than usual so that it carries a slight luff to prevent excessive heeling. Secondly, when carrying a large, overlapping jib, a certain amount of backwind can be expected, and this can cause the mainsail to luff slightly.

• Watch the jib's luff yarns, especially the leeward yarn, which indicates by twirling erratically that the sail is stalled. This means that the helmsman should head up higher or else that he should crack off the sheet.

• Use your senses of hearing and balance, and use visual signs, such as jibstay sag, as aids to good helmsmanship.

• Develop a tiller touch by sensing when the boat is traveling her best through the feel of varying pressures on the helm.

• Constantly experiment to see if you can't sail your boat higher without reducing her speed.

• Be conscious of rudder action. Larger boats should be turned more slowly than small ones. In light airs turn the boat slowly, with a gentle touch. In moderate to heavy breezes, a quicker action should be used in responding to headers and lifts. In heavy breezes, feather up sharply to prevent heeling. Slacken sheets only as a last resort.

• Sail full and by in rough seas and light airs, but point high in smooth waters and moderate winds.

Tacking

The rudiments of tacking and the problem of when to tack to fetch a windward mark were discussed in chapter 3. Now we will deal with the specific procedures and helmsmanship involved in coming about.

Figure 5-8 shows a typical small centerboard sloop being tacked. Most small Naval Academy boats do not have the kind of backstays illustrated. Those shown are called *running backstays* or *runners*, and every time a boat is tacked the stays must be changed, with the windward one being set up *taut* (tight) and the leeward one being slacked off. Obviously, if the boat is not equipped with these stays, tacking her is a much simpler procedure. Navy yawls and Navy 44s carry running backstays and set them up at certain times, and this will be discussed in chapters 8 and 9.

A
At the word
hard-a-lee

2 set up
new
windward
backstay

3 ease off
jibsheet
*when near
head to
wind*

helm
pushed
to leeward
slowly

3
slack off
new leeward
backstay
(may be done
by skipper)

B
Head to
wind

1 heads
low

2 shift
weight
to other
side

C
On new
tack

3 crack main sheet
momentarily

bear off a
little then
straighten
helm

1
trim
jib
hard

5-8. Tacking procedure.

In any kind of boat that carries a crew, certain tacking commands should be given by the helmsman so that the crew can know what to expect and when to carry out their duties. The first command should be "Stand by to come about." This is especially important in a large boat, because it alerts the crew and gives them time to get to their proper stations. Details on tacking a large boat will be given in chapter 8. The next command is "Ready about," and this is promptly followed by "Hard a-lee," or "Helm's a-lee." The latter expressions are said when the helm is actually moved. The tiller is pushed to leeward or a-lee (a wheel, of course, is turned to windward), and this naturally turns the bow into the wind. When the boat is head to wind, all crew members should keep their heads low and watch out for booms or flogging *fittings* (boat hardware) that could hit someone. Crew weight is usually shifted to the new windward side unless there is very light air (the technique of *roll tacking* will be discussed in chapter 7). Notice that in Step 3 of figure 5-8A, the leeward jibsheet is not released until the boat is almost head to wind. It is a very common mistake to release the jibsheet too soon. This results in loss of boat speed and less distance gained to windward when making the turn.

After the boat turns through the eye of the wind, the jib should be trimmed in immediately for two reasons. First, it is easier to trim before it completely fills with wind, and secondly, the trimmed jib will help pull the bow around onto the new tack. After the tack has been completed, the boat will have lost some way; therefore, the helmsman should bear off to very slightly below his normal windward course in order to get her moving again. It often helps to *crack* or slightly slack the mainsheet until speed is regained. As the boat picks up speed, the helmsman can begin to head up and trim in the mainsail.

Immediately prior to tacking, the helmsman should see that his boat is moving at her best close-hauled speed, for if the boat is tacked without sufficient way, she is liable to get *in stays* or *in irons*. This means that so much way is lost when the boat is head to wind that she is unable to complete the tack. In such a predicament, the boat drifts helplessly backwards with her sails flapping. Figure 5-9 shows how to recover after being in stays. If the boat has a jib, the jib may be backed, and this usually is sufficient to cause the bow to be blown off, away from the wind. In a cat-rigged boat, however, the helmsman must wait until the boat gains sufficient stern way so that the rudder may be used. The mainsail may be pushed to windward as shown in the illustration to accelerate the backward speed. Of course, the stern will follow the direction of the rudder when moving backward.

Proper rudder action is important to avoid getting in stays. If the rudder is jammed hard over, it will act as a brake and kill headway. On the other hand, if the rudder is turned too slowly, the boat may not have enough momentum to carry her through the resulting long, slow turn. As said be-

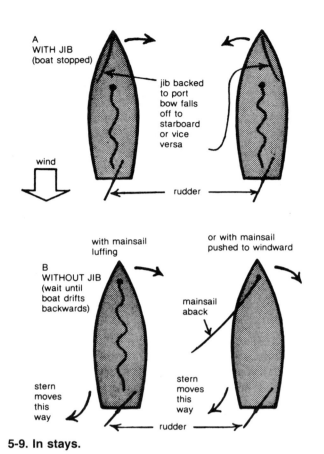

A
WITH JIB
(boat stopped)

jib backed
to port
bow falls
off to
starboard
or vice
versa

wind

rudder

with mainsail
luffing

or with mainsail
pushed to windward

B
WITHOUT JIB
(wait until
boat drifts
backwards)

mainsail
aback

stern
moves
this
way

stern
moves
this
way

rudder

5-9. In stays.

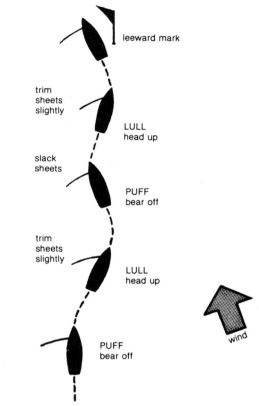

leeward mark

trim
sheets
slightly

LULL
head up

slack
sheets

PUFF
bear off

trim
sheets
slightly

LULL
head up

PUFF
bear off

wind

5-10. Working to leeward.

52

fore, have ample way on your boat before bringing her about. When tacking in a rough sea, wait for a relatively smooth spot before tacking, and be sure to trim the jib flat after passing through the eye of the wind.

Downwind helmsmanship

Getting the best performance from a boat that is broad reaching or running requires nearly as much skillful helmsmanship as getting the best windward performance. It might be said that sailing downwind requires rudder action that is almost directly opposite to that used when sailing to windward. The windward helmsman bears off in the lulls and heads up in the puffs, but the downwind helmsman bears off in the puffs and heads up in the lulls. This is illustrated in figure 5-10, which shows how a boat is properly worked to leeward. The boat in the diagram will surely reach the leeward mark before a boat that merely follows a straight course. The reason for this is that reaching is a faster point of sailing than running; thus, during a lull, the helmsman heads up from a running course to a broad-

reaching course in order to keep his boat moving despite the decrease in wind. During the puffs, he bears off to almost a dead run because he has sufficient power from the puff to retain his speed. Also, his boat will be less subject to speed-retarding heeling forces when the wind is from nearly dead astern. Furthermore, by heading far off during the puffs, the helmsman sails slightly below his course for the leeward destination and so compensates for the high heading he sailed during the previous lull.

Working to leeward is a constant weaving back and forth during the puffs and lulls to maintain boat speed. This principle applies when sailing slightly below a beam-reaching course, because as you approach a beam reach, the boat speed increases. In moderate to heavy winds when sailing higher than a beam reach, speed begins to decrease. In light airs, the best speed often occurs near the close-reaching point of sailing. Thus, it should be kept in mind that when sailing lower than a beam reach in moderate to heavy breezes or lower than a close reach in light airs, *the helmsman bears off in the puffs and heads up in the lulls.*

Sailing for longer than very brief periods with the wind from dead astern should be avoided if possible. As previously said, a dead run is a relatively slow point of sailing except perhaps in very fresh air. When the wind is dead astern, the after sails will have a blanketing effect, and the air flow will not move across the sails and stay attached on their leeward sides, thus causing a definite reduction in boat speed. To avoid this predicament, use the procedure called *tacking downwind*. It is illustrated in figure 5-11. Instead of running directly for the leeward mark, the boat shown in the illustration broad reaches towards the mark on one tack and then jibes over and broad reaches toward the mark on the other tack. Quite often the extra distance sailed to reach the mark is more than compensated for by the additional speed gained in broad reaching. It is easy to overdo this strategy, however, and to sail too high so that the extra speed does not make up for the extra distance sailed. Generally, a safe rule to follow is to sail as far off as possible and still keep the forward sails *drawing* or filled with wind. In puffy weather, of course, this strategy should be used with the previously mentioned "working to leeward" technique. Quite often, when tacking downwind, the boat can be headed (with her forward sails drawing well) closer to her desired course on one tack than on the other. In such a case, the helmsman should first take the tack that allows him to head closer to his destination. This will be discussed further in chapter 11, "Basic Racing."

Aside from the consideration of boat speed, there is another reason to avoid running with the wind flat aft or from dead astern. Since the wind is usually shifty or oscillating slightly in direction, a boat sailing dead before the wind is subject to a shift from the "wrong side," or a shift that blows from the leeward side instead of the windward side. When this happens the boat is said to be *running by the lee*. To put it another way, when a boat, sailing with the wind dead aft, turns to leeward as though to jibe but does not jibe, she is sailing by the lee. Of course, she can only turn to leeward so far before she is forced to jibe, but from a dead run to the point where her sails go aback and force her to jibe, she is by the lee. This is a dangerous point of sailing, because there is always the possibility she might have an accidental or unintentional jibe. More will be said about this in the next section when we discuss the technique of jibing.

Jibing

It is very important to understand the principles involved in jibing, because if improperly executed, a jibe can be a somewhat dangerous maneuver. A heavy boom swinging suddenly and unexpectedly across the boat can strike a crew member, cause damage to the rigging, or cause a centerboard boat to capsize. A properly executed jibe, however, is a completely safe maneuver. It should be respected but never feared.

As previously stated, a jibe is a downwind turn from one tack to the other. When the sails cross from one side of the boat to the other, they do not flap as when tacking, but they fill from the lee side and swing over rapidly.

When it is blowing so hard that a jibe would be dangerous, an alternative method of getting the boat on the other tack is to bring her up close-hauled, tack, and then head off to the desired course.

Figure 5-12 shows the proper procedure for jibing a small sloop. As with tacking, certain commands should be given prior to jibing in order to

53

5-11. Tacking downwind.

A
At the word
"stand by to
jibe"

1 Head off
directly
before the
wind.

2 Adjust
jib-
sheets
for new
tack.

B
Just before jibing

1 mainsheet hauled in,
boat held before
the wind. Belay
mainsheet with
turn on cleat
except in light air.

4 Boat turned
on to new
tack.

2 Backstays
shifted
for new
tack.

3 Heads
low
weight
shifted.

C
At the word "jibe-ho"
boom swings across
(jibe completed from
starboard to port tack).

1 Straighten helm.
Slack mainsheet
quickly. Then steer
on to new course.

2 Trim jib
for new
course.

5-12. Jibing procedure.

alert the crew. The helmsman first calls out, "Stand by to jibe." At this warning, the crew get to their proper stations and prepare to duck their heads to avoid being struck by the boom. The helmsman then calls out, "Helm's to weather," as he begins to steer off dead before the wind. The sheets may have to be slacked to effect this maneuver, especially if the wind is blowing hard and the boat is reaching. Once dead before the wind, the helmsman shouts, "Centerline the main," and he or a crew member begins to haul the mainsail in by its sheet. It is important that the sheet is pulled in as far as it will come before the boat is turned onto the new tack. A crew member changes the jibsheets, casting off the cleated sheet and cleating the windward sheet, which will be on the leeward side after the jibe has been completed. If the wind has much strength, avoid having both jibsheets cast off simultaneously, even for an instant, or the jib may blow out ahead and its flogging may quickly snarl the sheets. If the boat has running backstays, these must be changed so that the leeward stay on the new tack will be slack.

When the helmsman is ready to turn onto the new tack, he calls out, "Jibe-ho." This warns the crew that he is jibing at that moment. The crew duck their heads and shift their weight to the new windward side if the boat is a small one, while the helmsman steers slowly off to leeward until the main boom swings over. At this point the helmsman should straighten up his helm or steer almost dead before the wind until the mainsail is slacked off rapidly to where it should be for running. It is a common mistake, when it is blowing, to round up into the wind too quickly after jibing. This has led to the capsizing of many centerboarders. In a fresh breeze the mainsail must be slacked all the way off before rounding up. Unless this is done, the boat is exposing her beam to the wind with flattened sails, which

(more likely on gaff-rigged boat)

To recover jibe back to original tack.

Boom rides up from failure to shorten sheet.

5-13. Goosewing jibe. If rolling severely while running, a boat with low freeboard and a long boom might need her boom's end slightly lifted with the topping lift to prevent dipping the boom in the water. This may increase the tendency to goosewing. Gaffrigged boats are most susceptible to this kind of problem.

will cause extreme heeling, and furthermore she is heeled by the centrifugal force of her turn towards the wind. Immediately after jibing, most boats will have a natural tendency to turn into the wind. The helmsman must counteract this tendency by straightening his helm or even reversing it momentarily in order to hold his boat before the wind until the sheets are slacked.

When jibing a large boat in a fresh breeze, the mainsheet should have a turn around its cleat as illustrated in figure 5-7, because otherwise, the force of the boom crossing over the boat might cause the sheet to run through the hands of the one who is tending it. *Shortening sheet*, or pulling it all the way in, is particularly important when jibing in a strong wind. If the mainsheet is not shortened prior to jibing, the boom can swing up high in the air and result in what is called a *goosewing jibe*. This is illustrated in figure 5-13. Notice in the illustration that the lower half of the sail has jibed over while the upper half has not. The proper way to recover

from this predicament is to jibe back onto the original tack. A goosewing jibe can always be avoided if the sheet is properly shortened or some other means, such as a *boom vang*, is used to hold the boom down when jibing. The boom vang is a tackle, rod, or other device attached to the boom for the specific purpose of holding it down. The boom vang will be dealt with further in the next chapter when we discuss sails and sail trim.

As previously said, an improperly executed jibe can result in a mishap. The most common mistakes that cause poorly executed jibes and the means of avoiding these mistakes are listed below:

• *The accidental or unexpected jibe.* This can result in personal injury or damage to the rigging from the boom flying across the boat.

To avoid accidental jibes, do not sail excessively by the lee. When sailing nearly dead before the wind, watch the telltales or masthead indicator for a wind shift that puts you by the lee. Also watch the luff of the mainsail for the first sign of its beginning to fill from the leeward side, and especially watch the jib because it will nearly always jibe before the mainsail. When the jib swings over, head up so that the wind comes more from the windward quarter. When running before a following sea, which tends to make the boat *yaw* (turn from side to side), rig a jibing preventer. This is merely a line or lashing to hold the boom forward for the purpose of preventing an accidental jibe.

• *The goosewing jibe.* This can result in damage to the sail and rigging.

To avoid the goosewing jibe, shorten sheet. Be sure the mainsheet is pulled all the way in before the boom swings across. Use the boom vang, if your boat has one that fastens at or near the base of the mast (see figure 6-7). Set it up tight to prevent the boom from lifting. To recover from a goosewing, jibe back to the original tack.

• *The broaching jibe.* When a running boat suddenly makes an involuntary turn towards the wind so that she lies beam to the wind, she is said to *broach to*. This turn can be caused by a yaw-producing sea rolling under her quarter while the bow is simultaneously buried in another sea. Most boats are particularly susceptible to broaching to immediately after jibing when they develop the aforementioned strong tendency to turn into the wind. The dangers of a rapid turn towards the wind after jibing are that the boat will heel excessively

55

due to the centrifugal force of the turn and the fact that the boat lies beam to the wind and waves, her most vulnerable position to heeling forces. Excessive heeling can cause the shipping of water, a capsizing, or the breaking of the main boom if it *trips* (if its end dips into the water).

To avoid broaching to, reduce sail when the seas are steep and the wind is heavy. Take in the aftermost sails first. Move the crew aft. Their weight will keep the stern down and keep the rudder submerged for better helm control. If the boat is a centerboarder, she will be running with the board nearly all the way up when the waves are not steep, because in this position, the board offers little resistance and allows the fastest hull speed. However, in rough water or when the boat develops a tendency to yaw or broach to, lower the centerboard slightly. This will help prevent broaching to. Immediately after jibing, reverse the helm momentarily in order to counteract the strong tendency most boats

have to turn into the wind. Slack off the mainsheet quickly after jibing. Be sure the mainsheet is clear and does not foul. Keep the wind aft until the mainsheet is slacked. Prevent heeling to leeward by slacking the mainsail and moving the crew weight to windward. Heeling increases the tendency to turn into the wind. Trim the jib in flat when the boat shows a tendency to broach to. Flattening the jib will help hold the bow off before the wind.

Jibing in light airs usually presents no problems. Quite often the sheet tender can gather the mainsheet into a bunch and use a direct pull on the boom when he pulls it across the boat, rather than pulling on only a single line of the mainsheet tackle. In bunching the sheet, he obviously sacrifices power for speed, but this is perfectly permissible in light airs provided care is taken to see that the sheet does not foul. This same technique can be used in small dinghies in much heavier air if the boom vang is taut to hold the boom down.

6.
Sails and Rigging

Classification of modern sails

Yacht sails are traditionally grouped into three general classifications: *working sails*, *storm sails*, and *light sails*. The first group includes mainsails, mizzens, and moderate-sized jibs or forestaysails of moderate weight cloth, which are carried most of the time for everyday, shorthanded sailing. The working sail most commonly mentioned is the *working jib*. Normally, this is a medium-sized jib that slightly overlaps the mast and is sometimes called a *lapper*, or else it is a nonoverlapping jib attached to a boom. Storm sails are small, heavy sails used in heavy weather. These include the *storm trysail*, a small triangular sail, usually not attached to the boom, which is set in place of the mainsail, and the *spitfire*, or small, heavy, storm jib or staysail. Light sails are large sails intended for light to medium winds when maximum speed is desired, and they are usually made of lighter weight cloth than that used for working sails. The most common light sails are *Genoa jibs*, *spinnakers*, *reaching jibs*, *drifters*, *spinnaker staysails*, and *mizzen staysails*, or *mizzen spinnakers*, which are actually balloon-like mizzen staysails. All but the last of these sails are illustrated in figure 6-1.

The well-known Swedish yachtsman, Sven Salén, is given credit for inventing the Genoa jib. It was first shown to the sailing world at a regatta in Genoa, hence its name. The Genoa, or *Jenny*, has a long foot that overlaps the mainsail. It is an effective sail for reaching and beating to windward because of its great area and the efficient slot it creates due to its overlap. It comes in various sizes and weights and is carried when racing in all breezes, except perhaps in the very lightest airs or in very strong winds.

The spinnaker is a balloon-like, triangular sail carried when the true wind is abaft the beam. Made from very light cloth in a variety of shapes and cloth weights, it is an essential sail for racing. The spinnaker can be tricky to handle, trim, and steer by; therefore, chapter 10 will be devoted entirely to it.

The drifter or *ghoster* is a lightweight jib for reaching in very light airs. It is cut high at the clew so that it will fill easily in the lightest airs and so that it can be sheeted to main boom as shown in the illustration. The high clew also helps prevent excessive twist, a distortion of shape that will be discussed later in this chapter. The drifter is often cut

58

6-1. Light sails.

fuller or with a deeper belly than a Genoa, and the drifter's leech or after edge is nearly straight, having little concave curvature as does a Genoa's leech.

The spinnaker staysail is a balloon-like forestaysail of lightweight cloth that is set beneath the spinnaker as illustrated. In a good breeze, a well-designed spinnaker will rise or lift so that its foot or bottom edge is high above the deck. The spinnaker staysail, sometimes called the *cheater*, simply fills in the gap under the lifted spinnaker. In addition, there are tall, thin spinnaker staysails and Genoa jib–shaped staysails for specific points of sailing. These

sails will be discussed at the end of this chapter and at the end of chapter 10.

The mizzen staysail is, of course, carried only by boats having mizzens—yawls or ketches. It is set forward of the mizzen and is sheeted to the mizzen boom. This sail will be discussed in chapter 8. The mizzen spinnaker is set identically, but its shape is that of a spinnaker.

Sail materials

Virtually all of today's sails are made from synthetic materials, because they offer many advantages in strength, durability, stability, and low maintenance as compared with cloth made from natural fibers. The most commonly used synthetic is polyester, known as Dacron in America and Terylene in England, primarily because it provides good stretch resistance with excellent durability at a relatively economical price. Nylon, a polyamide cloth, is the material almost always used for spinnakers. Although it has low resistance to stretch and is more subject to deterioration from sunlight, nylon is suitable for full-draft, light air, downwind sails because of its strength and ultra-light weight, as light as one-half ounce per yard.

Some elasticity in a sail can be tolerated when sailing downwind, but upwind sails must be highly stable or resistant to stretch. Dacron is the normal choice for any sail that is carried to windward and subject to maximum loading, but for the most competitive racing sails, composite or laminated synthetics are often used for the greatest possible cloth stability. Commonly used in the construction of these ultra-stable sails are Mylar, a polyester film, and Kevlar, an aramidic polyamide fiber. Drawbacks of the latter synthetics are that they are relatively expensive, stiff and difficult to handle, while lacking in durability as a result of low tear resistance or susceptibility to fatigue. Some of these problems have been overcome by interweaving Kevlar with Dacron, laminating Mylar with Dacron, and other construction techniques.

Cut and draft of sails

Two typical modern sails, a jib and a mainsail, are shown in figure 6-2, along with their terminology and details of their fittings. The mainsail is *crosscut*, with its *cloths* (the narrow panels of material) running at right angles to the leech of the sail. This minimizes *bias stretch* (stretch that is diagonal to the direction of cloth weave) at the leech where it is particularly harmful. The jib shown in the illustration is *miter-cut* with the cloths at right angles to the leech and the foot, meeting at a diagonal seam, called the *miter seam*, which bisects the angle at the *clew* (the sail's after corner). All sails are variations or combinations of four basic patterns of construction. Aside from the miter and cross cuts, there is the *vertical cut*, with cloths running parallel to the leech, and *radial cut*, with cloths radiating inward from each corner or perhaps only the head and clew.

Modern mainsails usually have a *roach* or convex

curve to the leech, which adds to the sail's area. This requires that the leech be fitted with *battens* (strips of wood or plastic shown in figure 6-2) that hold out the leech, preventing it from curling inward. These battens fit into cloth pockets sewn to the leech. Two methods of securing battens in their pockets are shown in the illustration. There is another variation of the offset pocket, which has the opening at the side of the pocket instead of above the pocket on the leech.

As previously mentioned, sails must be made with a luff-to-leech curvature called draft, or camber, in order that they function as efficient airfoils. Correct draft is perhaps the prime requirement of a high-performance sail. Draft is built into a sail by either or both of two principal methods. The usual method is to give the foot and luff a slightly convex round. When these edges are stretched along a straight mast, stay, or boom, curvature is thrown into the material abaft the luff and above the foot. The second method of building draft into a sail is to taper slightly the cloths of a crosscut sail at the luff and the leech. In other words, every cloth panel will be narrower at each end than it is near the middle. This latter method is being used more and more as improvements are made in the stability of the newer sailcloths.

Figure 6-3 shows the draft curves of some typical sails. Good and bad cambers are shown for comparison. In general, a correct draft curve should have its points of maximum draft anywhere from one-third of the distance from the luff to the leech to almost halfway from luff to leech. The latter draft will work better in light airs and when sailing downwind. For upwind sailing, a draft curve should be flat in its after section. From the middle of the sail to the leech, the curve should gradually flatten until it is almost a straight line at the leech. For downwind sailing, the leech area should have a little more curvature. If a sail having excessive draft in the leech is trimmed in for beating, however, the leeside suction pull in the after part of the sail will tend to pull the boat backwards because this suction force acts approximately at right angles to the surface of the sail.

The efficient upwind sail should not have excessive draft nor should the draft be too far forward, because when the boat is sailing close hauled, the wind will blow against the leeward side of the draft curve and cause the sail to luff prematurely. This is

59

6-2. Working sails and related fittings.

especially true for a mainsail, particularly if the jib overlaps the mainsail. A jib tends to deflect the leeward airflow towards the lee side of the mainsail. Draft curves should be considerable for light airs or in a rough sea, but less for a strong breeze that is not accompanied by a steep chop. In other words, it is usually desirable to have a flat sail for a breeze and

a full sail for light airs or rough water. Unless a boat is equipped with two *suits* (sets) of working sails, one for light weather and another for heavy weather, her sails should be made for average conditions and with consideration for all points of sailing. For this kind of sail, draft should be average, with the maximum amount of draft (the distance,

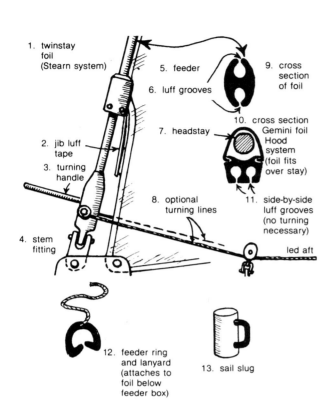

1. twinstay foil (Stearn system)
2. jib luff tape
3. turning handle
4. stem fitting
5. feeder
6. luff grooves
7. headstay
8. optional turning lines
9. cross section of foil
10. cross section Gemini foil Hood system (foil fits over stay)
11. side-by-side luff grooves (no turning necessary)

led aft

12. feeder ring and lanyard (attaches to foil below feeder box)
13. sail slug

A   Marconi Cross-cut Mainsail
(1) head (2) headboard
(3) foot (4) luff (5) leech
(6) clew (7) tack (8) seams
(9) roach (10) tabling
(11) cloths

B   Miter-cut Jib
(1) miter seam
(2) angle between foot
and miter seam is equal
to angle between leech
and miter seam
(3) corner patch

C   Sail Slide or Car
(1) track (2) slide (3) grommet
Small shackle may be used to
secure slide to grommet.
(4) mast (5) bolt rope

D   Battens and Batten Pockets
(1) conventional type with lanyards
(2) offset pocket sewn closed at (3)

E   Jib Hanks (two types)
(1) snap hook (2) piston hank
(3) headstay or jibstay
(4) jib (5) grommet

F   Slide Stops (two types)

to keep slides or cars from
sliding off track when you
wish to lower mainsail but
not remove it from mast

G   Jib Clew Shackles
(two types)
(1) snap shackle
(2) Brummel or Inglefield hooks
(hooks interlock when
placed at right angles
to each other)
(3) lashing cord (spring-loaded pin
on snap shackle should be lashed
in because it can open when
jib flaps violently)

H   Outhaul Fitting
(1) outhaul slide
(2) cheek block (3) clew pin

I   Headfoils (grooved to
accept jib's luff rope
or occasionally sail slugs)
used on some modern racer
cruisers in order that sail
can be changed without lowering
the jib that is flying before
its replacement is hoisted.

61

measured at right angles from a straight line running between luff and leech, to the deepest part of the curve) being about one-eighth of the sail's width (from luff to leech) at a height of slightly lower than halfway up the mast. This maximum draft's fore-and-aft location should lie forward of the halfway point between luff and leech but no farther forward than a third of the luff-to-leech distance abaft the luff (see A in figure 6-3).

Although draft is built into a sail, the curvature may be altered slightly by making certain adjustments. Of course, with only one suit of working sails for average conditions, the slight alterations in draft can be tremendously helpful in adapting the sail to varying wind conditions and different points of sailing. The principal draft-altering adjustments are: stretching or loosening the luff or foot of a sail, bending the mast, changing the angle of trim with the sheet, and the use of the boom vang. There are one or two special draft-changing devices, such as zippered or laced foot pockets that may be opened to increase draft or closed to decrease draft. When beating in a fresh breeze, a zipper may be difficult to close, so this should be done just before starting on the windward leg. Foot lacings, rarely seen today,

usually are used in conjunction with a *Cunningham cringle* (small hole just above the tack), which is pulled down with a line when it is desirable to flatten the draft and move it forward to the greatest possible extent.

The simplest and most often neglected draft alterations are the luff and foot adjustments. The foot is adjusted by tightening or slacking the *outhaul*, the line or device that pulls the clew out on the bottom (see figure 6-3). Tightening the outhaul stretches the sail's foot and in general flattens the sail, especially just above the foot. The outhaul is usually tightened in a breeze and when sailing to windward, but slacked in light airs and when sailing downwind. Some mainsails, especially those limited in the amount of outhaul adjustment, have a *flattening reef*. In this case, there is a leech grommet just above the clew through which a line is rove to haul the grommet aft and down to the boom (see chapter 8).

The luff is adjusted by either the halyard, Cunningham, or the *downhaul*, a line or tackle attached to the forward end of the boom that can pull it down. Of course this requires a sliding gooseneck (a gooseneck fitting that slides on a track) in order that the fore end of the boom can move up and down on the mast. The *tack* or forward corner of the sail is attached to the top of the gooseneck; so naturally when the gooseneck is pulled down, the tack will move down and stretch the sail's luff. Tightening the

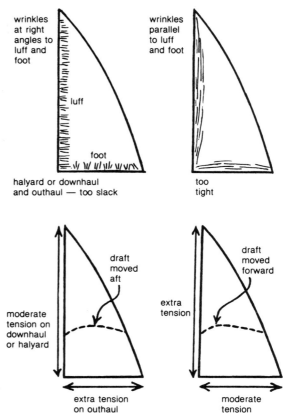

6-3. Sail draft and luff and foot adjustments.

62

halyard with the downhaul cleated accomplishes the same thing as tightening the downhaul, except that the halyard adjustment has more effect on the upper part of the sail. A racing boat often has a black band painted around the top of her mast and also a black band near her gooseneck to limit the hoist and the amount the luff can be stretched. Class rules or handicap rules forbid that the head of the sail be hoisted above the bottom of the upper black band and that the tack be pulled lower than the top of the lower band. Therefore, in such a case, it is custom-

ary to hoist the head to its highest legal limit and then to make luff adjustments with the downhaul down to the limit allowed by the lower band. Luff adjustments alter the fore-and-aft position of the draft. Stretching the luff tight will move the draft forward, and slacking the luff moves the draft aft. In heavy winds the draft is usually blown aft due to the stretch of the sail cloth; thus, it is wise to tighten the luff. In light airs, however, the luff should be quite slack especially when sailing downwind. It is a common mistake to overtighten the luff of a Dacron sail when the wind is light. In most breezes except heavy winds, the luff should be stretched just tight enough to smooth out the horizontal wrinkles along the luff. Heavy winds call for a very tight luff when beating, and this may require the use of the Cunningham.

The other methods of altering sail draft will be discussed later in this chapter. Draft changes made with mast bend will be dealt with briefly when we discuss rigging, and draft alterations through sheet trim and use of the boom vang will be dealt with in the next three sections.

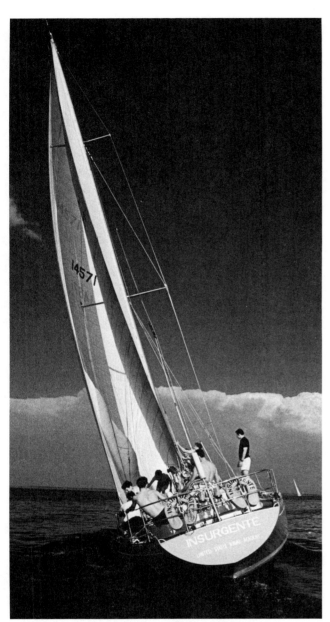

6-4. The PJ-48 *Insurgente*, which became available to the Naval Academy in 1975 following confiscation by the U.S. government for smuggling. The slot between the sails might be opened up a little more aloft if the jib lead were moved farther aft.

Sail trim

A sail is trimmed with its sheet. Let us review briefly the general sail positions for each point of sailing. When running, a sail is let all the way out; when beam reaching, it is about halfway out or somewhat closer; when broad reaching, the sail should lie somewhere between the running and beam-reaching positions; when close reaching, it should lie between the beam-reaching position and its closest point of trim; and when beating the sail should be trimmed in almost as far as it will come. These are only approximate positions. Exact positions will depend on the strength of the breeze, the design of the boat, the cut of her sails, the boat speed, and the size of the seas.

As said in chapter 3, sails are always trimmed to the apparent wind. The faster a boat travels, especially when she is beam reaching, the closer her sheets must be trimmed. When she is beating, the difference between the true and apparent wind will not be tremendous in terms of direction, but there will be a great difference in velocity. On this point of sailing the boat speed is added to true wind, which increases the apparent wind speed. When running, however, the boat speed wind is subtracted from the true wind to give a decreased apparent wind. There is no directional change in the apparent wind when a boat runs dead before the wind; therefore, in all breezes on this point of sailing the mainsail should be let out until the boom almost touches the after shroud. When trimming sails, always refer to the telltales or wind indicator, because these give the apparent wind direction.

The simplest way to obtain proper trim on a reach is to slack the sheets until the sail begins to luff, then pull the sheet in until the sail stops luffing. It is usually better to err on the side of trimming the sails too far out than too far in. A sail that is trimmed too far in will stall, as explained in chapter 3, and, in addition, will cause extra heeling. A sail that is trimmed too far out, although not correct, at least will be in such a position that the suction pull on the sail's leeward side has a more favorable angle with the boat's centerline to pull her ahead instead of sideways. It is usually advantageous to keep the sail *on edge*, so that it is just on the verge of luffing. This is when the sail is most effective. In order to do this while holding a straight course on a reach, the sheets must be tended constantly. Luff yarns, described in chapter 5, are a great aid in determining whether the sail is stalled through overtrimming. Especially when racing, the sheets should be *played* or adjusted for every wind shift and every puff or lull.

On the beat, sail trim is not changed as often as when reaching, because the helmsman changes his course more often to conform with changes of wind

63

direction and velocity. When there are great variations in wind speed, however, sheets should be slacked slightly during the lulls and tightened during puffs. There are two exceptions to this rule. In heavy breezes when the boat is *overburdened* (carrying too much sail), the mainsail should be eased so that it carries a slight luff. The other exception is that when sailing into a rough sea that tends to slow the boat, sheets should be started, and as said in the last chapter, the helmsman should bear off slightly to keep the boat footing.

Sheet leads

When we consider sail trim, we must consider not only the in-and-out adjustment of the sheet, but also the location of its *lead*. A sheet lead is usually a *block* (pulley) on the deck or rail through which the sheet is led. Most leads are mounted in such a way that their location (fore-and-aft and/or athwartships) can be changed slightly to give the sheet the most favorable angle of trim for various sailing conditions. This altering of location is usually accomplished by attaching the block to a slide on a track, although sometimes a lead block slides on a low, athwartships metal bar called a *traveler* or *horse*.

Figure 6-5 shows correct and incorrect leads for working jibs. Notice that the fore-and-aft location should be at a point where neither the foot nor the leech is stretched excessively tight. A tight leech, caused by a lead that is too far forward, almost closes the upper slot between the jib and the mainsail, thereby restricting the air flow, and the leech deflects the flow into the lee side of the mainsail producing harmful backwind. A loose leech, on the other hand, opens the slot aloft too much so that the space between the jib's leech and the mainsail's luff is too wide, thereby harming the efficiency of the slot. A correct jib lead is placed so that neither the jib's leech nor the foot is stretched excessively tight when the sail is trimmed in flat. It is often very helpful to gauge the fore-and-aft lead position by its relationship to a projection of the jib's miter seam as shown in figure 6-6 when the miter seam bisects the clew angle. The correct lead position for most working jibs lies slightly forward of the point where the miter seam projection strikes the deck. When the sheet of the average close-hauled jib is properly led, the sail will first begin to luff along the general area just above the miter seam (see figure 6-5). If the

jib's luff begins to shake below the miter seam, the lead is usually too far forward; if the luff shakes aloft near the sail's head, the lead is too far aft. When reaching, with the mainsail slacked off, it sometimes pays to move the jib lead slightly farther foreward than its normal position for beating. This is done to help prevent the upper part of the jib from twisting too much, which will cause the top of the sail to luff when the bottom is correctly trimmed.

In addition to the fore-and-aft sheet lead, we must consider the athwartships position, or how far inboard or outboard the lead is located. For a *lapper* jib, one that slightly overlaps the mast, the angle between the lead and centerline might be about 12 degrees, as shown in figure 6-6. A non-overlapping headsail should have a slightly wider angle, while a jib with considerable overlap needs a smaller angle of perhaps seven or eight degrees. Exact optimal angles will vary according to the strength of wind, sea conditions, and point of sailing. Outboard leads are most effective when reaching in strong winds and rough seas, while leads that are farther inboard are needed when beating in smooth waters and lighter winds.

The Genoa jib is most often led from an adjustable slide on a track that is mounted on or inboard of the rail; thus, there usually is no athwartships adjustment but only a fore-and-aft choice for the lead position. Occasionally, however, a *Barber hauler*, a control line used to alter a jib's lead, is rigged from the sheet to change the athwartship position. The Genoa nearly always lies outside the shrouds, and when it is trimmed in flat for beating in a fresh breeze its foot lies close to or snugly against the shrouds while its upper leech lies a few inches from the end of the *spreaders* (the struts that hold the shrouds away from the mast). Of course, the Genoa lead position will vary according to the size and shape of the particular jib, strength of the wind, position of the shrouds, the length of the spreaders, and the position of the lifelines around the boat. Some authorities say that the lead should be located slightly abaft the miter projection when the miter seam bisects the clew angle (see figure 6-6); however, some Genoas are more effective when the lead lies at the point where the projection strikes the rail or even slightly forward of this point. The after location is generally better in a fresh breeze in order to open up the slot aloft. As previously said, a little more backwind can be expected from a Genoa than

6-5. Jibsheet leads.

from a working jib; therefore, with a Genoa, it is not usually harmful to carry a very slight shake in the lower luff of the mainsail, especially in a fresh breeze.

As with a working jib, when the Genoa's lead is too far forward, the leech becomes tight, and when the lead is too far aft the leech becomes loose. It is usually better to favor the loose leech, because the tight leech will cause excessive backwind. A leech that is too loose, however, will often develop an annoying flutter. Some authorities say that a leech flutter does no real harm; nevertheless, it should be minimized or stopped if possible. Sliding the lead forward slightly will help. If your Genoa has a *leech line* (a light adjustable line sewn into the leech), this can be tightened slightly to help eliminate the flutter, but take great care not to over-tighten the leech line as this can cause a tight, curling leech that can be harmful aerodynamically.

Quite often chafing problems arise from constant sailing with a Genoa. If the spreader ends touch the sail, it should have a *reinforcing patch* over the spot that is rubbed. This is especially true if the spreaders touch a sail seam, because the stitching will soon chafe through. Also the spreader ends should be wrapped with felt or covered with rubber spreader boots. The Genoa foot will usually rub on the shrouds, therefore the outboard and forward shrouds should be equipped with *shroud rollers*. These are split tubes of wood or plastic that are taped closed on the shrouds in order that the tubes can turn or roll and minimize chafe to the jibs or sheets (see figure 6-6). Rollers will also speed up tacking because there is less friction when the jib wipes across the shrouds as the boat turns through the eye of the wind.

Mainsheet leads can only be adjusted athwartships because this sail is attached to a boom, and so there would be little point in having a fore-and-aft adjustment. When beating in light airs the mainsheet lead should be kept near, or even slightly to

6-6. Genoa lead and shroud roller.

windward of, the centerline of the boat. This will permit the boom to lift a little, which will give the sail maximum draft. At the same time, of course, the sheet should be eased. When beating in a fresh breeze, the mainsheet lead should be moved farther to leeward where the sheet can pull the sail down as well as in. This will tend to flatten the sail and give it a more desirable draft for a good breeze. One word of caution, however; don't lead the mainsheet very far to leeward if carrying a Genoa, because this will tend to close the slot and increase jib backwind.

The boom vang

The boom vang, sometimes called the *kicking strap*, has been mentioned, and it is illustrated in figure 6-7. This is an important device for shaping and controlling the mainsail. Its fundamental purpose is to pull the boom down, preventing it from riding up when the sheet is eased. When the boom rides up or lifts, the leech curves or sags off and the sail becomes twisted causing the bottom area to be trimmed closer than the top area. This is shown in figure 6-7. With the vang set up, however, the leech becomes straighter and the head and foot of the sail lie almost in the same plane. The boom vang is most effective when reaching in a fresh breeze, because this is when the boom will have the greatest tendency to lift. The lighter a boat's boom, the tighter

should be the vang adjustment to hold the boom down.

The value of a vang during a jibe has already been pointed out. It will ensure against a goosewing jibe. Some large boats with high cabin trunks, however, cannot carry a vang secured at the base of the mast (see fig. 6-7), because there is not enough space under the boom or the boom vang will foul the cabin top. In such a case, the vang must be fastened off-center to a through-bolted fitting to leeward on the side deck, perhaps a slide on the Genoa track. The disadvantage of this arrangement is that the vang must be adjusted every time there is a change of sheet trim, and obviously it must be removed before jibing. However, an off-center vang offers the advantage of a preventer to hold the boom steady in choppy seas and in the event of an accidental jibe.

It is often advantageous to carry the vang set up tight when beating in a good breeze. The vang will sometimes bend a limber boom down near its middle to help remove draft, and on many small boats it will help tighten the jibstay, which is definitely advantageous when beating. If the boat has a fixed, nonadjustable, mainsheet lead, a vang rigged to the side deck will help pull the boom outboard and give about the same effect as could be achieved with an adjustable traveler. In fairly light breezes when the sheets are slacked, the vang is often carried moderately taut in order to tighten the leech and remove sail twist. Usually, however, it should be slacked off when beating to windward in light airs. At this time the mainsail should have maximum draft, except perhaps in drifting conditions with motorboat swells when it is desirable to have a flat sail, and the vang will tend to flatten the sail. Figure 6-8 shows that a slight twist is desirable, because the wind near the head of a sail usually has a greater velocity than that at the foot. This causes the apparent wind aloft to be farther aft. Nevertheless, most sails, when trimmed for reaching in anything but light airs, have far too much twist and need at least some tension on the vang.

Handling and care of sails

Although sail construction and fitting details often vary with different boats, the procedure for *bending* sails (putting them on) is basically the same for all boats. When bending on a jib or staysail, start with the tack, which is fastened to the *stem head fitting* (a metal fitting with eyes at the top of the stem) or

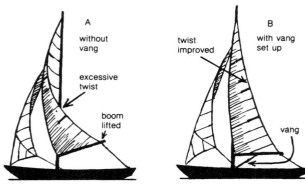

6-7. Boom vang. This type of vang requires a very strong gooseneck whose track should be bolted to the mast if possible. Boats with light aluminum booms require more frequent use of the vang.

some other eye fitting at the lower end of the jibstay. The tack is usually secured with a *shackle* (a U-shaped fastener) that is usually closed with a screw or twist pin or spring-loaded piston (see the *snap shackle* in figure 6-2G). The jib is most often hooked to its stay with *piston hanks* or *snap hooks* (see figure 6-2) unless it is *set flying* (set without being hooked to a stay), or it is used with a slotted headfoil (as shown in figure 6-2I). When snapping on the hanks or hooks, start at the sail's tack and work towards the head being sure that the hanks all face the same way so that they are not twisted. Then attach the sheets to the clew (with bowlines, normally, unless the sheets have clew shackles) and shackle on the halyard. After the sheets are run through their lead blocks, figure-eight knots should

be tied in the very ends of the lines to prevent them from accidentally being pulled back through the blocks.

On most boats the mainsail is held to the mast and boom by one of two means: slides on a track (shown in figure 6-2), or with grooved spars. When the spars are grooved, the sail's *bolt rope* (a rope sewn to the edge of the luff and foot) is fed into the boom groove as the clew is pulled aft, and then the bolt rope is fed into the mast groove as the sail is hoisted. In some cases, small plastic cylinders are fastened to a sail's luff or foot, and these are fed into the grooves. In any event, in bending on the luff of a mainsail, it is usually necessary to start with the head and work down towards the tack unless the track has a gate a few feet up from its bottom. Also, it is necessary to work from clew to tack when bending on the foot. The last edge of the sail (luff or foot) to be bent should first be run through the hands to see that the sail is not twisted before the bending is completed. Next the battens should be inserted. A sail equipped with batten pockets should not be used without the battens being inserted. Before hoisting the mainsail, be sure to set up the *topping lift* (the line that supports the boom when the sail is not hoisted). Failure to have the boom lifted up high when the sail is being hoisted or lowered may result in a crew member or deck gear being struck by the boom. After the sail is entirely hoisted, slack off the topping lift so that it gives no support to the boom. On some small boats without topping lifts, the boom can be lifted by hand.

Although Dacron sails are tougher and can stand more abuse than the cotton sails of former days, they are still vulnerable to certain mistreatment. Chafe is often a problem with synthetic sails, be-

67

cause the stitching does not sink down into the cloth but lies on the surface where it is susceptible to being rubbed. Any area of a sail that is constantly chafed should be protected with a reinforcing patch. Sun rot is also a problem, especially with nylon. Sails that are left bent on should be furled or *flaked* (accordion folded) on top of the boom, *stopped* (tied with cloth straps called *stops* or elastic shock cord), and protected with *sail covers* (specially fitted cloth covers that are lashed or snapped around the furled sail and its boom). Sail covers should not be entirely closed at the bottom, because lack of air inside the cover will encourage mildew, even on synthetic sails.

When furling a sail, pull the entire sail over to one side of the boom. Grab the leech of the sail and pull it aft so that the battens lie flat or parallel to the boom. Then bundle up the loose sail and neatly roll it up on top of the boom. After the roll is as tight as you can get it, secure it to the boom with stops. Before the sail is covered, slack off the outhaul.

If the sails are taken off and bagged, be sure the battens are removed, as they can be broken or permanently bent inside a bag. Don't bag a wet sail. Let it dry first. Sails can be dried by hoisting them while moored, but only if the breeze is very light. The violent flapping and flogging of sails in a wind can be very harmful to them. Before racing sails are bagged, it is a good idea to roll or fold them to minimize wrinkles. This is especially important with Mylar and Kevlar sails. Fold a sail so that a few unavoidable creases run horizontally. Horizontal creases will least disturb the airflow from luff to leech.

When sailing is done in salt water, sails should be washed fairly frequently to remove salt crystals that become lodged in the material. A salt-caked sail usually does not set well, because the salt absorbs any moisture in the air, even on a seemingly dry day. Sail washing should be done fairly gently and never with a strong detergent.

One of the greatest sources of damage to a sail is the cotter pin. This is a thin, bent metal pin that is put through a hole in a threaded screw fitting to prevent it from becoming unscrewed (see figure 6-15). Cotter pins have sharp ends that can easily snag and tear a sail. All these pins should be thoroughly wrapped in waterproof adhesive tape, and they should be inspected regularly to see that

they remain taped. Another frequent source of sail damage is from cigarette or pipe ashes. Synthetic sails will not burst into flames, but they can be holed from sparks very easily.

Balance

As previously mentioned, helm balance has to do with the ability of a boat to hold a straight course when her helm is left alone. If she tends to head up into the wind, she has a *weather helm*; if she heads away from the wind, she has a *lee helm*. A boat's helm balance primarily depends on the relationship of the *center of effort* (CE) of her sails to the *center of lateral resistance* (CLR) of her underwater profile. The point at the geometric center of the side view of a sail is commonly referred to as the center of effort, and a combination of the centers of effort of each sail concentrated at a single point, or the center of effort of the entire sail plan, is often called the *total center of effort* (TCE). The CLR is the central point on the hull's underwater side at which the boat can be pushed sideways (at right angles to her centerline) without turning. The fore-and-aft position of the CLR may be found by cutting from cardboard the silhouette of the immersed hull and hanging it in a level position from a pin, as shown in figure 6-8. Almost all boats are designed with the TCE slightly "leading" or ahead of the CLR, because it has been found that this gives the best average balance when considering all conditions of sailing. The amount of lead is generally between 10 and 20 percent of the boat's waterline length.

Although the fact that the TCE is forward of the CLR would apparently produce lee helm, several other forces acting on the boat tend to produce weather helm. For example, when the sheets are eased and the boat heels, the TCE is to leeward of the CLR, and this creates a moment arm that turns the boat to windward, thus giving her a weather helm.

Every boat should be *tuned* (properly adjusted) to carry a slight weather helm in all but the lightest breezes. A slight weather helm makes it easier for the helmsman to feel his boat, and also it is a built-in safety device; if the helmsman should happen to leave or lose his grip on the helm, the boat will automatically round up into the wind where she will lose headway and gain stability.

Furthermore, it has been found that a slight

A
Boat with
excessive
weather helm

vertical
lines through
CLR and TCE

TCE

CLR

To help correct

1 prevent heeling to leeward
2 move weight aft
3 raise centerboard slightly
4 rake mast forward
5 trim jibsheet (pull it in) or set larger jib
6 reduce area of mainsail or have it recut
   to reduce draft (fig. 6-3) near after edge

6-8. Helm balance.

B
Boat with
excessive
lee helm

C
To locate CLR:
waterline horizontal

CLR

pin

When hull's under
water silhouette
hangs level, pin
shows position
of CLR.

TCE

CLR

To help correct

1 heel to leeward
2 move weight forward
3 lower centerboard
4 rake mast aft
5 ease (slack) jibsheet or set smaller jib
6 enlarge main and/or tighten its
   leech (after edge)

69

weather helm when beating actually boosts a boat to windward. If a rudder that is attached to the trailing edge of a keel is held at an angle of from three to five degrees from the boat's centerline, depending on the design, the keel-rudder combination will act as a hydrofoil and create a lateral lifting force. This is illustrated in figure 6-10. Of course, excessive weather helm can be very harmful, because a rudder that is held over too far will partially stall and create a great amount of drag. When this happens, the rudder acts partially as a brake. Also, boats with spade rudders should be balanced to carry very little weather helm, because these rudders cannot alter keel lift, and they can quickly stall.

Improper balance is seldom extreme in a one-design-class boat or boats designed by recognized naval architects, as are all Naval Academy boats, but many individual boats have minor helm faults that can be corrected by various minor adjustments. These are shown in figure 6-8. Most of the adjustments, raking the mast, raising or lowering the centerboard, moving crew weight, and setting larger

or smaller sails forward or aft, change the boat's balance by changing the relation of the CLR to the TCE, as can be seen in the diagram.

There is a possibility, however, that one or two of these adjustments may be harmful to the boat's speed even though her helm is improved. For example, setting a smaller jib in light air to help correct a lee helm might cause a loss of speed. Therefore, care should be taken to see that helm balance is not improved at the expense of over-all performance. The first correction to be made when a boat is improperly balanced is to change the angle of heel. The severe weather helm often experienced when sailing in a blow is due mainly to an extreme heeling angle. This can be lessened by *hiking* or putting the crew as far as possible to windward and also by carrying a slight luff in the mainsail while the jib is trimmed reasonably flat.

The last balance correction listed in figure 6-8 (correction #6) mentions the tightening or slacking of the mainsail's leech. A tight leech will increase weather helm, while a loose leech will decrease it.

Drastic changes in the leech can only be made by a skillful sailmaker, and even then the changes may not be completely successful. Improving a sail's leech by recutting should be attempted only as a last resort to improve an original faulty draft. Slight, temporary changes in the leech can be made by adjustments to the boom vang. Tightening the vang will tighten the leech, and slacking the vang will slack the leech. Naturally, the sail's leech line should have very little tension when a slack leech is desired. Tighten the leech line just enough to keep it from flapping excessively.

Figure 6-11 shows how balance should be maintained when sail is reduced for heavy weather. As the diagram explains, there are various methods of shortening sail, and these will vary according to the boat's rig. *Reefing* is the method of reducing a sail's area by lashing its lower area to its boom or by winding its foot around the boom or by rolling the sail around its luff. It should also be remembered that reefing the mainsail not only reduces the angle of heel, but also moves the CE of that sail forward. Thus, reefing reduces weather helm in two ways. These procedures will be discussed in chapter 8. The purpose of figure 6-11 is to illustrate that the sail areas on either side of the TCE should be fairly equal when sail is reduced. In actual practice, however, most boats should carry slightly more sail forward of the TCE as the wind increases in order to compensate for the excessive weather helm caused by extreme heeling.

The Naval Academy now has a fleet of sailboards, which are not only fun for recreational sailing but useful in developing athletic agility and body balance as well as basic sailing skills. These boards, which are stood on and controlled by a *freesail* held upright by the sailor gripping a wishbone boom, perfectly demonstrate the relationship of the CE and CLR in determining helm balance. The mast is attached to the hull with a universal joint that allows pushing the mast from side to side or raking it aft or forward. When reaching, a sailboard is steered by changing mast rake. If the mast is pushed forward, the CE is positioned ahead of the CLR and the board bears off, turning downwind. But when the mast is pushed aft, the CE is positioned abaft the CLR, and the board heads up into the wind. The position of a sailboard's CLR is determined largely by its daggerboard and partly by a small skeg aft. Once a sailor learns the fundamentals of boardsailing, he can fully appreciate how a large vessel's helm is affected by changing her sail area forward of or abaft her underwater geometric center.

Standing rigging

A boat's rigging can be divided into two categories: running and standing. Running rigging refers to the movable lines or wires used to set or adjust sails, and this rigging includes halyards, sheets, downhauls, outhauls, and topping lifts. Standing rigging, on the other hand, is more or less fixed, and this includes various stays and shrouds that support the mast and control its bending. On modern boats this rigging usually consists of wire rope, usually 1×19 construction wire (one solid strand of 19 wires), which is particularly resistant to stretch. Occasionally, solid rod rigging is used on racing boats, but some authorities feel this is not quite as reliable, because it is more subject to fatigue failure—and failure is total, whereas the breaking of one wire in a 1×19 cable still leaves 18 wires for support. In recent years, however, rod rigging has been improved to the point where it is considered very dependable, except perhaps for continuous use offshore in the most rugged conditions.

Figure 6-14 illustrates two basic standing rigging plans with suggestions for tuning or adjusting the shrouds and stays. There are many standing rigging variations, but boats A and B in the diagram, *masthead* and *fractional* (specifically seven-eighths) rigs respectively, illustrate typical simple rigs and show the basic principles of tuning that can be applied to nearly all boats. Specific variations or departures from the norm, if any, will be pointed out when each individual Naval Academy boat is discussed.

Tuning the standing rigging can be a complicated and sometimes controversial procedure. We will not attempt a detailed study here but simply introduce the generally accepted rules. A common-sense rule is to adjust the shrouds so that the mast is held up vertically, at right angles to the deck, when the boat is viewed from her bow or stern. When the boat heels, of course, the mast will be supported by the windward shrouds only, and they will tighten, which will cause the leeward shrouds to slacken considerably. In this case, the mast will not be exactly at right angles to the deck, but it should be nearly so. From this same view (from the bow or stern), the mast should be kept straight. This re-

6-9. A J-24 beating to windward in a moderate breeze. Her Genoa jib seems to be trimmed about right, and she is being well sailed as shown by the leeward luff yarns streaming aft and the one to windward lifting slightly.

6-10. Keel-rudder hydrofoil action.

quires that the lower shrouds be kept slightly more slack than the upper shrouds, because the latter are longer, pass over a spreader, and therefore have more stretch when the boat heels. Lateral bends and "S" curves in a mast can be very harmful to the set of its sail.

Another fundamental of tuning is to keep the jibstay or headstay taught. This is essential to good windward performance. In order to keep these forward stays taut, the permanent backstay must be kept taut to counteract the pull of the forward stays; if the boat has running backstays, which pull directly behind the jibstay, these must be kept taut alternately when beating. Jumper stays on a seven-eighths rig (shown on boat B) should be kept taut if it is desired that the mast be straight when it is viewed from the side.

It has already been mentioned that there are certain occasions when masts are intentionally bent aft in order to alter draft. This is common practice with certain small-boat classes. The principle behind this bending or flexing of spars is shown by the bent mast (indicated by the dotted line) in figure 6-14. When a mast is bent so that its top bends aft and its lower portion, below the jibstay point of attachment, bows forward, then the sail is stretched fore and aft abaft the luff, and this flattens the draft. Boats with "bendy" rigs carry very full mainsails on straight spars in light airs or rough seas, but sail with bent spars in a good breeze to reduce the draft. If the boat is equipped with jumper stays and a permanent backstay, the former can be slacked while the latter is tightened to achieve a bend. In some very small boats with limber masts and few stays, bending the mast may be accomplished simply by tightening the boom vang or sheet.

Mast bending works very well in many cases, but there should be a few words of warning. Sails must be specially cut for flexible spars. If the sail is cut for

Broken lines are TCE under full sail.

A. full mainsail B. reefed main C. deeply reefed main D. jib
E. storm jib F. staysail G. mizzen H. reefed mizzen I. foresail

6-11. **Balance with reduced sail.**

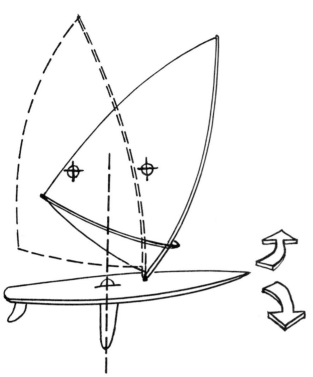

6-12. Steering a sailboard by changing her balance.

a straight mast, it will often be badly distorted if carried on a bent mast. A mast should rarely be bent in light airs, as this is when full draft is needed. Also, it is usually not wise to attempt more than a slight bend with a masthead rig, as greater flexing results in strength-reducing compression loading and often extra stress on the spreaders. One rule of thumb is that a masthead rig should be flexed no more than the amount necessary to move the luff of the sail forward by half the fore-and-aft sectional dimension of the mast.

Standing rigging is adjusted with turnbuckles (see figure 6-15). Once the shrouds are adjusted correctly, they should be left alone for most of the sailing season with only an occasional tightening if the rigging stretches; therefore, shroud turnbuckles should be locked with cotter pins as shown in the diagram. Don't forget to wrap the cotter pins with tape. Turnbuckles for stays, however, might need more frequent adjustment, and it is often convenient to use turnbuckles with locking handles or wheels or hydraulic adjusters to avoid constant removal of cotters (see figure 6-15). Headstays and jibstays often have a lot of lateral movement due to the side pressure of a jib or staysail; thus it is

especially vital on large boats that these stays are fitted with *toggles* as shown in the diagram. A toggle is a small fitting with a pin that makes a movable universal joint between the bottom of the turnbuckle and its eye, stemhead fitting, or other point of attachment. Without a toggle, the lower jaws of a turnbuckle are subject to breakage through metal fatigue.

The question of how tight to set up the rigging is an often debated one. Rigging that is too loose allows the mast to jump around and move too much in a seaway, but on the other hand, rigging that is too tight often seems to kill a boat's speed, and it puts unnecessary strain and stress on the hull. Almost everyone agrees that the jibstay or headstay should be taut for windward sailing in a fresh wind, but these should not be so taut that they put great strain on the stem or that they put compression bends in the mast. When tightening up the headstay, sight up the mast track on the after side of the mast to see that no adverse bend is developing. Sight from aft forward and also from the side.

For most boats, shrouds should not be any tighter than they have to be to hold the mast nearly at right angles to the deck (when viewed from the bow or stern) when the boat is heeled. In other words, the

73

6-13. Windsurfers reaching in very light air on the Severn River.

A. Masthead Rig   **B. Fractional Rig**

1. headstay	5. upper shroud	9. jibstay
2. permanent backstay	6. spreader	10. running backstays
3. forward lower shroud	7. jumper stay	11. mast bowed to flatten sail
4. after lower shroud	8. jumper strut	for heavy winds

6-14. Standing rigging and tuning.

mast should not be allowed to lean too far to leeward. As for the amount of rake in a mast (the amount it leans fore and aft when viewed from the side), most boats are designed to carry a slight rake aft. This usually makes the mainsail hang better, improves lift alignment, and it also causes the jibstay to stand better, allowing a minimum of sag. The question of rake, however, will depend primarily on the balance of the boat as mentioned in the last section. If the boat has too little weather helm or a lee helm, her mast should be raked fairly far aft. With too much weather helm, the mast should be almost vertical and in some rare cases raked slightly forward of the vertical.

A few last words of advice about rigging: a spreader should be adjusted so that the angles between the shroud and spreader above and below are exactly equal (see figure 6-14). Failure to do this could unduly strain the spreader and possibly cause slippage that could result in the loss of the mast. Get in the habit of checking fittings for cracks, wear, or fatigue. Particularly, check lock nuts, which often seem to come loose. It is far better to use cotter pins rather than lock nuts, as the latter put extra stress on the threads when they are set up tight. Avoid, or at least be very cautious about, making rigging

adjustments while underway. Rigging on the leeward side is normally quite slack when a boat is heeled, and it is easy to adjust it too tight, which can destroy the proper tune and put a great strain on the boat.

A summary of sail adjustments

In this chapter, a fair amount has been said about sail shaping and adjusting; therefore, a summary of the main points in outline form should be helpful. This will list the various adjustments for sailing to windward (beating) or off the wind (running and reaching) in different conditions of wind and sea.

To windward

In light airs or in rough seas, maximum draft is desirable. (Keep boat heeled slightly to leeward.)
- Slack outhaul and ease downhaul slightly.
- Ease sheets and lead mainsail from centerline of boat or slightly to windward for light airs, but slightly to leeward in rough seas.
- Ease boom vang, but keep it tight enough to hold the boom steady.
- Keep mast fairly straight.

- Keep jibstay moderately taut.
- Open foot zipper if there is one.

In a moderate breeze with smooth water, draft should be reduced.

- Tighten outhaul and downhaul.
- Close foot zipper.
- Flatten sheets and lead main from centerline or slightly to leeward.
- Boom vang should be moderately taut.
- Mast may be bent moderately if rig is flexible.
- Jibstay should be taut.

In a strong breeze with fairly smooth water, flatten draft, avoid a tight leech, and keep boat from heeling excessively.

- Tight on downhaul or Cunningham and fairly tight on outhaul, unless seas are rough.
- Close foot zipper or use flattening reef.
- Ease main, but flatten jib.
- Lead main farther to leeward.
- Boom vang should be tight.
- Mast should have considerable bend if rig is flexible.
- Jibstay should be taut.

Off the wind

In light airs, full draft with most draft farther aft is desirable.

- Slack outhaul and downhaul.
- Ease sheets to point of luffing when reaching.
- Jib leads might be moved slightly farther forward.
- Open foot zipper and slack off flattening reef.
- Boom vang should be only slightly taut unless boom is very light.
- Keep mast straight unless sail is cut for prebend.
- On some boats the backstays may be eased.

In a strong breeze, slightly less draft is desirable

- Ease outhaul and downhaul.
- Carry slight luff in main if there is a strong weather helm.
- Keep boom vang tight, but be ready to release it if the boom should start to dip in the water.
- Keep mast straight and particularly free from compression bends.
- Don't slack backstays.

Recent theory on rigging and sails

As a result of the most recent thinking by sailmakers, designers, handicap rule makers, and racing sailors, the following subtle changes or modifications to rigs and sails are in evidence: many new rigs have higher aspect ratios (they have become taller and more narrow at the foot); Mylar and Kevlar are being used to make sails lighter and more resistant to stretch; draft or camber in sails is somewhat deeper, more uniform from head to foot, and the greatest depth is farther aft; shrouds are being moved farther inboard; sheeting angles for jibs are becoming smaller; the mainsheet traveler slide is more often moved to windward of the boat's centerline; jib leads are often being moved slightly farther forward; and greater use is being made of staysails and *double slot* arrangements (one slot being between a jib and staysail and the other between staysail and mainsail).

One reason for the increased use of high aspect ratio rigs was the American acceptance of the International Offshore Rule (IOR) for handicapping racing-cruising boats. This rule and other modern handicap systems have not only encouraged the use of taller rigs, but also relatively smaller mainsails and larger *headsails* (those sails set forward of the forward mast). Nowadays, the trend, however, is a return to seven-eighths and three-quarter rigs.

Today, sails are often cut with a deeper draft that is located farther aft, because the newest sail cloth is more stable (less subject to stretching out of shape)

(1) shroud (2) clevis pin
(3) cotter pin (should be wrapped in tape)
(4) fork (5) threads
(6) barrel (turn to tighten stay)
(7) some turnbuckles have locknuts here instead of cotter pins, but these put extra stress on the threads
(8) toggle (at the bottom of every turnbuckle on large boats at least)

6-15. A turnbuckle.

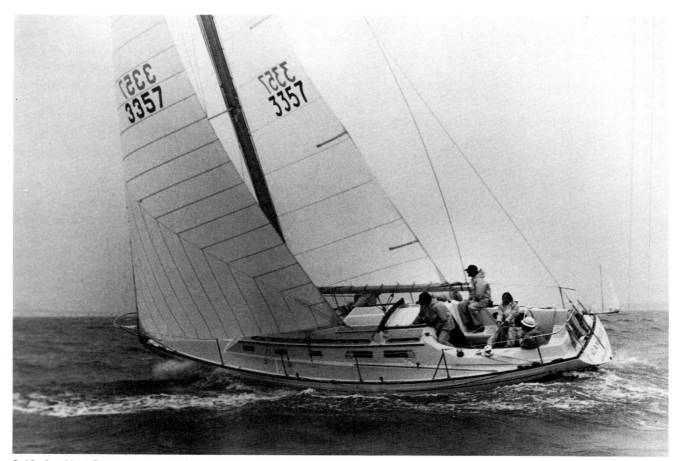

6-16. An Alan Gurney designed Islander 36 beating in heavy weather. Her inboard shrouds and deck track for the jib leads permit extra flat trimming of headsails. Notice the neatly laced reef in the mainsail. A lacing line may be wrapped around the boom as shown, but reef points should be tied under the sail's bolt rope whenever possible so that tension on the sail's foot can be more evenly distributed.

and a reasonably deep draft increases power. Having the sail's greatest depth farther aft increases pointing ability and often encourages the air flow to stay attached to the sail and thus delays stalling. Many of the modern mainsails have their greatest depth almost half way from the luff to the leech, while some Genoa jibs have their maximum draft 40 percent aft. Uniform draft curves from head to foot increase the effective area of a sail, and a typical modern jib has its foot as low as possible so that the deck becomes an aerodynamic end plate or *fence* to prevent the high-pressure air flow on the windward side of the sail from escaping under the foot to the low-pressure leeward side. Jib leads are being set moderately far forward to encourage adequate draft curvature at the foot. This is done also to prevent the leech of high-aspect-ratio jibs from falling off excessively.

Genoa jibs on many of the modern boats lead to tracks set well inboard of the rails, because many of these craft are exceedingly beamy by former standards, and also narrow sheeting angles permit high pointing. Of course, trimming an overlapping jib inside of the rail means that the shrouds must be set inboard (see figure 6-16). Boats with inboard shrouds often have two or more sets of spreaders in order that the spreaders can be short to permit the narrow sheeting angles and yet allow an ample angle between the mast and upper shroud. This latter angle should nearly always be at least 10 degrees to avoid extreme compression on the mast.

The mainsheet traveler slide is frequently positioned to windward of the boat's centerline in light to medium winds for several reasons. The more fully cambered jibs throw more backwind against the mainsail, especially when they are sheeted at very narrow angles, and this means that the mainsail must be sheeted extra flat with its boom far inboard to avoid the backwind. Although the traveler slide may be somewhat to windward of the centerline, rarely if ever should the boom itself be pulled to windward, because then the after part of the mainsail attempts to push the boat backwards. When the slide is to windward but the boom is slightly to leeward of the centerline, the boom lifts up somewhat, and this eases the mainsail's leech, which may help the air flow around the sail and relieve weather helm. Still another reason for sheeting the mainsail extra flat is to minimize backwind from a staysail carried with a high-cut Genoa jib or reaching jib when the boat is sailing close-hauled.

The carrying of special forestaysails with large jibs in light to moderate winds when beating or close reaching was a trend that has become less popular recently. The primary purpose of light-air double headsail arrangements is to obtain a maximum of sail area at a minimum cost of rating in handicap racing. The practice generally is most suitable in areas where light winds and close-reaching courses prevail. In heavy winds when beating to windward, a conventional *double head rig* with a heavy staysail and small jib topsail (a small jib set aloft on the headstay), as carried by the Luders yawls (see chapter 8), is far more effective. The most effective light-air double-slot arrangement, however, is probably a very light Dacron drifter or reaching jib, sheeted as far as possible aft, set over a low-cut *Genoa staysail* (a staysail shaped like a Genoa) that is tacked about 25 percent of the distance from the stem head to the mast abaft the stem head and is sheeted quite far inboard of the rail. With such a rig the boat will not point high, but in very light airs the boat will make good progress to windward by virtue of her faster footing. It may not be advisable, though, to carry the rig on short windward legs where a lot of tacking is anticipated, because such tacking requires extra crew effort, and it often takes a while to get the two headsails properly trimmed so that they don't interfere with each other.

7.
Small Sailboats

*I*n the preceding chapters, we discussed the general principles of sailboat handling without going into the many variations of rigs, sails, and hulls in the different classes of boats. In this chapter, moving from the general to the particular, we will discuss the principal small-boat classes used, or formerly used, at the Naval Academy—the knockabout, the 420, the Laser, and the J-24.

It is interesting to compare these boats, because each represents a slightly different concept of small, class-boat sailing. The knockabout is a modern fin-keel/spade-rudder boat primarily intended for elementary training and comfortable day sailing with a roomy cockpit and short rig. Also a fin keeler, the J-24 is a fast, highly maneuverable miniature cruising boat. The 420 and the Laser, on the other hand, are high-performance, light-displacement, modern racing dinghies. Knockabouts make good trainers for the basic rudiments of sailing and preliminary big-boat handling. Intermediate between dinghies and ocean racers, J-24s are good trainers for keelboat racing, middle-distance tactics, light-sail handling, and for developing helmsmanship and a fine "tiller touch." The 420s and Lasers are good trainers for centerboard boat seamanship, round-the-buoy racing, and special techniques, such as planing and sailing with flexible spars. All these craft help develop not only general proficiency in boat handling and seamanship, but also teamwork and the ability to command.

Knockabout sloops

Plans of the Naval Academy knockabout are shown in figure 7-1. As can be seen, she is a sloop-rigged day sailer, partially decked, with a large open cockpit. This kind of cockpit drains into the bilge, but the boat is equipped with a large-capacity, fixed bilge pump for the removal of rainwater and spray. Some boats of this size or larger have *self-bailing* cockpits, with the *sole* (floor) level above the waterline and through-the-hull *scuppers* (drains).

With her short rig and cast-iron fin keel weighing 1,120 pounds, having most of its weight concentrated in a bulb at the keel's bottom, the knockabout is a very stable boat that is nearly impossible to capsize. Furthermore, she has flotation and is unsinkable if she should happen to become filled with water. Of course, it is possible for any open sailboat to be heeled over, held down, and swamped in choppy seas if she is badly handled. In a fresh, puffy breeze, knockdowns must be expected, and if the boat is not let right up, especially in rough water, she might possibly ship enough water to affect her stability. Such a predicament is extremely unlikely, however, if the knockabout skipper follows common-sense rules for heavy weather sailing—that is, if he reefs or shortens sail in very strong winds, luffs up in hard gusts (or bears off to a run when the wind is well abaft the beam), and slacks sheets when the rail buries. An effective feature for comfort and safety is the high coaming around the knockabout's cockpit, which helps keep waves from sloshing in when the boat is heeled. Should water accumulate in the bilge, it can easily be removed with the fixed diaphragm pump under the bridge deck at the forward end of the cockpit well.

These sloops are 24 feet 2 inches long overall, 17 feet 3 inches on the load waterline, 6 feet 3 inches beam, and 3 feet 6 inches draft. The knockabout is constructed of molded fiberglass, and her mast and boom are aluminum. She has a spade-type rudder (under-hung and not attached to the keel) made of bronze and fiberglass. Although her *working sail area* (the area of the mainsail plus a masthead non-overlapping jib) is a modest 218 square feet, it is sufficient for her easily driven, light-displacement hull. Produced by Tidewater Boats of Annapolis, the knockabout is a modification of the Rainbow-class sloop, which was designed by Sparkman and Stephens. Changes over the original Rainbow include a larger cockpit, removal of a *cuddy* (small cabin-trunk shelter at the forward end of the cockpit), additional ballast on the keel, and a slightly modified rudder (see figures 7-1 and 7-2).

The knockabout's jib is bent on with piston hanks that are snapped onto the headstay (see figure 6-2), and the mainsail is bent on with nylon slides sewn to the luff and a bolt rope on the foot that fit into grooves on the mast and boom. A cotter pin inserted into holes penetrating the mast groove just above the mainsail's tack prevents the slides from dropping out of the groove when the sail is lowered. The mainsail outhaul is a line that runs from a grommet in the sail's clew through an eye or shackle at the boom's end and then a short distance forward to a cleat on the side of the boom. It is better to have the line run through a shackle rather than the small eye in order to reduce chafe. The boom also moves a limited distance up and down on a slide that fits into the mast groove, and its position is controlled by a

downhaul line. The mainsail is hoisted until the head of the sail is at the bottom edge of a black band painted around the masthead; then the boom is pulled down with its downhaul, which is then made fast to a cleat near the base of the mast in order to adjust the sail's luff to the proper tension. As said earlier, tension will vary with the strength of wind. The luff should be tight in fresh breezes and slack in light airs but never so slack as to have very noticeable horizontal wrinkles along the luff. Before the sail is hoisted, however, four battens (stowed in the stern lazarette) must be inserted into pockets on the sail's leech. The battens are tapered and their thin ends are inserted first. The two longest battens go into the middle of the leech, while the short ones are at the sail's top and bottom.

The main boom is supported by a short wire strop called the *boom support pendant*, which is attached to the permanent backstay. It is important that the boom is held high above the deck while the mainsail is being hoisted so that the leech will not be strained and no one will be hit on the head with the boom. A better arrangement would be a topping lift running from the boom's end to the masthead so that the sail could be hoisted and lowered with the boom broad

length overall	24'2"
length load waterline	17'3"
beam	6'3"
draft	3'6"
mast height	28'3½"
keel weight	1120 lbs.
displacement	2250 lbs.
working sail area	218 sq. ft.

7-1. The knockabout sail plan and lines.

off when necessary. With the short strop lift presently used, however, the boom must be held up by hand unless the boat is headed almost directly into the wind when hoisting or lowering sail. Of course, during those operations it is nearly always desirable to have the boat headed directly into the wind, but there are times when such a heading is not possible, and then the boom should be unhooked from the strop and held by hand to one side of the boat in order that the sail itself can be headed, as closely as possible, into the wind. When hoisting the mainsail, look aloft and see that the battens do not foul the rigging and that everything up the mast is clear.

The jib halyard has a small winch on the port side of the mast. On the knockabouts winch handles are seldom carried because they are not really needed and, not being self-locking types, they can be lost overboard quite easily. In order to hoist the jib taut, therefore, it is necessary to *swig* or sway it up. This is a method of pulling on a halyard, which may be described as follows. After the sail is hoisted until it is as taut as possible by pulling down on the halyard, several turns are wrapped clockwise around the winch. With one hand tightly holding the halyard as it comes off the winch, the jib hoister uses his other hand to grip the standing part of the halyard a foot or so above the winch, and he pulls it away from the

mast. Then he hauls downward on the standing part and brings it back to the mast while slack is taken in at the winch. With two men, one can swig while the other takes in the slack. The jibsheets lead from the jib's clew to swivel lead blocks on each rail, then to small winches on each side farther aft, and finally to jam cleats just forward of the winches. Before getting underway, be sure the sheets are clear and that there are figure-eight knots in the ends of the jibsheets to prevent them from running through the lead blocks.

The mainsheet consists of a three-purchase tackle running from the boom's end to a deck swivel on the boat's centerline. There is no traveler, and the sheet is cleated in a cam-action jam attached to the lower end of the tackle. At the forward end of the boom there is a vang, similar to the vang shown in figure 6-7, running from the boom several feet abaft the mast to the base of the mast. The knockabouts do not have flexible rigs, and thus the vangs are not used for mastbending; they are used to hold the boom down and remove excess sail twist when running and reaching as explained in the previous chapter.

With her short keel (short from fore edge to after edge) and spade rudder located at the after end of the load waterline, the knockabout is highly maneu-

81

verable and can turn within a small radius. At a considerable angle of heel, however, when the boat develops a significant weather helm, the rudder may stall and lose its grip on the water, at which time she is apt to round up inadvertently into the wind. To alleviate this, the mainsheet should be slacked to help prevent heeling and to move the center of effort farther forward, which will lessen the weather helm. If the boat begins to knock down and lose steering control while broad reaching, the helmsman should immediately bear off to a run so that stability will be regained and the rudder will not stall completely. When not allowed to heel excessively, knockabouts

have good balance and they will even balance and sail reasonably well under jib alone.

Because of her light *displacement* (weight), a knockabout *forereaches* (carries way when shooting) for only a relatively short distance, especially when she is headed into a fresh breeze. Exactly how far she will shoot depends on the wind and waves, her speed, and how fast the rudder is turned. A dock, mooring, or *dolphin* (mooring post) should be approached with ample headway for steering control, but at moderately slow speed. A *boat hook* (a pole with a blunt hook at its end) should be handy to reach the objective if the shoot is too short. If the

82

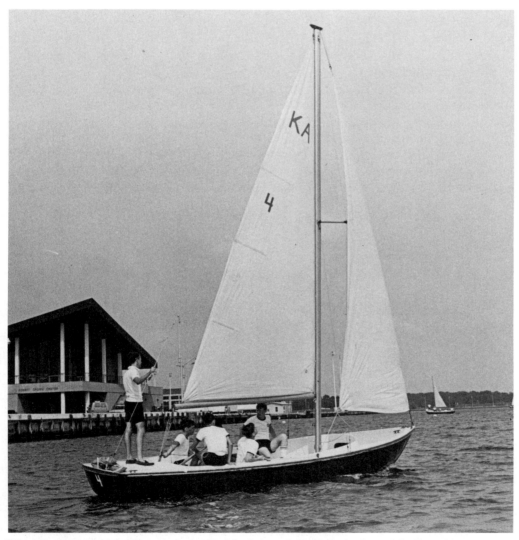

7-2. A knockabout sailing close-hauled in front of the Robert Crown Sailing Center at the U.S. Naval Academy. Among the boat's virtues are her sizable cockpit that can accommodate a large crew and her short rig that makes her quite stiff.

boat is moving a little too fast, a crew member can slow speed by backing the mainsail, pushing the boom broad off against the wind so that it brakes the boat's forward momentum.

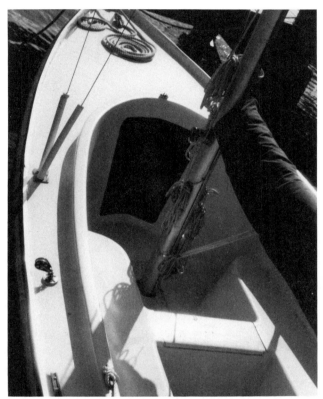

7-3. A knockabout's cockpit showing her forward locker, mast with boom vang, and after well. The bilge pump is under the bridge deck that divides the cockpit.

7-4. After deck of a knockabout showing mainsheet, lazaret hatch, and neatly flemished stern lines. On J-24s the stern lines are usually crossed.

The knockabouts and J-24s are kept moored to finger piers off the seawalls at Santee Basin. These boats are made fast with bow and stern lines and *springs*, those lines leading diagonally to the pier from the bow and stern that keep the boats from moving forward or astern. One side of each boat faces a finger pier, and on this side she is made fast in the manner illustrated in figure 13-8 (breast lines are not necessary). On the opposite side of each boat, bow and stern lines lead to dolphins in order to hold the boat away from her finger pier. Dock lines are made with spliced eyes that pass around the pilings. Unspliced ends are cleated to the boats, and when lines are cast off, they can be left coiled, if possible, on their pilings or the pier. Each slip is provided with a heavy hand line stretched between the hold-off dolphins to assist the crews in maneuvering the boats into their berths.

Careful planning is required to get underway and land at these berths. Exact procedure, of course, will vary according to the strength and direction of the wind and also according to whether the boat is moored bow-to or stern-to the main pier from which the finger piers project. Quite often the boats are moored in a staggered arrangement with one boat being in her slip bow first and her neighbor stern

83

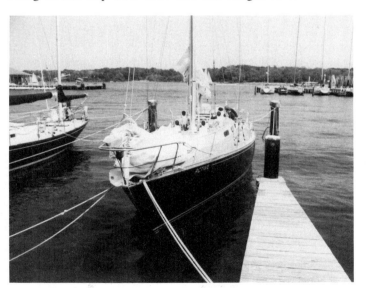

7-5. The standard mooring arrangement at the Naval Academy for the knockabouts, J-24s, yawls, Navy 44 sloops, and other offshore racing yachts. A finger pier permits access to boats on either side. The larger yachts with auxiliary engines are usually moored bow in to the pier. The knockabouts and J-24s are easier to get underway when moored with the stern into the pier.

first in order that their masts are not directly opposite. This is done to prevent possible contact in heavy swells when the boats are rolling. When there are sufficient crew or helpers on the pier, it is not difficult turning the boats end-for-end as the knockabouts and J-24s are quite light and easy to fend off or warp around.

Before getting underway care must be taken to see that the boat is shipshape with sails ready to hoist and running rigging in order. Knot the ends of sheets and halyards or otherwise ensure that they cannot escape. If the wind is astern with the stern facing the main pier, the jib can be hoisted first and the boat may be run out of her berth under jib alone. When she is turned the opposite way, she may be allowed to drift backwards until clear of the slip. Moving out of the slip against the wind is more difficult. The boat might be propelled from her berth with a simultaneous push and pull from crew members. She will have to be well clear of the slip before sail is hoisted. Remember the basic principles of heading into the wind when hoisting sail, hoisting the aftermost sail first (the mainsail in this case), and backing the jib to make the bow fall off in the desired direction.

When returning to her slip the knockabout or J-24 should normally approach the pier under mainsail alone and at slow speed. If the wind is from ahead, blowing out of the slip, or even abeam, the boat can be luffed up and landed bow first. But when the wind is blowing into the slip, it is best to sail close to windward of the slip, luff up and lower the main. Then you can either drift down on the finger pier *under bare pole* (with sail down), or in light airs sail into the slip under jib alone. In the latter case the jib should be dropped just before landing. A boat hook can be useful in reaching the heavy hand line stretched between the dolphins and also in grabbing the coiled dock lines off their pilings.

Proper orders for dropping sail are: "Let go the main (or jib) halyard; douse (drop) the main (or jib)." Before leaving the boat, see that she is well secured and shipshape. Dock lines should be hitched on their cleats; all lines are neatly coiled, battens are removed; sails are removed, folded, and bagged (knockabout mainsails are often furled and protected with sail covers); halyards are rigged so that they can't beat against the mast; the mainboom is secured to prevent if from swinging excessively; the tiller is lashed so that it can't swing and strike

anything; and the bilge is pumped dry. Keep the spring lines tight, but leave a little slack in the bow and stern lines.

In heavy weather, a knockabout's sail area may be reduced by reefing. The need for reefing should be determined by a careful evaluation of weather conditions before getting underway, because it is much easier to reef before sail is hoisted and in the calm waters of a mooring area. There are no hard and fast rules for when to reef, but generally a knockabout should be reefed when the wind blows about 18 knots (see Beaufort Scale, Appendix H). This will depend somewhat on the experience of the skipper. A novice skipper should reef sooner than a veteran sailor with previous knockabout experience. If it should breeze up after a knockabout has left her mooring area, the skipper should slack his mainsheet and carry a moderate luff in the mainsail. But if the boat still buries her rail and takes a lot of spray into the cockpit, it is definitely time to reef. These boats are stiffer than many boats of their size and type.

Knockabouts are provided with a simplified form of *roller reefing* whereby the boom can be rotated by hand to roll the foot of the mainsail around the boom, thus reducing the sail's area. The forward end of the boom has a square projection or spindle that fits into a square hole in the gooseneck fitting. To reef, the boom must be pulled aft far enough to remove the spindle from its hole, then the boom is rotated by hand until the sail is wound around it the desired amount, and finally the spindle is reinserted in its hole so that the sail will not inadvertently unwind. Of course, the halyard must be eased off as the boom is being turned. More will be said about roller reefing in the next chapter.

Knockabouts should be sailed with a minimum of two in the crew (the skipper plus two crew members) or a maximum of six. The sloops are provided with at least six life jackets that are stowed in the stern lazaret.

420 Dinghies

A great variety of sailboat types from basic trainers to sophisticated racers and seagoing racing-cruisers are almost constantly in use at the U.S. Naval Academy. The 420 represents the high-performance dinghy that is manned by a crew of two. Although the expression "high performance" is often over-

7-6. Getting underway on the knockabout requires planning and crew organization. The crew has pulled the boat clear of the finger pier and pilings and is preparing to set the mainsail. Note that the instructor is manning the tiller, which does have an effect as long as the boat is moving. As the mainsail is hoisted, the crew stands clear of the main boom. With the sail fully set and trimmed, the boat bears off to starboard to gain way and clear the basin.

used, it generally applies to a light displacement boat that will easily plane or exceed her hull speed as a result of dynamic lift (see chapter 3). A popular class on both the national and international scene, the 420 has achieved a degree of fame through intercollegiate competition. Midshipmen are active in this kind of racing, and they sail the so-called collegiate model. This is a beefed-up, slightly heavier than the standard fiberglass racing model, built by Vanguard of Pewaukee, Wisconsin, for rugged use by the leading universities.

Designed by Frenchman Christian Maury, the 420 is a sloop-rigged dinghy measuring 13 feet 9 inches in overall length. Her beam is 5 feet 5, and she draws 3 feet 2 inches with the centerboard down but only 6 inches with the board up. The collegiate model weighs 240 pounds and it is easily propelled by 120 square feet of sail area. Some boats even carry a 95-square-foot spinnaker, but those at the Academy are not so equipped. Large flotation tanks provide plenty of buoyancy in the event of a capsize. There are three scuppers through the transom, one at each corner of the cockpit and one near the boat's centerline. These are normally kept closed with twist plugs but are opened when the boats are hauled out of water.

Being an unballasted centerboarder, the 420 obviously can capsize, but having ample flotation under her gunwales, she will float high on her side when overturned. Every effort should be made for the crew of a capsized boat to immediately grab or stand on the centerboard to help prevent the boat from burying her mast or turtling (turning bottom-side up). Righting is not difficult when the boat is prevented from filling excessively or turning turtle. Usually it is not necessary to lower sail. The boat is brought around near the wind so that wind can get under the sail as the person on the centerboard leverages the boat upright. The crew member who is not on the centerboard can grab the traveler bar that crosses the cockpit, and he will be scooped into the cockpit as the boat rights. He can then counterbalance the boat as the crew on the centerboard scrambles onboard. Each boat is provided with a hand bailer that should be lashed in the cockpit.

As with any small centerboard dinghy, the 420 depends on crew weight for much of her stability. The boat is provided with *hiking straps* (web straps secured inside the boat near her bottom) in order that the crew and skipper may put their feet under these straps and lean far out to windward when the boat heels excessively. The inboard edge of the side

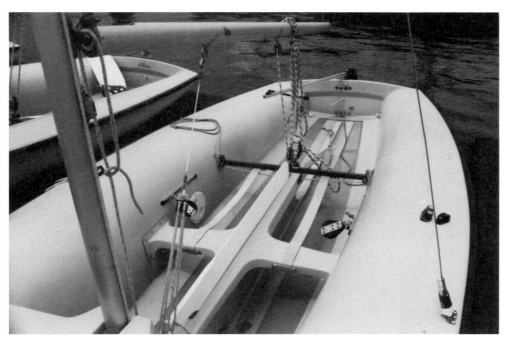

7-7. This view of a 420 dinghy shows her hiking straps, boom vang, mainsheet, and double jibsheet leads. The outboard lead uses a bull's eye fitting and jam cleat, while the inboard lead uses a block on a short track.

decking is well rounded for comfortable hiking, and there is a jam cleat at the after end of the straps to allow their adjustment to suit individual crew. The helmsman is provided with a *tiller extension* (a bar that pivots from the end of the tiller), which allows him to steer while sitting far out to windward. Hiking should be an almost instinctive reaction for the small-boat sailor. As with most dinghies, 420s should be kept as flat (without heel) as possible except in very light airs when they should be heeled slightly to leeward in order to reduce wetted surface area, utilize gravity to help keep the sails full, and provide a bit of weather helm. When running, it often pays to heel the boat slightly to windward to raise the sail's center of effort and reduce pressure on the rudder.

The 420 has a flexible sloop rig, with her aluminum mast supported by three stays (actually a jibstay and two shrouds). There are a set of swept-back spreaders that allow considerable mast bend to flatten the sail in a breeze. The rig is a rather floppy one with the rigging carried quite slack, but the shrouds should be sufficiently taut to keep excessive slack out of the jib's luff when beating in moderate to fresh winds. A slack luff may be beneficial in light airs to give the jib a fuller shape. Mast bend is

achieved by bowsing down the mainsheet and vang, which will pull the top of the mast aft and bow the lower part of the mast forward to flatten the mainsail. Each halyard is fitted with a becket block so that after sail is hoisted a three-to-one purchase (called a *jig*) may be rigged by leading the halyard under its cleat around the becket block and back to the cleat. There is a mainsheet traveller, but it is not used as such on the Academy boats, for the lower blocks are fixed on the centerline. This means that greater use must be made of the vang to hold the boom down when the sheet is eased. Vang controls are conveniently located on each side at the after end of the centerboard well.

It pays to carry considerable rake in the mast partly because this gives the boat some weather helm in light airs and partly because it causes the *lift line* to be more vertical so that it provides improved thrust alignment. The lift line is an imaginary line drawn through the centers of lift at all heights up the sail, and since there is great distance from luff to leech at the foot but very little distance at the head, the mainsail's lift line will slope forward when the mast is vertical. Maximum rake is achieved by pinning the base of the mast to the forward-most hole at the step. Be sure the jibstay is not so slack

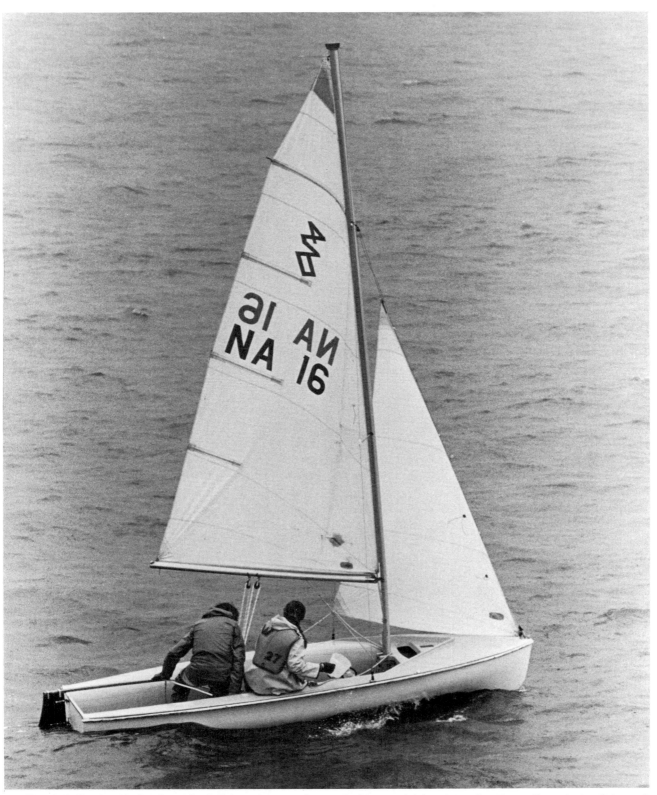

7-8. The 420 dinghy. Notice how the full-length upper batten holds out the leech to give the sail a substantial roach. The luff telltales on the jib seem to indicate that the sail is stalled as a result of being trimmed in too flat.

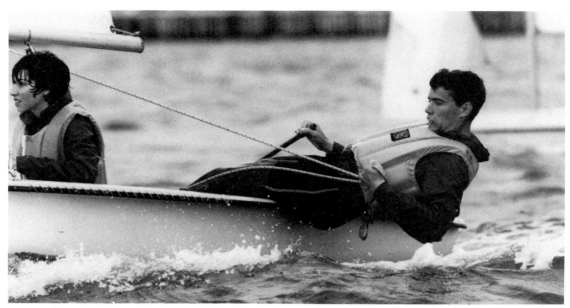

7-9. A 420 reaching on a plane. Note the skipper is trimming the mainsail directly (a 1:1 purchase). This technique eliminates the friction of the mainsheet block and tackle and permits rapid pumping and adjustment of the sail to maintain the boat on a plane. Permitted in intercollegiate sailing, this method of trimming is not legal in other USYRU or international regattas. (Courtesy Phil Hoffmann)

that it allows the mast to slip out of the partners channel at deck level. As a general rule, pronounced rake is most appropriate on *una-rigged* boats (those with one sail) or on sloops having large mainsails with small jibs, since the luffs of jibs are naturally well raked.

A somewhat unique feature of the 420's mainsail is its full-length top batten that holds out a sizable roach. This feature also prevents a crease from forming in the middle of the sail as it often does when the upper batten is short. It is helpful to attach ribbons to the mainsail's leech at the upper battens, since they indicate whether the upper area is stalled. As a general rule for average conditions, the after part of the top batten should be kept about parallel to the boom with the ribbon streaming aft. If the ribbon turns under the leech, this indicates the sail is overtrimmed or insufficiently twisted and stalled. Twist is controlled with the sheet and vang as described in the last chapter. Sail shaping is also controlled with a Cunningham and outhaul, which can be adjusted at the forward end of the boom. Remember that you want a full shape with minimal edge tensioning in light airs and a flatter shape with considerable edge tensioning in fresh winds. There are two sizes of jibs, a large one with slight overlap

for light to medium breezes and a smaller one for winds over about 18 m.p.h. On each side of the boat there are two jibsheet leads, one inboard on the side of the cockpit well and one outboard on the side deck. Regatta rules determine which lead position will be used. All boats must use the same position. The inboard lead is most advantageous for beating to windward, but sometimes the outboard lead can be improved by slightly tightening the windward sheet. Telltales on the jib's luff provide a good indication of proper jib trim. For the most part they should be kept streaming directly aft, although the windward telltale may be allowed to lift slightly when beating in smooth water.

As mentioned earlier, the 420 carries a two-person crew (skipper plus a crew member). Teamwork is required to sail any boat effectively, but this is especially true with this type of boat. The crew member does most of the hiking and shifting of weight for the purpose of correcting the angle of heel so that the skipper can be in the most comfortable and convenient position to concentrate on his helmsmanship. The skipper hikes or moves his weight inboard only if it is really necessary. The boat should be kept at a more or less consistent angle of heel. During a puff the crew should hike, but during

7-10. 420s running to the leeward mark with sails set "wing and wing." The mainsheet is slacked so that the sail is resting against the shrouds. The skipper is heeling the boat to weather and holding the jib sheet outboard of the shrouds to get the maximum sail area. NA 27 and NA 2 are in clear air with full sails. NA 25 is being blanketed by NA 26, which is being steered too far to port in an effort to prevent jib collapse. (Courtesy Phil Hoffmann)

the lulls he should move inboard or even to leeward in light airs. In heavy winds, of course, both skipper and crew must hike to keep the boat flat.

Duties of the crew are: to trim the jib, tend the centerboard, adjust downhaul, hike, shift his weight fore and aft to affect hull trim, keep a lookout for other boats, keep the bilge dry with the hand bailer, and be alert for any maneuvering situations that should be called to the skipper's attention. When the boat is on a beat, the jib should be trimmed flat most of the time except in light airs and in rough seas, at which times it should be eased. Cam-action jam cleats are provided for the jibsheets. The sheet is belayed by pulling it down into the cams, but a tug upward will release it quickly. When the boat is on a run, the board is pulled almost all the way up, but when on a beat it is usually all the way down. On a reach, the board should not be down any farther than is necessary to prevent the boat from making excessive leeway. Opinions differ somewhat as to the proper board adjustment when jibing a light dinghy in a breeze. Most authorities agree that the

board should not be all the way down because these boats have a tendency to trip on their board, which will encourage a capsizing. Many consider it dangerous to carry the board all the way up because of side slipping and the tendency of the boat to roll and yaw in a heavy seaway. As a general rule it is the best policy, when jibing in a breeze, to carry the centerboard about a quarter of the way down or slightly farther up.

Duties of the skipper are: to steer, handle the mainsheet and boom vang, instruct the crews as to sail adjustment when necessary, look around frequently to keep a lookout and size up maneuvering situations, and of course, make the major decisions during a race or in an emergency. When steering with the tiller extension, the extension arm must be kept almost at right angles with the tiller, because if the angle becomes extremely obtuse (the extension arm tending to make a straight line with the tiller), then the tiller might be unintentionally flipped in the wrong direction. The mainsheet should always be held in the skipper's hand unless, on some dinghies,

7-11. The Laser.

90

it is temporarily jammed in a cam-action jam cleat in such a way that the sheet may be released instantly with an upward pull. The skipper should always hold the helm in one hand. This leaves only one hand for tending the sheet, and it becomes awkward when it is necessary to trim the mainsail in very much. It is sometimes necessary for the skipper to hold the sheet in his teeth while he slides his hand up the rope for a higher grip when pulling in the sail. In a fresh breeze it is often necessary for the crew to help with this operation. The helmsman's hands should usually be in constant motion slacking or trimming the mainsheet and/or moving the tiller to weave the smoothest course through the waves and to respond to puffs or lulls. When the boat is beating in a moderate breeze, the tiller should not be jammed over violently, but it should be moved quite rapidly. In light airs, of course, a slower, smoother tiller action is used.

Planing in a small dinghy is an exhilarating experience. This is when the boat lifts up and breaks away from her speed-retarding wave system. Requirements for planing are a strong breeze and a light displacement hull having a flat run aft. Following seas are extremely helpful. A plane is usually attained most easily when sailing between a broad and a beam reach. To get on a plane the helmsman waits for a puff, heads up slightly if sailing low, and quickly trims in his mainsheet. As the boat begins to heel and pick up speed, he bears off but may have to trim in his sheets, because the apparent wind has been drawn forward due to the increased boat speed. At the same time, the skipper and crew should hike out to keep the boat flat and follow the rule for sailing to leeward: head up in the lulls, off in the puffs. The crew should be moved aft during a plane. This is particularly true when the bow begins to dig into the waves. The stern should not be allowed to bury, however. The boom vang is set up tight to remove sail twist, and the centerboard should usually be nearly all the way up. The jib should be kept full. On the other hand, the mainsail may be allowed to luff slightly when planing in a strong wind.

Laser

The single-handed dinghy raced in intercollegiate competition is the popular Laser. This cat-rigged, high-performance boat was designed in 1970 by Bruce Kirby. The first production boat was finished in 1971 with Ian Bruce as the builder and Hans Fogh as the sailmaker. The Laser's dimensions are: 13 feet 10½ inches length overall, 4 feet 6 inches beam, 130 pounds displacement (minimum sailing weight), 2 feet 4 inches draft (with the centerboard down), and 76 square feet of sail area. The hull is fiberglass, while the spars are of aluminum alloy. The hull has 350 pounds of positive flotation built in to provide buoyancy. As with the 420, the Laser is an unballasted centerboard boat fitted with a hiking strap and a tiller extension to allow the transfer of crew weight outboard. The rig is flexible but has no stays or shrouds. (See figure 7-11.)

Rigging the Laser is a simple job requiring only a few minutes. The mast is made up of two light-weight sections that slide together. The luff of the sail is sewn together to form a sleeve that slides completely over the assembled mast, and two Dacron straps at the top of the sleeve hold the sail aloft. The sail is fitted with three battens that are normally sewn into their pockets. After putting the mast together and attaching the sail, fit the mast into a loose step near the bow. Next, rig a Cunningham line to a jam cleat just forward of the centerboard trunk, as shown in figure 7-12.

Since the mainsheet is rigged permanently to the boom and traveler (a light line that can be slackened

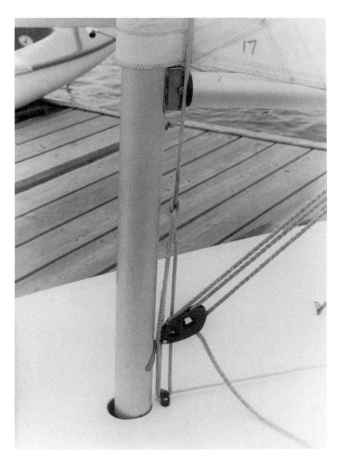

7-12. Laser Cunningham and vang. By tying a loop in the Cunningham line and leading the line back through the loop and the fairlead on deck, you get a 2:1 purchase to control luff tension.

or tightened with a jam cleat), ease the sheet completely off to allow the sail to luff while completing the remainder of the rigging operation. Fit the forward end of the boom onto a pin protruding from the gooseneck on the mast. Hold the boom up, walk aft, and secure the clew of the sail to the boom with the clew outhaul. Lead the outhaul forward along the boom and make it fast in its jam cleat. A small clew tiedown, consisting of a piece of *small stuff* (light line) led through the clew, is tied around the boom. This keeps the foot of the sail along the boom regardless of the foot tension set by the outhaul. The final step in rigging the sail is to attach the boom vang. The vang consists of a tackle attached to the mast by a clevis pin and securing ring. The top block of the vang tackle has either a swaged cylinder or a metal pin that slides into a keyhole slot on the bottom of the boom.

7-13A. Laser roll-tacking sequence. From close-hauled the tiller is pushed to leeward.

7-13B. The sailor hikes to weather rolling the boat toward him.

7-13C. The boat is head to wind, the tiller hard over. The sailor ducks under as the sail snaps across on the new tack.

7-13D. The sailor should be transferring the tiller and sheet behind his back.

7-13E. With the crew's weight outboard, the boat heads off from head to wind as a new tack is started.

With the drydocked Laser's transom hanging out over the water's edge, attach the rudder to the transom by fitting two *pintles* (pins) into *gudgeons* (brackets). Slip the tiller with its extension into the rudder head and secure it with a cotter pin. Rudder depth can be controlled with a small line that runs from the rudder through the rudder head, but since the rudder should always be fully extended while sailing, pull the rudder downhaul taut and secure it to a jam cleat mounted on the side of the tiller.

Now place the Laser in the water and insert the centerboard in its trunk. The top of the board has two rudder stops that prevent the board from sliding through the trunk. Most Laser sailors drill a small hole in the top of the board at the forward edge. A length of shock cord with a hook at its end is tied through the hole, and the end may be hooked to the mast or the Cunningham fairlead. The shock cord prevents the board from falling out in the event of a capsize and also holds the board up when on a reach or run. To facilitate board positioning, it is a good idea to drill another small hole in the after end of the board and insert a rope handle.

The Laser is a highly maneuverable boat that responds rapidly to her helm and changes in wind velocity. With her light weight and high performance characteristics, any errors in sail shape, sail trim, weight distribution, or helmsmanship are immediately evident as other boats rapidly pull away.

Roll tacking and roll jibing are two techniques that every racing dinghy sailor should master. While the techniques take a great deal of practice to perfect, once they are mastered the racing sailor will realize immediate results in faster, more controlled tacks and jibes.

Figure 7-13 shows the sequence for roll tacking the Laser. The same basic technique is also used successfully in the 420. When preparing to tack, trim the sheet in hard, ease the tiller to leeward, and hike to weather. Your after foot should be free of the hiking strap in preparation for moving to the other side. As the boat heads up, allow the boat to roll towards you. When the rail you are sitting on touches the water, the luff of the sail will become soft. Push the tiller all the way to leeward, push off against the side of the cockpit with your forward foot, and duck as you move across the boat. Immediately hook you new forward foot (former after foot) under the hiking strap. In light or medium winds be careful not to hike out too quickly; let the boat get going on her new tack. The tiller should now be behind your back. Transfer your grip on the tiller and sheet to the other hand behind your back as you sail off on the new tack. Hike quickly and hard if the wind is fresh. Roll tacking gives the boat an extra boost to weather as well as keeping the speed up. The sail should never actually luff; it should quickly snap over to the boat's opposite side.

Roll jibing begins with the Laser sailing on a dead run with the sail well out, the board about two-thirds of the way up, and the boat heeled to weather. The sailor in figure 7-15 is rolling the boat to weather as he pushes the helm to weather. As the boat rolls, the boom will lift slightly and the sheet should be jerked hard and the stern turned through the wind. Since the natural tendency of the boat is to round up to windward, the helmsman must steer the boat "down" (away from the wind) as he eases the sheet out on the new tack. The result is a course alteration in the shape of an "S". It is particularly important to get the boom up and jerk the sheet to prevent the sheet snagging on the transom. If this occurs the sail will be overtrimmed and the boat will

have a marked tendency to round up. In a breeze this can easily lead to a capsize. The position of the centerboard is also very important. If the board is all the way down, the boat can trip over the board and capsize. If the board is all the way up, the boat will be out of balance and lose directional stability during the jibe. The result is that it is difficult to steer the boat "down" at the completion of the jibe and again a capsize can result.

The following is a summary of helpful hints which will be useful when sailing the Laser.

Light winds

Helm—Make slow, very smooth alterations in course. Do not pinch the boat when beating to windward. Let her foot to keep the speed up. On a run bear off in a puff, head up in the lulls.

Weight—Keep weight well forward, but be careful not to bury the bow. Heel to leeward going to windward; heel to weather on the runs.

Sail Shape—Clew tie-down should be tight against the boom. Ease the outhaul and Cunningham to get maximum draft. Since mast bend is controlled by sheet tension and the vang rather than by stays and shrouds, the sheet should be trimmed in hard and the vang set up almost as tight as possible. Although this induces mast bend and tends to flatten the sail, it moves the draft aft. When going to weather the sheet should be eased slightly to allow the boat to foot. On a reach or run ease the vang slightly to ease the leech.

Traveler—Ease the traveler bridle a little to allow the boom to rise. Be careful not to allow excessive leech twist. Easing the traveler will also make the tiller action easier.

Centerboard—All the way down when going to weather. On a run get the board all the way up. Put it down about one-third just before a jibe.

Medium air

Helm—Respond quickly to wind shifts. Be careful not to overcorrect and jam the tiller over, as this will stall the rudder. Keep the boat pointing and sailing flat when going to windward. Once again, when on a run bear off in the puffs, head up in the lulls.

Weight—Keep your weight forward and hike to keep the boat flat. Heel the boat to weather on the runs. If marginal planing conditions exist, move your weight quickly forward when coming off a wave. Also, give the sail a few rapid trims. If the

93

7-14. Navy's All-American sailor Paul Van Cleve scrambles to prevent his Laser from capsizing after attempting a roll tack in a stiff breeze. In heavy winds it is not necessary to roll tack. Simply put the tiller over, trim the sheet, and hike out quickly on the new windward side as the boat comes through the wind.

94

boat gets up on a plane, shift your weight aft to keep the bow out, but do not bury the stern.

Sail Shape—Keep the shape basically the same as for light air. Tighten the outhaul and Cunningham to flatten the sail slightly. Keep the draft in the middle of the sail.

Traveler—Tighten the traveler as much as possible to keep the leech straight. Just before a jibe many good sailors ease the traveler to allow the traveler block to move freely across the boat.

Centerboard—Keep the board all the way down when going to weather unless the water is becoming sloppy, in which case move the board up about 2 inches. On a reach adjust the board to keep the boat *tracking* (holding a steady course). On a run the board should be all the way up.

Heavy air

Helm—Respond quickly to wind shifts and puffs. When going to windward keep the boat pointing. If you cannot keep the boat flat in the hardest puffs, head up slightly to gain distance to weather rather than allowing the boat to heel excessively (review feathering in chapter 5). If the boat is stopped by seas, bear off slightly and foot.

Weight—Hike hard and keep the boat flat. On reaches and runs, shift your weight aft when on a plane.

Sail shape—Get all sail controls as tight as possible. You can twist the vang to get extra tension and mast

bend. The sail should be flat with the draft well forward.

Traveler—Have the traveler as tight as possible. Again, it helps to ease it slightly before a jibe.

Centerboard—Put the board all the way down when going to weather. On a run it may be necessary to put the board down slightly while planing to help the boat track. Be sure to get the board down less than halfway before a jibe.

Capsize—It is not necessary to lower the sail on a Laser in order to get it upright after a capsize. The following technique will get the boat upright and sailing without spending time swimming the boat head to wind. Step up on the centerboard as shown in figure 7-16. As the sail clears itself of water and the boat begins to come upright, step off the board and "hug" it hard with both arms. Go under the boat holding on to the board. Swim out on the weather side, crawl aboard, trim, hike, and sail away. Another method, perhaps easier, of righting a Laser is shown in figure 7-16.

Miscellaneous tips for Laser sailors

• Keep the mast step clean. Soap chips make a good lubricant.

• When hiking on a long leg, cross your feet under the strap to give one leg a rest.

• Rig a short piece of shock cord at the after end of the hiking strap to keep it up. This makes it easier to hook your foot after a tack. Also rig a short "backup" securing line to the strap in case the primary securing line breaks.

• Wax the boom and mast to ease outhaul and Cunningham action.

• Use tape around the tiller to prevent any "play" in the rudder head. Use tape and twine to make a grip at the end of the tiller extension.

• Make sure that the battens are exactly the correct length and that they are sanded smooth or fitted with plastic end tips.

• Get extra purchase from the Cunningham by rigging a loop in the line as shown in figure 7-12.

• Install telltales. These may be ribbons taped to the sail or yarns threaded through the sail so that telltales show on each side at a distance of about 18 inches abaft the luff a little lower than halfway up the sail and also slightly higher than halfway up. In addition, yarns or ribbons are often attached to the leech at each batten. These telltales will indicate when the sail is stalled or when it is on the verge of

7-15A. Laser roll-jibing sequence. Sailing on a dead run, the boat is heeled to weather as the tiller is put over.

7-15B. As the stern passes through the wind, the tiller is pushed to weather and the sheet is jerked hard.

7-15C. As the sail jibes, the sailor ducks under and begins to bear off.

7-15D. The sailor continues to bear off. Note the correct position of the tiller behind the sailor's back.

95

7-15E. The Laser is heeled to weather on a run. The Cunningham and clew outhaul should now be eased to get more draft in the sail.

luffing. Try to sail with the telltales streaming directly aft. If the leeward luff yarns are hanging down or twirling, the sail is stalled, and you can point higher or else ease the sheet; if the windward yarns are twirling, the sail is luffing and you should bear off or perhaps trim in slightly. As said earlier, luff yarns are also effective on jibs, but they are usually located farther forward, perhaps a foot or less abaft the luff, because there is no mast forward of the sail to disturb the air flow (see figure 5-6). It is also helpful to attach ribbons to the ends of the upper battens as decribed in the section on 420s.

• Some Laser sailors mount wind direction indicators (a feather or Windex vane) atop the mast or on the bow. If the Windex is on the mast, care must be taken not to make any holes that would allow the mast to fill with water and thereby encourage the boat to turn turtle in the event of a capsize.

J-24 class

Since the third edition of this book, the Naval Academy has acquired a small fleet of J-24s. Said to be the most popular one-design keel boat in the

7-16. Righting technique for Laser.

world, J-24s are raced seriously in about every major yachting region in the United States and in many foreign countries as well. This boat might be called a midget cruising-racer, as it is primarily a racer with the accent on speed and maneuverability, but it has minimal cruising accommodations for overnighting or weekend cruising. Normally, it completes either as a one-design or in the MORC (Midget Ocean Racing Club) class against boats of similar type no longer than 30 feet overall. Occasionally, it races against boats of greater difference in size and design, as in the PHRF (Performance Handicap Racing Fleet). There is an active J-24 cruising one-design fleet on the Chesapeake with presently 17 seasonal races sanctioned by the Chesapeake Bay Yacht Racing Association.

Designed in 1974 by Rodney Johnstone, the J-24 prototype, named *Ragtime*, was home-built in the designer's garage. Soon after her launching in 1976, she began to dominate MORC racing, and the following year the design went into production. Tillotson-Pearson at Fall River, Mass., the builders of the new Navy 44s (see chapter 9), were the original builders of the J-24, although the boats are now being built elsewhere in the United States and in Europe, South America, Australia, and the Far

East. Their construction is fiberglass sandwich with a core of end-grain balsa. This offers stiffness with light displacement, which provides speed and ease of handling when it comes to warping (moving the boat with lines) or fending off during a fast landing at a dock. Her displacement is 2,600 pounds, of which 950 pounds are consigned to lead keel ballast. Her other particulars are: 24 feet LOA, 20 feet LWL, 8 feet 11 inches beam, 4 feet draft, and 261 square feet of sail area.

The J-24 has a five-sixths sloop rig with the upper shrouds as well as the jibstay secured to the mast a distance of about one sixth of the above-deck mast's length from the masthead. Both the upper and lower shrouds attach to chainplates slightly abaft the mast, and the spreaders are swept back so that the uppers will be straight from the *hounds* (where they join the mast) to the chainplates. This arrangement obviates any vital need for running backstays to control jibstay sag. A permanent backstay, attached to a sizable masthead crane aloft and controlled with rollers on a bridle and a four-part tackle at the lower end, makes it easy to bend the mast and flatten the upper part of the mainsail in a breeze. The most successful J-24 racing sailors usually agree that rake should be maximum with the shortest mast and

7-17. Rounding the mark during a Laser race. NA 1 is properly heeled to windward, while NA 4 is not. NA 8 is preparing to roll jibe around the mark.

longest jibstay allowed under class rules. This will provide the best balance and give the boat the right amount of weather helm in light airs.

In tuning the rig, the shrouds are adjusted for about two or slightly more inches of *prebend* (bend prior to hoisting sail), depending on the cut of the mainsail. Formerly, the top J-24 sailors set their shrouds, especially the uppers, very taut, but nowadays shrouds are generally carried with much more slack. Exact tension for racing should be varied for wind strength. Although tuning rules are complicated and experts don't always agree, a simplified rule of thumb is to set the uppers at about 400 pounds (using a Loos tension gauge) in light airs, 800 pounds in medium airs, (8 to 12 knots) and 1,200 or more pounds in heavier air. The lowers should be about half the tension of the uppers in

light airs, perhaps two thirds of the uppers in medium winds, and almost equal to the uppers in fresh winds. This tuning allows some jibstay sag for power when the wind is light but less sag for improved pointing and a slight masthead falloff for depowering the main in fresh winds with moderately smooth seas. Backstay adjustment also affects jibstay sag as well as the fullness of the main, and tension should be applied when the wind is about 8 knots or more. Unless the seas are very rough, the backstay rollers might be pulled down to where they are about even with the stern pulpit for maximum adjustment. Cleats for the backstay control lines are on each side of the boat just forward of the main sheet.

Class rules allow two jibs, a 100 percent working jib and a 150 percent Genoa. The former has an *LP*

7-18. The J-24.

lead blocks on tracks that are located just abaft the mast. The 150's tracks are located near the forward end of the cockpit well. Care must be taken not to overtrim the Genoa in light airs. Its foot should be just inboard of the lifelines when beating in light weather, but the sail is progressively trimmed in as the wind freshens until its foot is just off the shrouds. J-24 racing sailors seldom reef the mainsail nowadays, as it has been found that in heavy weather, sailing around the usual short race course, it pays to sail with the 100 percent jib and a slightly luffing main rather than with the 150 jib and reefed main.

Although a few J-24s carry luff foils for the jib, they do not avoid bald-headed changes when the boat is fitted with one jib halyard, and the sail is more difficult to control when hoisting or lowering, as its luff becomes detached from the foil. Navy boats have the more seamanlike arrangement of hanks on a wire stay. When windward legs are short, jibs are nearly always changed when sailing

(a perpendicular from luff to clew) equal to the foretriangle base (distance from stem to mast), while the latter sail has an LP that is 150 percent of the foretriangle base. The smaller sail, without overlap, is used when the wind is approximately 18 knots or more, and its sheets are trimmed through

7-19. A J-24 in her slip showing the berthing arrangement. Her boom is a bit droopy and the tiller might need lashing. Note the heavy dolphin line between the finger pier and port side of the boat to assist when warping the boat into her slip.

downwind with the spinnaker set. Halyard arrangements vary, but on the Navy J-24s and most of the hottest racers, the main and jib halyards, leading aft to the cockpit, are on the port side of the mast. This is the most practical arrangement (despite the fact that it is customary to have the main halyard of a large boat on the starboard side of her mast), because spinnaker lines (halyard, lift, and foreguy) are more easily handled on the "uphill" side when sailing the usual race course that requires that turning marks be left to port. The crew on a J-24 should always try to stay to windward when the boat is heeled, not only for balance, but because the "downhill" side of the high-crowned foredeck can be slippery and difficult to stand on. Chapter 10 of this book will cover the basic handling of spinnakers, but a few specific details of the way these sails are carried on J-24s should be mentioned here. Like some dinghies and other small racers, the J-24 is fitted with a *twing line* near and outboard of the shrouds on each side of the boat. This is a short line with a bullet block at its end through which a spinnaker guy or sheet is led. Each twing is adjustable, with its own lead and cam cleat, so that the sheet or guy can be allowed to lift up or be pulled down close to the deck, thus affording better control

over the spinnaker lines. Typical uses for a twing are: to pull the guy down and outboard so that it will not chafe against the shrouds, to choke down the sail in a breeze, to pull the lines within easy reach during a jibe, and to haul down on the sheet for quick trimming. Spinnaker jibing is done by the end-for-end method, which will be explained in chapter 10. The spinnaker pole has jaws at each end and bridles for the topping lift and downhaul (foreguy). There are no special winches for the spinnaker sheet and guy, since the sail is not huge and the boat carries a sizable crew when racing. If the last few inches of guy trim are difficult in a breeze, the twing can be used for leverage.

With respect to sailing technique, the J-24 falls somewhere between a dinghy and a moderately large cruising-racer. As does a big boat, she needs ample crew for efficient handling, but in responsiveness she is more like a dinghy. When sailing to windward or reaching in a breeze, the boat should be kept reasonably flat. The designer and others have noted that any heel beyond 15 degrees will cause too much weather helm and adversely affect the performance. Ideal crew weight is generally between 830 and 880 pounds, which normally means there is a crew of five. In light airs, however,

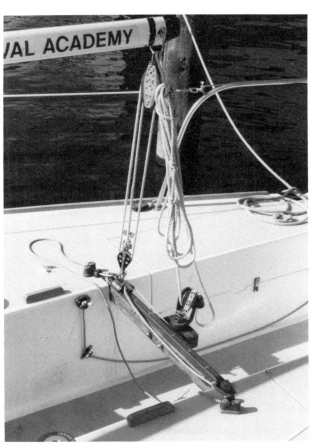

7-20. A J-24's mainsheet and traveler. The sliding block is shown in approximately the correct position for reaching or sailing close-hauled on the port tack in a fresh breeze. The backstay tackle is also controlled near the traveler.

7-21. The J-24's swept-back spreaders allow consider-able mast bend and permit the jibstay to be tightened with the shrouds.

101

the boat can be easily handled by four, and there is less chance of crew members getting in each other's way. For some regattas there is often a specified limit on crew weight. To keep the boat flat in a breeze, all crew should sit as far as possible to windward near the beamiest part of the boat, and lines that need adjustment should be led to the high side. Crew weight should be concentrated as much as possible to inhibit *hobbyhorsing* (violent pitch-ing). The main sheet has a traveler, and the lead block should be pulled slightly to weather of the boat's centerline (with the boom almost on the centerline) to minimize jib backwind in light to moderate air. In fresher air the traveler is centered or positioned slightly farther to leeward, and the vang can be used effectively. Some sailors use the twings, or similarly rigged lines, as Barber haulers (see chapter 6) on the jib sheets to pull the clew

farther outboard when backwind becomes a prob-lem.

The helm has a tiller extension that allows the helmsman to sit farther outboard, to windward in a breeze and to leeward when the wind is light. There is a fair amount of play in the J-24's tiller, so helm movement must be anticipated, with the helmsman moving the rudder just slightly before the time when he would normally move a firm tiller. Helm sloppi-ness often can be alleviated with shims in the rudder-head fitting or even a wrapping with duct tape. When beating to windward, the J should be sailed somewhat *full and by* (without pinching), especially in rough weather, for optimum *VMG* (velocity made good). Her VMG is also optimized by keeping the breeze fairly close to the quarter while sailing downwind. In light airs especially, avoid sailing with the wind dead aft. Wind shifts and sailing angles can be figured most easily by

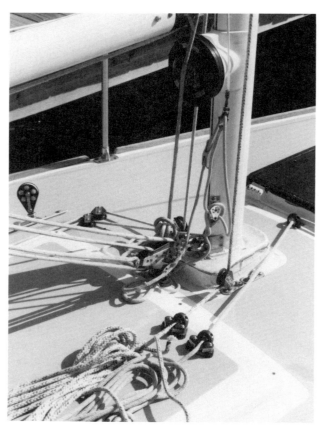

102

7-22. The base of a J-24's mast showing her spinnaker lines on the starboard side to facilitate setting the 'chute on a port-side mark rounding. Note the compass directly under the main boom's gooseneck.

offshore. In fact, the J-24 does not pass the United States Yacht Racing Union's basic *Capsize Screening Formula*, which is applied to a design by dividing the boat's maximum beam by the cube root of her displacement in cubic feet. To pass the screen, the result of the calculation must be two or less, but the J-24 is 2.6. One verification of the formula's accuracy is the case of the J-24 *Chubasco*, which capsized a few years ago and *turned turtle* (bottom-side up) after having been struck by a fierce squall while crossing the Gulf Stream during an ocean race. Fortunately, the boat remained afloat long enough for her crew to be rescued. Due to the fact that the J-24 is normally easy to handle and is initially *stiff* (not easily heeled), an eager racing crew might be lulled into a sense of false security and attempt to carry too much sail in heavy weather. When the boat is overburdened or when a squall is threatening, it is most prudent to reduce sail early. Also, it should not be considered sissy to don PFDs or flotation jackets in threatening weather. If there seems to be any danger of a capsize, insert the drop slide in the companionway and dog all hatches. The foregoing remarks are by no means intended as a condemnation of the J-24, which is a remarkably fast, responsive, and initially stable boat. The remarks are intended only as a reminder that it is important to know the capability of any boat and to exercise seamanlike judgment in threatening weather.

observing the compass, which is located on the mast just below the gooseneck.

J-24s have been touted for their seaworthiness, and according to some reports, they have handled gusts exceeding hurricane force, but skippers should be reminded that the boat is small, light, and beamy, Despite the fact that she has high *initial* stability and excellent sail-carrying power, she does not have the *range* of stability that many sailors might expect from a cruising-racing keel boat that is often sailed

Naval Academy J-24s are moored similarly to the knockabouts, yawls, and Navy 44s at the sea wall in the Santee Basin. This is a practical arrangement that allows easy use, but to be competitive in topflight international one-design racing, the boats should be *dry sailed*, i.e., kept out of water when not in use. This allows the cleanest and smoothest possible bottom. There is also a racing advantage in using Mylar jibs, but the Naval Academy favors dacron sails because of their greater durability.

8.
Luders Yawls

*I*n addition to having a fleet of small sailing craft, the Naval Academy owns and maintains a fleet of larger racing-cruisers including a number of nearly identical 44-foot Luders yawls. They offer the midshipmen a unique opportunity for training in large ocean-racing sailboats. These boats carry a full complement of light sails, and they may be used as a class (racing against each other), or they can compete against comparable boats of different designs under a handicap system. A safe and seaworthy design, the Naval Academy yawls have been raced in many ocean races, even across the North Atlantic.

These yawls were designed for the Naval Academy in 1939 by the Luders Marine Construction Company of Stamford, Connecticut. The original 12 boats, the last of which was completed in 1943, were built of wood. Commencing in 1963, however, the wooden yawls were gradually replaced by fiberglass versions. Although hull forms and rigs are nearly identical, there are certain differences between the wooden and fiberglass yawls. For instance, the wooden boats are engineless, while the fiberglass boats are fitted with diesel power; the old boats have wooden spars, while the new ones are fitted with aluminum masts and have improvements in the rigging, some of which will be discussed later. Accommodations below have been changed considerably, and the new boats carry slightly more keel ballast than the old boats. At present, the Naval Academy has fiberglass yawls only, but the original wooden yawls are still being used at various naval stations.

The dimensions of the Luders yawls are as follows: length overall, 44 feet 2½ inches; length water line, 30 feet 1 inch; maximum beam, 10 feet 10½ inches; draft, 6 feet ⅜ inch; mainmast height from deck to masthead, 52 feet 3 inches; displacement (light) (fiberglass), 22,260 pounds; keel ballast (fiberglass), 9,850 pounds; keel ballast (wood), 9,000 pounds; and working sail area (main, mizzen, and forestaysail), 722 square feet.

Photos on the opposite page show Luders yawls under sail. The shape of the Luders hull may be seen in figures 8-2 and 8-4. The interior layout for the fiberglass yawls is shown in figure 8-5, and that for the wooden yawls in figure 8-6. The sail and deck plans for the fiberglass yawls are shown in figure 8-7.

8-1. The Luders yawl under shortened sail. The yawl _Frolic_ under the well-balanced rig of mainsail and forestaysail. The photo was taken in 1953. Since then, anchor windlasses (shown on her foredeck) have been removed. The forestaysail halyard needs setting up, the main topping lift wants some slack, and the mizzen might be furled a bit more securely.

Yawl rigging

Figure 8-7 also shows the rigging of the Luders yawl. The rig is basically a masthead plan with a headstay and an opposing permanent backstay on the mainmast. At a distance of about 15 feet from the _truck_ (top of the mast) on the mast's fore side a forestay is attached. The forestay has two functions: to support the forestaysail, and also to help prevent fore-and-aft bending below the headstay. Runners (running backstays) are attached to the mast at the same point to prevent the mast from bowing forward at the forestay's point of attachment. Originally the yawls were designed to carry jumper stays and struts to eliminate the need for running backstays, but jumpers would have interfered with the tacking of large headsails, and it was decided that runners would be used.

Actually these stays are not used at all times but only when it is blowing hard enough to bend the mast or when the forestaysail is set. Likewise, the forestay is not usually set up in a light to moderate breeze. When not in use, it is released from its deck fitting by a lever and is brought aft, slack, and clipped to the shrouds. In this position, it will not interfere with the tacking of a large Genoa jib. The aluminum masts are stiffer than the wooden ones; therefore, on the newer yawls, forestays and backstays are usually not needed except when a Genoa is

8-2. Hull of a fiberglass Luders yawl.

carried in a fresh breeze. The need for these stays varies with individual boats. Some masts are more limber than others. The proper time for setting up these running stays should be determined by sighting up the mast. If it is bowing more than very slightly or pumping in a seaway, set them up. Don't take a chance on breaking the mast.

At their lower ends the running backstays on the yawls have *whips* (a single whip is a tackle with only one block. See figure 8-7). One end of the whip has an eye that fits on a hook secured to the deck, while the whip's other end is adjusted with a lever. On the fiberglass yawls, a tail of ¾" dacron braid is led through a snatch block attached to a pad eye located on deck between the primary and secondary Genoa winches. From there the runner may be led to either winch. When the runners are in use, naturally the one to leeward is slacked, while the one to windward is tightened with its lever or winch. However, when the runners are not in use, the eye ends of the whip are released from their hooks and the stays are brought forward, slack, and are secured to the after shrouds. The shrouds are provided with snap shackles for holding the runners.

The mizzenmast on a wooden yawl is provided with a backstay that is set up with a *pelican hook* (a

hinged hook that is held closed with a sliding ring). A mizzen backstay is usually not set up unless the mizzen staysail is carried in a moderate breeze. This sail has a strong tendency to pull the mast forward. Of course, the backstay must be released when tacking or jibing. Fiberglass yawls have the chainplates for the mizzen after shrouds located much farther aft than on the wooden yawls; therefore, on the newer boats, mizzen backstays are really not necessary. The wooden mizzenmast is fitted with a jumper stay running over a strut; it keeps the top of the mast from bending aft.

Looking at the rigging plan from the bow or stern, we can see that the mainmast has two sets of spreaders and has intermediate shrouds as well as upper shrouds and two sets of lower shrouds. Although the rigging seems complicated, it involves the same tuning principles as were discussed in chapter 6. The upper shrouds should always be kept taut, while the intermediates are slightly less taut, and the lowers are still less taut. The after and forward lowers are adjusted to keep the mast straight. Obviously, this is a masthead rig and the sails are cut for a straight mast; thus, the mast should be kept straight, both fore and aft and athwartships, at all times. The headstay and back-

105

8-3. A new rudder design for the Luders yawls. The new rudder is more efficient partly because there is more area at the bottom where the water is less aerated. Also, tank tests have shown that the sharp corner has a beneficial effect on the efficiency of the lateral plane. Yawls fitted with the new rudder are easier to control downwind, and windward performance may be slightly improved in moderate to fresh winds. The rudder design before change is shown on right.

stay should be quite taut for efficient windward sailing. It is a good idea to tighten the backstay slightly before a race but to slack it off again after the race. This keeps the strain off the boat most of the time. For cruising purposes it is recommended that the hydraulic backstay adjuster be tensioned no higher than 1,500 pounds per square inch as shown on the adjuster's gauge. The yawls are designed to carry their masts with a slight rake aft of about 26 inches, which gives them a slight weather helm. Of course, this may vary slightly with individual boats because of differences in trim and the condition of the sails.

Most of the running rigging consists of one-half-inch Dacron sheets and a combination of wire and Dacron for halyards. There are six halyards on the mainmast: one for the forestaysail and spinnaker staysail, which runs through a block just below the point of attachment of the forestay, a main halyard, two masthead jib halyards running through mast sheaves (pulleys set into the masthead as shown in figure 8-8) on the fiberglass yawls, and two spinnaker halyards running through blocks hung just above and forward of the point of attachment of the headstay. Also, there is a spinnaker pole lift that runs through a block hung on the fore side of the

length overall	44 feet 2½ inches
length water line	30 feet 1 inch
beam extreme	10 feet 10½ inches
draft	6 feet 3/8 inch
mast from deck to masthead	52 feet 3 inches
displacement (light)	22,260 pounds
ballast	
wood	9,000 pounds
fiberglass	9,850 pounds

8-4. Luders yawl, lines. The lines of the yawl show a successful compromise between an able, seakindly, fairly heavy displacement hull and one that is easily driven. The slack bilges (having a gradual as opposed to a sharp curve) and moderate deadrise lessen wetted surface for speed and give an easy motion in a seaway. These factors make for a boat that will heel quite easily initially, but that will become increasingly stiff as her ample keel ballast becomes effective at higher angles of heel. The keel is of sufficient length to give good directional stability, but it is sufficiently cut away forward to reduce wetted surface and to assure reasonably quick helm response. The keel is also of ample draft to assure good performance when beating to windward, and the deep draft allows the keel ballast to be placed low where it is most effective. With their long overhangs, moderate freeboard, graceful sheer, and sleek underbody, the Luders yawls are among the most aesthetically pleasing of sailing yachts. The designer, A. E. Luders, Jr., told the author that the Navy yawl's hull is a near sister to Luders's famous sloop *Storm*, which all but dominated big-boat racing for more than a decade on Long Island Sound.

mast some distance below the upper spreaders. All these lines belay near the base of the mast. The wooden yawls have a double purchase or tackle arrangement for their main halyards on a Number 2 ratchet main halyard winch on the mast. The halyard is wrapped three or four times around the winch after the sail is almost hoisted. The fiberglass boats, however, have a different main halyard arrangement. Until fairly recently, these halyards were all wire that wound up on reel winches, similar in principle to fishing line reels. Presently, however, the yawls have main halyards that are wire with Dacron tails, and their winches are non-reel, number 16 Barients. The operation of winches will be discussed near the end of this chapter.

There is also a difference between the wooden and fiberglass yawls in their sheeting arrangements for most sails. On the former, there are adjustable forestaysail leads consisting of slides on tracks mounted on the side decks. On the fiberglass boats, forestaysail sheets are led to one of two pad eyes on each side, to which lead blocks are fastened. Both wooden and fiberglass yawls have mainsheet travel-

ers abaft the cockpit, but on the wooden boats, the sheet runs along the underside of the boom to a block near the gooseneck, and then it is led back to a cleat and winch atop the cabin house near its after end on the starboard side. On the fiberglass boats, however, the sheet is led internally through the boom to a block at the gooseneck, and then back to a cleat and winch atop the cabin house near its after end on the port side. Genoa sheets are essentially the same for all boats. These sheets lead outside the shrouds through blocks on adjustable slides that attach to tracks mounted on the rails. They are then taken to winches through *turning blocks* (blocks used to change the direction of a line), as shown in figure 8-9.

The mizzen running rigging includes the mizzen halyard, which has a Number 10 Barient winch on the starboard side of the mast. Both the wooden and fiberglass yawls have mizzen staysail halyards, but only the wooden boats have a Number 2 winch on the port side of the mast for this halyard. The fiberglass boats are fitted with a cleat only for making fast the staysail halyard. All yawls have a

8-5. Luders fiberglass yawl, accommodations plan and inboard profile.

triple-purchase mizzen sheet that leads to a winch mounted on the lower, after side of the mizzen mast. The sheet's cleat is just below the winch. The mizzen staysail sheet is led through a block at the end of the mizzen boom and belays to a cleat on the boom.

Yawl sails

Yawl mainsails are made of heavy dacron and have an area of 487 square feet. They are usually left furled and stopped on the boom when the boats are not in use. The sails are secured to their spars with tracks and slides. On the wooden boats the main boom's gooseneck may slide up or down on the mast, and all luff tension adjustments are made with the boom downhaul. The fiberglass boats have a fixed gooseneck, and luff tension adjustments are made with a combination of a *jack line* (a line fitted through the bottom ten slides of the luff), a Cunningham line, or halyard tension. The sail is hoisted until the top of the headboard (the plate in the head of the mainsail) is even with the bottom of the black band at the masthead, and then the downhaul (or Cunningham) is adjusted to give the proper luff

tension appropriate to the wind velocity or a particular point of sailing. When sighting aloft to align the headboard with the black band, remember that you are sighting from directly beneath, and the extreme perspective will make it appear that the headboard is higher relative to the band than it really is. Once a mainsail is hoisted to its proper height, it is often possible to mark the halyard with a piece of tape, or preferably a *serving* (tight winding) of twine around the halyard that can be aligned with another tape mark on the mast for future reference. It is important to hoist the mainsail as high as possible for two reasons: in light airs there is usually more wind aloft, and the maximum distance between upper and lower black bands may be utilized fully to tighten the luff in a fresh breeze.

The clew outhaul on the main boom of the fiberglass yawls consists of a slide on a track mounted along the top of the boom. The outhaul line runs from the slide internally through the boom and exits along the forward starboard side of the boom. The mainsail clew on any yawl should never be pulled abaft the forward edge of the black band at the boom's end. Never forget to *slack the outhaul*

8-6. Luders wooden yawl, accommodations plan and inboard profile.

of any furled sail left bent on its boom. Before hoisting or lowering the mainsail, be sure that the boom topping lift (see figure 8-7) is set up, and that it is slacked off when underway. Sailing with a taut topping lift is nearly always harmful to the set of a sail.

Mainsails on the wooden yawls were originally reefed in the conventional way, as shown in figure 8-10. Now the yawls have a newer simplified system, which will soon be described, but first it is well to discuss the older system as it involves basic principles, and in the interest in becoming a complete seaman, every sailor should be familiar with all the fundamental forms of reefing. Notice that before the sail is reefed there is a row of eyelets with lanyards (short lines) hanging from them. These are called *reef points*, and they hang down on each side of the sail. In line with the reef point eyelets at the luff, there is a reinforced hole in the sail called the *luff cringle* and at the leech a similar hole called the *leech cringle*. When reefing the sail, these cringles are lashed down to the boom with short, stout lines called *earings*. Each yawl is supplied with a clew and tack earing. The luff cringle should be lashed down before the leech cringle is pulled aft. The clew earing must not only hold the leech cringle down, but the line must pull the cringle aft as well. The earing should run from the cringle aft through the clew outhaul fitting (or some other reefing point at the boom's after end), and then be led forward to the cringle again. The sail is hauled aft until it is tight along the boom, and then the leech cringle is lashed down to the boom with the remaining end of the earing. After both cringles are lashed, the loose lower part of the sail below the reef points, which is called the *bunt*, is rolled up neatly and placed on top of the boom where it is tied with the reef points. Notice in figure 8-10 that the reef points are not tied around the boom, but they pass between the boom and the sail. Were they tied around the boom, unequal tension on different reef points could cause harmful stretching or even tearing of the sail.

If reefing is done while underway, the mainsail can be lowered entirely. The topping lift is set up, the boat is luffed into the wind, and the sail is lowered. This requires that the boat be a sufficient distance from the *lee shore* (downwind shore) before the operation is begun because the boat may make considerable leeway while the reef is being tied in. The boat can jog along under jib and mizzen

until the reef is tied in. While reefing, the boom should be in its crutch and the mainsheet must be *bowsed down* (pulled tight) to hold the boom in place. Since some yawls are equipped with more than one row of reef points, it is very important, before hoisting sail, to check that all the tied reef points are from the same row. A sail could be seriously torn if some points were tied from the first row while others were tied from the second. If a mainsail is not equipped with reef points but only a row of eyelets, then a long, continuous reefing line may be rove through the eyelets and around the foot of the sail or around the boom in a spiral manner when there is no space between the foot and boom. If a reef is taken in using the conventional points method, it is often easier and the sail flaps less if it is lowered, but racing boats seldom if ever lower their mainsails. Also, in rough seas when there is a large Genoa set, lowering the main can put excessive strain on the mast. To reef without lowering sail, set up the topping lift and sail close-hauled with a slight luff in the mainsail; ease the halyard until the luff cringle comes down to the boom, set up the tack earing and then the clew earing, tie in the reef points, hoist the sail until the luff is taut, and slack the topping lift.

Shaking out (untying) a reef is usually easier than tying one in. This is one reason why it is better to reef before getting underway when there is doubt as to the need for reducing sail. Should it be found, when underway, that conditions don't warrant a reef, it is not difficult to shake it out. This can usually be done without lowering the sail. First the topping lift is set up. Then the reef points are untied, the clew earing is cast off, and finally the tack earing is unlashed. The helmsman then luffs slightly and another crew man stands by the halyard to hoist the sail up hard as soon as the tack earing has been released.

The fiberglass yawls were equipped with roller reefing until 1976. With this reefing method, the mainsail is rolled up on its boom, which may be rotated with a gear and crank handle at the gooseneck. Figure 8-11 shows a worm-gear roller reefing mechanism similar to that formerly used on the Navy yawls. For clarity, the illustration shows the gears exposed, but in actuality they lie within a metal housing so that the sail will not get caught in the gears. With roller reefing, sail is rarely lowered entirely before reefing. The halyard is simply eased

109

off as the crank is turned. The bottom four slides on the mainsail are attached to the jack line. Before reefing, the jack line is unrove from the slides allowing them to remain on the track when the sail is wound around the boom. If a deeper reef is required, the upper slides must be removed from the track, one at a time, when they are pulled down to the bottom of the track by the boom's rotation. It is nearly always necessary to have one or two crew members pulling aft on the sail's leech near the clew, in order that the roll be kept smooth all the

way along the boom. The mainsheet is attached to a swivel fitting at the end of the boom. Someone should check to see that this fitting is swivelling smoothly as the boom is turned. When unrolling a reef, the procedure is reversed. The boom is turned in the opposite direction unwinding the sail, while the halyard is taken up and the slides are fed back onto the track and the bottom slides are secured to the sail.

In 1976 the Navy fiberglass yawls received new aluminum booms that converted the reefing to a

110

Approximate Sail Areas

mainsail	487 square feet
mizzen	94 square feet
forestaysail	141 square feet
working jib	170 square feet
storm trysail	135 square feet
Genoa jibs	
No. 1	642 square feet
No. 2	566 square feet
No. 3	410 square feet
mizzen staysail	257 square feet
spinnaker	1080 square feet
spinnaker staysail	444 square feet
tri-radial staysail	1080 square feet

8-7. Luders fiberglass yawl, sail, rigging, and half-deck plans.

"jiffy" or "slab" reefing system. The sail is lowered onto the boom and secured with a single earing and hook, and the bunt is gathered and tied up with small stuff or a spiral lacing line through relatively few reef eyelets. With this system the yawls have a flattening reef, first reef, and second reef.

The flattening reef does little to reduce sail, but it removes excessive draft, particularly in the lower third of the sail. To set the flattening reef, the mainsheet is eased while the flattening reef line is winched in until the leech cringle lies close to the boom. The luff of the sail is not adjusted for this reef.

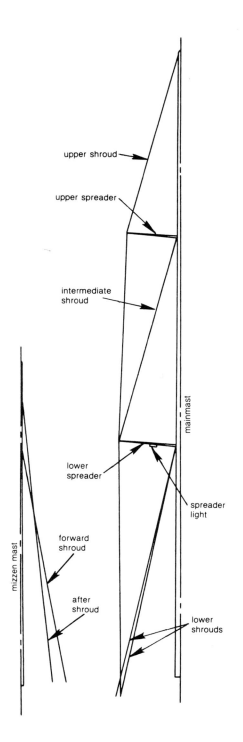

112

1 1/4" R

1/4"

4 1/2"

1/4"

pin & bushing same
as backstay

4"

1 1/4" R

16"

drill for 1/4"
RHMS

sail track

drill tang for
3/4" bolt

2 3/16" plates,
cres. type 316

13/16"

1"

4"

3/16"

drill for
5/8" dia.
pin

3/16"

13/16" R

5/8"

view from STBD

3/4" I.D. alum. pipe
threaded for VHF antenna

8 1/2"

5"

5/8" R

4"

5/8" pl

30°

5/8" pl

masthead light

Kenyon AWI 300
bracket

2 3/16"
plates, cres.

13/16" R

3/16"

2 3/4"

drill for 5/8"
dia. pin

backstay link

1 1/16" R

4"

7/8" R

drill for
3/4" bolt

drill for 5/8" dia. pin

3/16" plate, cres. type

alternate tang for shrouds
make 1 for each shroud

masthead plate

3/4" R

1/8"

7/16"

5/8"

7/16"

3 1/4"

1 5/8"

1 3/16"

7/16"

7/16"

5/8"

1/8"

drill for 5/8"
dia. pin

headstay toggle

8-8. Luders fiberglass yawl, mainmasthead detail.

113

8-9. A fiberglass Luders yawl on the wind. This close view of the *Fearless* working to windward full and by shows the Genoa sheeting arrangement. Note that the sheet runs through the sliding lead block on the track on the rail, through a turning block abaft the lead block, and then forward to the large winch. To get extra power, the crew can then lead the sheet across the boat to the weather winch. The helmsman is sitting to leeward where he can get a clear view of the jib. Observe the dinghy in her chocks and secured by crisscrossed straps.

The reef lines or earings that control the leech of the sail are led internally through the boom. The after part of each line exits the boom around a turning block, passes up through a reefing cringle in the leech, and then is led back to the boom where it is made fast. The forward part of the reef line leaves the boom at the gooseneck as shown in figure 8-13. Also note the internal mainsheet. The reef line is then led to a fairlead block, through a jam cleat, and to one of the #16 Barient winches at the aft end of the cabin house.

When the reef line is winched up, the leech of the sail is held firmly along the boom. The luff of the sail is secured through the use of a grommet (cringle) in the luff and one of the two hooks at the gooseneck, one hook for each of the two full reefs.

Steps for inserting a full reef in the mainsail while beating to windward are as follows: luff the sail by slacking its sheet. The helmsman bears off slightly to

maintain speed. Ease the main halyard until the appropriate reef grommet on the luff can be fitted onto the tack hook above the gooseneck. After hooking on the grommet, rehoist the main to tighten its luff. Simultaneously, the appropriate reefing line is taken in and tensioned with its winch to pull the clew down to the boom. When both the leech and luff have been secured, the mainsail is trimmed, and the helmsman heads up to a close-hauled course. The crew can then tie up the bunt of the sail with small stuff or a lacing line that is wound spirally around the boom and inserted through the reef point eyelets. A well-trained crew should be able to clap in a reef and get the boat back on her course in 15 to 20 seconds. A jiffy reefing sequence is shown in figure 9-19.

The mizzen on a Navy yawl is quite similar to the mainsail except, of course, that it is much smaller, with an area of 94 square feet. For this reason it is not provided with any means of reefing. The clew outhaul is a slide on a track controlled with a purchase, but the gooseneck is fixed, so luff tension must be controlled with the halyard. The mizzen's primary function is to act as a balancing sail. When the sail is sheeted in flat, weather helm is increased, but when the sheet is eased, weather helm is lessened. Because the mizzen is usually backwinded by the mainsail when sailing close-hauled, some sailors feel that the mizzen is of little value on a beat. Actually, it has considerable value as a balancing

114

FULL MAINSAIL

REEFED MAINSAIL

8-10. Conventional reefing.

On many roller reefing devices of this type the gears are entirely housed within the fitting to protect the sail.

8-11. Roller reefing.

sail, particularly in light airs, giving the boat a little weather helm. As said previously, this helm is important to give the keel hydrodynamic lift and especially to give the helmsman a "helm feel." In a strong breeze, when weather helm is excessive, the mizzen can be lowered, and this will nearly always relieve the boat's strong tendency to round up into the wind. Don't be too hasty in lowering the mizzen when beating against head seas, as the sail can help hold the bow up when it is being pushed to leeward by the seas. One of the advantages of the yawl rig is that in a sudden squall the mainsail may be lowered and balance will be maintained under forestaysail and mizzen. Also, unless the boat is heeled excessively, reasonable balance can be had under mainsail and forestaysail, or even under mainsail alone, if it is desired that the jib and mizzen be lowered (see figures 6-11 and 8-1).

The forestaysail is a fairly small (141 square feet), heavy sail with battens, and it is hanked on to the forestay. It is the basic, working headsail on a yawl. Usually this sail is set in a strong breeze only, or when squalls threaten, or when a yawl is undermanned in a moderate breeze. The most usual sail combinations that include the forestaysail are as follows:

• Main, mizzen, forestaysail, and a high-cut working jib hanked on to the headstay. This combination of sails forward of the mainmast is known as the double head rig, and it is sometimes carried when beating to windward in a fresh breeze. This combination can be very effective. Some boats with a double head rig carry a larger high-cut jib called a *yankee* in moderate weather.

• Main and forestaysail, or reefed main and forestaysail. The latter is an especially well-balanced plan for a strong breeze.

• Mizzen and forestaysail for a sudden squall.

• Forestaysail alone in a strong gale. If the boat is heeled severely, this sail will balance the boat reasonably well even though it is well forward of the normal total center of effort (see figure 6-11).

• Forestaysail set in combination with a Genoa jib, mainsail, and mizzen in squally weather, so that if a squall hits, Genoa and mainsail may be dropped quickly and the boat will be under a very short, balanced rig.

Light sails used on the yawls include three sizes of Genoa jibs, spinnakers (to be discussed in chapter 10), spinnaker staysails, mizzen staysail, and

8-12. The Luders yawl *Swift* with a shallow reef rolled in her mainsail. Notice how the boom vang must be attached with a claw ring. The reef is not sufficiently deep to necessitate removing all the slides from the jack line. The mizzen is furled primarily to relieve weather helm.

drifter. The large Genoa, called the number one Genoa, with an area of 642 square feet, is the "work horse" of a yawl in light weather. It supplies the principal driving power in a light breeze on all points of sailing, except when the wind is abaft the beam—at which times the spinnaker comes into prominence. The number one is probably carried more often than any other sail except the main and mizzen. (See figure 8-15).

The number two is the next smaller size Genoa, and it has an area of 566 square feet. This is carried when the wind is too strong for the number one. When jibs should be changed will depend on whether the boat is being raced or cruised, whether the main is reefed, how many and how skilled are her crew, the cut and condition of the particular jibs involved, and the stiffness of the boat. To be very general, however, when the boat is racing, the

number one should probably be replaced with the number two when the wind velocity is between 16 and 18 knots.

When a boat begins to be overburdened with the number two Genoa, the number three should be used. The modern version of this sail has an area of only 410 square feet. In a breeze that would warrant carrying this sail, perhaps 25 to 30 knots, there would be an option between the number three and the aforementioned double head rig. In heavy seas, the latter might be preferable, because the lower-cut Genoa often takes heavy spray and solid water against its foot, and this could obviously damage the sail. Notice, however, that the number three shown in figure 8-7 is cut with a high clew to minimize damage from the bow wave. Another factor to take into consideration is the trend of the weather. If it seems likely that the breeze will increase and de-

8-13A. Luders fiberglass yawl slab or jiffy reefing sheave box. From left to right: first reef line; mainsheet; flattening reef; second reef line. All lines are lead internally along the boom.

8-13B. Deck layout showing reefing arrangement. From starboard to port: the second reef line is coiled and hanging just beneath the sheave box; the flattening reef line is lead aft through a jam cleat.

velop into a gale, the double head rig will be preferable because the forestaysail is already set and the jib can be quickly doused if the wind becomes overpowering. When it comes to carrying only one headsail in a gale, the forestaysail is nearly always easier to manage than a long-tailed overlapping jib.

The drifter has been discussed very briefly in chapter 6. It is a light-weather sail, and therefore it should have a lightweight sheet so that its clew will lift in the slightest zephyr. If it is cut high in the foot, its sheet can be led to a block on the end of the main boom when sailing between a beam reach and a close reach, so that the sail is trimmed a maximum distance outboard (see figure 6-1). Of course, when racing with the wind abeam or abaft the beam, the drifter is not carried because this is when the spinnaker is the most effective sail. These two should rarely be carried simultaneously, because they will interfere with each other's wind. Drifters are rarely carried on a beat except, perhaps, in the very lightest airs. On the wind, it is usually better to carry a lightweight number one Genoa, because the boat will not be able to point very high with a drifter.

The yawls carry three spinnaker staysails, the first of these is a "low boy" having an area of 250 square feet. This sail is carried on broad reaches and runs, although frequently it is blanketed by the mainsail

on a nearly dead run. It is designed to fill the area beneath the spinnaker. A new, very large spinnaker staysail was added in 1977. This sail has an area of 432 square feet and is most effective on a reach. Having a very long luff, the staysail is set on a jib halyard and tacked down with a tack line to a pad eye on the foredeck. Since this is such a large sail, it must be properly trimmed to prevent spoiling the airflow to the spinnaker, which could cause the spinnaker to collapse. The third staysail used with the spinnaker is a "tall boy" with an area of 250 square feet. This sail is most effective on the closer spinnaker reaches. It is also set on a jib halyard and tacked to the foredeck with a tack line. It can be carried when running by tacking it down to the weather rail not far forward of the mast.

The mizzen staysail can be an effective sail on certain points of sailing because its area of 257 square feet is more than two and one-half times that of the mizzen. The most effective point of sailing for the mizzen staysail is the broad reach. When the wind draws abaft the quarter, the sail begins to be blanketed by the mizzen, but when the wind draws forward of the quarter, the staysail begins to back-wind the mizzen. The mizzen staysail can almost never be carried on a dead run, and it can rarely be carried effectively when sailing higher than a beam reach. On this latter point of sailing, it not only backwinds the mizzen, but it is backwinded by the mainsail, and it also blankets the lower after corner of the mainsail. The mizzen staysail is tacked down to a pad eye located on the windward side of the cabin top, or just inboard of the weather shrouds.

Remember always to secure the tack to windward of the boat's centerline. The sail must be hoisted to leeward of the permanent backstay. Its sheet runs outside the mizzen shrouds, through a block on the end of the mizzen boom, and then inboard (see figure 6-1).

8-14. The Navy boat *Ranger* showing her flattening reef. Notice how the reef lines lead internally through the boom. The helmsman is sitting where he can get a clear view of the jib's circular telltale window. Instrumentation includes apparent wind direction and speed indicators, inclinometer, and log. Rubber hoses on the lifelines allow the crew to lean against the wires in comfort.

As when trimming any sail on a reach, the mizzen staysail's sheet should be kept eased to the point where the sail begins to luff. In addition, there should be an ample slot between the leech of the staysail and the lee side of the mizzen. The clew of the staysail should never be pulled close to the mizzen boom when the mizzen is hoisted because of the problem with backwind. When pulling in on the staysail sheet, always watch the mizzen to see that it does not begin to bulge from the staysail's backwind. When this bulge occurs, the staysail's sheet must be eased or else the mizzen must be lowered. Occasionally it pays to lower the mizzen when it blankets the mizzen staysail or when the latter backwinds the former, because the staysail has the larger sail area. Once the mizzen staysail is basically well trimmed, it is often best to make fine trim adjustments with the mizzen sheet. Since the staysail sheet is led to the mizzen boom, then obviously the mizzen sheet will also affect the staysail's trim. Making the adjustments with the mizzen sheet will keep the slot between staysail and mizzen wide, and also the staysail will be led the maximum distance outboard. When sailing close to a beam reach, be sure the staysail's luff is taut. When jibing, the mizzen staysail must be lowered and removed entirely before the main boom swings across. Then the staysail may be reset on the new tack, again with its tack to windward and the halyard to leeward of the backstay.

The mizzen spinnaker is cut like a spinnaker but is set and sheeted like a conventional mizzen staysail. Unlike a conventional spinnaker set on the mainmast, the mizzen spinnaker is not equipped with a pole that holds the sail out to windward; therefore, the mizzen spinnaker is particularly subject to being blanketed by the mizzen when the wind is far aft. On a run it often pays to lower the mizzen to avoid this blanketing. Although by tightening its luff the conventional mizzen staysail can be carried when sailing almost as high as a beam reach, the mizzen spinnaker, with its full cut, cannot be carried that close to the wind. In a fresh breeze, the mizzen spinnaker should be allowed to lift to the maximum extent. This means that the sheet and tack should be eased liberally. When the sail is well lifted, it also often pays to slack the halyard slightly to let the head of the sail move away from the mizzen's wind shadow.

Stowable gear and equipment

Before getting underway in a Navy yawl (or any boat), it is important to know the location of her gear and equipment. For obvious reasons, all stowable gear should be returned to its proper location. Heed the old expression, "a place for everything and everything in its place."

Figure 8-5 shows the accommodation plan of a fiberglass yawl. The arrangement of the wooden yawls is similar (see figure 8-6), except that on these boats, the head is located aft on the starboard side, adjacent to the companion ladder. It is generally agreed that the fiberglass yawls have much more practical and comfortable accommodations for the crew.

Locations for stowable gear are as follows:
- Life jackets are evenly distributed throughout the boat in order that they may be reached from anywhere regardless of the type of emergency that requires them.
- Life rings and man-overboard gear (see chapter 12) are carried aft in holders attached to the stern pulpit. These rings should never be lashed in their holders.
- Sails are stowed forward under the foredeck in the wooden yawls, but on the forward bunks or in bins under the cockpit seats to port and starboard in the fiberglass yawls.
- Sheets are kept near the sail stowage area. In the wooden yawls, sheets are stowed in the labeled areas on either side of the mainmast. Genoa sheets are forward to starboard, spinnaker sheets aft to starboard, forestaysail sheets forward to port, and spare sheets and halyards aft to port. On the fiberglass boats, sheets are on the port side under the cockpit seat.
- *Snatch blocks* (removable, side-opening blocks) on the wooden yawls are stowed in drawers under the galley sink. When detaching a block from a rail slide, keep the sheet rove through the block until it is detached and has been moved inboard, so there is no possibility of dropping it overboard.
- Winch handles are stowed in drawers in the same area as the snatch blocks on the wooden boats. When under sail, if the handles are not in use, they are always kept in special holders in the cockpit.
- Snatch blocks and winch handles on the fiberglass boats are stowed in bins or drawers under the amidships bunks on the port and starboard sides.

• On all boats, reefing earings and sail stops are stowed in this same area, in the forward port drawers.

• These same drawers hold the tool kit, sail repair kit, and lead line.

• The fog horn is stowed in this area, although some yawls have it mounted on the cabin top.

• Flares are kept in the bottom locker of the navigator's table for easy access.

• The first aid kit is stowed in a shelf on the forward bulkhead near the head (on the port side).

• Fenders, a *fender board* (a plank hung over the side outboard of the fenders to protect the topsides when lying alongside a pier), a *bosun's chair* (a wooden or canvas seat used to haul a person up the mast), and certain cleaning gear is kept in the *lazaret* (space under the hatch on the after deck abaft the cockpit).

• Other cleaning gear is stowed in the galley.

• A 40-pound Danforth anchor is kept in the port side cockpit locker; 150 feet of ½-inch anchor rode, together with a 6-foot chain leader and a 12-pound Danforth, are stowed in the lazarette.

• Three fire extinguishers are on board: one in the forward cabin, one in the galley, and one in the port sheet locker. These are dry-chemical extin-

8-15. The number one Genoa jib. This picture shows the sail from two different views. Most Genoas have concave leeches (reverse roaches), because they are not fitted with battens. This leech curve is especially important with the Luders yawls in order that the leech will clear the upper spreaders. On the *Resolute* (starboard tack), the Genoa's foot seems to be stretched overly taut against the shrouds. This might be relieved by moving the lead farther forward, provided that the knot or splice in the sheet is not pulled into the lead block. In this light breeze, she might foot a little faster with the mainsheet started an inch or two.

guishers, and each crew member should be familiar with their operation. They should be checked frequently to be sure they are pressurized adequately.

- The inflatable rubber life rafts on the yawls are stowed on the cabin house abaft the mast before going offshore.

Each Luders yawl was originally equipped with one dinghy, a 7-foot 9-inch, unsinkable Dyer Dhow. Although these boats are no longer used at the Naval Academy, they are perhaps the most common dinghy used by private yachts. Such boats are primarily used for convenience in going to or from a yacht when she is anchored or moored offshore in a harbor away from home. However, a dinghy is also handy for such jobs as carrying out a kedge anchor in the event of a grounding, and the sailing model is great fun to sail in a small harbor. It can also be used as a lifeboat in calm weather, but it can only hold three or possibly four small people.

When not in use, a Dhow is usually carried upside down on the cabin top. The dinghies are lashed to special *chocks* (wooden blocks specifically designed to hold a boat or other equipment in place so that it will not shift during an extreme angle of heel or in rough weather). Usually one continuous line, often the boat's *painter* (bow line), is used to lash a boat in her chocks. If the painter is used, it is run through the eye in either forward chock and then the line is passed over the boat's bottom to the after chock on the opposite side. Here the line is passed through the chock's eye, back over the boat's bottom, through the handgrip hole in the boat's skeg, and through the eye in the other after chock. The line is then passed over the boat's bottom to the forward chock on the opposite side, and here the line is secured with two half hitches. It is a wise precaution to finish off this knot with a slippery hitch (see figure 2-9) for quick release in an emergency. As can be seen in figure 8-9, the lashing line will make a criss-cross pattern over the dinghy's bottom.

Oars, oarlocks, and a bailer should be lashed inside the dinghy.

A small Dyer Dhow, weighing slightly less than 70 pounds, can easily be lifted aboard a yacht by two people. One can lift the dinghy by her painter while another can lift her with a stern line made fast to the metal ring at her stern. An upward pull on these lines by two people at the yacht's rail will not only lift the dinghy but tilt her over so that her lower gunwale can be rested on the yacht's rail. From here she can easily be lifted over the lifelines, turned upside down, and placed on her chocks. When a dinghy is brought aboard in this manner, the yacht's topsides should be protected with fenders or lines draped over the side.

If a heavier boat is brought aboard, the main halyard can be used for lifting purposes. First a bridle is rigged from the stern ring to the bow ring, and then the halyard is shackled on to a loop in the center of the bridle. The bridle's loop should be in such a position that the boat is balanced or horizontal when she is lifted clear of the water. Obviously, a great deal of power can be had with the halyard when it is put on a winch.

The Dyer Dhows are cat-rigged and are fitted with a removable rudder and dagger board. The boats have very small sails and are a bit sluggish in light airs, but in a moderate to fresh breeze they are quite responsive and great fun to sail. (See figure 8-16.)

The Dhow's sail is attached to a spar that is hooked on to the top of a short mast. First the mast is stepped and then the sail is bent to the spar by sliding the sail's luff rope into a groove on the after side of the spar. Next the spar, with sail attached, is lifted up and hooked to the top of the mast. The sail is loose-footed and secures to the boom with a hook at the tack and a short outhaul at the clew. The boom's forward end has jaws that fit around the mast. The mainsheet is snapped to the traveler and rove through the sheet blocks.

The rudder is hooked to a vertical rod on the transom, and the dagger board, stowed under the thwart, is slid down its well. Then the boat is ready to sail.

Handling the yawl under sail

Although it is possible to sail a Navy yawl single-handed, the Naval Academy requires that there be a minimum crew of four. When sailing with this minimum, one man obviously will be at the helm. Another man should be assigned to the cockpit area forward of the helsman to tend the jib-sheets and sheet winches. The third man should be assigned to the foredeck to tend to the mooring line and halyards, and clear the jib if necessary when tacking. The fourth man should lend a hand either on the foredeck or in the cockpit. Sailing shorthanded

8-16. The Dyer Dhow. Crew weight is placed well so that the boat is not trimmed excessively by the stern. Notice that the mainsheet has fouled on its traveler on the fully shown boat.

requires careful planning ahead. The skipper should try to anticipate any difficulties that could arise as a result of having a small crew. A forestaysail or easy-to-handle jib should be carried in most cases.

The ideal racing crew for a Navy yawl generally numbers between seven and ten members (the fiberglass yawls have sleeping accommodations for nine). The yawls may be sailed with less than seven but not at maximum efficiency under all racing conditions, unless the crew is exceptionally skilled and experienced. When a crew numbers more than ten, some members are superfluous and they usually get in the way of each other and the working crew as well.

A crew should be divided into two groups, a foredeck crew and an afterguard. The latter group is concentrated in or near the cockpit, and it consists of the skipper who is the principal helmsman, a relief helmsman who may tend the mizzen and mizzen staysail, a navigator who may double as a mainsheet tender or help with other sheets or backstays, and the winch men. The foredeck group has a foredeck captain or person in charge of all activities forward of the mainmast, and he has at least two assistants. This forward group is particularly busy when the spinnaker is set.

The wooden yawls were moored offshore on permanent moorings. When under sail in a large heavy boat without an engine, such as a wooden Luders yawl, it is usually much easier to leave and return to a mooring than to leave and enter a slip similar to those in which the knockabouts and J-24s are kept. Fiberglass yawls are kept in slips, but because of their auxiliary power they are not difficult to maneuver. Maneuvering under power will be discussed in chapter 13.

Leaving and landing at a mooring under sail was discussed briefly in chapter 5, and of course the same basic principles apply to the Navy yawls. The skipper should size up the weather, estimate wind strength and direction, and determine which sails will be carried before boarding his yawl. This will prevent any apparent indecision on the skipper's part and allow him to give instructions to the crew immediately after going aboard. Any inexperienced crew members should be checked out on their particular duties and on the operation of deck gear they will handle. The mizzen is hoisted first, and it is sheeted flat so that the boat is held head to wind. Next, the mainsail is hoisted. But prior to this operation, both running backstays should be secured forward against the shrouds so that the mainsail will not foul them. Before casting off the mooring line, the mizzen may be backed (pushed to windward). This will cause the stern to move in the direction opposite to the sail. In other words, if the mizzen is pushed to port the stern will move to starboard, and the bow will fall away from the wind to port. When the bow has fallen away slightly, the jib may be hoisted. Care should be taken that the jib does not get aback in the wrong direction. After the mooring line's eye is taken off its bitt, the eye may be taken to the windward side of the bow and walked a short distance aft to ensure that the yawl will sail off in the desired direction. Then the mooring line is cast off, the jib is trimmed flat, or backed if necessary, and the mizzen is slacked until the yawl is on her proper course. Before casting off, be sure the halyards are coiled and all sheets are clear.

When picking up the mooring, the yawl is headed into the wind. It is usually the safest policy to approach the mooring about two or more boat lengths to leeward of it on a point of sailing between a beam and close reach at low speed with the sails luffing. If it is found that the speed is too slow, sails may be trimmed in a little; if the speed seems too fast, sheets can be slacked. When nearing the mooring buoy, the bow is turned slowly into the wind while all sheets are slacked. The mooring *pendant* (line) is picked up with a boat hook. If the boat should have slightly too much way, then the main boom may be pushed up to windward so that the sail will act as a brake. Be sure the runners are secured forward.

Another, but less desirable, mooring approach can be made directly downwind. The boat is sailed before the wind down to her mooring. She passes one or two boat lengths away from the buoy, leaving it on the windward side. When the buoy is less than half a boat length abaft the stern, the helm is put hard to leeward and the boat rounds up sharply coming to a nearly dead stop. Remember that a slowly turned rudder does little to kill speed, but a rudder jammed hard over acts as a brake.

It is usually best not to pick up a mooring with a Genoa jib set, because this sail restricts visibility and causes confusion on the foredeck when its long tail thrashes around as the boat heads into the wind. The mooring can be approached with a small jib or forestaysail set or without any headsail (under main and mizzen, or mainsail alone). If the mizzen is set, its sheet must be slacked off to maintain balance. After the buoy is picked up, the mizzen sheet should be pulled in to hold the boat's bow to the wind. Sails are doused from bow to stern, with the mizzen being the last sail lowered.

The procedures for tacking and jibing were discussed in chapter 5. It is important that all crew members understand the basic principles of these procedures, because maneuvering a Navy yawl requires teamwork. Before tacking, the skipper alerts his crew to stand by to come about. The crew take their stations. One man, or perhaps two if the forestay is set up, should take a position along the foot of the jib to see that the foot runs easily forward

and through the slot between stays during the tack. A man stands by to release the jibsheet and set up the running backstay if it is in use. Two men stand by the windward Genoa sheet winch that will be used to bring the jib in on the new tack. Another man stands by to pull back on the jib's clew when it is first being trimmed in, and this same man can then release the leeward running backstay if it is set up. It is usually easier to adjust the traveler before tacking. Be sure that every man has a station and knows his job.

At the command *hard-a-lee*, the helm is put over. The jibsheet is slacked when almost head to wind, and it is eased off. It is not suddenly released, because this will noticeably slow the boat and kill her momentum. The skipper often tells the man on the sheet when to release it. If the runners are being used, the man who releases the sheet can set up the new windward backstay. Some authorities advise setting up the runner before the jibsheet is released, because at this time it is often possible to get the stay very taut. The men stationed at the foot of the Genoa carry it forward while the bowman gathers in the slack. If the forestay is set up, the jib must be fed through the space between the forestay and headstay. When the boat swings past the head-to-wind position, the jib will be blown through the space between the stays, so the helmsman should momentarily bear away sharply onto the new tack to make the jib blow through quickly. After this, the helm is turned more slowly to give the sheet trimmers maximum help in winching in the jib. Of course, if the backstays are not in use, and especially if the forestay is not set up, tacking is a much simpler job.

Jibing involves essentially the same crew activity as tacking, except that not as many are needed to handle the jib and two men are needed to tend the mizzen and mainsheets. The man on the mainsheet has an especially important job because the mainsail is quite large and its boom has considerable weight. In a breeze, he must be sure that the sheet is pulled all the way in when the boom crosses over the boat's centerline, and he must never ease the sheet until the new leeward running backstay has been slacked. The helmsman does not actually turn onto the new tack until the mainsheet tender is ready and has the mainboom amidships. At the word *jibe-ho*, the helmsman turns the bow to leeward so that the boom swings across onto the new tack. Of course, all crew members must be well clear of the boom when it swings across.

It is important that all crew members be thoroughly familiar with the operation of winches. Crew members who are inexperienced should be given rudimentary winch instruction soon after boarding a yawl, because the improper operation of a winch can be dangerous and cause injuries. As previously mentioned, main halyards on the fiberglass yawls are now operated with number 16 Barients. With the wire halyards having Dacron tails, it is important to see that at least four turns of wire go around the winch. Never wrap the wire-to-rope splice around a cleat, as this could weaken the splice.

It might be well to include a few words about the operation of reel winches, even though they are no longer used on the Luders yawls, because they are so common on other boats. Many seamen consider the screw pin and toggle type of brake release (see figure 8-17) safer than the pull handle type, because if the screw pin is very carefully and slowly turned, there is seldom a necessity to insert the winch handle when sail is lowered or the halyard is slacked. Less modern types of reel winches had brake handles that could, on rare occasions, be tripped accidentally. Often, when the halyard was under great strain, the winch handle had to be used to ease the halyard's tension before the sail was lowered or the luff was slacked to adjust the sail's draft. According to the winch manufacturer's advertising literature, the screw pin brake can be released gradually and there is no need to ease off tension with the winch handle. One word of warning, however; some screw pin releases may slack off more quickly than the manufacturer's claims lead you to believe. If the handle must be used, it must be gripped firmly, because more than a few injuries have been caused by the handle slipping out of the operator's hand. Keep heads and arms well clear of the handle, and remember that tension on the halyard often can be eased by slacking the downhaul.

Another advantage of this screw toggle brake is that sail can be hoisted with the brake on so that if the handle should happen to slip out of the operator's hand, the winch will not spin around.

Other winches on the yawls are conventional top-action (with handle at the top) ratchet or geared winches. With these winches, several turns of a sheet or halyard are wound around the winch and

8-17. Reel winch for the main halyard. Notice the screw toggle brake release on the left side of the winch base, the handle lock switch, and the step-up rim to take the last few turns of wire in order to prevent them from jamming into less tightly packed earlier turns. Some time ago, Barient added the following warning to its reel winches: "Set brake before cranking" and "Remove handle before releasing brake."

the winch is turned around with its crank handle while the line's tail (that part of the line between the winch and its free end) is pulled upon. A tension must be kept on the tail or else the line will slip on the drum. The man or men who pull on the tail are often called *tailers*, and their job is *tailing the sheet*. With winches on the Navy yawls, and on nearly all American boats for that matter, *lines are wound around the winches in a clockwise direction*. (See figure 8-18.) Some of the newer winches are self-tailers with a line-gripping channel and lifting arm at the top. The line is wrapped around the drum, then over the lifting arm and around the gripper, thus avoiding the need of a person tailing.

The yawls are equipped with powerful geared winches for the Genoa. Good teamwork is required the drum speed but increases power. Low gear is obtained by reversing the rotation direction of the winch handle. Ratcheting is obtained by flipping a switch on top of the winch handle. There is even a three-speed winch with an extra low gear that can be engaged by rotating a switch on top of the winch. Of course, low gears are only used for the last few feet of trim when there is too much strain to flatten the sail with higher gears or direct drive.

The following are a few tips on handling winches. Handles are always removed when the winch is not being used. When winching in a sheet, never throw on too many turns at first, as they can override each other and jam. When easing off a winch under strain, carefully unwrap one turn at a time while keeping tension on the tail; then ease off slowly until most of the strain has been relieved. When taking turns off a ratchet halyard winch, keep tension on the tail in such a way that it is pulled at right angles to the drum axis or else at a slight angle toward the mast, otherwise the line is liable to slip off the drum. When winching in a jib after tacking, be sure the windward sheet is completely clear to run through its lead blocks. When winding a wire-to-rope splice around a winch (some halyards are part wire and part rope), see that the splice is not left bent around the winch. This can harm the splice and cause wire snags to appear through the rope. Crank the winch a little farther, until the splice clears the drum. Never wrap the splice around the cleat, and never stand or sit with your head near a winch handle while it is being cranked, because the handle could slip out of the operator's hand. Be very cautious about placing fingers near a winch drum under strain. Be particularly cautious with wire on a winch. And once again, don't forget that a line is wrapped around a winch in a clockwise direction.

When sailing a yawl off the wind, especially during a race, a main boom vang is often used. This consists of a tackle that fastens to a strap that is put around the middle part of the boom. The bottom of the tackle does not secure at the base of the mast but at various points on the side deck, depending on the trim of the sail. This type of vang is sometimes called a *go-fast*. It can be hooked to any through-bolted fitting, such as a pad eye, the base of a lifeline stanchion, or Genoa car when the track is well bolted. Naturally, the vang must be removed before jibing.

When sailing a yawl (or any boat), a lookout must

8-18. Genoa sheet winch in operation. Notice that the tailer is keeping the sheet low, almost at right angles to the winch axis, so that the crank clears the sheet when the crank is turned all the way around. The trailer is looking up to call the jib's distance from the spreader, while the man on the foredeck is setting up the spinnaker pole.

to trim this jib rapidly when tacking in a breeze. When the jib swings over and begins to fill after the boat has tacked, the Genoa sheet tailer winds two or three loops of the sheet clockwise around the winch; then he pulls in on the sheet, hand over hand, as quickly as he can before the jib completely fills. The helmsman should be bearing away very slowly. When the tailer no longer has strength to pull in the sheet by hand, he wraps another turn or two around the winch, and the cranker (who cranks the winch) inserts the handle. He then cranks the winch, turning the handle all the way around making complete circles until he no longer has the strength for this, and then he ratchets with the handle, or moves it back and forth so that the winch turns spasmodically. Winch cranking can be a tiring task if tacks are frequent, so it is usually wise to have the cranker and tailer alternate or to have other crew members spell the cranker. If the line begins to slip on the drum as it is being winched in, the cranker must quickly remove the handle, while the tailer puts another turn or two around the drum.

Some sheet winches are two-speed with a direct drive that gives fast speed and a low gear that slows be kept at all times. Of course, this is primarily the helmsman's responsibility, but when a low-cut Genoa jib is set, it is very difficult for the helmsman to see off the lee bow. Therefore, a lookout should be stationed to leeward where he can see under or around the jib. The lookout should make constant reports to the helmsman concerning the location of approaching boats or obstructions that lie in this "blind" sector.

Electrical and water systems of the wooden Luders yawl

Although the wooden Luders yawls are no longer at the Naval Academy, they are still being used at various naval installations. Therefore, it is appropriate to describe here their electrical, and fresh- and salt-water systems, since detailed knowledge of these systems is required of any wooden-yawl skipper.

The electrical system of the wooden yawl has at least one 12-volt or two 6-volt wet-cell batteries connected in series to obtain 12 volts. These batteries are located in a lead or fiberglass battery box (to protect the boat from acid) abaft the companionway ladder. These batteries provide power for cabin lights, running lights, spreader lights, the binnacle, and a Kenyon light (in boats where Kenyon speed indicators are installed). The cabin lights are controlled by switches on the fixtures, in addition to switches on the control panel located abaft the companion ladder. The appropriate switch on the control box must be turned on before the fixture switches will work. The other lights are controlled solely by the switch on the control panel. On deck, two electrical jacks are provided for connecting emergency running lights and spotlights. When not in use, these jacks should be capped to ensure that salt water does not short the circuit.

The freshwater system has two 50-gallon tanks, located under the lower bunks amidships. Connecting valves are located beneath the cabin sole and are reached by removing a portable section of the cabin sole. The tanks are filled from the deck. The freshwater fill pipe deck plate is on the port side amidships. The boat's tool kit should include a spanner wrench for removing the plate. Each tank has a vent on its top. There are two freshwater pumps in the boat, one at the galley sink and one at the head sink. The head sink drains into the toilet bowel. The galley sink drains via a globe valve, pump, and sea

cock overboard through the hull. The icebox drains via a separate valve into this same drain line, so that the pump below the icebox can be used to empty either the icebox or the sink. To do so, the appropriate valve must be open, and the valve not in use should be shut. Both these valves are in the locker next to the icebox.

Before using any pump, check that both intake and discharge valves are open. If the intake valve is shut, only useless effort is expended, but if the discharge valve is shut, *pumping can rupture the pump or discharge line.*

Included in the saltwater system is the piping for the bilge pumps, cockpit scuppers, and the head. On all the boats there are two bilge pumps. One is located just abaft the head, to starboard of the companionway. The other is beneath the cockpit and is operated from the cockpit. The intake strainers for both these pumps are in the bilge beneath the companionway. Both these pumps discharge through the hull through sea cocks, which should be opened for use and shut immediately afterwards. A sea cock is opened by paralleling the handle with the piping; when the handle is perpendicular to the piping, the valve is shut. All through-hull fittings on the Luders yawls are equipped with sea cocks, and familiarity with their location and use is a must. If a bilge pump seems hard to operate, first check to make certain that the discharge valve is open. Second, check the intake strainer in the bilge to see if it has been clogged. For this very reason, it is important to keep all foreign matter out of the bilge. On some of the wooden yawls, a third bilge pump is installed. It is a high-capacity diaphragm pump located beneath the cabin sole. The intake for this pump is beneath it in the bilge, and it discharges over the side via a length of fire hose led out through the hatch. This length of fire hose and the handle needed to operate the pump should be stowed with the pump. If they are lost, the pump cannot be operated.

The head has two sea cocks, one at the hull on the intake side (this one is the smaller of the two), the other at the hull on the discharge side. The intake (hull) valve is beneath the cabin sole next to the head, and the discharge valve is in the locker just outboard of the head. Both must be open to use the head. To operate the head, open the valves, depress the pedal on the foot-operated intake valve, and pump. This action pumps water both in and out.

125

8-19. The Westerbeke Model Four-107 diesel.

After the head has been pumped clear, pump ten more strokes to clear the discharge line, then release the foot pedal and continue to pump until most of the water has been removed from the bowl. In a rough sea, remove all water from the bowl. Before leaving, *shut the valves. Never* put solid objects or large quantities of paper in a marine toilet, as they will not fit through the rubber diaphragms. These rules apply to most marine toilets, but if there is any question about operation, ask before using one.

The cockpit scuppers drain overboard through pipes located beneath the cockpit. These pipes are fitted with sea cocks at the through-hull fittings that are abaft the ice box on the port side and under the quarter berth on the starboard side. These valves should always be left *open* so that the cockpit will drain.

As has been mentioned, it is good practice to shut other sea cocks that are near or below the waterline, if not after every use, at least when securing the boat. The reason for this is that pumps and the head often will siphon water back into the boat after use. Bilge pump outlets close to the waterline have allowed dangerous flooding, and a few boats with their head bowls below the waterline have sunk at their moorings after their valves had been left open.

All of the Luders yawls are equipped with alcohol-burning galley stoves. To the uninitiated, these stoves are hard to operate and seem dangerous. An alcohol stove must be filled before it is operated. Be very careful not to spill the alcohol while filling the stove. Once the tank is filled and the cap secured, the tank must be pressurized. There is a pump for this purpose and a pressure gauge that is very clearly marked. When the tank is full, it is very easy to *over*-pressurize the tank. A pressure of about 10 pounds per square inch is recommended. Be sure to watch the gauge while pumping. Also, remember that pressure must be maintained during use. This will require occasional pumping while the stove is in use.

After the stove has been filled, it must be primed. First some alcohol must be collected in the small basins below the burners. This is done by opening the burner valves *very* briefly. About three seconds will be all that is necessary. If the valves are left open too long, raw alcohol will spill onto the tray under the stove and when the stove is lighted there will be a conflagration. If alcohol has spilled, wait for it to evaporate before lighting. If a flash fire does occur, as it will whenever excess alcohol is allowed to collect on the tray beneath the burners, it can

127

often be put out by smothering it with a wet towel or garment. Water can be used to extinguish an alcohol fire if care is taken to see that all the fire is thoroughly extinguished and not merely washed to a new location. Be sure to use enough water to prevent smoldering. Do not use the dry-chemical fire extinguisher unless it is absolutely necessary, because it will cover the galley with a white powder that takes hours to clean up.

The alcohol in the basins under the burners is lighted to heat the burners. After a burner has been adequately pre-heated, when the primer fire almost dies out, the burner valve should be opened again, and the alcohol will vaporize and burn as a gas.

If a proper gas flame cannot be obtained, turn off the valves and start the whole process of priming again after the burner has cooled.

Diesel auxiliary engines

The fiberglass yawls are equipped with four-cylinder Westerbeke Model Four-107 diesel engines (see figure 8-19). They are direct drive and have hydraulic transmissions. The engines are controlled from the cockpit by Morse single-lever controls (see figure 8-20). These engines are reliable and easy to operate, as are the controls, but there are a number of *essential* checks that must be made prior to operation in order to ensure continued reliability. Remember, the more you know about the operation of the auxiliary, the less likely it is to give you trouble. The checks that are necessary for the Westerbeke are similar to checks required before getting underway with any auxiliary. In every case, the cooling system, oil level in the engine, fuel supply, and shaft lock, if there is one, should be checked.

The Westerbeke engine has a self-contained freshwater cooling system. The freshwater tank is atop the forward end of the engine and must be checked before starting. It should be filled to three-quarters of an inch below the opening. The fresh water, which recirculates, is kept cool by a heat exchanger on the after end of the engine, which in this system uses salt water. In addition, the salt water cools the lubricating-oil heat exchanger and the exhaust pipe. The saltwater cooling system has two valves, an intake and a discharge, and *both must be open when the engine is running*. The saltwater intake valve is abaft the engine shaft coupling on the port side. The discharge valve is in

the exhaust line and is in the lazarette. The discharge valve should always be shut when under sail in a seaway, because it then keeps salt water from entering the engine via the exhaust line. Both valves are shown in figure 8-21.

The lubricating oil sump on the Westerbeke has a maximum capacity of five quarts of oil. For proper engine operation the oil level in the sump must be kept between four and five quarts. The engine sump dipstick must be pulled and inspected to ensure that the lubricating oil is at the required level. The dipstick on the Westerbeke is on the starboard side of the engine, down quite low. Be sure to push it all the way into the sump when checking the oil level. As already mentioned, the engines are equipped with hydraulic reverse gears. Because of this, the reverse gear has a separate oil sump that must also be checked. The reverse gear dipstick is on top of the gear box at the after end of the engine on the port side. If oil is needed in the main sump, only Navy symbol 9250 oil or a high-quality, heavy-duty, 30-weight detergent oil should be used. The gear box uses special, light, hydraulic oil, and *only* this should be used if oil is needed. These dipsticks are located as shown in figure 8-19.

Fuel is supplied by one 40-gallon tank, which is amidships below the cabin sole. As indicated in figure 8-21, it is the forward one of the two tanks in this area. It is reached by lifting the forward removable section of the sole in the main cabin. The fuel gauge is on top of the tank or at the side of the companionway ladder. The fuel tank is filled from the deck with the fill pipe deck plate forward in the cockpit. The valve in the fuel supply line is on the bulkhead abaft the companionway just forward of the first fuel strainer; it should be left open. On boats with a gasoline auxiliary, because of the very explosive nature of the fuel, it is good practice to shut the gasoline supply valve when leaving the boat. More on this subject will be discussed in chapter 13.

One last item remains on the checklist. This is the shaft lock, which is used to keep the propeller in a vertical position for minimum drag when sailing. It must be released before the engine is run. It is on the shaft beneath the cockpit. You are ready to start the engine once the following items have been checked: (1) freshwater tank, (2) saltwater exhaust and intake valves, (3) oil supply in sump and reverse gear,

128

(4) fuel gauge, and (5) shaft lock. You are now ready to start the engine.

The first step in starting the engine is to energize the electrical system. This is done by switching the battery selector switch from "off" to position "1" or "2." The battery selector switch is abaft the companionway. It is a Perko circular switch, and it determines which of the yawl's two 12-volt batteries is going to be used for power. One should note that between positions "1" and "2" on the switch there is a position marked "ALL." When the switch is moved to this position, power is drained from both batteries simultaneously. The "ALL" position should not be used unless neither battery has sufficient power by itself to start the engine. If both batteries must be used to start the engine, switch to position "1" or "2" immediately after starting, as any short circuit in the electrical system will discharge both batteries if the selector switch is left on "ALL."

The next step is to prime the engine. This is done by pushing the hand prime pump shown in figure 8-19 three or four times. A diesel cannot be flooded, so overprime rather than underprime.

The rest of the starting operation is conducted from the cockpit. The engine is put in neutral, by putting the Morse control handle in the vertical position. This control is both gear shift and throttle. It is on the starboard side of the cockpit and is illustrated in figure 8-20. Once in neutral, the knob below the handle must be pulled out to disengage the gear shift, and then the throttle is advanced forward about one-half speed. The starter is a button, which must be depressed. The starter switch is on the panel at the after end of the cockpit, or on the starboard side of the cockpit. As soon as the engine starts, move the throttle back to the idle position and let the engine warm up for at least five minutes. Remember to push in the knob below the handle to engage the gear shift. To start the engine in cold weather, it must be preheated. This is done by pushing in the button labeled "preheat" and

129

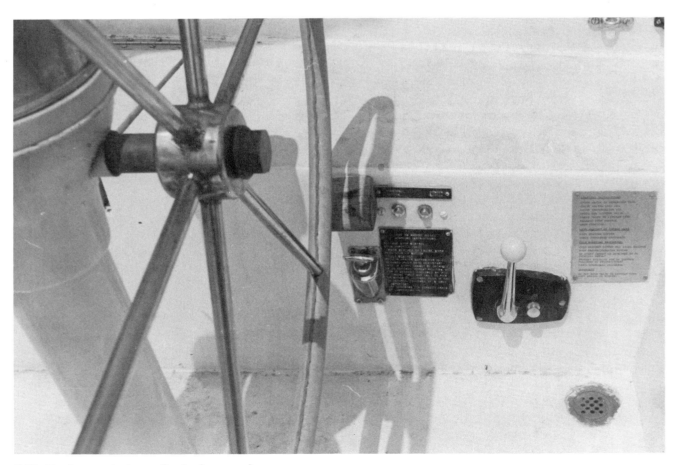

8-20. Engine controls on the Luders yawl.

holding it in for about 15 seconds. After the engine is heated, start in the normal manner. In each yawl, there are starting instructions posted in the cockpit near the starting panel.

Once the engine has started, check the oil pressure. The gauge is in the instrument panel at the forward end of the cockpit, and should read 40 pounds or more. Then check over the stern to see if water is coming out of the exhaust. If it is not, the saltwater cooling system is not working properly. If the oil pressure is low, or if water is not being pumped out the exhaust, shut down the engine immediately.

While running the engine, periodically check the oil pressure and the water temperature. The water-temperature gauge is beside the oil-pressure gauge.

Table 8-1. Luders fiberglass yawl, performance characteristics under power.

Engine RPM	Speed in Knots	Fuel Consumed in Gallons Per Hour
1,000	3.0	0.39
1,500	4.5	0.48
1,750	5.5	0.57
2,000	6.0	0.66
2,250	6.3	0.75
2,500	6.5	0.82
2,750	6.6	1.00

The oil pressure should be 40 pounds or higher (never below 30 pounds), and the water temperature should never go higher than 190°F. An alarm will sound when this temperature is reached and also when the lube-oil pressure drops below 10 pounds. *Never run the engine faster than 3,000 RPM.* Proper cruising speed for the Luders yawls is six knots at about 1,800 RPM. It should be noted in Table 8-1, that for engine RPMs greater than 1,800, fuel consumption goes up much faster than speed. When running the engine for several hours or more, shut it down periodically, and check the oil.

To secure the engine, put the throttle in neutral and pull out the engine "STOP" handle. Remember to push the stop handle back in, because it cuts off engine fuel and unless it is reset, the engine cannot be restarted. Once the engine has stopped and when power is no longer needed, switch the battery selector switch to the "OFF" position. Check fuel, oil, and fresh water to ensure that the engine will be ready for use when next needed.

Table 8-2 has been included to help troubleshoot the Westerbeke diesel engine. It does, however, offer many suggestions to the owner of any diesel-powered auxiliary who is trying to determine the cause of engine malfunction. It is for use primarily by trained mechanics, but also includes probable faults that can be checked by even the most inexperienced operator. The most common causes of en-

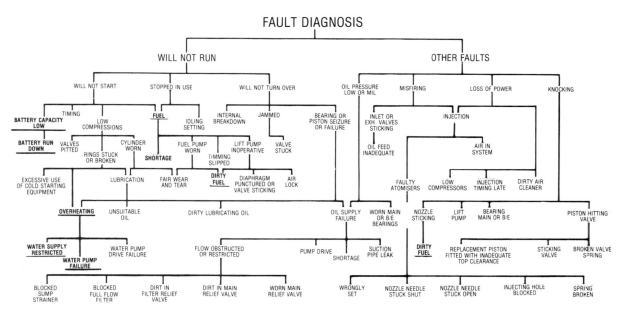

Table 8-2. Troubleshooting the Westerbeke diesel.

gine failure—such as low battery, loss of cooling water, and dirty fuel (dirt or water in the fuel)—have been underlined.

On the Westerbeke engine, overheating is often a problem. It can be caused by closed saltwater cooling system valves or an empty freshwater tank.

Often overheating is caused by the malfunction of either the fresh- or salt-water pump. These pumps are mounted on the front of the engine and are belt-driven. If the drive belts are too loose, they will not function. There are adjustments on both pumps that can be altered to increase tension.

8-21. Luders fiberglass yawl; freshwater, saltwater drainage, fuel, and exhaust systems.

Electrical and water systems of the fiberglass Luders yawl

In addition to knowing how to run the engine on the fiberglass yawls, the skipper and crew must know the location of the valves in the fresh- and saltwater systems and the switches in the electrical system (see figures 8-21 and 8-22). The fiberglass yawls formerly carried 100 gallons of fresh water in two tanks, one in the forepeak with a capacity of 40 gallons, and one amidships in the main cabin abaft the fuel tank under the cabin sole with a capacity of 60 gallons. Now, in lieu of the bow tank most boats carry a polyethylene bladder under the port 'midships berth. Each receptacle is filled by means of direct access on top of the tank or bladder. The system has two pumps, one at the head sink and one at the galley sink. Both these sinks drain overboard through a sea cock in the hull. The valve in the head is below the sink. The valve for the galley sink is located in the port cockpit locker and is also the valve for the port cockpit scupper. For this reason it must be left open. To keep seawater from backing

8-22. Luders fiberglass yawl, electrical system.

up into the galley sink when under sail, there is an additional stop valve in the sink drain line in the locker just below the sink. This valve should be shut when the sink is not in use.

The icebox drains into the bilge. Since there is no check valve installed in the drain line, it is important to keep the bilge free of water.

The fiberglass yawls have two manually operated bilge pumps installed. The intake strainers are in the bilge beneath the companionway ladder. The port pump is a GUSHER 10 (discharges 10 gallons per minute) and is located inside the port sheet locker in the cockpit. The starboard pump is a GUSHER 25 (25 gallons per minute), which is located over the navigator's berth. There is an access port for each pump on either side of the cockpit. The starboard pump may also be operated from below decks. Both pumps discharge through the side above the water-line. While there is no sea cock installed, the diaphragm in each pump acts as a check valve to prevent water from backing up into the bilges when the yawl is heeled.

The marine toilet in the head is installed with sea cocks on both intake and discharge lines. The intake valve is beneath the sink, and the discharge is in the locker behind the toilet. The operating procedure for the head is the same as that for the wooden yawls. It should be noted that the fiberglass yawl heads have hand-, rather than a foot-operated intake valve.

Power for the electrical instruments and lights aboard the fiberglass yawls is supplied by two 12-volt storage batteries located aft and to starboard of the engine. The engine is equipped with a 60-amp, 14-volt, battery-charging alternator-rectifier system. This system rapidly charges the batteries until they reach capacity and then shuts itself down and provides only a trickle charge to keep them fully charged. All control switches and fuses are installed in the control panel above the navigator's chart table on the starboard side of the main cabin, with the exception of the engine starter, binnacle, and engine panel light switches, all of which are in the cockpit.

Battery-powered equipment aboard the fiberglass yawls includes cabin lights, running lights, spreader lights, masthead lights, stern light, anchor light, binnacle light, fathometer, and radio. The entire system is diagrammed in detail in figure 8-22.

Boarding and securing procedures

The following are rough checklists of what should be done after a yawl is boarded, before getting underway, and what should be done before securing or leaving her.

Before getting underway

- Check the bilge. Pump it into the harbor only if you are certain there is no oil in the bilge. The Naval Academy and most marinas have pumping stations for removing oily water from the bilge.
- See that the head is almost dry and that both its water intake and discharge valves are shut.
- See that halyards are clear aloft and that sheets are bent and led properly.
- Remove the *binnacle* (the compass housing) cover and wheel cover and stow these below.
- Set up the topping lift and detach the boom strap. Stow this and the boat hook below.
- Bend on the desired jib and check to see that it is correctly bent.
- Set jib leads to correct position for the headsail that will be carried.
- Break out winch handles and place in their proper holders.
- If aboard a fiberglass yawl, see that the engine's fuel and water valves are opened and that the main battery switch is on. Check oil and cooling water.
- Unstop furled sails and tighten their outhauls just before hoisting.
- See that all loose gear below is properly stowed and that all opening lockers are closed so that gear will not spill out when the boat heels.
- See that ports are shut unless it is a calm, hot day with clear weather.

Before leaving the boat

- Be sure mooring pendants are properly secured on the bow cleat. It is wise to put a short, stout lashing through the mooring pendant eye and the center part of the cleat, so that even should the eye jump off the cleat, it would be held by several turns of lashing.
- If on a mooring, put up the anchor light.
- If moored in a slip, secure the boat so that she lies straight fore and aft in the slip and as nearly as possible in the slip's center. Be sure that there is some slack in the mooring lines to allow for a

change in tide, and that the lines are protected against chafe and properly secured with tail ends coiled.

• Pull boarding plank in and leave it on the pier. Coil the hose over its proper rack.

• See that bent sails are properly furled, or flaked, well stopped, and that outhauls are slacked. Tie down the heads of furled sails.

• See that sails are properly bagged and stowed. Wet or torn sails should be bagged and taken ashore to be dried or repaired.

• Halyards should be secured in such a manner that they do not chafe the rigging or mast. On the Luders yawls all headsail halyards are led forward to the foredeck and secured to the bow pulpit and stanchions. Another method is to pull them somewhat away from the mast by lashing them to the shrouds with short lengths of line, often called *gilguys*. They should be securely belayed to their proper cleats. The main halyard should be unshackled from the head of the mainsail and shackled into a rubber strop or cloth *belly band* provided for the purpose, which is led under the main boom at about its midpoint.

• The mainsheet should be taut enough to hold the boom steady.

• The mizzen topping lift should be set up enough to tilt the mizzen boom slightly upward, and then the mizzen sheet set up taut enough to keep the boom from swinging. A drooping mizzen boom makes the boat look droopy, while a topped up mizzen gives her a cheerful look.

• Lines should be coiled and, if not removable, should be hung off the deck.

• All removable sheets, blocks, winch handles, and other gear should be stowed in their proper places.

• Set up runners, but not overly taut. No line should be pulled overly taut. Some allowance should be made for shrinkage in wet weather.

• Strike and stow ensign and burgee.

• Replace covers on the wheel and binnacle.

• See that the main electrical and other switches are off and that the engine is properly secured.

• See that the bilge and sink are dry and that the bilge pump discharge valve is shut.

• The head should be clean and the intake and discharge valves shut.

• The icebox should be drained, and all ice, food, and beverage should be removed. Prop open the icebox door.

• All lockers below should be opened to allow adequate circulation of air. All deck ventilators should be turned the correct way. The aft end of the companionway should be left open, but other hatches and ports should be shut, except the port in the head. The after end of the lazaret hatch should be propped open about three inches.

• Secure lower extension berths in outboard position.

• A yawl should be left shipshape and in a cleaner condition than when she was boarded.

• Remove all trash, sweep down cabin sole, clean out sinks, wipe off bunk cushions, and wash down decks. Use hoses and fresh water when available, but otherwise use a bucket and Bay water. If possible, hose down topsides to remove salt deposits. Stow cleaning gear.

• Note any discrepancies—negative reports are required—in the log and sign it (please print). Don't forget to enter engine hours. Leave the log aboard on the chart desk.

Most of the essential information on the Luders yawls has been covered in this chapter, but other subjects related to these boats will be discussed later. Chapter 12, will cover emergencies such as man overboard and rigging failures. It will also discuss the changing of headsails and heavy-weather sailing.

9.
The Navy 44s

*I*n the late spring of 1987 an impressive 44-foot cutter named *Audacious*, bearing the sail insignia NA1, arrived at the U.S. Naval Academy. She was the prototype of a brand new class of racing-cruiser that would be used primarily to instruct the midshipmen in the fine points of offshore sailing and seamanship. Formally designated as 44-foot offshore sail training craft (OSTC), the class is more commonly referred to as Navy 44s. *Audacious* underwent a considerable period of trials and testing before her sisters were built, in order that the finest possible boat for its purpose could be developed. Although modifications to the prototype turned out to be minor, the trial period provided a valuable opportunity to eliminate most of the "bugs" that are common in every new design.

Dimensions and other important particulars of the Navy 44s are as follows: length overall, 44 feet; length waterline (measurement trim), 34 feet 6 inches; beam, 12 feet 4¾ inches; draft (measurement trim), 7 feet 2½ inches; displacement (measurement trim), 27,900 pounds; keel ballast, 12,310 pounds; sail area 946 square feet; bridge clearance, 65 feet; fuel capacity, 50 gallons; water capacity, 163 gallons; IOR rating, 32.94 feet; IMS rating (GP), 526.0 sec./mi.; and PHRF rating, 084 sec./mi.

The ideas of many authorities went into the concept of the Navy 44s. Naval personnel with offshore experience sailing Luders yawls and other Navy yachts had definite thoughts on improving accommodations, and many expressed great admiration for *Constellation*, a Sparkman and Stephens–designed Swan 48 donated to the Academy, which became the benchmark or comparison design. Basic specifications, as well as a number of individual details, were suggested by the Fales Committee, a group of knowledgeable civilian yachtsmen appointed by the Navy Academy superintendent to advise him on the sailing program. While it has been said that a camel is a horse designed by a committee, the Navy 44 does not suffer from the amalgamation of many different ideas. Rather, it benefits from the initial input and consolidation of thought by experienced offshore sailors prior to the actual execution of the design by a firm of professional naval architects. The firm selected by the Naval Academy Sailing Foundation, following a design-proposal competition, was McCurdy and Rhodes Incorporated, a highly respected company noted for the design of conservative, seaworthy, yet fast and handsome sailing yachts.

After inviting thirteen builders to submit bids, the Navy received three detailed proposals from topflight firms. Construction was awarded to Tillotson-Pearson, a company with considerable experience working with fiberglass-reinforced plastic, the

material from which the Navy 44s are built. Although the Tillotson-Pearson company specializes in sandwich construction that utilizes a core of end-grain balsa, the Navy specifications call for a hull core of Airex foam, which has greater resistance to damage from possible water penetration. The deck core material is Termanto R75, similar to

136

9-1. Sail plan of the Navy 44. The plan shows the mainsail's two reefing positions, the number 1 and 3 Genoas, and storm sails (spitfire staysail and storm trysail). (Courtesy of McCurdy & Rhodes, Inc.)

Divinycell, which is not as subject to softening from extreme heat. Cored construction provides hull rigidity and resistance to flexing without the need for excessive surface curvature or weight. Vinylester resin is used in the layup to inhibit osmotic blistering and water penetration into the laminate. All specifications are top grade, and the boats are very strongly built in compliance with the American Bureau of Shipping standards.

During her trial period, *Audacious* was sailed more than a thousand miles offshore, and she was thoroughly tested under the supervision of Captain John Bonds, formerly director of Navy Sailing and presently executive director of the USYRU. At the end of the trials, Captain Bonds concluded in his written report: "The test period confirmed our preliminary judgment that this is an exceptionally able sailing craft. From the lowest end of the wind spectrum up to the point at which she will normally heave to under authentic storm conditions, she remains tractable, predictable and controllable by relatively inexperienced sailors." Off the cuff, Bonds

9-2. A Navy 44 sailing under reduced sail in a fresh breeze. She is carrying a number 2 Genoa jib and jiffy-reefed main. Notice that the main is well eased. This relieves weather helm for two reasons: it helps keep the boat on her feet and moves the center of effort farther forward. When shaking out the reef, care must be taken to untie the reef points before the clew earing is released.

9-3. Downwind in light air, the Navy 44 enjoys the advantage of a large main and spinnaker.

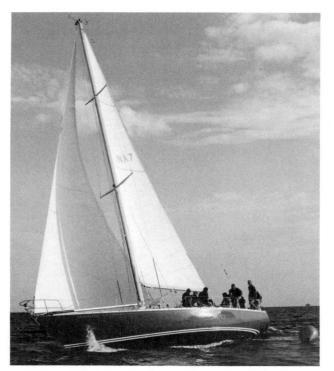

9-4. Rounding the mark: *Dauntless* **has cleared the spinnaker from her foredeck and is clear to tack as she rounds a leeward mark during a weekday practice session on the bay. To sharpen sail-handling skills, the Navy team frequently uses very short race courses in practice so that the crew is constantly in motion.**

commented, "This is the sweetest sailing boat I have ever sailed." This favorable report helped to provide the go-ahead to build seven more, slightly modified, Navy 44s. These are presently at the Naval Academy, and it is hoped that eventually there will be thirty-six of these craft. All of them will be almost identical in every respect for equitable class racing and so that crews can easily transfer from one boat to another.

Although the Luders yawls have been superb in serving as offshore sailing trainers since 1939, and they will continue being used by the naval stations and the Coast Guard Academy for some time to come, the Navy 44s have certain advantages. With greater length on the waterline and more beam for sail-carrying power, they are considerably faster in fresh winds, while light-air performance is improved by virtue of the taller rig and greater sail area. A fin keel reduces wetted surface area while providing greater maneuverability. The Navy 44's rudder, hung on a small skeg as far as possible aft, provides improved steering control when running with the spinnaker set in strong winds. (See figure 9-7.) These features and some others make the new trainer more competitive for racing and more forgiving for novice sailors who have had little if any experience at sea. Generous freeboard helps keep the boat dry, while the broad beam and greater waterline length allow more room below and adequate accommodations for a sizable crew. Offshore, the Navy 44s normally carry a crew of eight midshipmen and two coaches.

Stability and Displacement

One drawback of a very wide beam is its harmful effect on ultimate stability, but this is not a problem with the Navy 44, for she can be heeled slightly more than 130 degrees before capsizing. Her stability curve, calculated by McCurdy and Rhodes, is illustrated in figure 9-6. Notice that the greatest resistance to capsizing occurs at around 65 degrees of heel, and the righting arm decreases with greater heel until positive stability is lost at 130.6 degrees of heeling angle. The curve shown under the baseline is negative stability or resistance to righting, and the small area enclosed by the curve indicates that the boat is not apt to remain inverted for more than a few seconds in the unlikely event that the boat should happen to capsize. The 44's respectable range of stability, considerably higher than many of today's racing yachts, is largely due to her generous displacement and low ballast, which is more than 44 percent of her displacement. A further benefit of her adequate displacement is that it provides a relatively easy, sea-kindly motion in rough waters. Still another plaudit for moderately heavy displacement is that the boat can be heavily loaded with supplies for an ocean voyage without excessively detracting from her performance. The Navy 44s have molded-in flotation marks to help assure against overloading.

Performance

In addition to the stability curve for the Navy 44, the designers have supplied a *polar diagram*, derived from their velocity prediction program. The boat's performance polar, seen in figure 9-12, shows speed curves for six different strengths of wind ranging

from 8 to 20 knots. Each of the six curves predicts the boat's speed on every point of sailing from hard on the wind to running dead before it. The straight lines radiating from the center of the semicircles indicate sailing angles with respect to the true wind, and the tick marks on the radial lines show boat speeds from 2 to 10 knots. The farther a speed curve bends away from the center, the faster the boat's speed. It can be seen that the maximum speed shown on the diagram is 9 knots sailing in a 20-knot breeze at an angle of 120 degrees. It should be borne in mind that in stronger winds and ideal waves allowing the boat to *surf* (partially plane on a wave), a Navy 44 can sail much faster. *Audacious* was once clocked at 12.63 knots during a squall.

The small arrows shown at the beating and running ends of the speed curves indicate optimum heading angles when hard on the wind and sailing off the wind. Each angle, marked by an arrow and shown to the left of the diagram in digital form, provides the optimal *Vmg* (*velocity made good*), which is the best progress made upwind or downwind when the boat is changing tacks. Notice that when the boat is beating in 8 knots of wind, her optimum Vmg comes at a heading of 46 degrees to the true wind, but she may be sailed progressively higher as the wind increases until it reaches 16 knots, at which time the optimum heading is 40 degrees. Tacking downwind, the optimum heading

139

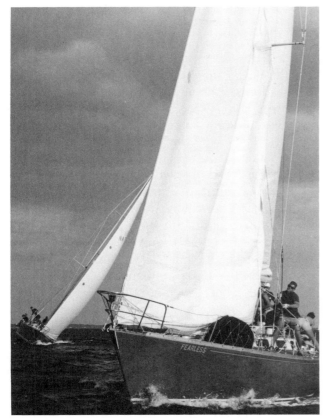

9-5. Tacking ahead to cover: *Fearless* has just tacked directly in front of NA 7, *Dauntless*, during racing practice. In order to prevent losing further ground as a result of sailing in bad air, *Dauntless* should tack immediately. The Navy 44s can be used for class competition or boat-for-boat racing, as well as handicap racing.

9-6. Stability curve for the Navy 44. Positive stability is represented by the large hump above the base line and negative stability by the small hump beneath the base line. Notice that the positive range extends to slightly more than 130 degrees of heel. This shows that in the highly improbable event of a capsize from an exceptionally steep breaking sea, the boat should right herself within a few seconds. (Courtesy of McCurdy & Rhodes, Inc.)

9-7. A view of a Navy 44 (left) and a Luders yawl hauled for winter maintenance. Note the skeg rudder and fin keel of the 44 compared with the more traditional keel and rudder of the yawl.

occurs at 144 degrees in an 8-knot breeze, but the boat can be sailed progressively lower in freshening winds until reaching 169 degrees in a 20-knot wind.

Optimum Vmgs are particularly useful when racing downwind with the spinnaker set. Another useful polar for tacking to leeward, which is included in an IMS Performance Package when a boat is measured to the IMS rule, can be obtained from the United States Yacht Racing Union. Although the USYRU polar does not show close-hauled Vmgs, there is an apparent-wind diagram for downwind headings, which enables the helmsman to sail headings shown by the electronic apparent wind indicator. Under good conditions, however, the true wind polar shown here can be used just as effectively by taking compass bearings on wind patterns (ripple lines) as they move across the water. The helmsman can merely sight with his hand across the top of the steering compass, and if he is reasonably experienced, his wind-pattern bearing may be more accurate than the instrument's reading.

Standing Rigging

There are two criteria for classifying a single-masted boat as a cutter rather than a sloop. The first is that the mast be stepped at least two fifths of the load waterline abaft the LWL ending, and the other is that the boat is double-head rigged, i.e., there are two headsails, a jib and forestaysail, in the foretriangle. The Navy 44 meets both these criteria, as the centerline of the mast is exactly two fifths aft, and she has an inner forestay for a staysail.

The latter feature is particularly valuable for sailing in heavy weather when the jib can be lowered and the boat sailed under a forestaysail and reefed main. In exceptionally heavy weather she will sail well or can be hove to under a 120-square-foot storm trysail and a 140-square-foot spitfire (storm staysail) set on the inner stay. This sail plan preserves balance and allows more efficient proximity of the sails while affording a safer working area around the forward sail. There is a separate track on the mast for a storm trysail, and at sea the sail can be carried in its bag permanently bent on its track. This greatly facilitates shifting from reefed main to storm trysail. The lower end of the forestay is fitted with a quick release lever in the form of a pelican hook so that the stay may be easily detached from the foredeck in light to moderate weather when a large Genoa jib is carried. With the stay released and secured aft in its stowed position, the fore triangle is opened to allow faster and more efficient tacking of the Genoa. To stow the stay after it is released, it is fitted into a curved channel on the port side of the

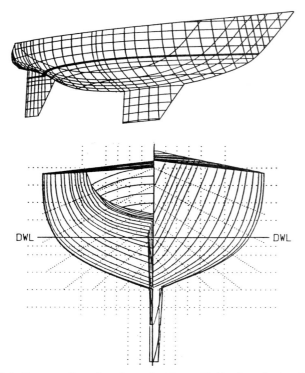

9-8. Perspective drawing of a Navy 44 (top) and a body plan. The rather slack bilge not only reduces wetted surface but also encourages a sea-kindly motion. Ample flair and freeboard forward keep the decks dry. (Courtesy of McCurdy & Rhodes, Inc.)

mast, and the pelican hook is attached to an eye on the cabin top abaft the mast.

Although most modern racers have grooved foil luff support systems for jibs primarily to avoid bald-headed sail changes (the need to lower one sail before a replacement is hoisted), the Navy 44s have solid rod headstays. This is the more seamanlike arrangement, as it allows jibs to be hanked on, and therefore the entire luff is always firmly attached to the headstay when sail is hoisted or lowered. This means the sail is easier to handle and cannot easily blow overboard when sails are changed in heavy weather. The tradeoff for this arrangement is that during a sail change more speed is lost, but very little when the operation is well organized and often practiced. To save time the replacement jib is hanked on under the jib that is flying. When beating to windward the change is best made when coming about. As the boat rounds up into the wind, the jib flying is lowered and unhanked as it comes down, then the replacement sail is hoisted as the boat fills away on the new tack. Properly executed, this evolution will cause little loss of headway. Downwind sail changes, of course, can often be made when the spinnaker is set, thus avoiding the need for a bald-headed change. On a close reach when the

141

9-9. The Navy 44s demonstrate their excellent Vmg or velocity made good to windward, illustrated graphically by this figure. The sloop *Dauntless* (left) under a full main and number 1 Genoa jib. Note the horizontal wrinkle in the mainsail caused by too much tension on the Cunningham. In light air the luff of the main should be just taut enough to hold the sail's shape without introducing stress wrinkles along the luff.

spinnaker cannot be carried, the forestaysail might be set as an interim sail to prevent excessive loss of speed when the jib is lowered.

Running backstays are provided to oppose the pull of the forestay. In light or moderate weather they need not be set up and can be secured to the after shrouds where they won't interfere with the main boom. In fresh winds, however, especially when the mast is pumping or there is a sail hoisted on the forestay, the running backstays should be used.

The permanent backstay is fitted with a NAVTEC hydraulic adjuster that allows an easy variation of tension even when the stay is under load. It is generally desirable to tighten the backstay so that it pulls the masthead aft, thereby tightening the head-stay for optimal pointing when beating to windward in moderate to fresh winds. On the other hand, a slacker headstay is preferable to give the jib power in light airs and/or when reaching, especially in choppy seas. Normally, the stay is well slackened by racing skippers when running before the wind. The variation of headstay tension is especially important when modern sails of stable materials such as Mylar and Kevlar are used, because these do not respond as well to shaping through edge tensioning. Thus, the luff-supporting stay should be coordinated with halyard tension. A word of warning about using the hydraulic backstay adjuster: this device can exert tremendous power that can put undesirable strain on the boat and her rig, so it is advisable to use restraint when tightening the stay. About 3,000 pounds of pressure as shown on the gauge seems a reasonable limit for maximum tension.

Running Rigging

The concentration of running rigging near the base of the mast necessitates keeping the various lines orderly at all times, properly coiled, and correctly led to their respective winches and cleats. Neatness is not only important for appearance but most especially for safety and good seamanship. Halyards

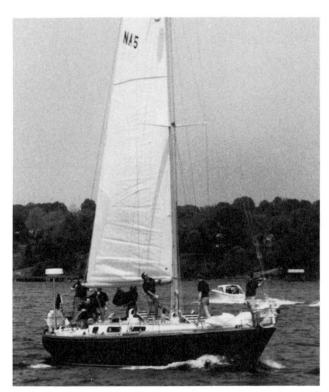

9-10. NA 5, the Navy 44 *Active*, prepares to enter port. Maneuvering under power, the boat is head to wind, and the jib is already on deck as preparations are made to lower the mainsail.

9-11. With her excellent balance and large main, the Navy 44 can be sailed effectively under main alone in a fresh breeze. This is often a good tactic to enhance visibility prior to the warning gun at the start of a race.

McCurdy & Rhodes, Inc.

Velocity Prediction Program

Polar Diagram

Boat Speed as a Function of
True Wind Velocity & Angle

Design No. 85
Final Lines w/Inclining Data
Measurement Trim is the Datum
Waterline + 1.5 in. (DWL + 1.5 in.)

Wind	Optimum Vmg Beat	Optimum Beat ∠	Optimum Vmg Run	Optimum Run ∠
8kt	3.852	46°	4.318	144°
10kt	4.411	45°	5.206	145°
12kt	4.784	43°	6.022	159°
14kt	5.022	41°	6.710	164°
16kt	5.177	40°	7.217	167°
20kt	5.332	40°	7.980	169°

85_F_D_1

6/3/87

9-12. Velocity prediction polar diagram for the Navy 44. The irregular curved lines represent speeds in six different wind velocities. Each curve shows speed on a dead run at its bottom left (where the wind velocity numbers are located), and the curve progresses from a run through a broad reach, beam reach, close reach, and hard on the wind. The farther a curve is from the center of the semicircular lines, the faster the speed. Small arrows near the tops and bottoms of the curves show optimal headings upwind and downwind. Numbers around the outer semicircle are heading angles with respect to the wind, which is blowing from top to bottom. (Courtesy of McCurdy & Rhodes, Inc.)

9-13. Looking aft at the base of the mast, there are six winches for the yacht's halyards. The forward winches are the port and starboard spinnaker halyards, the middle two are for port and starboard jib halyards, the aft winch on the starboard side is for the main halyard, and the aft port-side winch is a spare.

are internal but they exit at the lower end of the mast and run through ball-bearing lead blocks on the cabin top and thence to nearby winches. On the starboard side just abaft the mast there is a group of three winches, the forward one being used for a spinnaker halyard, the next aft for a jib halyard, and the after one for the main halyard. A similar arrangement is on the port side, with the forward winch used for another spinnaker halyard, the next aft for another jib halyard, and the aftermost intended as a spare for a reef earing or some other line. These winches are #28 Barients, and they are now all self-tailers. (Refer to figure 9-13.) Just forward of the mast on the cabin top there is a low securing rail to which the halyards not in use can be hooked.

Other gear near the lower part of the mast includes a Cunningham hook and tackle, boom

vang, spinnaker pole slide, and a combination pole lift and forestaysail halyard. The former is used to vary tension on the mainsail's luff, allowing it to be fairly slack in light winds for power and to be tightened in fresher winds to help flatten the sail and keep the draft forward. The boom vang, a Hall Quik-Vang (size D-40), is a mechanical type consisting of an aluminum spar with a heavy internal spring controlled with a powerful tackle that leads aft to a jam cleat on the cabin top next to the companionway. This kind of vang obviates the need for a main boom topping lift by holding up the boom and relieving the load on the mainsail's leech when setting, lowering, and reefing, With any on-center vang, however, a jibing preventer is needed to hold the boom forward when running before the wind. The spinnaker pole slide has roller bearings and runs on a track on the fore side of the mast. It is

144

9-14. A Navy 44 in her mooring slip. Notice that the bow lines are crossed for better fairleading. Perhaps they could be more neatly coiled.

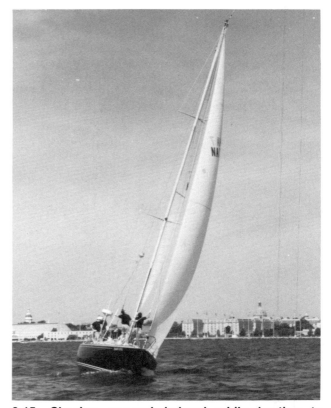

9-15. Clearing crossed halyard while beating to weather. This chore can generally be avoided by a careful selection of spinnaker and jib halyards prior to changing sails. Note the correct shape of the number 1 Genoa jib under these conditions. Sufficient jib halyard and backstay tension keeps the draft of the jib well forward.

9-16. The Hall Quik Vang on a Navy 44, which may be controlled from either side of the boat. A stout spring inside the vang is sufficiently powerful to hold the boom up and obviate the need of a topping lift, although it is advisable to rig an emergency lift before going offshore.

used to adjust the height of the pole's inboard end so that the pole may be kept approximately horizontal or cocked up slightly. The pole's lift is led aft to the port side of the companionway. On both sides of the mast, about two feet above the cabin top, are fittings to attach the *reaching strut*, which is used to hold the spinnaker guy outboard, thus reducing compression on the pole. Two spinnaker halyards are led through blocks on a masthead crane to avoid chafe. Two wire halyards with rope tails service the jibs. The largest jib, the number one Genoa, has an overlap of 150 percent of the foretriangle base.

Reefing is accomplished with the jiffy system similar to that now used on the fiberglass Luders yawls. Each of two reefs will remove about 25 percent of the mainsail's full area. In the mainsail's leech there are three reef grommets, a lower one just above the boom for a flattening reef, a first reef grommet about halfway between the boom and lower spreader, and a second reef grommet about level with the spreader for maximum sail reduction. The latter two grommets are out of reach from the deck, of course, so they should have the reef lines or messengers permanently rove through them. These lines lead to the after end of the boom, through the

boom to sheaves near the gooseneck, then down to the cabin top and aft to a self-tailing winch.

The Cockpit

Almost any cockpit layout involves some trade-offs, but the Navy 44's is well arranged for the boat's intended use. The mainsheet leads to a self-tailing winch and cleat on the after end of the cabin top. This location is out of the helmsman's reach, so during sailing maneuvers that require slacking the mainsheet, there always should be a crew member standing by just abaft the sheet ready to slack or trim on orders from the skipper or helmsman. A traveler runs across the bridge deck, and the sheet's sliding lead block is positioned with tackles running parallel with the traveler. When close-reaching or beating in fresh winds, the lead block is carried well to leeward of the boat's centerline. In lighter winds when close-hauled, the lead may be slid to windward to minimize headsail backwind, but the boom should never be pulled to windward of the centerline.

Slightly abaft the traveler on each side of the cockpit are large primary winches for headsail sheets and the spinnaker guy, and abaft these are

9-17. A foredeck spinnaker takedown: With the number 1 Genoa jib up and drawing on a beam reach, the spinnaker pole is eased forward to the headstay and the sheet is eased slightly, permitting the spinnaker to collapse. As the halyard is eased, the foredeck crew gathers the sail under the jib onto the foredeck. Note that the spinnaker guy and sheet are not fully eased to ensure that the sail does not fall into the water. The final steps in the takedown are to lower the pole, clear the topping lift back to the base of the mast, and ensure that the jib sheets are clear of the spinnaker so that the boat can tack.

9-18. The spinnaker pole foreguy, sometimes called the downhaul, has a two-part mechanical advantage. The line controlling the foreguy leads aft through fairleads to a jam cleat on the after end of the cabin top.

smaller secondary winches for spinnaker sheets or changing sheets when making a headsail change. The headsail sheets lead from adjustable sliding blocks on deck tracks. Foot blocks aft are used to alter lead direction to a winch for the sake of improving lead angle and fairness to avoid overrides and/or chafe. Sheets run through their lead blocks and thence to the foot blocks. The spinnaker foreguy (downhaul) consists of a two-part tackle forward that leads aft to cam cleats on the port and starboard sides of the cabin house at the forward end of the cockpit. Primary sheet winches are Barient 736s. All winch handles have locks to assure they will stay in place.

Cockpit volume is fairly large, and on some boats this could cause a safety problem if the well should happen to fill during heavy weather. But the Navy 44 has generous freeboard aft to discourage filling, her stern is very buoyant, and she is fitted with large scuppers for relatively quick drainage. Furthermore, the life-raft canister stowed under the bridge deck reduces volume. The high companionway sill helps prevent downflooding into the cabin. The companionway drop board can be locked in place, and there is a pad eye for life-line attachment in rough weather when entering or leaving the cabin. Outboard of the

cockpit on each side, a plastic-coated jack line leading forward is shackled to the rail. These allow the crew to hook on their safety harness tethers for uninterrupted travel when going forward and returning to the cockpit in heavy weather or at night.

The T-shaped well allows crew movement around a steering wheel having sizable diameter. It is highly desirable to have a large wheel so that the helmsman can sit far to leeward or far to windward in fresh winds to get a good view of the jib's luff and its telltales. An elkhide cover on the wheel inhibits the wheel from slipping in the helmsman's hand during wet weather. The wheel's pedestal not only supports the helmsman's binnacle with compass but also a sturdy grab rail just forward of the pedestal. This offers security for a standing crew member in rough weather, allows foot bracing when sitting near the rail, and provides protection against someone off-balance grabbing the helm.

Engine instruments and controls are just to starboard of the helm. They consist of a Morse single-lever throttle/clutch control (see chapter on Luders yawls), preheat and starting buttons, and gauges showing RPMs, engine hours, water temperature, oil pressure, and battery condition. Other instruments are at the forward end of the cockpit on the

9-19. Reefing sequence: The main sheet and the halyard are eased off until the reefing grommet is fitted on the hook above the gooseneck. Simultaneously, the crew winches the first reef clew cringle down to the boom. The halyard is then taken back up to the correct amount of luff tension, and the sail is retrimmed. The final step is to tie up the bunt, preferably with a spiral lacing line, to more evenly distribute the strain.

9-20. The bridge deck of a 44 showing her mainsheet traveler and the life-raft stowage beneath. The raft is not difficult to slide out, but it cannot be fitted with a hydrostatic release.

after side of the cabin trunk. These include digital repeaters for boat speed, wind direction, wind speed, and water depth. There is also another compass for on-deck use by the navigator/tactician or any other crew member.

Sizable lockers are under the cockpit seats, and they are used to stow gear such as extra sheets, dock lines, fenders, PFDs, and so forth. The locker lids are hinged, gasketed, and held closed with hasp-type fasteners. It is important that the lids be securely fastened in heavy weather, otherwise they could fall open during a knockdown and allow flooding of the boat's interior. In the port seat locker there is an Edson diaphragm bilge pump that can be operated manually by the helmsman without opening the locker lid. The pump's handle is on the after side of the seat locker. LP gas bottles for the galley stove are installed under the after cockpit seat on the starboard side. This locker is vented and has drains to prevent a build up of gas in the event of a gas leak, and it is very important not to stow anything in a gas locker that could possibly block the drains. A pressure regulator and gauge is installed in the locker. An aluminum emergency tiller, designed to engage the squared end of the rudder stock above

the after coaming, is stowed in chocks in the lazaret. (See figure 9-23.)

The life raft, stowed under the bridge deck, is a 10-man Avon packed inside a fiberglass canister. This stowage location prevents the use of a hydrostatic device that automatically releases the raft, but it can be slid out into the cockpit without too much difficulty and then thrown overboard. Inflation is effected with a CO_2 bottle inside the canister activated by pulling on a sturdy lanyard that is attached to the vessel. The raft is well equipped, but there also should be an easily accessible grab bag packed with extra emergency supplies when sailing offshore. It is well to bear in mind the old saying that an abandoning crew should step *UP* into a life raft. In other words, don't abandon ship until the last possible moment when there is not the slightest doubt that the vessel is really sinking (or that a fire cannot be controlled). Abandon-ship instructions are posted on the locker door near the companionway ladder.

On the stern pulpit there is one yellow horseshoe buoy with a man-overboard pole attached. Also carried on the stern pulpit is a packed Lifesling and a throw sock to assist in recovering a man who has

9-21. A crossing situation near the starting line: The bow of the J-44 *Quintessence* shows that she is on starboard tack crossing in front of a Navy 44 on port tack. In a stiff breeze such as this, the main on the Navy 44 should be eased to decrease the weather helm and permit the helmsman greater steering control should he have to bear off quickly to pass clear astern.

fallen overboard. This device will be described under *Emergencies* in the chapter on distance racing and offshore sailing.

Below decks

Though not intended as luxury yachts, the Navy 44s are very comfortable below decks and well planned to contend with difficult living conditions for a sizable crew at sea. There is plenty of light and ventilation with three Lexan hinged hatches, six port lights (one opening), and six ventilators (five Dorades), as well as the companionway hatch that can be protected from rain or spray with a folding dodger. The cabin has an open layout, a key requirement for ease of inspection and accessibility to all wiring, piping, structural members and fasteners. Incidentally, all nuts should always be kept tight.

There are adequate sleeping facilities, with four folding pipe berths in the forward cabin, two transoms and two removable pilot berths in the main cabin, and a quarter berth aft. Bunks are fitted with *lee cloths* (side flaps) and/or tackles that can be adjusted to keep them level on the windward side when the boat is heeled. For heavy weather there are plenty of grab rails, handholds, and steel pipes that not only serve as grabbing posts for the crew but also as sturdy supports for the cabin top. Drawers and locker doors are designed to be latched or locked in rough conditions. Similar to the main deck, the cabin sole has been skidproofed with sheets of Treadmaster, and it is made with removable sections to allow complete access to the bilge for inspection and cleaning. The bilge has been gel-coated for smoothness in order to greatly simplify cleaning.

There is one head in an enclosed compartment near the companionway. The compartment is fitted with a wash basin and two shower heads, one for fresh water and the other for seawater, to be used offshore to conserve fresh water. Corners in the head have been rounded to simplify cleaning. A wet-clothes locker is provided for foul-weather gear. Its location just forward of the head compartment near the companionway ladder prevents water from being tracked into the middle of the cabin and helps keep the bunks dry. A scupper in the bottom of the locker allows water from wet clothes to drain into

9-22. Trimming the jib: The tailer is keeping the jib sheet parallel to the base of the winch as the grinder trims the sail. The tailer must also look aloft to watch the distance off the spreaders as the boat is brought to a close-hauled course.

9-23. Looking aft through the steering wheel of a 44. Note the elk-hide covering on the wheel's rim that gives the helmsman a secure grip in wet weather. Abaft the wheel is a curved helmsman's seat (advantageous when the boat is heeled), the rudder stock head that accepts an emergency tiller, and all the way aft, the lower end of the permanent backstay with hydraulic line for the adjuster.

the bilge. See that these scuppers don't become clogged with loose gear.

The galley is L-shaped for convenience and security, and it features refrigeration, two sinks, and a gimballed three-burner gas stove with oven. The sinks are well inboard for good drainage and to prevent flooding when the boat is heeled. They are fitted with swiveling spouts for fresh water and seawater as well. Care must be taken not to drink from the latter spout, especially in polluted harbors. The fresh water comes from two 70-gallon tanks that have gauges under the transom berths to monitor the supply. Another small 23-gallon water tank is located under the cabin sole. The gas stove is most convenient to use, but it can create an explosive hazard if valves are left open or there is a leak in the line, since LP gas is heavier than air and can sink into the bilge (refer to subhead "Fire" in the emergencies section in chapter 12). There is an automatic stove fuel shutoff mounted in a recess in the galley counter and a control valve in the previously mentioned gas-tank stowage compartment. A rather

novel feature is the fiberglass garbage container secured between two steel posts in the galley area. The container has a teak lid and can be used as a seat.

Directly across from the galley is an unusually large navigation station that allows side-by-side instruction. It has a sizable chart table, comfortable seat, and an array of electronic instruments. Navigation and communications equipment includes a Northstar Loran-C receiver; Raytheon R20 radar (with scanner mounted on an aluminum mast on the after deck); and two radio telephones, an Icom VHF/FM set for short-distance communications and a Stephens SEA 222 single-sideband radio for long distance. In addition, there are two Brooks and Gatehouse instruments with full alarm capabilities and dual sensor/transducers with gravity change-over switches activated when tacks are changed: a Hornet Depth Monitor and a B & G Hydra 330 sailing monitor that provides boat speed, wind speed, and wind direction. As previously noted, both these instruments have digital repeaters in the cockpit. The vessel's electrical system switchboard is located on the port side (to the left of the seated navigator). It has approximately 36 labeled switches for all electrical components, electricity monitoring instruments, and circuit breakers. The board is hinged on one side for access to its back. Three

151

9-24. The cockpit bilge pump under the port seat of a Navy 44. The pump lever is located aft on this seat so that the pump can be operated by the helmsman with the seat lid closed.

9-25. Arrangement and profile plans of the Navy 44. Note the nearly horizontal propeller shaft just forward of the rudder for optimum efficiency and steering control under power. (Courtesy of McCurdy & Rhodes, Inc.)

deep-cycle batteries are located under the navigator's seat. They are charged with two alternators belted to the engine.

Auxiliary power is supplied by a Westerbeke 40NA diesel engine located in a box under the companionway ladder. Accessibility to the engine from every side was a prime requirement, and this aspect is unusually good. Formerly called the 4-107, the 40NA produces 33 horsepower at 2,500 RPM. The 4-107 is the auxiliary used in the Luders yawls, and for the most part, what was written about the yawl engines in the preceding chapter also applies to the 40NA. The Navy 44's engine is fueled from a 50-gallon tank under the cabin sole. It is filled by way of a screw plate on deck that is plainly marked "DIESEL" to avoid any inadvertent filling of the tank with water. The engine box is provided with an automatic halon fire extinguishing system with an indicating light. There are also three portable dry-chemical and one five-pound carbon-dioxide fire extinguishers. A unique feature is that, should it be necessary to remove the engine in a faraway port

lacking facilities, it can be lifted out through the companionway hatch using the main halyard as a hoist. The auxiliary drives a Martec folding prop, which not only minimizes drag under sail but prevents propeller rotation when the engine is not running. In the event that one blade should fail to open when the engine is first started and run in forward gear, momentarily shift into reverse to open the blade so that possible damage will not be done as a result of excessive vibration.

All valves, sea cocks, and pumps are labeled with plastic tags for identification. Each plumbing pipe and hose that penetrates the hull is controlled by a sea cock having a lever handle that needs only a quarter of a turn to open or close the line. Attached to each sea cock is a tapered, wooden damage-control plug to be used in the event a hose cracks or slips off and the valve cannot be closed.

Most of the bulky gear such as sails and heavy lines and the like are stowed in the forward cabin, often with pipe berths folded up. Anchors carried in the Navy 44s are: one 20-pound Hi-Tensile Dan-

9-26. Lee cloths and tackles on a 44's pilot berth to prevent crew from rolling out during a knockdown or severe roll. Note that all nuts on the overhead are accessible. They should be kept tight.

9-27. A view of the Navy 44's cabin looking aft from near the inboard galley sink. Note the hand rails near the companionway, the hand grip on the semi-bulk-head abaft the nav. station, and the three pipe supports, all of which contribute to crew security in heavy weather. A nice feature is the curved companionway ladder steps that provide good footing when the boat is heeled.

9-28. The 44's galley showing her double sinks close to the centerline to avoid flooding when the boat is heeled and the metal bar in front of the stove to protect the cook. Note the two metal posts that support the garbage container with a seat on its top. Abandon- ship instructions are posted to starboard.

9-29. A view of the 44's cockpit repeater instruments, which include a magnetic compass with inclinometer, apparent wind angle dial, and a Brooks and Gatehouse Hydra sailing monitor providing magnetic apparent wind, trip log, and wind speed.

154

9-30. Breaker and switch electrical panel near the navigator's seat. All switches are labeled, and the panel can be opened to allow inspection of wiring on its back side.

9-31. The Navy 44's auxiliary engine located under the companionway ladder. Note its excellent accessibility. It may be removed if necessary with the main halyard through the companionway.

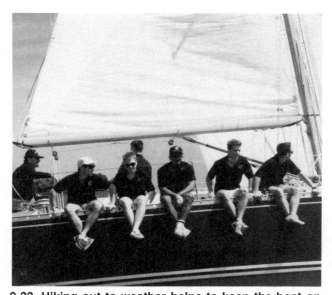

9-32. A through-hull seacock on a Navy 44 with a damage-control plug lashed to the fitting so that it will not have to be searched for in the event of an emergency.

9-33. Hiking out to weather helps to keep the boat on her feet, which improves speed and pointing ability. Note that the crew is as far outboard as permitted by the racing rules, which require that each person's torso be behind the lifeline. The rules now allow one's head to be outboard of the top lifeline if the torso is inboard of the lower lifeline.

9-34. Two Navy 44 sloops broad-reaching under a full main and the number 1 Genoa. Both sails on the lead boat could be eased much more than they are to provide increased sail area and better thrust alignment on this point of sail. Also, the jib sheet might be led farther forward.

forth for temporary anchoring in favorable weather; a 35-pound Hi-Tensile Danforth for longer periods of anchoring or in windy or more difficult conditions; and a 75-pound Paul Luke, fisherman-type storm hook that can be disassembled into three pieces for stowage.

In summary, the Navy 44s are ideal for their purpose. They are wholesome boats, safe and seaworthy, with few if any concessions to racing rules for the sake of achieving the most favorable handicap rating. Yet they are fast, well mannered, and have proven competitive when well sailed. They are also low-maintenance boats with a minimum of woodwork needing upkeep. Their equipment is generally first class, and it provides ample opportunity for training in many different aspects of navigation and seamanship. In addition, these boats are a joy to sail, and they should help instill in the inexperienced midshipman a love for just plain "messing about in boats," an element that is highly desirable if not necessary for developing the very best seamen.

155

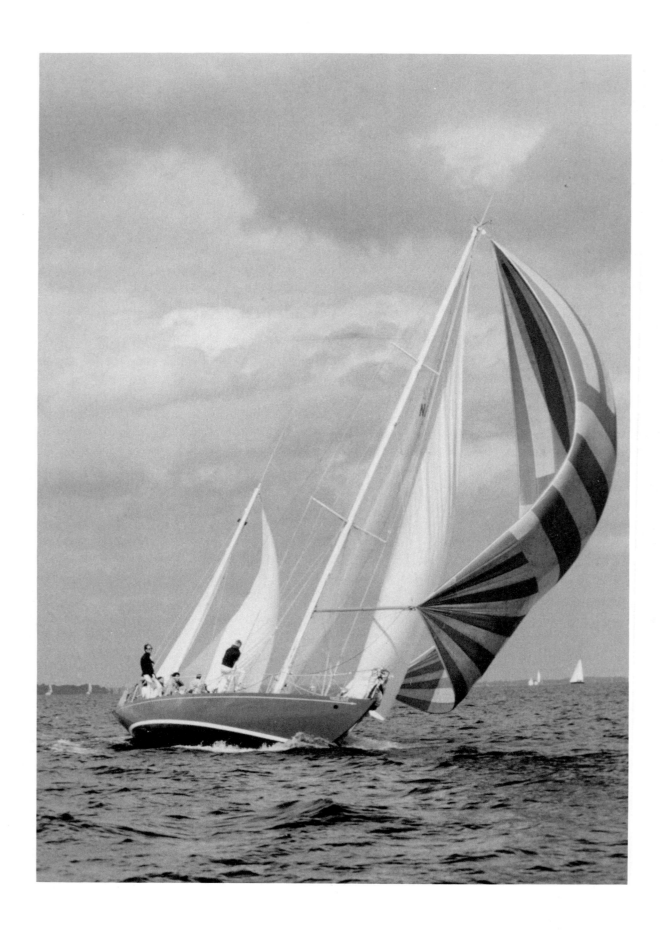

10.
The Spinnaker

Description

The Luders yawls, Navy 44s, J-24s, a few knockabouts, and the donated Naval Academy ocean racers are equipped with spinnakers. These sails are essential for racing and are often difficult to handle; therefore, this entire chapter will be devoted to them.

The spinnaker derives its name from the fact that the first version of the sail was carried by the British yacht, *Sphinx*. It is said that rival crews called the sail a "Sphinxer" and sometimes referred to it as "Sphinx's Acre." These names soon evolved into our present term for the sail.

The modern racing spinnaker, the type carried on the Navy boats, is properly termed a parachute spinnaker. It is shaped like a ballooned isosceles triangle, the upper corner of which is called the head and the lower corners both called clews. When set, the sail is supported at these three corners only. Either clew may be fastened to the end of a boom called the *spinnaker pole*, which is carried on the fore side of the mast, and the clew on the pole would then actually be called the tack. The clews are interchangeable; that is, either may be used as the tack, depending on whether the sail is set to port or to starboard. Figure 10-1 shows a typical parachute spinnaker with its lines and fittings. The line attached to the tack and pole is called the *after guy* (or often just *guy*), while the line attached to the clew is the sheet. Of course, the head is supported by the halyard. Another line shown in the illustration is attached to the pole to hold it down and forward, and this line is called the pole *downhaul* or *foreguy*. Still another line shown in the illustration is the *pole topping lift*, or simply *lift*, and this holds the pole up.

Pole adjustments

At its inboard end, the pole is attached to a slide on a track that is fastened to the fore side of the mast. The outboard end of the pole may swing forward until it touches the headstay or aft until it touches the forward shroud. The after guy controls the pole's fore-and-aft position. When beam reaching, the pole is carried all the way forward; when running, the pole is all the way aft. But when broad reaching, the pole is about halfway between the running and beam-reaching positions. These positions are illustrated in figure 10-2. Notice that the pole is always about at right angles to the direction

A   Spinnaker Sheet
B   Guy (sheet & guy
    lead outside shrouds)
C   Spinnaker Pole
D   Pole Lift
E   Pole Downhaul (foreguy)
    (may be attached to the
    bridle under the pole)
F   Sheet and Guy
    Lead Blocks
G   Pole Fitting and Slide
    (1) pole fitting (at each
    end of pole)
    (2) pole (3) spring loaded pin
    (4) lanyard (pull to open pin)
    (5) adjustable slide
    (6) track (on mast's fore side)
H   Spinnaker Halyard Swivel
    Shackle (often at each end
    of halyard) (sometimes
    a swivel is permanently
    attached to the spinnaker
    head)

I   Spinnaker Tack
    (1) metal ring lashed to
    tack grommet (optional)
    (2) Swivel ring shackle
    (same arrangement
    at clew)
    (3) pole snapped on guy
J   Alternate Method
    (pole snapped to ring
    on shackle)
K   Middle of Pole
    (1) lift (2) downhaul
    (3) wire or rope strop
    (4) eye strap
    (5) continuous lanyard
L   Alternate Method
    (1) lift (may lead to end of
    pole for dip-pole jibing)
    (2) downhaul (3) bridle
    (4) lanyard

10-1. The parachute spinnaker.

of the apparent wind. This holds true no matter what the point of sailing. Most spinnakers cannot be carried effectively when the true wind comes from forward of the beam or when the boat is on a point of sailing that is slightly higher than a beam reach.

The pole may be raised or lowered at either end. The height of the outboard end is controlled with the lift, and the inboard end is controlled with the adjustable slide on the mast track. Given a good breeze, a well-designed parachute spinnaker will lift, and it should be encouraged to do so. The pole

should be carried as high as possible when the 'chute is lifting, but the tack should not be allowed to lift any higher than the clew. In other words, the tack and clew should be kept at about the same level, almost horizontal or with the tack slightly lower than the clew. Then also, the pole should not be cocked up very much with its outboard end a great deal higher than its inboard end.

Proper up and down pole positions are shown in figure 10-3. In a light breeze, the pole should make an approximate right angle with the mast, with the

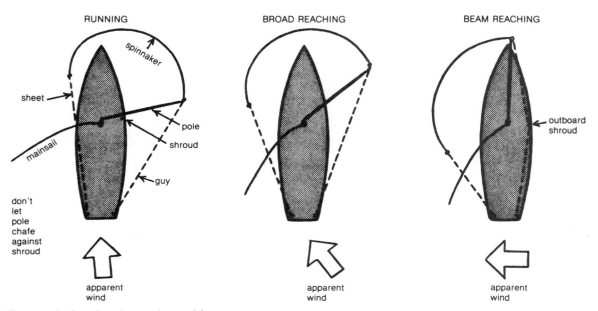

10-2. Fore-and-aft spinnaker pole positions.

10-3. Pole lift adjustments. Tack should not be lifted above height of clew. Keep spinnaker's foot horizontal.

inboard end at the highest position that will keep the tack level with the clew. In very light airs, the clew will not lift; therefore, the inboard pole end must be kept low. As the breeze freshens, the inboard end can be pushed higher up the mast until,

in a moderate breeze, the pole is near the top of its track. If the clew is lifting sufficiently in this much breeze, the pole can be raised with the pole lift until the outboard end is slightly higher than the inboard end. As the breeze continues to freshen, the pole's

10-4A. Setting the spinnaker on a Navy 44. A bow man and mast man prepare for hoisting. Pole is attached to mast and guy run through its outboard end. Downhaul and lift attached. Bagged chute has been secured at mid foredeck.

10-4B. Halyard and sheet have been attached to chute, and the pole is being raised.

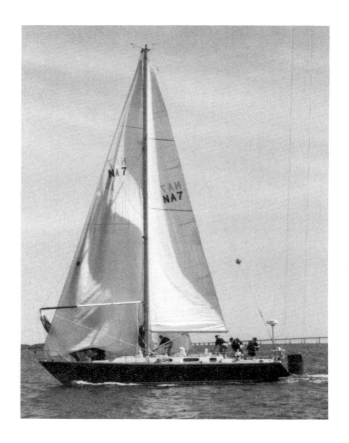

10-4C & D. The chute is being hoisted behind the jib.

outboard end can be lifted until the pole comes in line with the angle of the after guy, as shown by position B in the diagram. In this position, the sail is lifted and the pull of the after guy doesn't exert an extra strain on the downhaul or the pole lift. Position A, shown in the diagram, is usually bad even when the spinnaker lifts in a fresh breeze. Although the pole is lifted, its outboard end is too close to the mast, putting an extra strain on the downhaul, which already has a great deal of upward strain from the lifting 'chute. It is advantageous to keep the pole's outboard end away from the mast so that the spinnaker is held out in cleaner air, away from the blanketing effect of the mainsail. In a very strong breeze, the spinnaker should be kept flatter for better steering control, and this calls for a lower pole setting at both the inboard and outboard ends.

10-4F. Jib being dropped to prevent blanketing, and pole guyed farther aft.

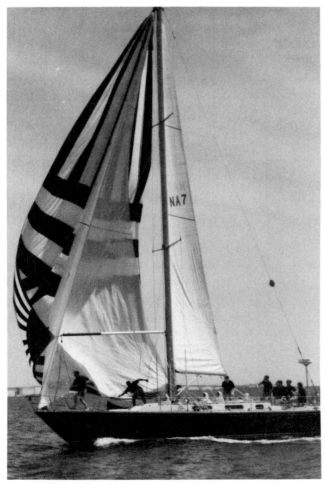

10-4E. Spinnaker hoisted with sheet being trimmed in to prevent hourglassing. Jib's foot being brought inboard preparatory to lowering.

10-4G. Boat is on course with chute drawing and sheet trimmer keeping the luff on edge.

The spinnaker pole may be rigged with its lift and downhaul in one of several ways. Two of these are shown in figure 10-1. Illustration K shows the lift rigged to the middle of the pole with the downhaul at the under side of the pole, directly beneath the lift. Illustration L shows the downhaul rigged from the outboard end of the pole and the lift attached to the middle of a *bridle* or wire span running from one end of the pole to the other. Of course, the lift may also be rigged directly to the pole end if the method of jibing called dip-poling (see figure 10-12 and accompanying text) is used exclusively. A pole rigged by method K is usually somewhat easier to handle, especially when end-for-end jibing. Sometimes a bridle is rigged at both the top and bottom of the pole to alleviate bending strains. This arrangement is often used on small boats and sometimes on fairly large boats in a moderate breeze. The other method, L, however, is most often used by large boats and in a strong breeze. With this arrangement there is less chance of breaking the pole. In a strong breeze, the spinnaker usually exerts a strong upward pull that can bend the pole up if the downhaul is secured in the pole's middle. This can be counteracted by putting the after guy into a forward lead, but usually the most effective way to stop the upward bending is to secure the downhaul to the pole's end. When it is desirable to use a forward lead, it is often best to use a twing as described in chapter 7 in the discussion of the J-24. A bridle transfers the pull of the lift or downhaul from the pole's middle to its end. No matter how a pole is rigged, it is wise to have the lift fastened directly above the pole downhaul. J-24s are rigged with double bridles, but the large Navy boats are normally rigged with the lift secured directly to the pole end.

Setting the spinnaker

There are three common ways to set a spinnaker: by stopping it, setting it from a turtle, or setting it from its bag. Actually, however, the latter two methods are practically the same. The turtle is a special container that holds the folded or bundled spinnaker on deck prior to hoisting. These containers are often quite varied in design, depending on the fancy of each particular skipper or foredeck captain. One type of turtle is shown in figure 10-5. Notice that the three corners of the sail emerge from the container's top, which is held almost closed with a piece of

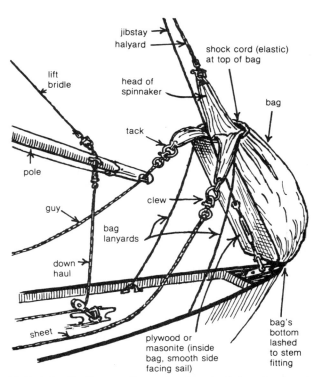

10-5. A turtle (for medium-size boat). Spinnaker ready to hoist (pole to port). Be careful that the leeches are not twisted around each other when sail is put into bag. Spinnaker may be hoisted while jib is set, but after spinnaker is up, jib is normally lowered.

elastic shock cord (sometimes rubber is used). Each corner is rigged to its proper line: the head to the halyard, the guy to the tack, and the sheet to the clew. Figure 10-5 shows the pole hooked onto the guy (the line itself), but the pole may be hooked onto the ring of the swivel shackle as shown in figure 10-1J. The first method (the pole on the guy) is preferable for short races in sheltered waters, but the second method (the pole on the ring) may be better for distance and offshore sailing because there is less chafe.

When setting the 'chute from its bag, the bag becomes a simplified turtle. About the only difference between the bag and the turtle is that the latter is more elaborate, and it is usually (though not always) designed to be secured forward of the headstay or jibstay as shown in figure 10-5. Sometimes the turtle is equipped with snap hooks that snap on to the bow pulpit if the boat has one. When the spinnaker is set from its bag, however, it is usually secured to the foredeck abaft the headstay. The bag must have a lanyard at its bottom so that it

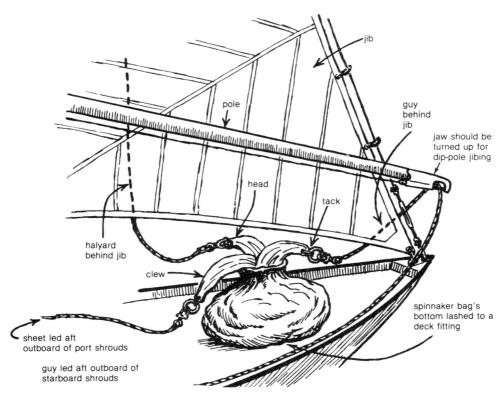

jib

pole

guy
behind
jib

jaw should be
turned up for
dip-pole jibing

head

tack

halyard
behind jib

clew

spinnaker bag's
bottom lashed to a
deck fitting

163

sheet led aft
outboard of port shrouds

guy led aft outboard of
starboard shrouds

10-6. Setting the spinnaker from its bag.

can be lashed to the bow cleat or some other fitting on the foredeck. Figure 10-6 illustrates the usual manner of rigging the spinnaker bag. The sail's three corners hang out of the bag's top, which is closed with the bag's draw string and tied with a slip knot. Immediately prior to hoisting the spinnaker, the slip knot is pulled to release the sail. Notice that figure 10-6 shows the jib hoisted. Usually, the jib is not lowered until after the spinnaker has been hoisted, at which time the jib is *quickly* dropped, so it will not blanket the spinnaker.

As figure 10-6 shows, with dotted lines, that part of the halyard that fastens to the sail's head must lie to leeward of the jib. The hoisting part of the halyard is, of course, to windward of the jib, next to the mast. When the halyard straddles the headstay aloft, be careful not to wrap the stay when snapping it onto the sail's head. The leeward end of the halyard that snaps on to the head must be put to leeward of the jib by running it aft, outside the shrouds, to the sail's leech. Then the halyard is put behind the leech and the halyard's end is worked forward under the foot of the jib until it is opposite the spinnaker bag where the end can be snapped onto the sail's head. Putting the halyard to leeward

of the jib by running the line forward and around the headstay will often cause the halyard to make a wrap around the stay. More will be said about this later when we discuss spinnaker problems. Always look aloft to see that all is clear before hoisting the spinnaker.

It should be noticed in figure 10-6 that the after guy runs around the headstay and to leeward of the jib tack where it is snapped onto the spinnaker's tack. If it is desired that the pole be snapped to the guy's shackle ring, then the spinnaker's tack corner must be carried to leeward of the jib and around the headstay where the ring can be fastened to the pole's outboard end, which is resting up against the head-stay.

The sheet leads outboard of the lee shrouds and snaps into the clew.

On large boats with *lifelines* (lines forming a safety railing around the outboard edge of the deck), it is especially important to check the sheet, guy, and halyard that are to leeward of the jib to make sure they are not fouled in the lifelines. The spinnaker sheet, guy, and halyard are always led *over*, or outboard of the lifelines.

It is very important that the spinnaker be "made

up" or properly prepared before it is stuffed into its turtle or bag prior to hoisting. This preparation consists of folding the two spinnaker leeches together before the sail is bagged so that the sail will not be twisted when it is hoisted. A simple method is to dump the loose sail on the cabin sole where it is protected from the wind; then starting at the head, each leech is located and folded one against the other. The man doing this works his way down towards the sail's foot, *flaking down* or folding the sail accordion style with the leeches together. When almost at the foot, the two clews are separated and pulled out in opposite directions. The loose bulk of the sail is stuffed into the bag followed by the folded leeches. The head and the two clews are left hanging out of the bag or the turtle's top with the head in the middle between the two clews. When the spinnaker is being hoisted on large boats, a man should "see" it out of the bag or turtle. He should let the spinnaker run through his hands or arms while looking aloft to see that the sail does not foul on a stay or spreader and that it does not become twisted. More will be said about this when we study spinnaker problems later in this chapter.

The remaining method of setting a spinnaker is to hoist the sail while it is rolled up and tied with light stops. After the sail is hoisted, the stops are then broken. This method is illustrated in figure 10-7. In former days, before the advent of the turtle, stopping a spinnaker was the usual practice, but now this is not often done except on a big boat in a strong wind. In most instances, using a turtle or bag is simpler and quicker.

When a spinnaker is stopped, its leeches are put together in much the same manner as when preparing the sail for a turtle. The sail should be stretched tight between its head and foot, and then the loose part of the sail between the leeches is rolled or bunched up so that it makes the appearance of a long, thin sausage. A rolled sail is usually more difficult to break out than one that is bunched. The sail is then stopped tightly at about every two or three feet with rotten twine or light cotton thread that may be broken very easily. The tighter the twine is tied the easier it will break. It is usually a good practice to make "frog's legs" at the foot as shown in figure 10-7. As can be seen, the lowest stops are not put around the two leeches but around the foot and leech so that each clew forms the end of a leg. It is important that the upper stop not be tied too

164

10-7. A stopped spinnaker. Pull on sheet to break it out.

close to the spinnaker's head because this stop is often difficult to break. Upper stops are usually tied with one turn, while lower stops may have two. The lower the stop, the more force can be applied to it by a pull on the sheet.

Occasionally a special line is tied under the stops in such a way that the line may be pulled from the deck after the sail is hoisted to facilitate breaking the stops. Usually, however, a breaking line is not necessary. The leg stops can be reached and broken by hand, and a hard pull aft on the sheet will break the higher stops. When the stops begin to break, the wind will fill out the lower portion of the sail and help break the upper stops. The important thing in preparing a spinnaker for hoisting (whether it be in a bag, turtle, or stops) is to have the leeches running continuously together in order to assure that the sail is not twisted.

After the sail is hoisted, in a moderate or stronger breeze ease the halyard slightly (about 12 to 18 inches) so that the head is blown slightly out and away from the mast. In light airs, however, the head should be as high as possible.

Spinnaker trim and helmsmanship

There are two ways a boat can be sailed with the spinnaker set. The first is to trim the sail properly and leave it alone while the helmsman changes course to conform with changes in the velocity and direction of the wind. The second is for the helmsman to hold a steady course while the spinnaker's trim is changed to match every change in the wind. On most top racing boats, however, a combination of these two techniques is used.

When the first method is used, the helmsman must be able to watch the spinnaker's luff (the forward edge from masthead to the outboard end of the pole). When the sail begins to collapse, he must quickly alter course. When sailing between a beam reach and a broad reach, the helmsman bears off if the spinnaker starts to *break* (to luff, beginning to collapse). But if the boat is running and the spinnaker begins to collapse, it is often difficult for the helmsman to know which way to turn. The sail could be luffing on account of a wind shift that is more on the beam, or the sail might be blanketed by the mainsail because of a shift that comes from astern and puts the boat by the lee (see chapter 5). This can become a real problem even for an experienced sailor in a rapidly shifting wind. The best way to overcome the problem is to look at the windward telltales or a masthead wind indicator. These will tell which way the wind is shifting. The helmsman should remember that the pole should be kept at right angles to the apparent wind. Of course, the wind indicators will give the apparent wind direction; thus, when an indicator makes an acute angle (less than 90 degrees) with the pole, the helmsman should *head up* to make the angle 90 degrees, but when the indicator makes an obtuse angle (more than 90 degrees) with the pole, he should *bear off* to make the angle 90 degrees. This is explained in figure 10-8.

An experienced helmsman can often (but not always) tell what is causing a spinnaker to break by simply looking at the sail. If it suddenly shakes and begins to collapse all over, it is probably blanketed by the mainsail. But if the sail first curls or bulges in near the luff edge, then the sail is probably luffing because of being on a point of sailing that is too high for the sail trim. The feel of the wind on the back of his neck aids the helmsman also. Nevertheless, experienced sailors have caused a complete spinnaker collapse by steering the wrong way at the first sign of the sail's breaking. This can usually be avoided by referring to the wind indicators. In shifty conditions, it is sometimes wise to station a man near the telltales who can call their direction to the

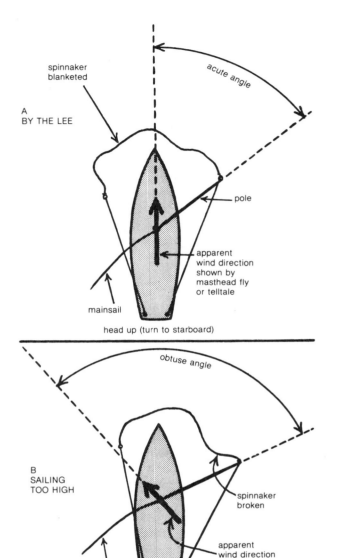

165

10-8. Spinnaker helmsmanship. Masthead flys often swing from side to side if boat is rolling severely. In such a case, it is usually better to watch the telltales.

helmsman with the words "beamy" or "by the lee," or some such designation.

The second method mentioned (changing the sail's trim for shifts while the helmsman holds a straight course) requires a lot of action and coordination on the crew's part, because the guy as well as the sheet must be constantly tended. The responsibility for preventing a spinnaker collapse lies primarily with the sheet tender instead of the helmsman.

At most times it is best to use a combination of the two methods discussed, whereby the helmsman alters course to keep on the fastest point of sailing while a man stands by the sheet to prevent a collapse in the event of a sudden wind shift. With this technique, the fore-and-aft pole position is not often changed. The most frequent adjustments are with the helm and sheet. The helmsman should sail according to the principles discussed in chapter 5. He should bear off in the puffs and head up in the lulls, and unless there is a good reason for not doing so, he should *moderately* tack downwind. It is nearly always harmful to run dead before the wind with the spinnaker set, because this is a slower point of sailing and there is the danger of the spinnaker collapsing from being by the lee. Of course, the helmsman should steer as low as possible but with the sails, especially the spinnaker, drawing at maximum efficiency. On a yawl, the mizzen staysail can be an effective guide to the helmsman. If he steers too low, this sail will collapse because of being blanketed by the mizzen. A simple rule of thumb for sailing a yawl downwind is to sail as low as possible without collapsing the mizzen staysail.

Principles for trimming the spinnaker sheet are essentially the same as for any other downwind sail. The sheet should be eased as far as possible without the sail beginning to bulge in at the luff. The sail should actually be carried "on edge," with the luff just beginning to curl. The person who tends the sheet is the key to successful spinnaker sailing. Since the wind and the boat's heading change almost continuously, he must follow with almost continuous experiments to try to ease the sheet more and more until the luff curls too much, then quickly trim in just enough to straighten the curl, then try to ease it out again, and keep on repeating this cycle. He must be stationed far enough forward, often on the windward side, so that he can watch the luff of the sail continuously. At times he may be able to put several turns around the winch with the sheet and then lead it forward to a position just forward of the main boom. At other times, on a large boat such as a Navy yawl, he may stand at the shrouds and reach outboard to the sheet to give it frequent inward tugs while another sheet trimmer backs him up aft at the winch. If the man at the shrouds cannot reach the sheet with his hand, he may use a short piece of line looped over the sheet. This short line is sometimes called a *snatch line*. The man at the

shrouds should watch the luff continuously and give the sheet a jerk when the luff edge begins to curl too much. On small boats the same kind of trimming is achieved with the twing lines as described in chapter 7 in the discussion of J-24s. In light airs, light sheets with lightweight shackles (or no shackle at all) should be used so that the clew will lift as high as possible. This sheet should be played by hand every moment.

When running, the spinnaker sheet should be led far aft where it is a maximum distance outboard. On many boats this lead point is at the top corners of the transom, but on the Navy yawls and 44s the lead blocks are somewhat farther forward because these boats have such narrow sterns. When reaching, it sometimes pays to lead the spinnaker sheet through a block at the end of the main boom in order to move the lead outboard. This has been effectively done on the Navy yawls. In strong winds it is usually best to lead the sheet farther forward.

Jibing the 'chute

There are two principal methods of jibing a parachute spinnaker: the *end-for-end* method and the *dip-pole* or *free-wheeling* jibe. Since the 'chute is symmetrical with leech and clew being identical, the sail can merely be shifted bodily from one side of the boat to the other without turning it around leech for leech.

The first jibing method mentioned, end-for-ending, requires that the spinnaker pole be reversible, that there be identical fittings on each end of the pole. Actually, the vast majority of poles are made this way. Opinions vary as to which is the best method of jibing. But generally speaking, end-for-ending seems to be more suitable for small boats and even medium-sized boats in light airs when the lift and foreguy are rigged from the middle of the pole (as in figure 10-1K). Dip-poling is more often favored on large boats, especially when jibing in a fresh breeze and when jibing from a broad reach on one tack to a broad reach on the other tack. Dip-poling is usually done on the Navy yawls and the 44s.

Figure 10-9 explains the end-for-end spinnaker jibe. The procedure is divided into three steps. In the first, Step A, the guy and lift are slacked slightly. The pole should be about horizontal and low enough to be within easy reach of the foredeck man. The inboard end of the pole is unhooked from the

10-9. Jibing the spinnaker.
A. Lift and guy slacked slightly. Foredeck man unhooks pole from mast. On small boats one man can handle sheet and guy. Each line should be led to and snubbed on (wrapped around) a winch.
B. Sheet slacked slightly. Pole end snapped on sheet. Pole now on both corners of sail and at right angles to wind. Helmsman holds boat before wind and jibes the main. On some small boats foredeck man can work in fore end of cockpit.
C. Pole unhooked from former guy. New guy (port side) is slacked. Pole end hooked to mast. New sheet trimmed in. On small boats, guy can be hooked or pulled down with a twing forward near shrouds (shown by dotted line) to hold pole down, eliminating need for downhaul.

mast, and in Step B, this same pole end is hooked onto the spinnaker sheet or swivel shackle. At this point, midway in the jibe, the pole is attached to both lower corners of the spinnaker, the sail is directly ahead of the bow and is kept full, the pole is at right angles to the boat's centerline, the boat is headed directly before the wind, and the main boom has been pulled in amidships. In the final Step C, the pole end that was formerly the outboard end is detached from the sail and is hooked onto the mast while the new guy is being eased off and the new sheet is trimmed in as the boat turns onto her new course, and finally the lift is readjusted.

One advantage of this jibing technique is that it is usually not difficult to keep the spinnaker full and drawing during the entire operation, because the clews are held apart by the pole. Nevertheless, it is important that the helmsman turn from one tack to the other very slowly. He should hold the boat dead before the wind until he is sure that the foredeck crew has everything under control and that the guy and sheet tenders are ready to slack and trim. Also, the mainsail should be held amidships and jibed very slowly in a light breeze; if it is slacked too soon, it will blanket the spinnaker and perhaps cause the 'chute to collapse before it is properly trimmed for the new course.

A spinnaker pole of the type in figure 10-1 is frequently rigged with a continuous lanyard or trip line that connects the pull pins of the pole-end fittings as shown in the illustration. With this arrangement, the foredeck man can release the sail from the end fitting by pulling the lanyard at any point on the pole.

Although it is customary to dip the poles of large ocean racers, they can be jibed using the end-for-end method when they have poles with proper jaws at both ends. This can be very effective in a light

10-10. Spinnaker pole fitting on mast of a fiberglass Luders yawl. The jaws at the end of the pole fit around the pin in the bracket. Inboard pole height is controlled by adjusting the position of the fitting using the block and tackle arrangement fitted to the slide. Two jam cleats are provided to prevent the line from slipping.

breeze, especially when jibing from a run on one tack to a run on the other tack. The procedure is the same as shown in figure 10-9 except that two crew should be used to disconnect and connect the pole with the mast and another is needed to help connect the new guy to the pole end and disconnect the former guy.

A dip-pole jibe is shown in figure 10-12. With this method, the outboard end of the pole is un-hooked from the after guy or tack shackle, and the lift is slacked in order to lower (almost to the deck) the outboard pole end, which is then passed under the headstay and across to the boat's other side where it is attached to the spinnaker's new guy or other clew. This method usually requires the in-

10-11. Dip-pole jibing. Yawl at midpoint during dip-pole jibe. Pole end released from guy, lowered, passed under headstay, and hooked to former sheet (new guy).

board end of the pole to be slid up to the highest position on the mast track so that the pole will be short enough, when its outboard end is lowered, to clear the headstay. When dip-pole jibing, the spinnaker sheet and guy should be eased. The crew member who stands by the pole lift should trip the outboard end of the pole with the tripping lanyard, and perhaps another will be needed to help remove the tack from the outboard pole end fitting. The pole is dipped by slacking the lift, and it is swung inboard and ducked under the headstay. A crew member grabs the old sheet that will become the new guy and hooks it to the outboard end of the pole. Tension should be put on the new sheet immediately to prevent the sail from collapsing. At one point during this jibing procedure the spinnaker is, of course, completely detached from the pole. This is a crucial time and the helmsman must be careful not to put over his helm too suddenly before the pole is attached, the sheet trimmed, and the main boom is swung over. Also the mainsail should not be slacked off so rapidly that it blankets the 'chute while it is guyed far forward and before the helmsman heads up onto his new course.

Dip-pole jibing is usually the best method in a strong breeze because the pole does not have to be removed and refitted to the mast, a considerable task in a blow. In heavy weather, on big boats especially, an extra pair of sheets can be bent to each

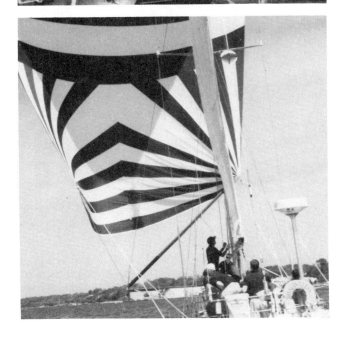

10-12A. Dip-pole jibing on a Navy 44. Beginning to jibe. The bow man has the "lazy" (unused) guy in hand ready to insert it into the pole end when it swings over. The mast man is ready to release the pole from the spinnaker's clew with the tripping lanyard.

B. Pole is tripped while the boat turns downwind with her main centered. Pole end is lowered so that it will swing under the headstay.

C. Pole is attached to new guy and is being raised.

D. Boat turned onto port tack while main is jibed and pole raised to clew.

E. Jibe completed and main slacked off. The downhaul needs tightening and main's foot should be slacked.

spinnaker clew. This will greatly facilitate the handling of the sail because it gives extra lines to control the sail, and during the dip-pole jibe, the pole can be attached to the extra sheet (sometimes called a lazy guy) when it is slack and inboard, within easy reach. This extra sheet to which the pole is fastened then becomes the new guy after the jibe has been completed.

On small boats during a race, consideration should be given to keeping extra weight off the foredeck. To some extent this is even true with boats as large as the Navy yawls. When jibing, therefore, no extra crew should be on the foredeck, because this can have a harmful effect on the boat's fore-and-aft trim. Small racers need only one person to rig the spinnaker, getting it ready for hoisting. He may stand on the foredeck when jibing, but as far aft as possible, near the mast. End-for-end jibing, especially when done with a tripping lanyard on the pole, usually keeps weight on the foredeck to a minimum. There are conflicting schools of thought on whether the sliding pin on the pole-end fitting should be up or down. This is a matter of personal preference. The pole is usually easier to engage and disengage from the mast during an end-for-end jibe if the pin is down (as illustrated in figure 10-1), but it is much easier to trip the end fitting with its lanyard to release the guy or tack if the pole is upside down with the sliding pin on top. Since dip-poling is used on the larger Navy boats, the pole should normally be carried with the jaws up on these boats.

Handing the spinnaker

Handing or taking in the spinnaker is not difficult if the job is done properly and carefully, but poor helmsmanship and sailhandling during the lowering operation can mean trouble aplenty. On large boats in nearly all cases, the Genoa or some other jib is set before the spinnaker is taken down. This will provide continuous sail power during a race, and the jib will help blanket the spinnaker and thereby make it easier to handle when it is being lowered. After the jib is hoisted, the guy is slacked all the way forward until the pole lies against the headstay or jibstay. Then the spinnaker's tack is released from the guy snap shackle so that the sail's luff flies free.

It is better to head the boat nearly dead before the wind when the tack is released in order that the spinnaker is blanketed to the greatest extent. At this point, one or two crew members are standing by the clew and sheet. When the crew on the sheet are ready, the person on the halyard slowly lowers the sail. The sheet tenders, who are usually stationed abaft the main shrouds, pull in on the sheet and gather in the sail as it is lowered, either smothering the sail to keep it from blowing overboard or stuffing it out of the way (see figure 10-13). It can often be stuffed under the fore end of the cockpit on an open boat or down the companionway hatch on a boat with a cabin. The halyard man must be sure he doesn't lower the spinnaker faster than it can be taken in; otherwise, the sail will blow overboard and possibly scoop up water, which could tear the sail and make it very difficult to haul it back aboard. In the rare instance that no jib is hoisted, the boat should be headed dead before the wind so that the spinnaker can be lowered in the lee of the mainsail. On dinghies and other small centerboarders, the spinnaker often can be dropped on the windward side, and this may be beneficial in keeping crew weight to windward.

10-13. Dousing the spinnaker. The tack has been released from the pole end, and the sail is being handed under the lee of the mainsail. The crew is keeping the sail tightly muzzled so it cannot fill with wind, which is especially important when it is blowing hard.

A frequently encountered spinnaker-lowering situation occurs when approaching a leeward turning mark during a race, when the next leg of the course is closer than a beam reach. The 'chute should be lowered in advance of reaching the mark. Unless sailing with an experienced crew who have worked together, it is far better to be too soon than too late getting the spinnaker off. If the mark can be approached on a broad reach, the Genoa can be hoisted early to substitute for the 'chute, and not a great deal of speed will be lost if the jib is not blanketed by the mainsail. When jibing around the mark, try to jibe early or else hoist the jib, lower the spinnaker, and then jibe. If the mark is rounded sharply and the boat heads onto a close reach before the spinnaker has been lowered, the sail will blow quite far aft when its tack is released from the guy, and the dousing operation may be difficult because the 'chute will be partly out of the mainsail's wind shadow. In this case, the 'chute must be brought in under the after end of the main boom. On a yawl, great care must be taken to see that the sail does not foul the mizzen mast or its rigging. This has happened. When the 'chute is being lowered, it should be gathered in by the clew edge of the sail. Hand only one leech. If both leeches are pulled on, the sail will fill with wind and become very difficult to handle. The person lowering the spinnaker should always keep a turn of the halyard on its cleat or winch so that the sail cannot get away.

Spinnaker problems

In certain conditions of wind and sea, spinnakers can cause many problems even when they are reasonably well handled. Many experienced offshore sailors feel that the modern 'chute is not a completely safe and seamanlike sail to carry at sea. There is no doubt, however, that it is a very fast sail, and a boat racing without a spinnaker has little chance of doing well in a downwind race. Furthermore, troubles can be minimized with practice, careful sail handling, advanced planning, and a general knowledge of what to expect.

The most common spinnaker problems with brief solutions or suggestions as to how to avoid them are as follows:

The hour glass—This is a spinnaker twist about halfway between head and foot that prevents the middle of the sail from filling, but above and below the twist, the sail balloons out in such a way that it

171

10-14. An hour-glassed spinnaker. Crew members are pulling on both leeches in an attempt to make the swivel at the sail's head turn. The twist is so low, however, that it is doubtful that this attempt will succeed. The sail will probably have to be lowered to clear it, or if the breeze is light, the tack and clew could be detached and the lower half of the sail untwisted.

gives the appearance of an hour glass (see figure 10-14). It is usually caused by improperly preparing the sail before hoisting or by not spreading the clews as the sail is hoisted. The best way to prevent the twist is to see that the *leeches* are not twisted about each other when the sail is bagged, turtled, or stopped. Also, as said before, a crew member should see the sail out of its turtle or bag during the hoisting. He can often clear a twist before it develops by tugging on a leech. In addition, the sheet trimmer should keep tension on the sheet as the sail goes up. If an hour glass occurs near the spinnaker's head, the twist might be removed by tugging on the sheet or leech or by jerking on the halyard, because there is always a swivel at the head that might turn to allow the sail to untwist. An hour glass near the middle or bottom of the sail will probably make it necessary to lower and untwist it by interchanging the tack and clew.

A fouled halyard—Spinnaker halyard blocks are mounted on a swivel above the headstay (or jibstay with a fractional rig). The halyard will either lie entirely on one side of the stay, or will straddle the stay (with one part of the halyard on either side of the stay). Some spinnaker halyards have snap shackles at both ends, but the usual 'chute halyard on a Navy boat has a shackle at one end of the line only. If a single-shackle halyard straddles the headstay and the shackle end of the line lies to leeward of the stay, then, as explained earlier, the leeward part of the halyard should be taken to leeward of the jib by passing the line aft around the jib's leech. Do *not pass the leeward part of a spinnaker halyard around the headstay to get it behind the jib*, because this will cause the halyard to wrap the stay. On the other hand, if this halyard's shackle end lies to windward of the stay, then the shackle end of the line must be taken forward where it is passed around the headstay to the jib's leeward side. Of course, it is then passed under the foot of the jib, and the shackle is snapped onto the spinnaker's head. With a double-shackle halyard (a shackle on each end) straddling the headstay, one has a choice: to take the *leeward part* of the halyard *aft*, around the jib's leech, or take the *windward part forward* around the headstay. In the first case, the hauling part of the halyard is to windward of the headstay, and in the second case, the hauling part is to leeward of the stay. The latter solution is better in the interest of chafe prevention when the spinnaker is carried for lengthy periods.

One method of simplifying halyard preparation is to fasten the halyard's shackle end (or both shackles on a double-shackle halyard) to the bow pulpit ahead of the jib on a Navy yawl. It is then in a position to be easily rigged on either tack. However, it is not advisable to leave the halyard permanently hooked to the pulpit, because the whipping line will cause some windage and turbulence that will interfere with the jib's luff when beating to windward. The spinnaker halyard should be hooked forward only just prior to setting the 'chute.

Some good general rules for rigging the halyard are: *Determine well in advance of setting the spin-*

naker on which side the sail will be carried. Of course, this is determined by noting the wind direction and estimating what the spinnaker-carrying course will be. Another vital rule is *always to look aloft just prior to hoisting the spinnaker to see that its halyard is clear*. See that the line is not wrapped around the headstay, and see that the block above the stay has properly swivelled.

Spinnaker knockdowns—In a fresh breeze, it is not uncommon to see boats with spinnakers set take sudden *knockdowns* (extreme heelings) to either windward or leeward. (See figures 10-15 and 10-16.) Quite often these knockdowns will cause a loss of rudder control because the rudder will be acting in more of a horizontal than a vertical plane. A knockdown to windward can cause an accidental jibe, while a leeward knockdown can cause the main boom to break if it is broad off and vanged down. Either kind of knockdown can make the boat broach to or turn, out of control, broadside to the wind and seas.

The most seamanlike solution to this problem is to take the spinnaker off when there is real danger of a knockdown. In a race when competitors are carrying 'chutes successfully, however, it is desirable to carry the spinnaker as long as possible. It is often difficult to determine the exact time the spinnaker should be handed. To a large extent this will depend on the experience and skill of the crew and on the condition of the weather, sea, and boat. By and large, when the boat is at hull speed, when she is yawing and rolling violently, when there is a steep following sea, or when extreme heeling commences and the helm is very hard to control, the spinnaker should be doused. Under these conditions the boat will be safer, handle much easier, and perhaps will not lose any speed carrying a poled-out Genoa jib. When poling out a jib, the spinnaker pole is rigged to windward, the jib is kept blanketed by the main, and then the jib's clew is hauled out to the pole's outboard end with the windward sheet run through the pole-end fitting.

If caught by a sudden puff that causes a knockdown to leeward when the spinnaker is set, release the sheet to spill the wind from the sail. Some sailors don't believe in knotting the ends of spinnaker sheets, because a knot may prevent sufficient slack; but when the sheet is sufficiently long, at least two times the length of the boat, enough slack should be available, and the knot will prevent the sheet from

10-15. Spinnaker knockdowns to leeward. This picture illustrates examples of the troubles that can be had when trying to carry spinnakers in too much breeze. Obviously, both boats are overpowered, and they would have been safer—and would be sailing faster—with boomed-out jibs. The lead boat appears to have tripped on her main boom while it was vanged down. This could break the boom. The spinnaker pole has escaped its bell fitting and is flailing dangerously. The mizzen is trimmed in flat making it very difficult for the helmsman to bear off. The after boat should have slacked her spinnaker sheet and borne off. The mizzen staysail is doing no good and is only adding to the confusion.

running out of its lead block. It is often wise to rig two sheets, one with a few feet of slack, so that when the taut sheet is slacked, the loose sheet will take the strain but still allow the spinnaker to go out enough to spill its wind. With a knockdown to leeward, the helmsman should try to bear off immediately so that the boat will gain stability.

If caught by a sudden puff that causes a windward knockdown, the sheet should be flattened quickly and the boat headed up, if possible. This kind of knockdown can be avoided by overtrimming the spinnaker sheet and by not sailing too low, by reaching instead of running.

Breaking the spinnaker pole—Breaking a pole is not a common occurrence, but it does happen occasionally. As previously said, the lift/downhaul arrangement that secures these lines to the end of the pole (either directly or with bridles) is generally considered the strongest rig. However, with this arrangement, there is still a great compression load on the pole when it is guyed far forward because the after guy pulls almost straight aft.

One solution to this is the *reaching strut*, which is often used by large boats on distance races but not as often on short, closed-course races. This strut is a short extra pole that is rigged to windward to hold the guy a few feet out from the windward shrouds. While the pole is guyed forward, the strut sticks out horizontally at a near right angle to the boat's centerline. The length of the strut is equal to approximately three-quarters of the boat's maximum beam. The strut lies against the fore side of the forward shroud and it is usually lashed to the shroud. The strut's inboard end hooks onto a pad eye or similar fitting on the mast, while the outboard end usually has a large sheave to accept the guy. Advantages of the strut are three-fold: to keep the pole from pressing too hard against the headstay, to

10-16. The Luders yawl *Lively* under reefed mainsail and tri-radial spinnaker takes a roll to weather. Weather knockdowns can be prevented by heading up slightly, moving the sheet lead well forward, and overtrimming the spinnaker in gusts.

reduce compression on the pole, and to prevent the guy from chafing against the outboard shroud. On the other hand, the strut does cause extra complications on the foredeck, and both setting it up and removing it take extra time; so it is not always used on short races in protected waters, especially if the boat has outboard shrouds that hold the guy fairly far away from the boat's centerline.

Whether or not the strut is used, care must be taken to see that the pole does not exert too much pressure against the headstay. The guy must be kept tight enough to hold the pole just off the stay even on a beam reach. In a strong wind the outboard pole end should be lowered slightly for two reasons. First, if the pole does hit the headstay, due to the guy stretching, the lateral strain will be near the pole's end where the spinnaker will not have the leverage to break the pole (by pulling it sideways against the stay). Secondly, by keeping the pole end low, the after guy will pull the pole down to help counteract the strong upward pull of the spinnaker. Of course, in winds less than those which threaten to break the

pole, the spinnaker should be allowed to lift for the greatest efficiency and drive. But in strong winds it is best to control and tame the 'chute somewhat by overtrimming the sheet and lowering the pole.

The spinnaker wrap—One of the most difficult troubles to clear up is the spinnaker headstay wrap. This is most likely to occur in a seaway when the spinnaker has collapsed and its loose middle section lies against the headstay. Occasionally, a current of wind from the side will cause the loose folds of the sail to start spinning around the headstay. The boat's motion from the seas will often initiate or add to the twisting. This is most likely to happen if the sail collapses from sailing by the lee, during a jibe, or as the 'chute is hoisted without the jib being set. Of course, if the jib is kept up until after the spinnaker is hoisted and sheeted, then there is little chance of a wrap. The 'chute cannot wind around the stay as long as the jib is hoisted. For this reason many ocean racers carry *spinnaker nets*, which are basically jibs made from bigmesh nets instead of cloth. In fact, the British often refer to spinnaker nets as *phantom jibs*. Nets vary greatly in design, but they are usually composed of the least number of lines or tapes that will do the job of preventing a wrap. Of course, a cloth jib should not always remain hoisted because it might blanket the spinnaker.

Spinnaker nets are seldom used in short races or in protected waters because the nets take time to rig, and they are easy to tangle. Many small boats carry one or two *antiwrap lines* that are permanently rigged. An antiwrap line (usually of shock cord) is one permanently fastened to the mast at about a third or more of the mast's length down from the masthead (if the boat has a masthead rig). This line is slightly shorter than the distance from its point of attachment on the mast to the masthead. The other end of the line (the end not attached to the mast) is fastened to a sliding ring on the headstay. When no jib is set, the line hangs loosely between the mast and the stay where it will help prevent a spinnaker wrap; but when the jib is hoisted, the ring slides up to the top of the stay, and the line will be stretched tight against or near the fore side of the mast. Of course, effectiveness is increased if two such antiwrap lines are used.

With boats rigged like the Navy 44s or yawls, the forestay may be set up, and a jib halyard may be wound back and forth between the forestay and the headstay so that the halyard makes a kind of net. This is not recommended for short races but only on long spinnaker courses and when there is danger of a spinnaker wrap. At all other times when the spinnaker is carried, the forestay should be detached and secured at the mast or shrouds. The foredeck should always be kept as clear as possible (stripped of anchors, boathooks, etc.) to minimize the possibility of lines becoming fouled.

Once the spinnaker becomes wrapped, it is usually very difficult to clear. The first action to take is to jibe over as soon as the wrap occurs, so that the wind current that caused the wrap will come from the opposite side. After jibing, the boat should be held almost dead before the wind. She should not be let up to a broad reach. This may promptly cause the sail to unwrap, but if not you may be in for some trouble. Sometimes the wraps can be cleared by sailing by the lee and then luffing the boat in a series of swoops that reduce the wraps one turn per swoop. But if this doesn't work and the sail is badly

wrapped, a crew member may have to go aloft in a bosun's chair to clear the twists.

Some general tips on spinnaker wraps are as follows. Try to avoid letting the sail collapse against the headstay, especially in a seaway. Keep the jib set until after the spinnaker is hoisted and trimmed. Try to keep the spinnaker full when jibing. After the jib has been lowered, unshackle its halyard and bring it aft to the mast, because if a wrap occurs, the sail can get pinched between the stay and halyard. Also, the halyard may have to be used to hoist a man up in the bosun's chair. When there is danger of a wrap, keep tension on the spinnaker's sheet or pull on the leech, or both; anything that can be done to flatten the sail will be helpful. If the sail begins to wrap, a sharp change of course may stop it, but if not, jibe over and perhaps the sail will unwrap.

Recent spinnaker theory

In recent years some subtle improvements have been made in the design of spinnakers. Many of these sails have become more highly specialized for particular points of sailing and certain strengths of wind. Great strides, especially, have been made in the development of reaching spinnakers, and some of the modern designs can be carried when the boat is sailing considerably higher than a beam reach.

Specialized reaching spinnakers vary from flat, crosscut 'chutes to *spankers* (symmetrical jib-like spinnakers with narrow shoulders—see figure 10-17) to the more recent *star-cut* reachers. The latter design has cloth panels that radiate inwards from each corner towards the center of the sail to form a star-shaped pattern. This radial construction minimizes bias stretch (distortion from pull that is diagonal to the direction of the cloth's weave) and thus allows the sail to better hold its shape on a reach. The first spankers usually had mitered seams at the clews, and the sails were carried jib-style with the outboard end of the pole lowered to the stem head to tighten and thereby straighten the luff (racing rules forbid detaching the sail from the pole and tacking it to the stem). Many newer spankers and star-cuts are designed to be carried with the pole fairly low but horizontal, so that the sail's tack is slightly forward of the headstay, and, although there is some sag in the luff, it will have a flatter draft curve forward to allow reasonably high pointing. On many spinnakers over-tightening the luff will cause very deep draft forward that will be

10-17. Contrasting spinnaker types. Two Britton Chance—designed 30-footers racing with different spinnakers. The lead boat, a Chance 30-30, is flying a conventional cross-cut chute, while the following boat, a PT-30, is carrying a type of spanker. Notice the high-aspect ratio rigs favored by the IOR handicap rule and the double-spreader rig, clearly seen on the PT-30, which allows inboard shrouds without much sacrifice to the shroud angle.

detrimental to close reaching. As a rule, when reaching it is well to experiment with the pole level on every individual sail to test its pointing abilities, because optimal shaping of the sail will depend on its particular cut. Spinnakers intended for close reaching, being made of medium weight cloth, having narrow shoulders aloft, and being cut relatively flat, are also highly suitable for running in strong winds.

Those 'chutes intended for running or broad reaching in light airs are made of the lightest weight nylon, one-half ounce or three-quarters ounce, depending on the size of the boat. Such spinnakers are cut with deeper draft, and except for those intended for drifting conditions, they have fairly broad shoulders aloft. In very light airs, the pole is carried quite

low but horizontal, partly to deepen the draft curve from the luff to leech. In medium winds, however, the pole is raised and the sail is allowed to lift all it can, and the shoulders are encouraged to spread apart. When only one spinnaker is on board, it must quite obviously be a very versatile sail, reasonably good in all conditions. Such a 'chute might be a three-quarters- or 1.2-ounce *radial head crosscut* (having horizontal panels in the lower half and vertical radial panels in the upper half) with only moderately deep draft and substantial shoulders. Another versatile 'chute, very popular today, is the *tri-radial*, which is crosscut in the middle but has radial panels at all three corners (see figure 10-18).

Staysails carried under spinnakers also have become more specialized. Sailmakers and expert sail-

10-18. The ex-Academy boat *Patriot* flying a tri-radial spinnaker. The radial seams at the head and clews help prevent bias stretch and thus distortion on a reach. The round patch just above the numbers is a "belly button" for the attachment of a retrieving line, which helps in handing the chute. With the retrieving line, the chute is lowered in the usual manner behind a jib, but it is normally not necessary to release the tack initially, because the sail is hauled down by the line attached to its middle, and this will effectively spill the wind.

10-19. A C&C 35 flying a cross-cut chute and tallboy staysail. Notice the battens in the tallboy to stabilize its leech. The sail might be tacked down a little farther to weather. The mainsail is well vanged and its luff slacked to increase draft and move it aft, but the sail might be hoisted a bit more for better advantage in such light air.

ors do not always agree about what staysail is most effective for each set of conditions, but by and large, taller staysails with shorter foot lengths are now being used. Very tall, narrow sails, often called *tallboys* or *ribbon staysails*, are tacked to the windward rail not far forward of the mainmast when running (see figure 10-19). For broad reaching with the apparent wind about on the quarter or somewhat farther forward, a low spinnaker staysail with a long foot (similar to the one illustrated in figure 6-1) is probably more effective to minimize blanketing the spinnaker. On this same point of sailing a few boats carry *topless* or *baldheaded staysails*

(those having their tops cut off to avoid blocking off the spinnaker's wind). Most broad-reaching staysails are tacked down a third or more of the distance from the stem head to the mainmast abaft the stem head. When the wind is closer to being on the beam or slightly forward of the beam, larger, taller staysails can be used, and generally they are tacked down farther forward. An effective sail for this point of sailing is a large Genoa staysail (a staysail shaped like a Genoa jib) with its tack about a quarter of the stem-to-mast distance aft and its luff about parallel to the headstay. On a very close spinnaker reach in moderate winds and smooth water, a full-size Genoa or reaching jib often can be carried under the 'chute to give a very noticeable increase in speed. Double slot arrangements with large staysails or jibs under the spinnaker are most effective when *penalty poles* (spinnaker poles longer than the distance

178

10-20. Hoisting the chute on the former Navy boat *Guerrière*. The spinnaker bag is secured quite far abaft the stem, and the sail is being hoisted under the foot of the jib. This may help prevent hourglass twists, because it allows the clews to be spread a maximum distance apart while hoisting. Care must be taken, however, to see that the sail does not drag in the water too much. Note that the halyard man is wearing sailing gloves to guard against rope burn.

between the stem head and mast that slightly increase the boat's racing handicap) are carried. Also, it will pay to ease the spinnaker halyard a foot or so in fresh breezes to get the 'chute as far as possible away from the jib.

Summary

A brief summary of the main points in this chapter in list form may be helpful. Several of these points are illustrated in figure 10-21 and other illustrations. If any of the tips are not clear, they should be looked up in the preceding text where they are dealt with in more detail.

Spinnaker tips

• Plan ahead. Lay out sheet and guy, prepare the 'chute, and set up pole with lift and downhaul well in advance of hoisting.

• Bag, turtle, or stop spinnaker with both leeches untwisted.

• Look aloft before hoisting. Be sure halyard is not wrapped around the headstay.

• Be sure that the sheet, guy, and halyard are led over the lifelines.

• Consider hooking spinnaker halyard on bow pulpit while getting the sail ready to hoist.

• Hoist spinnaker behind the jib whenever possible, and hoist fast.

10-21. A spinnaker problem. NA 2 is successfully hoisting her chute behind the lee of the jib, but it appears that NA 9 has not kept her spinnaker blanketed, and the halyard has gotten away from the crew doing the hoisting. The spinnaker should be pulled aboard by one sheet only; otherwise it will act like a sea anchor.

- Ease halyard slightly in a moderate or stronger breeze unless spinnaker begins to oscillate, in which case halyard should be *two-blocked* (hauled all the way up).
- Start trimming the sheet immediately while the 'chute is being hoisted.
- Keep pole at right angles to apparent wind.
- Keep tack and clew at same level.
- Keep inboard end of pole high in a moderate breeze but low in a light air.
- Keep pole horizontal in a light air but cocked up slightly in a moderate breeze.
- Keep pole's outboard end low in a strong breeze.
- Keep spinnaker "on edge" with the sheet.
- Station the sheet trimmer where he can see the luff.
- Use a sheet snatch line or twing in a strong breeze.
- Make maximum use of wind indicators when steering with the 'chute set.
- Avoid sailing low, or by the lee.
- Use a combination of course changing and sheet adjusting when sailing with the 'chute in a shifting breeze.
- Use the mizzen staysail as a guide to spinnaker steering.
- Jibe the mainsail slowly when the 'chute is being jibed.

- Consider dip-poling when jibing from reach to reach or in a strong breeze.
- Consider end-for-ending pole when jibing from run to run or in a moderate breeze on a small boat.
- Keep excess crew off the foredeck.

- Slack the sheet during a spinnaker knockdown to leeward, slack the main, and head off.
- Flatten sheet during a windward knockdown. Also head up and/or guy the pole farther forward.
- Lower the 'chute in the lee of a jib.

10-22. Setting the chute after rounding the windward mark. It is the safest policy, especially in a fresh wind, to keep the spinnaker blanketed until after it is fully hoisted. Crew members who are not busy should check for lines dragging overboard.

• Cast off tack and hand the 'chute by one leech only.

• Keep a turn around the winch or cleat with the halyard when the 'chute is lowered, and lower slowly.

• Continue steering before the wind, if possible, until the 'chute has been entirely lowered.

• Keep the pole from bearing hard against the forestay.

• Consider using a reaching strut and some form of spinnaker net when distance racing in a rough sea.

• When beginning to lose helm control, douse the 'chute and pole out a jib.

11.
Basic Racing

*A*lthough there are many excellent seamen who seldom race, there is no doubt that sailboat racing is a sport that develops and sharpens all the aspects and skills of good seamanship—team work, organization, the power to concentrate, the ability to make quick decisions, and the desire to learn and improve. Volumes have been written on racing, and we cannot hope to cover all the fine points of the subject in one chapter. We have already put a good deal of emphasis on a very important aspect of racing, however—that of getting the best speed and performance from a boat through helmsmanship, sail trim, and the duties of the crew. Therefore, a large part of competitive sailing has been dealt with. What remains to be covered may be roughly divided into three parts: racing rules, starting, and course tactics.

Introduction to racing

When a group of sailboats race against each other as individuals (not as a team), there can be two forms of competition: handicap or class (sometimes called one-design) racing. The latter is boat-for-boat racing between nearly identical boats. In this case, the boat with the fastest *elapsed time* from start to finish, or the first boat over the finish line, wins the race. In handicap racing, however, boats of different sizes and types compete against each other. The larger, faster boats are given time handicaps. Under this system, each boat is given a *measurement* or *performance rating* that attempts to predict her speed potential. This rating is assigned a time allowance in seconds per mile. To find out how much time a particular boat would receive from a larger, higher-rated boat, subtract the allowance of the larger boat from the allowance of the smaller one, and multiply this difference by the distance in miles of the particular race. The winning boat is the one with the best *corrected time*, or the best time for sailing the course after handicap corrections have been made.

While many small boats are raced as a class, the Navy 44s, Luders yawls, and J-24s may be raced either as a class, when racing among themselves, or under a handicap system when racing against boats of different sizes and designs. The Navy 44s are rated in three different handicap divisions: IOR (International Offshore Rule), IMS (International Measurement System), and PHRF (Performance Handicap Racing Fleet). The first two rules are measurement systems whereby certain vital measurements such as length, beam, draft, displacement, sail area, etc. are taken and applied to a handicap formula. The PHRF, however, uses a rating based on observed boat performance. Ratings are assigned by local handicappers after a study of race results nationwide. IMS and PHRF ratings are assigned seconds per mile, but the IOR is given in feet, which is then converted to seconds per mile with the use of time-allowance tables.

Race courses are of two general types: the point-to-point course and the closed course. The former is literally from one geographic location to another. This type of racing may turn out to be a reach, beat, or run the entire way, or it may be some combination of these points of sailing depending on the wind direction with respect to the particular course. Certain aspects of this kind of racing will be discussed in the next chapter. Unlike the point-to-point course, the closed course has its start and finish in the same, or approximately the same, location. This type of race is deliberately planned to have a variety of points of sailing, and at least one beating leg is considered essential. Most closed courses are *windward-leeward, triangular*, or some combination of the two.

The simplest windward-leeward course has its first leg a near dead beat to a windward turning mark and then a run back to the starting point. Some windward-leeward courses have an initial short windward leg to the mark, then a long run to another mark to leeward of the starting line, and finally a short beat back to the starting area, which then becomes the finish line. In a triangular course, three major marks are involved so as to make each leg of the course the side of a triangle. This kind of course is usually arranged so that one leg is a beat, another a run, and the other a reach. Combinations of windward-leeward and triangular courses make the *Gold Cup, Modified Gold Cup,* and *Olympic* courses. The Gold Cup is a windward-leeward followed by a triangular course, the Modified Gold Cup is a triangle followed by a windward-leeward course, and an Olympic course is a triangle followed by a windward-leeward course with an extra windward leg.

A first look at the racing rules

The principal racing rules in this country and those under which all Navy boats race are the International Yacht Racing Union Rules as adopted by the United States Yacht Racing Union (USYRU). Included in these rules are the right-of-way principles for all converging situations. Remember that these are not rules of the road. The USYRU rules govern boats racing among themselves only; however, their right-of-way principles now closely agree with those of the Rules of the Road as discussed in chapter 4.

It is important for all racing skippers to know the rules. Of course, the newcomer cannot be expected to know all the fine points of the rules or the outcome of all protests resulting from different interpretations of the rules, but all skippers should at least be thoroughly familiar with the main points expressed in Part IV of the USYRU rules, which is "Right of Way Rules, and Rights and Obligations When Yachts Meet." This and other parts of the rules are printed verbatim in appendix C. Knowledge of these rules not only gives racing skippers confidence to exercise their judgment and to make split-second decisions, but their knowledge considerably lessens the chance of a dangerous collision on the race course. Racing terms used in the rules are defined in Part I of the USYRU rules and this is also printed verbatim in the appendix.

It is important first to learn the Basic Rules, Numbers 36 and 37 in Part IV of the USYRU rules; Number 36 is the *opposite tack rule*, and Number 37 is the *same tack rule*. Rule 36 is the most simple basic rule, and it states that: "A *port-tack* yacht shall keep clear of a *starboard-tack* yacht." There are but three exceptions to this rule. First, if you have crossed the starting line too early and must return to restart, you do not have the right of way even if on the starboard tack. This is expressed in Rule 44.1 (a). The second exception has to do with overlapping boats when rounding or passing a mark, and it is expressed in Rule 42.1 (a). We shall discuss the subject of rounding marks later in this chapter. The other exception has to do with yachts re-rounding after touching a mark (see Rule 45).

Rule 37 deals with boats converging when they are on the same tack. This states that: "1. A *windward yacht* shall keep clear of a *leeward yacht*. 2. A yacht *clear astern* shall keep clear of a yacht *clear ahead*. 3. A yacht that establishes an *overlap* to *leeward* from *clear astern* shall initially allow the *windward yacht* ample room and opportunity to keep clear." In defining clear astern, clear ahead, and overlap, the rules say, "A yacht is *clear astern* of another when her hull and equipment in normal position are abaft an imaginary line projected abeam from the aftermost point of the other's hull and equipment in normal position. The other yacht is *clear ahead.* The yachts *overlap* when neither is *clear astern;* or when, although one is *clear astern,* an intervening yacht *overlaps* both of them. The terms *clear astern, clear ahead,* and *overlap* apply to yachts on opposite *tacks* only when they are subject to Rule 42, (Rounding or Passing Marks and Obstructions).'' The term proper course is defined as follows: ''A *proper course* is any course which a yacht might sail after the starting signal, in the absence of the other yacht or yachts affected, to *finish* as quickly as possible. The course sailed before *luffing* or *bearing away* is presumably, but not necessarily, that yacht's *proper course.* There is no *proper course* before the starting signal.'' (Words printed in italics in the quoted parts of the rule, are terms that are defined in Part I of the rule. For those terms not already defined, see appendix C.) Examples of the opposite tack rule and the same tack rule are shown in figures 11-1 and 11-2. More will be said about the racing rules later in this chapter.

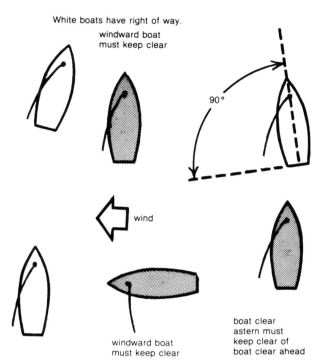

White boats have right of way.
windward boat must keep clear

90°

wind

boat clear astern must keep clear of boat clear ahead

windward boat must keep clear

185

11-2. Same tack rule.

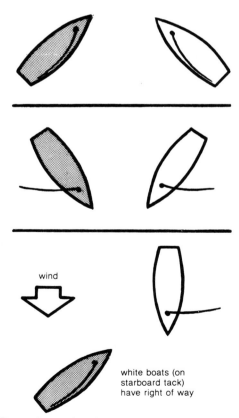

wind

white boats (on starboard tack) have right of way

11-1. Opposite tack rule.

The start

The start is often the most difficult and unnerving part of a race, especially for the novice skipper; but in a short race, getting a good start is tremendously important. Races have been won and lost at the start.

The starting line is an imaginary line between two points, usually a mark and an orange flag on a committee boat. The mark may be a fixed channel marker or buoy or a special mark, often a sizable orange inflatable buoy, temporarily put into position by the organization sponsoring the race. The committee boat may be any kind of craft with a mast from which flags and shapes (usually balls, cylinders, or cones) can be hoisted. The boat must be large enough to accommodate several members of the race committee from the sponsoring yacht club. Usually, but not always, the starting line marker is placed so that it is passed on the same side as the course turning marks as passed. In other words, all marks are usually left on the same side. Very often, turning marks are left to port and the starting mark is at the port end of the line. Course instructions are usually given in the form of a race circular mailed or handed to each contestant before the race; sometimes the course is given at a preliminary skipper's meeting, or often the course is posted with large signs on the side of the committee boat. In the latter case, the signs are often a combination system of single letters or numbers, and the system is explained in the race circular.

The ideal starting line is one that is set approximately square (90 degrees) to the wind. If there is any variation, the left-hand end of the line should be set slightly closer to the first mark than the right-hand end. This variation should rarely exceed 5 degrees, with the first leg of the course (the direction to the first mark) being nearly a dead beat to windward. This is theoretically possible to achieve with a closed-course race, but it is usually not possible on a point-to-point course unless the wind happens to blow from exactly the right direction. Of course, the first mark may not always lie dead to windward, but it is important that the line be about square to the wind. The object of such a line is that neither end of the line is favored, so that competitors will not be bunched or jammed together at one end. If the current or some other factor makes one end of the line more attractive, then the line should be slanted slightly away from the right angle to the wind in order to make both ends equally attractive. This principle holds true on reaching and running starts as well. It is highly desirable to have the starting boats evenly spread out along the line no matter what the point of sailing. Windward starts are preferable, because all the boats rarely arrive at the first mark at almost the same time, as so often happens with reaching and running starts.

Even on a closed course, the ideal starting line is often very difficult to set because of last minute wind shifts that cause the line to be slanted away from the 90-degree angle to the wind. In fact, even though the race committee makes a great effort to set a perfect line, more often than not one end will be slightly more favored than the other.

The following system is customarily used to start a race: at precisely ten minutes before the start, a *warning* signal is given from the committee boat. This signal is given audibly, with a gun or horn, and at the same time it is given visibly with the hoisting of a flag or shape, usually white or yellow. Exactly four minutes later, the warning shape, which is usually white, is hauled down; and one minute later another signal is given audibly and visibly with a gun or horn and the hoisting of another flag or shape. This is called the *preparatory* signal, and the flag or shape is usually colored blue. Four minutes

later, the preparatory shape is hauled down; and one minute after this, the *start* signal is given with the hoisting of the starting shape or flag, usually colored red, and the sounding of the horn or gun. Actually, the visual signal gives the exact time of the start, because a starting gun can misfire.

Racing skippers try to reach the starting line just as the starting signal is made. The ideal or perfect start is one that is made at the favored spot on the line, with the boat sailing at top speed and just touching the line as the signal is hoisted and the gun is fired. Of course, this is an ideal that is very difficult to achieve.

Choosing the favored spot on the line is one of the keys to successful starting. There is a simple rule for choosing the favored end when the line is not square to the wind. With the boat near the center of the starting line, luff up until the boat is headed directly into the eye of the wind, and the bow will point closer to one end of the line than the other. *The end that is closer to the boat's heading when she is head-to-wind is the favored end of the line.* This is illustrated in figure 11-4. A boat making a well-timed start at the favored end is always ahead of boats making well-timed starts anywhere else on the line. In choosing the favored end, however, one has to be careful about a last minute wind shift that might favor the opposite end. If you are ahead but to leeward of a competitor, you gain if the shift is a header, but you lose if the shift is a lift. This can be seen in figure 11-4.

Notice in the diagram, the starting boats are on the starboard tack. This is a fundamental rule. *Start on the starboard tack*, because you have the right of way and can force port tack boats about in converging situations. Of course, there are exceptions to every rule, and occasionally a perfectly timed port tack start will pay off. But there is no question that starting on the starboard tack is the safest policy, and it is most certainly recommended for beginners. You can certainly *approach* the starting line on port tack, but come about before closely converging with starboard tackers.

When choosing the favored starting spot on the line, there are factors to be considered other than what position will put you ahead of your competitors at that particular moment. The racing skipper must decide where he wants to go immediately after the start. He may, for example, wish to go offshore if the current is favorable and there appears to be a

11-3. Getting ready to start. Everyone seems to be in his proper position, with the timer informing the helmsman of time remaining, the bow man keeping a lookout and sighting down the line, and other crew members standing by the sheets.

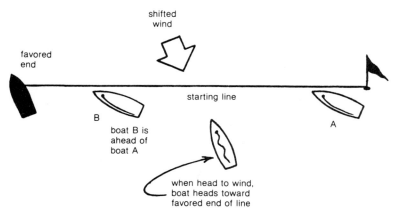

11-4. Favored end of starting line.

better breeze away from the land, or he may want to tack inshore to get into smoother water and to escape a foul current. If he knows where he wants to go, he must plan the kind of start that will allow him to reach his strategic course in the quickest time. For instance, if he starts to leeward on the starboard tack but wishes to stand inshore on the port tack, he might be boxed in or trapped by boats to windward that could prevent him from coming about. In this hypothetical case, it might be the better plan for him to take a late start to windward so that he could go over on the port tack immediately after crossing the line.

Another tremendously important consideration is where the starter should go to get clean, undisturbed wind. A boat's speed can be greatly harmed by the disturbed air (backwind and wind shadows) from other boats, and this is particularly true in the vicinity of a crowded starting line. A boat that makes a well-timed start at the line's favored end will usually get clean air. At the windward end of the line (when on the starboard tack of a windward start), a boat can usually get clear wind even if she gets a bad start, because she can promptly tack into undisturbed wind soon after crossing the line. If she gets a bad start at the line's leeward end, she may not be able to tack, but she may be able to bear off slightly and foot into clean air. Of course, if all the starting boats are headed, this will put the leeward boat in the most favored position. In the event that the line is square to the wind and the starters are bunched at each end, there might be cleaner air in the middle; but when starting in the line's middle, it is usually difficult to bear off into less disturbed air and also difficult to tack for clean air.

Figure 11-5 shows just how a boat can disturb the air of other boats in her vicinity. The black boats in the diagram have their wind disturbed by boat A,

wind

wind
direction

A

A's
wind
shadow
(it extends
5 to 7 times
height to mast)

A's backwind
(it is deflected
far to windward
of A)

11-5. Disturbed air. White boats have their wind clear with respect to boat A. Black boats' winds are disturbed by boat A.

while the white boats have their wind clear. Notice that black boat 3 is getting some backwind even though she is to windward of A. This is due to the draft curve of A's mainsail , which deflects the backwind to windward. To clear her air, black 3 should pinch up in an attempt to work farther to windward of A. Black boat 2, to leeward, is sailing in A's wind shadow. To clear her air, black 2 should try to drive off slightly to leeward with eased sheets until she sails out of the wind shadow. Black boat 1, dead astern of A, is getting backwind and also disturbed water from A's wake. The chances are that she cannot pinch up or drive off enough to clear her air without dropping far astern. Probably, her best alternative is to tack. If her skipper wants to remain on the starboard tack, then he can tack again as soon as he gets into undisturbed air. White boat 1 in the diagram is in the most enviable position, because she is actually lifted slightly by the deflected air flowing to leeward of A's jib. White 1 is said to have a *safe leeward position*. Of course, she has her wind clear and is throwing backwind against the lee side of A's sails.

Once the starting spot on the line is selected, the next problem to cope with is how to hit the line with sufficient headway when the starting gun is fired. There are five fundamental techniques for arriving at the line as the starting signal is made: (1) the timed start, (2) sitting on the line, (3) running the line, (4) the dip start, and (5) the barging start (see figure 11-6). There are certain special occasions when any of these techniques or a combination of some of them might be used, but by and large, the timed start is generally the most effective and the safest, for large boats at least.

The most commonly used method with this kind of start is known as the Vanderbilt system. This system suggests that you cross the line on the port tack heading in the wrong direction (away from the first turning mark) while, as nearly as possible, beam reaching with very roughly 2 minutes to go before the starting gun. A timer, a crew member with a stopwatch, takes the time as you cross the line and notes the time remaining until the starting gun. You add the time it takes to turn (tack or jibe) to the time remaining and divide by 2. This figure gives the proper time to begin your turn to head back for the starting line. Theoretically, you should return to the line as the gun fires.

An example is shown in figure 11-7. The boat crosses the line going the wrong way when there are 2 minutes and 20 seconds to go (until the start). The skipper estimates that it will take him 10 seconds to tack. He adds 10 seconds to 2 minutes 20 seconds and divides by 2, which gives 1 minute 15 seconds. He sails the boat on a steady course until there is 1 minute 15 seconds to go, and then he tacks and heads straight back to the spot where he formerly crossed the line. In the absence of a current, interference from other boats, and if the wind is steady, he should reach the line at gunfire. This method usually works well when there are not a great number of boats racing. A crowded starting line can throw off the timing because of necessary course alterations. Also, strong currents and light or spotty winds can disrupt this kind of start.

The second starting technique, sitting on the line, is sometimes used when racing small, light dinghies—420s or Lasers, for instance. In this case, a skipper approaches the line early, perhaps a minute before the gun, lets his sails luff to kill speed, and then trims them in immediately prior to gunfire. This can be dangerous when right-of-way boats establish an overlap to leeward. This starting method is not recommended with large, heavy boats (Navy yawls, for instance), because they are slow to pick up speed after the sails are trimmed. Even in small boats that will accelerate rapidly, care must be taken that speed is not altogether killed, because then the boat has no rudder control. If there is open water around the boat using the sitting start, she might be sailed on a slightly weaving, up and down course while her sheets are only slightly slacked.

The other three starting techniques should be used rarely and with great caution. When running the line, a boat arrives at the line early and to

11-6. Five types of starts.

1 timed start
2 sitting on the line
3 running the line
4 dip start
5 barging start (see fig. 10-7)

11-7. A timed start.

11-8. Barging. In both cases *B* is barging illegally because she is trying to get room at the starting mark. *A* does not have to give room to *B*, but *A* cannot head above her course to the first mark (or her close-hauled course when beating) after the starting signal before she crosses the starting line.

windward of the desired starting spot. Her sheets are then eased, and she reaches along parallel to the line until just before the gun fires at which time her sheets are trimmed and she is headed up onto her proper course. This method has the advantage that the boat has good headway when she hits the line as the gun is fired. The method is dangerous, however, because boats to leeward have the right of way. Never attempt this unless there is plenty of open space to leeward, and if attempting it, always keep a constant lookout to leeward for converging boats. Also, run the line a safe distance away from the line.

The dip start can also be dangerous. In this case, you stay on the wrong side of the line and dip back across to the right side of the line just before the gun fires. This start is sometimes used when there is a strong foul current (flow of water against you) and when the other starters are late getting to the line. The dip starter must be very cautious and dip into a clear open spot, for he usually has no rights. This kind of start is certainly not recommended for beginners at a crowded start, especially in large boats. When code flag I has been displayed on the committee boat, it signifies the "Round-the-End Starting Rule" is in effect. If a boat is on the course side of the starting line or its extensions during the minute before the starting signal when the I flag is displayed, she shall sail to the pre-start side of the line across one of its extensions and start (Rule 51.1(c)).

The barging start is also dangerous. When a boat illegally barges, she attempts to force her way

between the starting mark and another competitor as illustrated in figure 11-8. However, it is perfectly legal to start on the wrong side of the danger line, as boats B are doing in the diagram, provided there are no boats close or overlapping you to leeward. The danger lines shown in the diagram represent the course to the first mark for a reaching start and the close-hauled course for a windward start.

In order to understand the barging start thoroughly, it is necessary to learn Racing Rule 42, which deals with rounding or passing marks or obstructions. Rule 42.1 covers various rounding situations when boats are overlapped, the Rule 42.4 is the Anti-barging Rule. In most cases, when two boats are overlapped rounding or passing a mark, the outside boat must give the inside boat room to pass the mark on the correct side. An important exception is the Anti-barging Rule, which says that the windward boat *cannot* claim room from an overlapping leeward boat. The rule goes on to say, however, that the leeward boat may not sail above her course to the first mark on a reaching or running start or luff above a close-hauled course on a windward start after the starting signal has been made. Before the signal, the leeward boat may sail higher, and if she is close enough to the mark, she may squeeze out windward boats after the signal provided she doesn't sail above her course to the next mark or above close-hauled on a windward start. Of course, this prohibition against luffing applies only before reaching the starting line and after the starting signal has been made.

The following is a list of tips for getting good starts:

- Get to the starting area early (a half hour before your start or earlier if other classes are starting ahead of you).
- Study the race circular, the wind, current, and position of the starting line.
- Luff head-to-wind to determine favored end of the line.
- Just before starting, sight along the line at an object on shore to establish a range and thus facilitate judging your distance away from the line when boats block your view of the line's other end.
- Run the entire length of the line and time your run.
- Decide where you want to go after the start. (This should be based on such factors as wind, current, and where you think your competitors will go.)
- Try to determine the most probable area of undisturbed air. (This may be done by watching your competitors to see which end of the line they favor and by watching them make practice runs at preselected starting spots.)
- Stay close to the line, especially in light airs.
- If other classes are starting ahead of you, watch their starts closely to see which boats profit and which do not in their various starting tactics, but stay clear of them.
- Use a timed start in most cases.
- The timer should start his stopwatch at the warning signal and call out the time remaining to the helmsman.
- If you are a little late for the start, properly trim your sails immediately, bear off slightly, and drive for the line.
- If it seems you will be a little too early slack sheets and/or luff up slightly to kill speed.
- Never kill speed to the extent that it affects helm control.
- Start on the starboard tack unless there is no doubt that you will be entirely clear on the port tack or can find a gap through the starboard tack boats and if there should happen to be a great advantage to starting on the port tack.
- If the windward end of the line is favored on a windward starboard tack start, plan to start not exactly at the mark but a boat length or two to leeward of the line's windward end. In this position,

there is little chance of your being forced into a barging position by boats to leeward.

- If the leeward end of the line is favored on a windward starboard tack start, plan to start not exactly at the mark but a slight distance to windward of the leeward end; otherwise, a heading wind shift might keep you from fetching the leeward mark. Also, if the committee boat is at that end, you may, at the last moment, become trapped in what is often called the "coffin corner." A boat in this predicament cannot bear off at the last moment because she may hit the committee boat; she cannot tack if there are boats close to windward because she will then be on the port tack with no rights, and Rule 41.1 says that a yacht tacking must keep clear of a yacht on a tack.
- If headed when approaching the coffin corner, do not try to pinch by the mark; but bear off, jibe around, and pass under the stern of the starboard tack boats.

The foregoing discussion of starting has been primarily concerned with the windward start, the usual start for closed courses. The next chapter will deal with distance racing involving point-to-point courses, so in this chapter there will be little more said about the tactics of reaching and running starts.

Basic course tactics

After the start, we are concerned with three general factors: boat speed, the fastest course, and the whereabouts of competitors. Of course, boat speed depends on what has already been discussed—helmsmanship, tuning, sail adjustment, and boat handling. The fastest course primarily depends on the wind and current if we discount the presence of other competitors. As the race progresses, competitors will have a definite influence on strategy, but to begin with there should be a basic preliminary plan, and this should mainly be based on wind and current. This section, therefore, will first touch on wind and current tactics and then on tactics relative to the competition.

Many sailors use the words current and tide interchangeably, but actually tide is the alternating, vertical rise and fall of water, while current is the horizontal movement of the water. Tidal currents are the currents caused by the tides. Before every race, the current should be looked up in the *Tidal Current Tables*, which give the velocity of flow and the time of *slack water*, maximum *ebb*, and maximum *flood* in the general locality of your race. Slack water means no flow, while ebb means to flow outward and flood means to flow inward. Current tables should not be relied on absolutely because certain weather conditions can throw them off. The flow of water should continually be checked visually, by looking at buoys, fish stakes, channel markers, anchored boats, crab or lobster pots, and so forth. Tall objects that are anchored, such as spar buoys, tend to lean in the direction of flow. Stationary objects in a strong current will leave a definite wake and appear as though they are moving through the water. Anchored boats in light air and ships especially will often swing into the current so that their bows will point in the direction from which the current is flowing. Incidentally, if we speak of a southerly wind we mean that the wind is blowing *from* the south, but a southerly current means that the current is flowing *towards* the south.

Figure 11-9 shows how land and bottom contours affect the current. In deep water and particularly in channels, the current flows fast, but the flow is slow in shallow water. The current changes first in shoal areas, however. If we have foul current (against us), then we should usually sail near the shore where the water is shallow, but if the current is fair (with us), we should probably go offshore where the water is deep. Of course, we also want to go where the current will first change to favor us. The current is often accelerated when it flows past a point, land spit, or constricted channel because of the venturi principle; and behind a point or spit there will often be eddies or contrary flows as shown in figure 11-9. Tide rips are streaks of ruffled waters that usually mark the dividing line between a fast current and a slow current moving in the same direction or two currents moving in opposite directions. Usually it is wise to stay out of the rip, but obviously you should stay to its favorable side.

When beating to windward against the current, try to take the tack that will allow a directional change of the current to push against the lee side of your bow. This is called *lee-bowing* the current and will give the boat a push to windward. Sometimes a lee-bow current can be had by tacking into the mouth of a river when the river's current meets the main current (of the bay or principal body of water) at a wide angle. This is illustrated in figure 11-10.

When sailing across a current, nearly at right angles to the current, allowance must be made for

11-9. Current. To determine current's direction, watch buoys and fixed objects in water such as fish stakes. Buoys usually lean in the direction of flow. Current causes buoys and fixed objects to make rippled wakes.

193

its sidewise push. If we continually aim our boat directly at the mark or destination, our course will resemble an arc, but if we steer above the mark (toward the direction from which the current is flowing), our course will be closer to a straight line. Obviously, the latter course is the shortest, and the stronger the current the higher above the mark we should steer. This course can often be determined by ranging the mark against the shore. If the mark does not appear to move against the shore, the boat should arrive precisely at the mark.

Wind is far more difficult to predict than current. It is always a good plan to get the latest weather report before a short race and to obtain frequent weather reports during a distance race. But no one knows better than a sailor that these reports are not entirely dependable. Quite often the reports are accurate, but the weather does not follow the pre-

direction of
main current
offshore

wind

river current

river

11-10. Lee bow current.

more than the water. This causes the hot air over the land to rise and leave a partial void that sucks in the cooler air from over the water; thus, we have a sea breeze. On the other hand, after dark the land begins to cool, and the thermal activity is reversed, with the warmer air over the water rising and the cooler land air being sucked towards the sea. In this case we have a land breeze. Sea breezes are most likely to be strong in the late afternoon on a clear, hot day after a cool night, while land breezes often occur late at night or in the early morning. Land and sea breezes are affected by such factors as the directional changes of the shoreline, the clearness of the weather, and the surface of the land. Flat plains, beaches, pavements, and open fields heat up faster than wooded areas. The land and sea breezes may not dominate the prevailing winds but only exert an influence on them. For instance, if a south wind (the most frequent summer breeze in the Chesapeake area) has been blowing steadily and a sea breeze comes in from the east, the two winds will most likely combine to form a southeaster.

Surface winds blowing across the land will be affected to a much greater extent by frictional drag than by wind blowing across the water. This causes the wind coming from a shore in the Northern Hemisphere gradually to *veer* (shift clockwise) often a half mile or so after it has left the shore. The reason for the shift is that the wind is affected by the *coriolis force* (a force created by the earth's rotation that deflects a free-moving object to the right in the Northern Hemisphere). Often called a shore slant or wind bend, the shift sometimes can be used to

dicted timetable. An expected breeze may arrive hours later than expected, a front as much as a day later than originally predicted, and so on. Also, something resembling the predicted weather may be taking place high above us, but there may be entirely different conditions at our location on the earth's surface. Forecasts of the general weather pattern are of far greater significance for the offshore, distance racer than for the closed-course, round-the-buoys racer. A two hours' difference between a predicted and an actual wind change may not be crucial during a race that lasts five days, but the same time lag will be crucial on a three-hour race. The short-distance racer is interested in the local weather only over a limited period of time—the time it takes to get around the course.

The local weather picture is very much influenced by the geography and topography of the land. The uneven heating of land and water cause the diurnal and nocturnal sea-land breezes. In the daytime, on a hot summer's day, the land heats up considerably

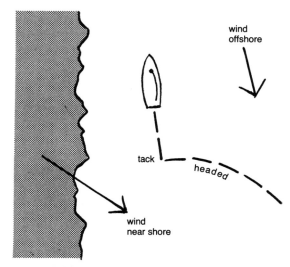

wind
offshore

tack

headed

wind
near shore

11-11. Taking advantage of a shore slant.

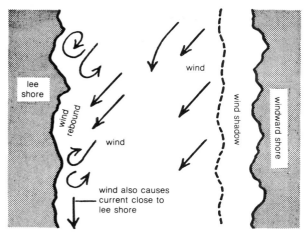

11-12. Wind and high shores.

advantage by a boat sailing upwind if she tacks under the windward shore as illustrated in figure 11-11. Notice that the boat approaching the shore on the starboard tack is headed when she makes contact with the unbent shore slant, at which time she comes about and then can sail almost parallel with the shore on the port tack.

Another benefit from this strategy is that there may be smoother water under the shore, but if the shore is high (with high banks or woods) it should seldom be approached very closely because of the harmful effect of its wind shadow (see figure 11-12). Even high lee shores should be approached with caution because the wind can rebound, causing turbulence and even an adverse current near the shore. Needless to say, charts should be carefully examined before approaching any shore to avoid running aground. Wind shifts will often occur near the mouth of a river because of the wind bending to blow directly into or out of the river. Crossing the river diagonally, the wind tends to shift so that it follows the course of the river.

In light airs look for streaks of wind on the water. The skipper should be concentrating on his sailing continually; so it is often a good idea to assign the puff-watching job to a capable crew member. When the wind is spotty, do not worry about sailing a direct course, but get into the breeze even if at first it appears you are going quite far off course to do so. Very often when the breeze is light, zephyrs will not come to you; you must go to them.

In heavy winds look for smooth water on the windward leg. There is nothing that will slow a boat more than driving into a steep head sea. Usually the smoothest water will lie under the windward shore. Current will make a difference in the seas also. When a strong current sets against the wind, the seas become very steep.

When a threatening thunderhead is seen in the west on a hot, calm afternoon be prepared for the worst, but consider a tack towards the cloud. Those boats closest to the squall when it hits will get the wind first. Don't take chances with an ugly looking storm, however. Be ready to drop the sails in an instant. If the storm appears to be a severe frontal type, if it is particularly dark and ragged, and especially if it has a preceding roll cloud or if weather reports have given warnings of severe thunderstorms, reduce sail and take all precautions.

Of particular importance to the racing sailor is an understanding of wind shifts. He cannot predict exactly when the wind will shift, but he can be in the right place to take advantage of it. Constantly steady breezes are rare. Of course, some are steadier than others. Winds that blow across the land are often shifty. In the Chesapeake Bay area, the southerly is generally the steadiest breeze, while northwesters are the least steady. Nevertheless, even southerlies can fluctuate in direction to some extent.

The following are three general rules for beating in a shifty wind: (1) take the tack that brings you closest to the windward mark, (2) tack on each major header, and (3) don't sail out to the lay line (or fetch line) until close to the windward mark. The first rule is explained in figure 11-13. It can be seen that the boat taking the close tack to the mark profits whether lifted or headed by a wind shift. If well lifted, the boat sailing the correct course can fetch the mark without tacking; and if headed severely, the boat tacks and can fetch on the opposite tack. Although the illustration shows how taking the close tack to the mark pays off when beating in shifty winds, the same principle applies when tacking downwind. Take the best sailing angle course (the downwind tack that lets the sails draw at maximum efficiency) that brings you closest to the mark. If the wind shifts so that it is flat aft, you can jibe and head directly for the mark on an efficient sailing angle; and if the wind shifts the opposite way (so that it is closer to the beam), you can head directly for the mark on an efficient angle without jibing.

Figure 11-13 also illustrates the second rule, tacking on major headers. This is clearly shown by

195

11-13. Windward strategy illustrating the advantage of first taking the closer tack. Whenever a boat is severely headed by a wind shift, she should tack.

the boat sailing the correct course in situation B. This strategy, however, will vary somewhat with the kind of boat that is being sailed. Small, light boats that pick up speed very quickly after tacking can be tacked far more often than large, heavy boats that are complicated to tack (the Navy yawls, for instance). With a large boat, a great deal of time is often lost tacking, so tacks should be limited. The tacking-on-headers strategy still holds true for a large boat, but care should be taken to see that she is well into a major, definite shift before tacking. It is especially damaging to tack a large, heavy boat too often in very light airs.

The third tactical rule for beating in shifty winds is to stay away from the lay line until close to the mark. If you sail out to the lay line far from the windward mark, any shift is bound to hurt you. When you are heading for the mark on the lay line, a lifting shift means that you have overstood the mark, and a heading shift means that you have wasted at least part of the time you spent reaching the lay line.

Although these aforementioned tactical rules apply most of the time, all rules have exceptions. For example, it might pay not to take the close tack to the mark first if this meant you had to sail in the backwind of boats ahead of you or if there were better wind and current on the other tack. Before forming any final tactical judgment, look at the whole situation and take every influencing factor into account.

Up to this point, our discussion of basic tactics after the starting gun has been concerned with sailing the fastest course as though there were no other boats in the race. The presence of competitors, however, creates tactical situations of a different sort that we might term competition tactics.

Most competition tactics involve *covering* situations. When one boat covers another, the covering boat keeps herself in a relatively advantageous tactical position with respect to the other. To cover another boat, you must be ahead or at least even with her. Actually, there are two ways of covering a competitor—with a loose cover and a tight one. The latter method has to do with keeping close to a rival boat and maneuvering into a position where you can give her disturbed air (either backwind or wind shadow). The loose form of covering means that you simply try to stay in such a position with respect to your competitor that she gets no beneficial wind or current that you won't get also. Unless you have only one important competitor to beat (as in a match race or if you are tied in a series standing), it is generally wiser to use loose covering tactics. *Because if you become preoccupied with one boat, the rest of the competition may leave you behind.* Loose covering tactics are based on a simple principle: *keep between your competitor and the next mark.* With this strategy, you will not do the competitor any particular harm unless he gets close enough to be affected by your disturbed air, but you will have reasonable assurance that you will be able to hold your lead position when boat speeds are the same.

With a tight cover on a beat to windward, you try to place yourself directly to windward of your competitor, attain a safe leeward position, or else put your rival in your wake where he will be affected by backwind and perhaps by disturbed water to some extent. These tactics are quite often used with small class boats, but they are often not practical in large handicapped boats. In handicap races, the boats are not equal in speed or ability to point. Thus, if a leading boat were trying to tight-cover a faster more close-winded boat, the latter could not be held back; and if it were the other way around, with the faster boat ahead, she would simply leave the slower boat behind. In races involving small, light-displacement boats, it is common practice to tack under a competitor's lee bow so that the tacking boat attains a safe leeward position and can throw disturbed and deflected backwind against her opponent's sails. But this is a dangerous maneuver with large, heavy boats, because they are slow to gain headway after tacking. The rules forbid tacking too close to another boat (Rule 41.1); furthermore, the boat that has not tacked will carry good momentum and will probably pass right by the boat that has tacked just ahead.

Occasionally two boats become engaged in a tacking duel when the boat that is being covered tries to tack away from the covering boat. In this case, the covered boat attempts to break away from the leading boat's backwind by tacking, but the lead boat counters by tacking in an attempt to blanket her rival and keep her covered. The leeward boat tacks again, and the windward boat also tacks again to cover. Such tacking duels come under the head-

ing of becoming preoccupied with one competitor and should be avoided unless it is a match race (only two boats racing).

When a boat is being overtaken by a boat close to windward, the lead boat may luff to prevent the overtaking boat from passing (see figure 11-14). The rules define luffing as "Altering course towards the wind." The maneuver is explained under Rule 38, Same Tack—Luffing after Clearing the Starting Line. This rule should be studied carefully in its entirety.

"Luffing Rights" are given in the first part of the rule, 38.1 This says that after she has started and cleared the starting line a yacht clear ahead or a leeward yacht may luff as she pleases, subject to certain limitations which are explained in rule 38.2. An important limitation is 38.2(a) which states: "*A leeward yacht* shall not sail above her *proper course* while an *overlap* exists if, when the *overlap* began or, at any time during its existence, the helmsman of the *windward yacht* (when sighting abeam from his normal station and sailing no higher than the *leeward yacht*) has been abreast or forward of the mainmast of the *leeward yacht*." The "mast abeam" line is illustrated in figure 11-15. When the leeward boat is ahead of the mast abeam line, she may luff, but behind this position, she cannot luff. Ordinarily, when a leeward boat luffs one to windward, the windward boat must respond by luffing also in order to avoid contact. If the leeward boat luffs when she is abaft the mast abeam line, however, the windward boat may not be able to luff without throwing her stern into the leeward boat's bow.

Competition tactics become very important at turning marks, because this is where the competitors often bunch together. When you are converging with other competitors on a windward mark to be left to port, try to approach the mark on the starboard tack. The reason for this obviously is that the starboard-tack boat has the right of way, and if she can fetch the mark, she will not have to tack again whereas a port tacker will have to tack around the mark. When the mark is to be left to starboard, however, a port-tack boat can often beat a starboard tacker around if the port tacker slows down slightly to allow her bow to be crossed by the other boat; then, while the starboard tacker must partially kill her way with an additional tack, the port tacker can simply drive for the mark. This is explained in figure 11-16.

In most cases when rounding a mark with other boats, try to maneuver to be on the inside at the mark so that you have the right of way. (See fig. 11-17.) However, if you plan to squeeze into the inside position on a boat ahead of you, be very careful not to establish your overlap when the boat ahead is very close to the mark. Rule 42 deals with rounding or passing marks or obstructions, and should be studied carefully. Rule 42.3 says in part that a yacht clear astern may establish an inside overlap and be entitled to room only when the yacht clear ahead is outside two of her overall lengths of the mark.

There is a definite technique to rounding marks.

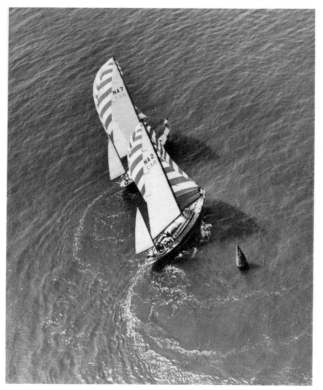

11-14. Rounding the mark. This photograph clearly shows the wakes of the yawls *Alert* (No. 2) and *Dandy* (No. 7) as they round a nun buoy. No. 2 is trying to blanket her rival, while No. 7 counters by luffing (the course to the next mark lies well off the port bow of both boats). If No. 7 had made a wider approach, then cut closer to the buoy's leeward side and afterwards headed as high as she could without breaking the spinnaker, she might have discouraged the blanketing tactics attempted by No. 2. Notice that No. 7 is able to keep her spinnaker full while No. 2 cannot, because No. 7's spinnaker tack has been slacked off so that it is a considerable distance from the end of the pole. This technique, however, is forbidden under USYRU racing rules.

A turn that is too sharp will kill your boat's way; thus, the turn should be fairly gradual. This is truer for big boats than for small ones. If you are not overlapped by other boats, do not approach the mark very closely when first beginning to make your turn, but cut close to the mark after the turn has been almost completed. This is important when turning onto a windward leg, in order that boats behind cannot sail up on your windward quarter in an attempt to go to weather of your backwind. You should try to keep boats following you directly behind you or slightly to leeward. When turning onto a leeward leg, keep to windward of your close competitors so that you can blanket them. Be very careful not to touch the mark when passing or rounding it. The penalty for this is making two complete 360 degree turns (720°) when well clear of

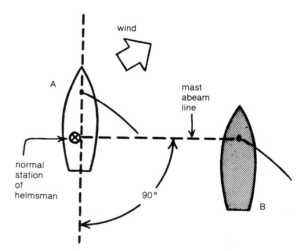

11-15. Mast abeam. *A* is passing to windward of *B*. Before reaching this mast-abeam position, *B* could have luffed. Now, or if *A* pulls farther ahead, *B* cannot luff. If *B* is the faster boat and is attempting to pass to leeward of *A*, *B* cannot luff even if she draws ahead of the mast-abeam line so long as this overlap exists.

11-16. Windward mark left to starboard.

11-17. 505s at the turning mark. It appears that the lead boat has gotten on a plane quickly with the help of the crew on the trapeze to help keep the boat on her feet. Normally, it is best to make a wide approach to the mark and then cut close as you are leaving it.

all other yachts. Details are given in rule 52.

The following is a list of tactical and strategy tips to be used on the race course:

- Make use of the current tables.
- Observe current constantly during the race by watching buoys, stakes, marks, etc.
- Whenever possible take advantage of a lee-bow current. The lee-bow effect is advantageous relative to a competitor only if the current changes direction.
- Stay in shoal water when the current is against you; conversely, stay in deep water and channels when the current is with you.
- Try to take advantage of eddies and counter currents behind points or near river mouths.

- Stay where you get a favoring current for the maximum length of time, and stay where you get a foul current for the minimum length of time.
- Stay to the most favorable side of a tide rip.
- Allow for sideways push when crossing a current.
- Do not always play the current at the expense of wind strategy. Unless the current is strong, it may be better to go where there is the best wind.
- Obtain marine weather forecasts before the race, but don't depend absolutely on the forecasts, especially during a short race.
- Look for the influence of a sea breeze during the afternoon of a hot, clear, summer day; look for the influence of a land breeze in the early morning.

- On calm days play the wind streaks. Go to them; don't wait for them to come to you.
- On hot, calm summer days, look westward for rising cumulus clouds that could develop into thunderheads. If a thunderstorm develops, be cautious, but in most cases work towards the storm.
- When the wind blows diagonally across a shore, look for wind slants. Also look for slants near the mouth of a river.
- Do not sail too close under a windward shore because of the shore's wind shadow.
- Make a study of local weather. Take mental or actual notes of local conditions during each race. These conditions often repeat themselves.
- In a strong breeze and rough sea, look for a smooth lee near the windward shore.
- In shifty winds when beating, take the close tack to the mark first.
- Tack on major headers.
- Do not sail out to the lay line until close to the windward mark.
- Do not tack more than is necessary, especially in a large boat.
- Constantly keep track of your competitors, particularly the best ones.
- Use loose covering instead of tight covering tactics most of the time unless in a match race, or unless you are tied in a series.
- Keep between your competitors and the next mark whenever possible.
- In most cases, do not engage in tacking duels or prolonged luffing matches, especially when running or reaching.

- Keep your wind clear.
- If well clear of a competitor, consider tacking under his lee bow if you are sailing a small, light boat, but don't try this in a large, heavy boat.
- When beating, luff to prevent a boat from passing close to windward, but don't luff if you are abaft the mast abeam line.
- Approach a windward mark that is to be left to port on the starboard tack in most cases.
- Round a turning mark fairly slowly so that you do not kill your boat's speed.
- Do not sail close to the mark when first beginning to turn, but cut close to it after nearly completing the turn if turning onto a windward leg.
- Try to round a mark in such a way that competitors behind are placed in your backwind on windward legs and competitors abeam or ahead are in your wind shadow on running or reaching legs.
- Try for the inside position at a mark.
- Learn the racing rules.
- Stay out of trouble. Try to avoid crowds of boats jammed together, and anticipate conditions or maneuvers that could lead to a collision.
- Don't be a wild, tactical gambler. Play the percentages. If you are behind, don't split with the rest of the fleet on the wild hope that you might get a break, when you are fairly certain you would be doing the wrong thing.
- If converging on the finish line with other boats, try to be on the starboard tack.
- Head for the closest end of the finish line.

12.
Distance Racing and Offshore Sailing

Distance racing and offshore sailing are, for the most part, done by seaworthy cruising-racing yachts, making a passage or racing on a handicap basis, usually under the IOR, IMS, or PHRF rules. The Navy 44s, Luders yawls, and other large boats at the Naval Academy participate in several night races on the Chesapeake Bay and quite a few ocean races. Long-distance races have included numerous events from local overnights such as the Cedar Point and Governor's Cup races to classic ocean events such as the Annapolis to Newport, Marblehead to Halifax, Newport to Bermuda, and even transoceanic races. In addition to conventional racing, there is the Circumnavigation of Delmarva Training Cruise, an exercise in seamanship, navigation, and sailboat handling held every May in preparation for the Summer Sail Training Program. Details of the training cruise and the exercise drills to be done are given in appendix D.

Safety at sea

The primary consideration in any offshore cruise, night race, or ocean race should be safety. It is easier than you might think to lose a man overboard at night in a rough sea, and if accidents happen offshore, prompt help is all but impossible to get.

Lists of required yacht equipment are compiled for most ocean races. Most race sponsors now use the Offshore Racing Council lists shown in appendix F. These lists include such safety equipment as: life jackets, harnesses, jackstays, fire extinguishers, bilge pumps, buckets, a suitable first-aid kit with instruction book, double lifelines with through-bolted *stanchions* (vertical posts supporting the lifelines), bow and stern *pulpits* (metal railings), *a radar reflector* (folding, or housed geometric shape containing numerous right angles made of light metal, which is hoisted in the rigging), a suitable binnacle and light, running lights meeting legal requirements, flares, heaving line, at least one large life ring equipped with water light, and perhaps an additional lifebuoy with whistle and dye marker, a properly buoyed pole weighted so it will float upright with a highly visible flag at the top at least six feet above the water, extra water, two compasses, one fog horn, two waterproof flashlights, transmitting radios, two anchors, two chains or rodes, safety belts for each crew member, rafts capable of taking off the entire crew, proper covers for all openings, navigation instruments, rigging cutters, a spare tiller or suitable auxiliary steering arrangement, heavy-weather sails, etc. Of course, many of these items should be aboard your boat whether or not you are going to sea. Exact equipment requirements for an ocean race must be obtained from the sponsoring yacht club. Remember, however, that equipment required is not all the equipment needed. A great deal of preliminary planning should go into preparing for a long ocean race. Plans should be made to meet all possible emergencies, and a complete set of tools and spares for almost every part of the rigging and fittings should be carried. A list of medical and

damage-control supplies as well as a bluewater underway checklist is included in the appendixes.

Some of the equipment listed above deserves brief comment. The large life rings should be placed in holders, usually on the lifelines or pulpit near the helmsman, since there is always someone stationed at the helm. Never lash a life ring to its holder. The horseshoe life buoy is generally thought to be the best type (see figure 12-1). The buoyed pole with a counterweight and flag is a very important item at sea where there are large waves, because the flag can be seen above the wave tops. The pole should be attached to a life ring, and if a man falls overboard, both pole and ring are thrown over the side instantly. The weighted pole will also tend to prevent the life ring from drifting excessively. It is always important to attach a small *drogue* (a cloth, cone-shaped sea anchor) to a life ring even if it is attached to a pole, in order to decrease drift. Obviously, water lights attached to life rings are essential at night. Electric water lights vary in design, but the usual type is equipped with a battery-powered light that shuts off when it is hung up-side down (near the life ring on the lifelines, or on the stern pulpit). The light is buoyed and weighted in such a way, however, that when it is thrown overboard, it rights itself and the light turns on (figures 12-1 and 12-2). The *Lifesling*, a towed horseshoe-type buoy, which will be described in the next section, is a particularly

ring buoy

holder

never lash buoy to holder (a small drogue is secured to buoy to lessen drift)

a waterlight (when turned upside down, light goes off)

float

battery case

lanyard attaches light to buoy

horse shoe buoy

holder

buoy can be lifted out of holder quickly

Note: A handy device is an inflatable pocket life preserver pack.

12-1. Lifesaving devices.

12-2. Close quarters. This photo shows a close view of the yawl's stern pulpit, the ring buoys resting in their holders, and the inverted waterlight abaft the port ring buoy. Notice that the aftermost slide on the mizzen has parted its lashing.

effective device for a shorthanded rescue of a man overboard.

Safety belts or harnesses are indispensable for the crew in rough weather at sea, especially at night. It is generally agreed that the best belt is basically a sturdy one that fits on the chest and is equipped with shoulder straps. Attached to the front of the belt is a short, stout line, sometimes called a *tag line* or tether, with a large snaphook at its free end. The belted crewman snaps the hook onto a convenient part of the rigging or a fitting when he needs to work with both hands. A tether should be attached to the belt with another snaphook so that the wearer can release himself if he should happen to be held underwater. The crew should always use safety harnesses when they leave the cockpit at night and in heavy weather.

The radar reflector is very important at night and especially in fog. Its purpose is to warn large ships, or any radar-equipped vessel, of your presence. Obviously, the reflector is essential in or near shipping lanes.

The crew of an ocean racer should always be conscious of the watertightness of the hull. In bad weather or even in fair weather, a boat can be rolled over on her beam ends by a sudden squall. If deck openings that are not on the boat's centerline are not closed and *secured*, the boat can quickly fill with water and perhaps sink. This has happened. Sea cocks and valves on all through-hull openings except scuppers should be shut in bad weather. Hinged cockpit seat-locker lids should be latched shut, because during a severe knockdown, they can fall or float open. Portholes and hatches should be dogged in bad weather, and vulnerable ventilators should be provided with a quick means of closing, even if they are only covered with small canvas bags.

Of course, all stores and equipment should be properly stowed so that they cannot go adrift in any kind of a knockdown. It is especially important that heavy gear, and particularly any anchors, batteries, or loose ballast in the bilge, is wedged in place or secured so that it cannot possibly shift position during the most severe heeling. Care should be taken to see that gear cannot fall against pipes, electric wires, or the handles of sea cocks.

Every person in the crew of an ocean racer should know where all the vital gear is stowed. He should also be thoroughly familiar with the operation of emergency equipment such as flares, fire extinguish-

ers, and lifesaving devices. He must know the proper and safe way to operate winches, and he must be thoroughly familiar with the rigging. A new crew member should study the halyards, sheets, leads, and cleat locations so that he can find them quickly in the dark.

Before sailing in an ocean race, a boat should be thoroughly surveyed and inspected. Most sponsoring yacht clubs require a superficial inspection, but most such inspections are far from complete. The hull should be checked for soundness, seams carefully inspected to see that they are tight and well caulked, metal parts and fittings checked for fatigue or corrosion, the fastenings of fittings should be checked, the nuts on all bolts should be tightened, the sea cocks and bilge pumps especially should be checked to see that they operate properly, and so forth. Electrical equipment, wiring, piping, water systems, steering cables, and all mechanical gear must be checked.

The spars and rigging should receive particular attention. Look for hairline cracks or signs of wear and strain in turnbuckles, tangs, terminal fittings, or any metal parts of the rigging. Look for the shifting or bending of tangs, for bent bolts, worn pins, or any deformation of wood or metal. See that all tracks on the mast, deck, and rail are securely fastened. All tracks should be through-bolted wherever possible at major points of stress. Also, wherever possible, all cleats and other fittings should be through-bolted. Inspect the spreaders, their sockets, and the masthead very carefully. See that the spreaders are securely fastened and that wire halyards cannot possibly jump out of their sheaves. Double-check the spinnaker halyard blocks and swivels, because these take tremendous strain. It is always wise to have spare halyards rigged in case one parts from chafe. See that all stays and shrouds are fitted with toggles. Also see that most halyards or at least the essential ones are fitted with downhauls (light lines attached to the halyard ends so that they can be pulled down in case a halyard shackle breaks or the head pulls out of a sail and leaves the halyard end aloft).

As said before, an important inspection that relates to speed rather than safety is an examination of the boat's bottom surface; the hull should be as smooth and fair as possible. Slime and marine growth on the bottom, especially barnacles, are disastrous to boat speed. A foul bottom can make a

203

difference of many hours on a distance race. Before racing in a major ocean race, the boat should be hauled and her bottom cleaned. Particular attention should be given to the bottom of the keel as this is an area that is often neglected. If the boat cannot be hauled, the crew should scrub her bottom with stiff brushes (or with a towel if the paint is soft). Before racing, be sure to see that the two blades of a solid propeller are lined up directly behind the keel, in the position of least drag. The shaft should be marked so that the propeller position for sailing can be noted by looking at the shaft from aboard the boat. Quite often this position can be noted by looking at the shaft keyways. If the propeller is out of position, it can be corrected by turning the shaft by hand. Once in position, the shaft must be locked (with the gear shift or shaft lock) to prevent inadvertent turning. Folding propellers should be aligned in such a way that the pin on which the blades hinge is exactly vertical so that the blades will not fall open when the boat heels.

Emergencies

Man overboard—If an ocean racer is properly inspected and equipped, and if her crew takes common-sense safety precautions, it is not likely that emergency situations will arise, but nevertheless, certain emergencies should be prepared for. Every crew member should be given instruction on what to do if a man falls overboard, and man overboard drills should be practiced before going offshore.

The method of recovery currently favored at the Naval Academy is the so-called quick-stop technique that is illustrated in figures 12-3A and 12-3B. The main advantage of this method is that it allows the boat to stay close to the overboard victim while allowing the on-board crew time to get organized for the rescue. Proximity of boat and victim is particularly important in conditions of low visibility. Figure 12-3A shows how the boat maneuvers after losing a man overboard (indicated by the X) when beating or close reaching, and figure 12-3B illustrates the maneuvering required for recovery when sailing downwind with a spinnaker set.

Notice in diagram A that immediately after the man falls overboard the boat is luffed into the wind and her jib is allowed to go aback. Then, before all headway is lost, she is turned downwind, the jib is dropped, and the mainsail centered. After the victim

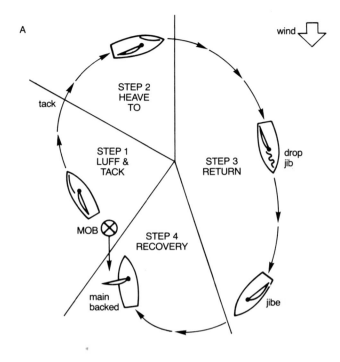

QUICK STOPPING based on U. S. Naval Academy techniques

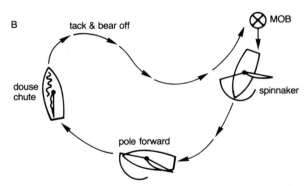

12-3. Quick stopping based on U.S. Naval Academy techniques.

is abaft the beam, the boat is jibed and rounded up to a close-hauled course. At this point the engine may be used to aid in maneuvering, but be sure there are no lines overboard that could foul the propeller. The victim is approached on a course of 45 to 60 degrees off the wind with the boat slightly upwind. When alongside the victim, the boat can be slowed by pushing or pulling the main boom forward (with a line led from the boom to the foredeck). If the engine is being used, it should be shifted into neutral not only to slow the boat but to assure that the victim cannot be cut by the propeller.

A line is thrown to the victim, and if there are plenty of able-bodied crew aboard, the victim can usually be lifted or hauled aboard without too much difficulty provided he is not injured or disabled from fatigue or hypothermia.

When the man falls overboard while heading downwind with the spinnaker set, the pole is eased forward and the boat is turned toward the wind until the sail breaks (flaps) and can be lowered onto the foredeck. Then the boat tacks and bears away to gain some headway so that she can be luffed up just to windward of the victim.

Miscellaneous tips to facilitate rescue are as follows:

• As soon as a person is seen falling overboard, the witness should yell "Man overboard, starboard (or port) side," while keeping his eyes glued on the victim and pointing to him.

• At the same time, the helmsman or anyone else on deck should throw PFDs (personal flotation devices) just to windward of the victim (previous practice is needed in throwing seat cushions, as they can "sail" in a fresh breeze). Then the man-overboard rig (buoy with drogue and pole) is deployed at once.

• The helmsman begins his quick-stop turn immediately while calling all hands on deck. All crew members must keep low so as not to block the vision of the helmsman and pointer. Be sure a capable helmsman is steering.

• In conditions of poor visibility particularly, the compass course should be noted (if possible before the boat is turned), and the Loran position should be stored in the Loran set if it is operating. Maintain navigation plot.

• After handling the sails, the crew should ready the engine for starting and assemble rescue gear such as heaving line, ladder, sling, and tackle for hoisting victim aboard.

• When coming alongside the victim, keep a little distance away from him, as the boat will drift down on him. Be sure to stop prop rotation, and as quickly as possible get a line around his body attaching him to the boat. If he is unconscious or injured, it may be necessary to put a tethered swimmer over the side. In the absence of a hoisting sling, consider using a bowline on a bight as illustrated. The victim puts one loop under his arms and the other under his seat or bent legs.

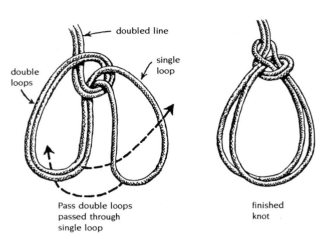

12-4. Bowline on the bight.

• If the victim cannot be lifted, use a tackle and/or winch. The tackle can be attached to the main boom or main halyard as illustrated.

• Once the victim is back on board, check his physical condition, and if necessary, provide first aid for bleeding, restore breathing and pulse, treat for hypothermia and shock.

When the boat is shorthanded, an effective method of rescue makes use of the Lifesling developed by the Sailing Foundation of Seattle, Washington. The Lifesling is a buoyant, flexible horsecollar attached to the stern by a long floating line. It is deployed immediately after a person falls overboard, and the boat circles the victim until the floating line comes within his grasp. The recommended method of recovering the victim is illustrated in figure 12-5. Notice that in the initial phase the method is similar to quick-stopping in that the boat is luffed up until her jib goes aback, and then she comes about, turns downwind, and jibes. The boat passes close to leeward of the victim and continues to circle him so that he can be encircled with the tether of the Lifesling, which is being towed astern. As soon as the victim can grab the sling he puts it under his arms, and then he is hauled close to the boat where he is temporarily secured. If he cannot climb or be lifted aboard by muscle power only, he can be hoisted with a tackle and/or a winch as illustrated. Notice that the halyard that supports the tackle is premarked to show when its end is sufficiently far off the deck to allow ample take-up for the tackle. Bear in mind that the success of any rescue system cannot be guaranteed without practice.

Advice for a man-overboard victim is as follows:

205

206

12-5A. MOB recovery with Lifesling.

• Yell a warning when you first begin to fall in order to alert the crew, but close your mouth before hitting the water.

• Try not to enter the water face first to minimize shock.

• If you are attached to a fast-moving boat with a safety line try to make your body plane in such a way as to get your face in the air. When you can't get your mouth above water try to release the safety line. It should be secured to your harness with a snaphook.

• Don't panic. Remember that your eyes are very close to the water surface and you may not be able to see the boat even if it is close by.

• Look for floating PFDs and swim to the closest one. Put it on or at least hold onto it. Conserve energy, especially if the water is cold. Don't try to swim after the boat.

• If you see a man overboard pole, swim slowly toward it. You should be able to reach it without undue loss of energy if its drogue is deployed.

• Don't waste energy by shouting, but use your whistle and pocket strobe light if you have one. Leave your clothes on to retain heat.

• When help arrives, be ready to receive a retrieval line thrown at you or floating in the water. Attach the line to your belt or harness or put the line around you under your arms. Be alert for instructions from the boat.

Fire—Some thought should be given to fire at sea. Of course, the Navy boats are relatively safe in this respect with their diesel engines. Fuel for these engines does not have the explosion potential of gasoline, but nevertheless a close check should be kept to see that there are no drips or leaks in the fuel lines or tanks. Bilges ought to be clean. Do not allow grease and oil to accumulate in the bilge, as this can become a definite fire hazard.

Potentials for fires or even explosions are the ship's batteries. Be sure they are properly filled, secured, protected against corrosion, and checked with a hydrometer. Look for cracks in the casing, check cables and connections, and be sure there is a ventilated lid on the top of the battery boxes.

Another potential fire hazard on many boats is the galley stove. The Navy yawls are equipped with relatively safe, gimbled alcohol stoves, but certain precautions should be taken. Garments and towels

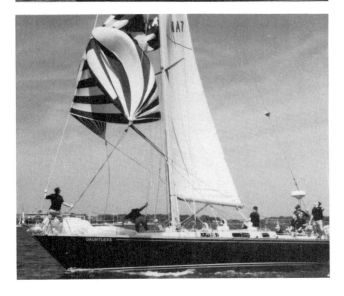

12-6. A practice quick stop with spinnaker to rescue a man overboard (MOB).

A. Life jacket with bucket (to prevent drift) is dropped to simulate MOB. Helmsman is already turning while a crew member keeps eyes on MOB.

B. Pole eased forward and main trimmed in as boat rounds up. A man is at the spinnaker halyard.

C. Spinnaker has collapsed, but the downhaul needs tightening.

D. Chute lowered and boat has lost most headway as she turns through wind. Note MOB at extreme right.

E. MOB is close aboard under lee bow, as crew muzzles chute and prepares to retrieve MOB.

12-7. Hoisting a man aboard using the Lifesling and the main halyard. Midshipmen demonstrate the use of the Lifesling harness for man overboard recovery. Note the crew member on deck holding the halyard and 3:1 Lifesling tackle outboard to prevent the person in the water from being injured against the side of the boat.

should not be hung too close to open flames, woodwork and painted surfaces around the stove must be protected or insulated from flames, the stove should be kept clean and grease-free, and care must be taken when filling or priming not to spill fuel. A dry chemical fire extinguisher is hung near the stove. Minor fires can be smothered with a towel or by pouring salt on the flames. Some people advocate pouring water on flaming alcohol, but this could be dangerous when the boat is heeled, because a small amount of water may simply float the burning alcohol, and the fire may flow to a new location. If water is used, be sure to use plenty of it, because alcohol fires have a tendency to smolder and reignite. If the cook has a good harness to hold him in his cooking location, there will be less chance of his spilling foods or being thrown against the stove in rough weather.

The following paragraphs on kerosene stoves and LP gas stoves were reprinted with permission from *Sea Sense* by Richard Henderson, published by International Marine Publishing Company, Camden, Maine.

Kerosene stoves, which are similar to the alcohol type we have been discussing, are also quite safe, but they require a fire extinguisher (rather than merely water) to put out a flare-up that is out of control. Regardless of the fuel, however, a fire extinguisher should always be mounted in or near the galley. The ABYC (American Boat and Yacht Council) does not recommend wicktype burners, because their performance may be adversely affected by the boat's motion. All accepted standards warn against the use of gasoline for stove fuel aboard boats. With any kind of stove, the woodwork around it, especially overhead, should be well protected with sheet metal over insulation. Also, it is important to keep all stoves clean, because accumulations of grease from cooking can be highly flammable.

Many boats are fitted with liquified petroleum (LP) gas stoves because of their convenience in not needing to be primed. These appliances can be extremely dangerous if they are not properly installed and carefully handled. They should be given the same respect as a gasoline engine and its fuel system, because LP gas and the gasoline vapors have the same dangerous characteristics: both are heavier than air, and both are potentially explosive. In some respects, LP gas, which includes propane and butane, may be even more hazardous than gasoline, because it is easily diffused and is difficult to dispel by overhead ventilation, and, furthermore, it is relatively odorless. In fact, the ABYC and NFPA (National Fire Protection Association) require the odorizing of LP gas used on boats. It is therefore important that LP gas cylinders be carried on deck or in a ventilated deck box fitted with a drain at the bottom that leads overboard. Thus, any possible leakage of gas will escape well clear of the boat's interior. LP gas systems should have a pressure gauge to allow a periodic (at least biweekly) convenient means of checking for leaks. The pressure should be read with the main cut-off valve and the cylinder valve open, while the appliance valves are shut. If the pressure remains constant for ten minutes after the cylinder valve is shut, this indicates there are no leaks. Of course, a drop in pressure would indicate a leak. The application of soapy water to all connections is an effective means of locating the leak.

• Always keep the cylinder valve shut unless the appliance is actually in use. Be sure that the valve is shut in any emergency.

• See that the appliance valves are shut before the cylinder valve is turned on.

• When lighting the stove, apply the lighted match (or lighter) to the burner *before* its valve is opened.

• Watch the stove while it is being used to see that the flame does not go out. If it should go out (from a sudden draft, a pot boiling over, etc.), shut the valve immediately.

• In order to ensure that minimal gas will remain in the fuel line, shut the cylinder valve first and allow the fuel to burn out of the line before shutting the appliance valves.

• Test for leaks in the system, in the manner previously described, at least every two weeks.

• Never use a flame to look for leaks.

• Be sure flexible fuel hoses near the stove are fire proof, as a stove-top fire could burn through the hose and cause a serious explosion.

Obviously, precautions should be taken against smoking around flammable materials, against smoking in bunks, and so forth. A fire at sea is usually a lot more dangerous than a fire in one's home.

Rigging breaks—Another potential emergency for which the crew of an ocean racer should prepare is the breaking of vital rigging. At sea when sailing continuously for days at a time, rigging gets a lot more wear than one would ordinarily think. Metals can become fatigued from the constant motion, and lines that are rubbed can soon chafe through. Chafe is a major enemy at sea, and chafing gear must be applied to any running rigging where it touches anything. Chafing gear must be checked and adjusted continually.

If the headstay should part while beating, bear off immediately so that you are running dead before the wind. Don't lower the jib right away because its wire luff will help hold the mast forward. Set up the forestay at once, if it is not already rigged. Fasten one or two masthead halyards to the stem head, and tighten these halyards so that they pull the masthead forward. Lower the mainsail and reef it to the point where its head is no higher than the forestay's point of attachment to the mast. If a spare headstay is carried, then this may be rigged when the weather permits. Otherwise, perhaps the wire jib halyard can be rigged as a *jury* (makeshift) headstay. The upper end of the halyard might be held to the masthead with wire clamps, and in moderate or light weather a large jib could be hoisted with a spinnaker halyard. Needless to say, spare turnbuckles and also bulldog clamps, a hacksaw or rigging cutters, and short lengths of chain to extend the rigging should be carried.

If any of the main shrouds should break on the boat's windward side, tack immediately so that the strain will be put on the opposite shrouds. This maneuver, quickly done, might save the mast. If the mast should happen to break (a very unlikely occurrence if the rigging is regularly inspected), the mast will usually fall over the side. In this case the broken spar should be hauled aboard or cut away as soon as possible, because in rough seas it can pound a hole in the hull. This is where the required rigging cutters will come in handy. Some experienced sailors advise using bronze cotter pins that are short and only slightly bent to facilitate removal, but stainless cotters have higher sheer strength. At sea in heavy weather it is always a good idea to glance at the lee shrouds immediately before tacking to see that none are loose. Masts have been lost needlessly because of failure to check the lee rigging before tacking.

Should the permanent backstay break, round up into the wind at once. Simultaneously set up the running backstays and haul the mainsail in flat. Then lower the jib to take the strain off the head of the mast. If a jury backstay is rigged, don't set the spinnaker, as this can put a great strain on the backstays.

There is much less chance of breaking a stay if the rigging is thoroughly inspected. It is not enough to do this before going to sea. Inspections should also take place regularly while at sea. On a long passage, when weather permits, a man should be hauled up to the head of the mast in a bosun's chair occasionally so that he can check stays, mast sheaves, blocks, pins, tangs, splices, swages, halyards, etc. Hauling a man up the mast at sea when the boat is rolling can be a dangerous operation. Every precaution should be taken. It is important that the man going aloft is lashed into his seat in such a way that he cannot fall even if he is knocked unconscious. There should be a downhaul or tag line tended by a crew member on deck to steady the man aloft.

A chafed rope halyard should be replaced long before it has a chance to chafe through. It is often possible to replace a halyard without going aloft by *marrying* the new halyard to the old one. This is done by placing the ends of the two halyards together, end-to-end, (after melting the ends with heat when the lines are synthetic) and sewing them in that position. Then the old halyard can be unrove from the deck, and the new halyard will follow the old one through the block.

Spinnaker halyards are particularly susceptible to chafe aloft, but this chafe may be reduced by taking the hauling part of the halyard to leeward of the headstay so that the halyard will not cross the headstay and chafe on it.

Helmsmanship at night

One of the keys to successful distance racing is the ability to keep a boat moving at her best at night. This is not easy. In the dark, some competent daytime helmsmen become disoriented, and sail trimming is often neglected.

On downwind courses at night, steering is done primarily by the compass. In this case, the helmsman usually tries to steer the straightest course; at least he should not let his heading wander excessively. It is not easy to steer a straight compass course with a following or quartering sea, when the boat has a tendency to yaw. The helmsman must attempt to "catch" the boat before she swings past her proper heading. The common mistake of beginners is to turn the helm too late and to overcorrect. This kind of steering takes practice and the helmsman's full attention.

Beginners often become disoriented when steering with a compass at night, because of the lack of distant visible reference points. On a clear night it is sometimes wise to pick out a star somewhere ahead that can be lined up with the mast or rigging for a check point. Sometimes a beginner becomes almost hypnotized by the compass so that it seems as though the compass card moves while the boat remains stationary. However, it must always be kept in mind that the card stands still and the *lubber line* (the mark or thin post on the compass bowl that corresponds to the boat's heading) is what really moves.

The binnacle light should not be too bright, because this can be blinding to the helmsman when he has to look away from the compass. Red binnacle

12-8. The wheel, binnacle, compass, anemometer, and apparent wind indicator on a Luders fiberglass yawl. The compass is clearly marked in degrees as well as points. Courses may be referred to by points, as for example, southeast (SE), or by degrees, as 135°, which is more customary. The thin white line on the forward side of the compass bowl is the lubber's line. The knob on the starboard side of the pedestal locks the wheel when screwed in clockwise.

lights are the least damaging to night vision. Those crew members in the cabin should be careful to use a minimum of light so as not to blind the helmsman (and, of course, so that they won't disturb off-watch sleepers or use more electrical power than necessary).

When sailing to windward at night, the helmsman must depend to a lesser degree on his sense of sight and to a greater degree on some of the senses discussed in chapter 5—sound, feel, balance, and the helm touch. He must determine when the boat is moving at her best to windward by listening to the bow wave, sensing the liveliness of the boat, and feeling the balance of the helm. He senses when to bear off or head up by listening to the rattling of the sail slides, by feeling any wind changes on his face, and by using his sense of balance in detecting any changes in the angle of heel.

Although there is less emphasis on the visual aspects of helmsmanship when sailing at night, the sense of sight should not be discounted altogether. When there is a moon, sails can often be seen fairly well. Also, the luff of a sail can be checked occasionally with a flashlight that is not overly bright. Although black luff yarns are most easily seen against white sails, white or bright yellow ribbons are best for shroud telltales at night. The compass is not used as much when beating, but it should constantly be consulted both to see that you are sailing the generally proper course and to detect wind shifts. If you were headed southeast on the starboard tack, for example, you should be sailing roughly southwest on the port tack, barring any permanent wind shift. Also, of course, the navigator is usually interested in your "average" heading for his *dead reckoning* (the figuring of the boat's position by recording or estimating the distance over a known course). There is a normal tendency to pinch a boat at night, because the boat's speed is apt to seem greater than it actually is, and heavy night air can cause you to misjudge the wind strength. Of course, instruments are a great help to a helmsman at night, and these will be discussed in the next section.

When one helmsman relieves another, the new man coming on watch should have plenty of time to get oriented and to let his eyes become adjusted to the dark. The new helmsman should watch at least ten minutes before taking the wheel for reasonable eye adaptation and to see how the boat is being steered and to study how the compass heading averages. The helmsman to be relieved should give the new man all pertinent information, such as the course he is trying to make good, the location of other boats, the steering characteristics, what sails are set, what preventers are rigged, and any special problems that might arise.

Sails should constantly be trimmed at night just as they are in the daytime. It is easy to become complacent in this respect after dark, but boat speed will suffer far more than one might think from apathetic attention to trim. Sails can be checked by stationing a man forward to check the headsails (when weather permits), by occasionally shining a dim flashlight on the sails and luff yarns, and by noting the proper daylight trim points and lead positions. It is often a help to mark the sheets with pieces of white tape at proper positions of trim for various points of sailing.

When carrying the spinnaker at night, keep the wind well on the quarter, so there is little danger of the sail being blanketed by the mainsail. On this point of sailing in a good breeze, the sheet should be trimmed a little more than usual to guard against the sail collapsing at the luff. A man should be standing by the sheet at all times, ready to give it a quick pull in the event of collapse. Naturally the helmsman should be ready to bear off when the sail first begins to break at the luff. Navy boats usually carry striped spinnakers and these are relatively easy to see or at least to interpret in the dark. When these sails begin to break, one can see a distortion in the contrasting striped pattern.

Instrumentation

Nearly all modern ocean racers are fitted with mechanical or electronic instruments to help the helmsman achieve optimal sailing speed and efficiency. A typical list of instruments would include: a speedometer, apparent wind indicator, *anemometer* (wind speed indicator), inclinometer, and a depth finder. Of course, the latter might be considered primarily a navigation instrument, but it can also be helpful in attaining the best possible speed, because it shows the fastest course through shallow water when there are adverse tidal currents and through deep water when the current is favorable. Instrument dials are located in or near the cockpit where they can be viewed easily by the helmsman, and in many cases there are repeater dials below

211

12-9. Two sailboat speedometers. Type A utilizes a rotator and transducer. The particular instrument shown is a self-powered Sims Yachtspeed. Notice that the underwater unit is designed to deflect seaweed. The Kenyon KMX speedometer (B), a log measuring speed but not distance that uses a strut or wand type underwater sensor. The control box has a switch that increases sensitivity and in effect expands the scale so that very slight changes in speed can be easily noted.

near the chart table in order that the navigator can also read the instruments.

Before proceeding further with this discussion, it should be said that instruments should not be considered a substitute for the instincts and judgment of a skilled helmsman. They should be thought of as aids only. In most cases, they should not be stared at continuously but merely checked frequently during daylight hours. There are many other things the helmsman ought to be looking at, such as the luffs of his sails, puffs on the water, waves approaching the windward bow, and nearby competitors during a race. Furthermore, overdependence on the instruments may partially atrophy a helmsman's feel of the boat and his "tiller touch," and this could not only adversely affect the boat's speed, but also take some of the fun out of sailing her. This is especially true in light airs when the instruments usually are least helpful. At night, however, a speedometer, inclinometer, and wind indicator are invaluable, and the helmsman should watch them attentively. The dials of these instruments should be illuminated with red lights, so that the helmsman will not be momentarily blinded when he looks away from them.

Speedometers, sometimes called knotmeters, come in a variety of styles. Some types register speed by measuring water pressure, either with a drag sensor such as a hinged, spring-loaded wand mounted on the boat's bottom or with a protruding, underwater pitot tube, although the latter type may be of limited value in rough seas or very light airs. Other speedometers use a free-turning rotator of the propeller (or impeller) or paddle-wheel type to indicate speed or distance traveled (figure 12-9). When distance alone or distance together with speed is recorded, the instrument is generally called a *log*, but sometimes the term log is used as a synonym for speedometer. Underwater parts of speedometers—rotators or sensors—can be linked to their indicators mechanically, hydraulically, or with a transducer that converts the physical movement of the submerged element to an electric signal that moves the indicator's pointer. It is advisable that a sensor or rotator be a removable type that can be withdrawn into the boat while she is afloat via a through-hull fitting provided with a valve or at least a watertight cap. In most saltwater areas, marine growth can rather quickly foul the underwater elements of speedometers or logs; thus, they should be cleaned frequently. Also, some types should be protected from being fouled by floating seaweed with a streamlined weed deflector.

The real value of a speedometer, aside from its usefulness to the navigator in calculating distance traveled, is its ability to show differences in speed when sails are changed, sheets are retrimmed, or headings are altered. Some sailboat speedometers have indicator dials with expanded scales showing readings in tenths of a knot in order that very subtle changes in speed can be observed. It should be kept in mind, however, that speed changes result not only from the manner in which the boat is handled and sailed, but also from changes in wind velocity and sea conditions. During a race, therefore, it is important to judge speed by watching competitors as well as by looking at the speedometer.

Changes in wind speed, of course, may be observed on the anemometer dial. This is a useful instrument for determining the need for sail changes, but bear in mind that a boat's anemometer measures the velocity of the apparent wind, not the true wind. The former may be considerably stronger than the latter when beating to windward, but the contrary will be true when running before the wind.

Wind strength also can be judged by the vessel's angle of heel when beating or reaching, and small changes in heel can be noted by reading the inclinometer. This is usually a simple mechanical instrument that consists of a curved scale marked in degrees of heeling angle and a pointer, which may be in the form of a ball in a curved tube filled with liquid or a rigid plumb bob that hangs at right angles to the surface of the earth regardless of the boat's heel. Every sailboat has some angle of heel beyond which (on heeling further) she will begin to slow. With most conventional deep-keel ocean racers this angle might lie between twenty and twenty-five degrees, but, of course, it will vary with individual boats and often with different conditions of the sea or weather. Narrow boats with long overhangs can generally be sailed effectively at greater heeling angles than short-ended beamy boats with relatively flat bilges. Every effort should be made to determine the various optimum heeling angles, primarily by comparing the inclinometer and speedometer readings. Optimum inclinometer readings should rarely be exceeded even if this means reducing sail.

Apparent wind indicators, sometimes called relative wind indicators, show the direction of the apparent wind. They consist of vanes, usually located above the masthead, electronically connected to dials located near the helmsman. These instruments serve the same purpose as masthead flies or wind socks, but the better electronic indicators have certain advantages. They obviate the need for helmsmen to stare aloft, and they are constructed so that wild oscillations of their wind vanes caused by

pitching and rolling are damped. In addition, many indicators are provided with pairs of dials for easier reading on the beat when the detection of minute changes in the apparent wind angle is very important. Each pair of dials has a general indicator, which shows wind direction through 360 degrees (180 degrees on the left side of the dial and 180 degrees on the right) and a close-hauled indicator that amplifies the scale on the close-hauled headings, showing zero to 45 degrees on both the starboard and port tacks. The ideal close-hauled heading for a typical modern ocean racer might lie between 30 and 25 degrees in favorable conditions of wind and sea. Of course, just how high a boat will point effectively will depend on her hull design, rig, and the cut of her sails. Here again, the pointing angle should be compared with the speedometer reading while leeway is noted to determine optimal close-hauled angles. Leeway can be estimated when trying to fetch a mark and observing the mark's apparent movement against a shore or some other object in the background when the current is slack.

As said earlier, depth sounders are especially handy for boats racing in shoal waters against a foul current. The instrument performs the same function as an old-fashioned lead line, but it has the great advantage of giving more continuous readings with less physical effort expended. In simple terms, a depth sounder operates by bouncing high-frequency sound waves off the bottom of the sea and measuring the time it takes for them to reach the sea bed and return to the boat. A transmitter feeds electric signals to a transducer, usually mounted on the boat's bottom, which sends and picks up the sound waves. The return waves or echoes are converted back into electric signals by the transducer, and they are amplified by a receiver and visually presented on an indicator or depth recorder. The latter system supplies a permanent record of depth on paper that is motor-moved at a constant rate under an inscribing stylus. A recorder can be of great value to a navigator in making a *chain of soundings* (finding one's position by matching a series of soundings to depths marked on a chart).

There are several types of nonpermanent indicators. Some types show depths in easy-to-read numbers (digits), but a popular and traditional indicator is the one that has a flashing neon light at the end of an arm that rotates rapidly around a circular scale. The light flashes when the sound waves leave and

213

12-10. Learning the elements of navigation is an important part of boating. Here a midshipman navigator takes a bearing using a hand-bearing magnetic compass.

214

return to the transducer, thus showing depth on the scale. With this type, however, a certain amount of interpretation of the indicator reading is required, because different types of bottoms will change the character of the flashes somewhat, and intervening subsurface flotsam or schools of fish will show a less deep and usually weaker signal than that bouncing off the sea bed. On some boats with long keels, there may be two transducers, one on each side of the boat, and in this case the leeward transducer should be used when the boat is heeled. Flashing light indicators on deck should be provided with sun shades for easy reading.

A final word on instruments is that the compass is not only indispensable to the navigator and to the helmsman for steering in poor visibility, it is also useful as a tactical instrument when beating to windward. As said in the last chapter, it often pays to tack on major heading wind shifts, but sometimes they occur so gradually that the helmsman, lacking clear landmarks, is not aware that he is being headed or of the extent of the shift. Obviously, an occasional reference to the compass can tell whether the boat is being headed or lifted and how much.

The crew

Although all racing is a team effort, in short races the skipper is the most important member of the crew. His start is important, his quick tactical decisions often form the strategy, and he usually has

the helm for most of the race. In distance racing, however, there is less emphasis on the start, and other members of the crew gain importance. Most crew members must take their trick at the helm, and although strategy is the skipper's responsibility, other members of the crew are conferred with and consulted before major decisions are made. In fact, it is usually the judgment of the weather expert or the navigator that influences the skipper's decisions the most.

Signing on a qualified crew is vital to the success of a distance race. A few inexperienced crew members may be taken if there are an ample number of veterans aboard, but the novices should be thoroughly investigated for susceptibility to seasickness, and they should be given ocean-racing instruction and training before the race. All new crew members, whether experienced in offshore sailing or not, should be thoroughly familiar with sail handling, all gear, and every aspect of the boat. An attempt should be made to acquire a number of good helmsmen, because no one helmsman, regardless of his skill, should be allowed to steer for too long a period of time. If so, he will become fatigued and lose concentration and effectiveness.

Certain members of the crew have definite specialities—for example, the navigator and the cook. Other members should be able helmsmen, skilled sail handlers, and seamen; but even these men should have knowledge of, or should be encouraged to specialize in, one or more useful subjects. For instance, there should be a weather specialist, a medic, or one with a good knowledge of first aid, at least one member with mechanical and electrical aptitude, a carpenter, an expert on marlinspike seamanship, and so forth. Of course, the perfect crew is hard to find, but regardless of experience and skills the single most important ingredients for an ocean-racing crew is probably enthusiasm and eagerness to excel.

When there are not other competitors around, it often helps to build up a sort of competition between watches to see which watch can log the greater number of miles or keep above a certain speed. Of course, such contests are not really meaningful and are contrived, to a large extent, in the spirit of fun, but often they do help keep the crew on their toes.

On most ocean races, the deck watch is on duty four hours and off four hours. This is commonly referred to as the "two-watch" or "watch-and-watch" system. In order to avoid the rotation sequence that would bring the same watch on duty at the same times each day, one of the four-hour periods is divided into two *dog watches*. These are two-hour watches, customarily from 1600 to 1800 and from 1800 to 2000, for the specific purpose of alternating watch hours each day. Another popular watch schedule is the *Swedish system*, which divides the day into five watches: 0200-0600, 0600-1200, 1200-1800, 1800-2200, and 2200-0200. This method gives six-hour watches during daylight, four-hour watches at night, and automatically alternates watches daily. Quite often the navigator is not required to stand watches, and in some cases the skipper does not stand regular watches. Each watch should have a capable watch officer.

Soon after the start of a long-distance race, although excitement is high, it is a good idea to settle down into a regular routine. It is important from the outset to combat fatigue. This is the ever-present enemy of the blue-water sailor. Fatigue causes carelessness, poor judgment, and laziness, which can lose races, cause accidents, and even endanger lives. When racing especially, an adequate crew should be carried so that the boat can be tacked and her headsails changed without rousing out the watch below. It is important that the crew get plenty of rest and sleep. If anyone has trouble sleeping, he might try using ear plugs or an eye mask or perhaps even a mild sedative. Ample carbohydrates in the form of sweets and starches and high-protein foods provide energy.

Another enemy of the offshore sailor is seasickness. As said before, any person particularly prone to this malady should not be allowed on an ocean race, but most sailors, even veterans, can expect to be at least mildly afflicted at times. Many sailors are subject to stomach queasiness the first day or so at sea, and then they become accustomed to the boat's motion and feel well for the rest of the passage, unless exceptionally rough weather is encountered. It is generally agreed that greasy and acid foods as well as excessive use of alcoholic beverages should be avoided a week or ten days before the beginning of an offshore race. If you should begin to feel mildly seasick or queasy, stay as much as possible on deck in the fresh air, try nibbling on dry soda crackers or biscuits, do not use your eyes excessively for close work such as compass or chart reading, and keep

warm and dry. In rough weather, smoking in the cabin, especially cigar smoking, should be forbidden. Care should be taken to see that odorless alcohol is used in the galley stove. The galley should be ventilated as much as possible commensurate with safety. There will be the least amount of motion in the aftermost bunks. Certain seasickness remedies such as Dramamine and Bonamine are a real help, but they should be taken well before rough weather is encountered. Also, they are apt to make some people very drowsy. Scopolamine stick-on patches (Transderm) can be effective, but there are apt to be side effects. Bucladin S, a prescription drug, can be effective if you have waited too long before taking the conventional remedies. Bucladin pills can be held under the tongue and absorbed into the body, thus avoiding the problem of losing a seasickness medicine through vomiting.

The most valuable personal item for the offshore crew is good foul weather gear. This not only keeps him dry, but warm. It should be of medium weight and colored bright orange or yellow for best visibility. It is generally agreed that the jacket should open at the front with snaps or with zipper or velcro. This type is the easiest to put on and take off in rough weather. Be sure of a proper fit, because foul weather gear that is too small restricts movement and may allow water penetration, while oversized gear may snag or cause tripping. Rubber boots are a great comfort in bad weather, but they should be short, light, have skidproof soles, and be designed so that they can be kicked off easily. There is a great tendency for the crew to peel off their clothes in fair weather, but overexposure to the sun should be avoided. This can not only produce bad burns, but it can be enervating. It is important for any sailor to carry a knife and wear nonskid deck shoes, but it is doubly important for the offshore sailor. Deck shoes not only help prevent skidding, but they also protect against stubbing toes.

Distance racing strategy

The strategy and tactics involved in a distance race are basically similar to those of a short race, but there are subtle differences. The start of a distance race is, of course, important, but it is not as crucial as in a short, closed-course race around the buoys. In long ocean races there is a greater dependence on general weather forecasts. Navigation plays a

215

greater role in the distance race, and there is less boat-for-boat racing or covering tactics. By and large, each skipper sails his own race.

Although the start is not as vital in a 600-mile race as in one 20 miles long, the start is always important. Distance races have been won and lost by minutes and even seconds. Nevertheless, it seems ridiculous to attempt a split-second start at the risk of fouling (as happened to more than one famous ocean racer) when there are perhaps four or five days of racing to come. The important thing is to start in clear air. More often than not, a distant point-to-point race will have a reaching start. In such a case, the smaller boats or late starters will often be subjected to the disturbed wind of the leaders. Don't follow in the wakes of those boats ahead unless they are far ahead. It is usually best to drive off or head up until you reach clear air. Quite often when there is a long starting line with competitors bunched at the windward end, it pays to try a leeward-end start with a "full head of steam." In this way, perhaps you can get a safe leeward position, and if you are overtaken by a large boat close to windward, you can usually bear off below her wind shadow. It seldom pays to split tacks on a reaching start. Even if your wind is disturbed temporarily, boats will soon disperse.

The general weather picture certainly must be carefully considered in a distance race. Before the race obtain a five-day forecast, and carefully study the latest weather charts. Forecasts based on the information available just before the start can predict weather over the following few days with reasonable accuracy. These predictions can be substantiated or modified offshore by tuning in, as often as possible, to high-seas radio broadcasts (times and frequencies available from the publication *Worldwide Marine Weather Broadcasts*). Some ocean racers carry weather facsimile equipment that can supply up-to-date synoptic and prognostic charts.

On many long ocean races, contestants can benefit greatly from passing barometric lows (cyclones), which move in a general west-to-east direction in the middle latitudes. In the Northern Hemisphere, the winds rotate counter-clockwise around a low and blow inward towards its center. Lows usually follow more or less definite tracks, and by staying in the favorable quadrant of a low, of course, a boat can get the benefit of its favoring winds. Keeping a continuous record of wind direction and barometer

readings can help determine where your boat is located with respect to the low. Of course, natural signs of the weather, such as the color of the sky at dawn and dusk and especially the clouds, should be studied.

Weather forecasts are fallible, and strategy should be based on percentages (your best chance of getting favorable weather). Don't make a drastic alteration in a normally sensible course to gamble on a possible weather change. If you are behind and the risk is such that a predicted change that fails to materialize costs you only a few miles or even hours, it may pay to take the risk. But if the failure to materialize could seriously damage your chances of doing well in the race, don't take the risk. In other words, where the weather is concerned, don't climb out on a limb. Consider making slight alterations in the course in an attempt to take advantage of a possible beneficial change, but don't risk everything.

Any course alterations on the *rhumb line* (the straight-line course on a Mercator chart) will not amount to any great change in the total distance to be covered if you are far from your destination, but a similar course alteration close to your destination will add considerably to the total distance remaining. Another thing to keep in mind if you are attempting to follow a rhumb-line course, is that your *present* rhumb line is a straight line from where you are, at the moment, to the finish line. Don't feel that you necessarily have to get back to the original (start to finish) rhumb line. This original course may have been the shortest one at the time of the start, but it is not the shortest later on in the race if you are not located on that line.

With some skippers, the desire to stick to the rhumb line becomes almost an obsession. Don't become overly concerned with a straight-line course, especially in the early stages of the race. The important thing is to keep your boat moving even if it is not in the exact direction of the finish line. If, for example, you have a close-hauled course to the finish and you pinch up in an attempt to fetch, a competitor near you who cracks sheets and sails full and by on a non-fetching course will almost always beat you. The reason for this is that there will probably be a general wind shift later on that will either lift and allow your competitor to fetch, or else will head you both, allowing neither of you to fetch. In the latter case, this shift will put you directly

12-11. Under reduced sail. The skippers of the four Luders yawls shown in this photo have all decided on different reduced sail combinations. From left to right these are: No. 2 Genoa, reefed main and mizzen; No. 2 Genoa and mizzen; No. 1 Genoa and trysail; and No. 3 Genoa and full main. The extreme left and right boats have the more effective rigs for beating to windward, and they seem to be sailing a bit faster than the other two boats.

astern of your competitor, because (as you will recall from the last chapter) a heading shift favors the leeward leading boat. The same principle often applies when you are reaching or running. If you are sailing a course that gives you an effective angle with the wind, especially when the spinnaker is set, don't worry about straying from the rhumb line, because the chances are that the wind will shift or change velocity later on. Use the wind you have to best advantage while you have it. In light airs, it generally pays to sail toward wind streaks. Don't wait for the wind to come to you.

One of the keys to successful distance racing is the ability to maintain the best possible speed, not only by choosing the right course, but by paying constant attention to such factors as sail trim and helmsmanship. It is easy to let down on these matters when there are no other competitors in sight, but an attempt should be made to sail the boat just as though she were racing around the buoys. Not only sheets, but also outhauls, downhauls, and

leads, should be adjusted for every wind change. It is of the utmost importance that the boat be reefed when necessary and that appropriate headsails are carried. There is a common tendency to procrastinate when it comes to sail changes; sails are usually reefed and unreefed too late, and headsails are not changed often enough. (See figure 12-11.)

When the wind moderates while you are carrying a Number 3 Genoa, it is easy to be lazy and rationalize that the wind will freshen again after a while, but in most cases the No. 1 or 2 Genoa should be set. If properly done, a headsail change does not waste much time. Jib changes on boats without double slotted head-foils were briefly discussed in chapter 9. A few details of this operation when close reaching are presented here: On a Navy 44 or any double-head-rigged boat that has hanked-on jibs, the forestaysail can be set as an interim sail to prevent excessive speed loss while the jib is down. Before the original jib is lowered, its lower hanks are unsnapped and the substitute jib is hanked onto the headstay beneath the original jib. A new set of sheets are bent to the substitute jib and properly led. Then the original jib is lowered, and its hanks are unsnapped as it comes down. The halyard is quickly shifted to the substitute jib and this is immediately hoisted. In a strong breeze, it sometimes pays to stop the substitute jib with light thread, similar to the way a spinnaker is stopped. Then after the jib is hoisted, the stops can be broken by hauling back on the sheet, and the forestaysail may be lowered if so desired. On a short closed-course race, it is often not advisable to change jibs, because the time wasted is too great when compared with the time spent on a course leg; but on a distance race, the best sails for the conditions of the moment should be used, and this often means reasonably frequent sail changes.

One sail change that is important, even though it is not often required, is a change from a reefed mainsail to the storm trysail, or vice versa. On some boats, the slides on the luff of the trysail are fitted into a short separate track alongside the track for the mainsail. The trysail track connects into the main track on the mast via a switch about four feet above the gooseneck. This arrangement allows the trysail to be bent onto its track while the mainsail is still set, and then to be hoisted as soon as the mainsail is lowered below the switch and the main halyard has been shackled onto the head of the trysail. On most of the fiberglass yawls and the Navy 44s, the separate trysail track runs up the mast alongside the main track far enough so that the trysail can be set on its own track. Most of the wooden yawls and many private yachts have no separate track, and the mainsail must be unbent before the trysail is bent on. Recently, a number of the yawls have had gates added to their sail tracks so that the trysail can be left bent on under the gate. When sail is reduced, the mainsail is lowered and its slides are run off the track through the gate, and then the trysail can be hoisted immediately after the halyard is transferred.

The trysail has a tack line that is shackled into the gooseneck fitting and allows the tack of the sail to ride up the mast about six feet when the sail is set.

Sheets are permanently attached to the trysail. The sail is normally sheeted like a headsail, with one sheet led on each side. The lead is through a block shackled into the base of the stanchion just forward of the forward mizzen shroud. Alternatively, the clew of the trysail may be lashed to the main boom after the mainsail has been lowered and the sail trimmed by using the mainsheet. In this case, the clew of the trysail must be lashed strongly aft, as well as down. Also, the main topping lift should be set up to take some of the weight of the boom.

The questions as to how hard to drive a boat and how long to carry on in bad weather are very difficult to answer. When these questions arise, the skipper must carefully consider the trend of the weather, the behavior of his boat, the condition of the boat and her equipment, and the ability of his crew. If the weather appears to be growing worse, if the boat is becoming difficult to manage and there have been a number of gear failures and jury repairs, or if some of the crew are sick, tired, or inexperienced, then it is time to reduce sail drastically. As weather conditions get worse, sail should be reduced accordingly. At first you might shift to a smaller Genoa, then to a double head rig, (working jib and forestaysail) with reefed mainsail. When smaller jibs are used, it is customary to use head and tack pendants, the former so that a wire and rope halyard can be extended to allow at least three turns of wire around its winch. Tack pendants are used to raise the sail's foot to keep it above seas breaking over the bow, for better visibility, or to improve the lead. (Incidentally, *pendant* is pronounced pennant but should be spelled with a "d". A pennant is a flag). A further wind increase might call for a deep-reefed main with the forestaysail, storm jib, and mizzen. If it blows even harder, you might lower the jib and mizzen. This is the smallest rig under which the boat will perform well to windward. If even further sail reduction is necessary, you would have the choice of either storm trysail and small forestaysail, or forestaysail and reefed mizzen. The boat will balance well under either of these minimum rigs, but cannot be expected to drive to windward in heavy seas with so little sail. In prolonged exposure to heavy weather with rough seas, the trysail and forestaysail might be the preferable rig, because the sails are concentrated just forward of the center of effort, and the trysail should help support the main mast and hold it steady, provided the sail is kept full and not allowed to flap excessively.

Under conditions that would warrant such sail

reduction, the boat should be eased along and held on course as closely as possible. But if she shows any alarming tendencies to bury the lee rail, or broach to when running or reaching, or if she frequently takes solid green water on deck she should be put on the easiest, most comfortable course, and slowed down even more.

Boat management in gale-force winds offshore

In the heaviest weather at sea, preparedness must be the first consideration. When it becomes evident that the weather is deteriorating and the vessel will face a real blow, the following precautions should be taken: don foul weather gear if it is not already being worn; put on safety belts and life jackets or flotation jackets (if safety belts will not fit around the jackets); dog all hatches and ports; stow un-needed deck gear below; lash securely all other gear remaining on deck; check stowage of all gear below; remove ventilators and replace them with screw caps (*Dorade*-type vents should be the last to be removed); insert heavy slides in the after end of the companionway; see that the bilge pumps are working properly; see that all gear that might be needed (flares, horn, flashlights, storm sails, drogues, buckets, stops, lashing lines, heavy lines to be used as drags, etc.) is readily available; hoist the radar reflector; shut off all sea cocks except those on the cockpit and deck scupper drains; shut off the valve on the engine exhaust outlet; and set up backstays and forestays (provided they do not interfere with any sail that is being carried). Of course, seasickness remedies should have been taken, meals and hot drinks for thermos bottles should be prepared, and as much rest as possible should be obtained well in advance of the bad weather. Make every effort to keep clothing and blankets dry, perhaps by stowing them in plastic bags. Check weather reports and navigation position. Get ready for bad weather early; the simplest task on deck becomes extraordinarily difficult in a gale, and an undone rigging chore may lead to a serious casualty. While sailing, as the weather gradually deteriorates, it is important that the condition of the vessel be checked frequently. See that the mast is not bending or whipping excessively, that lines or sails are not chafing, that gear is not breaking, and so forth. Periodically, check the amount of water in the bilge.

Heaving to

If the boat appears to be taking a serious battering from the seas, she should be *hove to* (her headway nearly stopped with her bow held fairly close to the wind under counteracting sails). This might be accomplished under a storm trysail and a *spitfire* (storm jib) backed (trimmed to windward) with the helm lashed down. When the boat has an inner staysail stay that secures to the deck slightly forward of the mid foredeck, as on the Navy 44s, a better plan is to set the spitfire on the staysail stay. This will improve balance, centralize the rig, and provide deck space surrounding the stay and lessen motion for the crew working forward. Finding the best means of heaving to will take a little experimentation. The boat should lie reasonably comfortably, and she should not be allowed to *forereach* (move ahead) with any speed (see figure 12-12). Do not allow the sails to flog in the wind, as they could easily become damaged.

If the wind freshens to such an extent that the boat no longer behaves well while hove to under storm sails, or if the sails are being damaged, it is advisable to lower them. Alternative storm tactics are *scudding* (running off before the wind under little or no sail) or *lying a-hull* (lying beam to the wind and seas under bare poles). In deciding which tactic to use, a major consideration will be the boat's position with respect to a lee shore. Obviously, scudding will take a boat quite rapidly towards a lee shore, so there must be ample sea room to leeward. Related considerations are that the boat should be headed away from the storm and away from shoal waters or a strong current flowing against the wind that could produce dangerously short, steep, breaking seas.

Lying a-hull

Lying a-hull, with the boat being allowed to fend for herself, is a somewhat controversial course of action, as it subjects her to beam seas that could possibly roll her over, but under the right conditions the tactic has proven highly effective in coping with gales offshore. Several advantages in hulling are that the boat lies in a position of maximum buoyancy, and she yields to the seas, much like a boxer rolls with the punches. Furthermore, she will remain fairly stationary with respect to a lee shore (most boats will make about two knots or less of leeway),

exaggerated
track of
the bow

nearly
square
drift
(wake to
windward)
helps to
smooth
seas

wind

spitfire or
reefed jib
sheeted to
windward

storm
trysail

helm
down

boat
ranges
ahead
very
slowly
(should not
be allowed to
move fast)

bow falls
off

220

helm lashed
part way down
with nylon line
or heavy shock
cord to take the
strain off rudder

tack pendant to lift tack
high off the deck.

12-12. Heaving to under sail.

and there is no need to man the helm. Except for a lookout, the crew members of a boat lying a-hull can close themselves in the cabin, where they should secure themselves in their bunks to guard against being thrown about when the vessel rolls.

There are several requirements for the hulling tactic: (1) the boat should have a high range of stability (preferably over 130 degrees); (2) she must have a strong cabin trunk well crowned (curved) and supported and with small "unbreakable" windows or ports (storm shutters may be needed); (3) there must be sturdy companionway storm slides that can be locked in place; and (4) all objects below must be capable of being secured so they cannot come loose no matter how far the boat is rolled or knocked down. This tactic should not be used when seas are high and extremely short with a predominance of *plunging* rather than *spilling breakers*. The latter type, more often associated with deep water, break gradually at the top of their crests leaving trails of foam streaming behind. In contrast, plungers, normally associated with shallow water or *overfalls* (breakers caused by an irregular bottom or the convergence of currents) have nearly vertical crests that tumble or fall forward with considerable force.

The helm is usually lashed down (with the rudder to windward) when lying a-hull. If the bow blows off or is knocked downwind by a wave, causing the boat to make headway, the rudder will turn her back toward the wind. It is preferable that the boat lie slightly higher than beam to the wind provided she doesn't damage her rudder by backing down on it. The helm can be lashed with shock cord to relieve severe strain on the rudder. Some yawls have had success hulling with the mizzen hoisted and sheeted flat to hold the bow up slightly, but the mizzen should be cut very flat to avoid excessive flogging. Some experimentation is usually necessary to find out how the boat lies most comfortably.

Scudding

Scudding requires a helmsman to hold the bow off and keep the stern more or less square to the seas. The boat should be running under bare poles or possibly a very small storm jib sheeted flat to help hold the bow off provided the sail does not cause too much speed. Of course, some speed is necessary in order that the rudder can be effective, but a speed faster than that necessary for adequate steering control could be dangerous for the following rea-

12-13. A sea coming aboard. This dramatic shot was taken by Norris Hoyt aboard the ocean racer *Figaro III* (later named *Foolscap*) during heavy weather in the mid-Atlantic. It clearly illustrates the value of a small self-draining cockpit on an offshore boat and also why it is important for the helmsman to be secured to the boat with a safety line in very heavy weather.

sons: the bow might be pushed deeply into a hollow in an irregular, confused sea, which might encourage a tendency to *broach to* (suddenly and inadvertently turn sideways to the seas), or else, in the very worst conditions, to *pitchpole* (turn end over end). The faster a boat is moving, the more dangerous a broach can be, because when the boat turns, her forward momentum is converted into a lateral force, which may cause excessive heeling. Furthermore, her forward speed lessens her ability to make leeway when she first turns sideways to the waves, and thus she will lack the same ability to yield to breaking seas that she would have if she were lying a-hull. Although broaching to at high speeds is not always dangerous in moderate winds and seas, in extreme

weather conditions there is considerable risk. Another argument for scudding at low speeds is that a displacement hull such as a Luders yawl might create a fairly sizable hull resistance wave system at high speed, which could cause the stern to *squat* (sink slightly) or possibly could reinforce the following seas and cause them to break over the stern. A further argument for running off slowly is that the boat spends less time on the crests of the waves, at which time she has less steering control and less stability because her ends are relatively unsupported by the water's buoyancy force forward and aft.

In recent times, some yachts have had success running off at fairly high speeds in heavy weather to benefit from maximum rudder control so that the quite often a crew member looking aft to inform the helmsman of an overtaking plunger and to suggest a change in course for avoidance. The forward facing helmsman must watch for abnormally deep troughs ahead so that the boat doesn't dig into a hole and bury her bow. High-speed scudding seems to work best for light-displacement racers that do not create a large drag wave system, that don't have a high range of stability (making lying a-hull too risky), and are manned by a large racing crew with plenty of competent helmsmen. The tactic could be dangerous, especially at night, for heavy-displacement craft with a tendency to squat or yaw, manned by a small, tired crew.

It is not always easy to slow a boat when she is rapidly scudding before great following seas, because she may tend to surf on the wave faces. The usual practice is to tow drags—long cables, docking lines tied together, extra sails (be sure they can be spared), fenders, buckets, and so forth. A better practice is to use a *drogue*, a small sea anchor that allows some drift, such as the *Galerider*, a modern drogue having a parabolic shape and open web construction to allow some steering control and minimize shock loading. Another promising design is the *series drogue* (consisting of numerous small cloth cones on the rode) as developed by Donald Jordan and successfully tested by the U.S. Coast Guard. Large conventional *sea anchors* such as the cornucopia type (a large single cone of canvas attached to an iron ring) or the parachute type are not often recommended by today's most experienced offshore sailors except for the more easily capsizable boats (such as open boats, centerboarders, or multihulls) that must be held end-to the seas,

or else when it is imperative to slow drift toward a lee shore. Sea anchors that do not afford some give can impose severe strains and overly tether a boat so that she cannot retreat from the force of the seas. Most modern yachts do not behave well when a sea anchor is streamed from the bow, as the bow blows off and the boat ranges about, yawing and jerking on her rode and often exposing her beam to the seas. It is usually better to stream a smaller sea anchor or drogue astern when the boat has ample freeboard aft, a small cockpit with large drains, a high companionway sill, and storm slides for the companionway.

When it is necessary to control the downwind speed by towing drags astern, a trick that may improve steering control is to tow a drogue from a stern bridle or with drag lines fastened at the rail amidships close to the boat's turning axis. Whether scudding at fast or slow speeds, there is always the possibility of being *pooped* (having a sea break over the stern), so it is essential that the helmsman is held securely to his post with a stout safety line (figure 12-13).

During the storm the navigator must do his best to keep track of the boat's position with dead reckoning or radio navigation. When scudding, the helmsman should try to keep track of his compass headings and also the speed on the speed indicator or distance on the taffrail log or other distance-recording device. When hulling, leeway will generally be about 1½ or 2 knots, and the boat will make some headway. It is important that one of the crew keep a lookout at all times, especially when near the coast or in steamer lanes.

13.
Boathandling Under Power

*T*he secret to success when handling a power-driven vessel is a thorough understanding of each of the forces affecting her travel. The Naval Academy uses several different types of power vessels (see chapter 14) to teach midshipmen the principles of shiphandling. Whether the craft is a 14-foot outboard skiff, an auxiliary-powered sailboat, or a 400-foot steam-powered frigate, these principles are the same. Once they are mastered, you are well on your way to becoming a competent boat or ship handler.

Uncontrollable forces

Every skipper must appreciate the significance of the effects of the wind and current. When they are understood, these forces can actually assist the skipper in completing a maneuver. Ignored, the wind and current can force even a powerful boat into a collision or out of the channel and onto the shallows of a lee shore.

The shape of the boat both above and below the waterline determines the degree to which the wind and current act on the craft. A deep-keeled sailboat maneuvering under auxiliary power is pushed around quite a bit by the current. This is because there is so much underwater surface area that is exposed to this force. The effect of wind will depend on the height of freeboard and superstructures, wind velocity, and boat speed. On boats with very low freeboard, the wind does not usually cause much difficulty except when the boat is traveling at very slow speeds. A modern motor cruiser with an ordinary "V" bottom and a high superstructure often reacts to the wind more than to a weak current. (See figure 13-1 for representative hull shapes.)

While there is no fixed relationship between the wind and current, a good rule of thumb is that 1 knot of current will have about the same effect as 15 to 25 knots of wind. It is very easy to overestimate the effects of the wind and underestimate the effects of the current. It is important, therefore, to know the precise direction and strength of the wind and current. This will assist you in making the correct decision when handling the boat in restricted waters.

Often the wind and current will not be from the same direction, and in such cases it is best to dock into the dominating force. For example, in a 10-knot breeze, you should dock into a 2-knot current, and,

flat bottom

V bottom

round bottom (sail)

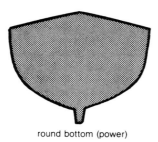

round bottom (power)

13-1. Representative hull shapes.

conversely, in a 25-knot breeze with a slight current of 1 knot or less, the docking should be made into the wind, if possible. The advantage of maneuvering into a strong current is that steerageway is maintained, while with a fair current you lose steerageway even though the boat is still making way over the bottom.

Most motor yachts, including the Naval Academy's Yard Patrol (YP) craft, are shallow draft with most of the "sail area" or *windage* (surface of the vessel exposed to the wind) well forward. When

underway, but with no way on, the boats will tend to lie with the beam almost perpendicular to the wind (the bow will be blown downwind slightly more than the stern). If not understood, this can ruin a good landing at a dock. As the boat approaches the pier with her engines stopped, the force of the wind becomes more noticeable and the boat starts to present her beam to the wind. Large amounts of rudder are required to keep the boat on course. If it becomes necessary to add power to correct the boat's heading, the initial movement will be to continue downwind, not straight ahead. The reason for this is that as the boat is seeking to present its maximum sail area to the wind, the bow will "sail" downwind faster than the engines and rudder can force the boat's head up into the wind.

It is not possible to describe the maneuvers required in every combination of wind and current. Later sections in this chapter will present additional examples that will assist the beginner in understanding the effects of wind and current. There is, however, no better way to learn than to take your boat to sea and practice handling her under a wide variety of weather conditions.

Controllable forces

There are five controllable forces available to you while handling under power: (1) your engines, (2) the rudder, (3) mooring lines, (4) anchors, (5) and tugs or pusher boats. Of course a tug or pusher boat is only used for larger vessels, but you should always consider each of these forces when maneuvering any type of power-driven vessel.

Before beginning a discussion of these forces, a word should be said about safety and the proper operation of power boats. Too many serious accidents are caused by the failure of skippers to operate and maintain their engines in accordance with the manufacturer's instructions. Engines and engine compartments should be kept clean and dry. You should never allow fuel or lubricating oil to accumulate in the bilges of the boat. This is particularly important if the boat has a gasoline engine. Gasoline and air combine to form an extremely dangerous vapor that can easily explode and possibly destroy the boat. According to Coast Guard literature, one cup of gasoline has the explosive potential of 15 sticks of dynamite. Fuel and electrical systems should be carefully inspected on a regular basis to ensure that hoses, pipes, and cables are securely

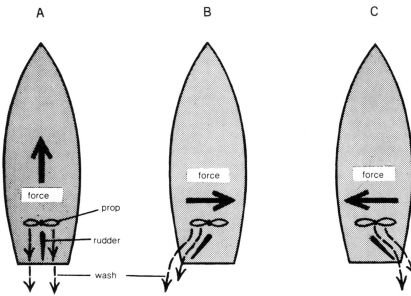

A   B   C

13-2. Effects of propeller wash on rudder of stationary boat. In all three cases the engine is going ahead. In case _B_ and _C_, there is an ahead component in addition to the lateral one.

fastened and that no deterioration has occurred that could lead to a fire on board. Battery stowage spaces should have adequate ventilation to allow the escape of gas that may build up during charging. Bear in mind that hydrogen gas (generated by the batteries) rises. All through-hull fittings, sea cocks, and hose clamps should be checked to make sure that there is no possibility of flooding.

There should be a set of operating instructions and a maintenance manual on board the boat for every piece of equipment. Midshipmen at the Naval Academy use two systems to ensure that boats are operated and maintained correctly. The first is called Engineering Operating Sequencing System (EOSS). This is a detailed checklist system for starting and securing engineering equipment aboard large vessels. The same simplified system is effectively used, however, as a one-page checklist on board smaller boats. The second system is the Planned Maintenance System (PMS). Each piece of equipment on board the boat has periodic maintenance checks. These checks range from a detailed technical inspection of the engines to the routine cleaning of air and fuel filters. Most manufacturers include instructions for the standard operation and recommended maintenance of their equipment. It is up to the conscientious boat owner to follow these recommendations so that he has a complete knowledge of all the equipment installed on board his boat.

Engines and rudder

The boat's engines are the most obvious source of power and sometimes cause the greatest difficulty to the novice as he attempts to "power" his way out of a tight spot. The expert _understands_ his engines and knows how to combine them with external forces to maneuver his craft skillfully into the tightest slip even during bad weather.

The engine drives a propeller that forces water astern when the engine is going ahead. This force not only drives the boat ahead, but it also acts on the rudder, which is generally directly behind the screw. When deflected by the turned rudder, the wash from the propeller will move the stern of the boat in the direction opposite to that of the rudder (figure 13-2). It should be obvious that if the engine is turning in the astern direction there is no wash directed onto the rudder. Thus, while the boat is easily maneuvered when going ahead, there is not as much control over her direction while going astern.

A second force generated by the propeller is a "side force", sometimes called _wheel effect_ or, more commonly but less correctly, _torque effect_. Figure 13-3 shows how this force is generated. Notice that there are two explanations, one having to do with the water being more aerated and thus less solid

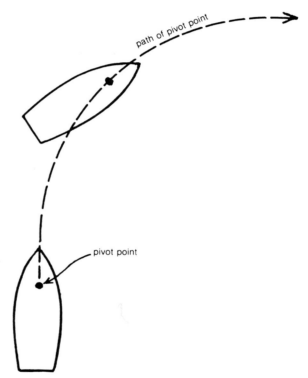

13-3. Explanations of wheel effect on propeller side force.

near the surface, and the other having to do with the fact that the projected area of the propeller pitch is greater on one side than on the other due to the shaft angle. On a single-screw boat with the usual "right-hand" propeller, one that turns clockwise when going ahead, the side force will drive the boat slightly to port with the rudder amidships. When backing, the side force has a very pronounced effect on the single-screw boat. When there is no wind and as yet no sternway, the boat will back to port regardless of the position of the rudder. (Remember that there is no wash being deflected by the rudder). Until there is sufficient sternway on the boat, the rudder will remain ineffective and the side force generated by the screw will be the dominant force.

An important factor affecting the handling of a vessel is the location of her *pivot point* (the point about which she turns). When the vessel is underway, but has no way on, the pivot point is located along the axis of the center-line and some distance, usually between 25 and 40 percent of the boat's length, abaft the bow. Figure 13-4 shows a vessel making a turn to starboard. Notice that the bow is slightly inside the path made by the pivot point while the stern is well outside this line. As the vessel gains headway the pivot point shifts forward. As the speed increases, the pivot point will shift slightly farther forward. When the boat backs down, the pivot point shifts aft.

Advance and transfer data is important in that it gives the boathandler information about the turning characteristics of his craft under various speeds and rudder angles. When the rudder is put over, say to starboard, the boat does not immediately pivot to the right and steady on the new course as shown in

13-4. Pivot point.

figure 13-5. Movement perpendicular to the original course is called transfer.

When one of the uncontrollable forces, wind, is present, the boat handles quite differently. Going ahead we have seen that the wind may force us off course but that this can be corrected with the engines and rudder. It is while backing that the wind and propeller side force can cause problems. As we have noted, on most boats "sail area" is forward of the pivot point. As the boat backs down, the wind tends to force the bow downwind while the force of the engine turning astern pulls the stern up into the wind. Figure 13-6A shows the course a single-screw vessel might make while backing into a berth in calm weather. Here the side force causes her to back to port. Figure 13-6B shows the same boat making the same approach with a moderate wind coming from the starboard side. In this example the wind is partially canceling the tendency to back to port caused by the side force. Notice that in each example it is not until sternway is gathered that the skipper is able to control his boat with the rudder.

Mooring lines

Mooring lines are a valuable asset to the skipper when handled safely and properly by the crew. On a small boat a spring line rigged amidships can settle the boat neatly into her berth. If handled poorly, however, the bow can swing around suddenly and crash into the pier.

The advantage gained from mooring lines is that the position of the pivot point is known precisely. Figure 13-7 shows the use of mooring lines along-side a pier. In each case the pivot point of the boat is near the point at which the line is belayed on deck.

Figure 13-8 shows the mooring line arrangement used on the Naval Academy YP. Figure 13-9 illustrates the use of mooring lines required to securely moor a much larger vessel such as a destroyer.

Safety on deck is an important consideration when handling lines on any vessel. Heavy strains are frequently placed on the lines as the boat maneuvers

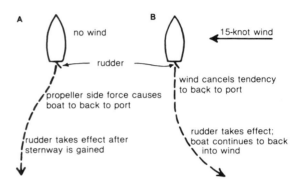

13-6. Effects of side force when backing a single-screw vessel.

227

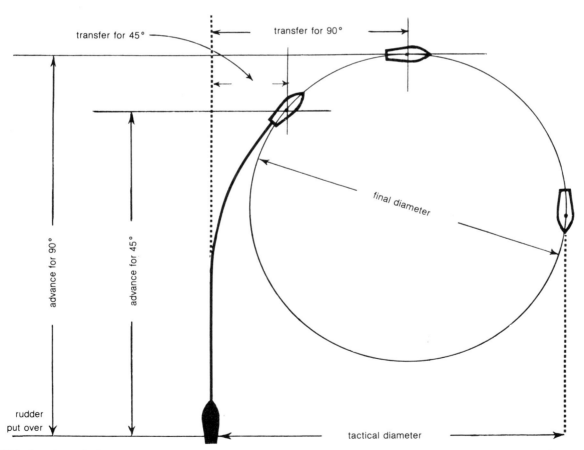

13-5. Ship turning circle.

around the pier. When new line is obtained, the manufacturer's label should be carefully checked to ensure that the right line is being used for the job. A line that is too small for the loads placed on it may part suddenly and recoil with tremendous force.

(arrows show screw wash)

13-7. Use of mooring lines when maneuvering alongside. (Arrows show screw wash.)
A. A bow spring can be used to bring a vessel alongside, in this case by going ahead on the starboard screw while using left rudder.
B. Twisting against a bow line with starboard ahead, port backing, and left rudder; once alongside, stop the twist and back starboard.
C. Twisting against a quarter spring is much less efficient, since the pivot point is aft near the screws.

The lines must be cared for properly if they are to last and perform safely under all conditions. They should never be allowed to chafe and become frayed. Sand, grease, rust, and chemicals can quickly ruin the most expensive mooring lines, and the lines should be inspected frequently for excessive wear or discoloration. If a line shows signs of deterioration, get rid of it; don't try to get through one more season with gear that might be unsafe.

The skipper and crew must communicate effectively if mooring lines are to be used to advantage. The command "Put that line over there!" leads to confusion and accidents even on small boats. The command "Hold the bow line!" means precisely that, even if it risks parting. Correct line-handling commands are simple, easily understood, and lead to smart, safe maneuvers. Table 13-1 lists a few of

13-8. Dock lines.

1. bow line
2. after bow spring
3. forward bow spring
4. after quarter spring
5. forward quarter spring
6. stern line

13-9. Mooring lines for large vessel.

the most common line-handling commands and their meanings.

Lines should be coiled, *faked down* (coiled flat, figure-eight fashion), or *flemished* (see fig. 13-10) so that they are ready for use at any time. This also ensures that there are no lines that can become fouled or wrap the screw. The crew must take care never to stand in a line's *bight* (loop or turn) that will come taut when the line is put under strain. The line should always be tended with a turn around a cleat or bitt, and handlers should keep their hands one or two feet away from the cleat to provide a

Table 13-1. Line-handling commands.

Command	Meaning
"Hold the bow line"	Hold the bow line even if it risks parting the line.
"Check the stern line"	Keep a heavy strain on the stern line, but do not allow the line to part
"Ease 2"	Ease tension on the number 2 line, but it should not be slacked.
"Slack 3"	There should be no tension on the number 3 line.
"Cast off"	Command to someone on the pier to cast off your lines.
"Take in ____"	Command to the crew to take aboard the lines cast off from the pier.
"Take a strain on ____"	Put tension on the line.

13-10. Lines faked down (left), flemished (lower middle), and coiled.

safety margin in case the line suddenly comes under strain and slips.

On most small boats the mooring lines are light enough to pass to the pier without the use of a *heaving line*. The latter is made of lightweight line and is fitted with a weight, usually a monkey's fist knot or a leather pouch filled with lead at the end of the line. On large vessels, however, a heaving line makes it easier to pass large mooring lines or a towing hawser. Figure 13-11 shows the proper way to prepare to use a heaving line. It is neatly coiled and the coils evenly separated into the left and right hands. When you heave the line, both coils are released at once. They will uncoil without forming knots or kinks. It takes a little practice, but soon you will be right on target with each throw. Don't forget to compensate for the wind when you take aim.

Anchors

The fundamentals of anchoring in open water were described in chapter 2. In this chapter we will discuss the use of an anchor in handling alongside. Many people are reluctant to use it while maneuvering in the vicinity of a pier, because they claim that it is too much trouble. Actually, the opposite is often true. Used correctly, the anchor provides excellent control at the bow with a minimum of effort.

As with mooring lines, the pivot point is moved to the hawse pipe or chock through which the anchor rode is led. With the bow under control, the stern can be easily maneuvered by using the engines and rudder, or by just letting the boat drift with the wind and current.

If strong wind and current are perpendicular to the pier, the experienced seaman prefers to moor on the lee side where the wind and current keep the boat away from the pier. If the approach must be made on the upwind side of the pier, an anchor will prevent the boat from crashing into the pier as it makes the landing. Figure 13-12 shows a wide approach in a single-screw boat. When abreast the desired berth, headway is killed and the anchor let go on the weather bow. The rate of approach to the pier is controlled by a combination of paying out the anchor rode and exerting short, strong bursts of power from the engine.

If the same conditions prevail when getting underway, the anchor set to windward can again be helpful. In the event the anchor has not been set, the only solution is to row one out to weather. Once the anchor is set, the boat is warped around head to wind (or current) and powered up to retrieve the hook before proceeding out of the harbor.

Another landing using an anchor is the Mediterranean moor. Figure 13-13 shows the steps for a single-screw boat making a stern-first landing using one anchor. Larger ships will use two anchors, which are set as shown in Figure 13-14. This is a difficult maneuver, especially if there is a strong wind or current running parallel to the pier. An alternative method is to approach the pier bow first, put a line ashore (on the pier), then back off and turn until the stern is facing the pier. Drop your anchor from the bow, transfer the shore line to the

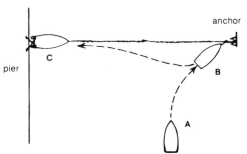

13-11. Using the heaving line. Note the weighted monkey's fist knot at the end of the coil in the sailor's right hand.

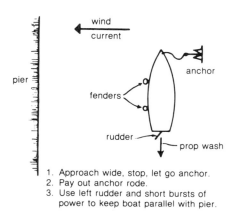

wind
current

pier

anchor

fenders

rudder

prop wash

1. Approach wide, stop, let go anchor.
2. Pay out anchor rode.
3. Use left rudder and short bursts of power to keep boat parallel with pier.

13-12. Using an anchor to moor on a weather pier.

anchor

pier

C

B

A

1. Approach parallel to the pier about 4 or 5 boat lengths away. When boat is opposite berth, turn rudder away from pier and back engine. After headway is checked, drop the anchor.
2. Continue backing and pay out anchor rode.
3. Steer with rudder after sternway is gained. Use engine ahead and a strain on the anchor rode to check sternway.
4. Pass two stern lines, place fenders on the stern.

13-13. Mediterranean moor.

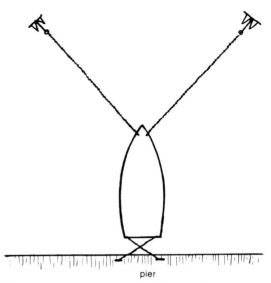

13-14. Mediterranean moor for large ship.

stern, and haul on the shore line while paying out the anchor rode until the stern reaches the pier.

A final use of the anchor is to "snub" it underfoot when attempting a landing with an onsetting wind. The anchor is let go to windward so that it just touches bottom beneath the bow. In this case, the anchor does not hold; it drags just enough to keep the bow from "sailing" downwind faster than the stern. With the anchor controlling the bow, the engines and rudder are used to maneuver the stern during the landing.

Tugs, towing, and freeing a grounded vessel

The use of tug boats is generally restricted to large ships in crowded harbors or narrow channels. Occasionally, a very large yacht might use a "pusher boat" (a work boat with fenders) to assist in a difficult maneuver such as a Mediterranean moor. Most yachts of this size have twin screws, however, and as we will see later in this chapter, they can be easily handled by using their engines, rudder, lines, and anchor.

There is one maneuver in which your powerboat may do the work of a tug—that is, when towing a vessel in distress or a sailboat that is becalmed. Towing safely is not easy, and every step must be very carefully planned well in advance to assure success.

When towing, there are no hard and fast rules. Analyze each situation before taking action, but never try to tow a capsized boat unless, perhaps, she

has been righted. Assisting capsized boats will be discussed in more detail in the next chapter. If the vessel requiring assistance is not aground, you may approach her from either her windward or leeward side. When approaching from the windward side, you provide a lee for the disabled boat that may be helpful, but the boats will tend to be blown together while the tow line is passed. Usually the better approach is from the leeward side. Before starting your approach, be sure the tow line is made fast, properly led, and ready for passing. Make your approach at an angle across the bow of the disabled vessel, and pass the tow line to the disabled vessel as it's bow is crossed. Once the tow line has been passed, pay it out slowly, allowing your boat enough slack to come up into the wind before taking a strain.

Coming head to wind is important, because it allows your boat to maintain her position while waiting for the tow line to be secured on the disabled vessel. Take great care while paying out the tow line not to let it foul your propeller.

If the tow line should foul the propeller, put the gear in neutral immediately and then try reversing the engine slowly. If this fails, the line will have to be cleared by a diver who can unwrap it, or cut it away. Another tow line will have to be passed, and it might be wise to anchor while the old tow line is being cleared.

When the tow line has been secured on the disabled vessel, take up the strain very slowly. It is at this point, when the inertia of the vessel under tow is greatest, that the danger of parting the tow line becomes critical. Increase speed slowly until both vessels have adequate steerageway. Maximum towing speed will be determined by wind and sea conditions and by the size of the vessels, but it should always be moderate. More than a few displacement yachts have been lost by large vessels towing them above their hull speed (see chapter 3). Remember that towing another vessel puts a double load on the engine and severely reduces the maneuverability of your boat.

The amount of tow line will vary with the sea condition. In calm water, several boat lengths should separate the boats, but in a rough sea, considerably more scope should be used. The more scope, the more spring and the less sudden strain on the tow line and towed boat. Although it is desirable to have the two boats in the same position relative to

231

crests and troughs, the seas are seldom regular enough to achieve this.

Assisting a vessel that has gone hard aground presents many additional problems. First, you must determine how hard she is aground. Taking soundings around the boat with a fathometer, a lead line, or any light line rigged with a weight and marked with strips of cloth or string to indicate depth, will give the quickest indication of the depth of water around the boat. Also check the nautical chart carefully, and accurately fix your position. A thorough inspection below decks will determine if the boat has maintained its watertight integrity. If the boat has been holed, you should attempt to plug or repair any leaks before continuing action to remove the boat from a shoal. Successful repairs of this nature have been made using mattresses, life jackets, sails, boards, table tops, or wooden plugs. The idea is to slow the flow of water into the boat to the point that a bilge pump can keep up with any flooding. If she is high and dry, any efforts to dislodge her will end in parted tow lines or damaged gear. Offer to set an anchor to windward and let the tide take care of the rest. If, however, she is not too hard aground, you may render towing assistance with caution. Most often, the grounded vessel will be on a lee shore, with the wind pushing her farther onto the shoal. In this situation, your approach must be made directly downwind, and you must take great care not to run aground in the process. To prevent this, set an anchor well to windward and ease back towards the grounded vessel, using the anchor to hold the bow into the wind. Once the tow line has been passed, increase the strain gradually while still using the anchor to keep from being blown broadside to the wind. After the grounded vessel has been freed, pick up the anchor, and if the vessel can proceed under her own power, cast her off when she is ready. If not, take her in tow, remembering the precautions mentioned in the preceding section.

If the situation is reversed and you have run aground, there is an excellent chance that you will be able to get off if you act quickly enough. When the boat has power, it should be used whether the boat is under sail or power at the instant of grounding. If under sail, lower the sails immediately. Try to back the boat off in the direction from which she came, as there is always good water astern. Put the engine in full reverse and move the entire crew,

perhaps even the helmsman, to the bow. As most sailboats are deepest aft, this tends to lessen the draft. The wash from the reversed engine will tend to free the keel from mud or sand. The crew can help by rhythmically jumping in unison on the bow. If this procedure does not free the boat in a few minutes, do not continue it, because prolonged running of the engine in full reverse will overheat it. Whether this action gets the boat off or not, be sure to check the saltwater cooling system intake strainer for weeds and sand before proceeding. You may have to go overboard to check the through-hull fitting for the saltwater system.

If the boat has not been freed by the above method, other steps, such as kedging or heeling the boat, will have to be taken. Review *Shoal Water* in chapter 2. Two points should be reemphasized. If you accept help from another boat, you must remain in charge of the situation as it affects your boat, and you should be ready to take immediate action to avoid having a would-be rescuer inadvertently damage your boat. In this regard, it is well to convey your exact intention to the boat rendering assistance before any maneuvering starts, as once engines begin to strain, communications may be difficult. Secondly, it is much better to wait for the tide to rise than to damage a boat while trying to get her off.

System of shiphandling

Midshipmen at the Naval Academy study an excellent book, *Naval Shiphandling*, by Captain R. S. Crenshaw, Jr. In this classic work on naval vessels, Captain Crenshaw provides a simple three-step system for shiphandling that is worth repeating. The beginner must understand that these steps are based on his having a very sound knowledge of his craft and how it reacts to a variety of weather conditions. Once these factors are understood, a systematic approach to each problem can begin. The three steps listed below are reprinted with permission from pages 6 and 7 of *Naval Shiphandling*.

1. Measure the situation. Measure the ranges and bearings important to the maneuver. Measure the ship's speed, the depth of water, the velocity of the wind.

2. Calculate the maneuver. Calculate the ranges at which to turn, the bearings at which the speed should be changed, the time to maintain a course.

3. Check and correct. As the maneuver

progresses, continual revaluation of the situation is required. At each opportunity the accuracy of the maneuver should be checked and corrections made as required. There are too many variables to expect the initial solution to hold good throughout an extended maneuver.

Every experienced skipper instinctively goes through these three steps each time he maneuvers his craft. The beginner should make a conscious effort to remember the steps and learn boathandling as a precise science. Once again, shiphandling can be studied from books, but it can only be learned by practicing at sea.

Single-screw boats

In discussing the forces acting on power-driven vessels thus far, most of the examples have referred to a single-screw boat. This section will build on these examples. When the single-screw craft is thoroughly understood, the understanding of a twin-screw craft is a logical extension of this knowledge and experience.

Since the most difficult maneuvers for the shiphandler usually occur in restricted waters or around the pier, the following examples of docking situations should be studied carefully. In preparing for a docking maneuver, it is important that the entire evolution be worked out ahead of time, including an alternative plan to be used if the initial approach fails at any point in its execution. The experienced seaman always tries to keep himself from getting into a situation from which he cannot recover. He makes elaborate preparations even for a simple maneuver. An anchor should always be ready for use in any situation where engine failure would endanger or embarrass the boat. Under some circumstances, a ready stern anchor may also be necessary. In every case, dock lines should be ready and led. Fenders should be out, but preferably not over the side until near the pier. Most important, the crew should be briefed on the skipper's plan and exactly what their individual jobs will be. Confusion at the last minute is the cause of most unseamanlike docking maneuvers. The crew, once briefed, should keep out of the skipper's way, and out of his line of vision.

As noted earlier, a single-screw boat (having a right-hand propeller) with rudder amidships tracks slightly to port when going ahead and backs very

13-15. Back and fill, turn to starboard.

noticeably to port with sternway. With this in mind, a few additional examples will provide a basic understanding of single-screw characteristics.

One of the operating parameters you should be familiar with is the turning circle of the boat. Knowing the boat's advance and transfer is enough in open water. But suppose you have to turn the boat around in a very tight space, such as a harbor or narrow channel? The maneuver is not usually difficult, although it does take practice.

Turning to starboard is easier since the tendency to back to port will assist the maneuver. Figure 13-15 shows how to "back and fill" in a tight spot. Notice that the rudder remains to the right throughout the maneuver. *Don't forget to determine the effects of wind and current.*

Turning to port is more difficult since each 10 degrees of compass heading gained while going ahead is quickly lost as the boat backs to port. Figure 13-16 shows a very easy method, using the anchor snubbed underfoot on the port bow.

When making a landing, it is easier to dock port side to the pier because the stern will swing toward the pier when the engine is reversed. Figure 13-17A shows a line of approach of about 15 degrees. Make the approach at the slowest speed possible. Continually think ahead and develop alternative actions so that you are prepared if you should suddenly lose power or rudder control.

13-16. Snubbing an anchor.

233

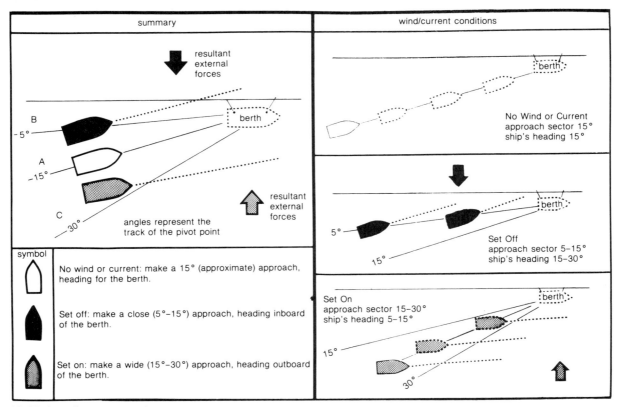

13-17. Landing approaches.

Backing away from the berth while moored port side to the pier is more difficult than backing away would be if the boat were moored on the starboard side. The text accompanying figure 13-12 discussed a method of getting underway if there is a strong wind or current pinning the boat against the pier. If the wind is not very strong, the boat may be maneuvered by springing the stern away from the pier.

First, the bow line, stern line, and quarter spring are taken in; then a crewman with a fender is stationed forward to fend off the bow. The engine is put ahead slowly and the rudder put over toward the pier. The boat pivots slowly against the bow spring. Power is kept on until the bow comes in against the forward fender and the stern swings away from the pier. When the stern is well away from the pier, the engine is reversed smartly, the rudder is shifted, and the bow spring is taken in. If the wind is not too strong, the boat can be backed rapidly away from the pier. When the wind is strong, there is the danger that the bow will scrape along the pier before the boat can be backed clear. If this is the case, the rudder should not be shifted immediately,

allowing the boat to back in a direction more parallel to the pier, until the bow is well clear. In this maneuver, it should be remembered that the torque effect of a right-hand screw tends to walk the stern to port. In all cases the boat should be backed smartly to avoid being blown back against the pier. Again, practice is essential.

Landing downwind can be one of the most challenging and frustrating maneuvers faced by beginners and experts alike. The situation is made even more difficult if the boat is running with a fair current during the approach. Needless to say, if there are no other boats alongside the pier, the problem is somewhat easier. Figure 13-18 shows a very flat approach in which you must take great care not to get the stern stuck out too far into the wind or current. You will have to maintain power throughout the maneuver since steerageway will be

13-18. Approach for downwind landing.

lost while the boat is still making some speed over the ground. Just as the berth is reached, you must undertake three actions quickly. Place the rudder hard left *and* back down hard. The left rudder will move the bow toward the pier, while the side force from the backing screw forces the stern to port. The result is that the boat slows down and moves parallel to the berth. Adjust the engine speed so that the boat's position is maintained. When the boat starts to back down, the crew must pass a line from the stern or port quarter to the pier. This keeps the stern into the pier and prevents the boat turning end for end, which could occur had a bow line been passed first. This after spring line also allows the wind and current to settle the bow into the berth. Note that the engine, not the line, is used to kill headway.

If the same situation exists and the landing must be made with the boat's starboard side against the pier, again the stern line is the secret to success. You must make a very flat, slow approach. Just *before* reversing the engine, put the rudder over hard left to push the stern toward the pier. After the stern line is passed, reverse the engine to cause the boat to back to port and prevent the starboard quarter from striking the pier. If other boats are fore and aft of the desired berth during a downwind landing, the approach should still be as flat as possible without risking a collision with the boats already moored. In some cases, of course, it may be possible to turn the boat around and bring her into the berth against the wind and current. Upwind landings are normally much easier.

Getting underway by backing clear or using the anchor with an onsetting wind was described earlier. Frequently the boat must get underway by going ahead. If the boat is on the leeward side of the pier, this is an easy maneuver. The spring lines are taken in followed by the bow and stern lines at the same time. Remember that the bow will blow downwind faster than the stern. It may be necessary to steer back toward the pier for a few seconds to keep the boat straight before proceeding out ahead. In any case, you should not make a sharp turn away from the pier until the stern is well clear. This could result in the stern striking pilings or boats moored at the pier. In the event of wind and/or current against the bow, the boat can be backed against a forward quarter spring (with fender at the stern) to move the bow away from the pier.

Twin-screw boats

Once you understand the forces involved in handling a single-screw boat, a twin-screw boat will seem relatively easy. The two shafts are offset some distance from the centerline, and most boats have twin rudders, one directly behind each screw. The two screws rotate in opposite directions so that when going ahead the starboard screw rotates clockwise and the port screw counterclockwise. Each screw generates a side force, but since the directions of these forces are opposite, a twin-screw boat will track straight ahead and astern with the rudders amidships and no wind present (see figure 13-20). With the rudders amidships and only the starboard engine turning ahead, the boat will make a slow turn to port. This is a result of the side force and the offset screw. Conversely, the side force and offset propeller will cause the boat to track slowly to starboard when going ahead on the port screw with the rudder amidships.

Turning a twin-screw boat in a narrow channel or harbor is very simple. The boat is "twisted" around to starboard by placing the port engine ahead and the starboard astern. These two opposing forces act through a moment arm to the centerline of the boat, causing the boat to twist around in its own length. It is not necessary to use the rudder while twisting, although the rate of turn can be increased by placing the rudder over in the direction of the turn (see figure 13-21). Notice that only the port rudder is effective, since it is the only rudder that has propeller wash being directed across it. Also, notice how the wheel effect helps accelerate the turn.

If there is wind present, the twin-screw boat will

235

13-19. The helm and controls on a 42-foot, twin-engine, diesel-powered offshore yacht. Clutches are on the left and throttles on the right.

Sail and Power

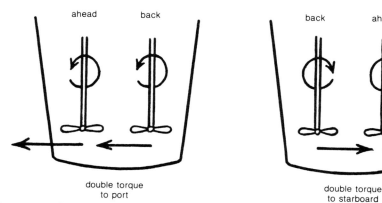

both engines going ahead

torque port screw

torque starboard screw

port cancels starboard with resulting zero wheel effect

both engines going astern

port cancels starboard with resulting zero wheel effect

236

ahead   back

double torque to port

back   ahead

double torque to starboard

13-20. Wheel effect on vessels with opposed twin screws.

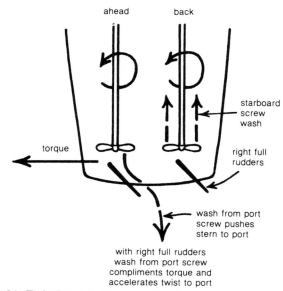

ahead   back

torque

starboard screw wash

right full rudders

wash from port screw pushes stern to port

with right full rudders wash from port screw compliments torque and accelerates twist to port

13-21. Twisting a twin-screw boat.

be affected in the same manner as the single-screw vessel. It will back into the wind since on most boats the "sail area" is concentrated forward of the pivot point. However, this is easily overcome by using the engines, the rudders, or a combination of the two. Figure 13-22 shows a twin-screw vessel backing into the wind when the skipper wants to go straight back toward point A. The course can be corrected by stopping the port engine or speeding up the starboard engine. The rudders can also be placed over full left to achieve positive course control since a

prop wash from screws

wind

actual course

desired course

point A

Correction alternatives:
1. Stop the port engines; or
2. turn rudders left; or
3. speed up the starboard engine.

13-22. Backing with twin screws.

13-23. A small, retrieve-only electric capstan on a Hatteras 42-foot motor yacht. The motor controller is the rubber-covered button in the foreground. Note the neatly flemished mooring lines.

twin-screw boat will respond quite well to the rudders when backing. Remember there is no dominating side force causing the boat to back to port.

Landing at the pier may be accomplished easily on the port or starboard side with the twin-screw boat. As the boat nears the berth during a port-side landing, and the headway slows, the rudder is placed right and the starboard engine is backed to kill headway and swing the boat parallel to the pier. The same procedure is followed if the landing is on the starboard side except that the rudder is turned left and the port engine is backed. The first line to be passed ashore is the after bow spring. It should not be used to stop the boat's headway. If the line is "held" before the headway is killed, the bow will be brought too violently into contact with the pier.

Getting underway from the berth is normally accomplished by taking in the bow line, the forward quarter spring, and the stern line. The boat is then twisted about the after bow spring so that the stern is moved out into the stream. One of the crew should place a fender along the bow to prevent scraping the side during the twisting. Once the stern is clear, the bow spring is taken in and the boat backed smartly into the channel. If there is an onsetting wind it is important to get the line on deck and commence backing before the boat has a chance to settle back down on the pier.

If there is clear space astern (about four boat lengths) and the pier is solid, the boat can be backed out of the berth without a spring, using only the inboard engine. All lines are taken in and the boat

lies on her fenders against the pier. The inboard engine is backed down smartly and the rudder is turned away from the pier. This forms a cushion of water for the bow. The inboard engine and outward-turned rudder bring the stern away from the pier while the rapidly building wash lets the bow ride the cushion of water without striking the pier. Nevertheless, a fender should be used at the bow.

When going out ahead, the twin-screw boat can often be "walked" away from the pier by alternating twists. Care must be taken to maneuver slowly so that neither headway nor sternway is gathered. Once the boat is clear of the pier, both engines are placed ahead, and the rudders control the course into the channel. An alternate method is to spring the bow out around a fender placed on the stern. With all lines taken in except the stern line, the engines are used to twist the stern into the pier while the quarter is protected by a large fender. This twisting action is not nearly as efficient as when twisting around the bow spring since the propellers are so close to the pivot point of the boat. When the bow is turned clear, the stern line is taken in, and the boat goes ahead on both engines. Do not turn the boat away from the pier until the stern is well clear. The rudders must remain amidships or be turned slightly toward the pier to prevent the quarter from striking the pier as the boat gets underway.

Just as the sailboat skipper should practice docking under sail, the twin-screw-boat skipper should practice handling his craft with two propellers and then with one propeller only. Use either the port or starboard screw under a variety of weather conditions. Also try steering using the engines alone. It takes some extra time for these practice sessions, but they are well worth it if you should suddenly lose an engine or suffer a steering casualty.

Backing into slip—single- and twin-screw boats

With the large number of boats on the water today, most marinas offer slips instead of a berth alongside a dock. A slip is a space at right angles to the pier with piles set to seaward as shown in figure 13-24A. The slip may also have a small finger pier or catwalk built from the pier to facilitate access to the boat.

Entering a slip bow first is a simple procedure as long as you remember to maneuver slowly. There is little margin for error in most slips and having your

237

13-24. A. Backing into a slip.

238

13-24. B. The flexibility offered by twin screws makes backing this boat into a slip a relatively easy task. The effects of wind and current may be overcome with the proper use of the engines and lines. Normally the rudder may be left amidships while the skipper uses the engines to maintain position as the boat is backed into the slip.

engine fail as you approach the seawall can obviously be disastrous if the boat is moving too fast. To make the job of entering a slip easier, most owners attach mooring lines permanently to the piles so that they may be picked up by hand or with a boat hook as the boat passes between the piles. Properly tended around cleats, the lines may be used to check the boat's forward progress in the event that there is a problem with the engine. If the boat is entering the slip with excessive headway, the load placed on lines, deck fittings, and the line handler's hands may be too great to check the boat's forward progress.

If the slip does not have a finger pier, many skippers prefer to back into the slip since it is easier to offload passengers and gear over the stern. Backing into a slip with a single-screw boat may appear difficult at first, but with practice this becomes

another routine maneuver. A thorough understanding of how your boat handles while backing in various wind and current conditions is necessary before entering a crowded marina. You should also take time to brief the crew on their duties and what you desire in the way of line handling or tending a fender.

When the wind is from dead ahead or dead astern, the boat must simply be backed straight into the slip. It is when there is a strong beam wind or current that the process of backing into the slip can become a real challenge for the boathandler.

If your boat will only back straight down with the rudder over hard right, you should position it to windward of your slip before backing. This allows room to leeward as you maneuver at slow speed into position. Fenders should be rigged on both sides of the boat and your crew should be in position to handle lines without obstructing your view. As you enter the slip, the windward lines should be picked up first and the boat held up to weather until you are positioned fore and aft in the slip. The leeward lines may be passed and adjusted later.

There are some slips where there is not enough room around them to position the boat to weather before backing in a strong beam wind. If this is the case, you may have to back upwind at right angles to the slip. Since most boats back into the wind you should have excellent directional control. Maneuver the stern up to the windward pile. The leeward pile will now be amidships. Make sure that you have the crew hold a fender in between the hull and this pile to prevent damage to the sides. The boat now can be backed against a line led from the quarter to the leeward pile. This force, together with manually pulling the stern around the windward pile, will twist the boat into the slip stern first. You may now use slow bursts of astern power to bring the boat farther into the slip. Backing down will also help keep the stern from blowing down toward the slip to leeward. The crew must remember to constantly adjust the fender on the lee bow as the boat maneuvers around the leeward pile into the slip. As the stern nears the seawall, the windward stern line is passed and the boat is held to windward in the slip. Taut lines permanently rigged between outer pilings and pilings at the pier are a help in that they give the crew who are stationed at the rail something to haul on.

Sailboats under power

The examples presented earlier apply to both motorboats and auxiliary-powered sailboats such as the 44s and Luders yawls. There are, however, some significant differences that the skipper must be aware of when handling a sailboat under power.

To begin with, auxiliary engines are just that: a secondary source of power. The sailor should practice difficult maneuvers under power as well as under sail until he is completely comfortable with the boat under all conditions. Auxiliary sailboats have small propellers, because they have small engines and also because of the need to minimize drag when under sail. Many sailboats are equipped with *feathering* or *folding* propellers that fold into a streamlined shape when not in use. While these are excellent for reducing underwater resistance, they may not provide much power for a large sailboat.

Most auxiliary sailboats with long, deep keels will track straight with a beam wind much longer than a shallow-draft boat with a short keel. The large longitudinal area of lateral plane reduces the amount of leeway and yaw when underway. Handling smaller centerboard boats that have either an outboard motor or a small inboard auxiliary can be very difficult in adverse weather conditions. The skipper should always plan ahead and allow a margin for error when there is a strong wind in the vicinity of the pier.

A final factor that is often remembered only after the skipper hears a loud, disturbing noise, is that sailboats have standing rigging and spreaders to support this rigging. Look aloft when making an approach alongside another sailboat. Before making fast you may have to adjust the boat's position forward or aft several feet in order to maintain safe clearance between the rigs.

Gasoline auxiliary engines

Although most Navy auxiliaries are diesel powered, gasoline engines are found on the majority of small- to medium-sized sailboats that are not owned by the

13-25. A smart Alden ketch that might be described as an 80-20 motor-sailor type. This boat can perform very well under power as well as under sail. Note that everything on deck is neatly stowed. Sail handling is simplified with the roller-furling jib, self-tending staysail, and gallows frame that supports the main boom. The dinghy is conveniently carried in stern davits, but it might need stowing on deck in heavy weather at sea.

LIFTING EYE

WATER OUTLET
⅜″ PIPE SIZE

SHIFTER LEVER

TEMPERATURE CONTROL
THERMOSTAT

NAME PLATE

EXHAUST FLANGE

BREATHER PIPE AND
OIL FILLER

MANIFOLD DRAIN PLUG

THROTTLE LEVER

THRUST BEARING

OIL SEAL

FUEL INLET

FUEL PUMP BOWL

OIL PRESSURE ADJUSTMENT

FUEL PUMP

HAND PRIMER

OIL PRESSURE
GAUGE CONNECTION

CHOKE LEVER

OIL DRAIN HOLE

FLAME ARRESTOR

MAIN FUEL VALVE ADJUSTMENT

IDLE NEEDLE VALVE

13-26. A. The Universal Atomic Four gasoline engine.

DISTRIBUTOR

ALTERNATOR

TRANSISTORIZED REGULATOR

COIL

OIL LEVEL
DIP STICK

WATER INLET
⅜″ PIPE SIZE

STARTER SOLENOID

THRUST BEARING

OIL SEAL

STARTING MOTOR

SHAFT HALF
COUPLING

ENGINE HALF
COUPLING

WATER PUMP

DRAIN PLUG

WATER PUMP
GREASE CUP

TACHOMETER
TAKE-OFF

CYLINDER BLOCK
DRAIN COCK

DRIVE BELT

OIL DRAIN PLUG

BELT TIGHTENER ARM

13-26. B. Opposite side view of the Universal Atomic Four gasoline engine.

240

Navy. The principal advantage of a diesel engine is that it uses a relatively safe fuel that will not readily explode. Also, diesels are generally considered more reliable due to the fact that they have no electrical ignition systems that can be affected by dampness. On the other hand, gasoline engines are considerably cheaper in initial cost, though their fuel is more expensive and is consumed faster than diesel oil. They are lighter in weight, and are less seriously affected by a major source of engine failure—water in the fuel. This is because fuel mixed with air usually is fed into the cylinders through a gasoline engine's carburetor, which is more forgiving of water than the injectors that introduce fuel to the cylinders of a diesel engine. Then, too, there is sometimes greater condensation in diesel tanks because some heated fuel (not consumed by the injectors) is often returned to the tank. As for the safety disadvantage of gasoline, engines using this fuel need not be dangerous so long as proper safety precautions are taken. These safeguards will be discussed in some detail later in this section. The most commonly used gasoline engine in the typical small- to medium-sized U.S. auxiliary sailboat has been the Universal Atomic Four, illustrated in figure 13-26. This is a compact, four-cylinder engine, designed specifically for marine use, that develops 30 horsepower near top speed, at about 3500 RPM. Average fuel consumption is approximately two quarts per hour at 1000 RPM, four quarts per hour at 2000 RPM, and six quarts per hour at 3000 RPM. On a light-displacement boat with a small propeller that causes little drag under sail, the engine's drive is usually direct, but on a heavy boat with a larger propeller, a reduction gear is often used with a ratio of perhaps two to one. In other words, with this ratio the engine will be turning over twice as fast as the propeller.

More often than not, these engines are cooled with seawater, but they may be had with a closed, freshwater cooling system similar to that used with the Westerbeke diesel. The principal advantage of a closed system is that it prolongs the engine's life, especially in areas where the water is very salty or polluted with chemicals. Exhaust pipes should be water jacketed or well insulated to prevent the possibility of hot metal starting a fire. The exhaust system should have a high loop or "swan neck" in the line to stop seawater from being forced back into the manifold during heavy weather when the

engine is not running. Of course, it is desirable that there be an outlet shut-off similar to that on a Luders yawl (see figure 8-21), but great care must be taken to see that the valve is open before the engine is started.

The fuel system of any gasoline engine should be very carefully installed so that no leaks can develop, as these could cause a definite explosion hazard. Some important points concerning the gas tank installation are shown in figure 13-27. Other points

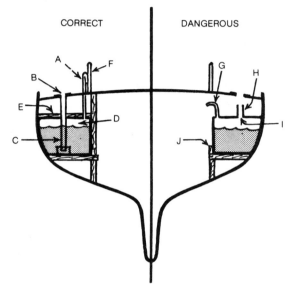

13-27. Gas tank installation.
A—Vent pipe above deck (opening bent down and facing aft, with pipe well secured and bent into a circle to assure that no water will enter).
B—Fill pipe connected to deck plate with a flexible section electrically connected (normally with a wire) to the metal part of the fill pipe just above the grounded tank.
C—Fill pipe preferably running to bottom of tank with well to form liquid seal.
D—Tank with baffles (avoid soldered seams). There should be a fuel line shut-off valve near tank with control outside tank's compartment.
E—Padded supports or straps at top as well as sides and bottom of tank.
F—Vent fastened to coaming or cabin side, but bent or looped to keep water out.
G—Vent pipe below deck. Fumes escape below.
H—Fill pipe not attached to deck plate. Gas can spill and fumes escape when fueling.
I—No fill pipe to bottom of tank. Tank can possibly explode from ignited fill pipe.
J—Tank not adequately supported.
(***Note:*** Storage battery should be in ventilated lead-lined or fiberglass box with a cover to prevent metal objects falling on battery terminals.)

Table 13-2. Troubleshooting procedures for the Universal Atomic Four gasoline engine.

Trouble	Probable Cause	Correction
Starter will not crank engine	Discharged battery	Charge or replace battery.
	Corroded battery terminals	Clean terminals.
	Loose connection in starting circuit	Check and tighten all connections.
	Defective starting switch	Replace switch.
	Starter motor brushes dirty	Clean or replace brushes.
	Jammed Bendix gear	Loosen starter motor to free gear.
	Defective starter motor	Replace motor.
Starter motor turns but does not crank engine	Partially discharged battery	Charge or replace battery.
	Defective wiring or wiring of too low capacity	Check wiring for worn acid spots. See manual for proper size wire.
	Broken Bendix drive	Remove starter motor and repair drive.
Engine will not start	Empty fuel tank	Fill tank with proper fuel.
	Flooded engine	Remove spark plugs and crank engine several times. Replace plugs.
	Water in fuel system	If water is found, clean tank, fuel lines, and carburetor. Refill with proper fuel.
	Inoperative or sticking choke valve	Check valve, linkage, and choke rod or cable for proper operation.
	Improperly adjusted carburetor	Adjust carburetor.
	Clogged fuel lines or defective fuel pump	Disconnect fuel line at carburetor. If fuel does not flow freely when engine is cranked, clean fuel line and sediment bowl. If fuel still does not flow freely after cleaning, repair or replace pump.
Engine will not start (Poor compression and other causes)	Air leak around intake manifold	Check for leak by squirting oil around intake connections. If leak is found, tighten manifold and if necessary replace gaskets.
	Loose spark plugs	Check all plugs for proper seating, gasket, and tightness. Replace all damaged plugs and gaskets.
	Loosely seating valves	Check for broken or weak valve springs, warped stems, carbon and gum deposits, and insufficient tappet clearance.
	Damaged cylinder head gasket	Check for leaks around gasket when engine is cranked. If a leak is found, replace gasket.
	Worn or broken piston rings	Replace broken and worn rings. Check cylinders for "out of round" and "taper."
Excessive engine temperature	No water circulation	Check for clogged water lines and restricted inlets and outlets. Check for broken or stuck thermostat. Look for worn or damaged water pump or water pump drive.
Engine temperature too low	Broken or stuck thermostat	Replace thermostat.
Engine will not start (ignition system)	Ignition switch "off" or defective	Turn on switch or replace.
	Fouled or broken spark plugs	Remove plugs and inspect for cracked porcelain, dirty points, or improper gap.

242

Table 13-2. (con't.)

Trouble	Probable Cause	Correction
Engine will not start (ignition system)	Improperly set, worn, or pitted distributor points. Defective ignition coil.	Remove center wire from distributor cap and hold within 3/8 inch of motor block. Crank engine. Clean, sharp spark should jump between wire and block when points open. Clean and adjust points. If spark is weak or yellow after adjustment of points, replace condenser. If spark still is weak or not present, replace ignition coil.
	Wet, cracked, or broken distributor	Wipe inside surface of distributor dry with clean cloth. Inspect for cracked or broken parts. Replace parts where necessary.
	Improperly set, worn, or pitted magneto breaker points (magneto models only)	Remove spark plug wire and hold within 3/8 inch of engine block. Clean, sharp spark should jump between wire and block when engine is cranked. If spark is weak or not present clean and adjust breaker points. Remove spark plug wire and hold within 1/8 inch of engine block. A clean spark should jump between wire and block when engine is cranked. Clean and set timer points. If spark still is not present when engine is cranked, replace coil.
	Improper timing	Set timing.
No oil pressure	Defective gauge or tube	Replace gauge or tube.
	No oil in engine	Refill with proper grade oil.
	Dirt in pressure relief valve	Clean valve.
	Defective oil pump, leak in oil lines or broken oil pump drive	Check oil pump and oil pump drive for worn or broken parts. Tighten all oil line connections.
Loss of RPM (Boat or associated equipment)	Damaged propeller or barnacles	Repair propeller and clean.
	Bent rudder	Repair.
	Misalignment	Realign engine to shaft.
	Too tight stuffing box packing gland	Adjust.
	Dirty boat bottom	Clean.
Vibration	Misfiring or pre-ignition	See correction under misfiring and pre-ignition.
	Loose foundation or foundation bolts	Tighten nuts.
	Propeller shaft out of line or bent	Check that both blades of folding prop are open.
	Propeller bent or pitch out of true	
Pre-ignition	Defective spark plugs	Check all spark plugs for broken porcelain, burned electrodes or electrodes out of adjustment. Replace all defective plugs or clean and reset.
	Improper timing	See engine manual.
	Engine carbon	Remove cylinder head and clean out carbon.
	Engine overheating	See correction under "Engine Temp" portion of this table.

Table 13-2. (con't.)

Trouble	Probable Cause	Correction
Back-firing	Insufficient fuel reaching engine due to dirty lines, strainer, or blocked fuel tank vent. Water in fuel	See correction under "Engine will not start" portion of this table.
	Poorly adjusted distributor.	See correction under "Engine will not start" portion of this table.
Low oil pressure	Too light body oil	Replace with proper weight oil.
	Oil leak in pressure line	Inspect all oil lines. Tighten all connections.
	Weak or broken pressure relief valve spring	Replace spring.
	Worn oil pump	Replace pump.
	Worn or loose bearings	Replace bearings.
Oil pressure too high	Too heavy body oil	Drain oil and replace with oil of proper weight.
	Stuck pressure relief valve	Clean or replace valve.
	Dirt or obstruction in lines	Drain and clean oil system. Check for bent or flattened oil lines and replace where necessary.
Sludge in oil	Infrequent oil changes	Drain and refill with proper weight oil.
	Water in oil	Drain and refill. If trouble persists check for cracked block, defective head gasket, and cracked head.
	Dirty oil filter	Replace filter.

are that the tank should be grounded, the fuel line should lead from the top of the tank, and there should be a shut-off valve at the tank connection. Fuel lines should be well secured and protected from vibration by flexible connections at the engine. Furthermore, there should be shut-off valves on the fuel line to allow the engine to be serviced without spilling fuel. Also, of course, there must be an adequate ventilation system meeting Coast Guard approval, and a sparkproof blower located high up in the air exhaust outlet.

Atomic Four engines, like the Westerbeke, can have Morse controls. It is preferable that cockpit controls be recessed so that they will not be fouled by lines or be bumped into accidentally, but one type of Morse control has removable handles that make recessing of the throttle unnecessary. The throttle, which regulates the engine's speed and is often susceptible to being moved inadvertently, can be controlled very easily on the Morse model by turning its notched hub when the handle is removed.

Starting procedure for the Atomic Four or a similar gasoline auxiliary engine is as follows:

• Check the lubricating oil with the oil-level dip stick (see figure 13-26B).

• Check the fuel in the tank to see that there is an ample supply. Turn on the fuel supply valve located at the tank and any other valve in the fuel line. These valves are usually manual lever types that can be opened by turning the handle a quarter of a revolution. When the handle is perpendicular to the fuel line, the valve is closed, but when it is parallel to the line the valve is open.

• Open the seawater intake valve and exhaust valve, if there is one, at the exhaust pipe outlet.

• Turn on the main electric switch. Usually this will be a three-way master switch similar to the Perko used with the Westerbeke, which has "All," "Battery one," and "Battery two" positions. Caution should be exercised in switching from one battery to the other when the engine is running because of the possibility of damaging the alternator. Don't pass through the "Off" position to change from battery one to two, and be sure the engine is idling if it is running when changing from one battery to the other.

• Before starting the engine, sniff the engine compartment for gas fumes. Turn on the blower and let it run for about five minutes. Sniff the air exhaust outlet for fumes before shutting off the blower. Be sure, incidentally, that the air exhaust hose runs

13-29. A three-bladed prop on an inboard-outdrive boat. Note the steering arm that rotates the outdrive unit for steering control. Also note the twin trim tabs on either side of the stern. These are controlled from the cockpit to keep this planing hull craft at optimum trim.

13-28. Outboard mounting and steering systems. The outboard engine is mounted to the transom of the boat using two screw clamps. The cables mounted to the spring-and-pulley arrangement inside the transom are linked to the steering wheel to provide a simple mechanical steering system. The bottom photo shows a small outboard that has the throttle control installed in the hand tiller, which is used to steer the boat.

from the deepest part of the bilge, because gas fumes sink to the low point. If there is water in the bilge it may be high enough to block the hose's intake; thus the bilge must be pumped almost dry.

• Check to see that the shaft lock is released if the boat has one, and insert control handles if they are removable.

• After all possible fumes have been exhausted, put gearshift clutch lever into neutral (normally the vertical position), pull the choke rod all the way out (if engine is cold), place the throttle lever at one quarter open position, turn on the ignition, and start the engine. If the engine has not been run for a long

time, fill the fuel pump bowl with the hand primer on the fuel pump (see figure 13-26A) before starting it.

• Immediately after starting the engine, push the choke in gradually until it is all the way in.

• Let the engine warm up at idling speed between 600 and 1000 RPM.

• Check the oil-pressure gauge and the exhaust outlet to see that it is emitting water. Oil pressure should show about 50 to 55 pounds for normal speeds when the engine is cold, but the pressure may go as low as 15 pounds at idling speed when the engine is hot. If water is not coming out of the exhaust, stop the engine and check the intake valve to be sure it is turned on.

• When getting underway, shift into forward at idling speeds only. When going ahead, the Morse shift lever is pushed ahead, and it is pushed aft when going into reverse.

• Should there be a lot of vibration after shifting into forward, shift back into neutral at once. Such vibration is often due to the failure of a blade on a folding propeller to fully open. The usual remedy is

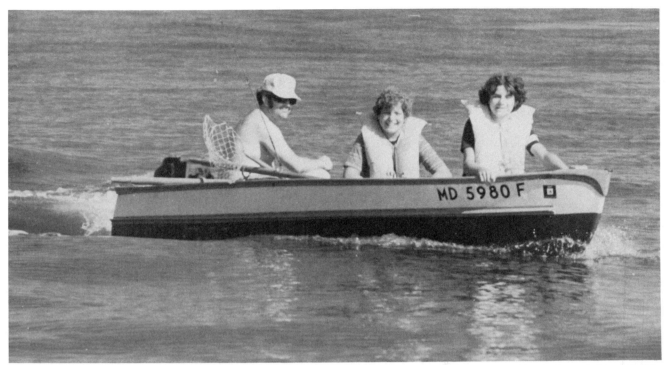

13-30. A well-operated outboard motorboat. 1. Proper weight placement fore and aft, as well as athwartships. 2. Life jackets properly used. 3. Boat has oars in case of power failure, although the oars might be better stowed.

to shift momentarily into reverse and then to shift into forward again. Allowing the vibration to continue can seriously damage the *stern tube* and *shaft log* areas (at the point where the propeller shaft penetrates the hull).

To secure the engine, simply shift into neutral, let the engine idle for a few minutes, and then turn off the ignition. The reason for letting the engine run for a short while at idling speed is to permit gradual cooling. A common mistake is to cut power suddenly when the engine is hot after it has been running at high speeds. Of course, this shuts off the cooling water, and residual heat builds up rapidly, which could be harmful to the engine, especially in locations where the water is very salty. Shut off the fuel valve, and before leaving the boat, turn off the main switch and cooling water intake.

Table 13-2 is a trouble shooting chart taken from the Universal Atomic Four engine manual. The chart covers almost every type of malfunction, and it will be most helpful to mechanics or at least mechanically minded owners with proper tools and spare parts. Unskilled boat owners should bear in mind a few simple principles when it comes to preventing engine troubles. Many problems that can

be easily prevented or corrected by the owner will have to do with moisture, dirt, or corrosion—corroded battery terminals, water or dirt in the fuel, damp ignition system, and so forth. Keep the engine and all connections (mechanical and electrical) clean and tight. Keep the fuel tank almost full to discourage condensation, and see that a good marine-type filter is installed in an accessible location on the fuel line. See that no water can enter the gas tank air vent, and be sure that the fill pipe cap is leakproof. See that the engine compartment is leakproof but well ventilated. Change the oil at regular intervals, every 40 to 50 hours according to Universal's recommendation.

Most engine ailments, aside from the ones already mentioned, come from broken or worn parts. The answer to this problem is to carry spares. The Universal Motor Division (of Medalist Industries) sells an on-board spare parts kit that includes such items as distributor points and rotor, condenser, distributor cap, coil, an extra spark plug (there should be several), water pump seal and impeller with pin, fuel pump diaphragm kit, and an alternator belt. In addition, it is a good idea to carry an ignition spray (used to protect wiring against moisture), extra lube oil (SAE 30 for the Atomic Four), several lengths of insulated electrical wire, some extra hose and hose clamps, and a small "junk" box with screws, bolts, nuts, washers, etc. Also, of course, be sure to carry an engine manual.

Although it often takes a skilled mechanic to repair a malfunctioning engine, very simple remedial actions can work surprisingly often. These actions include tapping, tightening, and drying. Tapping with a hammer is done gently to the carburetor when its valves are clogged with dirt particles, and sometimes a stuck Bendix gear can be loosened by tapping the starting motor. Tightening can often provide better electrical contacts, stop fuel leaks, and improve compression (by tightening spark plugs and intake manifold connections). Drying the ignition system can be done most simply by wiping the spark plugs and their wires and the inside of the distributor with a clean, dry rag. If spark tests are performed as suggested in the troubleshooting chart, hold the high-tension (large) wires by their insulation to guard against shocks, and be especially careful that the engine compartment is clear of gasoline fumes. When draining the gas filter, carburetor, or fuel pump, be sure to close the appropriate fuel line valves, drain into a container, wipe up any spills, and thoroughly air out the compartment and bilge before the engine is started or any electrical repairs are attempted.

Fire is an ever-present danger on any boat with an engine, whether gasoline or diesel powered. At sea, fire is a most dangerous emergency. Bilges should be kept clean. Never allow gasoline, diesel oil, or lubricating oil to accumulate. The engine room should be ventilated properly in accordance with the latest Coast Guard regulations. When the engine is running for long periods, inspect it frequently for fuel and lubricating oil leaks. To guard against broken fuel lines caused by engine vibration, flexible hose should be used between the engine and any unflexible connection. If a fire occurs, stop the engine and head off the wind to minimize relative wind velocity.

With a gasoline auxiliary, the times for *extra* caution are when fueling and when starting, especially starting after fueling or after a prolonged absence from the boat. (Figure 13-27 indicates proper and improper fuel tank installations.) Before fueling, shut off all power, turn off the stove, and stop smoking. Try to fuel up with the boat heading

so that the tanks are to leeward of the companionway. Then the gasoline fumes will be blown away from the boat, *not* down below. Remember that gasoline fumes are heavier than air and will displace the air in the cabin and engine room. When fueling, keep the nozzle of the gasoline hose in contact with the fill pipe to prevent a possible static electric spark. A static electric spark can also be caused by running water, so do not fill water tanks at the same time or immediately after filling fuel tanks. Do not spill fuel, and be very careful not to overflow the tank. After fueling, air the boat and, as mentioned earlier, run the engine room blower for at least five minutes before starting the engine. The higher the humidity and the lighter the breeze, the greater the danger from accumulated gasoline fumes. Open the engine compartment and smell for fumes *in the bilge* before starting. Also sniff the blower vent.

When securing gasoline engines prior to leaving the boat, shut off the fuel at the tank. This ensures

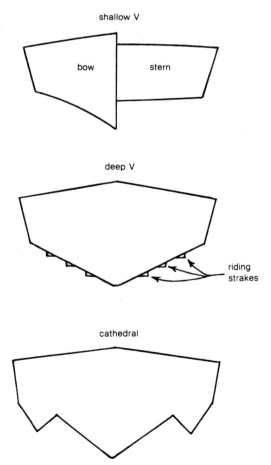

13-31. Variations on the V hull.

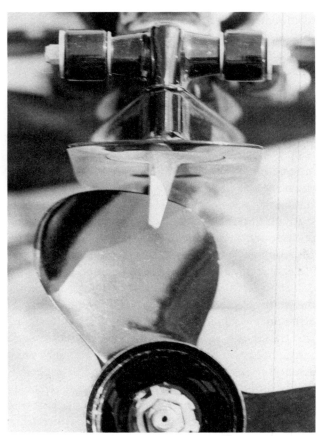

13-32. Outboard cavitation plate and trim tab. The left view shows the location of the cavitation plate above the propeller. The plate is properly called an "antiventilation" plate since it prevents air from being drawn down into the propeller from the surface. The right photograph shows the trim tab offset to port. This small steering correction counteracts side force developed by the propeller at high rotational speeds. The trim tab is also made of zinc. The zinc is sacrificed to galvanic corrosion, thus protecting the remainder of the lower unit.

against significant leakage from the carburetor into the bilge while the boat is at the mooring.

When starting a gasoline engine after a long shut-down period, it is especially important to open the engine room hatch and smell for gasoline fumes in the bilge before energizing any of the systems. Most important of all, incorporate these precautions into a routine that is *never* varied. Overconfidence and haste are the most usual causes of boat explosions and fires.

Outboard and inboard/outboard drive boats

The previous sections have discussed the handling characteristics of boats with inboard engines, rudders, and, for the most part, displacement hulls. In this section we will describe the characteristics of the most popular type of small boat found on the water today: the outboard drive. These boats generally are 12 to 24 feet in length and have aluminum

or fiberglass hulls. Supplied with modern engines, these sturdy hulls provide simple, inexpensive boating pleasure. Power for these small boats is provided by either a gasoline outboard engine or an *inboard/ outboard* (I/O) drive. The outboard engine is mounted on the boat's transom as shown in figure 13-28. The I/O drive has the engine mounted inboard with the drive, or lower, unit located outside the hull at the stern (figure 13-29).

Before beginning a discussion of the handling of these boats, it is worth repeating that it is very important for the boat owner to understand fully the operation of the craft. United States Coast Guard statistics indicate that the largest percentage of boating accidents resulting in serious injury or death occur during operation of outboard or inboard/ outboard boats. Excessive speeding, reckless operation, and the hazards associated with gasoline engines are only partly to blame. One of the most frequent accidents is capsizing or swamping the boat as a result of overloading. Also, accidents frequently result from operating in weather conditions that are beyond the capability of the boat. Troubles of this nature can be avoided with a watchful weather eye and by maintaining and operating your boat in accordance with the manufacturer's recommendations. In addition, all required safety equipment should be on board and fully operational. To assist you in learning about your boat and how it operates, both the USCG Auxiliary and the U.S. Power Squadrons offer inexpensive safe-boating classes. The USCG Auxiliary also offers a free safety inspection, the Courtesy Motorboat Examination.

Handling the small outboard drive boat is not exactly like handling the larger inboards described earlier in the chapter. The beginner should fully appreciate the differences before getting underway for the first time. Some obvious physical differences are in freeboard, displacement, and hull form. Figure 13-31 shows typical hull forms for boats from about 12 to 24 feet in length. A fourth type generally used for fishing or utility purposes is the flat-bottomed skiff shown earlier in figure 13-1. Each of these hulls has its own advantages and disadvantages, and you should find out which hull best suits your needs. Note that each hull is lightweight and has shallow draft. With the proper engine installed, these boats will get up on a plane very quickly in open water. Once on a plane and free of much of the water's resistance, speed increases rapidly. The speed produced by the planing hull and engines with high rotational speeds is another characteristic of the outboard boat. The boat will handle quite differently at planing speed than it does alongside the pier. Only practice on the water will tell you exactly how your boat handles through the wide range of speeds available.

Despite their light weight and shallow draft, most outboard boats are very stable prior to submerging their gunwales. They handle well in a moderate seaway and are normally equipped with positive buoyancy. This means that they will not sink unless perhaps very badly holed by collision. Some boats are somewhat tender initially, however, and they will respond quickly to any outside force such as a wave or shift of weight on board. For this reason, you should not step on the gunwales when boarding. The boat will not "tip over," but it may roll

toward you rapidly. This may cause you to lose your balance and fall overboard. To get on board, step, never jump, into the boat and move your weight to the centerline. The placement of passengers, as well as the battery, gasoline tanks, and other equipment, will have a significant effect on the boat's performance and handling. Normally, the boat should be trimmed so that her bow is up slightly, and of course she should not be listed or heeled.

Proper trim is very important if the outboard boat is to operate safely and achieve the performance intended by its designer. Not only must weight on board be properly placed, but also the outboard or I/O drive unit must be correctly aligned. Both vertical position and angle of the propeller have an important effect on the boat's trim and performance.

Another major difference between the inboard and the outboard boat is that the latter has no rudder. The entire engine, or drive unit, pivots so that the boat is turned by directing the propeller wash in the direction of the desired turn. This ability

249

13-33. Method of adjusting tilt for outboard engines. The pin and hole arrangement built into the mounting bracket provides the means of adjusting the tilt of this outboard engine. The tilt of the lower unit should be set so that the bow rides slightly bow up (2° to 3°) at cruising speeds. Normally this will occur when the cavitation plate is positioned parallel to the keel. Improper engine tilt and poor weight distribution can cause the boat to trim down by either the bow or stern. In both cases the hull and engine will not perform at design efficiency.

13-34. Contrasting uses of marine engines. Two uses of the same six-cylinder marine diesel are illustrated in the two top photos. The top left photo shows a Volvo-Penta engine as it would appear in an inboard mounting. In the top right photo, the engine is mated to an outdrive unit. Steering the inboard-outdrive (I/O) is accomplished by rotating the entire outdrive lower unit. Notice the cavitation plate and trim tab installed above the propeller in the top right-hand and bottom photos. The bottom photo shows a gasoline-powered inboard-outdrive marine engine.

to turn by controlling the wash moves the position of the pivot point well aft.

Every outboard and I/O drive has a cavitation or antiventilation plate (see figure 13-32) installed just above the propeller. Antiventilation is the less commonly used but more accurate term, since the plate does not prevent propeller *cavitation*. (Cavitation is the formation of a partial vacuum along the tips of the propeller when it rotates at very high speeds, a problem not normally encountered on pleasure boats if the correct propeller for the boat and engine is used.) The purpose of the cavitation plate is to prevent the propeller from drawing air down from the surface of the water into the propeller blades. When air is sucked down, the propeller meets with much less resistance. This allows the engine to race at very high speeds, which may damage the engine or drive shaft. When the transom is too high for the outboard being used, or if the engine is tilted too far

aft, the cavitation plate cannot perform its function, since the propeller is too close to the surface. Ventilation can also occur if the boat banks excessively in a hard turn so that the propeller is brought close to the surface. Properly aligned, the cavitation plate should be about an inch or so below the keel or skeg.

Figure 13-33 shows a typical method of adjusting the angle of an outboard engine using a pin and hole arrangement on the mounting bracket. The propeller shaft should be adjusted so that it is aligned horizontally with the surface of the water when the boat is on a plane. If the shaft is not adjusted so that the water flow runs parallel to the cavitation plate, the boat will either squat by the stern or hog down by the bow. Incorrect trim makes steering difficult and also slows the boat, since the planing hull is not meeting the water at the proper angle. Figure 13-29 shows trim tabs installed on the transom of an I/O

13-35. Basic damage control training during the midshipman's first summer includes becoming familiar with CO_2 fire extinguishers and standard Navy fire hoses, nozzles, and spray applicators. Here a midshipman demonstrates the use of the CO_2 fire extinguisher.

251

boat. These are adjusted, usually remotely from the helmsman's position, to keep the boat in trim with various loading and sea conditions.

When the propeller shaft is correctly positioned, there is little if any propeller side force due to the shaft angle discussed earlier in this chapter. However, many high-speed engines do generate a noticeable pull on the steering as a result of wheel effect, which is due perhaps to the lower blade being in more solid water (see figure 13-3). This is easily corrected by placing a small, adjustable vertical trim tab such as the one shown in figure 13-32 just below the cavitation plate. An alternative method is to offset the engine exhaust outlet. In both cases the slight amount of offset produces enough force at high speeds to counteract side force and keep the boat tracking straight.

Handling a small outboard or I/O alongside a pier is somewhat easier than handling larger vessels, but even if the boat is moving at slow speeds, her trim, propeller alignment, and the location of her pivot point must all be considered. You will notice that a boat with shallow draft is pushed around easily by the wind. The skillful skipper will use the directed thrust of the propeller in combination with lines and perhaps even a small anchor in very

difficult conditions to overcome the uncontrollable forces of wind and current.

A simple method of getting underway is to use a spring line as was described earlier and back clear of the pier. Bear in mind that the outboard-drive boat has excellent handling characteristics while backing. Since these small craft are very light and are often handled by one person, an even simpler method is to take in all lines and push the boat away from the pier. This will give you enough room to maneuver. Turn the boat slowly away from the pier when going out ahead. An abrupt turn of the wheel will only force the stern into the pier.

Landing alongside a pier is accomplished in the same manner as with larger craft. Get your mooring lines and fenders ready well in advance. Approach the pier at an angle of 20 to 30 degrees. Here is where you will notice an important difference in the small outboard as compared with larger displacement hulls. Without a rudder and having a shallow draft, the boat will not hold her course very well when the engine is in neutral. By shifting back and forth from ahead to neutral you can easily maintain your heading at slow speed. As the bow approaches the pier, turn the wheel all the way towards the pier and apply just enough reverse power to stop the boat. This will also bring the boat parallel to the pier. You should be close enough to the pier to step ashore with the bow line.

Since the lower unit of the engine is completely exposed, it is generally preferable to enter a slip bow first. This protects the propeller and does not pose a problem when getting underway since, as we have noted, the outboard handles so well when backing.

In boats of any size you should always check the official weather forecasts before getting underway. Once clear of the harbor, be alert for changes in the weather that could produce high winds and seas. This is particularly important in boats of the size we have been discussing. Also, keep a careful eye on your fuel supply. While it may seem overly conservative, leave at least two-thirds of your fuel supply in reserve for the trip back home. A small outboard or I/O is not much fun in a storm and even less so without power to help ride out the blow.

If you are caught by a threatening storm, one option is to try to outrun it. Make certain that you have the required fuel and that you are headed for a safe harbor before picking this course of action. If the seas pick up quickly and the boat is slamming badly from one wave to the next, slow the boat and head into the waves at a slight angle. The "Deep Vee" and cathedral hulls will be reasonably com-

fortable and will make headway against the storm. The shallow "V" and flat bottom boat will probably be better off idled down just enough to hold the boat's head almost into the waves.

When the storm is so bad that the boat cannot be comfortably controlled, it is time to set a sea anchor (see chapter 12). The sea anchor may be set either from the bow or stern, but in the latter position be sure there is ample freeboard aft. If you need to make distance to leeward but cannot control the boat in the following seas, some lines or drags, such as boat cushions or a bucket streamed astern, will help hold the stern into the seas. A word of caution should be added about going downwind in this manner. The transoms of most small boats are relatively low and the risk of taking a wave over the stern is great. The boat could be "pooped" by a large wave, filling it with water as well as flooding the engine. The preferred method is to set the anchor from the bow if it will hold the bow into the wind and seas. By careful adjustment of the throttle with the gear in reverse the boat will move slowly to leeward, for the most part sternfirst. Finally, keep weights low in the boat and keep her pumped out as much as possible. Try to rig a spray dodger from a piece of cloth to keep water from coming over the bow.

14.
Naval Academy Powerboats

*A*fter receiving their basic sail training in Lasers, windsurfers, and knockabouts, midshipmen at the Naval Academy are given instruction in powerboat handling. A midshipman, or young ensign, assigned to a ship for training or duty will soon be assigned responsibility as "boat officer" or, in effect, officer-in-charge of a boat and its crew and passengers. He will also stand watches as a junior officer of the deck under instruction on Navy ships. These are positions of great responsibility and require a detailed knowledge of seamanship and safety precautions. The Naval Academy's approach to instruction in both sail and power provides the midshipman with the fundamental knowledge and skills necessary to safely perform these duties while learning how basic principles are applied to large ships. The instruction also concentrates on teamwork and the importance of effective communications among the crew to accomplish various maneuvers.

Midshipmen are introduced to powerboat handling aboard small single-screw launches. With a crew of three midshipmen, instruction is provided in the fundamentals of handling under power, the effect of wind and waves, crew organization and teamwork, and the use of standard commands and naval phraseology. This experience prepares the midshipmen for duties in running utility or ship's boats and sets the stage for the next step in powerboat training aboard the Academy's twin-screw yard patrol (YP) craft. The YPs are 108-foot diesel-powered craft closely resembling in handling characteristics and equipment many of the ships in the fleet (see figure 14-4). The YP offers advanced seamanship training under conditions approximating those that will be encountered at sea by the newly commissioned ensign.

Professionally, YP training provides every midshipman with experience in seamanship, shiphandling, navigation, naval tactics and communications, naval phraseology, and standard shipboard procedures.

Naval Academy single-screw powerboats

After midshipmen have completed basic sail training, they use a converted mine sweeping launch (MSL) as an introduction to handling under power. These single-screw launches also afford opportunities to practice the rules of the road, chart reading and piloting, deck seamanship, handling the helm and throttles, and safe engineering practices.

14-1. MSL handling alongside.

The MSL is a 36-foot, shallow-draft, fiberglass boat (see figure 14-1). The source of power is a General Motors V-6 diesel that develops 216 horsepower at 2800 RPM. With the minesweeping equipment removed, the MSL is extremely light in weight for its engine and large 32-inch, three-bladed propeller. As a result, the MSL is very responsive to rudder and engine commands.

The MSL is capable of carrying ten passengers including the crew. Normally during training

14-2. MSL main engine components.

classes, this vessel is manned by a crew of five midshipmen and one instructor. The working crew consists of three midshipmen: a *coxswain* (the person in charge who steers the boat and runs the engine), and a *bow hook* and *stern hook* (persons in the bow and stern to handle mooring lines and fenders). Since the steering console contains all engine and electrical controls, it is not necessary to have an engineer on board.

Standard safety equipment includes life jackets for each member of the crew, two life rings, and a 15-pound CO_2 fire extinguisher. The boats do not have flotation installed and thus are suitable only for day training in the immediate vicinity of the Naval Academy.

As with most single-screw boats, the MSL has a tendency to back to port due to the effects of the propeller side force. Since the boats are so light and have a high freeboard relative to their shallow draft, they are also subject to the effects of the wind at slow speed. As noted earlier in chapter 13, wind effects can cancel the tendency to back to port, permitting a right-rudder command to take effect. This allows the coxswain to back straight or to the right once sufficient sternway is gathered.

Boat crew duties

The number of personnel in a boat crew will differ with the size of the boat. Figure 14-3 illustrates some of the small boats the midshipman is likely to encounter. These craft range from small 13-foot Boston Whalers to the large 50-foot motor launches. The Boston Whaler can be handled safely by a single individual. The majority of the other small boats carry a normal crew of four—the coxswain, an engineer, a bow hook, and a stern hook. The safety of the passengers embarked and the smartness of the boat depend to a great extent on how well these crewmen do their jobs.

Coxswain

The coxswain is in charge of the boat and is the helmsman, subject to supervision and possible relief by the boat officer or the senior line officer aboard the boat. It should be noted here that although the boat coxswain and assigned boat officer share in the responsibility for any mishap, Navy Regulations make it very clear that the final responsibility rests with the senior line officer aboard, even if that officer is only a passenger. *United States Naval Regulations* state: "When embarked in a boat the senior line officer (including commissioned warrant and warrant officers), eligible for command at sea,

14-3. Typical small boats.
(A) A Boston Whaler. All models of the Whaler boast planing hulls and high initial stability. Note that this model Whaler has a modified "V" entry at the bow that then leads to a nearly flat bottom. This model is very comfortable and safe at moderate speeds in choppy seas, although high speeds in such conditions may cause excessive pounding and spray.
(B) A 20-foot line handler and a 22-foot utility boat. The line handler is shown at full speed. Note the vertical steering lever on both boats.

(C) A 33-foot utility boat. This boat is shown running at full speed.
(D) A 50-foot motor launch and a 50-foot utility boat. Note the horizontal steering wheel on the utility boat and the tiller on the motor launch.

has authority over all persons embarked therein, and is responsible under all circumstances for the safety and management of the boat."

The coxswain is responsible for making certain that all necessary gear is aboard the boat and that it is in proper working order. The coxswain also enforces safety precautions and supervises the loading and unloading of the boat. Each boat has a posted capacity prescribing the maximum number of persons allowed aboard during good weather in a protected anchorage. The coxswain must ensure that these limits are never exceeded, and when weather is questionable or sea conditions become hazardous, the capacity must be reduced. In addition to these duties, the coxswain is responsible for proper helmsmanship and safe navigation of the boat. This includes obeying the rules of the road, careful piloting, and using common sense in handling the boat near piers, anchored vessels, and crowded channels.

Engineer

The engineer is responsible for the operation and maintenance of the engine. On the larger motor launches the engineer may control the clutch and throttles in response to *bell orders* given by the coxswain. Using the boat's bell, the coxswain has four signals to control the engines. One bell indicates ahead slow. Two bells means idle the engine in neutral. Three bells indicates back slow, and four bells means to use full throttle in whichever direction the boat is heading. In addition to these responsibilities, the engineer is responsible for the safe fueling of the boat.

Bow hook

The bow hook is the forward line handler and handles the bow line, *sea painter*, forward fenders, and the bow boat hook, from which the title is derived. The bow hook also functions as the forward lookout and should always be stationed in the forward part of the boat.

Stern hook

The stern hook handles stern lines, stern fenders, the stern boat hook, and acts as an after lookout.

The boat crew should always be in the uniform of the day, wear boat sneakers, and, when conditions warrant them, life jackets.

Boat officer responsibilities

The boat officer has a very delicate job in supervising the coxswain and crew without needlessly interfering with the coxswain's control of the boat, passengers, and crew. As noted earlier, the boat officer (or senior line officer) is ultimately responsible for the safety of the boat. As a safety observer, the boat officer should only take charge of the boat personally when absolutely necessary. In such a case, the boat officer should formally relieve the coxswain and report this fact immediately to the commanding officer upon return to either the ship or station from which the boat has embarked.

A summary of small-boat safety precautions

- All safety equipment, including life jackets, lights, fire extinguishers, and bilge pump, should be inspected regularly.
- The smoking lamp is always out.
- Passengers must always remain seated on thwarts and seats, with hands and fingers inside the gunwales.
- Boat crews must keep their stations, especially when weather conditions are unpleasant, for it is usually during these times that vigilance is most needed.
- Boats must always be properly loaded for the sea state. In heavy weather, the boat should be loaded slightly down by the stern and passengers and crew kept in life jackets.
- Bilges should be kept free of oil and debris.
- Shafts and engine equipment should be kept covered.
- All passengers should be kept clear of the boat when refueling.
- Boats should be loaded and unloaded in a safe, orderly fashion taking care to maintain an even distribution of weight.
- The coxswain and boat officer must adhere to the Rules of the Road and ensure that their boat is operated in a safe and courteous manner when in the vicinity of other craft.

The Naval Academy's approach towards developing seamanlike skills is based upon years of experience and emphasizes safety and smartness in both sailboat and powerboat handling. The skills of the seaman are based not only upon hands-on experience but also upon a detailed knowledge of the craft's handling characteristics and systems, weather, navigation, and the Rules of the Nautical Road. The next step in the midshipman's development takes place aboard the Academy's 108-foot yard patrol craft.

Yard patrol craft

The Naval Academy has twenty new yard patrol craft of the YP-676 class. The craft have replaced the older YP-654 craft and offer significant improvements in capabilities for training midshipmen in seamanship, navigation, fleet operations, and at-sea leadership and management. The new class offers improved habitability, cruising range and sea-keeping ability, and incorporation of up-to-date engineering, operations, and navigation systems. Much larger than the 80-foot 654 class, the YP-676 has an over-all length of 108 feet, a beam of 22'9", a full-load displacement draft of 8 feet, and a full-load displacement of 108 tons (figure 14-4). Table 14-1 lists the important characteristics of these craft. Many of these facts are required only occasionally, and this table can be referred to when necessary. Certain particulars, however, must be remembered for they are essential to proper shiphandling. Length, draft, *masthead height*, and rudder angles should be memorized.

The 20 YPs of this class were built by two different builders. Those with hull numbers of 676 through 682 were delivered by Peterson Builders, Inc., while hulls numbered 683 through 695 are from Marinette Marine Corporation. The latter craft are also identified as the YP-676 class, but are differentiated by referring to them as the 683 Series. Although identical in most respects, there are some subtle differences. The most obvious external difference is that two ladders lead from the forecastle to the bridge wing on the Peterson boats, while the Marinette boats have only a single ladder slightly to port of centerline (See figure 14-5). The differences in the location of equipment and the operation of certain systems will be highlighted throughout the remainder of this chapter.

When embarked on the YPs for training, it is particularly important to know which type of boat you are on (Peterson or Marinette) and to know precisely the minor differences in the locations of safety and firefighting equipment on these two classes. For some reason, most emergencies occur in bad weather and/or at night. This is not the time to try remembering where to find extra lengths of fire hose. Midshipmen may encounter similar situations when assigned to ships for training or duty upon graduation. There are frequently differences in equipment even on ships delivered by the same builder. The same holds true for civilian yachts. Do not assume that each and every craft of the same design will have the same equipment in the same location. The author spent several confusing moments trying to locate a spinnaker halyard during a storm at night only to finally remember that on this particular 42-footer, the halyards were not led aft to the cockpit but were instead at the mast. For the sake of familiarization, each individual boat should be checked out visually, preferably in broad daylight, by every new crew member before getting underway.

Typical crew positions and responsibilities

Each YP is assigned to an enlisted craftmaster. This senior petty officer is an experienced seaman and is responsible for all aspects of the YP's safe operation and maintenance until relieved by a qualified officer or midshipman. The craftmaster's crew consists of an engineer and one or two deck seamen. As will be described in a later section, the YP can be safely maneuvered by a single trained individual from the craftmaster's console in the pilothouse.

During the routine training in the vicinity of the Naval Academy, the YP is under the command of an instructor, and crew duties (with the exception of the engineer) are performed by midshipmen. The craftmaster and crew remain on board to assist the instructor as necessary and to monitor and control the craft's complex engineering equipment.

Crew positions and responsibilities vary with each training exercise or special circumstance such as piloting, mooring or anchoring, man overboard, collision, or fire. These positions are described in the *Ship's Bills* and *Watch Organization*. It is important to understand these positions and responsibilities and be able to respond quickly in the event of an emergency. The YPs also use standard Navy engineering and *casualty control* procedures. Engineering procedures for each piece of equipment aboard the YPs are detailed in the *Engineering/Electronic Operational Sequencing System (EOSS)* section of the *YP Standard Operating Procedures (YP SOP)*. The *Engineering Operational Casualty Control (EOCC)* section provides similar levels of details for dealing with equipment failures and

14-4. YP profile plan.

JACK STAFF

BOW TOWING CHOCK

DANFORTH ANCHOR

CALCULATIVE DRAFT MARKS P/S

LIFE RING W/FLOAT LIGHT
(Note: These have been relocated to the bridge wings.)

LORAN "C" ANTENNA PORT
HF ANTENNA STBD

SEARCH LIGHT

LOUD HAILER

SURFACE SEARCH RADAR

VHF ANTENNA PORT
VHF BRIDGE-TO-BRIDGE
ANTENNA STBD.

SIGNAL MAST

ENGINE ROOM
EXHAUST SCREEN

SATELLITE NAVIGATION
ANTENNA STBD
OMEGA ANTENNA PORT

PORTABLE LIFE LINES
AND STANCHIONS

FAN ROOM
INTAKE SCREEN

NAVIGATION LIGHT MAST

BULWARK ACCESS P/S

ENSIGN MAST

APPENDAGE DRAFT
MARKS P/S

DIESEL GENERATOR
EXHAUST P/S

AIRCRAFT FLOAT
LIGHTS P/S

PROPULSION ENGINE
EXHAUST P/S

BILGE KEELS

YP676

Table 14-1. YP 676-Class Characteristics

Length over-all	108'
Extreme beam	22'9"
Draft (navigational)	10'
Draft (light load)	7'
Draft (full load)	8'
Displacement	172 tons
Main Propulsion	(2) GM 12-71 diesels, 437 SHP each
Generators	(2) 440 volt, 50 kw, A.C., 3 phase
Propellers	Twin, 3-bladed, 52-inch blades
Fuel-oil capacity	6,550 gallons (6,222 gal @ 95%)
Lubricating-oil capacity	32 gallons (approximate)
Fresh water	1,532 gallons (1,133 forward storage tanks, 399 aft)
Fresh-water production capacity	50 gallons/hour (1,000–1,200 gals/day)
Maximum speed	13.25 knots (2100 rpm)
Cruising speed	10 knots (1460 rpm)
Maximum safe capacity	50 people
Rudder angles (Twin rudders)	
Standard	15 degrees
Full	25 degrees
Hard	35 degrees
Heights	
Masthead (yardarm to boot top)	42' (double for use with stadimeter)
Top of mast to boot top	48'
Height of eye—six-foot person standing at 0-1 level	22'

 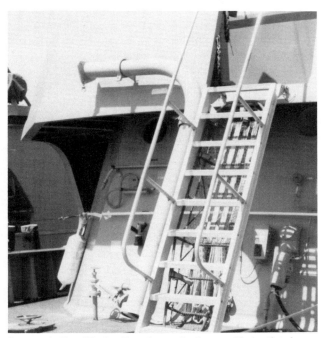

14-5. YP ladders. Two different models of the same class. The forecastle ladders are the most visible differences between YPs built by Peterson Builders and Marinette Marine. The Peterson craft have two ladders forward, the Marinettes have but one. Note the large "J" man-overboard davit stowed on the starboard side of the Marinette's ladder. The Peterson boats do not have such a davit.

14-6. YP main deck arrangement.

14-7. YP 01 level arrangement. The 01 level is the first level above the main deck.

on-board emergencies. The use of EOSS and EOCC is standard throughout the Navy and ensures consistency in training, operations, maintenance, and casualty control of major shipboard equipment.

The senior midshipman position is the *officer of the deck* (OOD). This individual is designated by the commanding officer as the one responsible for all aspects of the craft's operations. On board the YPs, the officer of the deck is also generally the *conning officer* and issues orders controlling the rudders and engines. On larger ships, the OOD is assisted by a *junior officer of the deck* (JOOD), who may act as the conning officer. In response to orders from the conning officer, the *helmsman* controls the operation of the craft's twin rudders while the *lee helmsman* controls the twin engines. Normally the engineering spaces are manned by the enlisted engineer. During summer cruises and YP Squadron training exercises, however, midshipmen also stand watch as *engineer* and *engineering officer of the watch*. *Line handlers* forward and aft respond to orders from the conning officer when mooring or getting underway from a pier. *Phone talkers* relay commands and information to various positions throughout the craft using the internal communications systems. For example, during a precision piloting exercise, phone talkers located on the bridge wings take visual bearings and relay these to the phone talkers of the navigation team located in the pilothouse and the *combat information center (CIC)*. The information is then relayed to the *navigator*, who plots the bearings and makes course and speed recommendations to the conning officer. Other positions include the *signalman* at the 01 level *signal flag bag*, the *radio telephone talker* in either the pilothouse or the CIC, and the *quartermaster* who assists the navigator.

General characteristics

Safe and seamanlike shiphandling depends upon a detailed understanding of the performance characteristics of the craft. These include turning circle (see figure 13-5), acceleration and deceleration figures, and the relationship between engine RPM and hull speed. Table 14-2 indicates the hull speed in knots compared to engine RPM. The speed of 3 knots is achieved by turning only one shaft. For all other speeds, both shafts are required. The engine order telegraph (EOT) settings are also indicated in this table. The YP-676-class ship-control equipment

Table 14-2. Speed and RPM

EOT Setting	RPM	Speed in Knots
Starboard (or Port) Engine Ahead 1/3	500*	3
All engines ahead 1/3	500*	4
All engines ahead 1/3	825	6
All engines ahead 2/3	970*	7
All engines ahead 2/3	1125	8
All engines ahead standard	1290*	9
All engines ahead standard	1460	10
All engines ahead full	1650*	11
All engines ahead full	1850†	12
All engines ahead flank	2060†	13
All engines ahead flank	2100†	13.25
All engines back 1/3	900	
All engines back 2/3	1200	
All engines back full	1500	

Note: * Maneuvering bells: These will be rung up whenever maneuvering combination is ordered.

† The main engines should not be run over 1800 rpm for extended periods.

also includes remote Panish engine controls located forward on the port side of the pilothouse at the craftmaster's console. These are marked with the same settings indicated for the EOT. The EOT, Panish controls, and the commands from the conning officer to the lee helmsman will be discussed later in the section on conning.

Table 14-3 provides essential *tactical data* necessary for shiphandling in formation with other YPs. This standardizes speeds and distances used in formation maneuvering. Of the data in this table, the most important to remember are the tactical diameters of 150 yards for *standard rudder (15 degrees)* and 80 yards for *full rudder (25 degrees)* when maneuvering at 9 knots. Also important are acceleration and deceleration rates. The YP will accelerate from 7 to 10 knots in 10 seconds. She will stop in 8 to 10 seconds when going from full ahead to backing full and will have a *head reach* distance of approximately 25 yards before becoming *dead in the water*. The YP's *surge rate* (the ratio of distance to speed that the ship travels when decelerating) is 16 yards for each knot of speed differential. This information permits a calculation of when to slow the vessel's speed when approaching an assigned station in formation. For example, a YP maneuvering to a new station at 11 knots must slow to the formation speed of 7 knots when 64 yards from her new station (speed differential: 4 knots × 16 yards/

Table 14-3. YP Tactical Data

Tactical speeds:	
Normal speed	8 knots
Cruising speed	10 knots
Stationing speed	12 knots
Operational speed	12+ knots
Tactical diameters and rudder angles at standard speed:	
Standard	150 yards (standard rudder—15 degrees at standard speed—9 knots)
Reduced	80 yards (Full rudder—25 degrees at standard speed—9 knots)
Distances:	
Standard distance	200 yards—line formations
Circle spacing	100 yards—screens and circular formations
Replenishment	Lifeguard—200 yards astern of transferring ship Waiting—100 yards astern of transferring ship
Acceleration	*Time (seconds)*
0 to 7 knots	16
7 to 10 knots	10

Surge is the ratio of distance to speed that a ship travels while decelerating. For the YP 676 class this ratio is 16 yards per knot of speed differential. This information permits a calculation of when to slow the vessel's speed when approaching an assigned station in a formation or making an approach to a mooring or pier. For example: If the YP is maneuvering to a new station at 11 knots and the formation speed is 7 knots, the YP should be slowed to 7 knots when she is 64 yards from the assigned station. Distances to other YPs or vessels may be obtained using the stadimeter or radar. It is also important, however, to develop a "seaman's eye" and be able to accurately estimate distances and relative motion.

Bare steerageway: This is the slowest speed at which the rudders will have an effect. For the YP this is about 1 knot, although this may vary slightly with wind and water conditions.

knot = 64 yards). The section on "formation ship-handling" provides an explanation of basic maneuvers and terms and more fully illustrates the necessity for understanding the handling characteristics of the YP.

Table 14-4 provides additional tactical data for the YP-676 class. This includes *advance and transfer* data (see figure 13-5) and tactical diameters for various speeds and rudder angles. When maneuvering in formation or when altering course and speed in restricted waters, it is essential that this data is understood.

Ship control equipment

As described in chapter 13, there are five controllable forces available to the seaman when operating under power: engines, rudders, mooring or warping lines, ground tackle, and tugs or pusher boats. With the exception of tugs, the YPs routinely make use of each of these forces to control the movement of the craft.

The main propulsion engines aboard the 676-class YPs are two 437-horsepower General Motors 12V71 diesels. These are fuel-injected, two-cycle engines. Each is connected to a shaft via a hydraulically activated reverse reduction gear with a 5.16:1 reduction ratio. Their maximum forward speed is 2100 RPM, and the maximum reverse speed is 1500 RPM. The engines should never exceed 1800 RPM for routine safe operations. The throttle and clutch are in the engine operations station (EOS) control booth in the engine room where they can be controlled by an engineer. Engine orders are transmitted to the engineer by the engine order telegraph (EOT) system located next to the helmsman's station in the pilothouse. This is an electro-mechanical system that links a signal device in the pilothouse to one in the EOS. The EOT has a handle for each engine and shaft combination and indicates direction and speed. The face of the EOT is divided into the following positions: Ahead 1/3, Ahead 2/3, Ahead Standard, Ahead Full, Stop, Back 1/3, Back 2/3, Back Full (figure 14-9A).

As engine speeds and direction are ordered by the conning officer, they are "rung up" on the EOT by the lee helmsman. The commands are answered manually by the engineer in the EOS control booth. A follow-up pointer under the EOT handle in both the EOS and pilothouse indicates when the commands have been answered. The lee helmsman will then report this fact to the conning officer (the commands and responses will be described in the

Table 14-4. Turning Characteristics for the YP-676 Class

Speed (RPM/KTS)	Rudder Angle (Deg)	Advance and Transfer 45° Turn Adv.	Advance and Transfer 45° Turn Tr.	90° Turn Adv.	90° Turn Tr.	Tactical Diameter (yards)
6/825	15°	117	55	135	85	170
	25°	67	40	55	55	120
10/1460	15°	80	45	125	80	150
	25°	45	30	75	50	80
13/2060	15°	125	85	150	125	180
	25°	100	75	80	55	130

Note: Advance and transfer are essentially the same for both left and right rudder commands on the YPs. This is not always the case, particularly for larger ships.

section on conning). The system is also equipped with a wrong-direction alarm. This feature provides a visual and audible warning if the engines have been operated in an opposite direction of that ordered. It should be noted that to safely shift from forward to reverse or vice versa, the engine must be slowed to idling speed in order to reverse the direction of the transfer gear. This takes several seconds. For this reason, unless an emergency exists, "Stop" should always be ordered before changing the direction of shaft rotation. As noted in table 14-2 *maneuvering bells* are normal RPM and speed combinations. Engine speeds other than these bells may be ordered by calling the engineer on the 1JV sound-powered telephone or the 1MC/6MC announcing system. These internal communications systems will be described in a subsequent section.

While the EOT system just described is the traditional method of transmitting and verifying engine orders, the YPs routinely use a remotely controlled engine order system. This consists of Panish controls mounted on the craftmaster's console, which is just to port of amidships and forward in the pilothouse. The controls are both clutches and throttles and are directly linked to the engine controls in the EOS. Thus, the YP's engines can be controlled from the pilothouse with the engineer acting only as a systems and safety monitor in the EOS. The Panish controls are shown in figure 14-9B.

The 676-class YPs have two rudders, one abaft each propeller for added maneuverability and control. The rudders are linked together and controlled by a mechanical/hydraulic power-steering system. A rudder angle indicator is located forward of the helm. The full throw of the rudders is 70 degrees, from 35 degrees port to 35 degrees starboard. *Hard rudder, 35 degrees* should be avoided except in an

emergency, because the mechanical linkage may jam in this position. The maximum rudder angle used under normal circumstances should be 30 degrees. When backing at speeds greater than two-thirds, never use more than 10 degrees rudder. Care must be taken when backing to hold the steering wheel firmly. If it is let go, it will spin hard over and the rudders will jam in the stops.

The steering system is activated in one of three ways: The pilothouse helm, the pilothouse *jog valve steering lever* mounted on the craftmaster's console, and the emergency wheel located on the forward bulkhead, port side in the lazaret. The helm is the normal method of steering (figure 14-10). Rotating the large wheel in a clockwise direction moves the rudders to the right while a counterclockwise rotation causes the rudders to turn to the left. The jog valve steering lever, seen above the Panish controls in figure 14-9B, facilitates "single-handling" opera-

14-7A. YP-676 class maneuvering in a column formation.

14-8. YP platform deck arrangement.

14-9A. YP Engine Order Telegraph.

265

14-9B. YP Panish controls. The traditional Engine Order Telegraph (EOT) is mounted on a pedestal to starboard of the helmsman's console. The more frequently used Panish remote engine controls are located forward on the port side of the pilothouse. Note the "jog valve steering lever" to the right of the Panish controls. From this position, the craftmaster can easily maneuver the YP single-handed.

tion by the craftmaster or when there are insufficient personnel on board to have both a helmsman and lee helmsman. To activate steering, the jog lever requires simple lateral motion, and the lever must be held in place. The rudders will remain at the last position "ordered" when the lever is released. A rudder-angle indicator located at the craftmaster's console indicates rudder direction and the number of degrees the rudders have turned. There is a slight delay with this system in that a movement of the jog lever to the left will cause the rudders to turn to the left after about 2 seconds. Moving the lever to the right is a "right" rudder command, and the same delay will be experienced. The jog lever will override the helm.

Emergency steering is accomplished in one of two

14-10. YP pilothouse. The top left photo is of a Marinette-built craft with a 30-inch diameter helm, the EOT and voice tube to starboard, and the surface-search radar repeater to port. Note the location of the wind, fathometer, and speed log instruments forward on the starboard side overhead. The VHF radio, searchlight control, and ship's whistle pull cord are mounted above the helm. The Peterson craft (bottom left) have all instruments and the VHF radios mounted in a single panel above the helm. The close-up of the Peterson's helmsman's console (right) shows three alarms (General, Collision, and Chemical) to the left, port and starboard engine tachometers, a centrally mounted rudder-angle indicator, and the craft's master gyro compass directly forward of the helmsman's position.

ways. In the event of an electrical power failure or the failure of the hydraulic actuators or pumps, a manual hydraulic pump is activated automatically. In this event, steering is still controlled by the helm located in the pilothouse. While the manual pump can provide full steering capability, more time and effort is needed. Under normal conditions, the full rudder range is achieved in about eight seconds using eight full revolutions of the helm. Using the manual hydraulic pump, full rudder range is achieved in about 15 seconds and 12 to 13 full rotations of the helm. The jog lever is ineffective in this mode of operation.

In the event of a failure of the pilothouse steering console, the emergency steering wheel unit in the lazaret can provide control. Precise valve position instructions are posted near this unit and must be strictly followed. Otherwise, the hydraulic fluid will be drained resulting in a total loss of the steering system. When using the lazaret emergency steering

wheel, orders must be relayed to the "helmsman" in the lazaret via the 1JV sound-powered telephone or the 1MC/6MC announcing system. Again, it will take more time than normal for rudder orders to have an effect on the ship's direction. Therefore, the YP should be maneuvered with caution until the systems can be repaired or you have reached a safe anchorage or port.

Conning

Midshipmen get hands-on experience in handling the YP soon after going aboard. With a basic understanding of the craft's engine and steering characteristics, simple conning exercises are conducted to build the midshipman's confidence and skills afloat. Early exercises include issuing and responding to helm, lee helm, and line-handling commands, getting underway from a pier, and handling alongside a pier.

The basics of handling under power were discussed in chapter 13. Quite often the conning officer (the officer doing the handling) will actually be both steering and controlling the engines himself. When this is the case, conning is analogous to driving a car—the person conning has the "feel" of the boat in his own hands, and can translate decisions directly into actions. The YPs can be conned in this manner from the pilothouse using the jog valve steering lever and the Panish engine controls located at the craftmaster's console.

On large ships, however, the conning officer does not handle the helm or engine order telegraph, for he must be free to move about on the open bridge to have the visibility necessary to do the job. When this is the case, a new dimension is added to the problem. The conning officer must now translate decisions into commands to the helmsman, lee helmsman, and line handlers (when maneuvering alongside a pier). A different sense of timing is needed by the conning officer when he is controlling the ship through others, rather than through his own actions. This is a skill requiring a great deal of practice. It is also a skill essential for all officers who go to sea in surface ships or submarines. It is for this reason that the YP, while on drills, is always conned from the open bridge as seen in figure 14-11.

With regard to steering, there are two distinctly different methods for conning a vessel from the bridge. The first, which can be called positive control, is recommended in all maneuvering situations when the conning officer wants direct control over rudder angle (as opposed to steering a compass course). For this method of conning, all steering commands relate to the positioning of the rudder. There is no reference to the compass or ship's head and, in fact, the compass is not required. This method of conning comes as close as possible to actually steering oneself. The standard commands for this method and their meanings are listed in figure 14-12A.

In the second method, a certain amount of helm control is relinquished by the conning officer to the helmsman, and his commands relate to ship's head and compass courses. Courses must always be given using this method, and once the helmsman receives a course, he will use the rudder control required to keep the vessel on the ordered heading. This second method is recommended for normal conning in channels and in formation. The standard commands

for this method are listed in figure 14-12B.

There are some general rules that apply to all standard conning commands. The most important is that *only* standard commands may be used. For this reason, the prospective conning officer must learn the commands and their meanings verbatim.

When conning by compass heading, a course order should always follow a rudder order. This ensures that the vessel will not swing past the desired course. Course changes up to 10 degrees should be ordered by giving the direction of turn followed by the new course. For example, when steadied on 050 degrees, the proper order of a change to 055 degrees would be, "Come right to zero five five." For course changes greater than 10 degrees, a rudder order should be given, followed by the new course. For example, to change course from 050 degrees to 090 degrees, the conning officer might say, "right standard rudder. Come right to course zero nine zero." The proper response from the helmsman is, "Right standard rudder, aye." When the rudder angle indicator shows that the rudder is right standard (right 15 degrees), the helmsman reports to the conning officer, "Sir, my rudder is right standard, coming right to new course zero nine zero." The conning officer then replies with, "Very well." When the helmsman is steady on the new course, this is reported to the conning officer by saying, "Steady on course zero nine zero." Again, the conning officer acknowledges with, "Very well."

Remember that the helmsman always goes by the last order given, and a change in rudder order will supersede a previous course given. Finally, the terms "belay my last," "negate my last," and "disregard" are never used. When an incorrect order has been given, simply correct it with a proper one. A skilled helmsman can alert a conning officer to an incorrect order by the tone of his voice. For example, with the ship steady on course 090 degrees, the the conning officer orders, "Right standard rudder, come right to course 050 degrees." The right rudder command will eventually get the ship around to 050 degrees, but it is a 320-degree turn and in the wrong direction. The helmsman must not ignore or delay in carrying out an order. He can, however, respond with "Right Standard Rudder!!?" as he puts the helm to the right. The intonation should alert the conning officer to the fact that he is taking the long

268

14-11. Handling alongside. "Fender drills" alongside the Naval Academy seawall provide the midshipmen with the opportunity to learn the handling characteristics of the twin-screw YPs, standard commands, and teamwork.

way around or that there is some other problem noticed by the helmsman. Issuing the command, "Shift your rudder, come left to course zero five zero" corrects the error.

Orders to the lee helmsman for control of the ship's engines and speeds also have a specified format. This is, "Engine, direction, and speed." For example, "All engines ahead full, indicate one six five zero RPMs for 11 knots." For astern speeds, orders do not include RPM or speed in knots. For a single engine command, the engine must be specified as in "Starboard engine back one-third, port engine stop." Emergency commands are given as "Emergency, all engines ahead (astern) full." When using the traditional EOT, the lee helmsman responds to the emergency command by ringing up "Ahead" (or "Astern") several times in rapid succession on the EOT. This signals the engineer to increase rapidly the speed of the engines to the maximum safe RPM in the direction indicated. When using the Panish controls, engine speeds and direction can be altered very quickly and directly by the lee helmsman in response to an "Emergency"

command. However, care must be taken not to increase the engine RPM above the safe maximum of 1800 RPM. The conning officer and lee helmsman must also be aware that it is unsafe to shift the direction of the shaft from ahead to astern (or vice versa) without first ringing up "Stop" and permitting the engines to come to idle speed (500 RPM).

As with commands to the helm, the lee helmsman repeats all commands verbatim and reports to the conning officer when the engine orders have been carried out. These procedures are the same when using either the Panish controls or the traditional engine order telegraph.

Ground tackle and basic anchoring procedures

Another important element of ship-control equipment to be mastered by the midshipman is the ground tackle. The YPs carry two 190-pound Danforth high-tensile deep-set anchors housed in *hawseholes* on either side of the bow. Each anchor has 70 *fathoms* (there are six feet in a fathom) of one-half-inch chain. The anchor chains on the YPs

Commands	Meaning
"Left (right)_____degrees rudder."	Put on the left (right) rudder ordered.
"Left (right) standard rudder."	Put on the previously specified amount of left (right) rudder required to turn the ship in her "standard tactical diameter."
"Left (right) full rudder."	Put on the previously specified amount of left (right) rudder to turn the ship in her "reduced tactical diameter."
"Hard left (right) rudder."	Use maximum left (right) rudder.
"Ease the rudder to_____degrees."	Decrease the rudder angle to_____degrees.
"Shift the rudder."	Change from left to right rudder (or vice versa) an equal amount.
"Rudder amidships."	Put the rudder amidships (to decrease the rate of swing).
"How is your rudder?"	Report the rudder's position.

14-12A. Standard commands—positive.

Commands	Meaning
"Steady on course_____."	Steady on course_____, using the amount of rudder previously ordered.
"Come left (right) to _____."	Put the rudder left (right), and steady on new course_____.
"Come left (right) handsomely to _____."	Use a small amount of rudder and come to course_____ (used when a very small course change is desired).
"Nothing to the left (right) of _____."	Do not steer to the left (right) of ordered heading.
"Steady," or "Steady as she goes."	Steer the course on which the ship is heading when the command is received. The helmsman's reply is "Steady as she goes; course _____, sir."
"Meet her."	Use rudder as necessary to check the swing.
"Mind your rudder."	Steer more carefully.
"How does she head?" or "Mark your head."	What is the ship's heading?
"Keep her so."	Steer the course that has just been reported as ship's heading.

14-12B. Standard commands—compass.

are color-coded by *shots of chain* to indicate the amount of chain paid out. On a large Navy ship, a shot of chain is 15 fathoms. Since the YPs are shallow-water craft, a shot of chain is 15 feet. The shots are marked with a standard Navy sequence of *red, white, and blue* paint. The first shot is marked with one white link on either side of the red 15-foot link (W-R-W), the second shot with two white links on either side of the white 30-foot link (WW-W-WW), and the third shot with three white links on either side of the blue 45-foot link (WWW-B-WWW). The fourth shot repeats the red link at 60 feet, and there are four white links on either side (WWWW-R-WWWW). The sequence repeats itself until the next to last shot, in which every link is painted yellow to indicate "danger." All links in the final shot are painted red. If for some reason the yellow shot appears on deck with the anchor still falling, all hands should immediately clear the forecastle before the final red shot appears. The final shot is fixed to the craft with a "weak link" that will part, permitting the anchor and chain to fall free without causing structural damage to the craft.

The anchor windlass pictured in figure 14-13 (top) is a power-driven, reversible, single-speed (34 feet per minute) model. The windlass is operated by the electric motor controls. On the Peterson boats (YPs 676–682), the switches are located on the after port side of the motor. These are button switches, the top being "hoist" and the bottom being "lower." There is a power indicator light in the center of the switch. On the Marinette boats (YPs 683–695), the "switch" is a lever mounted on a vertical stand located abaft the windlass (see figure 14-13 middle). Pressing the lever forward lowers the chain, releasing the lever to the upright position stops the motor, and pulling the lever aft is the hoist position. Both the push-bottom switches and the lever are "deadman" switches. This means constant pressure must be applied or the windlass operation will stop when the button or lever is released. On both the Peterson and Marinette boats, the windlass motor controller is located below the main deck on the forward bulkhead of the midshipmen berthing compartment.

The *wildcat* (a concave drum) over which the

chain is led, is engaged by the clutch handles located at the top of the windlass. In addition to the clutches, each wildcat has a mechanical friction handbrake controlled by the vertically mounted wheels on either side (figure 14-13 bottom). The brake is adjusted to obtain the proper amount of rotation when either raising or lowering the anchor. Turning the brake counterclockwise releases the brake and permits higher speeds. Clockwise rotation increases brake friction and slows shaft rotation. The *gypsy heads*, the two horizontally mounted smooth drums, may be operated independently of the wildcat. This is accomplished by disengaging the wildcat clutch and pinning the clutch handle to the inboard position with the clutch lock pin. By placing two or three turns of a line around the head and applying hand-held tension, each of the 9-inch heads can pull a maximum weight of 2,700 pounds at a rate of 44 feet per minute. Also illustrated in figure 14-13 bottom are the chain stoppers. Their use will be discussed in the next section.

271

Anchoring procedures

Anchoring is required during routine training cruises and for precision navigation and anchoring drills. There are two basic anchoring procedures for the YPs—for shallow-water anchorages (20 to 25 feet) and for deep-water anchorages (water over 25 feet deep). To ready the anchor for use in a shallow-water anchorage (most typical for YP anchoring exercises), loosen the brake slightly by turning the wheel counterclockwise. Disengage the wildcat clutch with the clutch handle in the inboard position and the lock pin inserted. The anchor is now being held in position by the chain stop. Remove the pawl from the chain stop so that the bail can open freely.

14-13. Anchor windlasses. The Peterson windlass (top) is operated by "Hoist" and "Lower" buttons located on the after port side of the windlass. The Marinette controller (middle) is a pedestal-mounted lever. Both types are "dead-man" switches, meaning the switch or lever must be held in position for the windlass to operate. Note the two vertically mounted handbrakes, the clutch levers just inboard of the brakes, and the gypsy heads to port and starboard of the wildcats. Two chain stoppers (shackles and locking pelican hooks) secure each anchor chain in the stowed position. The watertight scuttle forward of the windlass leads to the boatswain stores and chain locker compartment (bottom).

The anchor is now ready for letting go. A word of caution: During this exercise do not straddle or step over the anchor chain.

The forecastle crew should be informed by the bridge and navigation team when within 1,000 yards and then 500 yards from the anchorage. When the YP is head to wind or current, as the case may be, with all way off, the anchor is let go by striking open the chain stopper bail with a ball peen hammer. Again, it is of vital importance that no members of the crew stand near the anchor chain when it is let go. The crew member responsible for striking the bail should be outboard of the anchor chain and should step back immediately after releasing the bail. The anchor and chain will ride off the brake, thus the brake tension must be adjusted to permit a smooth rate of descent for the anchor. When the anchor chain has been paid out to the length specified by the navigator (a general rule of thumb is 5 to 7 times the water depth), and the anchor is holding, the chain stops should be put back in place with the bail closed and pawl inserted. The brake should be fully closed by turning the brake handle clockwise.

During the *casting* (letting go process), the forecastle crew should be reporting to the bridge the amount of chain to the water's edge, the direction the chain is tending, and the amount of strain (slack, light, moderate, or heavy). When the chain is snubbed, a report is given to the bridge that the anchor is holding or dragging. Often the conning officer will find it necessary to back down slowly to set the anchor. Prior to backing down, the chain stops should be put in place and the brake fully closed.

For anchorages in deep water, the YP anchor is first let go under the positive control of the wildcat. This is accomplished by engaging the wildcat clutch and inserting the lock pin. The wildcat motor is "bumped" with momentary pushes of the switch to ensure that the teeth of the wildcat are meshed with the motor shaft. The brake is fully released by turning the wheel counterclockwise, and the chain stop is removed. By pushing the "lower" button on the windlass controller, the anchor is slowly paid out until about 25 feet from the bottom. At this point the brake and chain stops are reset. After this is accomplished, the wildcat clutch is disengaged and locked in the inboard position with the pin. The

anchor is then let go using the shallow-water procedures described above.

When weighing anchor, it is usually "heaved around" to a *short stay* first; that is, the scope is shortened as much as possible without actually breaking the anchor free of the bottom. To bring the anchor to short stay, the wildcat is engaged by placing the clutch in the outboard position and inserting the locking pin. The motor is "bumped" briefly to ensure the wildcat is engaged, the chain stop is removed, and the brake is released by turning the wheel fully counterclockwise. The anchor chain is brought to short stay by pushing the "hoist" button (holding the lever forward on the Marinette boats) on the windlass controller. During this process, the crew takes the fire hose with an *all purpose nozzle* from the forecastle *fire station* and directs a stream of water into the hawsehole and onto the chain to clean it of mud and debris.

Once the command to "heave around" is given, the forecastle crew weighs anchor, reporting when the chain is *up and down* (vertical), when the anchor is *aweigh* (broken out and lifted clear of the bottom), *in sight, clear* or *foul, clear of the water*, and *to the hawsehole*. When the anchor is housed snuggly in the hawsehole, the chain stops and brake are reset and the chain made taut using the windlass. There should not be a heavy strain on the chain, however.

While anchored, the proper signals under the appropriate Rules of the Road must be observed: a black anchor ball hoisted at the yardarm by day, and a white, 32-point light shown by night.

Navigation equipment

Navigation is described as both an art and science and certainly elements of both are the talents and tools of the successful navigator. Safely planning and executing the safe passage of the craft from one point to another requires a detailed understanding of the principles and procedures necessary to determine the ship's position and to plan the next course. In addition to being an art and science, good navigation requires discipline. A typical summer afternoon near Annapolis will find at least one boat aground or in the wrong place simply because the skipper lost track of where he was and where he was going. A day trip such as one from Annapolis to Baltimore or an offshore passage from Annapolis to Newport both require constant attention to the craft's position, direction of travel, and position with respect to other vessels.

This section will introduce some of the equipment aboard the YPs (table 14-5) as well as some basic navigational terminology. There are any number of excellent books on navigation, and the midshipmen at the Naval Academy receive two full semesters of academic and practical instruction in this subject. For the civilian, the Coast Guard Auxiliary and the U.S. Power Squadrons offer basic courses in navigation. These are highly recommended for the beginner, and refresher courses are often beneficial to even the most experienced seaman.

The YPs depend upon a variety of methods for navigating safely. These include *piloting*, the use of visual landmarks or navigation aids to *fix* the position with accuracy; *dead reckoning*, calculating the position of the craft using courses and speeds made good from the time since the last fix; *electronic navigation*, the use of electronic signals to deter-

14-14. Magnetic compass and compass deviation card. The deviation should be calculated after any compass maintenance or major alteration in the craft's equipment.

Table 14-5. YP Navigation Equipment

Compasses & related equipment	*Location*
Magnetic compass—6-inch	Pilothouse
Sperry gyrocompass Mark 27, Model 1	Pilothouse
Gyro repeaters (7)	Helm, bridge wings (port, starboard), centerline forward, navigator's table in the pilothouse, and two in CIC
Peloruses	Bridge wing & centerline gyro repeaters
Electronic navigation equipment	
Kenyon DS-300 Fathometer	Pilothouse, repeaters at each CIC chart table
Epsco Plotters (2)	CIC
LORAN-C	Pilothouse
Magnavox MX1105 Satellite-OMEGA Receiver	Pilothouse
Radar—AN/SPS-64(V)9	Transceiver—CIC; antenna—mast
Radar repeaters	Pilothouse & CIC
Navigational lights	
One white 20-point masthead light	Mast
One white 12-point stern light	01 level—aft
One white 32-point anchor light	Mast
One 10-point green starboard sidelight	01 level, starboard bridge wing
One 10-point red port sidelight	01 level, port bridge wing
Three 20-point white lights	Vertically on the mast (towing lights)
Two 32-point red lights	Vertically on the mast (breakdown lights)
One yellow 12-point towing light	01 level—aft, vertically above the stern light
Miscellaneous equipment	
Air horn	Atop the pilothouse
Ship's bell	Signal bridge
14-inch sealed-beam navigational searchlight	Atop the pilothouse
Stadimeter—mechanical ranging device	Hand-held
Sextants (offshore cruises only)	Hand-held
Kenyon anemometer (relative wind direction and speed)	Pilothouse (instrument is mounted on the port yardarm)
Navigator speed log	Pilothouse & 2 repeaters in CIC (instrument is hull-mounted paddle wheel)

mine position; and *celestial navigation*, the use of the sun, moon, planets, and stars to determine position. Although each method uses different basic equipment, the principles of determining the ship's position are closely related and rely on accurate readings and records of course, speed, time, and bearings. Commonly used equipment includes an accurate timepiece, up-to-date nautical charts, simple plotting tools, and several sharp pencils (with erasers). Although modern electronic navigation displays provide crisp digital readouts of position, course, speed, and other useful data, the prudent navigator will maintain an "old-fashioned" paper plot to safeguard against an electrical or electronics casualty.

Compasses

Compasses are used to determine the ship's course or heading. The YPs have both magnetic and gyro compasses for this. The 6-inch magnetic compass provides course information relative to *magnetic north* and is installed immediately forward of the helm. A compass *deviation card* is posted next to the compass (figure 14-14). Deviation is the difference, in degrees, between magnetic north and "north" as indicated by each individual compass. These are referred to as *magnetic course* and *compass course*, respectively. Since the magnetic compass will be affected by its surroundings (being attracted by ferrous metals and electrical equipment), the deviation must be measured and compensated for when steering magnetic courses. Deviation is either added or subtracted depending upon whether it is East or West and depending on whether you are *correcting* (removing a compass error such as deviation when converting compass course to magnetic course) or *uncorrecting* (adding an error such as deviation when converting from magnetic course to compass course).

For example, to determine the magnetic course being made good by reading the compass course, the helmsman and navigator are "correcting" since they want to remove the deviation. If the helmsman is steering a compass course of 180 degrees and the deviation on the card for this course is 5 degrees East, the magnetic course is 180 + 5 = 185 degrees magnetic; if the deviation were 5 degrees West, the magnetic course would be 180 − 5 = 175 degrees. To convert from a desired magnetic course (from the nautical chart) to the compass course, the

navigator must add westerly error and subtract easterly error—"uncorrecting"—and the rule is reversed. For example, if the desired magnetic course is 180 degrees and the compass card indicates that for this course the deviation is 3 degrees East, the helmsman would subtract 3 degrees and steer a compass course of 177 degrees. Conversely, if the deviation was 5 degrees West the helmsman would add 5 degrees and steer a compass course of 185 degrees. Remembering the phrase *Correcting Add East* may assist in making the appropriate calculation. Another memory aid is to think of the letters AEC (as in the old Atomic Energy Commission), which stand for *Add East Correcting*. Regardless of the mnemonic, the correct calculation is critical, especially on a long run.

Another source of compass error is the difference (again in degrees) between *true geographic north* and *magnetic north*, which is slightly offset from the true North Pole. This is called *variation* and is generally marked on the *compass rose* printed on nautical charts (see figure 14-14). Variation is used when translating between magnetic courses and true courses. The rules are the same as with deviation. When correcting (i.e., from magnetic to true), add East, subtract West. When uncorrecting, reverse the rule. Piloting with a magnetic compass is simplified by working directly from the compass rose, when possible, in order to avoid the variation error.

A standard method of avoiding confusion when correcting for deviation and variation is to write down the letters CDMVT, which stand for Compass, Deviation, Magnetic, Variation, and True. One mnemonic to aid in remembering this is: "Can Dead Men Vote Twice." If you have trouble remembering the letter sequence for correcting, remember that you read from C to T in the word "correct" and also in the expression CDMVT; thus, reading from C to T is correcting, and obviously, reading the opposite way would be uncorrecting.

Gyro compass

Just forward of the helm, a Sperry *gyro compass* Mark 27, Model 1 is mounted (see figure 14-10). Modern gyro compasses are very accurate and when aligned to true north, no corrections are required when plotting or steering a course. However, the navigator must check each unit daily and should a *gyro error* exist, the method of correction (or uncor-

14-15. Two types of pelorus mounted to bridge-wing gyro repeaters. Each type provides the bearing taker with the ability to accurately record the true bearing to a navigational aid or another vessel.

rection) described above must be applied. One difference between a gyro compass and the magnetic compass is that the gyro error is constant on all headings.

The master gyro provides an input to radar plotting, the ship's dead-reckoning equipment (used with SATNAV and Omega), and to *gyro repeaters*. Pilothouse repeaters are located at the helm, centerline forward (craftmaster's console), and the navigator's table (aft port side). Additional repeaters are located on the bridge wings (port, starboard, and centerline forward) and at two locations in the Combat Information Center (CIC). The master control panel for the gyro is located in the pilothouse beneath the gyro. The YP has three *peloruses* (rotating circles marked in degrees with sights for taking visual bearings) mounted on the externally mounted gyro-compass repeaters. Figure 14-15 illustrates the two types of pelorus—a simple open pelorus with a rear sight and a "hairline" wire on which the object is centered, and a telescopic pelorus. The bearings taken from the pelorus are used in both navigation and formation shiphandling.

Fathometer

The Kenyon shallow-water digital *fathometer* indicates the depth of water beneath the keel from 1 foot to 300 feet. Its display is updated every 3 seconds and has an audible warning capability that can be set to warn of shallow water. The normal operating position of the unit is "Alarm" with a depth setting of 13 feet, 6 inches. Used in conjunc-

tion with other means of navigation and accurate bottom contour charts, the fathometer contributes to the overall accuracy of the ship's navigation.

Electronic navigation

The Magnavox MX1105 Satellite-Omega receiver combines two navigational technologies into a single system permitting extremely accurate, automatic position determination. The Satellite Navigation System (SATNAV), receives signals from navigation satellites placed in orbits about the earth's poles. *Lines of position* are determined by automatically measuring the "doppler shift" in successive broadcasts from either a single satellite or multiple satellites in succession. Normally four to seven 2-minute broadcasts from a single satellite are sufficient to provide a fix. With five satellites in the system, the YPs can obtain fixes at least every 100 minutes. In the interval between fixes, the system uses the dead-reckoning (DR) method of advancing the last known position based upon the ship's course and speed.

Omega is a terrestrial electronic navigation system that compares the electronic phase shift between two signals to determine lines of position. The system consists of eight stations around the world, with each broadcasting three very low frequency signals in time-sequenced 10-second patterns. A shipboard receiver can always receive three stations, thus permitting the calculation of three lines of position, the intersection of which determines a fix. The Omega system automatically determines which stations to use by comparing the

275

14-16. The navigator's table. The table is located aft on the port side of the pilothouse. The SATNAV and Loran-C are located above the table. Repeaters for the gyro compass and the wind instruments are located on the after bulkhead.

bearing, range, and strength of each signal being received. As with SATNAV, the dead-reckoning method of navigation is used between fixes.

The receiver operates in two modes—NAV1 and NAV2. NAV1 provides data based only on satellite and dead reckoning. NAV2, the preferred mode, combines data from SATNAV, Omega, set and drift, and dead-reckoning inputs. The ship's gyro compass and speed log can be set to provide automatic inputs to the system. These inputs provide the basis for the DR calculations, or the DR inputs can be made manually. The system can also supply additional navigational information such as course and distance to a destination point. This information is presented either as a *great circle route* (the shortest distance) or a *rhumb line* (a straight line on a *Mercator projection chart*). The system also computes the distance run, speed of advance, and course of advance. Both SATNAV and Omega are all-weather navigation systems.

Loran-C

Loran-C (Long Range Navigation) is another all-weather position-fixing system for both ships and aircraft. Using a nearly worldwide system of radio transmitting sites, the receiver located in the pilothouse measures the time differential between signals. The resulting lines of position provide latitude and longitude, calculations of the ship's speed and

distance, heading, and time to reach a preset destination. Figure 14-16 shows the navigator's station with the SATNAV, Loran-C, remote gyro repeater, and plotting arm.

CIC plotters

The EPSCO plotter in CIC is used as an aid to the navigator. The plotter consists of a computer and a mechanical plotter. There are two plotting tables used for both piloting and open-ocean navigation. In piloting, bearings to visual aids such as radio towers, water tanks, points of land, bridge towers, and lighthouses are transmitted from the bearing takers on the external peloruses to the *CIC plotting team* over the JW1 and JW2 *sound-powered telephones* (telephones that generate their own power through sound vibrations of the voice). For open-ocean transits such as those made during summer training cruises, the plotter is an invaluable aid to navigation, since it receives latitude and longitude inputs from Loran-C or the Satellite-Omega system. Figure 14-17 illustrates a portion of a track off the coast of Florida with the YP's position marked in 15-minute increments. The plotter may be set to match any chart scale and with automatic inputs from Loran-C or the SATNAV will automatically track the YP's progress with great accuracy.

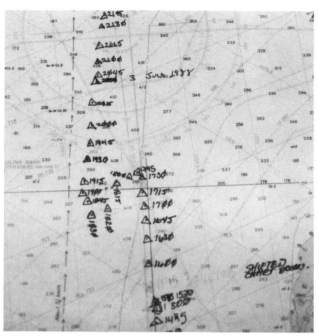

14-17. The EPSCO plotter in CIC. Taking inputs from either Loran-C or SATNAV, the plotter's compass rose is projected through the glass top onto the chart. The plotter is only an aid to navigation since it does not perform any dead reckoning or position determination functions without external inputs.

Speed log

Inputs for the craft's speed are provided to the navigation systems and plotters by the Loran-C or from SATNAV calculations. The YPs also have a Navigator's Speed Log to indicate speed through the water. The speed is measured by a simple paddle-wheel device in the hull, and the output is displayed in a monitor located in the pilothouse. The Speed Log's computer also calculates the distance run in nautical or statute miles, elapsed time since the computer was reset, average speed made good, and total distance traveled in nautical or statute miles. The dead-reckoning calculations from the Speed Log are provided as inputs to the SATNAV. Two remote speedometer displays indicating speed and distance are located alongside the plotting tables in CIC (see figure 14-18).

Radar

The final electronic aid to navigation is the surface-search radar. The AN/SPS-64(V)9 radar (the master unit is shown to port of the helm in figure 14-10) operates to a maximum range of 32 nautical miles.

The radar display consists of three 10-inch cathode-ray tubes (CRT), one in the pilothouse and two in the CIC. These displays permit the operator to determine the range and true bearing of other vessels, buoys, and points of land. The true bearings are obtained by coupling an output signal from the ship's gyro compass to the radar. Although radar bearings are not as accurate as visual bearings, radar ranges are extremely accurate and when combined with visual bearings in piloting, produce excellent fixes. The radar bearing and ranges obtained on other vessels are plotted over time to produce a calculation of the target vessel's true course and speed and the range, bearing, and time of the closest point of approach between the YP and target ship.

The navigator uses all of these sources of information to produce a *fix* or an *estimated position*. A fix is an accurate determination on a nautical chart of the craft's position. An estimated position is just that—an estimate of where the craft is located based on either *dead reckoning* or upon information of questionable accuracy. Figure 14-19 illustrates the basics of a fix in piloting, a dead reckoning position one hour after the fix, and an estimated position. Figure 14-20 illustrates the format of a navigator's

277

14-18. CIC chart table navigation and communications equipment. Navigation information is provided by the remote gyro repeater, fathometer, and speed log. Phone talkers pass visual bearings and radar ranges over the sound-powered telephones. There are also two remote UHF/HF radiotelephone units for external communications.

0950 estimated
position

C - 050 T
S - 8 kts

Turn at 0900

195°

TANGENT -
BEARING 300°

0840 DR
position

040°

C - 015 T
S - 10 kts

080°

0800 fix

14-19. Basics of a fix. Visual bearings provide a fix at 0800. Advancing this position along the course line at 10 knots provides a dead reckoning (DR) position at 0840. Continuing the DR plot and taking a single bearing at 0950 yields an estimated position (one of questionable accuracy).

report. As can be seen, the navigator comments on the quality of the fix, indicates where the craft is located relative to the planned track, and provides a series of recommendations to the officer of the deck.

Navigation lights

The YP-676s carry as navigational lights one white 20-point masthead light, one white 12-point stern light, one white 32-point anchor light, one 10-point green starboard sidelight and one 10-point red port

"BASED ON A (EXC., GOOD, FAIR, POOR) FIX, TIME
_____, NAVIGATOR HOLDS YOU _____ YDS
RIGHT/LEFT OF/ON TRACK.
RECOMMEND COURSE _____ TO MAINTAIN/
REGAIN TRACK.
NEAREST HAZARD TO NAVIGATION IS _____ , YDS
OFF YOUR _____ _____ (E.G., PORT BOW).
NEAREST AID TO NAVIGATION IS _____, _____
YDS OFF YOUR _____ _____. (E.G.,
STARBOARD BEAM)
FATHOMETER CONCURS (OR DOES NOT) WITH
CHARTED DEPTH.
DISTANCE REMAINING THIS LEG IS _____ YDS/NM.
TIME OF TURN WILL BE _____.
NEXT COURSE IS _____."

14-20. Navigator's report.

sidelight. There are three 20-point white lights arranged vertically on the mast as towing lights and two 32-point red lights for breakdown lights (vessel *not under command*, restricted in ability to maneuver, or aground). There is also a 12-point yellow towing light mounted vertically above the white stern light on the aft end of the 01 level. The control panel for the navigational lights is in the pilothouse. The ship's air horn is atop the pilothouse and is operated by a pull cord located on the overhead adjacent to the helm. The ship's bell is on the signal bridge. A 14-inch sealed-beam navigational searchlight is installed atop the pilothouse and is controlled from a handle on the overhead of the pilothouse. (See table 14-5.)

Communications equipment

The communications equipment on the YP-676 class falls into two basic categories, internal and external. Internal communications are accomplished by voice tubes, sound-powered phones, and electric announcing and talk-back systems. External communications equipment consists of three radios, two 12-inch signal searchlights, and two sets of standard Navy signal flags. The following sections describe both the equipment and the basic communications procedures to be used aboard the YPs.

Internal communications

Five voice tubes connect the bridge wings and signal bridge with the helmsman. The brass tubes provide a simple and reliable method of communications between each station. While it is not necessary to shout, a clear, steady voice ensures that commands and response are transmitted without distortion.

Internal communications between the many stations in a YP are essential to the smooth running and safe handling of the ship. These are conducted for the most part over sound-powered telephones that connect the various stations. Table 14-6 lists the internal communications circuits and the stations serviced by the circuits. Circuit "J" is the connection for a standard public-telephone system that can be hooked up when in port.

The sound-powered phone-jack boxes are clearly labeled, and the handset or headset (a combination of ear phones and mouthpiece) are stored nearby. To use the sound-powered phone handset simply push the button and talk clearly. The button does not need to be released to receive. When using the headset, push the button on the mouthpiece to talk and release to receive. As an example of proper procedures, the lee helmsman in the pilothouse calls the engineer in EOS to order an engine speed of 1,800 RPM. The calls would be made as follows over the 1JV circuit: "EOS, pilothouse, indicate 1800 RPM"; the engineer would respond with, "EOS, aye." If the message has not been received, the engineer would say, "Pilothouse, say again." The format is in the form of "called station" followed by "calling station" followed by the message. The response from the called station is to identify itself and acknowledge with "Aye."

As can be seen from the table, there will often be many stations on an individual circuit. For this reason precise phone-talking procedure and specific message format must be used by the telephone talkers to eliminate confusion and ensure efficient communications. Messages should never be transmitted while the circuit is busy. In an emergency, however, the command *"Silence"* spoken on any

Table 14-6. YP Internal Communications Circuits

	Circuit						
Stations	1JV	JW1	JW2	21JS	JX	6MC (2)	21MC (2)
Pilothouse	1 (E)	2	2		1	TB	1
EOS	1 (E)					TB	1
Bridge (port)	1 (E)	1	1				
Bridge (Center)	1 (E)	1	1				1
Bridge (Starboard)	1 (E)	1	1				
Replenishment at Sea (P/S)	2						
Instructor Stateroom	1 (E)					TB	
Quarterdeck	1 (E)					TB	
Lazaret	1					TB	
Fuel Station (P/S)	2						
Signal Bridge					1		1
CIC	2 (E)			2	2		2
Forecastle	1					TB (NOTE 4)	
Forward Crew Berthing	1 (E) (NOTE 4)						
Mess Decks						TB	

Notes:
1. E indicates an "E-call" station—a station that may be alerted to a call by means of a push-button buzzer.
2. The 1MC/6MC and 21MC circuits are electrically amplified announcing and calling networks.
3. TB indicates a "talk-back" position for the 1MC/6MC general announcing and communications network.
4. These communications capabilities are installed on the Marinette-built boats.
5. A patch panel in CIC permits the use of the following circuits with any other sound-powered circuit.

Outlet	Location
JX1, JX2	CIC (forward chart table)
JX3, JX4	CIC (after chart table)
JX5	Pilothouse chart table
JX6	Signal bridge

circuit is the command to cease all communications until the station originating the "Silence" command has conveyed the nature of the emergency.

The brief format used on the sound-powered telephone always takes concentrated attention on the part of the talkers, and initially, considerable practice. Familiarity with the general subject matter usually transmitted on a particular circuit is also a help to the talker. For example, phone talkers on the 1JV circuit should be familiar with commands related to ship control and engineering operations, whereas the JW phone talkers should be familiar with navigation terminology and procedures. Telephone talkers must not interpret messages they are given to send, or what they receive. Rather, these messages should be relayed verbatim. When vital messages between stations are so transmitted, there is little chance of misinterpretation.

The procedures for the YP's electric announcing and talk-back systems are similar to those described above for the sound-powered telephones. The systems offer amplification of the communications and do not require an individual dedicated to a particular circuit.

External communications

For external communications, the 676-class YP is equipped with three radios, two 12-inch signal searchlights, and two sets of standard Navy signal flags. The radios are used for ship-to-ship and ship-to-shore communications, while the flashing light and signal-flag hoists are for ship-to-ship, line-of-sight visual communications. Of the three methods, the radiotelephone and the signal-flag hoists are used to send most messages.

While the majority of communications aboard the YPs are with other YPs or naval units, there are occasions requiring communications with privately owned or commercial vessels. As will be discussed, the VHF radio is aboard most vessels, and this can be used to conduct "bridge-to-bridge" communications between the YPs and other vessels. Commercial ships of all nationalities also use the *International Code of Signals* (Defense Mapping Agency Publication Number 102). This publication uses simple one-, two-, and three-letter groups to encode and decode messages. Messages using the International Code of Signals may be sent by flag hoist, radiotelephone, semaphore, or on rare occasions by sound signal using Morse code. In this publication,

the single-letter groups are the most frequently used, for they have either very urgent or very common meanings. These signals are set forth in table 14-7. When flown by a naval vessel, they are always preceded by the special *Code pennant*.

Radiotelephone communications

The YPs are equipped with three radio *transceivers*—single units capable of both transmitting and receiving in a designated frequency band. The ultra-high-frequency (UHF) transceiver is located in the pilothouse. This gives the YP line-of-sight communications in the frequency range of 225–400 mega-

Table 14-7. International Code Single Letter Signals

A	I have a diver down; keep well clear at slow speed.
*B	I am taking in, or discharging, or carrying dangerous goods.
*C	Yes (Affirmative).
*D	Keep clear of me; I am maneuvering with difficulty.
*E	I am altering my course to starboard.
F	I am disabled; communicate with me.
*G	I require a pilot. When made by fishing vessels it means: "I am hauling nets."
*H	I have a pilot on board.
*I	I am altering my course to port.
J	I am on fire and have dangerous cargo on board; keep well clear of me.
K	I wish to communicate with you.
L	You should stop your vessel instantly.
M	My vessel is stopped and making no way through the water.
N	No (negative).
O	Man overboard.
P	In harbor—All persons should report on board as the vessel is about to proceed to sea. At sea—It may be used by fishing vessels to mean: "My nets have come fast upon an obstruction."
Q	My vessel is "healthy" and I request free pratique.
*S	I am operating astern propulsion.
*T	Keep clear of me; I am engaged in pair trawling.
U	You are running into danger.
V	I require assistance.
W	I require medical assistance.
X	Stop carrying out your intentions and watch for my signals.
Y	I am dragging my anchor.
*Z	I require a tug. When made by fishing vessels: "I am shooting nets."

Note: These signals may be made by any method of signaling. However, signals marked with an asterisk (*) may only be made by sound when they are in compliance with the requirements of the International Regulations for Preventing Collisions at Sea.

281

14-21. Ultra-high frequency and high-frequency radio-telephones. Located aft in the pilothouse, the UHF (left) is primarily for tactical ship-to-ship communications, while the longer-range HF (right) provides ship-to-ship and ship-to-shore communications.

hertz (MHz). The UHF is the primary ship-to-ship tactical communications system. It can be preset with twenty different frequencies and can "guard" one frequency while monitoring and using another (a guard frequency will provide an automatic interrupt—Navy ships typically "guard" the emergency UHF channel of 243.0 MHz). The UHF can also be used for radio direction finding giving a bearing to the transmitting station. There are remote speakers and transmitting stations on the bridge and in the CIC.

There is also one high-frequency (HF) radio located in the pilothouse. This transceiver gives the YP long-range communications capabilities from 1.5 MHz to 79.99 MHz. As with the UHF transceiver, there are remote speakers in the CIC and the pilothouse and a remote transmitting station in the

CIC. Both the UHF and HF radios are housed in a single rack at the after end of the pilothouse (figure 14-21).

Each YP is also equipped with a VHF marine transceiver, which is used for line-of-sight, bridge-to-bridge communications. Nearly all naval, commercial, and privately owned vessels are equipped with VHF communications equipment. Prudent usage of the bridge-to-bridge communications channels can greatly facilitate safe operations, particularly when operating in crowded waterways. Aboard the YPs, the VHF transceiver is located in the pilothouse. On the Peterson boats the location is on the overhead above the lee helm/EOT position, while the location is on an overhead panel at the forward starboard side of the pilothouse aboard the Marinette boats (see figures 14-22A and 14-22B).

There is a separate remote operation station near the open bridge centerline pelorus. The radio monitors either VHF channels 13 or 16 at all times and can scan up to 20 channels. Table 14-8 lists the common VHF channels and their use.

Radiotelephone procedures—As with internal communications, the radiotelephone operator must use proper procedures and recognized message formats. Radiotelephone circuit discipline is also extremely important, particularly when many ships are using a single tactical or administrative circuit.

Radiotelephone procedures call for the use of *message headings*, *message text*, and *procedure words* (*or prowords*—see table 14-9 for common prowords and their meanings). On tactical circuits, each message is "headed" by the *call sign* of the ship, or groups of ships, being called. As with internal communications, the format is "called ship," followed by "calling ship," the message, and ended with either "over" or "out."

Call signs are words or combinations of letters and numbers used for identifying ships, groups of

14-22. Pilothouse instruments and VHF radio. The Peterson craft (top left) have the fathometer, speed log, and the VHF radio in a single panel above the helmsman. The Marinette VHF (bottom left) is also above the helm, while the wind, fathometer, and speed log displays (right) are located forward on the starboard side overhead.

ships, and ship-group commanders. Many naval call signs are two letter alphanumeric groups that change daily as specified in a code book. On non-tactical circuits and all VHF communications, call signs are replaced by the YP hull number followed by the international call sign. Table 14-10 lists international call signs for the individual YPs. Commercial ships will use their international call signs, while civilian small craft and yachts will use the vessel's name followed by their VHF radiotelephone identification number.

To send tactical signals, the codes in *Allied Tactical Publication 1(B) (ATP1(B)), Volume II* are used. Signals encoded from ATP1(B), Volume II may be sent by UHF or HF radio, flashing light, or flag hoist. This volume takes standard tactical messages and encodes them for transmission using small groups of letters and numbers (e.g., "Bravo Zulu" means "well done"). While offering some degree of security, the code is primarily for purposes of brevity and standardization among all allied navies. As just illustrated with the "BZ" signal, individual letters of the alphabet are spoken phonetically (see table 14-11 for the phonetic alphabet).

Table 14-8. VHF Channels

VHF-FM Channels	Use
Channel 6	Intership safety. Mandatory worldwide on all marine VHF-FM-equipped vessels. This channel should only be used for safety.
Channel 12	Port operations. Intership and ship to shore.
Channel 13	Navigational channel. Used for bridge-to-bridge communications.
Channel 16	Distress, safety, calling. Intership and ship to shore. Common to all VHF equipped ships, U.S. Coast Guard, and marine operators.
Channel 26 28	Ship to Shore. The local marine operator monitors these channels and will connect the ship to a commercial telephone for a fee.
Channel 68	Working channel.
Channel 82A	U.S. Government use only. Monitored by Small Craft Harbor Control at the U.S. Naval Station, Annapolis.
Channel WX1	Weather broadcast. Frequency 162.400 MHz.
Channel WX2	Weather broadcast. Frequency 162.550 MHz.

Numbers are spoken digit by digit, except for multiples of hundreds and thousands, which are spoken normally. For example, 10 is spoken "one zero," while 100 is spoken "one hundred."

Tactical signals taken from ATP1(B), Volume II are most often used to direct the movements of multiple ships operating in formation. There are two methods for executing tactical signals over the radiotelephone—the *nonexecutive* and the *executive* methods. The former is used for information signals, while the latter is used to order an action such as a maneuver and consists of the *immediate executive* and *delayed executive* methods of signaling. Table 14-12 provides the format and also illustrates standard two-letter call signs as used by the YPs and naval ships during operations. If a signal is an emergency signal, the word "emergency" is in-

cluded in the text of the message, and the text of the message is repeated twice in succession.

The delayed executive method is used for signals that must be executed simultaneously by all ships, but need not be executed immediately. After the initial signal is sent and acknowledged as illustrated in table 14-12, another signal is sent at the time of execution. The delayed executive method provides time to decode signals and plan the required action in the interval between the receipt of the message and the time of execution. The immediate executive method is used for readily understood signals and requires simultaneous, immediate execution, as the name implies. Note that with the immediate executive format, the text must be repeated before it is executed. Signals sent by the immediate executive method should be in plain language or limited to

284

Table 14-9. Communications Prowords

Proword	Explanation
MESSAGE FOLLOWS	A message which requires recording is about to follow. Transmitted immediately after the call.
SIGNALS FOLLOW	The groups which follow are taken from a signal book. Not used on nets primarily employed for conveying signals. Intended for use when signals are passed on non-tactical nets such as the CI Net.
BREAK	I hereby indicate the separation of the text from other portions of the message.
CORRECTION	An error has been made in this transmission. Transmission will continue with the last word correctly transmitted.
DISREGARD THIS TRANSMISSION	This transmission is in error; disregard it, not used to cancel any message that has been completely transmitted and for which receipt or acknowledgement has been received.
NEGATIVE	Not received. No.
AFFIRMATIVE	Yes. Permission granted.
SAY AGAIN	Repeat all (or portion indicated) of your last transmission.
I SAY AGAIN	I am repeating transmission or portion indicated.
VERIFY	Verify entire message (or portion indicated) with the originator and send correct version.
I VERIFY	That which follows has been verified at your *request* and is repeated.
I SPELL	I shall spell the next word phonetically.
EXECUTE TO FOLLOW	Action on the message or signal which follows is to be carried out upon receipt of the proword "EXECUTE."
EXECUTE	Carry out the purport of the message or signal to which this applies.
ROGER	I have *received* your last transmission *satisfactorily*.
ACKNOWLEDGE	Let me know that you have received and understand this message.
WILCO	Reply to "ACKNOWLEDGE," meaning "I have received your message, understand it, and will comply." Must be authorized by the Commanding Officer (Officer-in-Charge).
OVER	This is the end of my transmission to you and a response is necessary. Go ahead; transmit. (Note: All transmissions must end with OVER or OUT.)
OUT	This is the end of my transmission to you and no answer is required or expected.
WORD AFTER	The word of the message to which I have reference is that which follows _____.
WORD BEFORE	The word of the message to which I have reference is that which precedes _____.

commonly used signals, because there is no opportunity for verification, repetition, or acknowledgment between receipt and execution.

It should be noted in table 14-12 that for both methods of execution, the same message format is used. This format consists of a heading, the call sign of the ship or unit signaled, and that of the ship or unit signaling. The heading indicates precisely whom the signal is to and whom it is from. The heading is separated from the text by the proword "break." This proword is used again to separate the text from the ending. The call signs in the ending indicate which ships should acknowledge the signal. This assignment of responsibility for acknowledgment must not be confused with the heading that indicates which ships are to take action on the signal. The ending is used by the originator to

ensure that the transmission has been received. If no specific call sign is used in the ending, all units called in the heading answer by call sign in alphabetical order.

Visual signaling

There are three methods of visual communication: flag hoist, flashing light, and semaphore. The YPs use the flag-hoist method extensively and flashing light only occasionally, usually in conjunction with a flag hoist to attract attention to it, or to relay the signal to a ship from which the flags cannot be seen. Semaphore is seldom used. Midshipmen are required to learn signal flags and flag-hoist procedures, but they are not required to learn semaphore.

The flashing light is used aboard the YP primarily as a back-up communication system. Nonetheless, international Morse code symbols and elementary flashing light procedures must be learned. For ease of learning, the Morse code has been broken down into five separate groups in table 14-13.

Flag-hoist signaling is a rapid, accurate, and secure system for handling tactical and information signals during daylight. The signals must be as brief as possible, and ships must be within easy visual

Table 14-10. YP International Call Signs

YP Hull Number	CALL
676	NAEF
677	NMGZ
678	NERL
679	NUDK
680	NHMO
681	NNZE
682	NABP
683	NTGE
684	NPAX
685	NQUD
686	NBDR
687	NZHO
688	NILA
689	NVGW
690	NCLH
691	NRKJ
692	NJLQ
693	NMYG
694	NGFO
695	NKLF

Table 14-11. Phonetic Alphabet

A	Alfa	J	Juliet	S	Sierra
B	Bravo	K	Kilo	T	Tango
C	Charlie	L	Lima	U	Uniform
D	Delta	M	Mike	V	Victor
E	Echo	N	November	W	Whiskey
F	Foxtrot	O	Oscar	X	X-Ray
G	Golf	P	Papa	Y	Yankee
H	Hotel	Q	Quebec	Z	Zulu
I	India	R	Romeo		

Table 14-12. Tactical Signal Execution

Methods of execution as spoken on tactical nets:

YP hull number	Two-letter call sign
YP 676	AB
YP 677	CD
YP 678	EF
Collective call	M6 (this addresses all three YPs)
Commander's call	C1 (the senior officer's call sign)

Nonexecutive method
Mike Six, this is Charlie One, break, (signal), break, Charlie Delta, Over.
This is Charlie Delta, Roger, Out.

Executive method—Delayed Executive
Mike Six, this is Charlie One, execute to follow, break, turn starboard zero seven five, break, over.
This is Alpha Bravo, Roger, Out.
This is Charlie Delta, Roger, Out.
This is Echo Foxtrot, Roger, Out.
Mike Six, this is Charlie One, turn starboard zero seven five, standby, execute, break, Echo Foxtrot, Over.
This is Echo Foxtrot, Roger, Out.

Executive method—Immediate Executive
Mike Six, this is Charlie One, immediate execute, break, turn niner, I say again, turn niner, break, Charlie Delta, over.
This is Charlie Delta, Roger, Out.

Table 14-13. International Morse Code Symbols

Group 1		Group 2		Group 3		Group 4		Group 5	
•	E	• —	A	— •	N	—	T	• — — — —	1
• •	I	• — —	W	— • •	D	— —	M	• • — — —	2
• • •	S	• — — —	J	— • • •	B	— — —	O	• • • — —	3
• • • •	H	• — •	R	— • —	K	— — •	G	• • • • —	4
• • —	U	• — • •	L	— • — •	C	— — • •	Z	• • • • •	5
• • — •	F	• — — •	P	— • — —	Y	— — • —	Q	— • • • •	6
• • • —	V			— • • —	X			— — • • •	7
								— — — • •	8
								— — — — •	9
								— — — — —	0

range. For flag-hoist signaling, the Navy uses standard international alphabet flags (square shaped), numeral pennants (triangular), numeral flags (square), and special flags and pennants (see end papers). As noted earlier, commercial ships also use the international signal flags.

In addition to the flags and pennants, *tacklines* are used in visual signaling. A tackline is a length of halyard about three feet long used between signals or groups of signals to avoid ambiguity and to indicate a break. It is also used when specified by the signal book. When a signal to be flown is so long that it cannot be bent onto one hoist, it should be broken where a tackline would normally occur and flown from more than one halyard.

Multiple hoists must be hoisted in the order in which they are to be read. Signals on the YP are flown from either the port or starboard yardarm and read from top to bottom, and from outboard to inboard on each side.

Flag-hoist procedure—The ship originating a flag hoist will hoist signals *close up* (with the top of the hoist touching the block on the yardarm). All ships respond by hoisting the identical signal, flag for flag, and fly it *at the dip* (three-fourths of the way up). Small vessels or vessels without a required flag may hoist the *answering pennant* at the dip instead of close up. The hoist should remain at the dip until the signal has been decoded and is fully understood by the conning officer and the officer in charge. When understood, the signal is *closed up* by each ship. The signal is executed when the originator hauls down his signal. If the signal commands a maneuver, the maneuver is begun when the originator hauls down his signal unless a time for the maneuver has been specified in the signal. When the signal is executed, all vessels haul down the signal. Signals preceded by

the "Emergency" pennant are executed as soon as they are understood.

Flag hoists originated by the *officer in tactical command (OTC)* are considered to be addressed to all ships unless a specific ship or ships are indicated in the heading. Ships are indicated by their visual call, a one-letter, type-of-ship designator and a numeral pennant. The numeral pennant will be the last digit of the ship's hull number. For example, the usual call for YP-678 would be Y8. Numeral pennants, not numeral flags, are used in these visual calls.

When ships are positioned so that the originator cannot be seen by all of them, such as in a column, a signal relay system is used. Ships nearest the originator have "visual responsibility" for those farther away in the same direction. The signal closed up on the originator is hoisted at the dip on the nearest ships. It is not closed up by them until the signal is both understood on board and the correct signal has been closed up on the next ship in line away from the originator. In this manner the originator knows that when the adjacent ship or ships close up the signal, it is ready for execution on all ships. If the originator should execute the signal before all ships have acknowledged, those ships which have answered should close up and execute the signal and then relay the signal by other means to the ships for which they are responsible.

Acknowledging ships may question a signal by hoisting "Interrogative" while leaving the questioned signal at the dip. Flag hoists are canceled by the originator by hoisting "Negative" on an adjacent halyard. If only one of many signals is to be canceled, it must be repeated and preceded by "Negative." When all ships have acknowledged the cancellation, the hoists are cleared.

Table 14-14. Passing Honor Procedures

OOD of Junior Ship	OOD of Senior Ship	Hand Whistle Signal
1. Sound "attention to (port/ starboard)"		1 whistle for attention to starboard
		2 whistles for attention to port
	2. Sound "attention to (port/ starboard")"	
3. Sound "hand salute"		1 short whistle
	4. Sound "hand salute"	
	5. (after approximately 3 seconds) sound "two"	2 short whistles
6. Sound "two"		
	7. Sound "carry on"	3 short whistles
8. Sound "carry on"		

When proceeding independently in or out of port, naval ships are obliged to fly speed information signals indicating the speed that they are making through the water. Speed is always indicated by two numeral flags (never pennants) flown at the dip. The special pennant "Speed" is never flown in conjunction with these speed indicator flags.

All ships that are designated as radio transmitting and receiving stations are assigned international radio call signs by the federal government (see table 14-10). These call signs are flown by Navy ships from the outboard port signal halyard while underway in inland waters. YPs hoist these international call signs smartly as soon as all lines are cast off when getting underway, and lower them leaving Annapolis Roads when red flashing bell buoy No. 8 on the port hand comes in line and forms a range with the fixed light of Greenbury Point. When entering Annapolis Roads, they will be hoisted at this same point and lowered when the first mooring line is put ashore.

Honors and ceremonies

The national ensign is flown from the gaff of the YP at all times while underway. When not underway, the national ensign and union jack are flown between 0800 and sunset from the flagstaff aft and jack staff forward, respectively. A ship changes status from underway to not underway when the first mooring line is put over or the anchor let go. At this moment colors are shifted with ceremony. Men are stationed at the flagstaff, jack staff, and the signal bridge. One blast on a hand whistle is sounded when the status is shifted, for example from underway to not underway, and the command, "shift colors," is given. At this command, the national ensign is lowered from the gaff and the international call sign from the yardarm. At the same time, the national ensign is run up on the flagstaff and the union jack raised on the jack staff. If the ship moors before 0800 or after sunset, the national ensign and the union jack are not raised, of course.

The ceremonial raising and lowering of the national ensign and union jack in port at 0800 and sunset is referred to as morning and evening colors. The procedure for carrying out morning and evening colors aboard the YP and other naval vessels is standard. All ships follow the timing of the senior officer present (SOP). Five minutes before the ceremony, Prep is hoisted by all vessels. Prep is hauled down and attention sounded (one long blast on the hand whistle) precisely at 0800 and at sunset. All hands face the national ensign and salute. When men are formed in ranks, only the officer or petty officer in charge salutes, while the rest remain at attention. The ensign and jack are hoisted smartly and lowered slowly. After the colors ceremony, "carry on" is sounded by three short blasts on a hand whistle.

When boarding a naval vessel between the hours of 0800 and sunset, naval officers face and salute the national ensign and then turn and salute the OOD. Civilians should face the national ensign before facing the OOD to ask permission to board. The reverse order is used when disembarking. The OOD returns the salute to both the national ensign and himself.

Salutes are rendered to naval vessels by private vessels underway by *dipping* (lowering halfway) the national ensign. When these salutes are received

A

Ahead (or astern) of the guide:
1. Range is a function of speed
2. Bearing is a function of course

guide

B

Abeam of the guide:
1. Range is a function of course.
2. Bearing is a function of speed.

Note: To regain station, it is necessary to remember that the ship maneuvers on a range "circle". It is almost always necessary to adjust both course and speed to improve on only one factor (range, bearing) of assigned station.

C

Positions between ahead and astern of the guide:

Range and bearing are a balance between course and speed.

14-23. Station keeping.

from vessels under the registry of nations formally recognized by the United States, naval vessels will return the salute, dip for dip. To return a dip, the ensign is lowered halfway, held momentarily, and then rehoisted. When the dip has been answered, the saluting ship rehoists her colors. Naval vessels never initiate dips; they only return them.

Appropriate honors are rendered to other naval vessels, both United States and foreign, and to embarked high-ranking naval officers and civilians when they are passed close aboard. These *passing honors*, as they are called, are accomplished by calling the crew to attention on the appropriate side and having them render a hand salute. This salute is then answered by the honored ship, and then both ships carry on. The precise steps in this procedure, together with the proper hand whistle signals, are found in table 14-14. Passing honors are not rendered before 0800 or after sunset, and they are not exchanged by YPs engaged in drills. Procedures for dressing ship, half-masting colors, entering a harbor, anchoring or using a guest mooring, and other points of etiquette afloat will be covered in the next chapter.

Typical maneuvers

In addition to receiving instruction in handling alongside and anchoring (as discussed earlier in chapter 13 and the section on conning), the midshipmen get training in: formation shiphandling, maneuvering alongside while underway, and emergency procedures.

Formation shiphandling

Operating with other ships in a formation presents the officer of the deck (OOD) with many problems not encountered when conning a ship that is maneuvering independently. In addition to a knowledge of basic shiphandling, a familiarity with formation shiphandling is required, particularly as described in *Allied Tactical Publication, ATP1(B)*, Volumes I and II. Also essential to the OOD maneuvering in formation is a thorough understanding of relative motion and the ability to work a maneuvering board. It is beyond the scope of this book to present a detailed explanation of Navy tactical publications or to attempt to teach the *maneuvering board* (a printed polar coordinate plotting sheet with convenient scales and a nomogram and logarithmic scale used to solve relative motion problems). It is possible and pertinent, however, to point out some of the problems encountered in formation shiphandling and their solutions.

When ships are operating in formation, they are all assigned specific positions relative to each other. One ship, usually the largest and when possible the one in the center, is designated the "guide." This ship is always assumed to be *on station* (in the correct position) and to be making precisely the signaled course and speed. All other ships keep their stations with reference to the guide. It is therefore essential that the OOD keep track of base course and speed and the range and bearing to the guide when maintaining station.

It is up to the OOD to keep his ship on station. Staying within 3 degrees in bearing and 50 yards in range is usually acceptable on the YP. The standard maneuvering-board scale used on the YPs is 100 yards per circle.

Station keeping is quite simple, as figure 14-23 indicates, but takes *constant* attention, requiring continued alteration of course and speed.

When stationed ahead of the guide, as in Situation A in figure 14-23, changes of speed affect range, and course changes alter bearing. When stationed on the beam, as in Situation B of figure 14-23, the effect is the opposite, with course alterations changing range, and speed changes affecting bearing. Usually, as in Situation C of figure 14-23, the station is neither directly ahead nor abeam of the guide, in which case station keeping is a function of combined course and speed changes. For example, if, in Situation C, the OOD wanted to keep the bearing to the guide constant, but decrease the range, he would have to alter course to the left to close the guide and thereby decrease the range, and at the same time increase speed in order not to fall behind while closing, and thereby change the bearing.

The best advice for station keeping is to work out a solution and then take action, using common sense backed up by a maneuvering-board solution to choose a course and speed that will produce the desired relative motion to move the ship from her actual to her desired position with respect to the guide. Course and speed changes should be gradual and with a constant check kept on the resulting change in position relative to the guide. An attempt

to regain station should never be made by radical course and speed changes, for when wrong, this type of solution is *very* wrong, and when right, before base course and speed can be resumed, the ship often will be as far from station as before, but in the opposite direction.

When station keeping, a constant check may be kept on the range to the guide by using the *stadimeter* (an optical range-finding device that computes distance to an object of known height once the angle between the bottom and top of the object is measured). The masthead height of the guide must be set on the stadimeter before accurate ranges can be determined. It should be remembered that the masthead height of the 676-class YP is 42 feet. Since the masthead-height scale on the stadimeter cannot be set this low, a setting of 84 feet (twice the height) is therefore used, and all ranges read from the stadimeter must be halved to get true ranges.

To stay on station, all movements of the guide must be followed precisely. All turns, unless otherwise indicated, should be executed when the guide turns and with standard rudder. The use of standard rudder ensures that all ships turn with the same tactical diameter, in this case 200 yards, and thus the range to the guide from each ship remains the same. When full rudder is prescribed, the result is the same, except that all ships turn with reduced tactical diameter, 80 yards for the YP (see table 14-3).

The safety of the ship is the paramount responsibility of the OOD. The OOD should never assume that all ships will act correctly on a given signal. For this reason, a constant check should always be kept on other ships in the formation, especially those toward which the ship is turning, to ensure that they are turning in the same direction.

When ordered to move from one station in a formation to another, the OOD at the earliest possible moment should acquaint himself with the new station number, the range and bearing to the guide from the new station, and the initial direction of turn if it has been prescribed. From this information, the OOD should be able to work out a rough course and speed solution to get to the new station. As soon as the maneuvering-board solution for the problem is available, it should be checked against this initial rough calculation.

It must be remembered that the maneuvering

board will often show solutions on paper that in reality are not practical. For instance, a speed increase from 7 knots to a stationing speed of 10 knots is not a practical solution for moving ahead 150 yards. In this case, the *three-minute rule* (speed, or relative speed, in knots times 100 equals distance traveled, or relative distance if relative speed was used, in yards in three minutes) would indicate that at 3 knots relative speed, it would only take 1½ minutes to travel the required relative distance of 150 yards. When it is remembered that it will take 16 seconds to accelerate from 7 knots to 10 knots, and that the 7-knot formation speed should be resumed when 27 yards from station, it will be realized that the 10-knot speed could only be kept for about one minute. Although this solution may at first be indicated on the maneuvering board, common sense suggests a more moderate one.

If a signal is executed before the precise course and speed solution to station is known, the best action is to turn in the correct direction and use the estimated rough course and speed. Course and speed can always be refined on the way to station.

The straight maneuvering-board solution does not allow for other ships that may be obstructing the direct route from one station to another. A YP should not be passed by another closer than 100 yards, and an attempt should be made to pass under the stern whenever possible. This is especially true when maneuvering close to the guide. While proceeding to station, a constant check must be kept on range and bearing to the guide. If the range and bearing are not changing as they should be, a return to base course and speed will at least maintain the status quo until the proper solution can be determined.

When proceeding to a new station, the number of the station should be indicated by an information signal flown from the yardarm. The proper signal is the Designation pennant followed by the numeral flag (never pennant unless out of flags) of the new station. This signal is flown *at the dip* (two or three feet below the yardarm) as soon as the new station is assigned. It is *closed up* (hoisted to the yardarm) while proceeding to station, and hauled down when on the new station. Station indicators are used to determine where other ships are going. If another YP is flying the same station number you are flying, assignments should be rechecked.

When maneuvering in formation:
- Always know the base course and speed of the formation.
- Know your ship's course and speed.
- Know the proper range and bearing of the guide.
- Know the actual range and bearing to the guide and check them continually.
- Always look before maneuvering and don't count on correct action from other vessels.
- Using all available information and a good deal of common sense, make decisions promptly and then take action.
- Most important, keep in mind that at all times the OOD's primary responsibility is the safety of the ship, and only a constant vigil will keep the ship out of danger. This is particularly important when operating in close company.

Maneuvering alongside: replenishment

The YP OOD will occasionally be required to maneuver alongside another YP while underway, either in a replenishment drill or to transfer a piece of equipment. In most cases, the delivering ship will act as control ship and guide. A replenishment course should be chosen that is into both wind and sea. When wind and sea are not from the same direction, the course should be into whichever element is the more significant. Replenishment speed should be the minimum speed required for responsive shiphandling. For the YPs, 8 knots is a good replenishment speed. Once signaled, the control ship should maintain replenishment course and speed. The ship designated to go alongside should, prior to her approach, steady on replenishment course and speed astern of the control ship. This gives the OOD an opportunity to check for gyro error and speed difference. For example, with the guide steady on course 175° T at 8 knots, the OOD on the approach ship determines that steering a course of 173° T is required to stay directly astern of the guide; that is, there is apparently 2 degrees of error between the two gyros. With this in mind and the YP in position to make an approach on the starboard side of the control ship, the OOD might issue a command of "Steer nothing to the left of one seven three." This assists in ensuring a safe approach. If approaching on the port side, the command would be, "Steer nothing to the right of one seven three."

Flag-hoist procedures used in Navy replenishment operations are found in *ATP1(B)*, Volume II, and are used during YP drills. Before an approach, fenders should be rigged along the appropriate sides of the delivering and receiving ships. On each ship, the most experienced helmsman and lee helmsman should be on watch. A helm error on either ship while alongside can cause a collision.

In making the approach, the OOD of the receiving ship should use a speed differential of from 3 to 5 knots. Three knots is recommended for the YPs. It should be kept in mind that surge for the 676-class YP is 9 yards per knot. This dictates that with a 3-knot speed advantage, the OOD should reduce speed when 27 yards from station alongside. A much higher speed advantage combined with an appropriate backing bell is often used in the fleet, but is not required or recommended for the YP.

The approach should be made from astern on the appropriate quarter. By the time the receiving ship begins to overlap the delivering ship, the approach course should be within two or three degrees of, or the same as, the course during replenishment. The separation between the two vessels at this point should never be less than the eventual desired separation. For the YPs this is not less than 20 feet. For the separation to be greater is merely to err on the safe side. It is during the approach and breakaway phases of the replenishment operation that the greatest danger of collision exists. The bow shape of the two ships as they come together acts to form a funnel. The water forced into this funnel increases in velocity as it passes between the two ships. As the velocity of the water between the ships increases, the pressure on their inboard sides is reduced relative to the pressure on their outboard sides. In effect, there is a force tending to pull them together (see illustration of Bernoulli's principle, figure 3-6). During the approach and breakaway phases of the operation, any rudder action that tends to swing the stern of the receiving ship towards the delivering ship causes an increase in this force that can result in the vessels being drawn together. This is why a near-parallel approach course is recommended. The same is true for breaking away. Speed should be increased to clear the side of the delivering ship, but course should not be altered significantly until the receiving ship is clear ahead. If, while alongside, the replenishment course must be changed, it should be changed very gradually, in 5-degree increments, and with great caution.

Emergency procedures

Emergencies can occur on any vessel at any time, but the watch officer who makes a habit of thinking ahead can foresee many emergencies and prevent them, or at least be prepared to meet them. The only way to prepare for emergencies is to be alert at all times and to know in advance exactly what action must be taken in a given situation. It is good practice for the watch officer, when conditions permit, to discuss emergency procedures with other members of the watch and with all hands whenever possible.

While not the only emergencies possible, man overboard, breakdown, collision, fire, and grounding are the most likely and pose the greatest threat to the YP or any other vessel. The proper procedures to cope with these emergencies must be known by the OOD. It is also his responsibility to keep the officer-in-charge of the YP informed of emergency situations and casualties, but action should precede reporting. It is obvious that this discussion is as pertinent to the skipper of a small auxiliary as it is to the OOD of a YP or the captain of a destroyer. All must know how to deal immediately with an emergency situation when it occurs.

Safety equipment

Lifesaving equipment for the 676-class YP includes 50 life preservers, 20 inflatable and 30 kapok, and two 25-man life rafts. The 30 kapok and 8 inflatable life preservers are stowed in the port and starboard life-jacket lockers on the 01 level. Twelve additional inflatable life jackets are stowed in the damage-control locker on the main deck, port side. Two 24-inch life rings with attached strobe-light markers are located on the port and starboard sides of the main deck amidships. There are two additional life rings located on the 01 level. Four "smoke floats" (floating markers that emit smoke) are located in racks on the 01 level just abaft the pilothouse doors, two on either side. Four are also located on the main deck amidships, two to port and two to starboard. There are two first aid kits—one located on the mess deck and the other in the passageway forward of the CIC. On the Peterson boats (YPs 676–682) there is an additional small first aid kit in a canvas bag in the pilothouse.

14-24. A 25-person life raft. Each life raft may be released manually or by the automatic hydrostatic release. Note the small sea painter extending from the life raft to the mounting stand. The sea painter should not be cast off until the raft is fully loaded and all equipment and supplies being taken from the YP are aboard the raft.

292

Life rafts

Two 25-person self-contained, encapsulated life rafts are stowed on the main deck fantail, one to port, the other to starboard (figure 14-24). These life rafts are equipped with an automatic hydrostatic release (triggered by water pressure when the main deck sinks below 10 to 15 feet) as well as a manual release. The life raft should only be inflated manually after the container has been launched and a check has been made to see that the 100-foot sea painter is securely fastened to the rail or the life raft stowage rack. Pulling on the sea painter will activate the manual inflation system. The life raft is equipped with a variety of safety equipment including hand pumps, bailer, sea anchors, radar reflector, sea markers, signal mirror, 50 cans of drinking water, and five desalinator kits.

EPIRBs

For offshore summer cruises the YPs are issued *Emergency Position Indicating Radio Beacons* (EPIRBs). These devices send automatic position signals that can be received by satellite and/or rescue aircraft. They should be activated only in the event of an extreme emergency. In the event that the crew has to abandon the YP, the EPIRBs should be taken aboard the life rafts. *Pyrotechnics*, visual emergency signaling devices, are also carried aboard during cruises. These consist of a Very flare pistol, day and night flares, and smoke floats. When aboard, these signaling devices are stowed in the pilothouse pyrotechnic locker or the 01 level smoke float locker.

Fire fighting and damage control

For fire fighting and damage control the YP-676 class has an extensive inventory of equipment as illustrated in table 14-15. Fire-fighting equipment includes standard Navy hoses and nozzles, portable CO_2 and PKP fire extinguishers, foam and foam pickup nozzles, an automatic or manually activated Halon fire-suppression system in the engine room and fuel tank compartment, and a manually operated PKP Gaylord Range Hood fire extinguisher above the galley stove. The primary saltwater firemain system is driven by the firemain pump on the starboard main engine. In addition, the YPs carry a portable P-250 gasoline-powered pump that can provide pressure to the firemain system. The P-250 is located aft on the port side of the fantail and is connected to the firemain through a firemain riser located on the after, port side of the deckhouse.

As illustrated in table 14-15, the YPs carry oxygen breathing apparatuses (OBAs) permitting fire fighters to enter smoke-filled compartments. Each YP also has one complete fire-fighting ensemble (see figure 14-25) stowed in the port side main deck damage control locker. This fire-fighting suit is made of heavy canvas and leather and affords a high degree of protection from heat and flame. In addition, there are small emergency breathing hoods attached to each bunk throughout the craft. These hoods provide the crew with fifteen minutes of emergency oxygen.

As mentioned earlier, there are some differences in the locations of fire-fighting and damage control equipment between the Peterson-built YPs (hull numbers 676 through 682) and the Marinette Marine–built YPs (hull numbers 683 through 695). Figure 14-26 illustrates the forward fire stations on each type YP. Note that in figure 14-26 (top) (the Marinette), the fire station includes a variable nozzle (commonly referred to as a "Veri" nozzle) and an NPU nozzle, while the Peterson station illustrated (bottom) does not have either. These nozzles are stowed in the port side, main deck damage control locker on YP 676 through 682.

In the Peterson engine room, the fire station includes hose, all-purpose nozzle, a 4-foot applicator, and a CO_2 and a PKP fire extinguisher mounted on the forward bulkhead of the EOS. The configuration on the Marinette boats is similar, except that the fire station also includes the Veri nozzle, the CO_2 is mounted on a bracket on a stanchion just forward of the starboard generator, and the PKP extinguisher is mounted on the stanchion just forward of the port generator. The mess decks first aid

Table 14-15. Safety and Damage-Control Equipment

Portable Fire Extinguishers—Locations and Quantities

Location	CO2	PKP
Pilothouse	1[1]	0
Main deck passage forward	1	1
CIC	2	0
Main deck passage aft	1	1
Each passage—platform deck, forward	2	0
Engine room[2]	1	1
EOS	1	1
Messroom	1	0
Galley	1	1
Lazaret	0	1

1. There are two CO_2 fire extinguishers on YPs 683 throuh 695—Marinette-built boats
2. On YPs 676 through 682 (Peterson-built boats), the extinguishers are located at the engine room fire station. On YPs 683 through 695 (Marinette-built boats), the CO_2 is mounted on a stanchion just forward of the starboard generator; the PKP is on a similar mount just forward of the port generator.

Fire Stations—Locations & Quantities YP 676/YP 683

Equipment	Forecastle	Fantail	Engine Room
4-foot applicator	1/1	1/1	1/1
1½-inch hose—50 ft.	2/2	2/2	0/0
1½-inch hose—25 ft.	0/0	0/0	1/1
All-purpose nozzle	1/1	1/1	1/1
Spanner wrench	1/1	1/1	1/1
Veri nozzle	0/1	0/1	0/1
NPU pickup nozzle	0/1	0/1	0/1

Note: The "Veri" nozzles and NPU pickups are stowed in the port side damage-control lockers on YPs 676 through 682 (Peterson-built boats).

Other Fire-fighting, Damage-control Equipment, and Safety Equipment

Oxygen-breathing apparatus—4 masks and 18 canisters, OBA locker, main deck passageway foward of CIC
15-minute emergency escape and breathing device—at each bunk throughout the YP.
Fire-fighting ensemble—1 suit with boots, port side, main deck damage-control locker
Foam—9 five-gallon cans. 6 cans in racks in the main deck passageway aft of CIC, 3 cans in the port side, main deck damage-control locker
Battle lanterns—portable and fixed (relay). All spaces except the fuel tanks and bilges.
Shoring, pipe patching, hammers, fire axes, DC plugs & wedges, hack saws, eductors, hammers, oakum, rubber sheets, extra fire hose, extra battle lanterns, extra battle lantern batteries, extra CO_2 life jackets—port side, main deck damage-control locker.
First aid kits—Kits are located on the mess decks and in the main deck passageway forward of CIC. On the Peterson-built boats there is additional small first aid kit in a canvas bag in the pilothouse.
Life jackets—60 Kapok and 16 CO_2 life jackets are stowed in the 01 level life jacket lockers on the port and starboard bridge wings. An additional 12 CO_2 life jackets are stowed in the port side, main deck damage-control locker.
Life rings—Two 24-inch life rings with strobe lights are located on the main deck, amidships, port and starboard sides. Two additional life rings are located on the 01 level bridge wings, port and starboard sides.
Life rafts—Two, 25-person, self-contained, fully encapsulated life rafts are located on the fantail, port and starboard sides.
Smoke floats & emergency signaling devices—Smoke floats, emergency pyrotechnics, and the Emergency Position Indicating Radio Beacon (EPIRB) are issued during training cruise. Smoke floats are mounted on the main deck and 01 levels, port and starboard sides. Pyrotechnics and the EPIRB are kept locked in the pilothouse pyrotechnic locker.

14-25. Fire-fighting ensemble. The heavy canvas and leather suit provides excellent short-term protection when used with the Oxygen-Breathing Apparatus (OBA). The suit is stowed in the port side, main deck damage-control locker.

kit on the Peterson boats is forward on the port bulkhead; it is on the starboard bulkhead on the Marinette boats.

The YP's *bilge system* is used to remove flood water resulting from grounding or a collision. The 35-gallon-per-minute bilge pump is driven by the port main engine. The bilge system consists of nine separate lines, each serving separate compartments below the main deck. In the event of a casualty to the port main engine, the P-250 can be connected to the bilge system providing a dewatering capacity of 250 gallons per minute with a suction lift of up to 20 feet. Should the bilge pump or port engine fail, the fire pump, driven by the starboard main engine, may be cross-connected to the bilge system for dewatering.

For a man overboard, the Marinette boats are fitted with a large J-davit to which a block and tackle and rescue sling can be fitted. This davit (see figure 14-5) is stowed under the ladder leading from the forecastle to the 01 level flying bridge and can be fitted in either port or starboard side mounting brackets located on the forecastle. The Peterson boats do not have this davit and bracket arrangement.

While these differences may seem minor, they are vitally important during an emergency. Each member of the crew must be aware of which type YP he is aboard, know precisely the location and function of all emergency equipment, and be able to make his

way from his bunk below decks to the main deck in conditions of smoke and darkness. Each midshipman is also assigned a specific responsibility in the ship's *Watch, Quarter, and Station Bill* for routine operations and shipboard emergencies. These specific responsibilities and duties must also be thoroughly understood to ensure the safety of the craft and her crew.

Man overboard

There are a number of man-overboard recovery methods. (Recovery methods for sailboats were discussed in chapter 11.) The three most common are: (1) Williamson turn for night or low visibility, (2) race-track turn for fastest recovery when proceeding at high speed in clear weather, and (3) Y-backing, for ships with large turning circles and great backing power proceeding at slow speeds. These three methods are illustrated in figure 14-27. Very large ships often use a small boat to recover a man from the water. Smaller vessels will use the small-boat recovery method as well when the sea is very rough, and the possibility of getting the man close alongside the ship is small. The principles mentioned earlier about launching a small boat in a seaway would apply if this method were used on the YP.

Regardless of which recovery method is used, the same basic principles and required action apply. Initially a life ring, life jacket, and floating light or smoke float is thrown overboard to provide flotation for the man and to mark his position. At the same time, the report is made to the OOD, "Man overboard, starboard (port) side." The OOD swings the stern away from the man with full rudder. If it is possible to stop the shaft on the side toward the man before he reaches the screws, this should be done. If it is not, which is likely, continue the recovery without attempting to stop the screw. The CIC must be informed immediately, in order that the EPSCO plotter can be shifted to the man-overboard mode of operations. In this mode, the automatic plotting head will move to the center of the table and the scale will be 1 inch equals 1 mile. When the plotter head is shifted, this position must be immediately marked as being the nearest position to the man in the water. The CIC plotting team will then continuously assist the officer of the deck by providing ranges and bearings to this position.

The general announcing system (21MC) is also

14-26. Differences in fire stations. The Marinette forward and aft main deck fire stations (top) have more equipment than the same fire stations on the Peterson craft (bottom). The foam pickup and variable flow ("Veri") nozzles shown at the Marinette stations are found in the port side, main deck damage-control locker on the Peterson craft. All fire stations are equipped with a sea strainer, valve, 1½-inch fire hose, spanner wrench, all-purpose nozzle, and a standard 4-foot spray applicator.

used to notify all crew members of the man overboard. Crew positions include swimmers, boat and grapnel hooks, and heaving lines and life rings. These positions are assigned in the YP's Watch, Quarter, and Station Bill. On the bridge, as many personnel as can be spared should be detailed to *keep the man overboard in sight*. Visual bearings and approximate ranges to the man should be sent to the CIC for cross-checking with the plotting team working on the EPSCO plotters.

Other ships in company must be informed of the emergency and be kept informed of recovery progress. Voice radio is the best method. In addition, six short blasts should be sounded at frequent intervals. As time permits, the Oscar flag should be hoisted during daylight, or the two, vertical, red 32-point lights turned on and pulsated at night.

The man should be recovered in the shortest possible time. For the YPs, in good weather this means the race-track method; at night or in low visibility, the Williamson turn—though not the fastest recovery method—must be used to bring the ship back along her track. With any method, the desired final position is beam to the wind slightly to

296

METHOD AND PRIMARY USE	DIAGRAM (SHIP ON COURSE 090; NUMBERS REFER TO THE EXPLANATION)	EXPLANATION	ANALYSIS	
			ADVANTAGES	DISADVANTAGES
WILLIAMSON TURN 1. USED IN REDUCED VISIBILITY BECAUSE IT MAKES GOOD THE ORIGINAL TRACK. 2. USED WHEN IT IS BELIEVED THAT A MAN FELL OVERBOARD SOME TIME PREVIOUSLY AND HE IS NOT IN SIGHT.	⊗ = MAN	1. PUT THE RUDDER OVER FULL IN THE DIRECTION CORRESPONDING TO THE SIDE OVER WHICH THE MAN FELL. STOP THE INBOARD ENGINE. 2. WHEN CLEAR OF THE MAN, GO AHEAD FULL ON ALL ENGINES, CONTINUE USING FULL RUDDER. 3. WHEN HEADING IS 60° BEYOND THE ORIGINAL COURSE, SHIFT THE RUDDER WITHOUT HAVING STEADIED ON A COURSE. 60° IS PROPER FOR MANY SHIPS, HOWEVER, THE EXACT AMOUNT MUST BE DETERMINED THROUGH TRIAL AND ERROR (50° FOR YPs). 4. COME TO THE RECIPROCAL OF THE ORIGINAL COURSE, USING FULL RUDDER. 5. USE THE ENGINES AND RUDDER TO ATTAIN THE PROPER FINAL POSITION (SHIP UPWIND OF THE MAN AND DEAD IN THE WATER WITH THE MAN ALONGSIDE, WELL FORWARD OF THE PROPELLERS).	1. SIMPLICITY, THE REASON WHY IT IS TAUGHT ON YP DRILLS. 2. MAKES GOOD THE ORIGINAL TRACK IN THE OPPOSITE DIRECTION, EXCEPT FOR THE EFFECTS OF WIND AND CURRENT.	1. SLOW 2. TAKES THE SHIP A RELATIVELY GREAT DISTANCE FROM THE MAN, WHEN SIGHT MAY BE LOST.
ONE TURN ("ANDERSON") USED BY DESTROYERS, SHIPS WHICH HAVE CONSIDERABLE POWER AVAILABLE AND RELATIVELY TIGHT TURNING CHARACTERISTICS.		1. PUT THE RUDDER OVER FULL IN THE DIRECTION CORRESPONDING TO THE SIDE OVER WHICH THE MAN FELL. STOP THE INBOARD ENGINE. 2. WHEN CLEAR OF THE MAN, GO AHEAD FULL ON THE OUTBOARD ENGINE. CONTINUE USING FULL RUDDER. 3. WHEN ABOUT TWO-THIRDS OF THE WAY AROUND, BACK THE INBOARD ENGINE 2/3 OR FULL. ORDER ALL ENGINES STOPPED WHEN THE MAN IS WITHIN ABOUT 15 DEGREES OF THE BOW, THEN EASE THE RUDDER AND BACK THE ENGINES AS REQUIRED TO ATTAIN THE PROPER FINAL POSITION (AS FOR THE OTHER METHODS). 4. MANY VARIATIONS OF THIS METHOD ARE USED, DIFFERING PRIMARILY IN RESPECT TO THE USE OF ONE OR BOTH ENGINES, AND THE TIME WHEN THEY ARE STOPPED AND BACKED TO RETURN TO THE MAN AND TIGHTEN THE TURN. THE VARIATION USED SHOULD REFLECT INDIVIDUAL SHIP'S CHARACTERISTICS, SEA CONDITIONS, PERSONAL PREFERENCES, ETC.	THE FASTEST RECOVERY METHOD.	1. REQUIRES A RELATIVELY HIGH DEGREE OF PROFICIENCY IN SHIPHANDLING BECAUSE OF THE LACK OF A STRAIGHT-A-WAY APPROACH TO THE MAN. 2. OFTEN IMPOSSIBLE FOR A SINGLE PROPELLER SHIP.
RACETRACK TURN (TWO 180° TURNS) USED IN GOOD VISIBILITY WHEN A STRAIGHT FINAL APPROACH LEG IS DESIRED.		1. A VARIATION OF THE ONE TURN METHOD WHICH PROVIDES A DESIRABLE STRAIGHT FINAL APPROACH TO THE MAN. 2. PUT THE RUDDER OVER FULL IN THE DIRECTION CORRESPONDING TO THE SIDE OVER WHICH THE MAN FELL. STOP THE INBOARD ENGINE. 3. WHEN CLEAR OF THE MAN, GO AHEAD FULL ON ALL ENGINES, CONTINUE USING FULL RUDDER TO TURN TO THE RECIPROCAL OF THE ORIGINAL COURSE. 4. STEADY FOR A DISTANCE WHICH WILL GIVE THE DESIRED RUN FOR A FINAL STRAIGHT APPROACH. 5. USE FULL RUDDER TO TURN TO THE MAN. 6. USE THE ENGINES AND RUDDER TO ATTAIN THE PROPER FINAL POSITION (SHIP UPWIND OF THE MAN AND DEAD IN THE WATER WITH THE MAN ALONGSIDE WELL FORWARD OF THE PROPELLERS).	1. THE STRAIGHT FINAL APPROACH LEG FACILITATES A MORE CALCULABLE APPROACH. 2. THE SHIP WILL BE RETURNED TO THE MAN IF HE IS LOST FROM SIGHT. 3. REASONABLY FAST. 4. EFFECTIVE WHEN THE WIND WAS FROM ABEAM ON THE ORIGINAL COURSE.	SLOWER THAN THE ONE TURN METHOD.
DELAYED TURN USED WHEN WORD IS RECEIVED THAT A MAN FELL OVERBOARD, MAN IN SIGHT AND CLEAR ASTERN OF THE SHIP.		1. A VARIATION OF THE ONE TURN METHOD. 2. PUT THE RUDDER OVER FULL IN THE DIRECTION CORRESPONDING TO THE SIDE OVER WHICH THE MAN FELL. GO AHEAD FULL ON ALL ENGINES. 3. HEAD TOWARDS THE MAN. 4. USE THE ENGINES AND RUDDER TO ATTAIN THE PROPER FINAL POSITION (SHIP UPWIND OF THE MAN AND DEAD IN THE WATER WITH THE MAN ALONGSIDE, WELL FORWARD OF THE PROPELLERS).	1. THE FASTEST METHOD WHEN THE MAN IS IN SIGHT AND ALREADY CLEAR ASTERN OF THE SHIP. 2. PROVIDES A STRAIGHT RUN IN THE CRITICAL FINAL PHASE. 3. EFFECTIVE WHEN THE WIND IS FROM AHEAD OR ASTERN OF THE SHIP ON THE ORIGINAL COURSE.	1. DOES NOT ENSURE RETURN TO THE MAN. 2. REQUIRES GOOD VISIBILITY. 3. TAKES THE SHIP FARTHER FROM THE MAN THAN THE OTHER METHODS.
Y BACKING USED BY SUBMARINES BECAUSE THE SHIP (LOW HEIGHT OF EYE) REMAINS COMPARATIVELY CLOSE TO THE MAN.		1. PUT THE RUDDER OVER FULL IN THE DIRECTION CORRESPONDING TO THE SIDE OVER WHICH THE MAN FELL. STOP THE INBOARD ENGINE. 2. WHEN CLEAR OF THE MAN, BACK THE ENGINES WITH FULL POWER, USING OPPOSITE RUDDER. 3. GO AHEAD. USE THE ENGINES AND RUDDER TO ATTAIN THE PROPER FINAL POSITION (SHIP UPWIND OF THE MAN AND DEAD IN THE WATER WITH THE MAN ALONGSIDE, WELL FORWARD OF THE PROPELLERS).	THE SHIP REMAINS COMPARATIVELY CLOSE TO THE MAN.	MOST SHIPS BACK INTO THE WIND/SEA, RESULTING IN POOR CONTROL OF THE SHIP WHILE BACKING.
BOAT RECOVERY 1. USED BY SHIPS LACKING SUFFICIENT MANEUVERABILITY TO MAKE A GOOD APPROACH FOR A SHIP RECOVERY. 2. USED WHEN THE SHIP IS DEAD IN THE WATER WITH THE MAN CLOSE ABOARD BUT NOT ALONGSIDE. 3. CAN BE USED IN CONJUNCTION WITH ANY OF THE METHODS SHOWN ABOVE.	BASIC BOAT RECOVERY METHOD:	BASIC BOAT RECOVERY METHOD: 1. PUT THE RUDDER OVER FULL IN THE DIRECTION CORRESPONDING TO THE SIDE OVER WHICH THE MAN FELL. STOP THE INBOARD ENGINE. 2. WHEN THE MAN IS CLEAR, BACK ALL ENGINES FULL TO NEARLY STOP THE SHIP. USE RUDDER TO THE SIDE OF THE READY LIFEBOAT TO PROVIDE A SLICK IN WHICH THE BOAT CAN BE LOWERED. STOP THE ENGINES WHILE THE SHIP STILL HAS VERY SLIGHT HEADWAY TO PERMIT BETTER CONTROL OF THE BOAT AND TO KEEP IT OUT OF THE PROPELLER WASH.	BASIC BOAT RECOVERY METHOD: 1. SIMPLE 2. FOR ANY GIVEN TYPE OF SHIP, THE SHIP WILL REMAIN CLOSER TO THE MAN THAN BY ANY OF THE OTHER METHODS. 3. DOES NOT REQUIRE THAT A PARTICULAR FINAL POSITION BE ATTAINED.	BASIC BOAT RECOVERY METHOD: 1. THE MAN MUST BE IN SIGHT. 2. SEA AND WEATHER CONDITIONS MUST BE SATISFACTORY FOR LOWERING AND RECOVERING THE LIFEBOAT AND FOR SMALL BOAT OPERATIONS.

14-27. Man-overboard recovery methods.

windward of the man with all way off. When in this position a lee is provided for the man, and since the ship will make more leeway than the man, she will drift toward, rather than away from him.

With the man overboard in the lee of the YP and *all engines stopped*, the actual recovery process begins. If the man is not injured, a heaving line or long boat hook may be passed and the man can pull himself aboard using the two large rubber "rub rails" attached outboard of the hull. Holding the line or boat hook, the victim can gain a foothold on the lower rub rail, then pull himself up to the upper rail, and climb aboard on the fantail. Another alternative in calm seas is to rig the Jacob's ladder on the quarter and let the man climb aboard. Again, it would be imperative to pass a heaving line to the man so that if he slipped from the ladder he would still be connected to the YP.

If the man overboard is injured, recovery is far more difficult, and swimmers must enter the water to assist. As can be appreciated, there will then be two or more "men overboard." If the original man overboard is unconscious or seriously injured, some form of sling must be rigged from the YP's mooring lines or replenishment-at-sea lines. A *Spanish bowline* or *bowline on the bight* may be tied in a line and the swimmers can place the double loops of either type of bowline around the man. The legs of the man go through each of the two loops on the Spanish bowline while the bowline on the bight provides a makeshift boatswain's chair with one loop being the seat and the second supporting the back. If the man is unconscious, additional hitches around the man's chest and arms must be made to prevent him from falling out of the sling. Figure 14-28 illustrates these two useful knots.

If the recovery is from one of the Marinette boats with the man-overboard recovery davit, a block and tackle is rigged on the outboard end of the davit, and the man is brought aboard on the forecastle. Again, a sling must be rigged to the lower block. If the recovery must be made from the Peterson-built boats, it is probably most advisable to make the recovery from the fantail since there is less freeboard over which to lift the injured man. The swimmers can either haul themselves aboard or use a Jacob's ladder as described earlier. If the water temperatures are cold, it is imperative that all hands be brought back aboard as quickly as possible to avoid hypothermia.

Man overboard maneuvering instructions for naval vessels involved in tactical evolutions can be found in ATP1(B), Volume I. Of specific importance to the YP OOD are the instructions for man overboard recovery from a column formation. In this situation, the ship that loses the man takes action to avoid him, and others do as well, with odd-numbered ships in the column clearing to starboard, and even-numbered ships clearing to port. The ship in the best position to recover the man does so, keeping the other vessels informed of her actions. All ships resume stations when clear.

In summary, when a man falls overboard, the following actions should be taken as rapidly as possible:

● Drop a life ring or jacket, and light or smoke float.
● Swing stern away from man.
● Inform CIC and ship's company.
● Keep man in sight.
● Inform other ships by radio, sound, and visual signals.
● Maneuver to recover man using race-track, Y-backing, or Williamson-turn method.
● Put your ship to windward of the man.
● Try to recover the man overboard from the deck using lines, recovery davit (Marinette boats only), or the Jacob's ladder.
● Assist the recovery with swimmers only as necessary.

Breakdown

Breakdowns that prevent the YP from maneuvering do not occur very frequently. However, when a breakdown occurs, the immediate reaction must always be to try to maintain control of the vessel. If there is a rudder casualty, the ship may be steered with the engines.

All ships in company should be notified of the casualty by voice radio. Six short blasts should be sounded, and during daylight the Five flag should be hoisted. At night, the six blasts should be sounded, the breakdown lights (red over red) turned on, and the running lights turned off if not making way (see Rule 27). The vessel should be anchored, if necessary.

When the nature of the breakdown has been determined, the senior officer present should be notified and given an estimate of repair time. If the

STEP
A

STEP
B

FINISHED
KNOT
(pull tight)

14-28. Spanish bowline (left) and bowline-on-the-bight (right).

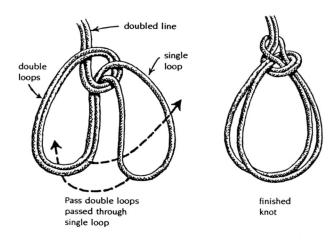

is used as a *messenger* to pass the tow line to the disabled vessel. In most situations, the towing vessel should approach the disabled one to windward and pass the line as she moves abeam at slow speed. If the disabled vessel is aground on a lee shore or shoal, the line may be floated to her on a life jacket with the towing vessel staying a safe distance to windward.

Each YP is equipped with a 235-foot towing hawser made of 4½ inch plaited nylon. One end of the hawser is fitted with a *thimble* (a metal *eye* spliced into the end) and the other with a *soft eye* (a spliced loop). The soft eye is large enough to fit over the *towing bitt* on the YP's stern. The thimble (or hard eye) is fitted to a *towing bridle* on the disabled vessel with a 1½-inch screw shackle (see figure 14-29). To form the towing bridle, every YP carries two, 55-foot, 4½-inch plaited nylon lines. Each line has a soft eye in one end that fits over the forecastle bitts on the YP being towed. The other end of each line has a hard eye with a thimble. With the two lines rigged port and starboard through the main-deck chocks, the two hard eyes are shackled into the hard eye of the towing hawser with a 1½-inch shackle, thus forming the bridle. This single hawser and bridle arrangement is satisfactory if the tow is of short duration and in calm seas. If the tow is of long duration (four hours or more) or if the seas are expected to be rough, the length of the tow should be doubled. This is accomplished by shackling the hawsers of both YPs together as illustrated in figure 14-29. For both short- and long-duration tows, the length of the hawsers is insufficient to provide for a *catenary* (a shock-absorbing dip or downward curve caused by the weight of the hawser). Therefore, it is most important to keep personnel clear of the lines

casualty cannot be repaired and the YP is without power, preparations for towing should be made.

Towing

It will occasionally be necessary for the YP to tow another vessel, and infrequently one may have to accept a tow. There are no hard and fast rules for towing, because wind and sea conditions and the size of the vessels involved are variable. Towing may be done astern or alongside. The astern method is preferred since it avoids damage caused when two vessels roll together while alongside. However, each situation must be evaluated before decisions are made (see chapter 13).

When preparing for towing astern, a heaving line

on both vessels to prevent possible injury should the tow line part.

If the disabled vessel is not another YP, the towing YP can pass one of its bridle lines and a shackle to rig the tow. If the vessel is large, both bridle lines can be passed and the tow is the same as with another YP. An alternative arrangement is to shackle the towing YP's hawser to the anchor rode of the towed vessel. In this event, it is extremely important that the towing vessel make the rode fast to bow cleats (or to the mast if a sailing vessel) and to keep personnel off the bow. As noted earlier, should the tow part, the rode and hawser may recoil and sweep across the bow of the disabled vessel.

Since normally there will be no catenary in the tow, the critical point in the towing operation is taking the strain on the lines and getting the tow underway. The towing ship must increase speed very gradually and overcome the inertia of the other vessel slowly in order to keep the tow line from parting. Once underway, speed may be increased gradually to the *hull speed* (see chapter 3) of the disabled vessel, conditions permitting. This is a very important fact to remember, particularly if the YP is towing another vessel with a hull speed less than 10 to 11 knots (the maximum safe towing speed for the YPs). Being towed at greater than hull speed can do considerable damage to a vessel.

When towing during daylight, no special shapes are required if the length of the tow is 200 meters or less. Towing vessels with a tow of more than 200 meters must carry a diamond shape where it can best be seen. At night, the towing YP will show two white towing lights mounted vertically on the mast. These lights have the same characteristics as the normal masthead light. For tows over 200 meters long, a towing vessel would show three white lights mounted vertically. In addition to the vertical white lights on the mast, a towing vessel carries normal sidelights and a yellow towing light mounted vertically above the white stern light. The rhymes "three white lights in a row, barge is in tow," and "white over white, a tow is in sight" assist in remembering the Rules. In conditions of restricted visibility, the towing vessel will sound one prolonged blast followed by two short blasts at intervals not to exceed

14-28 A & B. Two YP-676-class boats underway, the Marinette 683 series (top), and the Peterson 676 series (bottom).

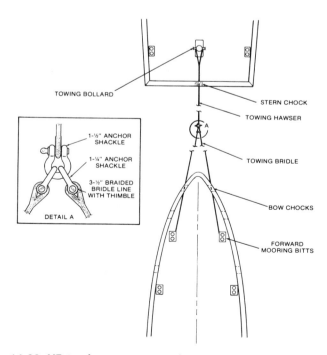

14-29. YP towing arrangement.

two minutes. For details of the Rules consult appendixes A and B.

Collision

Collisions at sea do not "just happen." They can usually be prevented by adhering to the signaling and maneuvering requirements of the Rules of the Road. The prudent seaman also learns to anticipate what might happen and constantly plays mental "what if" games to prepare for the unexpected. For example, "what if" the privileged vessel crossing close ahead experiences a propulsion or steering failure? Or, "what if" the sailing vessel now clear to starboard tacks early to clear shoal waters and comes back across my bow? Developing a plan of action for the unexpected will most often prevent a collision. As noted earlier in the section on communications, most vessels, even very small sailing and motor yachts, have VHF radios. In crowded waterways the VHF can be a valuable adjunct to the signals required by the Rules of the Road should another vessel's actions appear inconsistent or confusing.

Should the OOD of the YP or any other vessel find himself *in extremis*, however, the first two actions are to *reduce the relative motion* between the vessels and *sound the collision alarm* to alert the entire crew to potential danger. Given the power and maneuverability of the YP, reducing relative motion is fairly simple. The YP has great backing power, and the twin screws and rudders permit very tight turns in a short time. The simple construction and division of watertight compartments aboard the YPs also permit the crew to secure watertight doors and hatches rapidly to minimize flooding.

If a collision occurs, all compartments should be inspected for damage and flooding. The crew should be mustered at their assigned collision and flooding stations, and immediate action should be taken to prevent flooding. This may be accomplished by isolating watertight compartments, plugging holes using damage-control plugs, mattresses, pillows, buckets, etc., and removing water with the bilge and P-250 pumps. The fire pump, driven by the starboard engine, may also be cross-connected to the bilge system to give an increased dewatering capability. Even with substantial damage and flooding, the YP should be capable of staying afloat in a stable condition with forward berthing, fuel tank, and engine-room spaces flooded. In extreme conditions

when flooding takes place from damage above the waterline, limited counterflooding and/or pumping diesel fuel and fresh water overboard may raise the damaged area clear of the water and prevent further flooding. In the unlikely event that the flooding cannot be stopped and the vessel is at risk of sinking, abandoning ship or running the vessel aground are options of last resort. If the vessel is abandoned, the crew should take all available undamaged supplies and the EPIRBs into the life rafts.

Grounding

With the array of navigational gear aboard the YPs, it should certainly be possible to keep her in deep water. If a YP should run aground, the reaction should be exactly the same as it would be on any power vessel. (See the sections on grounding in chapters 2 and 13.)

In the event of a YP grounding, immediately stop the engines and inspect all below-deck spaces for damage and flooding. If the ship is holed and flooding is occurring, it may be safer to leave the YP aground until repairs can be completed and water removed from below-deck compartments. When no damage or flooding is evident, an attempt should be made to maneuver free by backing hard on both engines. Should this fail in the first few attempts, do not continue, as the engines may overheat. An alternative approach is to quickly twist the YP back and forth with one engine ahead standard and the opposite engine back full. Alternating the engines ahead and astern followed by a hard backing attempt may be sufficient to break any ground suction on the forward part of the YP. If these attempts fail, secure the main engines and signal for assistance. Some boats might be kedged off after setting out an anchor or two, but this is seldom a practical method for the YPs, as they carry very heavy anchors that must be carried out in fairly large boats.

If grounding has occurred at low tide, simply waiting for the tide to turn may be all that is required to refloat the YP. If, however, it is already high tide, or if the vessel is being damaged by wave action against a shoal, towing assistance should be requested. Throughout any actions to refloat the YP, continuous inspections must be made of below-deck compartments and the YP's main engines. Since the primary pumps (fire and bilge) are driven by the main engines, their loss due to overheating or a bent shaft or propeller would be doubly crippling to the safety of the vessel.

Fire

Fires at sea must be quickly brought under control and extinguished. Although YPs are better prepared for this emergency than many other small vessels, prompt action is required because of their small compartments, limited fire-fighting equipment, and abundance of combustible materials. As noted earlier, each member of the crew must know the precise location of all fire-fighting and damage-control equipment, how to use it, and their assigned responsibilities. The crew must also recognize there are multiple dangers associated with fire. The most obvious are the flame and heat. However, there are also hazards from smoke, noxious fumes (e.g., many plastics will produce a potentially lethal gas when burning), risk of explosion, and a general lack of oxygen.

Fires are classified according to the type of combustible material involved. There are four types of fire: Alpha, Bravo, Charlie, and Delta. Alpha-class fires are in solid combustibles such as wood, rags, mattresses, paper, or canvas. Class-A fires are fought with water, foam, CO_2, or PKP. Bravo fires involve petroleum products and flammables such as tar, grease, alcohol, paints, and solvents. These fires are fought with foam, PKP, Halon, or CO_2. When possible, the fuel supply should be shut off immediately. Charlie-class fires are electrical. The first action for a Class-C fire is to isolate the burning equipment from the power source by tripping a circuit breaker. CO_2 and PKP are also used, although PKP will most likely do considerable damage to the electrical or electronic equipment. Delta-class fires are metals such as magnesium and titanium—this class of fire is not a threat aboard a YP. There are also multiple-class fires resulting when one type causes another. A Class-B fire can easily result from a Class-A fire aboard the YPs, particularly in the engineering compartments. Likewise, a Class-C fire igniting cable insulation and then the wooden structure of the craft becomes a Class-AC fire. If in doubt as to the class of fire, always use the fire-fighting method prescribed by the higher (further in the alphabet) class fire. For example, fighting a Class-AC fire with water poses an electrical shock hazard, while CO_2 or PKP can be safely used against both the Class-A and Class-C

fires. A low-velocity water fog from the "Veri" nozzle or the standard four-foot applicator can effectively smother a Class-B diesel-oil fire, but Halon and foam are far more effective.

Class-A and -C fires can occur almost anywhere aboard the YP. Class-B fires are most likely in the engine room, fuel tanks, lazaret, and galley. The general fire-fighting procedures are: (1) locate the fire, report the fire to the officer in charge or craftmaster, and alert the entire crew by sounding the General Alarm and describing the emergency over the 21MC general announcing system or by sound-powered phones. (2) As all hands are proceeding to their assigned fire-fighting stations, the power and ventilation to the compartments on fire must be *secured* (turned off). Isolate and fight the fire. (3) *Overhaul* the area (cleaning all debris, breaking up any smoldering materials, saturating the area with water or foam, and dewatering the compartment). (4) Set a reflash watch.

While there are general procedures for fighting fires, they are only guidelines. The *on scene leader*, the officer in charge, and the craftmaster must be prepared to react immediately to unexpected situations that may occur while fighting a fire. These include the spread of the fire, conditions of reduced lighting and heavy smoke, injuries to members of the fire-fighting team, and reductions in fire-fighting capability as a result of damage to on-board equipment.

When approaching the compartment on fire, the crew must by very careful to first cool closed hatches or doors. This is accomplished by directing a stream of water from either the high-pressure hose or more generally a low-velocity fog from the four-foot applicator. It is also important to establish *fire boundaries* on adjacent compartments to ensure the fire has not spread. When the fire is under control, the crew must conduct a careful inspection and thoroughly overhaul all burned areas.

Special precautions with fire aboard the YPs

As noted earlier, the YPs are fitted with a Halon fire-extinguishing system in the engine room and fuel-tank compartments. The system is activated automatically by flame detectors that provide total coverage of both compartments. It may also be activated manually from the EOS or pilothouse control panels or from manual override "push-pull" levers and "T-handles" located in the EOS or in the main-deck passageway at frame 48 (the passageway just abaft the CIC and adjacent to the ladders leading down to the EOS and the mess decks). The pilothouse control panel is shown in figure 14-30. When activated, an audible alarm will sound in the pilothouse, the EOS, and the engine room.

Although generally safe, Halon can pose some special hazards. When the system is activated, the sudden release of Halon under pressure is extremely noisy and can move unsecured small objects. While such behavior is generally not damaging to the fire fighter, it can be unsettling and startling for him. Close contact with the discharging Halon can also cause frostbite to exposed skin. Again, this is not usually a problem since the liquid Halon vaporizes very quickly. Immediately after Halon release, there may be a fog in the compartment obscuring the crew's vision as a result of the high-velocity, low-temperature discharge. The fog should clear quickly and is not a hazard. The volume concentration of Halon does not exceed 7 percent, and a healthy individual can perform in this environment safely for up to five minutes maximum. The ventilation systems in the Halon-protected compartments are linked to the Halon system and will be de-energized automatically when the system is activated. With the ventilation systems off, Halon may produce toxic fumes in the form of hydrogen fluoride, hydrogen bromide, and free bromide in fires with temperatures above 900 degrees Fahrenheit. All of these vapors are colorless, although they all have a sharp acrid odor. To protect against injury from these chemicals, personnel entering a compartment in which Halon has been discharged should wear the Oxygen Breathing Apparatus (OBA) and protective clothing (either the fire-fighting ensemble shown in figure 14-25 or, as a minimum, long pants and long-sleeved shirts.) Direct contact with CO_2 can

14-30. Pilothouse Halon controller. When both the pilothouse and EOS controllers are set to automatic, a fire in either the engine room or the fuel-tank compartment will be sensed by the flame detectors, resulting in both spaces being flooded automatically with Halon gas. The system may also be activated manually from either the pilothouse or the EOS.

also pose a frostbite hazard if exposed skin is place directly in the path of the discharge.

To successfully prevent fires at sea, the craftmaster, officer in charge, and all members of the crew must exercise diligence on a daily basis to prevent conditions that could lead to a fire. This includes attention to details in equipment maintenance, proper cleaning and stowage of flammable materials, and the prompt reporting of potentially hazardous situations. All fire-fighting equipment must be regularly inspected and tested for proper operation. Finally, the crew must be drilled on a consistent basis to ensure that all hands thoroughly understand the proper use of emergency equipment and their role in fighting emergencies at sea.

15.
Etiquette Afloat

To most seamen, a love of boats and the sea is accompanied by a profound respect and admiration for those age-old traditions long associated with the sea. These often unwritten customs and traditions provide the basis of etiquette afloat.

When entering and leaving port, particular attention should be paid to the appearance of the vessel. For example, lines should never be left trailing over the side. Such sloppiness is not only unslightly, but also it creates a definite hazard in that a trailing line can become wrapped around the propeller. Shipshapeliness is important anytime, of course, but the lack of it is particularly noticeable in harbor. When a boat enters port, fenders and fender boards should be left on deck until nearing the dock. They should be taken aboard immediately after clearing the dock when leaving. Allowing fenders to dangle over the side while underway may seem a minor offense, but the practice certainly mars the appearance of a beautiful boat.

When entering harbor in a sailboat under power, sails should be furled neatly, sheets and halyards belayed and coiled properly, and loose gear, including clothes and towels, should be put below. The importance of presenting a seamanlike appearance when entering and leaving port cannot be overemphasized.

Once in the harbor, don't anchor too close to other boats already moored. Always allow for shifts in the wind and current, leaving room to swing a full 360 degrees around the anchor. Also keep in mind that deep-draft sailboats will sometimes swing to the current while shallow-draft boats swing to the wind. This means extra care and foresight when anchoring a sailboat in a harbor with many powerboats, and vice versa.

Often in a crowded anchorage there will be guest moorings provided by the community or local yacht club for visiting vessels. Do not pick up these moorings without first checking with the yacht club or harbor master. This is not only a courtesy, but also a precaution, since the mooring may be in disrepair or not heavy enough for your vessel.

When anchored or moored in a crowded anchorage, keep in mind that sound travels easily over the water. Late gatherings in the cockpit should be kept reasonably quiet. Boisterousness lasting until the early hours of the morning is not appreciated by others in the anchorage. Tying halyards away from aluminum masts will eliminate an objectionable source of noise on a windy evening. Keep radios turned low.

Never throw trash overboard in harbors or inland waters. The rule definitely applies to the Chesapeake Bay, since a Maryland law prohibits such pollution of its waters. All trash and garbage should be disposed of ashore or saved until well clear of the land when going offshore.

When under power, always respect the rights of boats under sail, and remember the effect that a large wake will have on them. Whenever possible, slow down when passing a sailboat, give her a wide berth, and try to pass astern. Occasionally, an ignorant or rude sailboat skipper will needlessly interfere with a powerboat navigating in a channel, or an inconsiderate motorboat operator will (deliberately?) come too close to a vessel under sail. Such conduct is not only extremely discourteous and irritating to the victims, it is also dangerous for obvious reasons. Sailboats racing should be given an especially wide berth, because wakes and wind interference left by powerboats or other sailboats can seriously affect the outcome of the race. This is especially true in light weather. When maneuvering around racing sailboats, reduce speed to minimize wake and always pass astern and to leeward of them, so their wind is not disturbed. Don't anchor near racing marks or starting or finish lines.

Channels, like roads, have two sides. Don't be a channel hog, keep to the right, and remember the proper whistle signals.

When in harbor, always proceed at a very slow speed, leaving little or no wake. In many areas, a maximum speed of six knots is allowed by law and will be posted. Whether posted or not, this rule of courtesy should be observed. This is especially important for heavy-displacement boats that make large waves.

When proceeding under sail, never interfere with a power vessel just to emphasize a sailboat's right of way. Try not to harass powerboats negotiating a crowded channel, and do not interfere with large steam vessels in restricted waters. Such prudent respect for size is common sense and also law under both International and Inland Rules of the Road.

Regatta protocol

There are many rules of etiquette afloat that are peculiar to regattas and sailboat racing in general.

Entry forms required for most regattas must be filled in accurately. They often provide the basis for handicapping and identifying the entrants, and all information contained on them is assumed to be correct. These entry forms usually stipulate conformance to racing instructions, liability releases, and, measurement requirements. These stipulations are honored without question. By the same unwritten rule of conduct, the skipper of the yacht racing under a handicap system is honor bound to race his boat loaded and trimmed as nearly as possible as she was when measured. Particularly important in this regard is the shifting of ballast, which is covered in Rule 22 of the USYRU Racing Rules.

If, after entering a race, the skipper finds he will not be able to race his boat, he should try to notify the sponsoring club of his change in plans before the date of the race. More importantly, he should notify the race committee as soon as possible when he drops out of a race.

Before starting a race, it is required by the racing rules (and it is also common courtesy) to keep clear of the starting area while other classes start. The same principle applies after finishing. It is also expected that boats that have not started or are not racing will keep clear of boats that are racing, regardless of who may have the right of way. Non-racers should be able to identify racers by the class flag nearly always flown on the backstay of competing boats.

When racing, keep clear of other racing classes whenever possible. It is considered poor sportsmanship to use racing tactics such as covering and blanketing, against boats of other classes that are not actual competitors. Luffing might be considered a reasonable tactic to discourage a larger boat in another class from passing you to windward.

All boats in a possible collision situation should of course seek to avoid collision. The boat with the right of way must hold course until in extremis, but must then maneuver to avoid collision, just as the other boat must. If the skipper of a racing yacht feels that another skipper is in danger of violating the racing rules, he should so inform him. If the rules are violated and a protest results, the protesting skipper should try to inform the protested skipper immediately. The racing rules require that the red protest flag be flown and the race committee be informed of the protest when finishing, or as soon as possible.

15-1. The former Naval Academy 60-foot sloop *Guerrière*. Notice that it is now accepted practice to fly the national ensign (or yacht ensign) from a stern staff while under sail. The boat would appear more shipshape if there were no lines hanging overboard.

Whenever a skipper of a boat being protested realizes that he is in fact guilty of an infraction of the rules, he should immediately withdraw from the race unless penalties are provided for the particular infraction. In the latter case when percentage penalties are applied, he should display code flag "I" in compliance with appendix 3 of the USYRU Rules. If, after withdrawal, he elects to continue to sail in the vicinity of the course, he must keep well clear of all racing yachts. The skipper that misses a mark or rounds a buoy the wrong way and cannot correct his mistake should immediately withdraw, regardless of whether or not any other boats are aware of his error.

It is not ethical to drop a protest just because the protested boat is eventually beaten in the race. If an infraction of the rules occurred, the case should be protested and decided. Withdrawing a written protest might not be allowed under Rule 68.9 of the USYRU Rules. Information given to the members of the protest committee should be as accurate as possible.

In summarizing these sections, it may be sufficient to note that, interestingly enough, most rules of etiquette afloat are also good rules of safety afloat.

Flag etiquette

The flying of flags or *colors* (the term may include all of the flags flown by a vessel or it may refer only to the national or yacht ensign) on sailing and power vessels is a subject governed primarily by custom and tradition. The right of private vessels to fly national colors stems indirectly from the Navy's long traditional use of the stars and stripes. When the Continental Congress established a national flag in June, 1777, it was immediately thereafter flown from naval vessels. As the Navy then and for some time thereafter was supplemented by large numbers of privateersmen, it became customary for these privately owned naval vessels to fly the national standard as well.

The yacht ensign, a Betsy Ross flag with a fouled anchor inside the circle of thirteen white stars, is usually flown from yachts instead of the national flag (see the end papers). It was designed by the New York Yacht Club and adopted in 1849 by the Secretary of the Navy as a signal to be flown by yachts and certain merchantmen, exempting them from entering and clearing at customs houses. Be-

Table 15-1. Sequence of Bunting for Full-Dress Ship

a. U.S. Navy FLAG BAG: (*starting from bow*)

3, 4, p1, S, 1st, A, Prep, C, M, Speed, J, p5, R, p9, Z, Corpen, 8, U, 6, X, Negat, 2, Port, N, p2, T, 2nd, B, D, Turn, 5, Station, K, p6, W, p0, 1, 0, 3rd, H, E, Emerg, L, p7, 0, Int, Div, p4, 9, 4th, P, Form, V, G, Stbd, I, F, Q, p8, Y, Desig, 7, p3, Squad, Ans.

b. Standard FLAG BAG: (*starting from bow*)

AB 2, UJ 1, KE 3, GH 6, IV 5, FL 4, DM 7, PO 3rd, RN 1st, ST 0, CX 9, WQ 8, ZY 2nd, Ans.

cause of its similarity to the national flag, it has become the yacht ensign and is today the customary ensign for yachts to fly. All U.S. Naval Academy vessels fly the national ensign, as they are naval vessels.

Colors are flown aboard yachts, as they are on naval vessels, from 0800 until sunset while in port. Underway, entering or leaving port, they may be flown whenever there is enough light to distinguish them, but before 0800 or after sunset, they should be hauled down immediately after anchoring. When underway offshore, colors may be flown whenever required, such as when meeting other vessels. They may also be flown as needed when approaching lightships or nearing foreign shores.

When making colors in the morning, if shorthanded, the ensign is raised first, then the *yacht club burgee* (flag, usually triangular, designating a specific yacht club). At sunset, colors are executed in the reverse order, if shorthanded. Whenever possible, however, all colors should be raised and lowered simultaneously. The Senior Officer Present should initiate morning and evening colors, all others following his timing and example.

If the ensign is to be flown at half-mast, it must first be mastheaded and then lowered to half-mast (actually about two-thirds of staff height). Before lowering from half-mast, colors should first be mastheaded and then lowered.

At anchor, all yachts should fly the yacht ensign from a staff aft. It should be noted that members of the *U.S. Power Squadrons* (an educational organization dedicated to safety afloat and good seamanship) are entitled to fly the U.S. Power Squadron ensign in place of the yacht ensign. The Power Squadron ensign is pictured on the end papers. Underway, the ensign is flown from a staff aft on a powerboat or a sailboat under power.

Traditionally, U.S. yachts have always flown the ensign from the leech of the after sail or from the after peak when the boat is gaff-rigged, but now it is permissible and proper to fly it from a staff at the stern when under sail.

The yacht club *burgee* is flown both at anchor and underway from a bow staff on powerboats, from the foremast truck of schooners, and from the mainmast truck of all other rigs.

On the Luders yawls and Navy 44s, the U.S. Naval Academy Sailing Squadron burgee (end papers) is flown from the mainmast head while under-

15-2. The *Fearless* in full dress. Notice that the signal flags extend below the rail at the bow and stern. The Union Jack is shown at the bow, the Naval Academy Sailing Squadron burgee at the masthead, and the Tango signal flag (launch requested) below the starboard lower spreader.

way (except when racing outside Chesapeake Bay) or at anchor.

Sailing Squadron members holding the ranks of commodore, vice commodore, and rear commodore should display the flag of their rank at the mizzen masthead in the Luders yawls, except when racing. These flags should be flown day and night.

On national holidays, at regattas, and when ordered or on other special occasions, a vessel may "dress ship" with signal flags and pennants of the International Code of Signals. In order to achieve the most colorful sequence of flags and pennants, the Navy method of two signal flags to one pennant is recommended. Table 15-1 gives the order of flags for dressing ship. The ship should be dressed at 0800 and should remain dressed until sunset. The signal flags should reach from the waterline forward to the heads of all masts, and down to the waterline aft (see figure 15-2).

When visiting in foreign waters, the *courtesy flag* (the national ensign of the host country) should be displayed from the starboard, lower mainmast spreader between 0800 and sunset.

It should go without saying that exemplary behavior and proper protocol are especially important in foreign countries, for you and your crew are in effect emissaries, or at least conspicuous representatives, of your country.

A. International Regulations for Preventing Collisions at Sea, 1972

Application

Rule 1. (a) These Rules shall apply to all vessels upon the high seas and in all waters connected therewith navigable by seagoing vessels.

(b) Nothing in these Rules shall interfere with the operation of special rules made by an appropriate authority for roadsteads, harbours, rivers, lakes or inland waterways connected with the high seas and navigable by seagoing vessels. Such special rules shall conform as closely as possible to these Rules.

(c) Nothing in these Rules shall interfere with the operation of any special rules made by the Government of any State with respect to additional station or signal lights, shapes or whistle signals for ships of war and vessels proceeding under convoy, or with respect to additional station or signal lights or shapes for fishing vessels engaged in fishing as a fleet. These additional station or signal lights, shapes or whistle signals shall, so far as possible, be such that they cannot be mistaken for any light, shape or signal authorized elsewhere under these Rules.[1]

(d) Traffic separation schemes may be adopted by the Organization for the purpose of these Rules.

(e) Whenever the Government concerned shall have determined that a vessel of special construction or purpose cannot comply fully with the provisions of any of these Rules with respect to the number, position, range or arc of visibility of lights or shapes, as well as to the disposition and characteristics of sound-signalling appliances, without interfering with the special function of the vessel, such vessel shall comply with such other provisions in regard to the number, position, range or arc of visibility of lights or shapes, as well as to the disposition and characteristics of sound-signalling appliances, as her Government shall have determined to be the closest possible compliance with these Rules in respect to that vessel.

Responsibility

Rule 2. (a) Nothing in these Rules shall exonerate any vessel, or the owner, master or crew thereof, from the consequences of any neglect to comply with these Rules or of the neglect of any precaution which may be required by the ordinary practice of seamen, or by the special circumstances of the case.

(b) In construing and complying with these Rules due regard shall be had to all dangers of navigation and collision and to any special circumstances, including the limitations of the vessels involved, which may make a

309

---

[1] Submarines may display, as a distinctive means of identification, an intermittent flashing amber (yellow) beacon with a sequence of operation of one flash per second for three (3) seconds followed by a three (3) second off-period. Other special rules made by the Secretary of the Navy with respect to additional station and signal lights are found in Part 707 of Title 32, Code of Federal Regulations (32 CFR 707).

departure from these Rules necessary to avoid immediate danger.

General Definitions

Rule 3. For the purpose of these Rules, except where the context otherwise requires:

(a) The word "vessel" includes every description of water craft, including nondisplacement craft and seaplanes, used or capable of being used as a means of transportation on water.

(b) The term "power-driven vessel" means any vessel propelled by machinery.

(c) The term "sailing vessel" means any vessel under sail provided that propelling machinery, if fitted, is not being used.

(d) The term "vessel engaged in fishing" means any vessel fishing with nets, lines, trawls or other fishing apparatus which restrict maneuverability, but does not include a vessel fishing with trolling lines or other fishing apparatus which do not restrict maneuverability.

(e) The word "seaplane" includes any aircraft designed to maneuver on the water.

(f) The term "vessel not under command" means a vessel which through some exceptional circumstance is unable to maneuver as required by these Rules and is therefore unable to keep out of the way of another vessel.

(g) The term "vessel restricted in her ability to maneuver" means a vessel which from the nature of her work is restricted in her ability to maneuver as required by these Rules and is therefore unable to keep out of the way of another vessel.

The term "vessels restricted in their ability to maneuver" shall include but not be limited to: (i) a vessel engaged in laying, servicing or picking up a navigation mark, submarine cable or pipeline; (ii) a vessel engaged in dredging, surveying or underwater operations; (iii) a vessel engaged in replenishment or transferring persons, provisions or cargo while underway; (iv) a vessel engaged in the launching or recovery of aircraft; (v) a vessel engaged in mineclearance operations; (vi) a vessel engaged in a towing operation such as severely restricts the towing vessel and her tow in their ability to deviate from their course.

(h) The term "vessel constrained by her draft" means a power-driven vessel which because of her draft in relation to the available depth of water is severely restricted in her ability to deviate from the course she is following.

(i) The word "underway" means that a vessel is not at anchor, or made fast to the shore, or aground.

(j) The words "length" and "breadth" of a vessel mean her length overall and greatest breadth.

(k) Vessels shall be deemed to be in sight of one another only when one can be observed visually from the other.

(l) The term "restricted visibility" means any condition in which visibility is restricted by fog, mist, falling snow, heavy rainstorms, sandstorms or any other similar causes.

Part B. Steering and Sailing Rules

Section I. Conduct of Vessels in Any Condition of Visibility

Application

Rule 4. Rules in this Section apply in any condition of visibility.

Look-out

Rule 5. Every vessel shall at all times maintain a proper look-out by sight and hearing as well as by all available means appropriate in the prevailing circumstances and conditions so as to make a full appraisal of the situation and of the risk of collision.

Safe Speed

Rule 6. Every vessel shall at all times proceed at a safe speed so that she can take proper and effective action to avoid collision and be stopped within a distance appropriate to the prevailing circumstances and conditions.

In determining a safe speed the following factors shall be among those taken into account:

(a) By all vessels: (i) the state of visibility; (ii) the traffic density including concentrations of fishing vessels or any other vessels; (iii) the maneuverability of the vessel with special reference to stopping distance and turning ability in the prevailing conditions; (iv) at night the presence of background light such as from shore lights or from back scatter of her own lights; (v) the state of wind, sea and current, and the proximity of navigational hazards; (vi) the draft in relation to the available depth of water.

(b) Additionally, by vessels with operational radar: (i) the characteristics, efficiency and limitations of the radar equipment; (ii) any constraints imposed by the radar range scale in use; (iii) the effect on radar detection of the sea state, weather and other sources of interference; (iv) the possibility that small vessels, ice and other floating objects may not be detected by radar at an adequate range; (v) the number, location and movement of vessels detected by radar; (vi) the more exact assessment of the visibility that may be possible when radar is used to determine the range of vessels or other objects in the vicinity.

Risk of Collision

Rule 7. (a) Every vessel shall use all available means appropriate to the prevailing circumstances and conditions to determine if risk of collision exists. If there is any doubt such risk shall be deemed to exist.

(b) Proper use shall be made of radar equipment if fitted and operational, including long-range scanning to obtain early warning of risk of collision and radar plotting or equivalent systematic observation of detected objects.

(c) Assumptions shall not be made on the basis of scanty information, especially scanty radar information.

(d) In determining if risk of collision exists the following considerations shall be among those taken into account: (i) such risk shall be deemed to exist if the compass bearing of an approaching vessel does not appreciably change; (ii) such risk may sometimes exist even when an appreciable bearing change is evident, particularly when approaching a very large vessel or a tow or when approaching a vessel at close range.

Action to Avoid Collision

Rule 8. (a) Any action taken to avoid collision shall, if the circumstances of the case admit, be positive, made in ample time and with due regard to the observance of good seamanship.

(b) Any alteration of course and/or speed to avoid collision shall, if the circumstances of the case admit, be large enough to be readily apparent to another vessel observing visually or by radar; a succession of small alterations of course and/or speed should be avoided.

(c) If there is sufficient sea room, alteration of course alone may be the most effective action to avoid a close-quarters situation provided that it is made in good time, is substantial and does not result in another close-quarters situation.

(d) Action taken to avoid collision with another vessel shall be such as to result in passing at a safe distance. The effectiveness of the action shall be carefully checked until the other vessel is finally past and clear.

(e) If necessary to avoid collision or allow more time to assess the situation, a vessel shall slacken her speed to take all way off by stopping or reversing her means of propulsion.

Narrow Channels

Rule 9. (a) A vessel proceeding along the course of a narrow channel or fairway shall keep as near to the outer limit of the channel or fairway which lies on her starboard side as is safe and practicable.

(b) A vessel of less than 20 meters in length or a sailing vessel shall not impede the passage of a vessel which can safely navigate only within a narrow channel or fairway.

(c) A vessel engaged in fishing shall not impede the passage of any other vessel navigating within a narrow channel or fairway.

(d) A vessel shall not cross a narrow channel or fairway if such crossing impedes the passage of a vessel which can safely navigate only within such channel or fairway. The latter vessel may use the sound signal prescribed in Rule 34(d) if in doubt as to the intention of the crossing vessel.

(e) (i) In a narrow channel or fairway when overtaking can take place only if the vessel to be overtaken has to take action to permit safe passing, the vessel intending to overtake shall indicate her intention by sounding the appropriate signal prescribed in Rule 34(c) (i). The vessel to be overtaken shall, if in agreement, sound the appropriate signal prescribed in Rule 34(c) (ii) and take steps to permit safe passage. If in doubt she may sound the signals prescribed in Rule 34(d). (ii) This Rule does not relieve the overtaking vessel of her obligation under Rule 13.

(f) A vessel nearing a bend or an area of narrow channel or fairway where other vessels may be obscured by an intervening obstruction shall navigate with particular alertness and caution and shall sound the appropriate signal prescribed in Rule 34(e).

(g) Any vessel shall, if the circumstances of the case admit, avoid anchoring in a narrow channel.

Traffic Separation Schemes

Rule 10. (a) This Rule applies to traffic separation schemes adopted by the Organization.

(b) A vessel using a traffic separation scheme shall: (i) proceed in the appropriate traffic lane in the general direction of traffic flow for that lane; (ii) so far as practicable keep clear of a traffic separation line or separation zone; (iii) normally join or leave a traffic lane at the termination of the lane, but when joining or leaving from either side shall do so at as small an angle to the general direction of traffic flow as practicable.

(c) A vessel shall so far as practicable avoid crossing traffic lines, but if obliged to do so shall cross as nearly as practicable at right angles to the general direction of traffic flow.

(d) Inshore traffic zones shall not normally be used by through traffic which can safely use the appropriate traffic lane within the adjacent traffic separation scheme. However, vessels of less than 20 meters in length and sailing vessels may under all circumstances use inshore traffic zones.

(e) A vessel other than a crossing vessel or a vessel joining or leaving a lane shall not normally enter a separation zone or cross a separation line except: (i) in cases of emergency to avoid immediate danger; (ii) to engage in fishing within a separation zone.

(f) A vessel navigating in areas near the terminations of traffic separation schemes shall do so with particular caution.

(g) A vessel shall so far as practicable avoid anchoring in a traffic separation scheme or in areas near its terminations.

(h) A vessel not using a traffic separation scheme shall avoid it by as wide a margin as is practicable.

(i) A vessel engaged in fishing shall not impede the passage of any vessel following a traffic lane.

(j) A vessel of less than 20 meters in length or a sailing vessel shall not impede the safe passage of a power-driven vessel following a traffic lane.

(k) A vessel restricted in her ability to maneuver when engaged in an operation for the maintenance of safety of navigation in a traffic separation scheme is exempted from complying with this Rule to the extent necessary to carry out the operation.

(l) A vessel restricted in her ability to maneuver when engaged in an operation for the laying, servicing or picking up of a submarine cable, within a traffic separation scheme, is exempted from complying with this Rule to the extent necessary to carry out the operation.

311

Appendix A

Section II. Conduct of Vessels in Sight of One Another

Application

Rule 11. Rules in this Section apply to vessels in sight of one another.

Sailing Vessels

Rule 12. (a) When two sailing vessels are approaching one another, so as to involve risk of collision, one of them shall keep out of the way of the other as follows: (i) when each has the wind on a different side, the vessel which has the wind on the port side shall keep out of the way of the other; (ii) when both have the wind on the same side, the vessel which is to windward shall keep out of the way of the vessel which is too leeward; (iii) if a vessel with the wind on the port side sees a vessel to windward and cannot determine with certainty whether the other vessel has the wind on the port or on the starboard side, she shall keep out of the way of the other.

(b) For the purposes of this Rule the windward side shall be deemed to be the side opposite to that on which the mainsail is carried or, in the case of a square-rigged vessel, the side opposite to that on which the largest fore-and-aft sail is carried.

Overtaking

Rule 13. (a) Notwithstanding anything contained in the Rules of Part B, Sections I and II any vessel overtaking any other shall keep out of the way of the vessel being overtaken.

(b) A vessel shall be deemed to be overtaking when coming up with another vessel from a direction more than 22.5 degrees abaft her beam; that is, in such a position with reference to the vessel she is overtaking, that at night she would be able to see only the sternlight of that vessel but neither of her sidelights.

(c) When a vessel is in any doubt as to whether she is overtaking another, she shall assume that this is the case and act accordingly.

(d) Any subsequent alteration of the bearing between the two vessels shall not make the overtaking vessel a crossing vessel within the meaning of these Rules or relieve her of the duty of keeping clear of the overtaken vessel until she is finally past and clear.

Head-on Situation

Rule 14. (a) When two power-driven vessels are meeting on reciprocal or nearly reciprocal courses so as to involve risk of collision each shall alter her course to starboard so that each shall pass on the port side of the other.

(b) Such a situation shall be deemed to exist when a vessel sees the other ahead or nearly ahead and by night she could see the masthead lights of the other in a line or nearly a line and/or both sidelights and by day she observes the corresponding aspect of the other vessel.

(c) When a vessel is in any doubt as to whether such a situation exists she shall assume that it does exist and act accordingly.

Crossing Situation

Rule 15. When two power-driven vessels are crossing so as to involve risk of collision, the vessel which has the other on her own starboard side shall keep out of the way and shall, if the circumstances of the case admit, avoid crossing ahead of the other vessel.

Action by Give-way Vessel

Rule 16. Every vessel which is directed to keep out of the way of another vessel shall, so far as possible, take early and substantial action to keep well clear.

Action by Stand-on Vessel

Rule 17. (a) (i) Where one of two vessels is to keep out of the way the other shall keep her course and speed. (ii) The latter vessel may however take action to avoid collision by the maneuver alone, as soon as it becomes apparent to her that the vessel required to keep out of the way is not taking appropriate action in compliance with these Rules.

(b) When, from any cause, the vessel required to keep her course and speed finds herself so close that collision cannot be avoided by the action of the give-way vessel alone, she shall take such action as will best aid to avoid collision.

(c) A power-driven vessel which takes action in a crossing situation in accordance with subparagraph (a) (ii) of this Rule to avoid collision with another power-driven vessel shall, if the circumstances of the case admit, not alter course to port for a vessel on her own port side.

(d) This Rule does not relieve the give-way vessel of her obligation to keep out of the way.

Responsibilities Between Vessels

Rule 18. Except where Rules 9, 10 and 13 otherwise require:

(a) A power-driven vessel underway shall keep out of the way of: (i) a vessel not under command; (ii) a vessel restricted in her ability to maneuver; (iii) a vessel engaged in fishing; (iv) a sailing vessel.

(b) A sailing vessel underway shall keep out of the way of: (i) a vessel not under command; (ii) a vessel restricted in her ability to maneuver; (iii) a vessel engaged in fishing.

(c) A vessel engaged in fishing when underway shall, so far as possible, keep out of the way of: (i) a vessel not under command; (ii) a vessel restricted in her ability to maneuver.

(d) (i) Any vessel other than a vessel not under command or a vessel restricted in her ability to maneuver shall, if the circumstances of the case admit, avoid impeding the safe passage of a vessel constrained by her draft, exhibiting the signals in Rule 28. (ii) A vessel constrained by her draught shall navigate with particular caution having full regard to her special condition.

(e) A seaplane on the water shall, in general, keep well clear of all vessels and avoid impeding their navigation. In circumstances, however, where risk of collision exists, she shall comply with the rules of this Part.

Section III. Conduct of Vessels in Restricted Visibility

Conduct of Vessels in Restricted Visibility

Rule 19. (a) This Rule applies to vessels not in sight of one another when navigating in or near an area of restricted visibility.

(b) Every vessel shall proceed at a safe speed adapted to the prevailing circumstances and conditions of restricted visibility. A power-driven vessel shall have her engines ready for immediate maneuver.

(c) Every vessel shall have due regard to the prevailing circumstances and conditions of restricted visibility when complying with the Rules of Section I of this Part.

(d) A vessel which detects by radar alone the presence of another vessel shall determine if a close-quarters situation is developing and/or risk of collision exists. If so, she shall take avoiding action in ample time, provided that when such action consists of an alteration of course, so far as possible the following shall be avoided: (i) an alteration of course to port for a vessel forward of the beam, other than for a vessel being overtaken; (ii) an alteration of course towards a vessel abeam or abaft the beam.

(e) Except where it has been determined that a risk of collision does not exist, every vessel which hears apparently forward of her beam the fog signal of another vessel, or which cannot avoid a close-quarters situation with another vessel forward of her beam, shall reduce her speed to the minimum at which she can be kept on her course. She shall if necessary take all her way off and in any event navigate with extreme caution until danger of collision is over.

Part C. Lights and Shapes

Application

Rule 20. (a) Rules in this Part shall be complied with in all weathers.

(b) The Rules concerning lights shall be complied with from sunset to sunrise, and during such times no other lights shall be exhibited, except such lights as cannot be mistaken for the lights specified in these Rules or do not impair their visibility or distinctive character, or interfere with the keeping of a proper look-out.

(c) The lights prescribed by these Rules shall, if carried, also be exhibited from sunrise to sunset in restricted visibility and may be exhibited in all other circumstances when it is deemed necessary.

(d) The Rules concerning shapes shall be complied with by day.

(e) The lights and shapes specified in these Rules shall comply with the provisions of Annex I to these Regulations.

Definitions

Rule 21. (a) "Masthead light" means a white light placed over the fore and aft centerline of the vessel showing an unbroken light over an arc of the horizon of 225 degrees and so fixed as to show the light from right ahead to 22.5 degrees abaft the beam on either side of the vessel.

(b) "Sidelights" means a green light on the starboard side and a red light on the port side each showing an unbroken light over an arc of the horizon of 112.5 degrees and so fixed as to show the light from right ahead to 22.5 degrees abaft the beam on its respective side. In a vessel of less than 20 meters in length the sidelights may be combined in one lantern carried on the fore and aft centerline of the vessel.

(c) "Sternlight" means a white light placed as nearly as practicable at the stern showing an unbroken light over an arc of the horizon of 135 degrees and so fixed as to show the light 67.5 degrees from right aft on each side of the vessel.

(d) "Towing light" means a yellow light having the same characteristics as the "sternlight" defined in paragraph (c) of this Rule.

(e) "All-round light" means a light showing an unbroken light over an arc of the horizon of 360 degrees.

(f) "Flashing light" means a light flashing at regular intervals at a frequency of 120 flashes or more per minute.

Visibility of Lights

Rule 22. The lights prescribed in these Rules shall have an intensity as specified in Section 8 of Annex I to these Regulations so as to be visible at the following minimum ranges:

(a) In vessels of 50 meters or more in length:
a masthead light, 6 miles;
a sidelight, 3 miles
a sternlight, 3 miles
a towing light, 3 miles;
a white, red, green or yellow all-round light, 3 miles

(b) In vessels of 12 meters or more in length but less than 50 meters in length:
a masthead light, 5 miles; except that where the length of the vessel is less than 20 meters, 3 miles;
a sidelight, 2 miles;
a sternlight, 2 miles;
a towing light, 2 miles;
a white, red, green or yellow all-round light, 2 miles.

(c) In vessels of less than 12 meters in length:
a masthead light, 2 miles;
a sidelight, 1 mile;
a sternlight, 2 miles;
a towing light, 2 miles;
a white, red, green or yellow all-round light, 2 miles

(d) In inconspicuous, partly submerged vessels or objects being towed:
a white all-round light, 3 miles.

Power-driven Vessels Underway

Rule 23. (a) A power-driven vessel underway shall exhibit: (i) a masthead light forward; (ii) a second masthead light abaft of and higher than the forward one; except that a vessel of less than 50 meters in length shall not be obliged to exhibit such light but may do so; (iii) sidelights; (iv) a sternlight.

(b) An air-cushion vessel when operating in the non-displacement mode shall, in addition to the lights prescribed in paragraph (a) of this Rule, exhibit an all-round flashing yellow light.

(c) (i) A power-driven vessel of less than 12 meters in length may in lieu of the lights prescribed in paragraph (a) of this Rule exhibit an all-round white light and sidelights;

(ii) a power-driven vessel of less than 7 meters in length whose maximum speed does not exceed 7 knots may in lieu of the lights prescribed in paragraph (a) of this Rule exhibit an all-round white light and shall, if practicable, also exhibit sidelights;

(iii) the masthead light or all-round white light on a power-driven vessel of less than 12 meters in length may be displaced from the fore and aft centerline of the vessel if centerline fitting is not practicable, provided that the sidelights are combined in one lantern which shall be carried on the fore and aft centerline of the vessel or located as nearly as practicable in the same fore and aft line as the masthead light or the all-round white light.

Towing and Pushing

Rule 24. (a) A power-driven vessel when towing shall exhibit: (i) instead of the light prescribed in Rule 23(a) (i) or (a) (ii), two masthead lights in a vertical line. When the length of the tow, measuring from the stern of the towing vessel to the after end of the tow exceeds 200 meters, three such lights in a vertical line; (ii) sidelights; (iii) a sternlight; (iv) a towing light in a vertical line above the sternlight; (v) when the length of the tow exceeds 200 meters, a diamond shape where it can best be seen.

(b) When a pushing vessel and a vessel being pushed ahead are rigidly connected in a composite unit they shall be regarded as a power-driven vessel and exhibit the lights prescribed in Rule 23.

(c) A power-driven vessel when pushing ahead or towing alongside, except in the case of a composite unit, shall exhibit: (i) instead of the light prescribed in Rule 23(a) (i) or (a) (ii), two masthead lights in a vertical line; (ii) sidelights; (iii) a sternlight.

(d) A power-driven vessel to which paragraph (a) or (c) of this Rule apply shall also comply with Rule 23(a) (ii).

(e) A vessel or object being towed, other than those mentioned in paragraph (g) of this Rule, shall exhibit: (i) sidelights; (ii) a sternlight; (iii) when the length of the tow exceeds 200 meters, a diamond shape where it can best be seen.

(f) Provided that any number of vessels being towed alongside or pushed in a group shall be lighted as one vessel, (i) a vessel being pushed ahead, not being part of a composite unit, shall exhibit at the forward end, sidelights; (ii) a vessel being towed alongside shall exhibit a sternlight and at the forward end, sidelights.

(g) An inconspicuous, partly submerged vessel or object, or combination of such vessels or objects being towed, shall exhibit: (i) if it is less than 25 meters in breadth, one all-round white light at or near the forward end and one at or near the after end except that dracones need not exhibit a light at or near the forward end; (ii) if it is 25 meters or more in breadth, two additional all-round white lights at or near the extremities of its breadth (iii) if it exceeds 100 meters in length, additional all-round white lights between the lights prescribed in subparagraphs (i) and (ii) so that the distance between the lights shall not exceed 100 meters; (iv) a diamond shape at or near the aftermost extremity of the last vessel or object being towed and if the length of the tow exceeds 200 meters an additional diamond shape where it can best be seen and located as far forward as is practicable.

(h) Where from any sufficient cause it is impracticable for a vessel or object being towed to exhibit the lights or shapes prescribed in paragraph (e) or (g) of this Rule, all possible measures shall be taken to light the vessel or object towed or at least to indicate the presence of such vessel or object.

(i) Where from any sufficient cause it is impracticable for a vessel not normally engaged in towing operations to display the lights prescribed in paragraph (a) or (c) of this Rule, such vessel shall not be required to exhibit those lights when engaged in towing another vessel in distress or otherwise in need of assistance. All possible measures shall be taken to indicate the nature of the relationship between the towing vessel and the vessel being towed as authorized by Rule 36, in particular by illuminating the towline.

Sailing Vessels Underway and Vessels Under Oars

Rule 25. (a) A sailing vessel underway shall exhibit: (i) sidelights; (ii) a sternlight.

(b) In a sailing vessel of less than 20 meters in length the lights prescribed in paragraph (a) of this Rule may be combined in one lantern carried at or near the top of the mast where it can best be seen.

(c) A sailing vessel underway may, in addition to the lights prescribed in paragraph (a) of this Rule, exhibit at or near the top of the mast, where they can best be seen, two all-round lights in a vertical line, the upper being red and the lower green, but these lights shall not be exhibited in conjunction with the combined lantern permitted by paragraph (b) of this Rule.

(d) (i) A sailing vessel of less than 7 meters in length shall, if practicable, exhibit the lights prescribed in paragraph (a) or (b) of this Rule, but if she does not, she shall have ready at hand an electric torch or lighted lantern showing a white light which shall be exhibited in sufficient time to prevent collision. (ii) A vessel under oars may exhibit the lights prescribed in this Rule for sailing vessels, but if she does not, she shall have ready at hand an electric torch or lighted lantern showing a white light which shall be exhibited in sufficient time to prevent collision.

(e) A vessel proceeding under sail when also being

314

propelled by machinery shall exhibit forward where it can best be seen a conical shape, apex downwards.

Fishing Vessels
Rule 26. (a) A vessel engaged in fishing, whether underway or at anchor, shall exhibit only the lights and shapes prescribed in this Rule.

(b) A vessel when engaged in trawling, by which is meant the dragging through the water of a dredge net or other apparatus used as a fishing appliance, shall exhibit: (i) two all-round lights in a vertical line, the upper being green and the lower white, or a shape consisting of two cones with their apexes together in a vertical line one above the other; a vessel of less than 20 meters in length may instead of this shape exhibit a basket; (ii) a masthead light abaft of and higher than the all-round green light; a vessel of less than 50 meters in length shall not be obliged to exhibit such a light but may do so; (iii) when making way through the water, in addition to the lights prescribed in this paragraph, sidelights and a sternlight.

(c) A vessel engaged in fishing, other than trawling, shall exhibit: (i) two all-round lights in a vertical line, the upper being red and the lower white, or a shape consisting of two cones with apexes together in a vertical line one above the other; a vessel of less than 20 meters in length may instead of this shape exhibit a basket; (ii) when there is outlying gear extending more than 150 meters horizontally from the vessel, an all-round white light or a cone apex upwards in the direction of the gear; (iii) when making way through the water, in addition to the lights prescribed in this paragraph, sidelights and a sternlight.

(d) A vessel engaged in fishing in close proximity to other vessels engaged in fishing may exhibit the additional signals described in Annex II to these Regulations.

(e) A vessel when not engaged in fishing shall not exhibit the lights or shapes prescribed in this Rule, but only those prescribed for a vessel of her length.

Vessels Not Under Command or Restricted in Their Ability to Maneuver
Rule 27. (a) A vessel not under command shall exhibit: (i) two all-round red lights in a vertical line where they can best be seen; (ii) two balls or similar shapes in a vertical line where they can best be seen; (iii) when making way through the water, in addition to the lights prescribed in this paragraph, sidelights and a sternlight.

(b) A vessel restricted in her ability to maneuver, except a vessel engaged in mineclearance operations, shall exhibit: (i) three all-round lights in a vertical line where they can best be seen. The highest and lowest of these lights shall be red and the middle light shall be white; (ii) three shapes in a vertical line where they can best be seen. The highest and lowest of these shapes shall be balls and the middle one a diamond; (iii) when making way through the water, a masthead light or lights, sidelights and a sternlight, in addition to the lights prescribed in subparagraph (i); (iv) when at anchor, in addition to

the lights or shapes prescribed in subparagraphs (i) and (ii), the light, lights or shape prescribed in Rule 30.

(c) A power-driven vessel engaged in a towing operation such as severely restricts the towing vessel and her tow in their ability to deviate from their course shall, in addition to the lights or shapes prescribed in Rule 24(a), exhibit the lights or shapes prescribed in subparagraphs (b) (i) and (ii) of this Rule.

(d) A vessel engaged in dredging or underwater operations, when restricted in her ability to maneuver, shall exhibit the lights and shapes prescribed in subparagraphs (b) (i), (ii) and (iii) of this Rule and shall in addition, when an obstruction exists, exhibit: (i) two all-round red lights or two balls in a vertical line to indicate the side on which the obstruction exists; (ii) two all-round green lights or two diamonds in a vertical line to indicate the side on which another vessel may pass; (iii) when at anchor, the lights or shapes prescribed in this paragraph instead of the lights or shape prescribed in Rule 30.

(e) Whenever the size of a vessel engaged in diving operations makes it impracticable to exhibit all lights and shapes prescribed in paragraph (d) of this Rule, the following shall be exhibited: (i) three all-round lights in a vertical line where they can best be seen. The highest and lowest of these lights shall be red and the middle light shall be white; (ii) a rigid replica of the International Code flag "A" not less than 1 meter in height. Measures shall be taken to ensure its all-round visibility.

(f) A vessel engaged in mineclearance operations shall in addition to the lights prescribed for a power-driven vessel in Rule 23 or to the lights or shape prescribed for a vessel at anchor in Rule 30 as appropriate, exhibit three all-round green lights or three balls. One of these lights or shapes shall be exhibited near the foremast head and one at each end of the fore yard. These lights or shapes indicate that it is dangerous for another vessel to approach within 1000 meters of the mineclearance vessel.

(g) Vessels of less than 12 meters in length, except those engaged in diving operations, shall not be required to exhibit the lights and shapes prescribed in this Rule.

(h) The signals prescribed in this Rule are not signals of vessels in distress and requiring assistance. Such signals are contained in Annex IV to these Regulations.

Vessels Constrained by Their Draft
Rule 28. A vessel constrained by her draft may, in addition to the lights prescribed for power-driven vessels in Rule 23, exhibit where they can best be seen three all-round red lights in a vertical line, or a cylinder.

Pilot Vessels
Rule 29. (a) A vessel engaged on pilotage duty shall exhibit: (i) at or near the masthead, two all-round lights in a vertical line, the upper being white and the lower red; (ii) when underway, in addition, sidelights and a sternlight; (iii) when at anchor, in addition to the lights prescribed in sub-paragraph (i), the light, lights or shape prescribed in Rule 30 for vessels at anchor.

(b) A pilot vessel when not engaged on pilotage duty

Appendix A

shall exhibit the lights or shapes prescribed for a similar vessel of her length.

Anchored Vessels and Vessels Aground
Rule 30. (a) A vessel at anchor shall exhibit where it can best be seen: (i) in the fore part, an all-round white light or one ball; (ii) at or near the stern and at a lower level than the light prescribed in sub-paragraph (i), an all-round white light.

(b) A vessel of less than 50 meters in length may exhibit an all-round white light where it can best be seen instead of the lights prescribed in paragraph (a) of this Rule.

(c) A vessel at anchor may, and a vessel of 100 meters and more in length shall, also use the available working or equivalent lights to illuminate her decks.

(d) A vessel aground shall exhibit the lights prescribed in paragraph (a) or (b) of this Rule and in addition, where they can best be seen: (i) two all-round red lights in a vertical line; (ii) three balls in a vertical line.

(e) A vessel of less than 7 meters in length, when at anchor, not in or near a narrow channel, fairway or anchorage, or where other vessels normally navigate, shall not be required to exhibit the lights or shape prescribed in paragraphs (a) and (b) of this Rule.

(f) A vessel of less than 12 meters in length, when aground, shall not be required to exhibit the lights or shapes prescribed in subparagraphs (d) (i) and (ii) of this Rule.

Seaplanes
Rule 31. Where it is impracticable for a seaplane to exhibit lights and shapes of the characteristics or in the positions prescribed in the Rules of this Part she shall exhibit lights and shapes as closely similar in characteristics and position as is possible.

Part D. Sound and Light Signals

Definitions
Rule 32. (a) The word "whistle" means any sound signalling appliance capable of producing the prescribed blasts and which complies with the specifications in Annex III to these Regulations.

(b) The term "short blast" means a blast of about one second's duration.

(c) The term "prolonged blast" means a blast of from four to six seconds' duration.

Equipment for Sound Signals
Rule 33. (a) A vessel of 12 meters or more in length shall be provided with a whistle and a bell and a vessel of 100 meters or more in length shall, in addition, be provided with a gong, the tone and sound of which cannot be confused with that of the bell. The whistle, bell and gong shall comply with the specifications in Annex III to these Regulations. The bell or gong or both may be replaced by other equipment having the same respective sound char-

acteristics, provided that manual sounding of the required signals shall always be possible.

(b) A vessel of less than 12 meters in length shall not be obliged to carry the sound signalling appliances prescribed in paragraph (a) of this Rule but if she does not, she shall be provided with some other means of making an efficient sound signal.

Maneuvering and Warning Signals
Rule 34. (a) When vessels are in sight of one another, a power-driven vessel underway, when maneuvering as authorized or required by these Rules, shall indicate that maneuver by the following signals on her whistle:
—one short blast to mean "I am altering my course to starboard";
—two short blasts to mean "I am altering my course to port";
—three short blasts to mean "I am operating astern propulsion."

(b) Any vessel may supplement the whistle signals prescribed in paragraph (a) of this Rule by light signals, repeated as appropriate, whilst the maneuver is being carried out: (i) these light signals shall have the following significance:
—one flash to mean "I am altering my course to starboard";
—two flashes to mean "I am altering my course to port";
—three flashes to mean "I am operating astern propulsion";
(ii) the duration of each flash shall be about one second, the interval between flashes shall be about one second, and the interval between successive signals shall be not less than ten seconds; (iii) the light used for this signal shall, if fitted, be an all-round white light, visible at a minimum range of 5 miles, and shall comply with the provisions of Annex I to these Regulations.

(c) When in sight of one another in a narrow channel or fairway: (i) a vessel intending to overtake another shall in compliance with Rule 9(e) (i) indicate her intention by the following signals on her whistle:
—two prolonged blasts followed by one short blast to mean "I intend to overtake you on your starboard side";
—two prolonged blasts followed by two short blasts to mean "I intend to overtake you on your port side".

(ii) the vessel about to be overtaken when acting in accordance with Rule 9(e) (i) shall indicate her agreement by the following signal on her whistle: one prolonged, one short, one prolonged and one short blast, in that order.

(d) When vessels in sight of one another are approaching each other and from any cause either vessel fails to understand the intentions or actions of the other, or is in doubt whether sufficient action is being taken by the other to avoid collision, the vessel in doubt shall immediately indicate such doubt by giving at least five short and rapid blasts on the whistle. Such signal may be supplemented by a light signal of at least five short and rapid flashes.

(e) A vessel nearing a bend or an area of a channel or fairway where other vessels may be obscured by an intervening obstruction shall sound one prolonged blast. Such signal shall be answered with a prolonged blast by any approaching vessel that may be within hearing around the bend or behind the intervening obstruction.

(f) If whistles are fitted on a vessel at a distance apart of more than 100 meters, one whistle only shall be used for giving maneuvering and warning signals.

Sound Signals in Restricted Visibility

Rule 35. In or near an area of restricted visibility, whether by day or night, the signals prescribed in this Rule shall be used as follows:

(a) A power-driven vessel making way through the water shall sound at intervals of not more than 2 minutes one prolonged blast.

(b) A power-driven vessel underway but stopped and making no way through the water shall sound at intervals of not more than 2 minutes two prolonged blasts in succession with an interval of about 2 seconds between them.

(c) A vessel not under command, a vessel restricted in her ability to maneuver, a vessel constrained by her draft, a sailing vessel, a vessel engaged in fishing and a vessel engaged in towing or pushing another vessel shall, instead of the signals prescribed in paragraphs (a) or (b) of this Rule, sound at intervals of not more than 2 minutes three blasts in succession, namely one prolonged followed by two short blasts.

(d) A vessel engaged in fishing, when at anchor and a vessel restricted in her ability to maneuver when carrying out her work at anchor, shall instead of the signals prescribed in paragraph (g) of this Rule sound the signal prescribed in paragraph (c) of this Rule.

(e) A vessel towed or if more than one vessel is towed the last vessel of the tow, if manned, shall at intervals of not more than 2 minutes sound four blasts in succession, namely one prolonged followed by three short blasts. When practicable, this signal shall be made immediately after the signal made by the towing vessel.

(f) When a pushing vessel and a vessel being pushed ahead are rigidly connected in a composite unit they shall be regarded as a power-driven vessel and shall give the signals prescribed in paragraphs (a) or (b) of this Rule.

(g) A vessel at anchor shall at intervals of not more than one minute ring the bell rapidly for about 5 seconds. In a vessel of 100 meters or more in length the bell shall be sounded in the forepart of the vessel and immediately after the ringing of the bell the gong shall be sounded rapidly for about 5 seconds in the after part of the vessel. A vessel at anchor may in addition sound three blasts in succession, namely one short, one prolonged and one short blast, to give warning of her position and of the possibility of collision to an approaching vessel.

(h) A vessel aground shall give the bell signal and if required the gong signal prescribed in paragraph (g) of this Rule and shall, in addition, give three separate and distinct strokes on the bell immediately before and after the rapid ringing of the bell. A vessel aground may in addition sound an appropriate whistle signal.

(i) A vessel of less than 12 meters in length shall not be obliged to give the above-mentioned signals but, if she does not, shall make some other efficient sound signal at intervals of not more than 2 minutes.

(j) A pilot vessel when engaged on pilotage duty may in addition to the signals prescribed in paragraphs (a), (b) or (g) of this Rule sound an identity signal consisting of four short blasts.

Signals to Attract Attention

Rule 36. If necessary to attract the attention of another vessel, any vessel may make light or sound signals that cannot be mistaken for any signal authorized elsewhere in these Rules, or may direct the beam of her searchlight in the direction of the danger, in such a way as not to embarrass any vessel. Any light to attract the attention of another vessel shall be such that it cannot be mistaken for any aid to navigation. For the purpose of this Rule the use of high intensity intermittent or revolving lights, such as strobe lights, shall be avoided.

Distress Signals

Rule 37. When a vessel is in distress and requires assistance she shall use or exhibit the signals described in Annex IV to these Regulations.

Part E. Exemptions

Exemptions

Rule 38. Any vessel (or class of vessels) provided that she complies with the requirements of the International Regulations for Preventing Collisions at Sea, 1960, the keel of which is laid or which is at a corresponding stage of construction before the entry into force of these Regulations may be exempted from compliance therewith as follows:

(a) The installation of lights with ranges prescribed in Rule 22, until four years after the date of entry into force of these Regulations.

(b) The installation of lights with color specification as prescribed in Section 7 of Annex I to these Regulations, until four years after the date of entry into force of these Regulations.

(c) The repositioning of lights as a result of conversion from Imperial to metric units and rounding off measurement figures, permanent exemption.

(d) (i) The repositioning of masthead lights on vessels of less than 150 meters in length, resulting from the prescriptions of Section 3(a) of Annex I to these Regulations, permanent exemption. (ii) The repositioning of masthead lights on vessels of 150 meters or more in length, resulting from the prescriptions of Section 3(a) of Annex I to these Regulations, until 9 years after the date of entry into force of these Regulations.

(e) The repositioning of masthead lights resulting from the prescriptions of Section 2(b) of Annex I to these

Appendix A

Regulations, until 9 years after the date of entry into force of these Regulations.

(f) The repositioning of sidelights resulting from the prescriptions of Sections 2(g) and 3(b) of Annex I to these Regulations, until 9 years after the date of entry into force of these Regulations.

(g) The requirements for sound signal appliances prescribed in Annex III to these Regulations, until 9 years after the date of entry into force of these Regulations.

(h) The repositioning of all-round lights resulting from the prescription of Section 9(b) of Annex I to these Regulations, permanent exemption.

Annex I

Positioning and Technical Details of Lights and Shapes

1. Definition

The term "height above the hull" means height above the uppermost continuous deck. This height shall be measured from the position vertically beneath the location of the light.

2. Vertical positioning and spacing of lights

(a) On a power-driven vessel of 20 meters or more in length the masthead lights shall be placed as follows: (i) the forward masthead light, or if only one masthead light is carried, then that light, at a height above the hull of not less than 6 meters, and, if the breadth of the vessel exceeds 6 meters, then at a height above the hull not less than such breadth, so however that the light need not be placed at a greater height above the hull than 12 meters; (ii) when two masthead lights are carried the after one shall be at least 4.5 meters vertically higher than the forward one.

(b) The vertical separation of masthead lights of power-driven vessels shall be such that in all normal conditions of trim the after light will be seen over and separate from the forward light at a distance of 1000 meters from the stem when viewed from sea level.

(c) The masthead light of a power-driven vessel of 12 meters but less than 20 meters in length shall be placed at a height above the gunwale of not less than 2.5 meters.

(d) A power-driven vessel of less than 12 meters in length may carry the uppermost light at a height of less than 2.5 meters above the gunwale. When however a masthead light is carried in addition to sidelights and a sternlight, then such masthead light shall be carried at least 1 meter higher than the sidelights.

(e) One of the two or three masthead lights prescribed for a power-driven vessel when engaged in towing or pushing another vessel shall be placed in the same position as either the forward masthead light or the after masthead light; provided that, if carried on the aftermast, the lowest after masthead light shall be at least 4.5 meters vertically higher than the forward masthead light.

(f) (i) The masthead light or lights prescribed in Rule 23(a) shall be so placed as to be above and clear of all other lights and obstructions except as described in subparagraph (ii).

(ii) When it is impracticable to carry the all-round lights prescribed by Rule 27(b) (i) or Rule 28 below the masthead lights, they may be carried above the after masthead light(s) or vertically in between the forward masthead light(s) and after masthead light(s), provided that in the latter case the requirement of Section 3(c) of this Annex shall be complied with.

(g) The sidelights of a power-driven vessel shall be placed at a height above the hull not greater than three quarters of that of the forward masthead light. They shall not be so low as to be interfered with by deck lights.

(h) The sidelights, if in a combined lantern and carried on a power-driven vessel of less than 20 meters in length, shall be placed not less than 1 meter below the masthead light.

(i) When the Rules prescribe two or three lights to be carried in a vertical line, they shall be spaced as follows: (i) on a vessel of 20 meters in length or more such lights shall be spaced not less than 2 meters apart, and the lowest of these lights shall, except where a towing light is required, be placed at a height of not less than 4 meters above the hull; (ii) on a vessel of less than 20 meters in length such lights shall be spaced not less than 1 meter apart and the lowest of these lights shall, except where a towing light is required, be placed at a height of not less than 2 meters above the hull; (iii) when three lights are carried they shall be equally spaced.

(j) The lower of the two all-round lights prescribed for a vessel when engaged in fishing shall be at a height above the sidelights not less than twice the distance between the two vertical lights.

(k) The forward anchor light prescribed in Rule 30(a) (i), when two are carried, shall not be less than 4.5 meters above the after one. On a vessel of 50 meters or more in length this forward anchor light shall be placed at a height of not less than 6 meters above the hull.

3. Horizontal positioning and spacing of lights

(a) When two masthead lights are prescribed for a power-driven vessel, the horizontal distance between them shall not be less than one half of the length of the vessel but need not be more than 100 meters. The forward light shall be placed not more than one quarter of the length of the vessel from the stem.

(b) On a power-driven vessel of 20 meters or more in length the sidelights shall not be placed in front of the forward masthead lights. They shall be placed at or near the side of the vessel.

(c) When the lights prescribed in Rule 27(b) (i) or Rule 28 are placed vertically between the forward masthead light(s) and the after masthead light(s) these all-round lights shall be placed at a horizontal distance of not less than 2 meters from the fore and aft centerline of the vessel in the athwartship direction.

4. Details of location of direction-indicating lights for fishing vessels, dredgers and vessels engaged in underwater operations

(a) The light indicating the direction of the outlying gear from a vessel engaged in fishing as prescribed in Rule 26(c) (ii) shall be placed at a horizontal distance of not less than 2 meters and not more than 6 meters away from the two all-round red and white lights. This light shall be placed not higher than the all-round white light prescribed in Rule 26(c) (i) and not lower than the sidelights.

(b) The lights and shapes on a vessel engaged in dredging or underwater operations to indicate the obstructed side and/or the side on which it is safe to pass, as prescribed in Rule 27(d) (i) and (ii), shall be placed at the maximum practical horizontal distance, but in no case less than 2 meters, from the lights or shapes prescribed in Rule 27(b) (i) and (ii). In no case shall the upper of these lights or shapes be at a greater height than the lower of the three lights or shapes prescribed in Rule 27(b) (i) and (ii).

5. Screens for sidelights

The sidelights of vessels of 20 meters or more in length shall be fitted with inboard screens painted matt black, and meeting the requirements of Section 9 of this Annex. On vessels of less than 20 meters in length the sidelights, if necessary to meet the requirements of Section 9 of this Annex, shall be fitted with inboard matt black screens. With a combined lantern, using a single vertical filament and a very narrow division between the green and red sections, external screens need not be fitted.

6. Shapes

(a) Shapes shall be black and of the following sizes: (i) a ball shall have a diameter of not less than 0.6 meter; (ii) a cone shall have a base diameter of not less than 0.6 meter and a height equal to its diameter; (iii) a cylinder shall have a diameter of at least 0.6 meter and a height of twice its diameter; (iv) a diamond shape shall consist of two cones as defined in (ii) above having a common base.

(b) The vertical distance between shapes shall be at least 1.5 meter.

(c) In a vessel of less than 20 meters in length shapes of lesser dimensions but commensurate with the size of the vessel may be used and the distance apart may be correspondingly reduced.

7. Color specification of lights

The chromaticity of all navigation lights shall conform to the following standards, which lie within the boundaries of the area of the diagram specified for each color by the International Commission on Illumination (CIE).

The boundaries of the area for each color are given by indicating the corner co-ordinates, which are as follows:

(i) *White*

x	0.525	0.525	0.452	0.310	0.310	0.443
y	0.382	0.440	0.440	0.348	0.283	0.382

(ii) *Green*

x	0.028	0.009	0.300	0.203
y	0.385	0.723	0.511	0.356

(iii) *Red*

x	0.680	0.660	0.735	0.721
y	0.320	0.320	0.264	0.259

(iv) *Yellow*

x	0.612	0.618	0.575	0.575
y	0.382	0.382	0.425	0.406

8. Intensity of Lights

(a) the minimum luminous intensity of lights shall be calculated by using the formula:

$$I = 3.43 \times 10^6 \times T \times D^2 \times K^{-D}$$

where I is luminous intensity in candelas under service conditions.

T is threshold factor 2×10^{-7} lux,
D is range of visibility (luminous range) of light in nautical miles,
K is atmospheric transmissivity. For prescribed lights the value of K shall be 0.8, corresponding to a meterological visibility of approximately 13 nautical miles.

(b) A selection of figures derived from the formula is given in the following table:

Range of visibility (luminous range) of light in nautical miles	Luminous intensity of light in candelas for K = 0.8
D	*I*
1	0.9
2	4.3
3	12
4	27
5	52
6	94

Note: The maximum luminous intensity of navigation lights should be limited to avoid undue glare. This shall not be achieved by a variable control of the luminous intensity.

9. Horizontal sectors

(a) (i) In the forward direction, sidelights as fitted on the vessel shall show the minimum required intensities. The intensities shall decrease to reach practical cut-off between 1 degree and 3 degrees outside the prescribed sectors. (ii) For sternlights and masthead lights and at 22.5 degrees abaft the beam for sidelights, the minimum required intensities shall be maintained over the arc of the horizon up to 5 degrees within the limits of the sectors prescribed in Rule 21. From 5 degrees within the prescribed sectors the intensity may decrease by 50 percent up to the prescribed limits; it shall decrease steadily to reach practical cut-off at not more than 5 degrees outside the prescribed sectors.

(b) All-round lights shall be so located as not to be obscured by masts, topmasts or structures within angular sectors of more than 6 degrees, except anchor lights prescribed in Rule 30, which need not be placed at an impracticable height above the hull.

10. Vertical sectors

(a) The verticle sectors of electric lights as fitted, with the exception of lights on sailing vessels shall ensure that: (i) at least the required minimum intensity is maintained at all angles from 5 degrees above to 5 degrees below the horizontal; (ii) at least 60 percent of the required minimum intensity is maintained from 7.5 degrees above to 7.5 degrees below the horizontal.

(b) In the case of sailing vessels the vertical sectors of electric lights as fitted shall ensure that: (i) at least the required minimum intensity is maintained at all angles from 5 degrees above to 5 degrees below the horizontal; (ii) at least 50 percent of the required minimum intensity is maintained from 25 degrees above to 25 degrees below the horizontal.

(c) In the case of lights other than electric these specifications shall be met as closely as possible.

11. Intensity of non-electric lights

Non-electric lights shall so far as practicable comply with the minimum intensities, as specified in the Table given in Section 8 of this Annex.

12. Maneuvering light

Notwithstanding the provisions of paragraph 2(f) of this Annex the maneuvering light described in Rule 34(b) shall be placed in the same fore and aft vertical plane as the masthead light or lights and, where practicable, at a minimum height of 2 meters vertically above the forward masthead light, provided that it shall be carried not less than 2 meters vertically above or below the after masthead light. On a vessel where only one masthead light is carried the maneuvering light, if fitted, shall be carried where it can best be seen, not less than 2 meters vertically apart from the masthead light.

13. Approval

The construction of lights and shapes and the installation of lights on board the vessel shall be to the satisfaction of the appropriate authority of the State whose flag the vessel is entitled to fly.

Annex II

Additional Signals for Fishing Vessels Fishing in Close Proximity

1. General

The lights mentioned herein shall, if exhibited in pursuance of Rule 26(d), be placed where they can best be seen. They shall be at least 0.9 meter apart but at a lower level than lights prescribed in Rule 26(b) (i) and (c) (i). The lights shall be visible all around the horizon at a distance of at least 1 mile but at a lesser distance than the lights prescribed by these Rules for fishing vessels.

2. Signals for trawlers

(a) Vessels when engaged in trawling, whether using demersal or pelagic gear, may exhibit: (i) when shooting their nets: two white lights in a vertical line; (ii) when hauling their nets: one white light over one red light in a vertical line; (iii) when the net has come fast upon an obstruction: two red lights in a vertical line.

(b) Each vessel engaged in pair trawling may exhibit: (i) by night, a searchlight directed forward and in the direction of the other vessel of the pair; (ii) when shooting or hauling their nets or when their nets have come fast upon an obstruction, the lights prescribed in 2(a) above.

3. Signals for purse seiners

Vessels engaged in fishing with purse seine gear may exhibit two yellow lights in a vertical line. These lights shall flash alternately every second and with equal light and occultation duration. These lights may be exhibited only when the vessel is hampered by its fishing gear.

Annex III

Technical Details of Sound Signal Appliances

1. Whistles

(a) *Frequencies and range of audibility.* The fundamental frequency of the signal shall lie within the range 70–700 Hz.

The range of audibility of the signal from a whistle shall be determined by those frequencies, which may include the fundamental and/or one or more higher frequencies, which lie within the range 180–700 Hz (± 1 percent) and which provide the sound pressure levels specified in paragraph 1(c) below.

(b) *Limits of fundamental frequencies.* To ensure a wide variety of whistle characteristics, the fundamental frequency of a whistle shall be between the following limits: (i) 70–200 Hz, for a vessel 200 meters or more in length; (ii) 130–350 Hz, for a vessel 75 meters but less than 200 meters in length; (iii) 250–700 Hz, for a vessel less than 75 meters in length.

(c) *Sound signal intensity and range of audibility.* A whistle fitted in a vessel shall provide, in the direction of maximum intensity of the whistle and at a distance of 1 meter from it, a sound pressure level in at least one $\frac{1}{3}$-octave band within the range of frequencies 180–700 Hz (± 1 percent) of not less than the appropriate figure given in the table below.

Length of vessel in meters	$\frac{1}{3}$-octave band level at 1 meter in dB referred to 2×10^{-5} N/m^2	Audibility range in nautical miles
200 or more	143	2.0
75 but less than 200...........	138	1.5
20 but less than 75..............	130	1.0
Less than 20........................	120	0.5

The range of audibility in the table above is for information and is approximately the range at which a whistle may be heard on its forward axis with 90 percent probability in conditions of still air on board a vessel having average background noise level at the listening posts (taken to be 68 dB in the octave band centered on 250 Hz and 63 dB in the octave band centered on 500 Hz).

In practice the range at which a whistle may be heard is extremely variable and depends critically on weather conditions; the values given can be regarded as typical but under conditions of strong wind or high ambient noise level at the listening post the range may be much reduced.

(d) *Directional properties.* The sound pressure level of a directional whistle shall not be more than 4 dB below the prescribed sound pressure level on the axis at any direction in the horizontal plane within ±45 degrees of the axis. The sound pressure level at any other direction in the horizontal plane shall be not more than 10 dB below the prescribed sound pressure level on the axis, so that the range in any direction will be at least half the range of the forward axis. The sound pressure level shall be measured in that one-third-octave band which determines the audibility range.

(e) *Positioning of whistles.* When a directional whistle is to be used as the only whistle on a vessel, it shall be installed with its maximum intensity directed straight ahead.

A whistle shall be placed as high as practicable on a vessel, in order to reduce interception of the emitted sound by obstructions and also to minimize hearing damage risk to personnel. The sound pressure level of the vessel's own signal at listening posts shall not exceed 110 dB (A) and so far as practicable should not exceed 100 dB (A).

(f) *Fitting of more than one whistle.* If whistles are fitted at a distance apart of more than 100 meters, it shall be so arranged that they are not sounded simultaneously.

(g) *Combined whistle systems.* If due to the presence of obstructions the sound field of a single whistle or of one of the whistles referred to in paragraph 1(f) above is likely to have a zone of greatly reduced signal level, it is recommended that a combined whistle system be fitted so as to overcome this reduction. For the purposes of the Rules a combined whistle system is to be regarded as a single whistle. The whistles of a combined system shall be located at a distance apart of not more than 100 meters and arranged to be sounded simultaneously. The frequency of any one whistle shall differ from those of the others by at least 10 Hz.

2. Bell or Gong

(a) *Intensity of signal.* A bell or gong, or other device having similar sound characteristics shall produce a sound pressure level of not less than 110 dB at a distance of 1 meter from it.

(b) *Construction.* Bells and gongs shall be made of corrosion-resistant material and designed to give a clear tone. The diameter of the mouth of the bell shall be not less than 300 mm for vessels of 20 meters or more in length, and shall be not less than 200 mm for vessels of 12 meters or more but of less than 20 meters in length. Where practicable, a power-driven bell striker is recommended to ensure constant force but manual operation shall be possible. The mass of the striker shall be not less than 3 percent of the mass of the bell.

3. Approval

The construction of sound signal appliances, their performance and their installation on board the vessel shall be to the satisfaction of the appropriate authority of the State whose flag the vessel is entitled to fly.

Annex IV

Distress Signals

1. The following signals, used or exhibited either together or separately, indicate distress and need of assistance:

(a) a gun or other explosive signal fired at intervals of about a minute;

(b) a continuous sounding with any fog-signalling apparatus;

(c) rockets or shells, throwing red stars fired one at a time at short intervals;

(d) a signal made by radiotelegraphy or by any other signalling method consisting of the group . . . — — — . . . (SOS) in the Morse Code;

(e) a signal sent by radiotelephony consisting of the spoken word "Mayday";

(f) the International Code Signal of distress indicated by N.C.;

(g) a signal consisting of a square flag having above or below it a ball or anything resembling a ball;

(h) flames on the vessel (as from a burning tar barrel, oil barrel, etc.);

(i) a rocket parachute flare or a hand flare showing a red light;

(j) a smoke signal giving off orange-colored smoke;

(k) slowly and repeatedly raising and lowering arms outstretched to each side;

(l) the radiotelegraph alarm signal;

(m) the radiotelephone alarm signal;

(n) signals transmitted by emergency position-indicating radio beacons.

2. The use or exhibition of any of the foregoing signals except for the purpose of indicating distress and need of assistance and the use of other signals which may be confused with any of the above signals is prohibited.

3. Attention is drawn to the relevant sections of the International Code of Signals, the Merchant Ship Search and Rescue Manual and the following signals:

(a) a piece of orange-colored canvas with either a black square and circle or other appropriate symbol (for identification from the air);

(b) a dye marker.

B.
Inland Rules of the Road

Part A. General

Application

Rule 1. (a) These Rules apply to all vessels upon the inland waters of the United States, and to vessels of the United States on the Canadian waters of the Great Lakes to the extent that there is no conflict with Canadian law.

(b)(i) These Rules constitute special rules made by an appropriate authority within the meaning of Rule 1(b) of the International Regulations.

(ii) All vessels complying with the construction and equipment requirements of the International Regulations are considered to be in compliance with these Rules.

(c) Nothing in these Rules shall interfere with the operation of any special rules made by the Secretary of the Navy with respect to additional station or signal lights and shapes or whistle signals for ships of war and vessels proceeding under convoy, or by the Secretary with respect to additional station or signal lights and shapes for fishing vessels engaged in fishing as a fleet. These additional station or signal lights and shapes or whistle signals shall, so far as possible, be such that they cannot be mistaken for any light, shape, or signal authorized elsewhere under these Rules. Notice of such special rules shall be published in the Federal Register and, after the effective date specified in such notice, they shall have effect as if they were a part of these Rules.[1]

(d) Vessel traffic service regulations may be in effect in certain areas.

(e) Whenever the Secretary determines that a vessel or class of vessels of special construction or purpose cannot comply fully with the provisions of any of these Rules with respect to the number, position, range, or arc of visibility of lights or shapes, as well as to the disposition and characteristics of sound-signalling appliances, without interfering with the special function of the vessel, the vessel shall comply with such other provisions in regard to the number, position, range, or arc of visibility of lights or shapes, as well as to the disposition and characteristics of sound-signalling appliances, as the Secretary shall have determined to be the closest possible compliance with these Rules. The Secretary may issue a certificate of alternative compliance for a vessel or class of vessels specifying the closest possible compliance with these Rules. The Secretary of the Navy shall make these determinations and issue certificates of alternative compliance for vessels of the Navy.

(f) The Secretary may accept a certificate of alternative compliance issued by a contracting party to the International Regulations if he determines that the alternative compliance standards of the contracting party are substantially the same as those of the United States.

---

[1] Submarines may display, as a distinctive means of identification, an intermittent flashing amber (yellow) beacon with a sequence of operation of one flash per second for three (3) seconds followed by a three (3) second off-period. Other special rules made by the Secretary of the Navy with respect to additional station and signal lights are found in Part 707 of Title 32, Code of Federal Regulations (32 CFR 707).

Responsibility

Rule 2. (a) Nothing in these Rules shall exonerate any vessel, or the owner, master, or crew thereof, from the consequences of any neglect to comply with these Rules or of the neglect of any precaution which may be required by the ordinary practice of seamen, or by the special circumstances of the case.

(b) In construing and complying with these Rules due regard shall be had to all dangers of navigation and collision and to any special circumstances, including the limitations of the vessels involved, which may make a departure from these Rules necessary to avoid immediate danger.

General Definitions

Rule 3. For the purpose of these Rules and this Act, except where the context otherwise requires:

(a) The word "vessel" includes every description of water craft, including nondisplacement craft and seaplanes, used or capable of being used as a means of transportation on water;

(b) The term "power-driven vessel" means any vessel propelled by machinery;

(c) The term "sailing vessel" means any vessel under sail provided that propelling machinery, if fitted, is not being used;

(d) The term "vessel engaged in fishing" means any vessel fishing with nets, lines, trawls, or other fishing apparatus which restricts maneuverability, but does not include a vessel fishing with trolling lines or other fishing apparatus which do not restrict maneuverability;

(e) The word "seaplane" includes any aircraft designed to maneuver on the water;

(f) The term "vessel not under command" means a vessel which through some exceptional circumstance is unable to maneuver as required by these Rules and is therefore unable to keep out of the way of another vessel;

(g) The term "vessel restricted in her ability to maneuver" means a vessel which from the nature of her work is restricted in her ability to maneuver as required by these Rules and is therefore unable to keep out of the way of another vessel; vessels restricted in their ability to maneuver include, but are not limited to:

(i) a vessel engaged in laying, servicing, or picking up a navigation mark, submarine cable, or pipeline;

(ii) a vessel engaged in dredging, surveying, or underwater operations;

(iii) a vessel engaged in replenishment or transferring persons, provisions, or cargo while underway;

(iv) a vessel engaged in the launching or recovery of aircraft;

(v) a vessel engaged in minesweeping operations; and

(vi) a vessel engaged in a towing operation such as severely restricts the towing vessel and her tow in their ability to deviate from their course.

(h) The word "underway" means that a vessel is not at anchor, or made fast to the shore, or aground;

(i) The words "length" and "breadth" of a vessel means her length overall and greatest breadth;

(j) Vessels shall be deemed to be in sight of one another only when one can be observed visually from the other;

(k) The term "restricted visibility" means any condition in which visibility is restricted by fog, mist, falling snow, heavy rainstorms, sandstorms, or any other similar causes;

(l) "Western Rivers" means the Mississippi River, its tributaries, South Pass, and Southwest Pass, to the navigational demarcation lines dividing the high seas from harbors, rivers, and other inland waters of the United States, and the Port Allen-Morgan City Alternate Route, and that part of the Atchafalaya River above its junction with the Port Allen-Morgan City Alternate Route including the Old River and the Red River;

(m) "Great Lakes" means the Great Lakes and their connecting and tributary waters including the Calumet River as far as the Thomas J. O'Brien Lock and Controlling Works (between mile 326 and 327), the Chicago River as far as the east side of the Ashland Avenue Bridge (between mile 321 and 322), and the Saint Lawrence River as far east as the lower exit of Saint Lambert Lock;

(n) "Secretary" means the Secretary of the department in which the Coast Guard is operating;

(o) "Inland Waters" means the navigable waters of the United States shoreward of the navigational demarcation lines dividing the high seas from harbors, rivers, and other inland waters of the United States and the waters of the Great Lakes on the United States side of the International Boundary;

(p) "Inland Rules" or "Rules" mean the Inland Navigational Rules and the annexes thereto, which govern the conduct of vessels and specify the lights, shapes, and sound signals that apply on inland waters; and

(q) "International Regulations" means the International Regulations for Preventing Collisions at Sea, 1972, including annexes currently in force for the United States.

Part B. Steering and Sailing Rules

Subpart I—Conduct of Vessels in Any Condition of Visibility

Application

Rule 4. Rules in this subpart apply in any condition of visibility.

Look-out

Rule 5. Every vessel shall at all times maintain a proper look-out by sight and hearing as well as by all available means appropriate in the prevailing circumstances and conditions so as to make a full appraisal of the situation and of the risk of collision.

Safe Speed

Rule 6. Every vessel shall at all times proceed at a safe speed so that she can take proper and effective action to avoid collision and be stopped within a distance appropriate to the prevailing circumstances and conditions.

In determining a safe speed the following factors shall be among those taken into account:

(a) By all vessels:

(i) the state of visibility;

(ii) the traffic density including concentration of fishing vessels or any other vessels;

(iii) the maneuverability of the vessel with special reference to stopping distance and turning ability in the prevailing conditions;

(iv) at night the presence of background light such as from shore lights or from back scatter of her own lights;

(v) the state of wind, sea, and current, and the proximity of navigational hazards;

(vi) the draft in relation to the available depth of water.

(b) Additionally, by vessels with operational radar:

(i) the characteristics, efficiency and limitations of the radar equipment;

(ii) any constraints imposed by the radar range scale in use;

(iii) the effect on radar detection of the sea state, weather, and other sources of interference;

(iv) the possibility that small vessels, ice and other floating objects may not be detected by radar at an adequate range;

(v) the number, location, and movement of vessels detected by radar; and

(vi) the more exact assessment of the visibility that may be possible when radar is used to determine the range of vessels or other objects in the vicinity.

Risk of Collision

Rule 7. (a) Every vessel shall use all available means appropriate to the prevailing circumstances and conditions to determine if risk of collision exists. If there is any doubt such risk shall be deemed to exist.

(b) Proper use shall be made of radar equipment if fitted and operational, including long-range scanning to obtain early warning of risk of collision and radar plotting or equivalent systematic observation of detected objects.

(c) Assumptions shall not be made on the basis of scanty information, especially scanty radar information.

(d) In determining if risk of collision exists the following considerations shall be among those taken into account:

(i) such risk shall be deemed to exist if the compass bearing of an approaching vessel does not appreciably change; and

(ii) such risk may sometimes exist even when an appreciable bearing change is evident, particularly when approaching a very large vessel or a tow or when approaching a vessel at close range.

Action to Avoid Collision

Rule 8. (a) Any action taken to avoid collision shall, if the circumstances of the case admit, be positive, made in ample time and with due regard to the observance of good seamanship.

(b) Any alteration of course or speed to avoid collision shall, if the circumstances of the case admit, be large enough to be readily apparent to another vessel observing visually or by radar; a succession of small alterations of course or speed should be avoided.

(c) If there is sufficient sea room, alteration of course alone may be the most effective action to avoid a close-quarters situation provided that it is made in good time, is substantial and does not result in another close-quarters situation.

(d) Action taken to avoid collision with another vessel shall be such as to result in passing at a safe distance. The effectiveness of the action shall be carefully checked until the other vessel is finally past and clear.

(e) If necessary to avoid collision or allow more time to assess the situation, a vessel shall slacken her speed or take all way off by stopping or reversing her means of propulsion.

Narrow Channels

Rule 9. (a)(i) A vessel proceeding along the course of a narrow channel or fairway shall keep as near to the outer limit of the channel or fairway which lies on her starboard side as is safe and practicable.

(ii) Notwithstanding paragraph (a)(i) and Rule 14(a), a power-driven vessel operating in narrow channels or fairways on the Great Lakes, Western Rivers, or waters specified by the Secretary, and proceeding downbound with a following current shall have the right-of-way over an upbound vessel, shall propose the manner and place of passage, and shall initiate the maneuvering signals prescribed by Rule 34(a)(i), as appropriate. The vessel proceeding upbound against the current shall hold as necessary to permit safe passing.

(b) A vessel of less than 20 meters in length or a sailing vessel shall not impede the passage of a vessel that can safely navigate only within a narrow channel or fairway.

(c) A vessel engaged in fishing shall not impede the passage of any other vessel navigating within a narrow channel or fairway.

(d) A vessel shall not cross a narrow channel or fairway if such crossing impedes the passage of a vessel which can safely navigate only within that channel or fairway. The latter vessel shall use the danger signal prescribed in Rule 34(d) if in doubt as to the intention of the crossing vessel.

(e)(i) In a narrow channel or fairway when overtaking, the vessel intending to overtake shall indicate her intention by sounding the appropriate signal prescribed in Rule 34(c) and take steps to permit safe passing. The overtaken vessel, if in agreement, shall sound the same signal. If in doubt she shall sound the danger signal prescribed in Rule 34(d).

(ii) This Rule does not relieve the overtaking vessel of her obligation under Rule 13.

(f) A vessel nearing a bend or an area of a narrow channel or fairway where other vessels may be obscured by an intervening obstruction shall navigate with particular alertness and caution and shall sound the appropriate signal prescribed in Rule 34(e).

(g) Every vessel shall, if the circumstances of the case admit, avoid anchoring in a narrow channel.

Vessel Traffic Services

Rule 10. Each vessel required by regulation to participate in a vessel traffic service shall comply with the applicable regulations.

Subpart II—Conduct of Vessels in Sight of One Another

Application

Rule 11. Rules in this subpart apply to vessels in sight of one another.

Sailing Vessels

Rule 12. (a) When two sailing vessels are approaching one another, so as to involve risk of collision, one of them shall keep out of the way of the other as follows:

(i) when each has the wind on a different side, the vessel which has the wind on the port side shall keep out of the way of the other;

(ii) when both have the wind on the same side, the vessel which is to windward shall keep out of the way of the vessel which is to leeward; and

(iii) if a vessel with the wind on the port side sees a vessel to windward and cannot determine with certainty whether the other vessel has the wind on the port or on the starboard side, she shall keep out of the way of the other.

(b) For the purpose of this Rule the windward side shall be deemed to be the side opposite to that on which the mainsail is carried or, in the case of a square-rigged vessel, the side opposite to that on which the largest fore-and-aft sail is carried.

Overtaking

Rule 13. (a) Notwithstanding anything contained in Rules 4 through 18, any vessel overtaking any other shall keep out of the way of the vessel being overtaken.

(b) A vessel shall be deemed to be overtaking when coming up with another vessel from a direction more than 22.5 degrees abaft her beam; that is, in such a position with reference to the vessel she is overtaking, that at night she would be able to see only the sternlight of that vessel but neither of her sidelights.

(c) When a vessel is in any doubt as to whether she is overtaking another, she shall assume that this is the case and act accordingly.

(d) Any subsequent alteration of the bearing between the two vessels shall not make the overtaking vessel a crossing vessel within the meaning of these Rules or relieve her of the duty of keeping clear of the overtaken vessel until she is finally past and clear.

Head-on Situation

Rule 14. (a) Unless otherwise agreed, when two power-driven vessels are meeting on reciprocal or nearly reciprocal courses so as to involve risk of collision each shall alter her course to starboard so that each shall pass on the port side of the other.

(b) Such a situation shall be deemed to exist when a vessel sees the other ahead or nearly ahead and by night she could see the masthead lights of the other in a line or nearly in a line or both sidelights and by day she observes the corresponding aspect of the other vessel.

(c) When a vessel is in any doubt as to whether such a situation exists she shall assume that it does exist and act accordingly.

(d) Notwithstanding paragraph (a) of this Rule, a power-driven vessel operating on the Great Lakes, Western Rivers, or waters specified by the Secretary, and proceeding downbound with a following current shall have the right-of-way over an upbound vessel, shall propose the manner of passage, and shall initiate the maneuvering signals prescribed by Rule 34(a)(i), as appropriate.

Crossing Situation

Rule 15. (a) When two power-driven vessels are crossing so as to involve risk of collision, the vessel which has the other on her starboard side shall keep out of the way and shall, if the circumstances of the case admit, avoid crossing ahead of the other vessel.

(b) Notwithstanding paragraph (a), on the Great Lakes, Western Rivers, or water specified by the Secretary, a vessel crossing a river shall keep out of the way of a power-driven vessel ascending or descending the river.

Action by Give-way Vessel

Rule 16. Every vessel which is directed to keep out of the way of another vessel shall, so far as possible, take early and substantial action to keep well clear.

Action by Stand-on Vessel

Rule 17. (a)(i) Where one of two vessels is to keep out of the way, the other shall keep her course and speed.

(ii) The latter vessel may, however, take action to avoid collision by her maneuver alone, as soon as it becomes apparent to her that the vessel required to keep out of the way is not taking appropriate action in compliance with these Rules.

(b) When, from any cause, the vessel required to keep her course and speed finds herself so close that collision cannot be avoided by the action of the give-away vessel alone, she shall take such action as will best aid to avoid collision.

(c) A power-driven vessel which takes action in a crossing situation in accordance with subparagraph (a)(ii) of this Rule to avoid collision with another power-driven vessel shall, if the circumstances of the case admit, not alter course to port for a vessel on her own port side.

(d) This Rule does not relieve the give-way vessel of her obligation to keep out of the way.

325

Responsibilities Between Vessels

Rule 18. Except where Rules 9, 10, and 13 otherwise require:

(a) A power-driven vessel underway shall keep out of the way of:

(i) a vessel not under command;

(ii) a vessel restricted in her ability to maneuver;

(iii) a vessel engaged in fishing; and

(iv) a sailing vessel.

(b) A sailing vessel underway shall keep out of the way of:

(i) a vessel not under command;

(ii) a vessel restricted in her ability to maneuver; and

(iii) a vessel engaged in fishing.

(c) A vessel engaged in fishing when underway shall, so far as possible, keep out of the way of:

(i) a vessel not under command; and

(ii) a vessel restricted in her ability to maneuver.

(d) A seaplane on the water shall, in general, keep well clear of all vessels and avoid impeding their navigation. In circumstances, however, where risk of collision exists, she shall comply with the Rules of this Part.

Subpart III—Conduct of Vessels in Restricted Visibility

Conduct of Vessels in Restricted Visibility

Rule 19. (a) This Rule applies to vessels not in sight of one another when navigating in or near an area of restricted visibility.

(b) Every vessel shall proceed at a safe speed adapted to the prevailing circumstances and conditions of restricted visibility. A power-driven vessel shall have her engines ready for immediate maneuver.

(c) Every vessel shall have due regard to the prevailing circumstances and conditions of restricted visibility when complying with Rules 4 through 10.

(d) A vessel which detects by radar alone the presence of another vessel shall determine if a close-quarters situation is developing or risk of collision exists. If so, she shall take avoiding action in ample time, provided that when such action consists of an alteration of course, so far as possible the following shall be avoided:

(i) an alteration of course to port for a vessel forward of the beam, other than for a vessel being overtaken; and

(ii) an alteration of course toward a vessel abeam or abaft the beam.

(e) Except where it has been determined that a risk of collision does not exist, every vessel which hears apparently forward of her beam the fog signal of another vessel, or which cannot avoid a close-quarters situation with another vessel forward of her beam, shall reduce her speed to the minimum at which she can be kept on course. She shall if necessary take all her way off and, in any event, navigate with extreme caution until danger of collision is over.

PART C—LIGHTS AND SHAPES

Application

Rule 20. (a) Rules in this Part shall be complied with in all weathers.

(b) The Rules concerning lights shall be complied with from sunset to sunrise, and during such times no other lights shall be exhibited, except such lights as cannot be mistaken for the lights specified in these Rules or do not impair their visibility or distinctive character, or interfere with the keeping of a proper look-out.

(c) The lights prescribed by these Rules shall, if carried, also be exhibited from sunrise to sunset in restricted visibility and may be exhibited in all other circumstances when it is deemed necessary.

(d) The Rules concerning shapes shall be complied with by day.

(e) The lights and shapes specified in these Rules shall comply with the provisions of Annex I of these Rules.

Definitions

Rule 21. (a) "Masthead light" means a white light placed over the fore and aft centerline of the vessel showing an unbroken light over an arc of the horizon of 225 degrees and so fixed as to show the light from right ahead to 22.5 degrees abaft the beam on either side of the vessel, except that on a vessel of less than 12 meters in length the masthead light shall be placed as nearly as practicable to the fore and aft centerline of the vessel.

(b) "Sidelights" mean a green light on the starboard side and a red light on the port side each showing an unbroken light over an arc of the horizon of 112.5 degrees and so fixed as to show the light from right ahead to 22.5 degrees abaft the beam on its respective side. On a vessel of less than 20 meters in length the sidelights may be combined in one lantern carried on the fore and aft centerline of the vessel, except that on a vessel of less than 12 meters in length the sidelights when combined in one lantern shall be placed as nearly as practicable to the fore and aft centerline of the vessel.

(c) "Sternlight" means a white light placed as nearly as practicable at the stern showing an unbroken light over an arc of the horizon of 135 degrees and so fixed as to show the light 67.5 degrees from right aft on each side of the vessel.

(d) "Towing light" means a yellow light having the same characteristics as the "sternlight" defined in paragraph (c) of this Rule.

(e) "All-round light" means a light showing an unbroken light over an arc of the horizon of 360 degrees.

(f) "Flashing light" means a light flashing at regular intervals at a frequency of 120 flashes or more per minute.

(g) "Special flashing light" means a yellow light flashing at regular intervals at a frequency of 50 to 70 flashes per minute, placed as far forward and as nearly as practicable on the fore and aft centerline of the tow and showing an unbroken light over an arc of the horizon of not less than 180 degrees nor more than 225 degrees and so fixed as to show the light from right ahead to abeam and no more than 22.5 degrees abaft the beam on either side of the vessel.

Visibility of Lights

Rule 22. The lights prescribed in these Rules shall have an intensity as specified in Annex I to these Rules, so as to be visible at the following minimum ranges:

(a) In a vessel of 50 meters or more in length:
—a masthead light, 6 miles;
—a sidelight, 3 miles;
—a sternlight, 3 miles;
—a towing light, 3 miles;
—a white, red, green or yellow all-round light, 3 miles; and
—a special flashing light, 2 miles.

(b) In a vessel of 12 meters or more in length but less than 50 meters in length:
—a masthead light, 5 miles; except that where the length of the vessel is less than 20 meters, 3 miles;
—a sidelight, 2 miles;
—a sternlight, 2 miles;
—a towing light, 2 miles;
—a white, red, green or yellow all-round light, 2 miles; and
—a special flashing light, 2 miles.

(c) In a vessel of less than 12 meters in length:
—a masthead light, 2 miles;
—a sidelight, 1 mile;
—a sternlight, 2 miles;
—a towing light, 2 miles;
—a white, red, green or yellow all-round light, 2 miles; and
—a special flashing light, 2 miles.

(d) In an inconspicuous, partly submerged vessel or object being towed:
—a white all-round light, 3 miles.

Power-driven Vessels Underway

Rule 23. (a) A power-driven vessel underway shall exhibit:

(i) a masthead light forward; except that a vessel of less than 20 meters in length need not exhibit this light forward of amidships but shall exhibit it as far forward as is practicable;

(ii) a second masthead light abaft of and higher than the forward one; except that a vessel of less than 50 meters in length shall not be obliged to exhibit such light but may do so;

(iii) sidelights; and

(iv) a sternlight.

(b) An air-cushion vessel when operating in the non-displacement mode shall, in addition to the lights prescribed in paragraph (a) of this Rule, exhibit an all-round flashing yellow light where it can best be seen.

(c) A power-driven vessel of less than 12 meters in length may, in lieu of the lights prescribed in paragraph (a) of this Rule, exhibit an all-round white light and sidelights.

(d) A power-driven vessel when operating on the Great Lakes may carry an all-round white light in lieu of the second masthead light and sternlight prescribed in paragraph (a) of this Rule. The light shall be carried in the position of the second masthead light and be visible at the same minimum range.

Towing and Pushing

Rule 24. (a) A power-driven vessel when towing astern shall exhibit:

(i) instead of the light prescribed either in Rule 23(a)(i) or 23(a)(ii), two masthead lights in a vertical line. When the length of the tow, measuring from the stern of the towing vessel to the after end of the tow exceeds 200 meters, three such lights in a vertical line;

(ii) sidelights;

(iii) a sternlight;

(iv) a towing light in a vertical line above the sternlight; and

(v) when the length of the tow exceeds 200 meters, a diamond shape where it can best be seen.

(b) When a pushing vessel and a vessel being pushed ahead are rigidly connected in a composite unit they shall be regarded as a power-driven vessel and exhibit the lights prescribed in Rule 23.

(c) A power-driven vessel when pushing ahead or towing alongside, except as required by paragraphs (b) and (i) of this Rule, shall exhibit:

(i) instead of the light prescribed either in Rule 23(a)(i) or 23(a)(ii), two masthead lights in a vertical line;

(ii) sidelights; and

(iii) two towing lights in a vertical line.

(d) A power-driven vessel to which paragraphs (a) or (c) of this Rule apply shall also comply with Rule 23(a)(i) and 23(a)(ii).

(e) A vessel or object other than those referred to in paragraph (g) of this Rule being towed shall exhibit:

(i) sidelights;

(ii) a sternlight; and

(iii) when the length of the tow exceeds 200 meters, a diamond shape where it can best be seen.

(f) Provided that any number of vessels being towed alongside or pushed in a group shall be lighted as one vessel:

(i) a vessel being pushed ahead, not being part of a composite unit, shall exhibit at the forward end sidelights, and a special flashing light; and

(ii) a vessel being towed alongside shall exhibit a sternlight and at the forward end sidelights.

(g) An inconspicuous, partly submerged vessel or object being towed shall exhibit:

(i) if it is less than 25 meters in breadth, one all-round white light at or near each end;

(ii) if it is 25 meters or more in breadth, four all-round white lights to mark its length and breadth;

(iii) if it exceeds 100 meters in length, additional all-round white lights between the lights prescribed in subparagraphs (i) and (ii) so that the distance between the lights shall not exceed 100 meters: *Provided,* That any vessels or objects being towed alongside each other shall be lighted as one vessel or object;

(iv) a diamond shape at or near the aftermost extremity of the last vessel or object being towed; and

(v) the towing vessel may direct a searchlight in the direction of the tow to indicate its presence to an approaching vessel.

(h) Where from any sufficient cause it is impracticable for a vessel or object being towed to exhibit the lights prescribed in paragraph (e) or (g) of this Rule, all possible measures shall be taken to light the vessel or object towed or at least to indicate the presence of the unlighted vessel or object.

(i) Notwithstanding paragraph (c), on the Western Rivers (except below the Huey P. Long Bridge on the Mississippi River) and on waters specified by the Secretary, a power-driven vessel when pushing ahead or towing alongside, except as paragraph (b) applies, shall exhibit:

(i) sidelights; and

(ii) two towing lights in a vertical line.

(j) Where from any sufficient cause it is impracticable for a vessel not normally engaged in towing operations to display the lights prescribed by paragraph (a), (c) or (i) of this Rule, such vessel shall not be required to exhibit those lights when engaged in towing another vessel in distress or otherwise in need of assistance. All possible measures shall be taken to indicate the nature of the relationship between the towing vessel and the vessel being assisted. The searchlight authorized by Rule 36 may be used to illuminate the tow.

Sailing Vessels Underway and Vessels Under Oars

Rule 25. (a) A sailing vessel underway shall exhibit:

(i) sidelights; and

(ii) a sternlight.

(b) In a sailing vessel of less than 20 meters in length the lights prescribed in paragraph (a) of this Rule may be combined in one lantern carried at or near the top of the mast where it can best be seen.

(c) A sailing vessel underway may, in addition to the lights prescribed in paragraph (a) of this Rule, exhibit at or near the top of the mast, where they can best be seen, two all-round lights in a vertical line, the upper being red and the lower green, but these lights shall not be exhibited in conjunction with the combined lantern permitted by paragraph (b) of this Rule.

(d)(i) A sailing vessel of less than 7 meters in length shall, if practicable, exhibit the lights prescribed in paragraph (a) or (b) of this Rule, but if she does not, she shall have ready at hand an electric torch or lighted lantern showing a white light which shall be exhibited in sufficient time to prevent collision.

(ii) A vessel under oars may exhibit the lights prescribed in this Rule for sailing vessels, but if she does not, she shall have ready at hand an electric torch or lighted lantern showing a white light which shall be exhibited in sufficient time to prevent collision.

(e) A vessel proceeding under sail when also being propelled by machinery shall exhibit forward where it can best be seen a conical shape, apex downward. A vessel of less than 12 meters in length is not required to exhibit this shape, but may do so.

Fishing Vessels

Rule 26. (a) A vessel engaged in fishing, whether underway or at anchor, shall exhibit only the lights and shapes prescribed in this Rule.

(b) A vessel when engaged in trawling, by which is meant the dragging through the water of a dredge net or other apparatus used as a fishing appliance, shall exhibit:

(i) two all-round lights in a vertical line, the upper being green and the lower white, or a shape consisting of two cones with their apexes together in a vertical line one above the other; a vessel of less than 20 meters in length may instead of this shape exhibit a basket;

(ii) a masthead light abaft of and higher than the all-round green light; a vessel of less than 50 meters in length shall not be obliged to exhibit such a light but may do so; and

(iii) when making way through the water, in addition to the lights prescribed in this paragraph, sidelights and a sternlight.

(c) A vessel engaged in fishing, other than trawling, shall exhibit:

(i) two all-round lights in a vertical line, the upper being red and the lower white, or a shape consisting of two cones with apexes together in a vertical line one above the other; a vessel of less than 20 meters in length may instead of this shape exhibit a basket;

(ii) when there is outlying gear extending more than 150 meters horizontally from the vessel, an all-round white light or a cone apex upward in the direction of the gear; and

(iii) when making way through the water, in addition to the lights prescribed in this paragraph, sidelights and a sternlight.

(d) A vessel engaged in fishing in close proximity to other vessels engaged in fishing may exhibit the additional signals described in Annex II to these Rules.

(e) A vessel when not engaged in fishing shall not exhibit the lights or shapes prescribed in this Rule, but only those prescribed for a vessel of her length.

Vessels Not Under Command or Restricted in Their Ability to Maneuver

Rule 27. (a) A vessel not under command shall exhibit:

(i) two all-round red lights in a vertical line where they can best be seen;

(ii) two balls or similar shapes in a vertical line where they can best be seen; and

(iii) when making way through the water, in addition to the lights prescribed in this paragraph, sidelights and a sternlight.

(b) A vessel restricted in her ability to maneuver, except a vessel engaged in minesweeping operations, shall exhibit:

(i) three all-round lights in a vertical line where they can best be seen. The highest and lowest of these lights shall be red and the middle light shall be white;

(ii) three shapes in a vertical line where they can best be seen. The highest and lowest of these shapes shall be balls and the middle one a diamond;

(iii) when making way through the water, masthead lights, sidelights and a sternlight, in addition to the lights prescribed in subparagraph (b)(i); and

(iv) when at anchor, in addition to the lights or shapes prescribed in subparagraphs (b)(i) and (ii), the light, lights or shapes prescribed in Rule 30.

(c) A vessel engaged in a towing operation which severely restricts the towing vessel and her tow in their ability to deviate from their course shall, in addition to the lights or shapes prescribed in subparagraphs (b)(i) and (ii) of this Rule, exhibit the lights or shape prescribed in Rule 24.

(d) A vessel engaged in dredging or underwater operations, when restricted in her ability to maneuver, shall exhibit the lights and shapes prescribed in subparagraphs (b)(i), (ii), and (iii) of this Rule and shall in addition, when an obstruction exists, exhibit:

(i) two all-round red lights or two balls in a vertical line to indicate the side on which the obstruction exists;

(ii) two all-round green lights or two diamonds in a vertical line to indicate the side on which another vessel may pass; and

(iii) when at anchor, the lights or shape prescribed by this paragraph, instead of the lights or shapes prescribed in Rule 30 for anchored vessels.

(e) Whenever the size of a vessel engaged in diving operations makes it impracticable to exhibit all lights and shapes prescribed in paragraph (d) of this Rule, the following shall instead be exhibited:

(i) Three all-round lights in a vertical line where they can best be seen. The highest and lowest of these lights shall be red and the middle light shall be white;

(ii) A rigid replica of the international Code flat "A" not less than 1 meter in height. Measures shall be taken to insure its all-round visibility.

(f) A vessel engaged in minesweeping operations shall, in addition to the lights prescribed for a power-driven vessel in Rule 23, exhibit three all-round green lights or three balls. One of these lights or shapes shall be exhibited near the foremast head and one at each end of the fore yard. These lights or shapes indicate that it is dangerous for another vessel to approach closer than 1,000 meters astern or 500 meters on either side of the minesweeper.

(g) A vessel of less than 12 meters in length, except when engaged in diving operations, is not required to exhibit the lights or shapes prescribed in this Rule.

(h) The signals prescribed in this Rule are not signals of vessels in distress and requiring assistance. Such signals are contained in Annex IV to these Rules.

Rule 28. [Reserved]

Pilot Vessels
Rule 29. (a) A vessel engaged on pilotage duty shall exhibit:

(i) at or near the masthead, two all-round lights in a vertical line, the upper being white and the lower red;

(ii) when underway, in addition, sidelights and a sternlight; and

(iii) when at anchor, in addition to the lights prescribed in subparagraph (i), the anchor light, lights, or shape prescribed in Rule 30 for anchored vessels.

(b) A pilot vessel when not engaged on pilotage duty shall exhibit the lights or shapes prescribed for a vessel of her length.

Anchored Vessels and Vessels Aground
Rule 30. (a) A vessel at anchor shall exhibit where it can best be seen:

(i) in the fore part, an all-round white light or one ball; and

(ii) at or near the stern and at a lower level than the light prescribed in subparagraph (i), an all-round white light.

(b) A vessel of less than 50 meters in length may exhibit an all-round white light where it can best be seen instead of the lights prescribed in paragraph (a) of this Rule.

(c) A vessel at anchor may, and a vessel of 100 meters or more in length shall, also use the available working or equivalent lights to illuminate her decks.

(d) A vessel aground shall exhibit the lights prescribed in paragraph (a) or (b) of this Rule and in addition, if practicable, where they can best be seen:

(i) two all-round red lights in a vertical line; and

(ii) three balls in a vertical line.

(e) A vessel of less than 7 meters in length, when at anchor, not in or near a narrow channel, fairway, anchorage, or where other vessels normally navigate, shall not be required to exhibit the lights or shape prescribed in paragraphs (a) and (b) of this Rule.

(f) A vessel of less than 12 meters in length when aground shall not be required to exhibit the lights or shapes prescribed in subparagraphs (d)(i) and (ii) of this Rule.

(g) A vessel of less than 20 meters in length, when at anchor in a special anchorage area designated by the Secretary, shall not be required to exhibit the anchor lights and shapes required by this Rule.

Seaplanes
Rule 31. Where it is impracticable for a seaplane to exhibit lights and shapes of the characteristics or in the positions prescribed in the Rules of this Part she shall exhibit lights and shapes as closely similar in characteristics and position as is possible.

PART D—SOUND AND LIGHT SIGNALS

Definitions
Rule 32. (a) The word "whistle" means any sound signaling appliance capable of producing the prescribed

blasts and which complies with specifications in Annex III to these Rules.

(b) The term "short blast" means a blast of about 1 second's duration.

(c) The term "prolonged blast" means a blast of from 4 to 6 seconds' duration.

Equipment for Sound Signals

Rule 33. (a) A vessel of 12 meters or more in length shall be provided with a whistle and a bell and a vessel of 100 meters or more in length shall, in addition, be provided with a gong, the tone and sound of which cannot be confused with that of the bell. The whistle, bell and gong shall comply with the specifications in Annex III to these Rules. The bell or gong or both may be replaced by other equipment having the same respective sound characteristics, provided that manual sounding of the prescribed signals shall always be possible.

(b) A vessel of less than 12 meters in length shall not be obliged to carry the sound signaling appliances prescribed in paragraph (a) of this Rule but if she does not, she shall be provided with some other means of making an efficient sound signal.

Maneuvering and Warning Signals

Rule 34. (a) When power-driven vessels are in sight of one another and meeting or crossing at a distance within half a mile of each other, each vessel underway, when maneuvering as authorized or required by these Rules:

(i) shall indicate that maneuver by the following signals on her whistle: one short blast to mean "I intend to leave you on my port side"; two short blasts to mean "I intend to leave you on my starboard side"; and three short blasts to mean "I am operating astern propulsion".

(ii) upon hearing the one or two blast signal of the other shall, if in agreement, sound the same whistle signal and take the steps necessary to effect a safe passing. If, however, from any cause, the vessel doubts the safety of the proposed maneuver, she shall sound the danger signal specified in paragraph (d) of this Rule and each vessel shall take appropriate precautionary action until a safe passing agreement is made.

(b) A vessel may supplement the whistle signals prescribed in paragraph (a) of this Rule by light signals:

(i) These signals shall have the following significance: one flash to mean "I intend to leave you on my port side"; two flashes to mean "I intend to leave you on my starboard side"; three flashes to mean "I am operating astern propulsion";

(ii) The duration of each flash shall be about 1 second; and

(iii) The light used for this signal shall, if fitted, be one all-round white or yellow light, visible at a minimum range of 2 miles, synchronized with the whistle, and shall comply with the provisions of Annex I to these Rules.

(c) When in sight of one another:

(i) a power-driven vessel intending to overtake another power-driven vessel shall indicate her intention by the following signals on her whistle: one short blast to mean "I intend to overtake you on your starboard side"; two short blasts to mean "I intend to overtake you on your port side"; and

(ii) the power-driven vessel about to be overtaken shall, if in agreement, sound a similar sound signal. If in doubt she shall sound the danger signal prescribed in paragraph (d).

(d) When vessels in sight of one another are approaching each other and from any cause either vessel fails to understand the intentions or actions of the other, or is in doubt whether sufficient action is being taken by the other to avoid collision, the vessel in doubt shall immediately indicate such doubt by giving at least five short and rapid blasts on the whistle. This signal may be supplemented by a light signal of at least five short and rapid flashes.

(e) A vessel nearing a bend or an area of a channel or fairway where other vessels may be obscured by an intervening obstruction shall sound one prolonged blast. This signal shall be answered with a prolonged blast by any approaching vessel that may be within hearing around the bend or behind the intervening obstruction.

(f) If whistles are fitted on a vessel at a distance apart of more than 100 meters, one whistle only shall be used for giving maneuvering and warning signals.

(g) When a power-driven vessel is leaving a dock or berth, she shall sound one prolonged blast.

(h) A vessel that reaches agreement with another vessel in a meeting, crossing, or overtaking situation by using the radiotelephone as prescribed by the Bridge-to-Bridge Radiotelephone Act (85 Stat. 165; 33 U.S.C. 1207), is not obliged to sound the whistle signals prescribed by this Rule, but may do so. If agreement is not reached, then whistle signals shall be exchanged in a timely manner and shall prevail.

Sound Signals in Restricted Visibility

Rule 35. In or near an area of restricted visibility, whether by day or night, the signals prescribed in this Rule shall be used as follows:

(a) A power-driven vessel making way through the water shall sound at intervals of not more than 2 minutes one prolonged blast.

(b) A power-driven vessel underway but stopped and making no way through the water shall sound at intervals of not more than 2 minutes two prolonged blasts in succession with an interval of about 2 seconds between them.

(c) A vessel not under command; a vessel restricted in her ability to maneuver, whether underway or at anchor; a sailing vessel; a vessel engaged in fishing, whether underway or at anchor; and a vessel engaged in towing or pushing another vessel shall, instead of the signals prescribed in paragraphs (a) or (b) of this Rule, sound at intervals of not more than 2 minutes, three blasts in succession; namely, one prolonged followed by two short blasts.

(d) A vessel towed or if more than one vessel is towed the last vessel of the tow, if manned, shall at intervals of not more than 2 minutes sound four blasts in succession; namely, one prolonged followed by three short blasts. When practicable, this signal shall be made immediately after the signal made by the towing vessel.

(e) When a pushing vessel and a vessel being pushed ahead are rigidly connected in a composite unit they shall be regarded as a power-driven vessel and shall give the signals prescribed in paragraphs (a) or (b) of this Rule.

(f) A vessel at anchor shall at intervals of not more than 1 minute ring the bell rapidly for about 5 seconds. In a vessel of 100 meters or more in length the bell shall be sounded in the forepart of the vessel and immediately after the ringing of the bell the gong shall be sounded rapidly for about 5 seconds in the after part of the vessel. A vessel at anchor may in addition sound three blasts in succession; namely, one short, one prolonged and one short blast, to give warning of her position and of the possibility of collision to an approaching vessel.

(g) A vessel aground shall give the bell signal and if required the gong signal prescribed in paragraph (f) of this Rule and shall, in addition, give three separate and distinct strokes on the bell immediately before and after the rapid ringing of the bell. A vessel aground may in addition sound an appropriate whistle signal.

(h) A vessel of less than 12 meters in length shall not be obliged to give the above-mentioned signals but, if she does not, shall make some other efficient sound signal at intervals of not more than 2 minutes.

(i) A pilot vessel when engaged on pilotage duty may in addition to the signals prescribed in paragraphs (a), (b) or (f) of this Rule sound an identity signal consisting of four short blasts.

(j) The following vessels shall not be required to sound signals as prescribed in paragraph (f) of this Rule when anchored in a special anchorage area designated by the Secretary:

(i) a vessel of less than 20 meters in length; and

(ii) a barge, canal boat, scow, or other nondescript craft.

Signals to Attract Attention

Rule 36. If necessary to attract the attention of another vessel, any vessel may make light or sound signals that cannot be mistaken for any signal authorized elsewhere in these Rules, or may direct the beam of her searchlight in the direction of the danger, in such a way as not to embarrass any vessel.

Distress Signals

Rule 37. When a vessel is in distress and requires assistance she shall use or exhibit the signals described in Annex IV to these Rules.

The distress signals for inland waters are the same as those displayed on the facing page for international waters with the following additional signal described:

PART E—EXEMPTIONS

Exemptions

Rule 38. Any vessel or class of vessels, the keel of which is laid or which is at a corresponding stage of construction before the date of enactment of this Act, provided that she complies with the requirements of—

(a) The Act of June 7, 1897 (30 Stat. 96), as amended (33 U.S.C. 154–232) for vessels navigating the waters subject to that statute;

(b) Section 4233 of the Revised Statutes (33 U.S.C. 301–356) for vessels navigating the waters subject to that statute;

(c) The Act of February 8, 1895 (28 Stat. 645), as amended (33 U.S.C. 241–295) for vessels navigating the waters subject to that statute; or

(d) Sections 3, 4, and 5 of the Act of April 25, 1940 (54 Stat. 163), as amended (46 U.S.C. 526 b, c, and d) for motorboats navigating the waters subject to that statute; shall be exempted from compliance with the technical Annexes to these Rules as follows:

(i) the installation of lights with ranges prescribed in Rule 22, until 4 years after the effective date of these Rules, except that vessels of less than 20 meters in length are permanently exempt;

(ii) the installation of lights with color specifications as prescribed in Annex I to these Rules, until 4 years after the effective date of these Rules, except that vessels of less than 20 meters in length are permanently exempt;

(iii) the repositioning of lights as a result of conversion to metric units and rounding off measurement figures, are permanently exempt; and

(iv) the horizontal repositioning of masthead lights prescribed by Annex I to these Rules:

(1) on vessels of less than 150 meters in length, permanent exemption.

(2) on vessels of 150 meters or more in length, until 9 years after the effective date of these Rules.

(v) the restructuring or repositioning of all lights to meet the prescriptions of Annex I to these Rules, until 9 years after the effective date of these Rules;

(vi) power-driven vessels of 12 meters or more but less than 20 meters in length are permanently exempt from the provisions of Rule 23(a)(i) and 23 (a)(iv) provided that, in place of these lights, the vessel exhibits a white light aft visible all round the horizon; and

(vii) the requirements for sound signal appliances prescribed in Annex III to these Rules, until 9 years after the effective date of these Rules.

ANNEX I—Positioning and Technical Details of Lights and Shapes

§ 84.01 Definitions.

(a) The term "height above the hull" means height above the uppermost continuous deck. This height shall be measured from the position vertically beneath the location of the light.

(b) The term "practical cut-off" means, for vessels 20

less than 2 meters, from the lights or shapes prescribed in Rule 27(b)(i) and (ii). In no case shall the upper of these lights or shapes be at a greater height than the lower of the three lights or shapes prescribed in Rule 27(b)(i) and (ii).

§ 84.09 Screens

(a) The sidelights of vessels of 20 meters or more in length shall be fitted with mat black inboard screens and meet the requirements of § 84.17. On vessels of less than 20 meters in length, the sidelights, if necessary to meet the requirements of § 84.17, shall be fitted with mat black inboard screens. With a combined lantern, using a single vertical filament and a very narrow division between the green and red sections, external screens need not be fitted.

(b) On power-driven vessels less than 12 meters in length constructed after July 31, 1983, the masthead light, or the all-round light described in Rule 23(c) shall be screened to prevent direct illumination of the vessel forward of the operator's position.

§ 84.11 Shapes

(a) Shapes shall be black and of the following sizes:
(1) A ball shall have a diameter of not less than 0.6 meter;
(2) A cone shall have a base diameter of not less than 0.6 meter and a height equal to its diameter;
(3) A diamond shape shall consist of two cones (as defined in Paragraph (a)(2) of this section) having a common base.
(b) The vertical distance between shapes shall be at least 1.5 meter.
(c) In a vessel of less than 20 meters in length shapes of lesser dimensions but commensurate with the size of the vessel may be used and the distance apart may be correspondingly reduced.

§ 84.13 Color specification of lights

(a) The chromaticity of all navigation lights shall conform to the following standards, which lie within the boundaries of the area of the diagram specified for each color by the International Commission on illumination (CIE), in the "Colors of Light Signals", which is incorporated by reference. It is Publication CIE No. 2.2. (TC-1.6), 1975, and is available from the Illumination Engineering Society, 345 East 47th Street, New York, NY 10017. It is also available for inspection at the Office of the Federal Register, Room 8401, 1100 L Street N.W., Washington, D.C. 20408. This incorporation by reference was approved by the Director of the Federal Register.

(b) The boundaries of the area for each color are given by indicating the corner coordinates, which are as follows:

(1) *White:*

x	0.525	0.525	0.452	0.310	0.310	0.443
y	0.382	0.440	0.440	0.348	0.283	0.382

(2) *Green:*

x	0.028	0.009	0.300	0.203
y	0.385	0.723	0.511	0.356

(3) *Red:*

x	0.680	0.660	0.735	0.721
y	0.320	0.320	0.265	0.259

(4) *Yellow:*

x	0.612	0.618	0.575	0.575
y	0.382	0.382	0.425	0.406

§ 84.15 Intensity of lights

(a) The minimum luminous intensity of lights shall be calculated by using the formula:

$$I = 3.43 \times 10^6 \times T \times D^2 \times K^{-D}$$

where I is luminous intensity in candelas under service conditions,

T is threshold factor 2×10^{-7} lux,

D is range of visibility (luminous range) of the light in nautical miles,

K is atmospheric transmissivity. For prescribed lights the value of K shall be 0.8, corresponding to a meteorological visibility of approximately 13 nautical miles.

(b) A selection of figures derived from the formula is given in Table 84.15(b).

Table 84.15(b)

Range of visibility (luminous range) of light in nautical miles D	Minimum luminous intensity of light in candelas for K = 0.8 I
1	0.9
2	4.3
3	12
4	27
5	52
6	94

§ 84.17 Horizontal sectors

(a)(1) In the forward direction, sidelights as fitted on the vessel shall show the minimum required intensities. The intensities shall decrease to reach practical cut-off between 1 and 3 degrees outside the prescribed sectors.

(2) For sternlights and masthead lights and at 22.5 degrees abaft the beam for sidelights, the minimum required intensities shall be maintained over the arc of the horizon up to 5 degrees within the limits of the sectors prescribed in Rule 21. From 5 degrees within the prescribed sectors the intensity may decrease by 50 percent up to the prescribed limits; it shall decrease steadily to reach practical cut-off at not more than 5 degrees outside the prescribed sectors.

(b) All-round lights shall be so located as not to be obscured by masts, topmasts or structures within angular sectors of more than 6 degrees, except anchor lights prescribed in Rule 30, which need not be placed at an impracticable height above the hull, and the all-round white light described in Rule 23(d), which may not be obscured at all.

§ 84.19 Vertical sectors

(a) The vertical sectors of electric lights as fitted, with the exception of lights on sailing vessels and on unmanned barges, shall ensure that:

(1) At least the required minimum intensity is maintained at all angles from 5 degrees above to 5 degrees below the horizontal;

(2) At least 60 percent of the required minimum intensity is maintained from 7.5 degrees above to 7.5 degrees below the horizontal.

(b) In the case of sailing vessels the vertical sectors of electric lights as fitted shall ensure that:

(1) At least the required minimum intensity is maintained at all angles from 5 degrees above to 5 degrees below the horizontal;

(2) At least 50 percent of the required minimum intensity is maintained from 25 degrees above to 25 degrees below the horizontal.

(c) In the case of unmanned barges the minimum required intensity of electric lights as fitted shall be maintained on the horizontal.

(d) In the case of lights other than electric lights these specifications shall be met as closely as possible.

§ 84.21 Intensity of non-electric lights

Non-electric lights shall so far as practicable comply with the minimum intensities, as specified in the Table given in § 84.15.

§ 84.23 Maneuvering light

Notwithstanding the provisions of § 84.03(f), the maneuvering light described in Rule 34(b) shall be placed approximately in the same fore and aft vertical plane as the masthead light or lights and, where practicable, at a minimum height of one-half meter vertically above the forward masthead light, provided that it shall be carried not less than one-half meter vertically above or below the after masthead light. On a vessel where only one masthead light is carried the maneuvering light, if fitted, shall be carried where it can best be seen, not less than one-half meter vertically apart from the masthead light.

§ 84.25 Approval. [Reserved]

ANNEX II—Additional Signals for Fishing Vessels Fishing in Close Proximity

§ 85.1 General

The lights mentioned herein shall, if exhibited in pursuance of Rule 26(d), be placed where they can best be seen. They shall be at least 0.9 meter apart but at a lower level than lights prescribed in Rule 26(b)(i) and (c)(i) contained in the Inland Navigational Rules Act of 1980. The lights shall be visible all around the horizon at a distance of at least 1 mile but at a lesser distance than the lights prescribed by these Rules for fishing vessels.

§ 85.3 Signals for trawlers

(a) Vessels when engaged in trawling, whether using demersal or pelagic gear, may exhibit:

(1) When shooting their nets: two white lights in a vertical line;

(2) When hauling their nets: one white light over one red light in a vertical line;

(3) When the net has come fast upon an obstruction: two red lights in a vertical line.

(b) Each vessel engaged in pair trawling may exhibit:

(1) By night, a searchlight directed forward and in the direction of the other vessel of the pair;

(2) When shooting or hauling their nets or when their nets have come fast upon an obstruction, the lights prescribed in paragraph (a) above.

§ 85.5 Signals for purse seiners

Vessels engaged in fishing with purse seine gear may exhibit two yellow lights in a vertical line. These lights shall flash alternately every second and with equal light and occultation duration. These lights may be exhibited only when the vessel is hampered by its fishing gear.

ANNEX III—Technical Details of Sound Signal Appliances

Subpart A—Whistles

§ 86.01 Frequencies and range of audibility.

The fundamental frequency of the signal shall lie within the range 70–525 Hz. The range of audibility of the signal from a whistle shall be determined by those frequencies, which may include the fundamental and/or one or more higher frequencies, which lie within the frequency ranges and provide the sound pressure levels specified in § 86.05.

§ 86.03 Limits of fundamental frequencies.

To ensure a wide variety of whistle characteristics, the fundamental frequency of a whistle shall be between the following limits:

(a) 70–200 Hz, for a vessel 200 meters or more in length;

(b) 130–350 Hz, for a vessel 75 meters but less than 200 meters in length;

(c) 250–525 Hz, for a vessel less than 75 meters in length.

§ 86.05 Sound signal intensity and range of audibility.

A whistle on a vessel shall provide, in the direction of the forward axis of the whistle and at a distance of 1 meter from it, a sound pressure level in at least one ⅓-octave band of not less than the appropriate figure given in Table 86.05 within the following frequency ranges (± 1 percent):

(a) 130–1200 Hz, for a vessel 75 meters or more in length;

(b) 250–1600 Hz, for a vessel 20 meters but less than 75 meters in length;

(c) 250–2100 Hz, for a vessel 12 meters but less than 20 meters in length.

Table 86.05

Length of vessel in meters	Fundamental frequency range (Hz)	For measured frequencies (Hz)	$\frac{1}{3}$-octave band level at 1 meter in dB referred to 2×10^{-5} N/m²	Audibility range in nautical miles
200 or more	70–200	130–180	145	2
		180–250	143	
		250–1200	140	
75 but less than 200	130–350	130–180	140	1.5
		180–250	138	
		250–1200	134	
20 but less than 75	250–525	250–450	130	1.0
		450–800	125	
		800–1600	121	
12 but less than 20	250–525	250–450	120	0.5
		450–800	115	
		800–2100	111	

Note: The range of audibility in the table above is for information and is approximately the range at which a whistle may usually be heard on its forward axis in conditions of still air on board a vessel having average background noise level at the listening posts (taken to be 68 dB in the octave band centered on 250 Hz and 63 dB in the octave band centered on 500 Hz).

In practice the range at which a whistle may be heard is extremely variable and depends critically on weather conditions; the values given can be regarded as typical but under conditions of strong wind or high ambient noise level at the listening post the range may be much reduced.

§ 86.07 Directional properties.

The sound pressure level of a directional whistle shall be not more than 4 dB below the sound pressure level specified in § 86.05 in any direction in the horizontal plane within ±45 degrees of the forward axis. The sound pressure level of the whistle at any other direction in the horizontal plane shall not be more than 10 dB less than the sound pressure level specified for the forward axis, so that the range of audibility in any direction will be at least half the range required on the forward axis. The sound pressure level shall be measured in that one-third octave band which determines the audibility range.

§ 86.09 Positioning of whistles.

(a) When a directional whistle is to be used as the only whistle on the vessel and is permanently installed, it shall be installed with its forward axis directed forward.

(b) A whistle shall be placed as high as practicable on a vessel, in order to reduce interception of the emitted sound by obstructions and also to minimize hearing damage risk to personnel. The sound pressure level of the vessel's own signal at listening posts shall not exceed 110 dB (A) and so far as practicable should not exceed 100 dB (A).

§ 86.11 Fitting of more than one whistle.

If whistles are fitted at a distance apart of more than 100 meters, they shall not be sounded simultaneously.

§ 86.13 Combined whistle systems.

(a) A combined whistle system is a number of whistles (sound emitting sources) operated together. For the purposes of the Rules a combined whistle system is to be regarded as a single whistle.

(b) The whistles of a combined system shall—

(1) Be located at a distance apart of not more than 100 meters,

(2) Be sounded simultaneously,

(3) Each have a fundamental frequency different from those of the others by at least 10 Hz, and

(4) Have a tonal characteristic appropriate for the length of vessel which shall be evidenced by at least two-thirds of the whistles in the combined system having fundamental frequencies falling within the limits prescribed in § 86.03, or if there are only two whistles in the combined system, by the higher fundamental frequency falling within the limits prescribed in § 86.03.

Note: If due to the presence of obstructions the sound field of a single whistle or of one of the whistles referred to in § 86.11 is likely to have a zone of greatly reduced signal level, a combined whistle system should be fitted so as to overcome this reduction.

§ 86.15 Towing vessel whistles.

A power-driven vessel normally engaged in pushing ahead or towing alongside may, at all times, use a whistle whose characteristic falls within the limits prescribed by § 86.03 for the longest customary composite length of the vessel and its tow.

Subpart B—Bell or gong

§ 86.21 Intensity of signal.

A bell or gong, or other device having similar sound characteristics shall produce a sound pressure level of not less than 110 dB at 1 meter.

§ 86.23 Construction.

Bells and gongs shall be made of corrosion-resistant material and designed to give a clear tone. The diameter of the mouth of the bell shall be not less than 300 mm for vessels of more than 20 meters in length, and shall be not less than 200 mm for vessels of 12 to 20 meters in length. The mass of the striker shall be not less than 3 percent of the mass of the bell. The striker shall be capable of manual operation.

Note: When practicable, a power-driven bell striker is recommended to ensure constant force.

Subpart C—Approval

§ 86.31 Approval. [Reserved]

ANNEX IV—Distress Signals

§ 87.1 Need of assistance.

The following signals, used or exhibited either together or separately, indicate distress and need of assistance:

(a) A gun or other explosive signal fired at intervals of about a minute;

(b) A continuous sounding with any fog-signalling apparatus;

(c) Rockets or shells, throwing red stars fired one at a time at short intervals;

(d) A signal made by radiotelegraphy or by any other signaling method consisting of the group . . . — ‘— — . . . (SOS) in the Morse Code;

(e) A signal sent by radiotelephony consisting of the spoken word "Mayday";

(f) The International Code Signal of distress indicated by N.C.;

(g) A signal consisting of a square flag having above or below it a ball or anything resembling a ball;

(h) Flames on the vessel (as from a burning tar barrel, oil barrel, etc.);

(i) A rocket parachute flare or a hand flare showing a red light;

(j) A smoke signal giving off orange-colored smoke;

(k) Slowly and repeatedly raising and lowering arms outstretched to each side;

(l) The radiotelegraph alarm signal;

(m) The radiotelephone alarm signal;

(n) Signals transmitted by emergency position-indicating radio beacons;

(o) A high intensity white light flashing at regular intervals from 50 to 70 times per minute.

§ 87.3 Exclusive use.

The use or exhibition of any of the foregoing signals except for the purpose of indicating distress and need of assistance and the use of other signals which may be confused with any of the above signals is prohibited.

§ 87.5 Supplemental signals.

Attention is drawn to the relevant sections of the International Code of Signals, the Merchant Ship Search and Rescue Manual and the following signals:

(a) A piece of orange-colored canvas with either a black square and circle or other appropriate symbol (for identification from the air);

(b) A dye marker.

336

C.
U.S.Y.R.U.
Racing Rules

Parts I and IV of the 1989–92 Yacht Racing Rules of the International Yacht Racing Union as adopted by the United States Yacht Racing Union.

Part I—Definitions

When a term defined in Part I is used in its defined sense it is printed in **italic** *type. All preambles and definitions rank as rules. Further definitions will be found at the beginning of Part VI.*

Sailing

A yacht is *sailing* when using only the wind and water to increase, maintain or decrease her speed, with her crew adjusting the trim of sails and hull and performing other acts of seamanship.

Racing

A yacht is *racing* from her preparatory signal until she has either *finished* and cleared the finishing line and finishing *marks* or retired, or until the race has been *postponed*, *abandoned*, *cancelled*, or a general recall has been signalled.

Starting

A yacht *starts* when, after fulfilling her penalty obligations, if any, under rule 51.1(c), Sailing the Course, and after her starting signal, any part of her hull, crew or equipment first crosses the starting line in the direction of the course to the first *mark*.

Finishing

A yacht *finishes* when any part of her hull, or of her crew or equipment in normal position, crosses the finishing line in the direction of the course from the last *mark*, after fulfilling her penalty obligations, if any, under rule 52.2(b), Touching a Mark.

Luffing

Altering course towards the wind.

Tacking

A yacht is *tacking* from the moment she is beyond head to wind until she has *borne away* to a *close-hauled* course.

Bearing away

Altering course away from the wind until a yacht begins to *gybe*.

Gybing

A yacht begins to *gybe* at the moment when, with the wind aft, the foot of her mainsail crosses her centre line, and completes the *gybe* when the mainsail has filled on the other *tack*.

Appendix C

On a tack

A yacht is *on a tack* except when she is *tacking* or *gybing*. A yacht is on the *tack* (*starboard* or *port*) corresponding to her *windward* side.

Close-hauled

A yacht is *close-hauled* when *sailing* by the wind as close as she can lie with advantage in working to windward.

Clear Astern and Clear Ahead; Overlap

A yacht is *clear astern* of another when her hull and equipment in normal position are abaft an imaginary line projected abeam from the aftermost point of the other's hull and equipment in normal position. The other yacht is *clear ahead*.

The yachts *overlap* when neither is *clear astern*; or when, although one is *clear astern*, an intervening yacht *overlaps* both of them.

The terms *clear astern*, *clear ahead* and *overlap* apply to yachts on opposite *tacks* only when they are subject to rule 42, Rounding or Passing Marks and Obstructions.

Leeward and Windward

The *leeward* side of a yacht is that on which she is, or, when head to wind, was, carrying her mainsail. The opposite side is the *windward* side.

When neither of two yachts on the same *tack* is *clear astern*, the one on the *leeward* side of the other is the *leeward yacht*. The other is the *windward yacht*.

Proper Course

A *proper course* is any course that a yacht might *sail* after the starting signal, in the absence of the other yacht or yachts affected, to *finish* as quickly as possible. The course *sailed* before *luffing* or *bearing away* is presumably, but not necessarily, that yacht's *proper course*. There is no *proper course* before the starting signal.

Mark

A *mark* is any object specified in the sailing instructions that a yacht must round or pass on a required side.

Every ordinary part of a *mark* ranks as part of it, including a flag, flagpole, boom or hoisted boat, but excluding ground tackle and any object either accidentally or temporarily attached to the *mark*.

Obstruction

An *obstruction* is any object, including a vessel under way, large enough to require a yacht, when more than one overall length away from it, to make a substantial alteration of course to pass on one side or the other, or any object that can be passed on one side only, including a buoy when the yacht in question cannot safely pass between it and the shoal or object that it marks. The sailing instructions may prescribe that certain defined areas shall rank as *obstructions*.

Postponement

A *postponed* race is one that is not started at its scheduled time and that can be sailed at any time the race committee may decide.

Abandonment

An *abandoned* race is one that the race committee declares void at any time after the starting signal, and that can be re-sailed at its discretion.

Cancellation

A *cancelled* race is one that the race committee decides will not be sailed thereafter.

Part IV—Right of Way Rules

Rights and Obligations when Yachts Meet

The rules of Part IV do not apply in any way to a vessel that is neither intending to **race** *nor* **racing***; such vessel shall be treated in accordance with the International Regulations for Preventing Collisions at Sea or Government Right of Way Rules applicable to the area concerned. The rules of Part IV apply only between yachts that are either intending to* **race** *or are* **racing** *in the same or different races, and, except when rule 3.2(b)(xxix), Race Continues After Sunset, applies, replace the International Regulations for Preventing Collisions at Sea or Government Right of Way Rules applicable to the area concerned, from the time a yacht intending to* **race** *begins to* **sail** *about in the vicinity of the starting line until she has either* **finished** *or retired and has left the vicinity of the course. (See Appendix 9).*

SECTION A—Obligations and Penalties

31   Rule Infringement

31.1 A yacht may be penalised for infringing a rule of Part IV only when the infringement occurs while she is *racing*.

31.2 A yacht may be penalised, before or after she is *racing*, for seriously hindering a yacht that is *racing* or for infringing the sailing instructions.

32   Serious Damage

32.1 AVOIDING COLLISIONS

When a collision has resulted in serious damage, the right-of-way yacht shall be penalised as well as the other yacht when she had the opportunity but failed to make a reasonable attempt to avoid the collision.

32.2 HAILING

Except when *luffing* under rule 38.1, Luffing Rights, a right-of-way yacht that does not hail before or when making an alteration of course that may not be foreseen by the other yacht may be penalised as well as the yacht required to keep clear when a collision resulting in serious damage occurs.

33   Contact between Yachts Racing

When there is contact that is not both minor and unavoidable between the hulls, equipment or crew of two yachts, both shall be penalised unless:

either

(a) one of the yachts retires in acknowledgement of the infringement, or exonerates herself by accepting an alternative penalty when so prescribed in the sailing instructions,

or

(b) one or both of these yachts lodges a valid **protest**.

34 Maintaining Rights

When a yacht that may have infringed a **rule** does not retire or exonerate herself, other yachts shall continue to accord her such rights as she has under the rules of Part IV.

SECTION B—Principal Right of Way Rules and their Limitations

These rules apply except when over-ridden by a rule in Section C.

35 Limitations on Altering Course

When one yacht is required to keep clear of another, the right-of-way yacht shall not alter course so as to prevent the other yacht from keeping clear, or so as to obstruct her while she is keeping clear, except:

(a) to the extent permitted by rule 38.1, Luffing Rights, and

(b) when assuming a *proper course*:

either

(i) to *start*, unless subject to rule 40, Same Tack, Luffing before Clearing the Starting Line, or to the second part of rule 44.1(b), Returning to Start,

or

(ii) when rounding a *mark*.

36 Opposite Tacks—Basic Rule

A *port-tack* yacht shall keep clear of a *starboard-tack* yacht.

37 Same Tack—Basic Rules

37.1 WHEN OVERLAPPED

A *windward yacht* shall keep clear of a *leeward yacht*.

37.2 WHEN NOT OVERLAPPED

A yacht *clear astern* shall keep clear of a yacht *clear ahead*.

37.3 TRANSITIONAL

A yacht that establishes an *overlap* to *leeward* from *clear astern* shall initially allow the *windward yacht* ample room and opportunity to keep clear.

38 Same Tack—Luffing after Clearing the Starting Line

38.1 LUFFING RIGHTS

After she has *started* and cleared the starting line, a yacht *clear ahead* or a *leeward yacht* may *luff* as she pleases, subject to the following limitations of this rule.

38.2 LIMITATIONS

(a) Proper Course Limitations:

A *leeward yacht* shall not sail above her *proper course* while an *overlap* exists, if when the *overlap* began or at any time during its existence, the helmsman of the *windward yacht* (when sighting abeam from his normal station and *sailing* no higher than the *leeward yacht*) has

been abreast or forward of the mainmast of the *leeward yacht*.

(b) Overlap Limitations:

For the purpose of rule 38 only: An *overlap* does not exist unless the yachts are clearly within two overall lengths of the longer yacht; and an *overlap* that exists between two yachts when the leading yacht *starts*, or when one or both of them completes a *tack* or *gybe*, shall be regarded as a new *overlap* beginning at that time.

(c) Hailing to Stop or Prevent a Luff:

When there is doubt, the *leeward yacht* may assume that she has the right to *luff* or *sail* above her *proper course* unless the helmsman of the *windward yacht* has hailed either:

(i) "Mast Abeam", or words to that effect, or

(ii) "Obstruction", or words to that effect.

The *leeward yacht* shall be governed by such hail and curtail her *luff*. When she deems the hail improper, her only remedy is to protest.

(d) Curtailing a Luff:

The *windward yacht* shall not cause a *luff* to be curtailed because of her proximity to the *leeward yacht* unless an *obstruction*, a third yacht or other object restricts her ability to respond.

(e) Luffing Rights over Two or More Yachts:

A yacht shall not *luff* unless she has the right to *luff* all yachts that would be affected by her *luff*, in which case they shall all respond, even when an intervening yacht or yachts would not otherwise have the right to *luff*.

39 Same Tack—Sailing below a Proper Course after Starting

A yacht that is on a free leg of the course shall not *sail* below her *proper course* when she is clearly within three of her overall lengths of a *leeward yacht* or of a yacht *clear astern* that is steering a course to *leeward* of her own.

40 Same Tack—Luffing before Clearing the Starting Line

Before a yacht *clear ahead* or a *leeward yacht* has *started* and cleared the starting line, any *luff* on her part that causes another yacht to have to alter course to avoid a collision shall be carried out slowly and initially in such a way as to give a *windward yacht* room and opportunity to keep clear. Furthermore, the *leeward yacht* shall not so *luff* above a close-hauled course while the helmsman of the *windward yacht* (sighting abeam from his normal station) is abreast or forward of the mainmast of the *leeward yacht*. Rules 38.2(c), Hailing to Stop or Prevent a Luff; 38.2(d), Curtailing a Luff; and 38.2(e), Luffing Rights over Two or More Yachts, also apply.

41 Changing Tacks—Tacking and Gybing

41.1 BASIC RULE

A yacht that is either *tacking* or *gybing* shall keep clear of a yacht *on a tack*.

41.2 TRANSITIONAL

A yacht shall neither *tack* nor *gybe* into a position

that will give her right of way unless she does so far enough from a yacht *on a tack* to enable this yacht to keep clear without having to begin to alter her course until after the *tack* or *gybe* has been completed.

41.3 ONUS
A yacht that *tacks* or *gybes* has the onus of satisfying the **protest committee** that she completed her *tack* or *gybe* in accordance with rule 41.2.

41.4 WHEN SIMULTANEOUS
When two yachts are both *tacking* or both *gybing* at the same time, the one on the other's port side shall keep clear.

SECTION C—Rules that Apply at Marks and Obstructions and other Exceptions to the Rules of Section B

When a rule of this section applies, to the extent to which it explicitly provides rights and obligations, it over-rides any conflicting rule of Section B, Principal Right of Way Rules and their Limitations, except rule 35, Limitations on Altering Course.

42 Rounding or Passing Marks and Obstructions
Rule 42 applies when yachts are about to round or pass a *mark* on the same required side or an *obstruction* on the same side, except that it shall not apply:

(a) between two yachts on opposite *tacks*:

   (i) when they are on a beat, or

   (ii) when one, but not both, of them will have to *tack* either to round or pass the *mark* or to avoid the *obstruction*, or

(b) when rule 42.4 applies.

42.1 WHEN OVERLAPPED
An Outside Yacht

(a) An outside yacht shall give each inside *overlapping* yacht room to round or pass the *mark* or *obstruction*, except as provided in rule 42.3. Room is the space needed by an inside *overlapping* yacht that is handled in a seamanlike manner in the prevailing conditions to pass in safety between an outside yacht and a *mark* or *obstruction*, and includes space to *tack* or *gybe* when either is an integral part of the rounding or passing manoeuvre.

(b) An outside yacht *overlapped* when she comes within two of her overall lengths of a *mark* or *obstruction* shall give room as required, even though the *overlap* may thereafter be broken.

(c) An outside yacht that claims to have broken an *overlap* has the onus of satisfying the **protest committee** that she became *clear ahead* when she was more than two of her overall lengths from the *mark* or *obstruction*.
An Inside Yacht

(d) A yacht that claims an inside *overlap* has the onus of satisfying the **protest committee** that she

established the *overlap* in accordance with rule 42.3.

(e) When an inside yacht of two or more *overlapped* yachts, either on opposite *tacks* or on the same *tack* without *luffing* rights, will have to *gybe* in order most directly to assume a *proper course* to the next *mark*, she shall *gybe* at the first reasonable opportunity.
Hailing

(f) A yacht that hails when claiming the establishment or termination of an *overlap* or insufficiency of room at a *mark* or *obstruction* thereby helps to support her claim.

42.2 WHEN NOT OVERLAPPED
A Yacht Clear Astern

(a) A yacht *clear astern* when the yacht *clear ahead* comes within two of her overall lengths of a *mark* or *obstruction* shall keep clear in anticipation of and during the rounding or passing manoeuvre, whether the yacht *clear ahead* remains on the same *tack* or *gybes*.

(b) A yacht *clear astern* shall not *luff* above *close-hauled* so as to prevent a yacht *clear ahead* from *tacking* to round a *mark*.
A Yacht Clear Ahead

(c) A yacht *clear ahead* that *tacks* to round a *mark* is subject to rule 41, Changing Tacks—Tacking and Gybing.

(d) A yacht *clear ahead* shall be under no obligation to give room to a yacht *clear astern* before an *overlap* is established.

42.3 LIMITATIONS
(a) Limitation on Establishing an Overlap
A yacht that establishes an inside *overlap* from *clear astern* is entitled to room under rule 42.1(a) only when, at that time, the outside yacht:

   (i) is able to give room, and

   (ii) is more than two of her overall lengths from the *mark* or *obstruction*. However, when a yacht completes a *tack* within two of her overall lengths of a *mark* or *obstruction*, she shall give room as required by rule 42.1(a) to a yacht that, by *luffing*, cannot thereafter avoid establishing a late inside *overlap*.

At a continuing *obstruction*, rule 42.3(b) applies.

(b) Limitation When an Obstruction is a Continuing One.
A yacht *clear astern* may establish an *overlap* between a yacht *clear ahead* and a continuing *obstruction*, such as a shoal or the shore or another vessel, only when, at that time, there is room for her to pass between them in safety.

42.4 AT A STARTING MARK SURROUNDED BY NAVIGABLE WATER
When approaching the starting line to *start* until clearing the starting *marks* after *starting*, a *leeward yacht* shall be under no obligation to give any

windward yacht room to pass to leeward of a starting *mark* surrounded by navigable water, including such a *mark* that is also an *obstruction*; but, after the starting signal, a *leeward yacht* shall not deprive a *windward yacht* of room at such a *mark* by *sailing* either:

(a) to windward of the compass bearing of the course to the next *mark*, or

(b) above *close-hauled*.

43 Close-Hauled, Hailing for Room to Tack at Obstructions

43.1 HAILING

When two *close-hauled* yachts are on the same *tack* and safe pilotage requires the yacht *clear ahead* or the *leeward yacht* to make a substantial alteration of course to clear an *obstruction*, and when she intends to *tack*, but cannot *tack* without colliding with the other yacht, she shall hail the other yacht for room to *tack* and clear the other yacht, but she shall not hail and *tack* simultaneously.

43.2 RESPONDING

The hailed yacht at the earliest possible moment after the hail shall either:

(a) *tack*, in which case the hailing yacht shall begin to *tack* immediately she is able to *tack* and clear the other yacht; or

(b) reply "You *tack*", or words to that effect, in which case:

  (i) the hailing yacht shall immediately *tack* and

  (ii) the hailed yacht shall give the hailing yacht room to *tack* and clear her.

  (iii) The onus of satisfying the **protest committee** that she gave sufficient room shall lie on the hailed yacht that replied "You *tack*".

43.3 WHEN AN OBSTRUCTION IS ALSO A MARK

(a) When an *obstruction* is a starting *mark* surrounded by navigable water, or the ground tackle of such a *mark*, and when approaching the starting line to *start* and after *starting*, the yacht *clear ahead* or the *leeward yacht* shall not be entitled to room to *tack*.

(b) At other *obstructions* that are *marks*, when the hailed yacht can fetch the *obstruction*, the hailing yacht shall not be entitled to room to *tack* and clear the hailed yacht, and the hailed yacht shall immediately so inform the hailing yacht. When, thereafter, the hailing yacht again hails for room to *tack* and clear the hailed yacht, give the hailing yacht the required room. After receiving room, the hailing yacht shall either retire immediately or exonerate herself by accepting an alternative penalty when so prescribed in the sailing instructions.

(c) When, after having refused to respond to a hail under rule 43.3(b), the hailed yacht fails to fetch, she shall retire immediately or exonerate herself by accepting an alternative penalty when so prescribed in the sailing instructions.

44 Returning to Start

44.1 (a) After the starting signal, a premature starter returning to *start*, or a yacht working into position from the course side of the starting line or its extensions, shall keep clear of all yachts that are *starting* or have *started* correctly, until she is wholly on the pre-start side of the starting line or its extensions.

(b) Thereafter, she shall be accorded the rights under the rules of Part IV of a yacht that is *starting* correctly; but when she thereby acquires right of way over another yacht that is *starting* correctly, she shall allow that yacht ample room and opportunity to keep clear.

44.2 A premature starter, while continuing to *sail* the course and until it is obvious that she is returning to *start*, shall be accorded the rights under the rules of Part IV of a yacht that has *started*.

45 Keeping Clear after Touching a Mark

45.1 A yacht that has touched a *mark* and is exonerating herself shall keep clear of all other yachts until she has completed her exoneration and, when she has *started*, is on a *proper course* to the next *mark*.

45.2 A yacht that has touched a *mark*, while continuing to *sail* the course and until it is obvious that she is exonerating herself, shall be accorded rights under the rules of Part IV.

46 Person Overboard; Yacht Anchored, Aground or Capsized

46.1 A yacht under way shall keep clear of another yacht *racing* that:

(a) is manoeuvring or hailing for the purpose of rescuing a person overboard, or

(b) is anchored, aground or capsized.

46.2 A yacht shall not be penalised when she is unable to avoid fouling a yacht that she is attempting to assist or that goes aground or is capsized.

46.3 A yacht is capsized from the time her masthead is in the water until her masthead is clear of the water and she has steerage way.

46.4 A yacht anchored or aground shall indicate the fact to any yacht that may be in danger of fouling her. Under normal conditions, a hail is sufficient indication. Of two yachts anchored, the one that anchored later shall keep clear, except that a yacht dragging shall keep clear of one that is not.

(Numbers 47, 48 and 49 are spare numbers)

D.
U.S.N.A.
Training Cruise

Circumnavigation of Delmarva

Sailing Instructions

1. Purpose. The objectives of this event are to provide offshore sailing experience for the midshipmen crews in preparation for the Summer Sail Training Program, and to enhance their professional development as Naval Officers in the areas of leadership, navigation, and seamanship.

2. Organization. The Sail Group shall consist of:

Insurgente	(US 14571)
Mistral	(NA–63)
Patriot	(US 7777)
Fair American	(US 17711)
Intrepid	(NA–1)
Alert	(NA–2)
Frolic	(NA–5)
Restless	(NA–6)
Fearless	(NA–8)
Flirt	(NA–9)
Lively	(NA–10)
Swift	(NA–11)
Vigilant	(NA–12)

3. Presail Conference. There will be a presail conference in Robert Crown Center at 1300 Friday, 26 May for all Coaches and Sailing Masters. All yachts shall be underway and proceed individually at 1600 Friday 26 May.

4. Course. The course will be down Chesapeake Bay, exiting through Chesapeake Channel. Leave the Chesapeake Tower (36° 54.3′N, 75° 42.8′W), R2JS fl. 4 sec. Whistle (38° 05′N, 74° 42.5′W), and Bell "5" fl. 2½ sec. at the mouth of Delaware Bay to port. Reenter Chesapeake Bay and return to Santee Basin. Thomas Point Light, Sharp's Island Light, Smith Point Light, Windmill Point Light, Wolfe Trappe Light, New Point Comfort, Nun 4 off Plum Point and Bell "38" off Worton Point must all be passed on the channel side. If prevailing winds dictate, MISTRAL may sail the course in reverse.

5. Safety. All safety equipment required by the Coast Guard must be on board and readily accessible. Fuel and water tanks must be filled to capacity. All yachts must have a full inventory of Category I equipment.

6. Time Limit. There is no time limit.

7. Rules. The USYRU Racing Rules shall apply in addition to the official Inland International Rules of the Road. Yachts approaching a large vessel in a channel shall yield the right of way to that vessel.

8. Special Requirements for Yachts. All participating yachts are required to perform the below-listed exercises during the Race. Each exercise may be performed at a time selected by the coach as long as the required static conditions are satisfied. Two drills may not be done simultaneously, but two or more could be done consecutively. Performance of each exercise and the time spent will be noted in the log.

Exercise Requirements

Exercise	Minimum static conditions	Mandatory minimum elapsed time
a. simulated man overboard drill (sea rough-day)	TRUE wind at least 12 knots; spinnaker must be set prior to commencing. Continue to practice pick-ups for remainder of drill time.	15 minutes
b. simulated man overboard drill (sea rough-night)	TRUE wind at least 10 knots; light and horseshoe with drogue must be in the water before timing is started. Continue to practice pick-up for remainder of drill time.	15 minutes
c. actual man overboard recovery	Static conditions optional to coach. Subject must be recovered by three different methods with minimal assistance by subject. 1) Simulating severe injury, use a jib and a halyard to scoop him aboard. Try shackling clew and tack of small genoa into a halyard. Tend head of sail aft in cockpit and lower the bight in the foot of the sail over the side to form a scoop. Attach a forward guy to halyard shackle to control fore and aft position of the sail. 2) Use vang at the end of the boom or relead a genoa sheet thru a block at the boom and a grinder to hoist subject aboard. You may need a preventer on the boom to triangulate it with the mainsheet. If you had to put another man in the water to assist (sea conditions permitting), how would you do it? 3) Practice putting a second man in the water to assist/rescue another. Always have rescuer attached. A bowline on a bight works well—one bight for rescuer, and the other to be slipped over head of subject.	30 minutes
d. storm jib/storm trysail	When on normal course, with wind over 20 knots. Tack and jibe a couple of times. Tack and jibe into a heave-to-condition.	Experiment for 20 minutes
e. heaving to	True wind greater than 15 knots. Enter with a fully reefed main (or simulated 3 reefs). Experiment with and without storm jib and with helm lashed at various angles.	20 minutes at near dead in the water
f. rig yacht for tow	Fully rig for a tow—include heaving line (messenger), chafing gear; determine fast way to secure line. *Have shroud cutters, sharp knife, or hatchet handy.*	None
g. emergency steering	True wind at least 10 knots. Tack/jibe at least twice. Think about how you would rig an emergency rudder. All boats experiment sailing and maneuvering without a rudder, just sails, or a drogue from the boom.	30 minutes under emergency steering conditions
h. abandon ship drill	Assign specific stations and exercise until all hands know their responsibilities.	None
i. discuss dismasting, broken boom, and rigging emergency spars, damage control and fire	Assign specific stations and plan ahead.	None
j. man aloft exercise	As a minimum, once in daylight in the ocean and once at night anywhere. In addition send a man up the headstay. In each case, rig the line to deck. Try securing reaching strut under bosuns chair and rigging two control lines to be tended from the deck.	None

343

9. Navigation Requirements. All yachts will determine their positions by RDF on at least two occasions. All boats are expected to home on the Chesapeake Tower with RDF. Their RDF-plotted positions will be verified by landmark references as soon as practicable. Both the RDF position and the geographic verifications will be entered in the log. Those yachts equipped with operative Loran and/or Omega will determine their position by that means on at least two occasions. At least one evening and one morning position will be determined by celestial navigation, weather permitting. A position will likewise be determined by advancing sunlines at least once. The ship's compass will be checked by celestial azimuth observation at least once on each leg. Coaches are responsible for review and critique of all charts after finishing race. Yachts are free to power as necessary to maintain a 4-knot average. All boats will use radar reflectors at night and in reduced visibility conditions.

10. Communications. All yachts will report exiting through Bay Bridge and Tunnel and entering Delaware Bay to the Naval Station Operations Office on SSB and VHF thru a local marine radio-telephone relay. SSB and VHF shall be used. Reverse charges to Naval Station operations (301) 267-3823. A listening watch will be maintained on VHF Channel 16 and SSB 2182 KHz in accordance with the following schedule:

Yacht	Watch commences
Insurgente	0100 and 1300
Patriot	0200 and 1400
Fair American	0300 and 1500
Intrepid	0400 and 1600
Alert	0500 and 1700
Frolic	0600 and 1800
Restless	0700 and 1900
Fearless	0800 and 2000
Flirt	0900 and 2100
Lively	1000 and 2200
Swift	1100 and 2300
Vigilant	1200 and 2400

As each yacht commences the watch, it should transmit an announcement identifying itself and stating that it is commencing radio watch.

E.
U.S. Navy Recreational Sailing Program

(*From* BUPERSINST 1710.11, 11 March 1974)

312. Navy Recreation Sailing Program.

Sailing is considered to be an ideal recreation activity for naval personnel. The responsibility for administration and operation of recreational sailing programs rests with the commanding officer administering the Recreation Fund which serves the installation on which appropriate facilities and equipment are maintained. He shall have custody of all such equipment procured with Recreation Funds. The U.S. Naval Sailing Association (USNSA) is recognized as an advisory group to assist in developing and conducting Navy sailing programs. Where established, continued recognition of its various branches as advisory groups is encouraged to assist commanding officers in the development and promotion of boating and sailing programs within their respective commands. When so recognized, the provisions of Chapter Two of this manual will be applicable.

345

1. Development

a. In determining feasibility of a Recreation Sailing Program, all assets should be considered. Alternatives to the acquisition of sailing craft include the use of privately owned boats and/or the use of Special Services craft belonging to shore commands with established programs. A vigorous instruction program will broaden the base of personnel qualified to sail and lead to increased utilization of Special Services sailing craft.

b. Standard qualification criteria as outlined in Appendix 3A will facilitate ready use of boats by newly arrived and transient personnel. In granting qualifications, Special Services Directors should require that knowledge and skill of each candidate be examined and qualifications demonstrated to ensure that he is qualified at the level indicated. When qualifications are comparable, each command should honor qualifications granted by another. However, each commanding officer should ensure that new personnel are given adequate familiarization of boats and sailing areas.

c. Instructional material for the Recreation Sailing Program includes the following: the American Red Cross Basic Sailing handbook, the American Red Cross Basic Sailing Instructors Manual, and the American Red Cross Sailing Instructors Visual Aids, developed by the American Red Cross and used at the Naval Academy. Sail and Power, published by the U.S. Naval Institute, is the text used by the Naval Academy in training midshipmen in ocean racing/cruising yachts. It is accepted as the basic instructional material for senior skippers and master skipper level of qualifications.

2. Program

a. Where established, recreational sailing will be included as part of the overall Recreation Program.

3. Funding

The procurement, operation, and maintenance of sailboats; the development of instructional programs in sailing; and the establishment of competitive events at local levels are the responsibility of the commanding officer of the installation on which the sailing facility is located. Appropriated fund support is authorized as specified by reference (d). Such support should be used to the maximum extent authorized. Financial support from nonappropriated recreation funds for recreational sailing is authorized when supported in accordance with Chapter Six of this manual. In general, sailing programs should be self-supporting from fees and charges levied for participation as specified in Chapter Six.

Appendix 3A. Standard Sailing Qualification Criteria

References

(a) American Red Cross Basic Sailing (ARC 2115) Stock No. 321143 (1966)

(b) American Red Cross Basic Sailing Instructors Manual (1967)

(c) American Red Cross Sailing Instructors Visual Aids (1969)

(d) Sail and Power (U.S. Naval Institute)

1. Levels of Sailing Qualification

a. Mate. Minimum qualification to crew on small sailing craft.

b. Skipper. Qualified to handle small sailing craft in local waters.

c. Racing Skipper. Qualified skipper who also has a thorough theoretical and practical knowledge of yacht racing rules and techniques.

d. Senior Skipper. Qualified to command a large sailing yacht in local waters.

e. Master Skipper. Qualified to command and race a large sailing yacht off shore under all conditions.

2. Details of Qualification Requirements

Each level shall include the requirements of all previous levels.

a. Mate. Fulfill present military requirements as swimmer 3rd class. (Enter water feet first from a minimum height of five feet and remain afloat for five minutes. During this time, swim at least 50 yards). Pass an oral examination on nomenclature and demonstrate ability to crew in a sailing craft.

b. Skipper. Successfully complete the course for Basic Sailing, reference (a), as taught in accordance with reference (b) by an approved instructor. This course includes classroom work using reference (c), completion of a Basic Sailing written examination and on-the-water instruction leading to a practical examination.

c. Racing Skipper. Demonstrate a thorough theoretical and practical knowledge of racing rules. Participate in several races as skipper and serve on a race committee.

Demonstrate superior boat handling and sail trimming capability to include use of the spinnaker where available.

d. Senior Skipper. Successfully complete a written examination based upon reference (d), including Rules of the Road. Be recommended by two established senior skippers after on-the-water demonstration of skills which should include:

(1) Ability to take charge of a watch at sea;

(2) Sound knowledge of regulations and procedures for preventing a collision at sea;

(3) Working knowledge of pilotage and tidal effects;

(4) Knowledge of when and where to anchor in safety, how to check for anchor drag, and how to clear a fouled anchor;

(5) Measures to be taken in bad weather, including fog, and the use of distress signals;

(6) Understanding simple first aid and lifesaving, to include recovery of man overboard and how to deal with cuts, bleeding, severe bruising, fractures, burns, shock, seasickness, sunstroke, sunburn, exposure and methods of artificial respiration;

(7) Emergency repair of boat and gear;

(8) Simple repairs to sails and maintaining the yacht's gear and standing rigging;

(9) Knowledge of courtesy and customs used at sea, including flag etiquette;

(10) Knowledge of simple meteorology;

(11) Practical knowledge of yacht engines;

(12) Preparing for sea;

(13) Taking charge of all phases of deck work;

(14) Handling a yacht competently under sail and power in confined water, getting underway, coming alongside berth, picking up mooring, and anchoring;

(15) Taking charge at sea; and

(16) Securing a yacht after mooring.

e. Master Skipper. Demonstrate ability and personal qualities requisite to taking charge of a yacht offshore including piloting, celestial navigation, visual signaling, and radiotelephone operation. Sail as a member of the afterguard in a major ocean race and be recommended by at least two established master skippers in that afterguard.

3. Availability of Training Material

References (a) through (c) are available from Red Cross field offices world-wide. Reference (d) is available from the U.S. Naval Institute, Annapolis, Maryland 21402.

4. Instructors

Each commanding officer must ascertain to his own satisfaction that the instructor(s)/qualifier(s) in his program are competent. Instructors do not necessarily have to be Navy personnel. It is envisioned that the U.S. Naval Sailing Association branches will assist in creating a nucleus of competent sailing instructors for various ships and stations. Acquisition of Red Cross certification for instructors is encouraged but not required.

5. Waivers

A commanding officer may waive specific requirements at his discretion, based upon past experience of a candidate, provided he is satisfied that the candidate can perform to the level indicated. Deviations from standard criteria should be documented on the certification form.

6. Disqualification

In the event a commanding officer considers that a qualified skipper should be reduced in qualification, he may do so at his discretion after appropriate investigation of circumstances leading to the action.

7. Certification

Certifications should be prepared at the local level and should include the following information:

Section I should be the sailing qualification. It should provide the individual's name and the sailing level for which qualifications have been completed. The qualification should be dated and signed by the instructor/qualifier and the commanding officer. Any deviations from standard criteria should also be noted on the qualification. Section II should be a record of the various sailing levels for which the individual is qualified. It should indicate the date, class boat, qualifier, and pertinent comments concerning each qualification.

F.
Offshore Racing Council January 1990

348

SPECIAL REGULATIONS GOVERNING OFFSHORE RACING*

1.0 PURPOSE AND USE

1.1 It is the purpose of these special regulations to establish uniform minimum equipment and accommodations standards for monohull yachts racing offshore.
N.B. Monohull: Hull in which the hull depth in any section does not decrease towards the centre-line.

1.2 These regulations do not replace, but rather supplement, the requirements of governmental authority and the Racing Rules. The attention of owners is called to restrictions in the rules on the location and movement of equipment.

1.3 The Offshore Racing Council strongly recommends the use of these special regulations by all organisations sponsoring offshore races. Race Committees may select the category deemed most suitable for the type of race to be sailed.

2.0 OWNER'S RESPONSIBILITY

2.1 The safety of a yacht and her crew is the sole and inescapable responsibility of the owner, or owner's representative who must do his best to ensure that the yacht is fully found, thoroughly seaworthy and manned by an experienced crew who are physically fit to face bad weather. He must be satisfied as to the soundness of hull, spars, rigging, sails and all gear. He must ensure that all safety equipment is properly maintained and stowed and that the crew know where it is kept and how it is to be used.

2.2 Neither the establishment of these special regulations, their use by sponsoring organisations, nor the inspection of a yacht under these regulations in any way limits or reduces the complete and unlimited responsibility of the owner or owner's representative.

2.3 It is the sole and exclusive responsibility of each yacht to decide whether or not to start or continue to race.

3.0 INSPECTION

3.1 A yacht may be inspected at any time. If she does not comply with these special regulations her entry may be rejected, or she will be liable to disqualification or such other penalty as may be prescribed by the national authority or the sponsoring organisation.

4.0 CATEGORIES OF OFFSHORE EVENTS

4.1 In many types of races, ranging from long-distance ocean races sailed under adverse conditions to short-course day races sailed in protected waters, five categories of races are established, as follows, to provide for the differences in the standards of safety and accommodation required for such varying circumstances.

4.2 *Category 0 race.* Trans-Ocean races, where yachts must be completely self-sufficient for very extended periods of time, capable of withstanding heavy storms and prepared to meet serious emergencies without the expectation of outside assistance.

4.3 *Category 1 race.* Races of long distance and well offshore, where yachts must be completely self-sufficient for extended periods of time, capable of withstanding heavy storm and prepared to meet serious emergencies without the expectation of outside assistance.

4.4 *Category 2 race.* Races of extended duration along or not far removed from shorelines or in large unprotected bays or lakes, where a high degree of self-sufficiency is required of the yachts but with the reasonable probability that outside assistance could be called upon for aid in the event of serious emergencies.

4.5 *Category 3 race.* Races across open water, most of which is relatively protected or close to shorelines, including races for small yachts.

4.6 *Category 4 race.* Short races, close to shore in relatively warm or protected waters normally held in daylight.

5.0 BASIC REQUIREMENTS

	RACE CATEGORY				
5.1 All required equipment shall: Function properly, Be readily accessible, Be of a type, size and capacity suitable and adequate for the intended use and size of the yacht	0	1	2	3	4
5.2 Yachts shall be self-righting (see I.O.R. Part XII). They shall be strongly built, watertight and, particularly with regard to hulls, decks and cabin trunks capable of withstanding solid water and knockdowns. They must be properly rigged and ballasted, be fully seaworthy and must meet the standards set forth herein. "Properly rigged" means (inter alia) that shrouds shall never be disconnected.	0	1	2	3	4
5.3 Inboard engine installations shall be such that the engine when running can be securely covered, and that the exhaust and fuel supply systems are securely installed and adequately	0	1	2	3	4

protected from the effects of heavy weather. When an electric starter is the only provision for starting the engine, a separate battery shall be carried, the primary purpose of which is to start the engine.

	RACE CATEGORY				
Each yacht fitted with a propulsion engine shall carry a minimum amount of fuel in a permanently installed fuel tank. This minimum amount of fuel may be specified in the Notice of Race but if not, shall be sufficient to be able to meet charging requirements for the duration of the race and to motor at $L(\sqrt{LWL})$ knots for at least 8 hours. Organising clubs are recommended to apply their own minimum fuel requirements.	0	1	2	3	4
5.4 Ballast and Heavy Equipment. All heavy items including inside ballast and internal fittings (such as batteries, stoves, gas bottles, tanks, engines, outboard motors etc.) and anchors and chains (see 8.31 and 8.32) shall be securely fastened so as to remain in position should the yacht be capsized 180 degrees.	0	1	2	3	
5.5 Yacht equipment and fittings shall be securely fastened.					4
5.6 Sail Numbers shall be in accordance with IYRR 25.	0	1	2	3	4

A yacht shall carry on all mainsails, all spinnakers and all jibs with LPG greater than $1.3 \times J$ (Longest perpendicular greater that $1.3 \times$ Base of foretriangle):

(a) A letter or letters showing her nationality except that National letters need not be carried in home waters, except in an international championship.

(b) A sail number allotted to her by her national or state authority.

The sail numbers and letters of the size shown on the mainsail must be displayed by alternative means if none of the numbered sails is set. (See SR 10.52)

6.0 STRUCTURAL FEATURES

Yachts shall have been built in accordance with ABS approved plans according to the ABS Guide for Building and Classing Offshore Racing Yachts.

	RACE CATEGORY	
Age or Series date (whichever is earlier) of 1/1986 or later.	0	1

349

	RACE CATEGORY				

Age or Series date (whichever is earlier) of 1/1987 or later and LOA of 40ft. (12.19m) and above. — **2**

Age or Series Date (whichever is earlier) of 1/1988 or later and LOA of less than 40ft. (12.19m). — **2**

Age Date is not otherwise specified shall be the month and year of launch and the Series Date shall be the launch date of the first yacht of the production series. — **0 1 2**

6.1 The hull, including deck, coach roof and all other parts, shall form an integral, essentially watertight, unit and any openings in it shall be capable of being immediately secured to maintain this integrity (see 5.1). For example, running rigging or control lines shall not compromise this watertight unit. Centerboard and daggerboard trunks shall not open into the interior of the hull. — **0 1 2 3 4**

6.12 Hatches. No hatches forward of the BMAX (maximum beam) station shall open inwards excepting ports having an area of less than 110 sq. in. (710 sq.cm.) Hatches shall be so arranged as to be above the water when the hull is heeled 90°. All hatches shall be permanently fitted so that they can be closed immediately and will remain firmly shut in a 180° capsize. The main companionway hatch shall be fitted with a strong securing arrangement which shall be operable from above and below. — **0 1 2 3 4**

6.13 Companionways. All blocking arrangements (washboards, hatchboards, etc.) shall be capable of being secured in position with the hatch open or shut and shall be secured to the yacht by lanyard or other mechanical means to prevent their being lost overboard. — **0 1 2 3 4**

6.14 Cockpit companionways, if extended below main deck level, must be capable of being blocked off to the level of the main deck at the sheer line abreast the opening. When such blocking arrangements are in place this companionway (or hatch) shall continue to give access to the interior of the hull. — **0 1 2 3 4**

6.21 Cockpits shall be structurally strong, self draining and permanently incorporated as an integral part of the hull. They must be essentially watertight, that is, all openings to the hull must be capable of being strongly and rigidly secured. Any bow, lateral central or stern well will be considered as a cockpit for the purposes of 6.21, 6.22, 6.23 and 6.31. — **0 1 2 3 4**

6.22 Cockpits opening aft to the sea. The lower edge of the companionway shall not be below main deck level as measured above. The openings shall not be less than 50% of maximum cockpit depth multiplied by maximum cockpit width. The requirement in 6.31 that cockpits must drain at all angles of heel applies. — **0 1 2 3 4**

6.23 Cockpit Volume

6.23.1 The maximum volume of all cockpits below lowest coamings shall not exceed 6% L × B × FA (6% loaded water line × maximum beam × freeboard abreast the cockpit). The cockpit sole must be at least 2% L above LWL (2% length overall above loaded water line). — **0 1**

6.23.2 The maximum volume of all cockpits below lowest coamings shall not exceed 9% L × B × FA (9% loaded water line × maximum beam × freeboard abreast the cockpit). The cockpit sole must be at least 2% L above LWL (2% length overall above loaded water line). — **2 3 4**

6.31 Cockpit drains.

6.31.1 For yachts 28 feet/8.53m length overall and over. Cockpit drains adequate to drain cockpits quickly but with a combined area (after allowance for screens, if attached) of not less than the equivalent of four .75in. (19 mm) diameter drains. Yachts built before 1-1-72 must have drains with a combined area (after allowance for screens, if attached) of not less than the equivalent of two 1 in. (25mm) drains. Cockpits shall drain at all angles of heel.
Yachts built before 1-1-77 may conform to 6.31.2 for races in Categories 3 and 4. — **0 1 2 3 4**

6.31.2 For yachts under 28 feet/8.53m length overall. Cockpit drains adequate to drain cockpits quickly but not less in combined area (after allowance for screens, if attached) than the equivalent of two 1 in. (25mm) diameter drains. Cockpits shall drain at all angles of heel. — **0 1 2 3 4**

6.4 Storm covering for all windows more than two square feet in area (1858 sq. cm.) — **0 1 2 3**

6.51 Sea cocks or valves on all through-hull openings below LWL, except integral deck scuppers, shaft log, speed indicators, depth finders and the like, however a means of closing such openings, when necessary to do so, shall be provided.

Does not apply in Category 4 races to yachts built before 1-1-76.

	0	1	2	3	4

6.52 Soft wood plugs, tapered and of the correct size, to be attached to, or adjacent to, the appropriate fitting. `0 1 2 3 4`

6.53 Sheet winches shall be mounted in such a way that no operator is required to be substantially below deck. `0 1 2 3 4`

6.54 Mast Step. The heel of a keel stepped mast shall be securely fastened to the mast step or adjoining structure. `0 1 2 3 4`

6.55 Bulkhead. The hull shall have a watertight bulkhead within 15% of the vessel's length from the bow and abaft the forward perpendicular. `0`

6.6 LIFELINES, STANCHIONS, PULPITS AND JACKSTAYS

6.61 For all yachts.

6.61.1 Life-line terminals and life-line material. All life-lines shall comprise 1 × 19 stainless steel wire or a stranded stainless steel wire of the same or greater strength (see also 6.62.1 and IYRR 62). A taut lanyard of synthetic rope may be used to secure life-lines, provided that when in position its length does not exceed 4 in. (100mm). The lanyard(s) and end fittings shall have an equivalent strength to that of the wire life-line. `0 1 2 3 4`

6.61.2 Stanchions shall not be angled at more than ten degrees from the vertical at any point above 50mm from the deck nor within the first 50mm from the deck, may they be displaced horizontally from the point at which they emerge from the deck or base by more than 10mm. For yachts with an Age Date of 1/1988 or later, stanchions shall be straight, except that one bend is permitted in the first 50mm above deck. For yachts with an Age Date of 1/1987 or later, stanchions, pulpits, and lifelines shall not be made of carbon fibre. `0 1 2 3 4`

6.61.3 Overlapping pulpits. Lifelines need not be affixed to the bow pulpit if they terminate at, or pass through, adequately braced stanchions 2 ft. (610mm) [18 in. (457mm) for yachts 28 feet/8.53 m length overall] `0 1 2 3 4`

above the working deck, set inside and overlapping the bow pulpit, provided that the gap between the upper lifeline and the bow pulpit does not exceed 6 ins. (152mm).

6.61.4 Pulpit and stanchion fixing. Pulpits and stanchions shall be securely attached. `0 1 2 3 4`

(a) When there are sockets or studs, these shall be through-bolted, bonded or welded. The pulpit(s) and/or stanchions fitted to these shall be mechanically retained without the help of the lifelines.

(b) Without sockets or studs, pulpits and/or stanchions shall be through-bolted, bonded or welded.

The bases of pulpits and stanchions shall not be further inboard from the edge of the working deck than 5% of BMAX (maximum beam) or 6in. (152mm), whichever is greater. Stanchion bases shall not be situated outboard of the working deck.

6.62 For yachts of 28 feet/8.53m length overall and over.

6.62.1 Taut double lifelines, with upper lifeline of wire at a height of not less than 2 ft. (609mm) above the working deck, to be permanently supported at intervals of not more than 7 ft. (2.13 m). When the cockpit opens aft to the sea, additional lifelines must be fitted so that no opening is greater in height than 22 in. (560mm). For yachts of 28ft./8.53m LOA or over, all life-lines shall comprise wire of minimum diameter 5mm. `0 1 2 3 4`

6.62.2 Pulpits. Fixed bow pulpit (forward of headstay) and stern pulpit (unless lifelines are arranged as to adequately substitute for a stern pulpit). Lower lifelines need not extend through the bow pulpit. Upper rails of pulpits shall be at not less height above the working deck than upper lifelines. Upper rails in bow pulpits shall be securely closed while racing. Any lifeline attachment point will be considered as a stanchion in so far as its base shall not be situated outboard of the working deck. Providing the complete lifeline enclosure is supported by stanchions and pulpit bases within the working deck, lifeline terminals and support struts may be fixed to the hull aft of the working deck. `0 1 2 3 4`

351

	RACE CATEGORY

6.63 For yachts under 28 feet/8.53m length overall.

6.63.1 Taut single wire lifeline, at a height of not less than 18 ins. (457mm) above the working deck, to be permanently supported at intervals of not more than 7 ft. (2.13m). If the lifeline is at any point more than 22 ins. (560mm) above the rail cap, a second intermediate lifeline must be fitted. If the cockpit opens aft to the sea additional lifelines must be fitted so that no opening is greater in height than 22 ins. (560mm). Lifelines shall comprise wire of minimum diameter 4mm. `0 1 2 3 4`

6.63.2 Pulpits. Fixed bow pulpit and stern pulpit (unless lifelines are arranged as to adequately substitute for a stern pulpit). Lower lifelines need not extend through the bow pulpit. Upper rails of pulpits must be at no less height above the working deck than upper lifelines. Upper rails in bow pulpits shall be securely closed while racing. The bow pulpit may be fitted abaft the forestay with its bases secured at any points on deck, but a point on its upper rail must be within 16 ins. (406mm) of the forestay on which the foremost headsail is hanked. `0 1 2 3`

Provided the complete lifeline enclosure is supported by stanchions and pulpit bases within the working deck, lifeline terminals and support struts may be fixed to the hull aft of the working deck.

6.64 Toe Rails. A toe-rail of not less than 1 in. (25mm) shall be permanently fitted around the deck forward of the mast, except in way of fittings. Location to be not further inboard from the edge of the working deck than one third of the local beam. `0 1 2 3`

A third lifeline (or second for yachts under 28 feet/8.53m length overall at a height of not less than 1 in. (25mm) or more than 2 ins. (50mm) above the working deck will be accepted in place of a toe-rail.

In yachts built before 1 January 1981 a toe-rail of 0.75in. (19mm) will be accepted.

6.65 JACKSTAYS

Jackstays must be fitted on deck, port and starboard of the yacht's centre line to provide secure attachments for safety harnesses. Jackstays shall comprise stainless steel 1 × 19 wire of minimum diameter 5mm, or webbing of equivalent strength. Jackstays must be attached to through-bolted or welded deck plates, or other suitable and strong anchorages. The jackstays must, if possible, be fitted in such a way that a crew member, when clipped on, can move from a cockpit to the forward and to the after end of the main deck without unclipping the harness. If the deck lay-out renders this impossible, additional lines must be fitted so that a crew member can move as described with a minimum of clipping operations.

A crew member must be able to clip on before coming on deck, unclip after going below and remain clipped on while moving laterally across the yacht on the foredeck, the afterdeck, and amidships. If necessary additional jackstays and/or through-bolted or welded anchorage points must be provided for this purpose.

Through-bolted or welded anchorage points, or other suitable and strong anchorage, for safety harnesses must be provided adjacent to stations such as the helm, sheet winches and masts, where crew members work for long periods. Jackstays should be sited in such a way that the safety harness lanyard can be kept as short as possible.

7.0 ACCOMMODATIONS

7.11 Toilet, securely installed `0 1 2`

7.12 Toilet, securely installed, or fitted bucket `3 4`

7.2 Bunks, securely installed `0 1 2 3 4`

7.3 Cooking stove, securely installed against a capsize with safe accessible fuel shutoff control capable of being safely operated in a seaway. `0 1 2 3`

7.4 Galley facilities. `0 1 2 3 4`

7.51 Water tank(s), securely installed and capable of dividing the water supply into at least three compartments and discharging through a pump. The quantity of water to be taken aboard is left to the discretion of the organising authority, but two gallons (nine litres) per person per one thousand miles shall be taken as the absolute minimum. `0`

RACE CATEGORY

7.52 Water tank(s), securely installed and capable of dividing the water supply into at least two compartments and discharging through a pump. — 1

7.53 At least one securely installed water tank discharging through a pump. — 2 3

8.0 GENERAL EQUIPMENT

8.1 Fire extinguishers, at least two, readily accessible in suitable and different parts of the boat. — 0 1 2 3 4

8.21.1 Bilge Pumps, at least two manually operated, securely fitted to the yacht's structure, one operable above, the other below deck. Each pump shall be operable with all cockpit seats, hatches and companionways shut. — 0 1 2

8.21.2 Each bilge pump shall be provided with permanently fitted discharge pipe(s) of sufficient capacity to accommodate simultaneously both pumps. — 0 1 2

8.21.3 No bilge pumps may discharge into a cockpit unless that cockpit opens aft to the sea. Bilge pumps shall not be connected to cockpit drains. — 0 1 2 3 4

8.21.4 Unless permanently fitted, each bilge pump handle shall be provided with a lanyard or catch or similar device to prevent accidental loss. — 0 1 2 3 4

8.22 One manual bilge operable with all cockpit seats, hatches and companionways closed. — 3

8.23 One manual bilge pump. — 4

8.24 Two buckets of stout construction each with at least 2 gallons (9 litres) capacity. Each bucket to have a lanyard. — 0 1 2 3 4

8.31 Anchors. Two with cables except yachts under 28 feet/8.53m length overall which shall carry at least one anchor and cable.

Anchors and any chain shall be securely fastened in the position recorded on the Rating Certificate when not in use. — 0 1 2 3

8.32 One anchor and cable.

Anchor(s) and any chain shall be securely fastened in the position recorded on the Rating Certificate when not in use. — 4

8.41 Flashlights, one of which is suitable for signalling, water resistant, with spare batteries and bulbs. — 0 1 2 3

8.42 At least one flashlight, water resistant, with spare batteries and bulb. — 4

8.5 First aid kit and manual. — 0 1 2 3 4

8.6 Foghorn. — 0 1 2 3 4

8.7 Radar reflector. If a radar reflector is octahedral it must have a minimum diagonal measurement of 18 ins. (457mm), or if not octahedral must have a documented "equivalent echoing area" of not less than 10 sq.m. — 0 1 2 3 4

8.8 Set of international code flags and international code book. — 0 1

8.9 Shutoff valves on all fuel tanks. — 0 1 2 3 4

9.0 NAVIGATION EQUIPMENT

9.1 Compass, marine type, properly installed and adjusted. — 0 1 2 3 4

9.2 Spare compass. — 0 1 2 3

9.3 Charts, light list and piloting equipment. — 0 1 2 3

9.4 Sextant, tables and accurate time piece. — 0 1

9.5 Radio direction finder or an automatic position fixing device. — 0 1 2

9.6 Lead line or echo sounder. — 0 1 2 3 4

9.7 Speedometer or distance measuring instrument. — 0 1 2 3

9.8 Navigation lights, to be shown as required by the International Regulations for Preventing Collision at Sea, mounted so that they will not be masked by sails or the heeling of the yacht. — 0 1 2 3 4

Yachts under 7m LOA shall comply with the regulations for those between 12m and 7m LOA (i.e. they shall exhibit sidelights and a sternlight).

Navigation lights shall not be mounted below deck level.

Spare bulbs for navigation lights shall be carried.

As a guide, minimum bulb wattage in navigation lights for yachts under sail should be as follows:

(a) yachts less than 12m (39.6 ft) LOA—10 watts

(b) yachts of 12m (39.6 ft) LOA and greater—25 watts.

Attention is drawn to Part C and Technical Annex I of International Regulations for Preventing Collisions at Sea, 1972.

10.0 EMERGENCY EQUIPMENT

10.1 Emergency navigation lights and power source. Emergency navigation lights shall have the same minimum specifications as the navigation lights in 9.8 and a power source and wiring separate from that used for the normal navigation lights. — 0 1 2 3

353

Appendix F

Emergency navigation lights shall not be used if the normal navigation lights (under Rule 9.8) are operable.

10.21 The following specifications for mandatory sails give maximum areas; smaller areas may well suit some yachts. Appropriate sheeting positions on deck shall be provided for these sails.

10.21.1 One storm trysail not larger than 0.175×P×E in area. It shall be sheeted independently of the boom and shall have neither a headboard nor battens and be of suitable strength for the purpose. The yacht's sail number and letter(s) shall be placed on both sides of the trysail in as large a size as is practicable. Aromatic polyamides, carbon fibres and other high modulous fibres shall not be used in the storm trysail. **[0 1 2]**

10.21.2 One storm jib of not more than 0.05×IG×IG (5% height of the foretriangle squared) in area, the luff of which does not exceed 0.65×IG (65% height of the foretriangle), and of suitable strength for the purpose. Aromatic polyamides, carbon fibres and other high modulous fibres shall not be used in the storm jib. **[0 1 2]**

10.21.3 One heavy-weather jib of suitable strength for the purpose with area not greater than 0.135×IG×IG (13.5% height of the foretriangle squared) and which does not contain reef points. **[0 1 2]**

10.22 One heavy-weather jib as in 10.21.3 (or heavy-weather sail in a boat with no forestay) and either:
(a) a storm trysail as in 10.21.1 or
(b) mainsail reefing equipment capable of reducing the effective luff to 60% P or less when aromatic polyamides, carbon fibres and other high modulous fibres shall not be used. **[3 4]**

10.23 Any storm or heavy-weather jib if designed for a seastay or luff-groove device shall have an alternative method of attachment to the stay. **[0 1 2 3 4]**

10.24 No mast shall have less than two halyards each capable of hoisting a sail. **[0 1 2 3 4]**

10.3 Emergency Steering Equipment

10.31 An emergency tiller capable of being fitted to the rudder stock. **[0 1 2 3]**

10.32 Crews must be aware of alternative methods of steering the yacht in any sea condition in the event of rudder failure. At least one method must have been proven to work on board the yacht. An inspector may require that this method be demonstrated. **[0 1 2 3 4]**

10.4 Tools and spare parts, including adequate means to disconnect or sever the standing rigging from the hull in the case of need. **[0 1 2 3 4]**

10.5 Yacht's name on miscellaneous buoyant equipment, such as life jackets, oars, cushions, lifebuoys and lifeslings, etc. **[0 1 2 3 4]**

10.51 Life-buoys, lifeslings, life-rafts, and life-jackets shall be fitted with marine grade retro-reflective material. **[0 1 2 3 4]**

10.52 Sail numbers, either portable or displayed on each side of the hull and meeting the requirements for mainsail numbers. **[0 1 2 3]**

10.61 Marine radio transmitter and receiver. If the regular antenna depends upon the mast, an emergency antenna must be provided.
Yachts fitted with VHF transceivers are recommended to install VHF Channel 72 (156.625 MHZ Simplex). This is an international ship-ship channel which, by "common use", could become an accepted yacht-yacht channel for all ocean racing yachts anywhere in the world. **[0 1 2]**

10.62 In addition to 10.61, a waterproof hand held VHF transceiver is recommended. **[0 1]**

10.63 Radio receiver capable of receiving weather bulletins. **[0 1 2 3 4]**

10.64 EPIRBs
Emergency indicator beacon transmitting on 121.5, 243 or 406 MHz. **[0 1]**

10.7 At least 2 gallons (9 liters) of water for emergency use carried in one or more containers. **[0 1 2 3]**

11.0 SAFETY EQUIPMENT

11.1 Life jackets, one for each crew member.
In the absence of any specification, the following definition of a life jacket is recommended:
"A life jacket should be of a form **[0 1 2 3 4]**

354

which is capable of providing not less than 16kg. of buoyancy, arranged so that an unconscious man will be securely suspended face upwards at approximately 45 degrees to the water surface."

11.2 Whistles attached to life jackets. — *Race Category: 0 1 2 3*

11.3 Safety belt (harness type) one for each crew member. — *Race Category: 0 1 2 3*

Each yacht may be required to demonstrate that two thirds of the crew can be adequately attached to strong points on the yacht.

11.4 Life raft(s) capable of carrying the entire crew and meeting the following requirements: — *Race Category: 0 1 2*

  A. Must be carried on the working deck or in a special stowage opening immediately to the working deck containing the life-raft(s) only.

  B. For yachts built after 1.7.83 Life-raft(s) may only be stowed under the working deck provided:

    (a) the stowage compartment is water tight or self draining

    (b) if the stowage compartment is not watertight, then the floor of the special stowage is defined as the cockpit sole for the purposes of rule 6.23.2

    (c) the cover of this compartment shall be capable of being opened under water pressure.

  C. Life-raft(s) packed in a valise and not exceeding 40kg. may be securely stowed below deck adjacent to the companionway.

  D. Each raft shall be capable of being got to the lifelines within 15 seconds.

  E. Must have a valid annual certificate from the manufacturer or an approved servicing agent certifying that it has been inspected, that it complies with the above requirements and stating the official capacity of the raft which shall not be exceeded. The certificate, or a copy thereof, to be carried on board the yacht.

11.51 Lifebuoy with a drogue, or lifesling, equipped with a self-igniting light within reach of the helmsman and ready for instant use. — *Race Category: 0 1 2 3 4*

11.52 In addition to 11.51. One lifebuoy, within reach of the helmsman and ready for instant use and equipped with a whistle, dye marker, drogue, a self-igniting light, and a pole and flag. The pole shall be either permanently extended or be capable of being fully automatically extended in less than 5 seconds. It shall be attached to the lifebuoy with 10ft. (3.048m) of floating line and is to be of a length and so ballasted that the flag will fly at least 6ft. (1.828m) off the water. — *Race Category: 0 1 2*

11.61 Distress signals conforming to the current International Convention for the Safety of Life at Sea (SOLAS) regulations (chapter III Visual Signals) to be stowed in a waterproof container or containers, as indicated. — *Race Category: 0 1 2 3 4*

11.62 Twelve red parachute flares. (SOLAS regulation 35) — *Race Category: 0 1*

11.63 Four red parachute flares. (SOLAS regulation 35) — *Race Category: 2 3*

11.64 Four red hand flares. (SOLAS regulation 36) — *Race Category: 0 1 2 3 4*

11.65 Four white hand flares. Although not specified by SOLAS, it is recommended that design criteria, excepting colour and candela rating, be in accordance with SOLAS regulation 36. — *Race Category: 0 1 2 3 4*

11.66 Two orange smoke day signals. (SOLAS regulation 37) — *Race Category: 0 1 2 3*

11.67 Distress signals which are more than 3 years old (as indicated by the date of manufacture) or of which the date of expiry has passed are not acceptable. — *Race Category: 0 1 2 3 4*

11.7 Heaving line (50 ft. (15.24m) minimum length) readily accessible to cockpit. — *Race Category: 0 1 2 3 4*

12. Weight jackets (IYRR 61.2) shall not be permitted. — *Race Category: 0 1 2 3 4*

G.
Sea State Codes

Hydrographic Office		International	
Term and height of waves, in feet	Code	Term and height of waves, in feet	Code
calm, 0	0	calm, glassy, 0	0
smooth, less than 1	1		
slight, 1–3	2	rippled, 0–1	1
moderate, 3–5	3	smooth, 1–2	2
rough, 5–8	4	slight, 2–4	3
		moderate, 4–8	4
		rough, 8–13	5

Hydrographic Office		International	
very rough, 8–12	5	very rough, 13–20	6
high, 12–20	6		
very high, 20–40	7	high, 20–30	7
mountainous, 40 and higher	8	very high, 30–45	8
confused	9	phenomenal, over 45	9

H.
Beaufort Scale

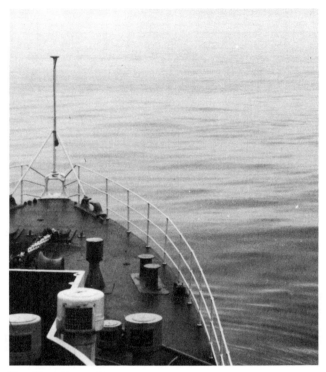

Beaufort Force 0.
Wind speed: Less than 1 knot.
Sea: Like a mirror.

Beaufort Force 1.
Wind speed: 1–3 knots.
Sea: Ripples with appearance of scales are formed, but without foam crests.

358

Beaufort Force 2.
Wind speed: 4–6 knots.
Sea: Small wavelets, still short, but more pronounced; crests have a glassy appearance and do not break.

Beaufort Force 4.
Wind speed: 11–16 knots.
Sea: Small waves, becoming longer; fairly frequent white horses.

Beaufort Force 3.
Wind speed: 7–10 knots.
Sea: Large wavelets; crests begin to break; foam of a glassy appearance. Perhaps some scattered white horses.

Beaufort Force 5.
Wind speed: 17–21 knots.
Sea: Moderate waves taking a more pronounced long form; many white horses are formed; chance of some spray.

Beaufort Force 6.
Wind speed: 22–27 knots.
Sea: Large waves begin to form; the white foam crests are more extensive everywhere; probably some spray.

Beaufort Force 8.
Wind speed: 34–40 knots.
Sea: Moderately high waves of greater length; edges of crests begin to break into the spindrift. The foam is blown in well-marked streaks along the direction of the wind.

359

Beaufort Force 7.
Wind speed: 28–33 knots.
Sea: Sea heaps up and white foam from breaking waves begins to be blown in streaks along the direction of the wind.

Beaufort Force 9.
Wind speed: 41–47 knots.
Sea: High waves. Dense streaks of foam along the direction of the wind. Crests of waves begin to topple, tumble, and roll over. Spray may affect visibility.

Beaufort Force 10.
Wind speed: 48–55 knots.
Sea: Very high waves with long overhanging crests. The resulting foam, in great patches, is blown in dense white streaks along the direction of the wind. On the whole, the surface of the sea takes on a white appearance. The tumbling of the sea becomes heavy and shocklike. Visibility affected.

Beaufort Force 12.
Wind speed: 64–71 knots, hurricane.
Sea: Air filled with foam; sea completely white with driving spray; visibility greatly reduced.

Beaufort Force 11.
Wind speed: 53–63 knots, violent storm.
Sea: Exceptionally high waves, sea covered with white foam patches; visibility still more reduced.

I.
Long-Established Olympic Classes

Finn, a planing, cat-rigged, centerboard dinghy for singlehanded racing. She has an extremely flexible, unstayed mast. Dimensions: 14′9″ L.O.A., 14′ L.W.L., 4′10″ beam, 2′3″ draft, 115 square feet sail area.

Soling, a modern fin-keel, spade-rudder sloop. She is fitted with hiking straps but not a trapeze. Her spinnaker is rounder looking than the typical cruising boat's spinnaker because class rules allow greater girth than most handicap rules. Dimensions: 26′9″ L.O.A., 20′ L.W.L., 6′3″ beam, 4′3″ draft, 233 square feet sail area.

362

Tornado. A catamaran that is extremely fast reaching even though she carries no spinnaker. Her wide beam and trapeze provide high initial stability, but her range of stability is low when compared with a keel boat. Dimensions: 20′ L.O.A., 19′2″ L.W.L., 10′ beam, 2′6″ draft (board down), and 272 square feet sail area.

Flying Dutchman, a very sophisticated, light displacement, planing centerboard dinghy. She carries a Genoa jib and spinnaker and has a trapeze for maximum advantage in hiking. Dimensions: 19′10″ L.O.A., 18′ L.W.L., 5′7″ beam, 3′7″ draft, 200 square feet sail area.

The 470, a centerboard dinghy similar to, but smaller than, the Flying Dutchman. She carries a spinnaker and is equipped with hiking straps and a trapeze. Dimensions: 15′6″ L.O.A., 5′6″ beam, 4′11″ draft (board down), 137 square feet sail area.

Star, an ancient class boat (80 years old) with a hard chine, fin keel, and separated rudder hinged on a skeg. She has a tall, flexible rig and is somewhat tender, but she does not carry a spinnaker. No special hiking devices are used. Dimensions: 22′7½″ L.O.A., 15′ L.W.L., 5′8″ beam, 3′4″ draft, 285 square feet sail area.

J. Bluewater Underway Checklist*

First LT:

1. Inspect all standing rigging from masthead to deck, ensuring cotters intact, taped as necessary, no cracks in swages or signs of broken strands in wire.
2. Inspect all running rigging. End for end as necessary, whip loose ends, install chafing gear as needed, change leads to prevent chafe. Note particularly areas under strain in heavy weather (reefing lines where they go through cringles, for example).
3. Bend on all storm sails, install sheets, and determine sheeting locations—mark with permanent felt-tip pen. Mark storm sails, with large letters for corners (e.g., *tack*, *head*, *clew*).
4. Mark all reef tack cringles on mainsail with numbers corresponding to reef number (e.g., #1, #2, #3, as appropriate).
5. Inventory sail ties. Ensure 3 times the normal number for racing.
6. Lay out safety lines on each deck and in cockpit. Check swages for cracks or unlaying indications. Run harness hooks fore and aft to ensure free travel and maximum utility.
7. Inspect and inventory all safety harnesses. Check for sprung clips, torn webbing, and inoperative lights.
8. Inspect and inventory all PFDs. Check whistles and other equipment, ensure ship's name is stenciled on the PFD.
9. Inspect liferaft(s) for seal and security of attachment.
10. Inventory sail repair kit. Ensure following supplies:
    4′–6′ heavy canvas for chafing gear
    min. 6 assorted sail needles
    min. 2 roping palms, right hand
    min. 1 yard 8–9-oz. sail cloth
    10″ reinforcing nylon tape
    min. 4 small rolls sailtwine
    complete set spare battens

Engineer:

1. Clean bilges completely, removing all debris, cleaning limberholes.
2. Clean bilge pump strainers.
3. Test all bilge pumps by pumping clean water, counting strokes required to empty one bucket, using each pump.
4. Ensure batteries and other equipment are secured against 180° rollover.
5. Ensure all batteries are fully charged, using hydrometer. Replace defective batteries.
6. Inspect steering carefully for correct cable size and tension, proper clamps and freedom from binding. Remove loose gear from quadrant area. If hydraulic steering, check reservoir and air charge, filling to specified level and pressure.
7. Find and test emergency tiller.

363

* Safety at Sea Symposium 1984

Damage Control Assistant (DCA):

1. Fit all washboards and other hatch devices. Ensure covers for large windows (greater than 2′ square) are on board and properly stored.
2. Cycle all through-hull valves through full travel. Lubricate as necessary. Check for DC plugs hung adjacent to each fitting of correct size. Ensure all below waterline hoses connected to thru-hulls are double clamped.
3. Check tightness of topsides by use of high-pressure hose applied to hatches, deck edge, windows, mast boot. Fill cockpit with tape over drains and determine time required to empty with drain covers and grates removed.
4. Inventory all covers for Dorade vents.
5. Inventory DC kit.

Navigator:

1. Ensure means of receiving HF/SSB weather information is in operation by copying at least one broadcast. Ensure copy of HO 118, or extracts for broadcast schedule is on board.
2. If possible, install WEATHERFAX receiver and test operate. Carry sufficient rolls of paper for 1.5 times anticipated need.
3. Ensure means of receiving time signals by checking and marking time signals on at least two frequencies.

4. Check barometer for accuracy against standard barometer.
5. Inventory emergency gear: Flares, EPIRB, survival mirrors, radar reflector, space blanket.
6. Ensure sufficient spare flashlight batteries for 1.5 times anticipated need.

Supply:

1. Prepare menu for possible 30-hour storm condition.
2. Ensure Seaswing stove and sufficient sterno on board.
3. Secure all stores for possible 180° rollover.
4. Rig all leecloths and check for adequacy of attachment.
5. Inventory all survival suits, removing from bags to determine condition.

Skipper/OinC:

1. Ensure all emergency bills are up-to-date, and personnel are assigned to functions by name.
2. Ensure HF-SSB radio is channelized to receive a range of frequencies from the USCG Portsmouth VA weather station. See HO 118 for frequencies.

Note: All hands should carry their own brand of seasick remedy, as no single type is adequate for every individual. Boat issue remedies vary widely in effectiveness and side effects, and are a poor substitute for a known solution.

K. Heavy-Weather Bill

Safety at Sea Symposium—1984

Purpose. To set forth procedures in *preparing* the vessel and crew for heavy weather.

Information. The heavy-weather bill shall be implemented upon the receipt of weather information that winds above 30 kts will be encountered within 24 hours, or when such action is required in the judgment of the Officer-in-Charge.

Action. Responsibilities are listed by billet:

First LT:

1. Inspect all running rigging. Replace or end-for-end frayed lines.
2. Inspect all standing rigging visible from deck.
3. Rig deck safety lines (jacklines), ensure firm attachment points.
4. Rig cockpit safety lines, ensure firm attachment points and utility in hooking up before emerging from cabin. On split rigs, consider rigging additional rope lifelines between shrouds of main and mizzen to protect cockpit area, fill gaps between horizontal lines with vertical Vs, using rolling hitches.
5. Set up running backstays and forestays as applicable.
6. Dig out storm sails and place in ready storage area.
7. Break out additional sheets and sail ties.
8. Strike below all unused sails, equipment, and anything which might be ripped from on-deck location.
9. Rig cockpit weather cloths if provided.
10. Check man-overboard gear for security and readiness for use.
11. Check liferaft(s) for security and seal.
12. Rig radar reflector and pad for chafe as necessary.

Engineer:

1. Get full battery charge, check with hydrometer.
2. Top off all liquid levels in engine and batteries.
3. Split fuel and water tank suctions, put fuel tank with most fuel on ready suction.
4. Check all bilge areas for cleanliness and freedom from debris, clean all pump strainers.
5. Pump all bilges completely, flush if necessary.
6. Doublecheck all storage in engine space—batteries, tools, spare parts, etc. Secure against 180° rollover.
7. Inspect steering gear for correct cable tension and remove any loose gear in area. If hydraulic steering installed, check reservoir level and air charge, correcting discrepancies.
8. Secure all engine through-hull fittings, including exhaust valve to prevent water entry into manifold. Remove key from starter lock and tag OOC in nav. table.

Damage Control Assistant (DCA):

1. Check all hatch-securing devices. Rig strongbacks if provided. Install heavy washboards.
2. Remove cockpit drain grates (if installed).

3. Break out and mark large window shutters where provided.
4. Place DC kit in readiness for use, including inventory. Position in cabin in secure but ready location. Centralize two buckets for emergency use as bailers.
5. Remove Dorade hoods and replace with covers.

Navigator:

1. Obtain best position using all inputs.
2. Establish DR on large-scale plotting sheet.
3. Monitor all available weather information (HO 118).
4. Increase barometer readings to 1/2 hour intervals.
5. Check time on navigational watch.
6. Replace batteries in flashlights.
7. Inventory emergency gear (flares, EPIRB).
8. Monitor VHF channel 16.

Supply:

1. Prepare hot, substantial meal before storm arrives. *Note:* Always wear foul weather gear trousers when cooking in heavy weather—use galley strap for support.
2. Prepare sandwiches for minimum 12-hour period, wrapped individually.
3. Secure regular stove before storm strikes, bleed off alcohol pressure or secure gas bottles at source as applicable.

4. Rig Seaswing stove, and position Sterno cans for easy access.
5. Place honey and peanut butter handily available, but secure.
6. Break out hand food for watches (granola bars or peanut butter and cheese crackers (one-handed food)), and place in convenient lockers.
7. Secure all storage compartments to prevent flying cans, etc. Use latches and back up with duct tape.
8. Supervise rigging of leecloths, storage of personal items and inspect entire living area for security and elimination of missile hazards.
9. Break out survival suits if temperatures indicate.

Skipper/OinC:

1. Adjust watchbill for necessary expertise on deck.
2. Ensure crew get maximum rest prior to storm.
3. Closely monitor weather conditions, evaluate situation as to possible diversion from storm.
4. Brief crew on storm tactics—precautions and procedures to be followed. Brief on sail changes, tacks, jibes, use of supplementary stays, man overboard considerations, flooding, dismasting and abandon ship.
5. Issue seasick remedies at least 4 hours prior to storm.

L.
Inventory—
Offshore
Medical
Supply Kit

1 18×3½ metal needle   1 18×1½ metal needle
1 20×3½ metal needle   1 20×1½ metal needle
1 14×1½ metal needle   1 21×1½ metal needle
2 1-ml ampuls Atropine (.4 mg 1/150 gr/ml)
2 1-ml ampuls Benadryl (.50 mg ea.)
3 1-ml ampuls Vosoxyl (methoxamine HCl) (20 mg ea.)
3 1-ml ampuls Epinephrine
2 5-ml ampuls Xylocaine (100 mg ea.)
1 2-ml ampuls Lanoxin (.5 mg/2 ml)
1 2-ml ampuls Compazine brand of Prochlorperazine (5 mg/ml)
1 100-tablet bottle Nitrostat (nitroglycerin tablets)
1 10-ml ampul Calcium Chloride (1 gr/10 ml)
1 10-ml ampul Calcium gluconate (1 gr/10 ml)
1 10-ml ampul Aminophylline (250 mg/10 ml)
1 2-ml mixovial Solu-cortef (hydrocortisone sodium succinate) (100 mg)
2 3-cc hypodermic needles
1 12-cc hypodermic plunger (no needle)
1 35-cc hypodermic plunger (no needle)
2 vaporole Amyl nitrite
2 vaporole Aromatic ammonia
1 2-ml mixorial Solu-medrol (methylpredrisolone sodium succinate (125 mg))
1 Endothracheal Tube w/15-mm connector
1 Blood-pressure cuff
1 Stethoscope
1 Laryngoscope
1 250-ml bottle lactated wringers
1 50-ml vial sodium bicarbonate (3.75 gm/50 ml)
1 50-ml vial dextrose (500 mg/ml)
3 various size artificial airway inserts
1 roll paper tape hypo-allergenic
1 pkg sterilized surgical equipment
2 long nose clamps (locking clamp)
1 short nose clamps (locking clamp)
1 pr. bandage scissors
1 pr. tweezers
1 pkg. sterile surgical sutures (silk, 18″) & (gut, 27″)
2 med. alcohol prep (70% isopropyl alcohol) (1 pad ea.)
1 Sterile disposable scalpel (stainless steel)
1 Rubber tourniquet strap
1 IV bottle extension rod
1 Intravenous injection set
1 instruction set and key

367

Appendix L

Inventory List for First Aid Kits

Meclizine tablets
Tigan suppository
Phenergan tablets
Ephedrine capsule
Transderm Scopolamine
Kaopectate powder
Lomotil tablets
Mylanta II liquid
Sudafed tablets
Drixoral tablets
Afrin nose spray

Robitussin DM liquid
Cepacol lozenges
Aspirin tablets
Tylenol tablets
Sunscreen lotion
Zinc oxide ointment
Hydrocortisone cream
Clotrimazole solution
Bacitracin ointment
Betadine scrub
Kwell cream

Desenex powder
Visine eye drops
Neosporin eye solution
Benadryl capsule
Ammonia inhalant
Tincture of benzoin
White petrolatum
Hydrogen peroxide
Isopropyl alcohol
Ace bandage 2″, 4″, 6″
Bandaids

Betadine swabs
Chapstick
Eye patches
Gauze
Sterile gloves
Steristrips
Telfa pads
Thermometer (Oral)
Tongue blades
Adhesive tape
Isopropyl alcohol pads

M.
Fire Extinguishers and Damage-Control Kit

Extinguishers

Type B-I	Type B-II
1 1/4 gal. foam	2 1/2 gal. foam
4 lbs. carbon dioxide—CO_2	15 lbs. carbon dioxide—CO_2
2 lbs. dry chemical	10 lbs. dry chemical
2 1/2 lbs. halon	10 lbs. halon

Boat Length	Required
26' or less	1 B-I
26' to 39'	2 B-I or 1 B-II
39' to 65'	3 B-I or 1 B-I & 1 B-II

Type Fire	CO_2	Dry Chemical	Halon
"A" Combustible solids	yes*	yes	yes
"B" Fuel, oil, grease, gas	yes	yes	yes
"C" Electrical	yes	yes[†]	yes

* Type "A" fires should be doused with water after extinguishing to prevent reflash.
† Dry chemical will extinguish but may cause damage unless equipment is well flushed.

Damage Control Kit

2 12" wooden squares (for hole patches)
1 Hatchet (sharp, sprayed w/silicone and wrapped)
2 Hacksaws (good number of blades for hacksaw) (Carbide-tipped rod blades are good on rod rigging, course-type blades are for wire rigging and heavy jobs)
2 Tubes of 5200 (pliable bonding that works underwater also—check for pliability as it hardens when old)
Caulking gun for 5200
Bag of self-tapping screws for fiberglass and aluminum boats (nails for wood)
Oakum or some other packing that swells when wet
Sheet of rubber for collision
Collision mat made of heavy material, wide seams with heavy grommets on each corner
Wooden wedges to use with shoring material
D.C. plugs, wooden plugs made of soft wood that swells when wet. These must be tapered and cut to fit each seacock and wired to seacock.
D.C. plugs of assorted larger sizes for hull holes
Duct tape (can never have too much)
Felco cable cutters (sharpened, siliconed, and protected)
Different size hose clamps. A few extra large come in handy when joined together.
Any of the new epoxies that cure underwater
Bilge-pump repair kits
Beckson (dinghy) bilge pumps—preferably long hoses
Well-stocked tool box

N.
*Sail Craft
Preventive
Maintenance/
Preparation for
Sea*

370

Preventive Maintenance System—PMS

1. A system used to ensure periodic inspection and maintenance on all boat systems and fixtures.
2. Intended to prevent equipment failure and identify discrepancies for repair prior to a sudden casualty.
3. Describes the maintenance procedures step by step as well as safety precautions to be taken and tools required to complete the job.
4. Determines the periodicity for each maintenance requirement—annual, quarterly, monthly, weekly

PMS Guidelines

Boat skipper to winch grinder responsibility

Boat cleanliness influences:
Personnel health
System casualty recovery
Ability to recognize pending equipment failures

PMS management
Designated PMS coordinator—organizes schedules & maintains PMS records
Secondary manager—Engineer—backs up PMS coordinator

PMS accomplishment
Knowledgeable mechanic
Instruct new members
Follow procedures
Observe safety precautions
Keep PMS records current

Maintenance follow-up
Notify skipper of deficiencies beyond the capability of boat crew or inability to complete (time constraint, lack of tools)

Sample Copy of Discrepancy Report

Notify sail craft repair officer of deficiencies using Discrepancy Report Form 4750/01.
When deployed, arrange commercial repair of deficiency during port visit.

Preparation

I. CREW
  A. Physically fit (stamina and strength)
    1. Rigorous activity
    2. Disrupted daily routine
    3. Unnatural sleeping patterns
  B. Individual safety equipment
    1. Cold-weather clothing
    2. Foul-weather clothing
    3. Sun glasses and sunscreen
    4. Knife, marlinspike, flashlight w/lanyards
    5. Safety harness
    6. PFD
    7. Good footwear
    8. Line-handling gloves

C. Training
  1. Skilled in sailing, navigation, watch routines
  2. Practiced in emergency procedures
     a. MOB
     b. Fire
     c. Flooding
     d. Abandon ship
     e. Collision
  3. Knowledgeable in boat systems and use
     a. Bilge pumps
     b. Loran
     c. Radios
     d. Battery charging
     e. Anchoring
     f. Ships stowage
        (1) Pyrotechnics
        (2) Fire extinguishers
        (3) DC kit

II. Many hours of instruction and practice are required to develop a crew capable of working as a team with an ability to interchange crew positions in emergency situations.

III. BOAT PREPARATION
Approach the entire preparation of the vessel with an organized checklist. Many factors and trial use develop an accurate preparation checklist.

Sample lists provided with handout:
  Preparation checklist
  Presail checklist
  Postsail checklist

Tools to complete offshore sailing preparation:
  Solid chain of command
  Standard operating procedures
  Emergency bills
  Training and practice

A. Deck inspection
  Topside fittings   Sails
  Running rigging   Hydraulics
  Standing rigging   Storm gear
  Ground tackle

B. Navigation inspection
  Charts/*Light Lists* w/corrections
  Performance instruments
  Communication equipment
  Electronic nav. gear
  Coast Pilots
  Deviation cards
  Celestial nav. pubs.

  Sextant kit
  Clocks and barometers

C. Electrical inspection
  Batteries—house and engine
  Battery-charging systems
  Portable equipment battery spares
  Navigation lights
  Internal boat lighting
  Lighting—spare bulbs or emergency backup
  Electric pumps and motors
  Circuit panel breakers and fuses
  Spares—breakers and fuses

D. Damage-control inspection
  Thru-hull DC plugs   MOB gear
  DC kit   Bilge pumps
  Liferafts   Cockpit drains
  EPIRBs   Personal strobe lights
  PFDs   Emergency steering
  Pyrotechnics   First aid equipment
  Safety harnesses   Drogues/sea anchors
  Jack lines/safety track Emergency bills

E. Engineering inspection
  Boat inspection/survey
  Valve labels
  Piping diagrams
  Engine spares
  Tank capacities
  Sounding rods/levelometers
  Hull valve operation
  Engine cooling and exhaust
  Engine gauge parameters
  Engine log
  Repair kits for heads/pumps
  Alarm ckt tests
  Refrigeration systems
  Repair manuals
  Tool boxes

F. Habitability
  Potable water tank chlorination
  Heads operational
  DC diagrams for PW, showers, heads
  Bunk lee cloths
  Cleaning equipment and consumables
  Stowage labeled throughout boat
  Wet gear hanging space
  Meal plans
  Galley-stove fuel systems
  Space ventilation
  Secure stowage boat-wide

371

This comprehensive index also serves as a glossary of terms and a list of illustrations. Defined terms are indicated by an italicized entry and page number; illustrations are indicated by a boldfaced page number.

Index

Index

375

Index

Index

389

Credits

Other books by Richard Henderson

First Sail for Skipper
Hand, Reef, and Steer
Dangerous Voyages of Captain William Andrews (Ed.)
The Racing-Cruiser
Sea Sense, 3rd ed.
The Cruiser's Compendium
Singlehanded Sailing, 2nd ed.
Better Sailing
East to the Azores
Choice Yacht Designs
Philip L. Rhodes and His Yacht Designs
John G. Alden and His Yacht Designs (with Robert W. Carrick)
Heavy Weather Guide, 2nd ed. (with William J. Kotsch)
53 Boats You Can Build
Understanding Rigs and Rigging
Sailing at Night
Sailing in Windy Weather
Encyclopedia of Sailing, 2nd ed. (with editors of *Yacht Racing and Cruising*)

THE NAVAL INSTITUTE PRESS

Sail and Power
Fourth Edition

Designed by Pamela L. Schnitter

Set in Simoncini Life and Helvetica by Byrd Data
Imaging, Richmond, Virginia

Printed on 60-lb. Finch Opaque Smooth
by The John D. Lucas Printing Company,
Baltimore, Maryland

Bound in Holliston Crown Linen
by American Trade Bindery, Inc.,
Baltimore, Maryland

ALLIED NAVAL SIGNAL FLAGS AND PENNANTS

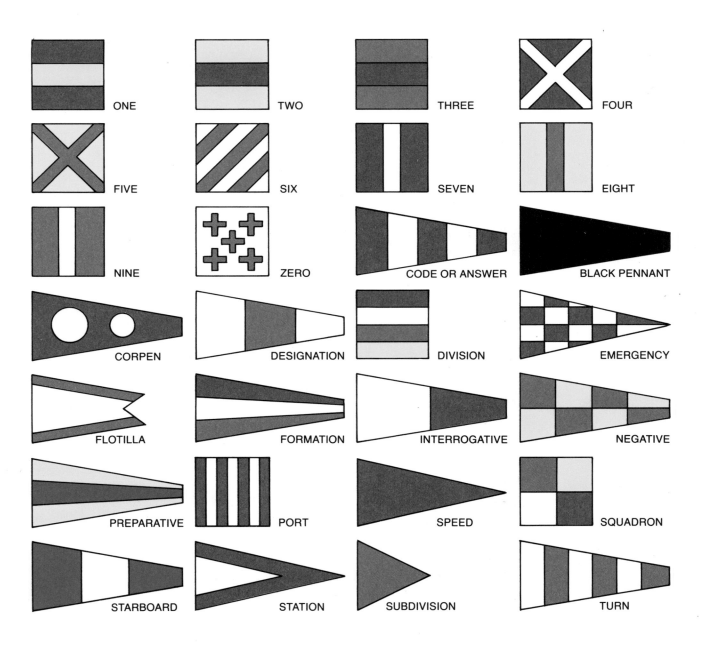

ONE

TWO

THREE

FOUR

FIVE

SIX

SEVEN

EIGHT

NINE

ZERO

CODE OR ANSWER

BLACK PENNANT

CORPEN

DESIGNATION

DIVISION

EMERGENCY

FLOTILLA

FORMATION

INTERROGATIVE

NEGATIVE

PREPARATIVE

PORT

SPEED

SQUADRON

STARBOARD

STATION

SUBDIVISION

TURN

U.S. YACHT ENSIGN

**U.S. NAVAL ACADEMY
SAILING SQUADRON**

U.S. POWER SQUADRONS